PETERSON'S
College Guide for
Visual *Arts*
Majors
2008

PETERSON'S

A **nelnet** COMPANY

PETERSON'S

A ⓝelnet COMPANY

About Peterson's, a Nelnet company

Peterson's (www.petersons.com) is a leading provider of education information and advice, with books and online resources focusing on education search, test preparation, and financial aid. Its Web site offers searchable databases and interactive tools for contacting educational institutions, online practice tests and instruction, and planning tools for securing financial aid. Peterson's serves 110 million education consumers annually.

For more information, contact Peterson's, 2000 Lenox Drive, Lawrenceville, NJ 08648; 800-338-3282; or find us on the World Wide Web at www.petersons.com/about.

© 2007 Peterson's, a Nelnet company

Previous editions published as *Peterson's Professional Degree Programs in the Visual & Performing Arts* © 1995, 1996, 1997, 1998, 1999, 2000, 2001, 2002, 2003, 2004, 2005 and as *Peterson's College Guide for Visual Arts Majors* © 2006

Editor: Linda Seghers; Production Editor: Jill C. Schwartz; Copy Editors: Bret Bollmann, Michael Haines, Brooke James, Sally Ross, Pam Sullivan, Valerie Bolus Vaughan; Research Project Manager: Jennifer Fishberg; Research Associate: Richard Neubeck; Programmer: Alex Lin; Interior Design: Katie Cordisco; Manufacturing Manager: Ivona Skibicki; Composition Manager: Gary Rozmierski; Client Relations Representatives: Janet Garwo, Mimi Kaufman, Karen Mount, Danielle Vreeland

ISBN-13: 978-0-7689-2423-7
ISBN-10: 0-7689-2423-5
ISSN 1552-7751

Printed in the United States of America

10 9 8 7 6 5 4 3 2 1   09 08 07

Thirteenth Edition

Contents

Foreword

There's a certain myth about the creative process that many high school students and aspiring artists have heard: Artists usually work best in unstructured, independent environments and without formal education in the arts.

This couldn't be farther from the truth. A college or university that specializes in the arts can offer a number of benefits to students—by helping them grow creatively, providing them with access to state-of-the-art equipment and facilities, and ultimately preparing them for successful arts-related careers. As members of a creative community, art students receive inspiration, encouragement, and feedback from peers, professors, and visiting artists—all of whom form a valuable network of creative and professional contacts.

Members of colleges and universities that specialize in arts education often make up a community that inspires and nourishes creativity. Students interact with peers who share a love of the arts and grow along with their classmates, who can provide critiques, offer tips, and share opportunities for collaboration, both within major programs and across disciplines. International students also add diversity and global perspectives to the community. A student body that collectively embraces difference, promotes curiosity, and explores questions permits aspiring artists to not only hone their specific craft but to develop an overall concept of the world and their place within it.

Faculty members at arts-related institutions serve as an invaluable resource to their students. These professors may be practicing artists or authors, curators, scholars, or theorists. The credentials they carry to the classroom—education and career experience, including publications, exhibitions, collaborations, and professional affiliations—impact their students, who benefit from knowledgeable critiques, answers to technical questions, and contacts in their field of study. To ensure that they choose an institution where they will receive maximum support from faculty members, prospective students may want to speak with both current students and professors. Office hours, availability outside the classroom, willingness to provide recommendations for internships or employment, and overall commitment to students all are important considerations. In addition, a combination of new and long-term faculty members often signals a mix of fresh ideas and seasoned professionalism.

Visual Arts

Effective arts colleges and universities offer their students ample opportunities to learn from guest speakers and artists. Whether they serve as artists-in-residence for a term, spend a few days providing individual critiques, or deliver a lecture or demonstration, professional artists share technical insight, innovative ideas, and market awareness through their communications with students.

In addition to the opportunities to interact with an array of artists, arts-centered colleges and universities offer students access to media, equipment, and facilities that individual artists may not be able to afford. The level of support for these resources varies from institution to institution, and prospective students may want to research whether and how this commitment affects opportunities in their area of interest. For example, a school that offers technology-dependent programs, such as animation, sound design, and visual effects, should regularly update software and hardware. Labs for disciplines such as metals and jewelry and industrial design should adhere to safety standards.

At an arts college or university, students also learn about potential areas of specialization that they might not otherwise have discovered. At Savannah College of Art and Design, for example, a student interested in computer art has the opportunity to explore a variety of focused majors, including animation, broadcast design and motion graphics, interactive design and game development, and visual effects, as well as sound design and film and television.

While students at many institutions of higher learning can experience off-campus programs and internships, at an arts-focused school, these opportunities are geared toward students' artistic growth and development. Internships help students get a foot in the door of their chosen industry, whether that means working at a high-end interior design firm or studying with a noted freelance artist. Professors, visiting artists, and even peers can prove valuable sources of internship leads, and schools also offer career services departments devoted to publicizing job openings for artists. Off-campus programs focused on arts can provide inspiration, motivation, and comprehensive understanding of creative industries. Arts-focused schools offer fashion students trips to New York during fashion week; offer art history students visits to Milan, Rome, and Venice; and offer painting and historic preservation students art history programs abroad—all of which let students experience diverse settings and explore other cultures, enhancing both the college experience and an artist's vision.

Ultimately, artists communicate through their work. They express their ideas, their dreams, their perspectives and their personal stories in forms that may endure for generations and speak to millions. An arts-centered educational community enables students to explore their talents and learn how best to articulate their unique perceptions to the world.

Sandra Reed
Former Dean of Graduate Studies
Savannah College of Art and Design

Visual

Arts

A Note from the Peterson's Editors

As a prospective art major, you probably know where your talent lies and can see yourself becoming a graphic designer, a photographer, a filmmaker, or maybe an art teacher one day. You are one of the lucky college-bound students who already know what they want to study and have one foot solidly on their career path. That part might have been easy.

But what's usually not easy is choosing a school and a program. You have some of the usual considerations: Do I want to be at a large school or a small school, in a busy city or on a quiet rural campus, 5 hours away from home by plane or 20 minutes away by car? But as an art student, you also have to decide if you want to attend a specialized art college or a liberal arts college or university and choose between a professional degree (B.F.A.) program and a liberal arts (B.A.) program. That's a lot to decide.

Peterson's College Guide for Visual Arts Majors will help you make the right decisions.

The first three sections of the guide, **The Right Program for You, Applying and Getting In,** and **You're In! What's Next?,** give you invaluable advice to help you assess your educational needs, discover what options are out there, navigate the admissions process, and learn what it's really like to be a serious art student. You'll learn the differences between B.F.A. and B.A. programs and what to expect at a specialized art college versus majoring in art at a liberal arts college. If you're in the early stages of college prep, you'll gain invaluable insight into how to prepare a portfolio—perhaps the most important part of the whole application process. Admissions directors at six top art colleges across the country reveal what they look for when reviewing students' portfolios. You'll also get advice from current art majors and a glimpse into what a typical day in art school is like. There are practical tips on making the most of your college visits and interviews and covering your college costs and a checklist to help you make sure you've found the right program for you. Finally, "Up Close and Personal with Professional Artists" gives you a look at some careers in the art field and what working artists say about art education.

When it's the nitty-gritty details you need, the **Profiles of Visual Arts Programs** section contains comprehensive, detailed descriptions of professional degree programs in art arranged alphabetically by name of school. Each profile provides all the need-to-know information on accredited art programs throughout the U.S. and Canada. Some schools have provided even more information about their facilities, faculty, alumni, and special programs in *More About the School* at the end of their profile. There isn't an easier or more efficient way to explore art programs. To get the most out of the **Profiles,** just turn to "How to Use This Guide." It provides in-depth explanations about each data element found in the **Profiles.**

For those who already have specifics in mind, the **Quick-Reference Chart** lists schools by state and lets you compare programs at a glance. The **Appendixes** include additional resources, including listings of summer programs and scholarships. The **Indexes** let you locate schools by their majors or concentrations or alphabetically by name.

Peterson's publishes a full line of resources to help guide you and your family through the college admission process. Peterson's publications can be found at your local bookstore, library, and high school guidance office, and you can access us online at www.petersons.com.

We welcome any comments or suggestions you may have about this publication and invite you to complete our online survey at www.petersons.com/booksurvey. Or you can fill out the survey at the back of this book, tear it out, and mail it to us at:

Publishing Department
Peterson's, a Nelnet company
2000 Lenox Drive
Lawrenceville, NJ 08648

Your feedback will help us make your educational dreams possible.

Remember, there is no "best" school—only the best school for you. Start examining your goals, your interests, your personality, your talents; and by all means, talk with your teachers and guidance counselors. The editors at Peterson's wish you the best of luck in your art school search!

The Right Program for You

Finding the right college art program is a challenge. What makes a program right for one person might make it very wrong for someone else. In order to find the perfect fit, you have to consider your needs, talents, and goals and then begin to explore your options.

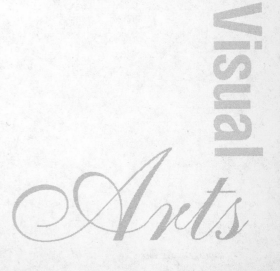

Liberal Arts Education vs. Specialized Education

Jon Fraser

If you are planning to major in art, it's important to choose the college art program that's right for you and an environment that nurtures you as an artist. That's what a good school can do for you: develop and nurture the talent you may already have and prepare you, in some cases, for a professional career.

The difference between a liberal arts education and a specialized education is significant. A specialized school usually awards a Bachelor of Fine Arts degree and offers intense training in your art form, with little emphasis on other subjects. A liberal arts education offers you a broad training that attempts to make you a well-rounded, well-educated member of society. Some programs offer a specialized approach in a liberal arts environment, where you'll study other subjects while receiving intense training in your art form. And some programs are highly specialized and preprofessional. Which one is best for you?

B.A./B.F.A./B.S.

Colleges offer three types of degrees in the visual arts: a general degree, called a Bachelor of Arts (B.A.), a preprofessional degree called a Bachelor of Fine Arts (B.F.A.), and a Bachelor of Science (B.S.) for areas such as art therapy. The main difference between the types of degree programs is the number of classes you will be required to take in your major. The goals of these various types of degrees are also different.

B.F.A. programs allow students to focus most of their studies in art—up to 70 percent of all course work—and don't usually permit as many electives in areas outside the major as B.A. programs. These programs are meant for those who intend to pursue a professional career in their field of study. The B.F.A. program in the visual arts at a university will be rigorous and professional, typically offering a broad range of courses and electives. Universities vary, though, as to whether or not areas for specialization are available.

The B.A. program is meant for those who want a broad-based education with plenty of room for electives and who may not be sure what they want to do after they graduate.

The B.S. is generally a more technically oriented degree in a subject like art therapy, where the career is related to art but requires other skills.

Some schools offer two or three degrees in the same subject and let you choose which program to pursue. Other schools have stricter entrance requirements for the B.F.A. or B.S. degree programs than for the B.A. program.

As a general rule of thumb, if you're not sure or you have to ask, it's probably best to pursue a B.A. degree. If you feel you have no choice, that your art form is what you must do for the rest of your life, the B.F.A. or B.S. is probably the right choice. Another thing to keep in mind is that in many schools with several degree programs, you may switch from one to the other once you get there.

LIBERAL ARTS COLLEGE OR SPECIALIZED COLLEGE

Once you've decided on a degree program, you need to decide which type of school is right for you. The choice between attending a liberal arts college and a specialized college is highly individual. It is not about which one will make you successful. Both types of school may or may not help you to become a success at what you do. You don't get a "better" education at one or the other. What you get is a different sort of education that may or may not serve your needs.

Competition within a specialized school tends to be more intense than in a liberal arts environment. Moreover, liberal arts schools may have a minimum grade point average requirement for staying in their programs. So, a word of warning: If you're planning on majoring in the arts, plan on working hard!

As someone who has worked for a liberal arts institution (Long Island University's C.W. Post Campus) for many years, I have my prejudice about which one you should choose. For most people, I feel that a liberal arts education makes a better artist, in the holistic sense that any art form is more than simply good technique. It requires intelligent inquiry and critical thinking about the world around you. A good liberal arts undergraduate education in the arts should develop not only your artistic skills and talent, but your intellectual and critical skills as well. Usually offered outside the department or school of art, liberal arts programs offer a wide range of electives from many disciplines, including business, languages, literature, and sciences. Art students interested in developing in-depth study in a liberal arts subject can often do so through the options of minors or dual majors.

In addition, keep in mind that graduate school is where there is plenty of time to focus your energies on developing career-related skills in your specific art form. Getting a Master of Fine Arts (M.F.A.) degree may be part of your future plans, and it won't matter so much where you went to undergraduate school, but how well you did as evidenced not only by grades, but by your portfolio.

That being said, the rule of thumb here is: If you have to ask or are not sure, go to the liberal arts school. If you have no doubt about your future, if art is the only thing you want to do, consider a specialized college. And remember, if you find yourself at the wrong school, you can always transfer.

Jon Fraser is Senior Associate Dean of the School of Visual and Performing Arts at Long Island University, C.W. Post Campus.

The Right Program for You

Choosing a Specialized School

Kimberly Stogner

Many people refer to college as the best time of their lives. But you may be wondering how you can achieve that experience if you enroll in a specialized school. What should you look for to make sure you get both a specialized education and the college experience you've always dreamed of?

MAKE SURE IT'S WHAT YOU LOVE

It may seem obvious, but before you commit to a specialized school, make sure you are really interested in that subject area. In other words, if you choose an art college and then decide you actually want to be a biomedical engineer, you will have to transfer to another college. However, if you love art, the more time spent in those courses, the better. And some specialized schools offer a wide range of majors and minors, allowing flexibility and cross-disciplinary study. So do your research on curriculum to know how limited or how broad a college's choices are.

VERIFY ACCREDITATION

Like money, you don't realize how important it is unless you don't have it. Accreditation is your thumbs-up that a college's curriculum, faculty, facilities, and resources are on par with other institutions and professionals in the field. In other words, accreditation is what qualifies a college to confer degrees. There are two basic types of accreditation: regional (such as the Southern Association of Colleges and Schools) and programmatic (like the National Architectural Accrediting Board). Lack of accreditation can keep you from transferring credits to other universities and becoming licensed in your field. When visiting colleges, ask them about their accreditation, talk to professionals in your intended field, and look online for licensure requirements. If you just want a certificate and some training and experience, you may not need to worry so much about accreditation. But make sure you know what you're paying for ahead of time.

CHECK REPUTATION

Once you know your college has the appropriate accreditation, you also want to look into its reputation in your field. What have the faculty members accomplished? What are alumni doing? Will potential employers recognize your school? Do companies actively recruit graduates? What are job placement rates? Is there a career placement office to assist with employment opportunities? Since you know the field you want to pursue, you can take a very close look at the faculty in that area. Your professors should have terminal degrees in their field (the highest degree possible), and they should have recent work experience. Equipment, software, and procedures are constantly changing in every industry, and you want the most updated knowledge and experience. You also want professors with contacts in your field. These are the people who will write recommendations for your internship and job applications, so the better their contacts, the better your odds of securing the job you want.

SHOW ME THE MONEY

Another important consideration, of course, is the cost. Don't be shy about asking for financial assistance. Apply for federal aid online at www.fafsa.ed.gov and check with your guidance counselor for local or state funding sources. Ask the college admission department about scholarships and need-based aid, as well as alternative loans, work-study assistance, and part-time jobs. A college education gets more expensive every year, but let's face it: You probably can't make a better investment in your future.

DON'T SACRIFICE STUDENT INVOLVEMENT

While the art program and academics are obviously your top priorities in choosing a college, the fun you have outside class may be the most important influence in keeping you there until you graduate. Maybe the swim team is your thing, or writing for the student newspaper. Whatever your interests, you are more than your major, and your college should recognize and encourage that. Ask about special events, clubs, and competitions, and if there aren't enough, ask if you can start your own. See if there are study-abroad opportunities. Look for a student body with the size and diversity to foster your needs and interests.

Other services may also be important to you, such as disability and counseling resources, career planning and placement, security, dining and residence life, health and fitness, learning assistance, religious organizations, and transportation and parking. All these should be available to the degree that you desire.

VISIT

Take a tour. Talk to students. See how far it really is from the residence hall to the grocery store. Sit in on a class. Go to a soccer game. See if you like the climate, the neighborhood, and the feeling you get walking around the campus. Visiting your top-choice schools is the best way to find a college that's right for you.

Kimberly Stogner is an admission representative at the Savannah College of Art and Design.

Visual

Arts

Making the Most of Your Campus Visit

Dawn B. Sova, Ph.D.

The campus visit should not be a passive activity for you and your parents. You will see many important indicators during your visit that will tell you a lot about the true character of the college and its students. Most organized campus visits include tours of such campus facilities as dorms, dining halls, libraries, student activity and recreation centers, and the health and student services centers. Some may only be pointed out, while you will walk through others. As an art student, you will of course be interested in seeing the facilities that pertain to your particular major, and those might be a major factor when considering a school. However, the general environment of the campus is important as well and merits close attention. Colleges do not train their tour guides to deceive prospective students, but they do caution guides to avoid unflattering topics and campus sites. Does this mean that you are condemned to see only a sugarcoated version of life on a particular college campus? Not at all—especially if you are observant.

VISITOR CENTER/ADMISSIONS OFFICE

Your first stop on a campus visit is the visitor center or admissions office. Begin your investigation with the visitor center staff members. As a student's first official contact with the college, they should make every effort to welcome prospective students and to project a friendly image.

- How do they treat you and other prospective students who are waiting? Are they friendly and willing to speak with you, or do they try their hardest to avoid eye contact and conversation?

- Are they friendly with each other and with students who enter the office, or are they curt and unwilling to help?

If the visitor center staff members seem indifferent to *prospective* students, there is little reason to believe that they will be warm and welcoming to current students.

SCHOOL NEWSPAPER

If time permits, look through several copies of the school newspaper, which should reflect the major concerns and interests of the students. The paper is also a good way to learn about the campus social life.

- Does the paper contain a mix of national and local news?

- What products or services are advertised?

- How assertive are the editorials?

- With what topics are the columnists concerned?

- Are movies and concerts that meet your tastes advertised or reviewed?

- What types of ads appear in the classified section?

The newspaper should be a public forum for students, and, as such, should reflect the character of the campus and of the student body. A paper that deals only with seemingly safe and well-edited topics on the editorial page and in regular feature columns might indicate administrative censorship. A lack of ads for restaurants might indicate either a lack of good places to eat or that area restaurants do not welcome student business. A limited mention of movies, concerts, or other entertainment might reveal a severely limited campus social life. Even if ads and reviews are included, you can also learn a lot about how such activities reflect your tastes.

BULLETIN BOARDS

Bulletin boards in the dorms and student centers contain a wealth of information about campus activities, student concerns, and campus groups. Read the posters, notices, and messages to learn what *really* interests students. Unlike ads in the school newspaper, posters put up by students advertise both on- and off-campus events, so they will give you an idea of what is also available in the surrounding community. Art exhibits, poetry readings, jam sessions, writers' groups, and other activities may be announced and show diversity of student interests on that campus. Even the brief bulletin board messages offering objects for sale and noting objects that people want to purchase reveal a lot about a campus. Are most of the items computer related? Or do the messages specify compact discs, audio equipment, or musical instruments? Don't ignore the "ride wanted" messages. Students who want to share rides home during a break may specify widely diverse geographical locations. If so, then you know that the student body is not limited to only the immediate area or one locale.

BUILDINGS

As you walk through various buildings, examine their condition carefully.

- Is the paint peeling, and do the exteriors look worn?

- Are the exteriors and interiors of the building clean?

- Do they look well maintained?

- Is the equipment in the classrooms up-to-date?

As an art major, you will of course be most interested in their art facilities. Check out as many of the studios and as much of the equipment as you can. Is the equipment up-to-date? Is there independent studio space for painting majors? What sort of computer equipment do they have? No matter what you're planning to major in, all disciplines overlap at some point—painters and sculptors may need photo equipment for slides, filmmakers may need access to costume design or model building facilities. Having access to state-of-the-art equipment is important.

Pay particular attention to the dorms, especially to factors that might affect your safety. Ask about the security measures in and around the dorms.

- Are the dorms noisy or quiet?

- Do they seem crowded?

- How good is the lighting?

- Are the dorms spread throughout the campus or are they clustered in one main area?

- Who has access to the dorms in addition to students?

- How secure are the means by which students enter and leave the dorm?

CAMPUS SAFETY

While you are on the subject of dorm safety, you should also ask about campus safety. Don't expect that the guide will rattle off a list of crimes that have been committed in the past year. To obtain that information, access the recent issues of the *Chronicle of Higher Education* and locate its yearly report on campus crime. Also ask the guide about safety measures that the campus police take and those that students have initiated.

- Can students request escorts to their residences late at night?

- Do campus shuttle buses run at frequent intervals all night?

- Are "blue-light" telephones liberally placed throughout the campus for students to use to call for help?

- Do the campus police patrol the campus regularly?

If the guide does not answer your questions satisfactorily, wait until after the tour to contact the campus police or traffic office for answers.

HEALTH SERVICES

Campus tours usually just point out the health services center without taking the time to walk through. Even if you don't see the inside of the building, you should take a close look at the location of the health services center and ask the guide questions about services.

- How far is the health center from the dorms?

- Is a doctor always on call?

- Does the campus transport sick students from their dormitories or must they walk?

- What are the operating hours of the health center?

- Does the health center refer students to the town hospital?

If the guide can't answer your questions, visit the health center later and ask someone there.

ACTIVITIES CENTERS

Most campus tours seem to take pride in showing students their activities centers, which may contain snack bars, game rooms, workout facilities, and other means of entertainment. Should you scrutinize this building as carefully as the rest? Of course. Outdated and poorly maintained activity equipment contributes to your total impression of the college. You should also ask about the hours, availability, and cost (no, the activities are usually *not* free) of using the bowling alleys, pool tables, air hockey tables, and other items.

STUDENTS

As you walk through campus with the tour, look carefully at the appearance of the students you pass. The way they act and dress communicate a lot more than any guidebook can. If everyone seems to conform to the same look, you might feel that you would be uncomfortable at the college, however nonconformist that look might be. On the other hand, you might not feel comfortable on a campus that stresses diversity of dress and behavior, and your observations now can save you discomfort later.

- Does every student seem to wear a sorority or fraternity t-shirt or jacket?

- Does everyone seem to be wearing expensive name-brand clothes?

- Do most of the students seem to be working hard to look outrageous in regard to clothing, hair color, and body art?

- Would you feel uncomfortable in a room full of these students?

Is appearance important to you? If it is, then you should consider very seriously if you answer *yes* to any of the above questions. You don't have to be the same as everyone else on campus, but standing out too much may make you unhappy.

As you observe the physical appearance of the students, also listen to their conversations. What are they talking about? How are they speaking? Are their voices and accents all the same, or do you hear diversity in their speech? Are you offended by their language? Think how you will feel if surrounded by these students for four years.

WHERE SHOULD YOU VISIT ON YOUR OWN?

Your campus visit is not over when the tour ends because you will probably have many questions yet to be answered and many places still to be seen. If you haven't seen any residential hall, health and student services center, gym or fitness center, dining hall, the library, or recreational center, visit them on your own and ask questions of the students and staff members you meet.

Eat lunch in one of the dining halls. Most will allow visitors to pay cash to experience a typical student meal. Food may not be important to you now while you are living at home and can simply take anything you want from the refrigerator at any time, but it will be when you are away at college with a meal ticket to feed you.

- How clean is the dining hall? Consider serving tables, floors, and seating.

- What is the quality of the food?

- How big are the portions?

- How much variety do students have at each meal?

- How healthy are the food choices?

While you are eating, try to strike up a conversation with students and tell them that you are considering attending their college. Their reactions and advice can be eye-opening. Ask them questions about the academic atmosphere and the professors.

- Are the classes large or small?

- Do the majority of the professors only lecture, or are tutorials and seminars common?

- Is the emphasis of the faculty career-oriented or abstract?

- Do they find the teaching methods innovative and stimulating or boring and dull?

- Is the academic atmosphere pressured, lax, or somewhere in between?

- Which are the strong majors? Which are the weak majors?

- Is the emphasis on grades or social life or a mix of both?

- How hard do students have to work to receive high grades?

Current students can also give you the inside line—the true highs and lows of campus life. Ask them about drug use, partying, dating, drinking, and anything else that may affect your life as a student.

- Which are the most popular club activities?

- What do students do on weekends? Do most go home?

- How frequently do concerts occur on campus? Ask them to name groups that have recently performed.

- How can you become involved in specific activities (name them)?

- How strictly are campus rules enforced and how severe are penalties?

- What counseling services are available?

- Are academic tutoring services available?

- Do they feel that the faculty really cares about students, especially freshmen?

You will receive the most valuable information from current students, but you will only be able to speak with them after the tour is over. And you might have to risk rejection as you try to initiate conversations with students who might not want to reveal how they feel about the school.

SURROUNDING COMMUNITY

Make a point of at least driving through the community surrounding the college, because you will be spending time there shopping, dining, working in a part-time job, or attending events. Even the largest and best-stocked campus will not meet all of your social and personal needs. If you can spare the time, stop in several stores to see if they welcome college students.

The Right Program for You

- Is the surrounding community suburban, urban, or rural?

- Does the community offer stores of interest, such as bookstores, craft shops, and boutiques?

- Do the businesses employ college students?

- Does the community have a movie or stage theater?

- Are there several types of interesting restaurants?

- Do there seem to be any clubs that court a college clientele?

- Is the center of activity easy to walk to, or do you need a car or other transportation?

REVIEW YOUR NOTES

You might feel that a day is not enough to answer all of your questions, but even answering some questions will provide you with a stronger basis for choosing a college. Many students visit a college campus several times before making their decision. Keep in mind that not only will you spend the next four years of your life at a college, but for the rest of your life you will be associated with that college. The effort of spending several days to collect information to make your decision is worthwhile.

FOLLOWING UP

Your connection with a college does not end when you return home, no matter what your impression might be. Whether or not you wish to attend the school, you should take the time to follow up. Write a letter to thank people specifically for taking the time to meet with you. Beyond common courtesy, this also leaves the college officials with a positive view of you, and the letter will most likely be placed in your file. Will it make the difference between being accepted or rejected? No one can say. Write to the visitor center to thank counselors for their time, even if your experience was less than pleasant. You may have contact with them in the future and there is no reason not to leave them with a good impression.

Dawn B. Sova is a former newspaper reporter and columnist who teaches creative and research writing as well as scientific and technical writing, newswriting, and journalism.

Searching for Art Programs and Scholarships Online

Choosing a college art program involves a serious commitment of time and resources. Therefore, it is important to have the most up-to-date information about institutions and their programs at your fingertips. The Internet can be a great tool for gathering that information, and one of the best sites to visit during the college selection process is Peterson's Visual & Performing Arts (VPA) channel at www.petersons.com.

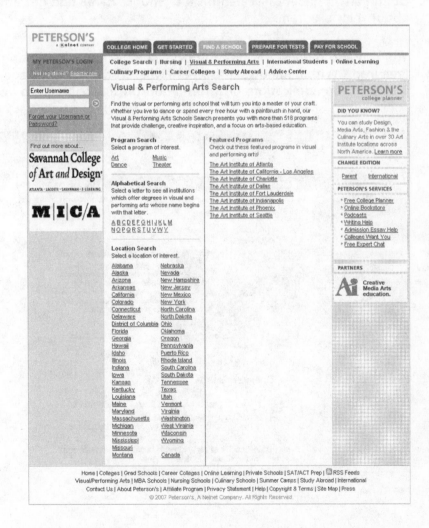

PETERSON'S VISUAL & PERFORMING ARTS CHANNEL

The VPA channel at Petersons.com is a one-stop source of information on college art programs in the U.S. and Canada. Just click on "High School Students," the "Find a School" tab, and then "Visual & Performing Arts" to access Peterson's comprehensive database of arts programs. If you know what area of art you're interested in, you can locate a school or program by clicking on "Art" on the Program Search pull-down menu, which gives you a list of art majors or concentrations. Simply click one of these and you will get a list of schools that offer a degree program in that field. Or, if you'd like to search by location, you can access lists of schools offering art programs in any state or in Canada. Finally, if you have a particular school in mind and want to see what art programs it offers, you can do an alphabetical search on the school's name and get information about their programs.

You can also request information from some schools by clicking on "Get Free Info." Within minutes, the school will receive your message and mail a catalog, an application, or information on financial aid to you. If you

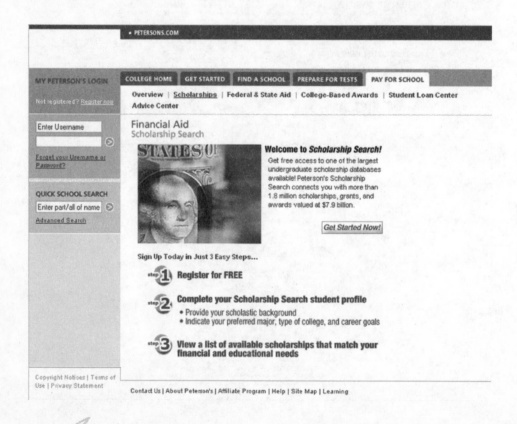

find the perfect school for a friend, you can even send the page to him or her with a message. There also are links to the school's Web site.

PETERSON'S FREE SCHOLARSHIP SEARCH

Petersons.com is a great site for any college-bound student. There is a wealth of information on undergraduate, graduate, online learning, and study-abroad programs and also some of the best financial aid advice available.

With Peterson's free Scholarship Search on the financial aid channel of Petersons.com (www.petersons.com/finaid), you can explore more than 1.7 million scholarships, grants, and prizes totaling nearly $8 billion and do an individualized search for awards that match your financial and educational needs. In just three easy steps, you can register and complete a customized profile indicating your scholastic and personal background, including intended major, work experience, and a host of other criteria that will allow you to access a list of scholarships that match your needs. Each scholarship is described in detail with eligibility and application requirements, contact information, and links to its e-mail address and Web site. Finding money for college couldn't be easier.

So, what are you waiting for? Log on to Petersons.com and let us help you with your college planning!

The Right Program for You

Covering Your College Costs

A college education is expensive: more than $150,000 for four years at some of the higher-priced colleges and universities and more than $50,000 at many lower-cost, state-supported colleges. Figuring out how you and your family will come up with the necessary funds to pay for your education requires planning, perseverance, and learning as much as you can about the options available.

For most families, paying the total cost of a student's college education out of savings is not possible. Clearly, the more your family has saved, the better off you will be and the less you will need to earn and borrow. But paying for college should not be looked at merely as a four-year financial commitment. While some of the money you need will likely come from funds that you and your parents have managed to save, some will come from a portion of your or your parents' current income. The rest will come from future earnings, through loans you or your parents will pay off later.

If your family has not saved the total amount or does not have sufficient current income to cover the costs, you can still attend college. That's where financial aid comes in. The amount you and your family will be expected to contribute toward your college expenses will be based upon your and your family's income and assets. But if this is not enough, the rest of the expenses can be met through various financial aid programs.

FINANCIAL AID BASICS: HOW FINANCIAL AID IS AWARDED

When you apply for aid, your family's financial situation is analyzed using a government-approved formula called the Federal Methodology. The result of this is the amount you and your family are expected to contribute toward your college expenses, called your Expected Family Contribution or EFC. If this is equal to or more than the cost of attendance at a particular college, then you do not demonstrate "financial need." However, even if you don't have financial need, you may still qualify for aid since there are many grants, scholarships, and loans that are not based on financial need.

If the cost of education is greater than your EFC, then you will be eligible for "need-based" assistance. The calculation of "financial need" is very simple:

Total Cost of Attendance
— Expected Family Contribution
Financial Need

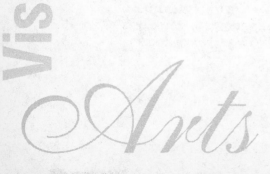

The total aid you are awarded by any one college will likely differ from the amount offered by other colleges you may be applying to because, among other things, the costs of attendance are different. Secondly, not all colleges have the same amount of funds available to offer their needy students. But, your EFC should remain about the same regardless of which college you attend. It is the goal of every financial aid office to meet the financial needs of its students and help all families find the information they need to finance the tuition, fees, room and board, and other costs.

SOURCES OF FINANCIAL AID

The largest single source of aid is the federal government, which awarded over $94 billion during 2005–06 (College Board, *Trends in Higher Education* series). More than 14 million people apply for financial aid each year. But the federal government is not the only source of financial aid. The colleges and universities themselves are the next-largest source of financial aid. Institutions award an estimated $24 billion to students each year. Some of this aid is awarded to students who have a demonstrated need based on either the Federal Methodology or another formula, the Institutional Methodology, which is used by some colleges to award their own funds in conjunction with other aid. Some aid is not based on need and is called merit aid. Merit-based aid is usually awarded based on a student's academic performance or specific talents or abilities, or to students the institutions most want to attract.

Another source of financial aid is from state governments, awarding more than $6.8 billion per year. All fifty states offer grant and/or scholarship aid, most of which is need-based, but some of which is merit-based. Most state programs award aid only to state residents attending college in their home state, although a few do allow their state aid to be "portable" from state to state.

Other sources of financial aid include private agencies, foundations, corporations, clubs, fraternal and service organizations, civic associations, unions, and religious groups that award grants, scholarships, and low-interest loans. Some employers provide tuition reimbursement benefits for employees and their families.

More information about these different sources of aid is available from high school guidance offices, public libraries, college financial aid offices, and directly from the sponsoring organizations. In addition, Peterson's offers an excellent source of scholarship leads at www.petersons.com.

The Right Program for You

APPLYING FOR FINANCIAL AID

Every student must complete the Free Application for Federal Student Aid (FAFSA) to be considered for federal aid. The FAFSA is available in your high school guidance office and many public libraries, or directly from the U.S. Department of Education. Students are encouraged to apply for aid on the Web by using the electronic FAFSA, which can be accessed at www.fafsa.ed.gov. If you apply online, you and one parent will need to obtain an electronic signature before filing. To get your Personal Identification Number, or PIN, go to www.pin.ed.gov.

To award their own funds, many schools require a second application, the CSS/Financial Aid PROFILE®. The PROFILE asks supplemental questions that some colleges and awarding agencies feel provide a more accurate assessment of the family's ability to pay for college. It is up to the college to decide whether it will use only the FAFSA or both the FAFSA and the PROFILE.

The first thing you will have to do is determine whether you will need to fill out only the FAFSA or whether you will also have to complete the PROFILE. The listings later in this book will tell you what forms are required. You should also read the schools' brochures, or speak to someone in the financial aid office to be sure. The PROFILE contains a list of schools and agencies that require the form.

If Every College You're Applying to in 2008 Requires Just the FAFSA

This scenario is pretty simple: Complete the FAFSA sometime after January 1, 2008, being certain to send it in before any college-imposed deadlines. (You are not permitted to send in the 2008–2009 FAFSA before January 1, 2008, which should not pose a problem because most college application deadlines are in February or March.) It is best if you wait until you have all your financial records for the previous year available, but if that is not possible, you can use estimated figures. It is critical to file by the published filing deadline. Filing late can mean the loss of thousands of dollars in assistance.

After you send in your FAFSA, either on paper or electronically, you'll receive a Student Aid Report (SAR) that includes all of the information you reported and shows your EFC. The SAR will be sent to you electronically if you provided an e-mail address. Otherwise, you will receive a paper-copy SAR in the mail. Be sure to review the SAR, checking to see if the information you reported is correct. If you used estimated numbers to complete the FAFSA, you may have to resubmit the SAR with any corrections to the data. The college(s) you have designated on the

FAFSA will receive the information you reported and will use that data to make their decision. In many instances, the colleges you've applied to will ask you to send copies of your and your parents' federal income tax returns for 2007 plus any other documents needed to verify the information you reported.

If a College Requires the CSS/Financial Aid PROFILE®

Step 1: Register for the PROFILE in the fall of your senior year in high school.

You can apply for the PROFILE online at http://profileonline.collegeboard. com/index/jsp.

Registration information with a list of the schools requiring the PROFILE is available in most high school guidance offices.

There is a fee for using the PROFILE application ($23 for the first college and $18 for each additional college). You must pay for the service by credit card when you register. If you do not have a credit card, you will be billed.

Step 2: Fill out your customized PROFILE.

Once you register, your application will be immediately available online and

- will have questions that must be completed by you and your parents (unless you are considered independent and the colleges or programs selected do not require parent information).

- *may* have supplemental questions needed by one or more of your schools or programs. If required, those will be found in Section Q of the application.

In addition to the PROFILE application, which you complete online, you may be required to complete a Business/Farm Supplement in a traditional paper format. Completion of this form is not part of the "online" process. Instead, instructions about how to download and print the supplemental form are provided if it is required.

If your biological or adoptive parents are separated or divorced and your colleges and programs require it, your noncustodial parent may be asked to complete the Noncustodial PROFILE.

Once you complete and submit your PROFILE application, your information is processed and sent directly to the colleges and programs that you requested.

FINANCIAL AID AWARDS

After you've submitted your financial aid application, and usually after you've been accepted for admission, each college will send you a letter containing your financial aid award. Most award letters show the college's budget, how much you and your family are expected to contribute, and the amount and types of aid awarded. Most students who are eligible for aid are awarded aid from a combination of sources and programs; hence your award is often called a "package." For first-year students, award letters are often sent with, or soon after, the letter of admission.

FINANCIAL AID PROGRAMS

There are three types of financial aid: scholarships (also known as grants or gift aid), loans, and student employment. Scholarships and grants are outright gifts and do not have to be repaid. Loans must be repaid, usually after graduation; the amount you have to pay back is the total you've borrowed plus an interest charge. Student employment is a job arranged for you during the academic year. Loans and student employment programs are generally referred to as self-help aid.

The federal government has two large grant programs, the Federal Pell Grant and the Federal Supplemental Educational Opportunity Grant; a student employment program called the Federal Work-Study Program; and several loan programs, including one for parents of undergraduate students. Students who are Pell Grant eligible and have completed a rigorous high school program may be eligible for the Academic Competitiveness Grant. Additional information on this new federal grant program is available from your college's financial aid office or high school guidance office. For juniors and seniors, there is another new federal scholarship program called National SMART grants. The grants are limited to Pell Grant recipients in selected majors—primarily science, math, and certain foreign languages.

The Subsidized Direct Stafford Student Loan, the Subsidized FFEL Stafford Student Loan, and the Federal Perkins Loan are all need-based, government-subsidized loans. Students who borrow under these programs do not have to pay interest on the loan until after they graduate or leave school. The Unsubsidized Direct Stafford Loan, the Unsubsidized

FFEL Stafford Student Loan, and the Parent Loan (PLUS) program are not based on need, and these loans accrue interest while the student is in school.

There are also a number of federal tax–based programs that help families with incomes up to $110,000. Additional information about the Hope Scholarship, Lifetime Learning tax credits, and other education assistance tax–based programs is available from the IRS. You should consult a tax adviser for other educational tax deductions, since income cutoffs can vary from program to program.

IF YOU DON'T QUALIFY FOR NEED-BASED AID

If you are not eligible for need-based aid, or the aid you have been awarded is not sufficient, you should look into three other funding sources.

First is the search for merit scholarships, which you can start during your junior year of high school at the initial stages of the aid application process. Merit-based awards are becoming an increasingly important part of college financing plans, and many colleges award these grants to students they especially want to attract. As a result, applying to a school at which your qualifications put you at the top of the entering class may be a good idea since you may receive a merit award. It is also a good idea to look for private scholarships and grants, especially from local service and community groups.

The second source of aid is employment, during both the summer and the academic year. The student employment office at your college should be able to help you locate a job in the area, either on or off campus.

The third source is borrowing through the Unsubsidized FFEL Stafford Student Loan or the Unsubsidized Direct Stafford Student Loan, both of which are open to all students. The terms and conditions are similar to the subsidized loans. The biggest difference is that the borrower is responsible for the interest while still in college, although most lenders permit students to delay paying the interest right away and add the accrued interest to the total amount owed.

After you've secured what you can through scholarships, work, and loans, your parents will have to figure out how they will meet the balance of the college bill. Most colleges offer monthly payment plans that spread the cost out over the academic year. For many parents, the monthly payments still turn out to be more than they can afford, so they can borrow through the Federal Parent Loan for Undergraduate Students

(PLUS) program, through one of the many private education loan programs available, or through home equity loans and lines of credit. This spreads the cost out over a longer time period and makes the monthly payments more manageable. The college financial aid office may offer a list of preferred lenders or banks and institutions they work with on a regular basis. Parents can select any lender they feel offers them the best terms and conditions and are not required to use a financial institution from the school's preferred lender list.

Students and parents who are interested in more information about financing a college education and in learning more about the financial aid application process should read *Peterson's College Money Handbook.*

How Do You Know It's the Right Program for You?

Putting together a list of eight or ten schools to apply to is the easy part. Waiting to hear if you've gotten in can be nerve-racking. But being admitted to more than one school and choosing the right one to attend can often be the hardest part of the college admissions process.

What makes an art program right for one person might make it very wrong for someone else. Here is a list of things to think about for each school you're considering:

- Are you happiest in a big school or small school? Do you prefer a big city or a small town? What is the overall environment of the school?

- How many people are majoring in the program you are interested in?

- What is the student-faculty ratio in your area of study? In the arts, you really shouldn't have studio classes with more than 15 or so students in the class. While the history of art or cinema may be taught in large sections, classes in, say, painting, photography, and film editing should have limited numbers of students.

- Where do the students in the program come from? Is this a regional school of commuting students, or does it attract students from all over the state—or country? What is the age group?

- Tour the facilities and ask which ones are available to you. Is there independent studio space for painting majors? Is there a foundry for sculptors? What kind of computer equipment does the school have?

- How many courses are offered in your area of interest?

- Try to attend a student exhibition. Is this the kind of work you hope to achieve?

- What opportunities will you have for professional exposure? Are there exhibition opportunities on or off campus? Are there student memberships in professional organizations? Are there opportunities for reality-based course work, such as designing a poster for a community group?

- Does the program feature visiting artists or critics so you can meet practicing professionals and learn the latest theories and techniques? Who are they? How many come each semester? Do they lecture in an auditorium, or do they come into the studios and talk and work with students?

- Does the program arrange job internships? Internships are one of the best tickets to a job following graduation. You'll want to have examples of recently awarded internships and find out with whom the students worked, as well as whether academic credit was given.

- Check out the faculty biographies in the college catalog or on the school's Web site. See what degrees faculty members have and from which institutions (look for a high percentage of M.F.A.'s or equivalent degrees) as well as their professional experience in terms of awards and exhibitions. Often, professional artists will have their own personal Web sites as well. And don't forget to check out the liberal arts faculty; liberal arts are part of the B.F.A.

- A good B.F.A. program should have a career development center that helps students in both placement and assessment. Are the opportunities local and/or national? Does the center help students assess their abilities, skills, and interests early on and assist them in putting together their programs of study?

- Try to find recent graduates of the program. Are they working in their chosen field? What kind of entry-level jobs did they get? What internships helped them? What aspects of their college curriculum helped them?

Later, you can use a pros and cons list and compare schools to see which one matches your needs, talents, interests, and goals the best. But don't forget to trust your first impressions—often a school just "feels" like home right away. When it's the right fit, you know it.

Applying and Getting In

Colleges and universities all compete for students, so don't let the college admission process intimidate you. Develop the best portfolio you can, select five to eight schools, and pay close attention to your applications. You might find that the hardest part of the process will be choosing which offer of admission to accept!

The College Admissions Process

THE APPLICATION

When you have finally narrowed your list to five to eight schools, it is time to approach the applications. Application forms have several components. When you decide to apply to a school, do not go immediately to the school's Web site, fill out the application online, and submit it quickly. Rather, either download a copy and sit down with the print-out of the application, or if you cannot get the entire document downloaded, start to fill it out as a DRAFT and save as you go along, but do NOT hit "submit" until you have truly reviewed the entire document for completeness. (Note that many colleges now strongly prefer that you use the online application, and in recent times more than half of all applicants have applied online.)

If you are applying with a hard copy and via "snail mail," first, read the application carefully. Then make a photocopy of the application and fill it out as your draft. It is important that applications be neat and legible, either typed or printed in black or blue ink. Never submit an application that has been filled out in pencil or an odd color ink or that has been scribbled in haste. Fill out the informational section first and then think about the essay questions, if required.

If you do apply electronically, be sure to do a spell check and to print out your draft to proofread before transmitting it. Always print and save a hard copy for yourself. Some schools will ask you also to send a hard copy with the application fee.

Academic Profile

Colleges will require a copy of your high school transcript(s). Be sure that you have checked your transcript for accuracy before it is sent by your high school. Many schools will also require college entrance examination scores. Some schools use standardized test scores for placement, and some use them as another indicator in the academic profile. If you plan to apply to schools that require the SAT, ACT, or SAT Subject Tests and have not received scores that you think are truly representative of your ability, you should consider doing some test preparation and retaking the test to raise your score.

In analyzing your scholastic record, colleges are trying to decide if you will be able to withstand the academic rigor of their environment. If you are applying to a specialized school, your academic profile is secondary in consideration to your demonstrated talent, but at liberal arts colleges and for joint programs, the academic profile is more important in establishing the match. If you want to leave all options open for college, the most prudent approach is to take the most challenging assortment of academic courses, including math, science, and foreign language electives. However, if you absolutely know that you are applying to an art college, taking an extra year of something in which you are not strong is probably not going to have any effect on an admissions decision, and by not taking it you may have more time to take an art course that could help you prepare material for your portfolio. Be sure to speak to your guidance counselor about this and, if necessary, to call a few admissions officers for opinions.

Personal Profile

The personal profile that a college gathers on you consists largely of information that is entirely in your control. This includes your list of extracurricular activities, your recommendations, essays, and any appropriate supplementary materials you send. Let's consider each of these.

Extracurricular Activities

This term refers to any activity outside of the classroom. Many colleges will ask you to put this information in a table, showing the activity, any position of leadership, hours spent in the activity, etc.

As an artist, you may not have joined many clubs in your high school, focusing all your time on artistic endeavors. That's great! Do not hesitate to acknowledge such dedication. If you have participated in many activities, draft a list including school activities, any jobs you've held, hobbies, community or volunteer activities, church groups, honors, and awards. The point is to make the list comprehensive, but not exhaustive. Depth in one activity is important, so don't try to pad the list.

Recommendations

Many colleges request teacher recommendations as well as the guidance counselor report. You should choose teachers who know you well as a student and as a person, who like you, and who write well. You should also choose teachers who will add balance and another dimension to your application. For instance, if you plan on majoring in photography, consider asking your language arts teacher for a recommendation. When you ask a teacher to write a letter of recommendation, remember to:

- ask politely;

- give the teacher the forms, with the top part filled out with your name, etc., well before the deadline;

- provide the teacher with stamped envelopes addressed to the colleges; and

- include a cover letter to the teacher that gives the deadlines for each school, a list of your extracurricular activities, or anything else that might be helpful to the teacher in writing your recommendation.

Guidance counselors are often also asked to fill out a counselor recommendation form that may include a checklist and narrative. If you attend a large school where the counselors have many responsibilities other than college advising, you would do well to establish a relationship with your guidance counselor. Schedule meetings, stop by the office to ask quick questions, and, in general, make yourself known to him or her. Additional letters of recommendation from a non–high school teacher or from a boss can be helpful.

Essays

While most admissions representatives say that an essay will not make or break an application, there have been applicants who essentially "wrote" themselves into acceptance. The essay is another opportunity for the admissions committee to get to know you better. Even if the essay is optional, it's a good idea to provide one. A well-written essay will make your application more memorable and distinctive.

You must plan to write several drafts of your college essay. Ask your parents, a trusted friend, your college counselor, and/or a teacher to read it and give their reactions. While some editorial help is not out of line, never allow anyone else to write your essay. Admissions counselors know when you have not submitted your own work. Also, do not allow someone to edit so much that the tone becomes stale or stilted. Do have someone proofread your final draft, however.

The best essays resonate with the personal voice of the applicant, describing ideas in very specific, reflective ways that may reveal fears, fantasies, or insecurities but are always thoughtful, fresh, and spontaneous. The worst essays present a factual, often chronological version of an experience—the art history class's tour to Europe, for example—in a way that is totally lacking in creativity or individuality. The trip to Europe essay that simply describes arriving in Paris, visiting the Louvre, and then taking a bus to the next place is hardly riveting. The same essay telling how you got lost on the Metro and how you dealt with that situation becomes specific and says something about you.

There is no "right" essay, but there are several approaches that you should avoid. For example, do not submit a poem as an essay. If you also have talent as a poet, consider submitting a few select samples of your poetry as supplementary material. Also, do not use the essay as a moment to make excuses for something in your background. If you have a special situation, consider writing about it in a separate letter or asking a teacher or your guidance counselor to mention it in his or her letter of recommendation. Do not repeat information from other parts of your application, and avoid writing about trendy topics, your religious beliefs, relationships, sex, drugs or alcohol, or the importance of a college education. Do not try to impress an admissions committee with your vocabulary, revealing that you have thumbed through the thesaurus. Rather, write simply about something you really care about in a personally specific manner.

Try to limit yourself to the space provided, or type your essay on separate sheets and write, "See essay attached." In general, it is the quality, not the quantity, that counts.

Personal Statement

Many colleges require students applying for their art programs to submit a "Personal Statement" or "Statement of Intent" in addition to, or instead of, the admissions essay. The schools usually ask you to write about why you are applying to their program, what you hope to gain from the program, and what your career plans are. Be honest and try to mention something about the particular school—but be original. Don't, for instance, go on about New York being the center of the creative universe, which they no doubt have read thousands of times. Above all, make sure your statement is personal and revealing and shows that you have a passion for your art.

Interviews and Portfolios

When you read the catalog, note whether an interview is optional or required. Because of staff restrictions, travel difficulties, and financial constraints, very few colleges make the interview mandatory. If you do decide to have an interview, never drop in; be sure to make the arrangements well in advance. Often, specialized colleges do not hold interviews but just require that you send in your portfolio. At liberal arts colleges the interview is usually with an admissions representative, who might ask you briefly about your work but does not see your portfolio, which is submitted directly to the appropriate art department or school of art for evaluation. For advice on having a successful college interview, see "Acing Your College Interview" in this guide.

When evaluating portfolios, liberal arts universities usually use faculty members from the department or school of art. Art colleges use trained admissions staff members who are usually artists themselves, as well as faculty members. Portfolio evaluators at the more selective art colleges and universities are looking for more than raw talent. They are looking for a particular level of competency and technical skill as well as conceptual ability. The emphasis placed on conceptual ability versus skill varies from college to college because each has a different philosophy of education and programmatic thrust and looks for students who are a good match for that institution. What all colleges look for, however, are students who demonstrate through their artwork that they are creative, intellectually curious, and seriously invested and committed—even compelled—to make art. For more in-depth advice on preparing a portfolio, see "Developing an Undergraduate Visual Portfolio" and "Portfolio Advice from Admissions Directors" in this guide.

Deadlines

You can do yourself and the admissions office a favor by submitting your application before it is actually due. Remember to proofread your application before you mail or transmit it and to keep a copy of it for your files. If sent by standard "snail mail," it is a good idea to include a postcard saying, "College X has received the application from Mary Jones. Signed by admissions: Date:" Also, watch for a canceled check or check the statement of the credit card you used. Things do get lost in "snail" and electronic mail, and you want to be sure that your application does not go astray. And, if you are using e-mail or otherwise filing electronically, remember to print out a hard copy of whatever you transmit to save for your files, too.

Refer to the College Admissions Timetable on pages 41–45 and use it as a guideline for the admission process.

ADMISSIONS OUTCOMES

After the application and portfolio review, admissions committees meet to determine whether to admit you, reject you, or place your name on a waiting list. Beware that the weight of the letter or size of the envelope does not necessarily indicate the admissions decision.

If you are admitted to more than one school, weigh the pros and cons of each institution, perhaps visit again, ask lots of questions, and try to respond to the Office of Admissions in plenty of time, before their acceptance deadline. Most institutions comply with the guidelines established by the National Association for College Admission Counseling (NACAC) and the College Board, which set the Candidate's Reply Deadline (CRD) as May 1. If a school requires you to make a decision before that deadline or before you have heard from all of your schools, you have every right to question that institution. If, in order to make an informed decision about your college choice, you need more information, or if your financial aid package has not arrived in time to meet the deadline, call the college and request an extension of the deadline. If you do not contact the college at all by the college's deadline, the admissions staff may assume that you have decided to attend another institution and offer your place to someone on the waiting list. Be certain to contact your college by the deadline stipulated.

The wait list is a positive place to be. It means that a college realized your strengths, but due to a limited number of openings was not able to offer you admission at this time. Your initial response will probably be disappointment and irritation, but wait a few days before you do anything. Then you will be more able to make a rational decision about whether to remain active on a wait list or to accept the offer of another college that admitted you.

If you want to be considered from the wait list, now is the time to be even more proactive in demonstrating your desire to attend. Call, send an e-mail, and/or write to the college to say that you want to be considered from the wait list. Include any new information about yourself since the review of your application. If it is true, let a college know that if taken off the wait list, you will enroll. Talk to your guidance counselor about any further steps you should take and then be patient. You should probably submit a deposit to your second-choice school to protect yourself, in the event that the first choice does not take anyone from the wait list. If you are admitted from the waiting list, however, and intend to accept the offer of admission and enroll, be sure to immediately contact the school where you gave your deposit so that they may possibly offer your place to someone else. You should never make a deposit at more than one school, as multiple deposits are considered unethical in college admissions.

If You Want To Defer Admission

Often, a student who has been admitted will want to take a year off to travel or work. Many colleges and universities are pleased to grant a deferral of a year. They may give you guidelines about what they will allow you to do with the year. For instance, attending another college usually is not allowed, and they may give a new deadline for committing to enrollment. Some schools may ask for an account of what you have done with your time off.

INTERNATIONAL STUDENTS' CHECKLIST

Any student who is not a citizen or permanent resident of the United States is usually considered an "international" or "foreign" student (the term varies at schools). Many schools recruit abroad and most schools welcome students from abroad. The admissions procedures at most schools are the same for international students as for U.S. applicants. However, there are a few additional aspects international students should take into account.

- Begin your search extra early. International mail takes additional time and catalogs cannot be faxed at this point.

- Take advantage of the Internet and e-mail in expediting your questions, but always print a hard copy for yourself.

- Determine from each college or university whether you must take the TOEFL (Test of English as a Foreign Language), if English is not your native language. Arrange to take the test, if necessary, so that your scores can be submitted at the required time. Contact www.TOEFL.org or ETS at 609-771-7760.

- Be sure to study English intensively. There are many good English as a Second Language (ESL) programs both in the United States and abroad and many summer programs in the United States. An Internet search should help you to discover ESL programs available to you.

- Investigate the visa process early. Many conservatories or colleges will issue you a letter to present to a consulate in order to obtain a B-2 Prospective Student Visa. An I-20 will be issued to admitted students only. Everything regarding visas does take time, so plan ahead.

- Determine a school's policy on financial aid for international students. Government or state loans are not available to students from abroad, and many schools reserve their limited scholarship funds for domestic students. Some schools will not admit a qualified international student who has applied for financial aid. Be sure to ask for the current policy, and do not hesitate to ask for clarification of the policy if you are in doubt.

- Find out whether the school requires a guarantee of financial support in advance.

- Ask about tape or application pre-screening or regional auditions in your country.

- Complete the application on your own, especially the essays. If your English is not good enough to write an acceptable essay, you probably won't be able to understand the lectures or complete the assignments at a U.S. school.

- Be sure that schools know about your academic history in terms of the grading and overall educational system in your country. For instance, if no one from your high school has ever applied to schools in the United States before, you should send a prospectus or profile of your school.

- Some colleges and universities may require that your official transcript be reviewed or translated by the World Education Service (WES). Ask about the requirements of the specific schools. The Web address for WES is www.wes.org.

- Find out whether it is possible for international students to work while attending the program.

- Ask whether there are quotas on the number of students from a certain country or on foreign students in general.

- Find out about advisers and other support services for students from abroad.

- Find out if the program is authorized to grant Practical Training status to international students.

FINANCIAL AID

Many art students considering postsecondary education need some form of financial aid. Do not eliminate a school from your list just because of the school's cost. Often, the most expensive schools have the largest endowments and are able to be particularly generous in financial aid. In order to qualify for financial aid, you must apply for it. Many middle-income families, in particular, assume that financial assistance is not available to them; this may not be true. Read the catalog and any financial aid information very carefully, and be sure to speak to a financial aid officer at the college to which you are applying. Ask questions about the financial aid process and find out exactly what forms you will need. It is essential that you submit all the required forms and documents and meet deadlines in applying for financial aid. For safety's sake, keep photocopies of every form you send, whether you file these via regular mail or electronically.

Aside from scholarships, there are a variety of grants, loans, and work-study opportunities to help you finance your education. The Foundation Center, http://foundationcenter.org; 79 Fifth Avenue, New York, NY 10003 (212-620-4230), is an excellent resource and has regional branches in the United States. There are also many helpful financial aid guides at libraries and in guidance offices. Do not overlook religious organizations, community and civic organizations, or state programs in your quest for funding. There are also many fine Web sites, such as Petersons.com, CollegeScholarships.com, or Collegetoolkit.com that have fine information about funding higher education, but beware of those Internet sites that advertise and request a fee for finding you funds. Ask your parents to check if they work for a company or belong to an association or union that sponsors scholarships.

Here are some questions that you will want to ask about financial aid:

- Are scholarships based on merit? On need? On a combination of both?

- Are financial aid decisions made separately from admissions decisions?

- What percentage of students receives scholarships? Other financial aid?

- What are the most common mistakes people make in filling out financial aid forms?

- Should I assume that if my parents make (some dollar amount) as their income I would not be eligible for any aid?

- Do you have payment plans?

- What happens if I do not meet deadlines in filing forms for financial aid?

- Do you give financial aid to applicants admitted from the waiting list?

Deadlines are very important when applying for financial aid. It is critical that the FAFSA (Free Application for Federal Student Aid) and the CSS/PROFILE® be completed and submitted as early as possible. Many colleges have January and February deadlines for submission of the PROFILE. If parents have not completed their income tax returns by February, estimate income as accurately as possible, and submit corrections later in the process.

If the financial aid package you are offered is not adequate, or if your first-choice school offers less than a second or third choice, call the admissions or financial aid office of your first-choice school and discuss this with them. Schools may reconsider their original financial aid offer. They may ask you to send a copy of the other school's offer and then make you a counter-offer. In general, there is a great deal more comparative shopping and negotiating in financial aid these days.

College Admissions Timetable

Below is a general outline of how to proceed and pace yourself in the college admissions process. Your actual timetable may differ slightly, depending on the deadlines at the schools you have chosen. Keep an up-to-date spreadsheet with deadlines and use this as a list of guideposts.

SOPHOMORE YEAR (TENTH GRADE)

September–October

- Make learning and your education a priority, along with developing your art. Aim for balance.

- Take a practice PSAT/NMSQT in October. This is good practice for junior year, when PSAT scores count toward National Merit® Scholarships. (National Merit Scholarships are based on the scores you achieve on this test when you take it in your junior year.) Note that many schools require that sophomores take a practice PSAT, some make it optional to take, and other schools do not offer it to tenth-graders at all. It can be a useful exercise to take it in tenth grade, and you should inquire in September about taking it if your guidance counselor does not have everyone register.

December

- Obtain your PSAT results. Review the answer sheet. Talk to your guidance counselor about the advisability of taking a test-preparation course.

January–April

- Begin your review of Web sites for colleges and universities.

- Write for college catalogs. Read them, noting portfolio requirements.

- Obtain a social security number if you do not already have one.

- Investigate the National Foundation for Advancement in the Arts (NFAA) or ARTS annual scholarship competition and National Portfolio Days.

- Meet with your guidance counselor. Discuss course plans—APs, honors, or additional art—and other plans for your future.

- Research taking and registering for any SAT Subject Tests in a course in which you have done well and which may be required by the school you're interested in attending. Speak to your teacher first.

- Start researching financial aid and scholarship opportunities.

- Keep a file of various documents. Keep reviews, copies of art exhibit programs, photos, and any papers you have written about art and received good comments and grades on.

- Attend college fairs. Find out all you can about schools you are considering.

- Plan your summer to expand your experience in art. Participate in a summer art program. Remember to ask for letters of recommendation.

JUNIOR YEAR (ELEVENTH GRADE)
September

- Meet with your guidance counselor or college adviser to renew or establish your acquaintance. Review plans; register for the PSAT/NMSQT.

- Do well in your classes this year.

October

- Take the PSAT (again). Remember that this time it counts for National Merit Scholarships.

- Obtain information. Surf the Internet and get catalogs and applications from all the schools you are considering.

- Continue to investigate financial aid opportunities.

- Keep your spreadsheet up-to-date.

Applying and Getting In

December

- Review PSAT/NMSQT results. PSAT scores indicate what areas you need to strengthen for the SAT.

- Register for the SAT or ACT. Also consider SAT Subject Tests and the TOEFL, if appropriate. Prepare on your own or take a review course.

March–June

- Meet with your guidance counselor and parents/guardians to discuss college plans, your testing schedule, course selections for your senior year, college application essay topics, and any other related matters.

- Start your college visits.

- Take the SAT, ACT, TOEFL, and any SAT Subject Tests, if necessary.

- Attend college fairs.

- Plan another enriching summer.

July–August

- Continue your college visits and interviews over the summer.

- Continue to surf the Internet, send for applications, visit colleges, and interview.

- Work on your portfolio.

SENIOR YEAR (TWELFTH GRADE)

September–October

- Continue your college visits and interviews. Keep notes of your impressions.

- Meet with your guidance counselor or college adviser. Discuss your college list and try to narrow it down.

- Consider applying Early Decision to your top-choice school. Check deadlines. November 1 and November 15 are common dates.

- Get letters of recommendation from teachers and former employers.

- Apply for the ARTS recognition scholarship through NFAA. (National Foundation for Advancement in the Arts, 444 Brickell Avenue, Miami, FL 33131; 305-377-1140; www.artsawards.org.)

- Be sure you have all application forms. Start drafting college application essays.

- Attend or make plans to attend National Portfolio Days.

November

- Meet Early Decision deadline, if appropriate.

- Fill out college application forms. Continue to revise and perfect your essays.

- Take any additional tests: SAT, ACT, TOEFL, or SAT Subject Tests.

- Complete and submit your applications. Proofread them thoroughly and photocopy them before mailing.

- Request that ETS or ACT send your test results to the colleges that require them.

- Continue developing your portfolio.

December–January

- Early Decision results are mailed. Celebrate if you were admitted and meet all deadlines for enrollment deposits. If you were deferred or rejected, submit other applications and move on.

- Obtain the FAFSA and CSS/PROFILE® (if applicable) if you are applying for financial aid. Start filling out financial aid forms and be aware of deadlines.

- Finalize your portfolio.

- Forward transcripts and test scores. Be sure to have your guidance counselor or college adviser send transcripts and test scores to the schools you've chosen.

- Last chance to take the SAT and ACT.

February–March

- Check to make sure that all your financial aid documents are in order.

April

- Make your decision. Consider with your parents and adviser the pros and cons of each institution.

- Revisit any college if your decision to attend is not crystal clear.

- Notify colleges of your decision by May 1. If a school asks for a decision response before May 1, you have a right to request an extension until the May 1 Candidate's Reply Deadline (CRD).

May

- Be sure to notify all colleges by May 1, even if you are on the waiting list.

- Take any AP exams, if applicable.

Applying and Getting In

COLLEGE ADMISSIONS CHECKLIST

Use this convenient checklist to remind yourself of individual college admissions requirements and to record the progress of your application procedures.

College Name								
College Address								
Application Deadline								
Application Fee								
Required Tests:	Registration Deadline	Testing Date	Registration Deadline	Testing Date	Registration Deadline	Testing Date	Registration Deadline	Testing Date
PSAT/NMSQT								
SAT								
ACT								
Others								
Course Requirements Fulfilled								
Personal Interview Required								
Interview Date								
Portfolio Required								
Portfolio Date								
Applications Requested								
References Required								
Names/Addresses of References								
References Completed								
Application Filed								
Transcript Forwarded								
College Reply Date								
Financial Interview Required								
Required Financial Forms:								
CSS/PROFILE								
FAFSA								
Other								
Housing Deadline								
Housing Fee								
Housing Application Mailed								

Acing Your College Interview

A college interview is your opportunity to be more than just a stack of papers in the admissions office; it's your chance to personalize the process. Interviews do not usually make or break admissions decisions, but you should try to have an interview at those schools that are of real interest to you and are realistic choices.

TIMING OF INTERVIEWS

If you are prepared, plan your interviews as part of your campus visit. Don't schedule your first interview to be at your first-choice school; you'll do better after you've had some experience in an interview situation. Also, try to avoid making your first-choice school your last interview, as you want to remain fresh and spontaneous in your responses.

Practice interviews are helpful to some students. Ask your college counselor to conduct a mock interview with you or have a family friend role-play with you.

Schedule all interviews well in advance. And, if you cannot attend an interview appointment, be sure to call and cancel. A cancellation will not be held against you, but a missed appointment probably will be. If you get hopelessly lost en route to an interview and are running late, be sure to call.

GETTING READY

Preparing for an interview is important. Be sure to read the school's catalog and write down a list of questions that you want to ask. Take time to think about your strengths and weaknesses, and be prepared to speak about them in a positive way. College interviews are not the time for modesty and monosyllabic answers. At the same time, you do not want to sound boastful or arrogant.

Take stock of the extracurricular activities in which you have participated, your hobbies, volunteer work, and other ways that you spend your time. If there are special circumstances in your life that have affected your academic record, you may want to bring them up at an interview. For instance, if you missed a great deal of school because your family went through a particularly grueling year, with divorce, unemployment, or sickness, you may want to talk about it with your interviewer. Be careful not to sound as though you are making excuses for yourself, but rather adding to the college's understanding of who you are.

And above all, be prepared to talk about art in general and your artwork in particular in an intelligent and meaningful way, whether you are interviewing with someone who sees your portfolio or someone who never sees it at all.

WHAT TO WEAR

Just as there are costumes for performances, there are interview "costumes." For women, a nice skirt (not too short) or pants and a blouse, possibly with a jacket, or a simple dress is recommended, worn with low to medium heels. Men should wear nice pants with a shirt, jacket, and tie, or a turtleneck or shirt with a collar. Be neat and clean.

TYPICAL INTERVIEW QUESTIONS

Every interviewer has his or her favorite questions, but there are some common areas that are covered in most interviews. These include:

- Your high school experience

- Your personal traits, relationships with others, and family background

- Your interests outside the classroom—hobbies, extracurricular activities, summer vacations, movies you've seen, etc.

- Your values and goals, and how you view the world around you

- Your impressions of the college you are visiting

- Answering your questions

You might anticipate questions like these:

- Tell me about your high school. How long have you attended? What are the students like? Do you like your high school? What would you preserve or change about it?

- Which courses have you liked most? Which least? Which have been the most challenging?

- How well do you think your school has prepared you for your future study?

- How would you describe yourself as a student?

- Do you know what you want to major in?

- What has been your most stimulating intellectual experience?

- What extracurricular activity have you been most involved in? How much time do you devote to it?

- Do you have hobbies or special interests?

- After a long, hard day, what do you enjoy doing most? What do you do for fun?

- How have you spent your summer vacations? Why did you decide to spend them that way?

- How would you describe yourself in five adjectives?

- What is your family like? Describe your upbringing. How has your environment influenced your way of thinking?

- How would your friends describe you?

- Which relationships are most important to you? Why?

- Have you ever encountered people who thought and acted differently from you? What viewpoints or actions challenged you the most? How did you respond? What did you learn about yourself?

- What do your friends and family expect of you? What pressures have you felt?

- If you had a year to go anywhere and do whatever you wanted, how would you spend that year?

- What magazines or newspapers do you read regularly?

- What books have you read recently? Are there any authors you particularly like?

Applying and Getting In

- What movie have you seen recently and what did you think of it?

- Who are your favorite artists? Why?

- How did you choose your particular area of art? Why do you want to pursue this art form?

- Who has been your most memorable teacher? Why?

- Why do you want to go to college?

- Why have you chosen this college to investigate? What first brought us to your attention?

- What do you picture yourself doing ten years from now?

- What do you think of the National Endowment for the Arts (or some current affair in the arts)?

- What distresses you most about the world around you? If you had the opportunity to change the world, where would you start?

- Are there any outside circumstances that have interfered with your performance in school? An after-school job? Long commute back and forth to school? Home responsibilities or difficulties? Illness? Parental pressure? English not spoken at home? Problems with course scheduling?

- What more do you want to know about us?

This last question is your opening to ask your questions. Do not be shy about taking out your list; no one expects you to memorize a list of questions, and you want to be sure that you are learning all that you can during your visit to make the decision as to whether or not this is a campus where you could be happy. Many of the questions regarding campus life were probably answered by your tour guide or student host. Here are some other general questions you may want to ask.

- Who teaches freshmen? Transfers?

- How does registration work? Is it easy to get the classes I want to take?

- What is the advising system like? What are its strengths and weaknesses?

- Are there any changes anticipated in the curriculum?

- Are there any departments that might be cut or discontinued? What departments have been discontinued in the past two years?

- Are there any planned cutbacks in faculty? Any new appointments scheduled?

- Are there any new programs being contemplated? What are they?

- What percentage of students receive financial aid?

- Are there jobs on campus for students? What is a typical work/study job? Are there jobs in the community?

- Are there any opportunities for internships? Study abroad?

- Are financial aid decisions made separately from admissions decisions? Will applying for financial aid influence admissions decisions?

- Do you have any merit-based scholarships?

- What is your policy on fee waivers, if I cannot afford the application fee?

- What is the overall financial security of the school? Is tuition increased annually? What additional fees might I anticipate?

- What is most important in admissions decisions?

WHAT NOT TO DO AT YOUR INTERVIEW

Here are some things you should *not* do at an interview:

- Smoke

- Chew gum

- Complain or make excuses

- Swear or use language that it too colloquial

- Exhibit a negative attitude (bored, arrogant, etc.)

- Answer in monosyllables or one-sentence answers

- Ask questions if you have no interest in the response

- Ask for an evaluation of another school you are considering

- Bring your scrapbook of reviews, articles, or term papers for the interviewer to read

- Dress in an inappropriate fashion

- Twitch, fidget, or slump in your seat

- Pretend to be someone you are not. Be yourself!

AFTER YOUR INTERVIEW

Be sure to write down your impressions of the interview for future reference. And, most important, write the interviewer a thank-you note. Mention something specific that came up in the conversation. Three lines on nice stationery or even a postcard should be sufficient.

Developing an Undergraduate Visual Portfolio

Heidi Vee Metcalf

WHAT IS AN UNDERGRADUATE VISUAL PORTFOLIO?

A visual portfolio can mean many things to many colleges, and you should always consult directly with the colleges to which you are applying to determine what you should include in your portfolio as well as how you should submit it—whether in slide form, in person, as prints, etc. However, there are standard things that most colleges require in an admission portfolio. Therefore, for the purpose of this article, a visual portfolio is defined as any collection of works that appeal to the sense of sight, including but not limited to the following: drawings, paintings, films, photography, computer imagery, ceramics, sculpture, and printmaking.

WHAT ROLE DOES CREATIVITY PLAY IN THE VISUAL PORTFOLIO?

A college entrance portfolio is a collection of your artwork; it should be personal and creative by nature. We all see the world differently, and what you choose to draw, say, from a given still life is not likely to be what your classmates draw. There will be common elements but your work will be infused with your touch, vision, and interpretation. Your portfolio should reflect you. It should show off your skill set at this particular time in your life and expression of the world. Therefore, creativity is important to the makeup of your portfolio and can be expressed in something as simple as an angle, position, subject, proportion, etc.

WHEN SHOULD YOU START DEVELOPING YOUR PORTFOLIO?

Developing a visual portfolio for college entrance typically begins in your sophomore or junior year of high school. Creating art is like playing an instrument. It takes time and practice. In music, you need to master the notes, and in art, you need to master the mark making. Every work you create, be it good or bad, will bring you closer to a finished body of work. The more time and energy you put into developing your skills, the better your chances will be of producing a college-level entrance visual portfolio.

WHY DRAW FROM OBSERVATION?

Once you start the process of looking at specialty art schools or programs, you most likely will begin to hear the phrase, "drawing from observation." In other words, you need to create works that are derived by observing. You look at an object or objects and you create a drawing, painting, sculpture, etc., from this direct observation. Those students who have been trained in high school to draw from observation know the importance of showing this concept in their portfolio. Observational work is an important part of a portfolio.

Most specialty schools do not encourage or will even not permit drawings done from two-dimensional photographs, magazine pictures, etc. The reason for this is quite simple: the physical process of reproducing a two-dimensional image to a two-dimensional surface is easy, but the physical process of translating the three-dimensional world (still life, landscape, people, etc.) onto a two-dimensional surface (your paper, canvas, etc.) is complex and requires really paying attention to how the components in your still life, landscape, etc. relate to each other, particularly how these components intersect.

How to Improve Your Drawing Skills

If you started late, you may need to improve or develop your drawing skills before you start putting together your portfolio. Or perhaps you started early but feel like you could use some help getting a new perspective on your skill level. We recommend taking a pre-college or college class while you are still in high school to both develop your skills and also assess your own level of commitment to art. Pre-college classes are offered at numerous specialized art schools and vary from once-a-week courses that run for several weeks to intensive summer programs that run five days a week for a month. These programs can kick-start a portfolio in your sophomore or junior year, often offer different majors or subjects, and give you an opportunity to sample a particular major.

Another option is teaching yourself, which is a bit more challenging but can be done with some good reference books. We recommend picking up a few "how to" books from your school library or local bookstore. Two good "how to draw" books are *Keys to Drawing* by Bert Dodson and *Drawing on the Right Side of the Brain* by Betty Edwards. If you need some help with color theory, check out *Color Theory* by Jose M. Parramon. And finally, if you want to teach yourself to improve or develop your drawing skills, master the "blind contours," drawing without looking at the paper.

WHAT SIZE SHOULD MY WORKS BE? WHAT SUBJECT MATTER SHOULD I INCLUDE IN MY PORTFOLIO?

Size is important to your portfolio, and concentrating on the larger rather than smaller work is always recommended in portfolio development. You want to experience drawing objects life-size or larger. You can learn faster and show off your skills more readily if your work is not too small to see. Schools usually don't make you stick to a particular size, but 18 × 24 is a good place to begin—working up and down from that size.

Many schools recommend or require a self-portrait and a pencil rendering of a still life. If you are stuck for ideas, here are a few tried-and-true drawing subjects for you to tackle.

Self-Portrait: Draw yourself from a mirror and do it often. Try different mediums and sizes. Life-size is always a good place to start.

Footwear: Footwear is a great subject. It's not only fun to draw but can have a great deal of character because shoes, boots, slippers, ice skates, sneakers, etc., take on the character of their owner's foot. Be creative and try to come at footwear from a different direction.

Glass Bottles/Cups/Vases: Translucent, transparent, or just a plain reflective surface, glass of any kind is challenging to draw and is a good way to flex your drawing muscles.

Metallic Objects/Pots/Pans/Chrome: If you really take a look at a metal teapot or cooking pan, you will understand the challenges that are to be found in reflective surfaces such as metal. At first glance it's just shiny, but through further investigation, everything in the room—including you—is now twisted and distorted across the metal surface.

Fabric: Michelangelo created an abundance of fabric studies in his day in order to master the flow of fabric over the human form. Fabric is metamorphic. It has its own texture and reflects light accordingly, but it's malleable and can contour to form its subject.

Paper Bags: Angular and crisp, paper bags seem easy enough to draw, but try getting your drawing to look, feel, and sound like paper.

Hard-boiled Eggs: Light is a beautiful subject, and watching light float across white hard-boiled eggs is eye-opening.

Objects in Nature: Nature is a good place to go searching for subjects to draw. Whether it's flowers, bugs, fruits, or plants, there is always something in nature that can add color, texture, and design to your portfolio.

Landscapes/Cityscapes: Pull up a piece of grass or slab of concrete; drawing the land or cityscapes around you can demonstrate your ability to create perspective on a grander scale than the common still life, pushing houses, buildings, and lines further into the page.

WHAT ABOUT SKETCHBOOKS AND UNFINISHED WORKS?

Most colleges accept and even want to see your sketchbook and unfinished works as part of your portfolio as long as you have enough other work to demonstrate the full range of your skills. A word to the wise: If you do have a sketchbook, make sure there is enough work in it to make it worth showing. In addition, if you have unfinished artwork or work in progress, make sure there is a reason for showing it. Perhaps the unfinished work is a great idea or is just coming out extremely well. Make an active choice to include or exclude works.

HOW MANY WORKS SHOULD BE INCLUDED IN A VISUAL PORTFOLIO?

The number of pieces required will vary from school to school, and you should research your prospective school(s) by looking at their admissions Web sites. Typically, however, you should have at least eight to twenty pieces in your portfolio. The majority of schools will require ten to eighteen works, and most will not accept more than twenty. A word of advice: Don't include the weak pieces just to have more work in your portfolio. Less truly can be more. If the school requires twelve and you have twelve strong pieces, stick with the twelve. Don't add works that are weak to reach the maximum number of works. Weak pieces can pull down the overall quality of your portfolio and should not be included if they are not required.

HOW CAN I GET SOME ADVICE ON MY WORK?

A preliminary review is important in order to understand what needs to be done to create a quality portfolio. You should take advantage of the many National Portfolio Days throughout the United States and Canada. For more information about the National Portfolio Day Association (NPDA), go to www.npda.org. These events are designed to help students understand what is required in a college entrance portfolio. Even if you only bring a few pieces, it is better to know up front what needs to be done in order to meet the portfolio requirement. If you wait until you are a senior to show someone your portfolio, you could be creating an unnecessary problem for yourself. So start early, and do your research at least in the beginning of your junior year.

WHAT MEDIA SHOULD I INCLUDE IN MY PORTFOLIO?

Most schools do not require you to present particular media. However, most do expect you to have a number of works in pencil and a few works done in other media. The most common media are pencil, charcoal (soft or hard), pastels (oil or dry), paint (oil, acrylic, watercolor, or colored inks or dyes), photography, computer-generated work, printmaking (block, etching, silk screen, or lithography), and collage. You are not required to have all, and the most important aspect of the media you choose is that you use them well and the works are strong. If possible, your portfolio should have works in black & white, color, and a few three-dimensional works. Variety and quality are the key points when deciding on media. If you cannot seem to master a particular medium, don't include it. Quality should not be compromised for variety.

WHAT IS A HOME EXAM/HOME TEST?

A home exam or home test is required at some college(s) in addition to the general portfolio. These home exams/tests give you a particular problem to solve and typically ask for this problem to be solved in particular dimensions. Some schools require that the original home exam/test work be mailed to them directly, and in some cases you cannot have this work back. Therefore, it is important that you document all of your work so that you have a record of your early works. You should check with all your potential school(s) to find out what requirements they may have for the home exam/test. These home exams/tests can get very detailed in terms of the particular requirements such as size, medium, etc. Pay close attention to the fine print.

HOW CAN I EDIT MY VISUAL PORTFOLIO?

When it comes to editing your work, there are many ways to get the job done. The first and most obvious way of editing your work is to have your high school art teacher help you out. The second way is to have a classmate or family member help you critique your work and edit using this information. The third way is to have a pre-review by one of your potential colleges. (See How Can I Get Some Advice on My Work?) The fourth way is to make sure you are not keeping works in your portfolio that are weak just because they have sentimental value. If you did a work in seventh grade and everyone thought it was the greatest work you'd ever done, don't assume it's still great. You have grown, and hopefully your work has grown too. Finally, the most important aspect of editing your work is you. After you have collected all necessary opinions, remember you have the final word on what stays in and what is left out.

HOW DO I PRESENT OR SUBMIT MY VISUAL PORTFOLIO?

Each school has its own requirements in regards to how you should and how you can submit work. Most schools do not require your work to be matted or framed and some even encourage you not to do so. Some schools will review your work in person and grade your portfolio and require no other reproductions. Other schools may review your work in person but also require reproductions to be sent with your applications. Still other schools may not offer personal interviews and may require all applicants to submit reproductions. Therefore, you need to get the details of what your potential school(s) requires. Don't wait to find out this information in your senior year. Do your research early and learn what will be expected of you.

However, no matter what the requirements of your potential school(s), it is recommended that you take slides of your visual work to keep as a visual record of your artwork history. To this day, I still have my slides from high school and I am grateful to my high school art teacher for stressing the importance of visual documentation. Most schools will accept slides and some even require them. However, some schools will accept images of your work either on a VHS, CD-ROM, DVD, via the Internet, or printed out, typically in an 8 × 10 format. It is extremely important that you find out the format required and/or accepted by your potential school(s). There may be size requirements and program requirements that are critical to the application process. At Pratt, we often receive CDs and DVDs with files that cannot be opened, and I am sure we are not alone.

Reproducing Your Work

35-mm Slides

You can take your own slides easily, provided you have or can borrow a 35-mm camera, a tripod, and daylight 200-slide film. Most high schools that offer photography have a 35-mm camera and tripod that you may be able to borrow or use at the school to take your slides. Even if your school doesn't have a photography department, you may want to talk to your art teacher or guidance counselor to see if there is any assistance or equipment available at your school.

Once you have your 35-mm camera, tripod, and daylight 200-slide film, the rest is pretty easy. First, set your 35-mm camera according to the instructions on the film. Then select a room that is evenly flooded with natural light. Do not use inside lighting, spot lights, etc. Use natural light only and not direct natural light. Then select a flat wall and place a large piece of black felt or board on the wall in an area larger than your largest two-dimensional works. Place each piece in the center of this black field individually, move in tightly on each image (close enough not to have too much excess space and not too close as to cut off part of your image) and take the number of slides you need of each work. Duplicates generally cost more than developing the slide directly from the film, so you should take multiple slides of the same artwork.

Three-dimensional works are shot by draping a piece of black felt or velvet over a box on a table. The goal here is to have the three-dimensional image completely surrounded by the black field.

Digital Images to Slides

With today's technology, it is possible to have digital images of your work converted into 35-mm slides. Generally, you will need to make sure you take the digital images using a similar ratio as the 35-mm slide film, such as 2 × 3 or 3 × 2, depending on the direction of your work. This translates into a pixel size of 1,200 × 1,800 or 1,800 × 1,200. Most companies that convert these images into slides accept the standard tif or jpeg files. You should also note that we don't recommend that you take images using a pixel size smaller than 600 × 900 as this will produce blurry results.

Digital Images on VHS, Photo Paper, CDs, DVDs, or Web Sites

No matter how you want to present your digital work, it is critical that you check with your potential schools for their requirements and restrictions.

Although stressful at times, creating your portfolio should be an enjoyable endeavor. The process alone should help your artwork improve and develop. Specialty schools require hard work once you're in, and getting into most of these schools requires putting the necessary time and energy into your portfolio.

Reprinted with permission of Heidi Vee Metcalf, Director of Admissions at Pratt Institute, Brooklyn, New York.

Portfolio Advice from Admissions Directors

Here is what some admissions directors at top art colleges across the country say about portfolios.

JANET SCHIPPER
Assistant Director of Admissions Operations
Otis College of Art and Design

One of the most important elements of the admission process is the portfolio. It demonstrates a student's artistic experience, education, and talent and helps us identify creative, talented students who will work hard at Otis and be successful.

What we look for in an admission portfolio is a balance between technical skills and creativity.

The B.F.A. program at Otis begins with the Foundation Year, during which students take four studio art classes: drawing and composition, figure drawing, second design, and third design along with their academic classes, such as English, art history, and social science. The idea is that studying basic drawing, design, and creative thinking will prepare students to enter any of Otis's seven majors.

Students applying to Otis directly from high school are applying to Foundation. Because of the Foundation Year emphasis on drawing, we like to see examples of "observational drawing," which is drawing by looking at a real object, person, or scene. A still life drawing with fruit and other small objects is a familiar kind of observational drawing. Other kinds of artwork, such as photographs, paintings, sculptures, digital prints, PowerPoint presentations, animations, etc., can be important in the admission portfolio and show different kinds of technical skills. For creativity, we suggest students submit the work they think is their best. It should show their ideas, personal expression, and passions.

For students who wish to transfer to Otis at the sophomore or junior level, the portfolio needs to show a higher level of experience—the same level and quality of skills that we expect from students who have attended Otis from the Foundation Year.

Visual

Arts

Students who are interested in Otis are always encouraged to visit the campus and bring their artwork. An admissions counselor can give feedback and suggestions for how to make the portfolio fit the criteria we use in making admission decisions.

JULIE HINGELBERG
Dean of Enrollment Services
College for Creative Studies

An acceptable portfolio is one that exhibits technical and conceptual preparation for college-level work at the College of Creative Studies. All portfolios must include a minimum of ten pieces representing your selected major or areas of strength.

General Guidelines

- **Edit your work.** Quality is more important than quantity. Ten great pieces are better than twenty that are inconsistent. Work completed within the last two years is usually the strongest.

- **Neatness counts.** Present your drawings and other work neatly on paper. Matted or mounted work is preferable, but not required.

- **Drawings.** If drawings are included in the portfolio, draw from observation of objects, scenes and people. Include good descriptive or representational drawings. Include accurate line drawings and good examples of fully-rendered compositions using a complete range of light, middle, and dark values. If possible, include figure drawings or partial-figure drawings (hands, feet, etc.) or portraiture.

- **Be original.** We would like to see work that expresses your ideas and feelings about a subject.

- **Consider the entire picture surface.** Try not to isolate one object in the center of the page.

For the following majors, portfolios should include:

- *Advertising Design:* A combination of conceptual or observational drawings, 2-D design (traditional or digital), short films or videos, software exploration (Photoshop, Illustrator, etc.), photography, lettering samples, and creative writing or any other conceptual thinking.

- *Animation and Digital Media:* A combination of photographs, 2-D design in either traditional or digital forms, live-action short films or animations, drawing, creative writing, or any 3-D work.

- *Crafts:* A combination of work from the following list: ceramics, glass, metals, fiber, painting, sculpture, prints, photography, video or digital, or drawings.

- *Fine Arts:* Five drawings of any kind. The remainder should represent solid examples of your best creative efforts in any medium; they may include, but are not limited to, painting, sculpture, prints, photography, crafts, video, or digital.

- *Graphic Design:* A combination of work from the following list: photographs, collages, software exploration (Photoshop, Illustrator, etc.), printmaking, lettering samples, drawing, creative writing, or any 3-D work.

- *Illustration:* At least five drawings from direct observation. The remainder can represent your selected major or areas of interest.

- *Industrial Design (includes Product and Transportation Design):* At least five drawings from direct observation. The remainder can represent your selected major or areas of interest.

- *Interior Design:* At least five drawings from direct observation. The remainder can represent your selected major or areas of interest.

- *Photography:* A combination of photographs and other forms of 2-D or 3-D design that expresses your creative potential.

- *Undeclared:* At least five drawings from direct observation. The remainder can represent your areas of interest.

THERESA BEDOYA
Director of Admissions
Maryland Institute, College of Art

Each art college has expectations and academic requirements particular to the program of study you choose. For most professional colleges, the evaluation of your portfolio will supersede the review of all other criteria for admission. The term "competitive" will have a different meaning if you are applying to a professional college specializing in art. The goal of the selective art colleges is to admit students of extraordinary talent. Many visual arts colleges even prescreen potential applicants through review of the portfolio prior to application in order to determine eligibility for admission.

In contrast, most comprehensive colleges and universities offering majors in art rely on academic criteria to make an admission decision. The portfolio, if required, plays a secondary role. You should take these factors into consideration when deciding whether or not to apply to a specialized art college.

That said, you should gain as much studio experience as possible in order to develop a strong portfolio. Take full advantage of your high school art program and enroll in extra Saturday or summer classes. Exhibit your artwork when the opportunity is provided. Become better informed as an artist by studying art history and the works of contemporary artists.

JON FRASER
Senior Associate Dean
School of Visual and Performing Arts
Long Island University, C.W. Post Campus

No school is expecting you to be Pablo Picasso when you walk in the door for a portfolio review. What they are all looking for is potential and talent. There are no standard portfolio requirements. They vary from school to school. Make sure that you know what each school is looking for, and adhere strictly to its requirements. It could be that one style of portfolio presentation will work for several schools, but be prepared to change and alter your portfolio to match a specific school's requirements. To find out what an individual school may want, check the Web site, or call directly to the department. If you call, simply tell the person answering the phone that you'd like to speak to someone about portfolio requirements. Then, ask them the questions below, along with any other questions you may have.

Your portfolio should be as professional as possible. It should also show you to your best abilities. Try to choose material that shows who you are as an individual. Make brave choices. Remember that the people viewing your work are seeing hundreds of potential students, so you need to stand out (in a good way) to be recognized.

How various schools look at your portfolio is entirely subjective. One school may love you and offer you a scholarship based on your portfolio; the next school will reject you entirely based on that same portfolio. There's no way to make sense of it, so just do the best you can. Try to maintain a positive attitude and make sure you know:

- How many pieces should be included

- Whether the school will accept slides, photographs, or CD-ROMs of your work

- What media the school is interested in seeing

- How to talk about your work intelligently

RITA GAGLIANO
Executive Director of Admission
Savannah College of Art and Design

Before formally submitting your portfolio for review, you will want to be sure you are clear regarding the submission formats required by each institution. Generally, traditional visual artwork is submitted in slide format. If slides are required, determine whether they must be included in a plastic slide sheet for viewing or whether they may be submitted in a box for later transference to a slide carousel. In any case, slides should always be properly cropped using film tape (available at most photo shops). Label each slide with your name and the title of the work. Give some indication of the orientation of the piece if it's unclear which side should face up.

More recently, some colleges are allowing students to submit visual artwork on CD-ROM. If submitting traditional work on CD-ROM, be sure to check your disk on a number of computers to be sure you have saved your work properly and that it can be easily opened by others. Most files should be saved as high-resolution JPEG files to allow for easy viewing on most computers.

Students submitting computer-generated artwork may submit the work in digital format on CD-ROM, DVD, or VHS videotape. If submitting a VHS tape, be sure it is NTSC formatted. Generally, all 2-D and 3-D images should be saved as high-resolution JPEG files, Adobe PDF files, or digital portfolios created in PowerPoint, Director, Flash, or HTML. Again, be sure you check for submission format specifications as required by the college to which you are applying.

Real-time animations and work with multimedia content may be submitted on DVD or in formats compatible with Quicktime, RealTime, or Windows Mediaplayer. Film and video work, along with performing arts auditions, may be submitted on VHS tape or DVD. Be sure these types of pieces are acceptable by the institution to which you are applying. If a college or university will accept your online portfolio, be sure to include all letters in the URL address and that the site is working. Have friends try it out from their home computers and get their feedback on ease of navigability. Keep in mind that schools receive a significant number of portfolio submissions each year and rely on your efforts to move efficiently during the review process.

Some colleges accept work in a wide variety of media, including photography, sound design, performing arts, and architectural viewbooks, among others. Be sure the various media are welcomed by the college and then ascertain the submission format requirements.

Regardless of format, all students should include an inventory sheet. The inventory sheet provides the opportunity to identify each piece by title or project, medium (or software/materials used), size, and date of completion. Some students include a description of the work and an explanation of the inspiration for the piece. This is a nice touch and allows the reviewer a glimpse of the artist's motivation and passion.

Applying and Getting In

National Events That Can Help You Prepare

NATIONAL PORTFOLIO DAYS

Each year, members of the National Portfolio Day Association sponsor National Portfolio Days in thirty-five cities across the nation and in Canada. These events provide an opportunity for students interested in pursuing undergraduate or graduate study in the visual arts to meet with representatives from some of the most outstanding colleges, universities, and independent schools that teach art and design. Attendees have their portfolio of artwork reviewed and gain guidance about their future artistic development. Participating institutions also provide information about programs of study, careers in art, admission requirements, financial aid, and scholarships.

Posters announcing dates and locations are mailed in September to high school art departments. You can also visit www.npda.org for more information.

ARTS RECOGNITION AND TALENT SEARCH PROGRAM (ARTS)

ARTS is a national program designed to identify, recognize, and encourage high school seniors and other 17- and 18-year-old artists who demonstrate excellence in dance, film and video, classical instrumental music, jazz music, voice, theater, visual arts, photography, and writing. ARTS is a program of the National Foundation for Advancement in the Arts (NFAA), an independent, nongovernmental institution dedicated to the support of young artists.

NFAA offers an award package of more than $1 million for ARTS applicants whose work has been judged as outstanding by a national panel of experts. Students selected for recognition share cash awards totaling more than $500,000, with individual awards ranging up to $10,000 each. Each January, up to 160 students are invited to participate in an all-expenses-paid ARTS Week in Miami. ARTS Week consists of master classes, performances, exhibitions, workshops, and final live adjudications. In addition, through the Scholarship List Service, NFAA provides the names of all ARTS applicants who are seniors in high school to colleges, universities, and professional institutions that are actively recruiting students in the creative and performing arts.

NFAA is also the exclusive agent for nominating selected ARTS winners to the Commission on Presidential Scholars, which names the Presidential Scholars in the Arts. For an application form and more information, contact the NFAA at 800-970-ARTS (toll-free) or apply online at www.NFAA.org.

PERFORMING AND VISUAL ARTS COLLEGE FAIRS

The NACAC (National Association for College Admission Counseling) Performing and Visual Arts College Fairs are events for college and college-bound students interested in pursuing undergraduate and graduate programs of study in the areas of music, dance, theater, visual arts, graphic design, and other related disciplines. Attendees learn about educational opportunities, admission and financial aid, portfolio days, audition and entrance requirements, and much more by meeting with representatives from colleges, universities, conservatories, festivals, and other educational institutions with specialized programs in the visual and performing arts.

For information about NACAC's Performing and Visual Arts College Fairs, call the national office at 800-822-6285 (toll-free). For a schedule, visit www.nacacnet.org.

Applying and Getting In

You're In! What's Next?

You have followed your dream and it has paid off. What will your life be like as a full-time art major? And what lies ahead for you if you decide to become a professional artist? Turn the page and find out from those in the know.

The Importance of Foundation Studies

Maureen Garvin

Foundation studies programs are an integral part of a visual arts education. These programs are a series of studio classes taken during the first year of study in an art college or program. The primary function of foundation programs is to prepare all students to be successful in their major programs.

The names of the foundation programs are variations on the terms "Visual Fundamentals" and "Preliminary Courses," which were used to describe the first year in the Bauhaus, a design school founded in Germany that migrated to Chicago in 1937. The structure and content of many of today's foundation programs developed from traditions established in the Bauhaus: material exploration and an understanding of form, color, and composition. More contemporary terms such as "Core Studio Practice" and the more common "Foundation Studies" are used to describe a sequence of classes that teach both the technical and conceptual skills needed to pursue any area of art and design.

LEARNING THE VISUAL LANGUAGE

While the sequence and titles of the foundation courses vary from college to college, the common goal is to teach visual literacy. Visual literacy is about understanding the language used in art and design. In the same manner that one learns French or Italian, one can learn about the elements of visual language: line, shape, value, color, and how to manipulate and compose these elements to visually communicate ideas. Georgia O' Keeffe said, "I found I could say things with color and shapes that I couldn't say any other way."

The elements and the principles of design are the language students use in their majors. In these first-year studio classes, students learn to handle a variety of media that can range from the traditional—charcoal, graphite, and gouache—to digital versions of these traditional tools. Foundation programs teach how to develop ideas, how to understand the terminology of visual language, and how to evaluate or critique the work. Most programs include drawing classes to train a student's eye and hand to see and translate information out in the real world into a visual representation or response. Learning to draw has been used as a method to train artists since the Renaissance.

Students often perceive foundation courses as something to get through to move on to "real" courses in the major. It can be a struggle to see the purpose of taking courses that appear unrelated to a major. The reality is that the visual language and skills learned in foundation courses are the common denominator in all the fields. Designing an ad, creating visual effects for a film, constructing a garment, and designing a building all begin with knowing how to manipulate visual language to relay content, an idea.

NEW WAYS OF SEEING

As a result of your foundation classes, you literally will begin to see in different ways. You will start to understand how artists and designers think—how one thought, sketch, or doodle leads to another and another and to a series of ideas that generate new designs or images. Another frequent outcome of taking foundation classes is that students accomplish what they never believed they could do. An example would be the drawing-phobic student who slowly realizes that he or she can actually draw and even reach a point where he or she wants to draw and enjoys the process of drawing. You will begin to make connections between the design principles you learn: balance, repetition, rhythm, emphasis, and why an image can look calm, boring, or comforting. You will look at an artist's work and understand what he or she was aiming to accomplish and how he or she went about it. (This can impress and amaze relatives.) New ideas will occur when looking at familiar objects. You might think, "The chair could be more comfortable and better-looking if the back was a different shape."

ADVANTAGES OF TAKING FOUNDATION COURSES

One advantage of beginning your career with the foundation courses is that you can picture yourself pursuing a variety of careers. You will be in classes with students who are interested in architecture, fashion, animation, furniture design, painting, and maybe a few majors you have never even heard of, such as sound design, broadcast design, or information architecture. Most first-year programs include the opportunity to take several electives to try out different areas of interest. Some students arrive with the desire to be a graphic designer and after taking an elective in ceramics or glass begin to see an entirely new future for themselves.

A second advantage of that first-year program is that you learn how to be disciplined, that good art and design come from practice and perseverance, and that creativity occurs with the willingness to go beyond what is obvious, to see, to visualize in new ways. Mary Stewart is a noted artist and author of a text frequently used in foundation studies courses, titled *Launching the Imagination: A Comprehensive Guide to Basic Design.* She writes about the seven characteristics of thinking: receptivity, curiosity, a wide range of interests, attentiveness, connection-seeking, conviction, and complexity. Throughout the sequence of foundation courses, you will learn not only the mechanics—the tools, techniques, and concepts— but how to think and see in new ways. You will be developing the ability to be a creative thinker.

A third advantage to foundation studies is that you will start to see the common language used in all the fields you could choose as a major. The edges of an architectural detail will remind you of lines in a drawing and a pattern on a fabric. This brings into play some of the characteristics to which Mary Stewart refers: connection-seeking, curiosity, and attentiveness.

SUMMING IT UP

- The primary function of foundation programs is to prepare all students to be successful in their major programs.

- The common goal is to teach visual literacy.

- Foundation programs teach how to develop ideas, understand the terminology of visual language, and how to evaluate or critique the work.

- "You are not only learning to draw but to see."

- One result of foundation classes is that you will begin to literally see in different ways.

- You will accomplish what you never believed you could do.

- A student can arrive with the desire to be a graphic designer and after taking an elective in ceramics or glass begin to see an entirely new future for himself.

- You will be acclimated to hard work and confident in your ability to learn. You will be ready.

Maureen Garvin is Dean of the School of Fine Arts, Savannah College of Art and Design

Typical First-Year Schedules

While all schools differ in their degree requirements, the following samples of first-year schedules for B.F.A. programs at a typical specialized college give you an idea of what a week in the life of an art major is like.

Computer Graphics

Mon	Survey of World Art	12:00–2:50
Tues	Imaging Techniques	9:00–11:50
Wed	Drawing	9:00–2:50
Thurs	Language and Literature	9:00–11:50
Fri	Introduction to Animation	2:00–6:50

Fine Arts

Mon	Painting	9:00–2:50
Tues	Sculpture	12:00–5:50
Wed	Drawing	9:00–2:50
Thurs	Free	
Fri	Survey of World Art	12:00–2:50
	Language and Literature	3:00–5:50

Photography

Mon	Free	
Tues	Digital Imaging	9:00–11:50
	History of Photography	3:00–5:30
Wed	Language and Literature	9:00–11:50
Thurs	Photo Workshop	9:00–2:50
	Studio Workshop	6:30–9:20
Fri	Free	

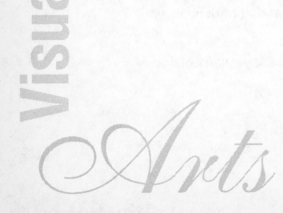

Visual Arts

Current Art Majors Tell All

ED MOORMAN
Comic Art
Minneapolis College of Art and Design

If you want to major in art, it's obvious to make sure that your portfolio is your focus; you want to have a variety of work, and you want to make sure that it's about something. Art is how you communicate, and you want to have something to communicate. The more specific your work is to you and the way that you feel, the more you'll stand out to admissions officers. Also, do as much work as you can outside of school and just push yourself. Sequester yourself in your room with your materials and follow all the ridiculous ideas you might have. Study history and artists that interest you and/or work within your chosen field. Trust your obsessions. Read, watch films, listen to music, and go to museums as much as you can. Everything you take in will feed and inform what you're doing.

When you go to Portfolio Days, pay attention to what the admissions officers are looking for. If, for example, they're looking to see if your proportions are dead-on or that you have included a landscape, a figure, etc., that says something about what the school cares about, because they're instructing their employees to find people who have these things. I went to a Portfolio Day and a popular school that shall remain nameless focused on those things alone while quickly sifting through my stuff. I went to the table for the Minneapolis College of Art and Design, and the admissions officer talked with me for a long time about my intentions and what I was doing, laughed at my comics, commented on my line quality, and generally seemed to be in tune with caring about me and how I was growing and would grow as an artist—instead of staunch criteria that has nothing to do with how a piece will affect the viewer. Lo and behold, MCAD is a great school.

As for once you're in school: I could advise you to learn how to manage your time, but you will learn through experience and stupidity (as we all do) that sleeping and eating are not negotiable enterprises.

Pay very close attention to selecting your teachers. Art school can cost your mortal soul in debts, and there's no reason you shouldn't have all fantastic instructors.

Watch out for debts! Don't pay for school on credit cards. There is a teacher at my school who lives part of the time in Ireland because he has been running from credit card bills ever since he left college.

If you're going to a good school, you will be amazed how easy it is to make friends, no matter how alienated or awkward you may have felt beforehand. As it always is, your friends will be your saving grace in art school, and what's more, they'll be your artistic peers. I always know that if I have trouble with a project and I need an objective viewpoint, there are certain friends of mine whose opinion I respect to the highest degree who will help out.

I'm majoring in comic art and will try my hand with independent publishers after college for awhile. Then, at some point, I'll go to graduate school and get a master's in art education, since I really want to be an art teacher.

As an artist, you may never make a great deal of money. You must make peace with this idea. My sculpture teacher talks about the janitors who are great novelists, the art museum guards who are great painters, etc., and there is always the possibility that that will be you. But if you think that your passion for art can drive you through school and life, you're blessed, because you will always have that and you will always be okay because of it.

DANIELLE SMITH
Film and Television, with a Minor in Sound Design
Savannah College of Art and Design

Visiting my sister who was attending a large university while I was still in high school allowed me to experience college life at an early age. I went to parties, football games, and sat in on a few of her classes—in an auditorium with hundreds of other students she barely knew. I can remember thinking, "Is something wrong with me or is this just not that appealing?" I mean, the only thing she did for fun was go to parties and sporting events. Right then and there, I promised myself I would make a different college decision—not for my parents, not for my friends, but for my future.

I requested catalogs from several different colleges with good film programs. I had decided I wanted to study film and that was that. By chance, I went with my video production club on a tour of the Savannah College of Art and Design and the rest is history. I brought my dad back for a visit and I remember thinking about it being the best college visit we had had out of the many colleges we visited up and down the East Coast. I applied, got in, and have never regretted my decision.

When I arrived at SCAD, I didn't know anyone. But that was a good thing. I knew that if I had gone to any of the other in-state colleges, I'd basically be living a rerun from high school. I knew that to grow I would need to expand my horizons by leaving my comfort zone. I can remember calling my friend during my first year of college to see how she was enjoying the new college life. The conversation went a little something like this:

"Hey, Jerry, what's going on? What are you up to?"

"Nothing much," she replied. "I'm just studying for this stupid science test I have tomorrow. What are you up to?"

"Oh, nothing really. I'm on a film shoot right now, so that's really cool. I got to work on a graduate student's film just yesterday too."

I wasn't trying to brag but I couldn't help but to express my excitement. She was amazed that I was already working in my major too.

At SCAD, it's like everyone is passionate about something. We love going to class and getting the chance to work with our favorite media. The best part about it is that our classmates love their work too, and they're excited to share it with you. It's never just busy work either. Every little thing you do can contribute to your portfolio if you want it to, and that makes students work even harder.

The networking possibilities are endless from the day you get here. From meeting graphic designers, architects, textile designers, and Hollywood directors, we experience it all. And we make connections with students in other majors. For instance, when I need an actor, I ask media and performing arts students. When they need headshots, they work with their photography friends. When photography students need to jazz up photos a little, they go to their graphic design friends.

I could seriously go on and on about how there's a tremendous networking cycle. I shot a music video for my senior project. If there's one thing you learn at SCAD, it's how to work in teams effectively. My roommate, who studies fashion, oversaw all of my costume design. A production design student was able to receive credit for being my art director. She took care of all my set design and worked closely with my production team and even had an assistant from the industrial design department help with the construction of the sets just because he was interested in helping. A metals and jewelry sophomore made a beautiful necklace with matching earrings for the singer to wear, and a sound design student came in to take care of the music playback. I couldn't have done it without them, not to mention the additional 11 film students who helped out in so many other ways.

A day in the life of an art student varies depending on the current projects on which he or she is working. The best advice I can provide is to make sure you're passionate about what you do. If you find yourself saying, "Well I guess that would be cool," then take a step back and really take into consideration what you enjoy doing and what you're good at. As a film and sound design student at SCAD, a typical day for me may start out attending an art history course, leaving there to grab a bite to eat, then going to recording studio class where I get to mix a film soundtrack. I might end my day as assistant director of a classmate's film project. That doesn't include my part-time job, studying, completing homework assignments, helping on other projects, and attending a Bahamian party or two. Yes, we party too! The next day could be completely different though. You need time management skills to survive.

My time is consumed by my passion for what I'm doing. I'm surrounded by people who love what they do, and that's important. It's never about making a grade. It's about producing my best work. With two internships under my belt, I feel even closer to the perfect career path: a job at an entertainment company in the music and television industry.

JOHN RENAUD
Fashion Design
Pratt Institute

It's 2:00 a.m. and I'm still in the studio, sewing machine buzzing away, and I have two more garments to make. I have been here since 9:00 a.m. Luckily, I have access to a 24-hour supply of coffee or I surely would be asleep on one of the cutting tables by now. I have to finish this collection; the fashion show is tomorrow. Some may think I have put myself in a dreadful situation, but I couldn't be happier. I am in bliss. I am creating. The hard work and long hours are worth the end result. The wave of relief and accomplishment that will come over me as my final model walks down the runway will be worth all the effort.

Many people think fashion design students sit around and draw pretty pictures all day. This is a common misconception. The truth is that fashion design, while it is my passion and I could never see myself doing anything else and being happy, is a tough, challenging, and very time-consuming major. At Pratt, fashion design students are constantly broadening their horizons through the many different classes they take. Classes in sportswear, knitwear, menswear, childrenswear, lingerie, tailoring, and numerous other subjects allow students to graduate with a more diverse knowledge of the multi-billion dollar fashion industry than any other school.

The required liberal arts classes give all art and design students the well-rounded education they need to get to the top of our fields. We are encouraged to expand our knowledge by taking our art electives in other departments. The professors in Pratt's fashion design department are fashion industry veterans. Many own their own lines, many have been head designers at major design companies, and all of them love teaching. Getting to work one-on-one with our teachers is a very important advantage we have over the larger, less-selective fashion design schools.

As I cut the final thread of the blouse I have been sewing, I glance at the clock. It's 3:34 a.m. I feel proud that I have finished this piece. It has taken all day. I then look to the cutting table at a pile of fabric and pattern paper. I still have two more to go.

KRISTEN SEGHERS
Art History
Rutgers University

Like a lot of students, I kind of fell into my major. I'd always had an appreciation for art and a critical eye, but I'd been planning on majoring in journalism in college. When it came time to register for spring classes during my freshman year I needed another course, and my adviser suggested I take art history. Luckily, I was on the crew team at the time and got to register early because art history courses usually fill up quickly; it's hard for a freshman to get in. It turned out to be my favorite class. So I took two more art history courses sophomore year and then knew I had found what I wanted to major in.

As I said, most introductory art history classes are popular and crowded. Some people think it's an easy way to satisfy a history requirement but later see they were mistaken. The large Intro to Art History lectures consist of those with an interest in art sitting in the front and those just trying to pass a history course in the back. So always try to sit with others who are engaged in the material and not just taking advantage of the dim lights (needed to view the slides) to catch up on sleep. And, as practically all my professors say, drink coffee: it's cheap and legal and will help combat the sleepiness that somehow befalls you in the dark. Or, take morning classes.

Most courses require you to go to a museum and write a paper on a selected work. While the papers may be required to be rather long, most professors are positive about any interpretation or response as long as you can back it up. Art is really about how you feel about something, and the trick is trying to find words to describe what you think the artist felt. Papers usually aren't a huge sweat, as there are ample resources available on all topics in art. The study of art history includes discussion of not only the art created in a period, but the history of when it was created, the philosophy of the people of the time, and the psychology behind an artist's work. You are rarely strapped for information. The hard part is fitting it together coherently.

I am extremely lucky to have the access to New York City that Rutgers offers. New York provides the perfect setting of world-class museums surrounded by an artistic culture. Any school in proximity to a major museum provides the best opportunity for special tours, internships, and other programs. Honestly, any art history professor will tell you that art needs to be experienced and seen up close and personal. The feeling you get knowing that there is only that one painting in the entire world and you are standing right in front of it, as the artist once did, is truly amazing. And check out a school's study-abroad programs. They should take you right to the source and offer something more than just a tour that any person could take. I am planning to do Rutgers' Summer in Paris program next year, where I'll be exploring the museums and architecture of Paris and its surrounding cities.

At this point, I am open to all career paths. I would like to work at a museum or a gallery and also further my interest in the developing field of art therapy. I would truly like to help change the world with my degree and reintroduce art as an important part of our culture. I remember that when I was growing up, art class was never considered as important as math or science class, and I think we need a serious overhaul of our values—especially in this country. I feel that many Americans take art (like everything else) for granted and really lack appreciation for it. I'd like to help bring some prestige and appreciation back to the study of art in this country.

Up Close and Personal with Professional Artists

SUSAN WHITE
Art Conservator

Susan White, owner of White Conservation Services—a New York–based art conservation business—received her B.A. in chemistry and art history from Duke University in 1982. As an undergraduate, White was interested in pursuing a career in medicine, but she longed to be involved in the visual arts as well. Unable to decide whether to choose a career in science or one dedicated to art, White elected to combine her interests by going into the then young field of fine art conservation. She attended graduate school at the University of Delaware/Winterthur Program, receiving an M.S. in fine art conservation with a specialty in objects restoration in 1985. She then went on to do internships at the National Gallery of Art, the National Museum of American History, and the Metropolitan Museum of Art. While she was at the Met, she published research in the study of ancient Egyptian goldworking technology in addition to working as a conservator for other museums, private dealers, and collectors in New York City.

In 1987, she visited China on a fellowship from the Met in order to learn more about restoration techniques used in that country. In 1988, she moved to Boston to study sculpture at the School of the Museum of Fine Arts, receiving a diploma in 1991. She subsequently attended the Massachusetts College of Art and received her M.F.A. in sculpture. After teaching at the college level and serving as artist-in-residence at a Boston-area private high school, she returned to New York City in 1997, where she now runs a private art conservation business.

White has worked on a wide variety of objects, from ancient Greek and Roman ceramics to contemporary sculpture. She works on porcelain, glass, stone, ivory, and wood—anything three-dimensional. She's repaired baby carriages for network executive wives and Outsider Art for Soho dealers. When asked what is the most interesting piece she has worked on, she says it's difficult to say. Was it the ninth-century life-size gold Buddha riddled with bullet holes that a dealer smuggled out of Nepal? Or perhaps the "ancient Chinese bronze" stork that turned out to be made from a collection of modern parts, including a toilet buoy and a brass dog bowl? White says that whatever crosses her bench presents new challenges, which is what she most loves about her work.

However, it's not only the art that White finds fascinating. She says that one of the most interesting aspects of her work are her clients, who range from modest, work-a-day folks to the powerful elite of the world of museums and collectors. She's particularly intrigued by the way some people attach to their works of art and says that many of her clients see their objects as "perfect reflections of themselves." When one of those objects breaks, she says, she has to "repair not only the object but the owner as well." She finds these to be the most interesting and the most challenging of jobs.

Owning her own business allows White unusual flexibility and freedom and is one of the great benefits of having chosen this field. "The work is not always steady, but when it comes, it is lucrative and interesting." And between jobs she is able to pursue her two creative loves: making art and writing. She is currently working on a manuscript about her work as a private art conservator, entitled *Objects and Their People*.

JEANNIE FRIEDMAN
Owner and President, Design Firm; Graphic Designer

Jeannie Friedman, owner and president of New York City–based graphic design firm Design Five, graduated from The Cooper Union School of Art with a degree in graphic design. Under Friedman's direction, the award-winning 15-person company produces classroom materials from pre-kindergarten through college for major U.S. educational publishers.

Having begun her college career as a painting major at the University of Chicago, Friedman's interests diversified once she arrived at Cooper. "I quickly discovered the silkscreen lab, the photography lab, and the typography lab," she says, and "that really turned me on to graphic design." Her interest in painting never waned, however, and one of the things she most enjoys about her current career is that "I'm still a painter and I'm financially supported by the work that I do as a graphic designer."

Friedman credits her real-world work experience with helping her to succeed both in school and in her field.

"I worked my way through school and I really recommend this to kids thinking of going to art school," says Friedman. "I was the art editor for a small magazine. This was how I supported myself while attending school. It was some of the best training I've ever had. I really learned how to put together a magazine from start to finish."

"Now that I'm the owner," Friedman says, "while I don't do the hands-on work, I'm still using the visual skills I learned at Cooper."

visual

Arts

LILI BERNARD
Painter
www.lilibernard.com

The arts played an integral role in my familial, native-Cuban upbringing. Fine art, music, and theater thrived in our household. When I was just a toddler, my family emigrated to the United States. In our little Brooklyn brownstone my mother gave me my first lesson in drawing. I was 4 years old. With great focus and joyful seriousness she showed me how to arrange circles and triangles to create a beautiful bird. I delighted at the complex simplicity of my mother's design. That moment was pivotal in my decision to become an artist. I was utterly fascinated by the living form that my mother was able to create, via the combination of two mere shapes.

Since I can remember, my mother used to always say that she knew I was going to grow up to be a famous artist one day. She and my father instilled in my siblings and me the knowledge that we could achieve any and every goal. My father, an electrical engineer, used to bring home discarded blueprints. My brothers and sisters and I squealed euphorically as he unrolled the huge papers on the kitchen table and spilled crayons on top of them. For hours we drew and colored on the back of those discarded blueprints. My father categorically saved our childhood drawings for each one of us to enjoy in our adulthood. I spent most of my time growing up in New Jersey. However, in the beginning of my junior year of high school, my family relocated to Tokyo, where I graduated from the American School in Japan. My art teachers in both New Jersey and Tokyo nourished my artistic capabilities. The uplifting nature of my teachers, coupled with the self-sacrificing love of my parents and their wonderful lessons in art, propelled me to study fine arts at Cornell University.

A visiting professor of painting at Cornell University named Patrick Webb taught me invaluable lessons on the derivation and arrangement of colors. Today, in my painting, I continue to incorporate many of the methods that I learned from Professor Webb as well as from many of the dynamic art professors at Cornell University. Along with fine arts, I also studied the sciences and acting at Cornell. My theater professor, Bruce Levitt, encouraged me to consider pursuing a career in acting and recommended that I study in New York City. After three years at Cornell, I left and started a successful acting career in New York, where I studied theater for three years, under the tutelage of Sonia Moore. My fine art continued to develop, alongside my thespian life. I used to come home from rehearsals and performances and paint. At my parents urging and with their support, I completed my bachelor's degree at the City University of New York.

My college education has been instrumental in my career as an artist, both in theater and in fine arts. It has given me the knowledge, skill, and fortitude necessary to forge through my occupation as an artist. Today, as a wife and a mother of five young boys, my vocational focus is more on fine arts. I paint prolifically while my children slumber or attend school. When they are home, they delight in watching me paint, often offering invaluable criticism and support. They boast about my art shows to their teachers and peers. My children tangibly benefit from my college education; I impart to them many of the invaluable lessons in art that I gained as a college student. Clearly, my college education has enriched my life, not only as an artist, but also as a mother.

My studio is in the premier art gallery district of Chung King Road in Chinatown, Los Angeles. The studio is large, over 2,000 square feet, with three levels—a "store front" level that is all windows, a large functional basement, and a loft. Upon my easels, taped in random order, are inspirational photographs and words, most smudged with paint and charcoal. The hardwood floors beneath my easels are splattered in paint. There is always music playing in the background that relates to the subject I am painting. I often dance when I paint and sometimes speak to the canvas, as if it has a life of its own. Painting is always a joy-filled experience. One of my goals is to share with viewers a small portion of the joy I am blessed to feel, all within the process of creating art.

The subjects of my paintings range from the spiritual, through the natural, to the ancestral. I paint in oils, sans thinning agents. One of the most time-consuming and yet therapeutic aspects in my painting is the mixing of colors on the pallet. I tend to derive hues that are brightly colored, which reflect, rather than absorb, light.

It is always rewarding to see how positively my paintings impact people. This is most evident at the opening of an art show. I measure the success of a painting by the length of time people stand in front of it and stare or by the questions they ask, regarding the work. My acting career has helped me with the Questions & Answers portion of art show openings when I have had to stand before more than 100 people and speak about my inspiration and creative process.

I look at every venue to display and sell my work as an utter blessing. This is particularly true in the context of relatively few women and people of color being represented in the art world. One of my most gratifying experiences as an artist is being able to commune with other artists, of all types. I enjoy the soul connection that invariably exists between artists and benefit from listening to the reflections and insights of artists who are more experienced in the professional world of art than I am.

Visual

Arts

In the eve of a career as a professional fine artist, my plans for the future involve applying to graduate school so that I may pursue a Master of Fine Arts (M.F.A.) for my own personal edification and fortification. I look forward to benefiting from the relationships I will form with other graduate students as well as with professors who themselves are experienced artists. Being equipped with an M.F.A. will also give me the option to pursue a career as an instructor of art at the college level, should I so desire. My other plans for the future involve my continuing to develop a nonprofit organization I recently incorporated called ¡HABLA! (Harvesting Asian, Black, Latino Artists). The purpose of ¡HABLA! is to provide a platform for the voices of Asian, Black, and Latino fine artists in the mainstream art world, where artists of color are grossly underrepresented. ¡HABLA! achieves this goal through its all-inclusive youth-mentoring programs and its scholarships for artists of color to graduate and undergraduate art schools.

You're In! What's Next?

How to Use This Guide

Peterson's College Guide for Visual Arts Majors offers detailed information on professional degree programs in art offered at institutions in the U.S., its territories, and Canada. The guide should be used as a first step toward identifying potential programs; students are encouraged to consult with their school counselors and arts teachers for additional guidance.

QUICK-REFERENCE CHART

If you want to find out quickly which professional degrees are offered by a specific school, turn to the **Art Programs At-a-Glance** chart. Organized geographically, the chart provides the most basic information about each school in this guide, including:

- *Institution name and location*

- *Professional degrees offered in art*

- *Total enrollment*

- *Tuition and fees for the 2007–08 or 2006–07 academic year*

- *Profile page reference*

PROFILES OF VISUAL ARTS PROGRAMS

This guide profiles professional degree programs only. The **Profiles of Visual Arts Programs** section is organized alphabetically by institution name.

Each profile consists of the following elements:

Institutional control: Private institutions are designated as *independent* (nonprofit), *independent/religious* (sponsored by or affiliated with a religious group or having a non-denominational or interdenominational religious orientation), or *proprietary* (profit-making). Public institutions are designated by their primary source of support, such as *federal, state, commonwealth* (Puerto Rico), *territory* (U.S. territories), *county, district* (an administrative unit of public education, often having boundaries different from units of local government), *city, state, and local* ("local" refers to county, district, or city), or *state-related* (funded primarily by the state but administered autonomously).

Student body type: Categories are *men* (100 percent of student body), *primarily men*, *women* (100 percent of student body), *primarily women*, and *coed*. A few schools are designated as *undergraduate: women only; graduate: coed* or *undergraduate: men only; graduate: coed*.

Campus setting: Setting is designated as *urban, suburban, small town*, or *rural*.

Degrees: Many of the degrees listed (both undergraduate and graduate) are purely professional in scope and definition. Institutions may also offer B.A., B.S., M.A., and M.S. degrees that are considered "professional" based upon the prescribed curriculum and course load within the discipline. In a professional degree program, the majority of the curriculum is made up of course work within the particular arts field, while the rest of the program involves traditional liberal arts course work. A professional degree program allows students to focus most of their studies in art and emphasizes professional training and acquiring professional skills. This section also lists program accreditation by national arts organizations.

Enrollment: This data element cites the number of matriculated undergraduate and (if applicable) graduate students in the arts program, both full-time and part-time, as of fall 2006 (or 2005 if 2006 information was not available).

Student profile: Whole-figure percentages are given for the total program enrollment broken down into the following categories: *minorities, female, male, international*.

Faculty: Numbers are given for undergraduate and (if applicable) graduate faculty members teaching full-time and part-time in the respective area of study. The percentage of full-time faculty members who have appropriate terminal degrees in their field is listed, as is the ratio of undergraduate students to faculty members teaching undergraduate courses. Finally, mention is made if graduate students teach undergraduate courses in the program.

Student life: This section lists program-related organizations and campus activities in which visual arts students may participate. The availability of housing opportunities designated solely for visual arts students is mentioned here as well.

Expenses: Figures are given for the 2007–08 academic year (actual or estimated) or for the 2006–07 academic year if more recent figures were not yet available at the time of data collection. Annual expenses may be expressed as a *comprehensive fee* (this includes full-time tuition, mandatory fees, and college room and board) or as separate figures for full-time *tuition, mandatory fees, college room and board*, or *college room only*. For public institutions where tuition differs according to residence, separate figures are given for area and/or state residents and for out-of-state residents. The tuition structure at some institutions is complex in that freshmen and sophomores may be charged a different rate from that for juniors and seniors, or a professional or vocational division may have a different fee structure than the liberal arts division of the same institution. In such cases, the lowest tuition appears in the profile, followed by the notation minimum. Also, in instances where colleges report room and board costs that vary depending on the type of accommodation and meal plan, the figures given are either for the most common room arrangement and a full meal plan or for the lowest figures, followed by the notation minimum. If the institution charges special program-related fees for students in the visual and performing arts, these are listed as well.

Financial aid: This section provides information regarding any college-administered award opportunities dedicated exclusively for undergraduate students in the program. Keep in mind that while these awards are only for students in the program, program students may qualify for other financial aid opportunities at the institution as well.

Application procedures: This section indicates if students are admitted directly into the professional program when they enroll for the freshman year or if they must apply for admission into the professional program at some point during their undergraduate career. Admission application deadlines and dates for notification of acceptance or rejection into the program are given either as specific dates or as *continuous* for freshmen and transfers. Continuous means that applications are processed as they are received, and qualified students are accepted as long as there are openings. Continuous notification means that applicants are notified of acceptance or rejection as applications are processed up until the date indicated or until the actual beginning of classes. Application requirements are grouped into either *required* or *recommended*. In addition to these requirements, an institution may indicate if *portfolio reviews* are held and where they are held (on or off campus).

Contact: Information includes the name, title, mailing address, phone number, fax number, and e-mail address of the person to contact for further information. Where applicable, a graduate contact is listed as well.

More About the School: A **Special Message** may be included for schools that wish to place additional emphasis on some aspect of their program offerings.

APPENDIXES

The **Summer Programs in Art** appendix lists names and contact information for summer programs that can help high school students develop their talent and skills and build their portfolio.

Scholarships for Artists contains a partial listing of private scholarships, grants, and prizes awarded to college-bound art students. The awards are based on data collected between January and April 2007 through survey mailings and phone interviews. Every effort has been made to provide up-to-date information. However, changes in particular program information may occur after this book is published. To make sure that you have the most current information, always contact the sponsors directly.

The **Additional Resources** appendix provide readers with lists of various art education organizations and resources that provide support to students in the arts.

INDEXES

The **Majors and Concentrations** index presents 267 major fields of study. The majors are listed alphabetically. The terms used for the majors are the most widely used. However, many institutions use different terms for the same or similar areas. In addition, while the term "major" is used in this guide, some schools may use other terms such as concentration, program of study, or field.

The **Alphabetical Listing of Schools** index lists every professional degree-granting institution in the guide alphabetically and gives the page number(s) on which its profile can be found.

DATA COLLECTION PROCEDURES

The data contained in the quick-reference chart, profiles, and indexes were collected through *Peterson's Survey of Professional Degree Programs in the Visual & Performing Arts.* Questionnaires were sent to the more than 1,100 programs that meet the criteria for inclusion outlined below. All data included in this edition have been submitted by officials (usually program directors, department heads, or admissions personnel) at the institutions themselves. In addition, the great majority

Visual

Arts

of institutions that submitted data were contacted directly by Peterson's editorial staff to verify unusual figures, resolve discrepancies, and obtain additional data. All usable information received in time for publication has been included. The omission of any items from an index or profile listing signifies either that the data were not applicable to that institution or that data were not available. Institutions that did not return a survey may be listed with an abbreviated profile in order to ensure a comprehensive reference product. We have every reason to believe that the information presented in this guide is accurate. However, students should check with a specific college or university to verify such figures as tuition and fees, which may have changed since the publication of this volume.

CRITERIA FOR INCLUSION IN THIS BOOK

Peterson's College Guide for Visual Arts Majors covers accredited baccalaureate-degree-granting institutions in the United States, U.S. territories, and Canada. Institutions have full accreditation or candidate-for-accreditation (preaccreditation) status granted by an institutional or specialized accrediting body recognized by the U.S. Department of Education or Council for Higher Education Accreditation. Recognized institutional accrediting bodies, which consider each institution as a whole, are the following: the six regional associations of schools and colleges (Middle States, New England, North Central, Northwest, Southern, and Western), each of which is responsible for a specified portion of the United States and its territories; the Association for Biblical Higher Education (ABHE); the Accrediting Council for Independent Colleges and Schools (ACICS); the Accrediting Commission of Career Schools and Colleges of Technology (ACCSCT); the Distance Education and Training Council (DETC); the American Academy for Liberal Education (AALE); the Council on Occupational Education; and the Transnational Association of Christian Colleges and Schools (TRACS). Program registration by the New York State Board of Regents is considered to be the equivalent of institutional accreditation, since the Board requires that all programs offered by an institution meet its standards before recognition is granted. A Canadian institution must be chartered and authorized to grant degrees by the provincial government, affiliated with a chartered institution, or accredited by a recognized U.S. accrediting body. There are recognized specialized accrediting bodies in more than forty different fields, each of which is authorized to accredit specific programs in its particular field. This can serve as the equivalent of institutional accreditation for specialized institutions that offer programs in one field only (schools of art, music, optometry, theology, etc.).

In addition, a profiled institution must grant one or more of the following undergraduate professional degrees in art:

Artist's Diploma
Associate in Occupational Studies
Bachelor of Architecture
Bachelor of Art Education
Bachelor of Arts
Bachelor of Arts/Bachelor of Education
Bachelor of Arts/Bachelor of Fine Arts
Bachelor of Arts/Bachelor of Science
Bachelor of Design
Bachelor of Education
Bachelor of Fashion Design and Merchandising
Bachelor of Fine Arts
Bachelor of Fine Arts/ Master of Arts
Bachelor of Fine Arts/ Master of Architecture
Bachelor of Fine Arts/ Master of Art Teaching
Bachelor of Graphic Design and Advertising
Bachelor of Industrial Design
Bachelor of Interior Architecture
Bachelor of Interior Design
Bachelor of Science
Bachelor of Science in Education
Bachelor of Science/ Bachelor of Fine Arts

Many of these institutions also offer advanced degrees at the master's or doctoral level:

Master of Architecture
Master of Art Education
Master of Art in Art Education
Master of Arts
Master of Arts/Doctor of Philosophy
Master of Arts/Master of Fine Arts
Master of Arts/Master of Science
Master of Arts in Education
Master of Arts in Teaching
Master of Design
Master of Education
Master of Fine Arts
Master of Humanities
Master of Industrial Design
Master of Interior Architecture
Master of Interior Design
Master of Landscape Architecture
Master of Professional Studies
Master of Public Art Studies
Master of Science
Master of Science in Education
Master of Science in Teaching
Doctor of Arts
Doctor of Education
Doctor of Philosophy

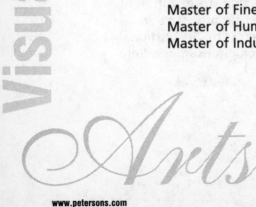

Quick-Reference Chart

Art Programs At-a-Glance

	Art	Enrollment	Tuition and Fees	Summer Programs	Page
U.S. AND U.S. TERRITORIES					
Alabama					
Birmingham-Southern College	BFA	1,256	24,300**		136
Jacksonville State University	BFA	8,957	5070**	Art	183
The University of Alabama	BFA, MA, MFA	23,838	5278*		283
University of Montevallo	BFA	2,895	5664*		303
University of North Alabama	BFA	6,810	4651*		305
Arizona					
Arizona State University	BFA, MFA, PhD	51,234	4688*		121
The Art Institute of Phoenix	BA	1,055	18,576*	Art	131
Collins College: A School of Design and Technology	BA	1,690	24,250*		155
The University of Arizona	BFA, MA, MFA, PhD	36,805	4766*		284
Arkansas					
Arkansas State University	BFA, MA	10,727	6010**		122
Harding University	BFA, BS	6,085	12,360**		176
University of Arkansas	BFA, MFA	17,926	6038**		285
University of Central Arkansas	BFA	12,330	6205**		286
Williams Baptist College	BA	629	10,370**		331
California					
Academy of Art University	BFA, MArch, MFA	9,483	14,680**	Art	111
American InterContinental University	BFA		NR		116
Art Center College of Design	BFA, BS, MA, MFA, MS	1,631	27,910**		123

* Expenses for 2006–2007.   ** Estimated expenses for 2007–2008.   NR = Not reported.
For public institutions where tuition differs according to residence, the in-state tuition and fees are shown.

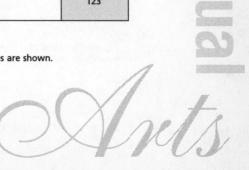

Visual Arts

	Art	Enrollment	Tuition and Fees	Summer Programs	Page
California—*continued*					
The Art Institute of California–San Diego	BFA	2,386	22,272**		127
The Art Institute of California–San Francisco	BFA, BS, MFA	1,624	20,640*	Art	128
California College of the Arts	BA, BARC, BFA, MA, MARC, MFA	1,622	27,914*	Art	140
California Design College	BFA		NR		143
California Institute of the Arts	BFA, BFA, MFA, MFA	1,349	31,865**		143
California State University, Chico	BFA, MFA	16,250	3690**		145
California State University, Fullerton	BFA, MA, MFA	35,921	3030*		146
Notre Dame de Namur University	BA, BFA	1,583	24,650**		226
Otis College of Art and Design	BFA, MFA	1,125	28,346**	Art	230
San Francisco Art Institute	BA, BFA, MA, MFA	652	27,235*	Art	255
Sonoma State University	BFA	7,749	3648*		269
Southern California Institute of Architecture	BARCH, MArch	438	10,696**	Art	270
University of Southern California	BFA, MFA, MPAS, MPAS/MA, MPAS/MPI	33,389	33,892*	Art	310
University of the Pacific	BFA	6,251	28,980**		317
Colorado					
The Art Institute of Colorado	BA	2,765	20,928**	Art	129
Colorado State University	BFA, MFA	26,723	4717*		156
Metropolitan State College of Denver	BFA	20,761	3,431*	Art	206
Rocky Mountain College of Art & Design	BFA	454	NR	Art	251
University of Colorado at Boulder	BA, BASA, BFA, MA, MFA	31,399	5643*		288
University of Denver	BFA, MA, MFA	10,374	32,232**		290

* Expenses for 2006–2007.   ** Estimated expenses for 2007–2008.   NR = Not reported.
For public institutions where tuition differs according to residence, the in-state tuition and fees are shown.

	Art	Enrollment	Tuition and Fees	Summer Programs	Page
Connecticut					
Albertus Magnus College	BFA, MA	2,186	19,390*		114
Lyme Academy College of Fine Arts	BFA		NR	Art	194
Paier College of Art, Inc.	BFA	248	12,380*		233
University of Bridgeport	BA, BFA, BS	4,018	22,860**		285
University of Connecticut	BFA, MFA	23,557	8842**		288
University of Hartford	BFA, MFA	7,308	26,996**	Art	292
District of Columbia					
American University	BFA, MFA	11,279	29,673*		117
Corcoran College of Art and Design	BFA, BFA/ MAT, MA	592	24,489*	Art	160
Florida					
The Art Institute of Fort Lauderdale	BS	3,058	19,940**	Art	129
The Art Institute of Jacksonville	BFA	53	NR		130
The Art Institute of Tampa	BFA	685	20,208*		132
Florida State University	BFA, MFA	39,973	3307*		173
International Academy of Design & Technology	BFA, MFA	2,405	NR		181
Jacksonville University	BFA	3,093	21,200*		183
Miami International University of Art & Design	BFA, MFA	1,406	18,960*	Art	206
New World School of the Arts	BFA	400	3000**		219
Ringling College of Art and Design	BFA	1,090	24,725**	Art	248
University of Florida	BA, BFA, MA, MFA, PhD	50,822	3206*		291
Georgia					
The Art Institute of Atlanta	BFA	2,694	20,064**	Art	125
Savannah College of Art and Design	BFA, MA, MArch, MFA	8,236	24,890**	Art	257
Shorter College	BFA	1,044	14,300*		269

* Expenses for 2006–2007.   ** Estimated expenses for 2007–2008.   NR = Not reported.
For public institutions where tuition differs according to residence, the in-state tuition and fees are shown.

	Art	Enrollment	Tuition and Fees	Summer Programs	Page
Georgia—*continued*					
University of Georgia	BFA, EdD, EdS, MA, MFA, PhD	33,959	5622**		292
Valdosta State University	BFA, MAE	10,888	3490**		322
Illinois					
Bradley University	BA, BFA, BS, MA, MFA	6,126	21,360**	Art	138
Columbia College Chicago	BA, BA, BA, BFA, BFA, MFA, MFA, MFA	11,499	16,788*	Art	157,158
Harrington College of Design	BFA	1,563	20,520**	Art	176
The Illinois Institute of Art–Chicago	BA, BFA	2,680	20,284**		177
The Illinois Institute of Art–Schaumburg	BFA	1,213	18,675*		178
Illinois Wesleyan University	BFA	2,144	30,750**		178
Millikin University	BFA	2,488	23,845**	Art	208
Northern Illinois University	BA, BFA, BS, MA, MFA, MSEd	25,313	7455**		224
Rockford College	BFA	1,426	22,950**		251
School of the Art Institute of Chicago	BA, BFA, BIA, MA, MArch, MDes, MFA, MIA, MS	2,873	31,020**		260
Southern Illinois University Carbondale	BFA, MFA	21,003	8071**		270
Southern Illinois University Edwardsville	BFA, BS, MA, MFA	13,449	7118**		271
University of Illinois at Chicago	BFA, MFA	24,654	9742*		294
University of Illinois at Urbana–Champaign	BFA, EdD, MA, MFA, PhD	42,728	11,130**		294
Western Illinois University	BA, BFA	13,602	8079**		328
Indiana					
Ball State University	BFA, BS, MA	17,082	6810*		134
Indiana State University	BFA, BS, MFA	10,568	6436*		179

* Expenses for 2006–2007.   ** Estimated expenses for 2007–2008.   NR = Not reported.
For public institutions where tuition differs according to residence, the in-state tuition and fees are shown.

	Art	Enrollment	Tuition and Fees	Summer Programs	Page
Indiana—*continued*					
Indiana University Bloomington	BFA, MA, MAT, MFA, PhD	38,247	7460*		180
Saint Mary's College	BA, BFA	1,527	26,872**		254
University of Evansville	BFA	2,879	22,980*		290
University of Indianapolis	BFA	4,389	19,730**		295
University of Notre Dame	BFA, MA, MFA	11,603	35,187**		308
Iowa					
Clarke College	BFA	1,201	20,297*		149
Drake University	BA, BFA	5,366	22,682*		166
Iowa State University of Science and Technology	BFA, MFA	25,462	6161**		181
Maharishi University of Management	BFA	931	24,430*		195
The University of Iowa	BFA, MA, MFA, PhD	28,816	6293**		296
Kansas					
Emporia State University	BFA, BSEd	6,473	3586*		170
Kansas State University	BA, BFA, MFA	23,141	5434*		188
University of Kansas	BFA, MFA	28,924	6153*		296
Washburn University	BFA	7,153	5312*		324
Kentucky					
Murray State University	BFA	10,298	5418**	Art	217
Northern Kentucky University	BFA	14,617	5448*		225
University of Louisville	BFA, MA, MAT, PhD	20,804	6252*		297
Louisiana					
Louisiana Tech University	BFA, MFA	11,203	4502*		193
Loyola University New Orleans	BA, BFA	4,604	26,508**		193
Northwestern State University of Louisiana	BFA	9,431	3553*	Art	226

* Expenses for 2006–2007.   ** Estimated expenses for 2007–2008.   NR = Not reported.
For public institutions where tuition differs according to residence, the in-state tuition and fees are shown.

VISUAL

Arts

	Art	Enrollment	Tuition and Fees	Summer Programs	Page
Maine					
Maine College of Art	BFA, MFA	409	26,615**	Art	196
University of Southern Maine	BA, BFA	10,478	6,326*	Art	310
Maryland					
Maryland Institute College of Art	BFA, BFA/MA, BFA/MAT, MA, MFA	1,866	28,670**	Art	200
Salisbury University	BFA	7,383	6412**		255
Massachusetts					
Anna Maria College	BA	1,200	23,234*		117
The Art Institute of Boston at Lesley University	BFA, BFA/MA, BFA/MEd, MFA	6,539	23,450**	Art	125
Boston University	BFA, MFA	31,574	33,792*	Art	137
Emerson College		4,324	25,894*		
Emmanuel College	BFA	2,340	24,200*		170
Massachusetts College of Art	BFA, MFA, MS	2,286	7450**		203
Montserrat College of Art	BFA	308	22,300**	Art	213
School of the Museum of Fine Arts, Boston	BA/BFA, MAT, MFA	733	27,970**	Art	264
Suffolk University	BFA, MA	8,863	24,250**	Art	275
University of Massachusetts Dartmouth	BA, BFA, MAE, MFA	8,756	8309*		298
Michigan					
Adrian College	BFA	1,051	21,620**		113
Albion College	BFA	1,941	26,122*		115
College for Creative Studies	BFA	1,302	26,375**	Art	152
Grand Valley State University	BFA	23,295	6588*		174
Hope College	BA	3,203	23,800**		177
Kendall College of Art and Design of Ferris State University	BFA, BS, MFA		NR		188

* Expenses for 2006–2007.   ** Estimated expenses for 2007–2008.   NR = Not reported.
For public institutions where tuition differs according to residence, the in-state tuition and fees are shown.

	Art	Enrollment	Tuition and Fees	Summer Programs	Page
Michigan—*continued*					
Lawrence Technological University	BFA, BIA, BS, MIntD	4,049	19,443*	Art	190
Michigan State University	BFA, MFA	45,520	9640**		208
University of Michigan	BFA, MFA	40,025	9798*		300
Wayne State University	BA, BFA, BS, MA, MFA	33,137	6,812*		326
Western Michigan University	BFA, MA	24,841	6866*		329
Minnesota					
The Art Institutes International Minnesota	BFA, BS	1,594	$18,336*	Art	133
College of Visual Arts	BFA		21,684**		155
Minneapolis College of Art and Design	BFA, BS, MFA	749	27,200**	Art	210
Minnesota State University Mankato	BFA, MA	14,148	6050**		211
St. Cloud State University	BFA	15,964	5718*		253
University of Minnesota, Twin Cities Campus	BFA, MFA	50,402	9173*		300
Mississippi					
Mississippi State University	BFA	16,206	4596*		211
University of Mississippi	BFA, MFA	15,220	4602*		301
University of Southern Mississippi	BA, BFA, BS, MAE	14,777	4714*		311
Missouri					
Columbia College	BFA	1,186	12,414*		156
Culver-Stockton College	BFA	869	16,600**		165
Kansas City Art Institute	BFA	674	25,680**	Art	185
Lindenwood University	BA, BFA, MA, MFA	9,525	12,700**		191
Maryville University of Saint Louis	BA, BFA	3,333	18,120*	Art	202
Missouri State University	BFA, BS, BSEd, MS	19,218	6606**	Art	212
Stephens College	BFA	964	20,500*	Art	274
Truman State University	BFA, MAE	5,762	6342*		280

* Expenses for 2006–2007.   ** Estimated expenses for 2007–2008.   NR = Not reported.
For public institutions where tuition differs according to residence, the in-state tuition and fees are shown.

Visual *Arts*

	Art	Enrollment	Tuition and Fees	Summer Programs	Page
Missouri—*continued*					
University of Missouri–Columbia	BFA, MFA	28,253	7308*		301
Webster University	BA, BFA, MA	7,840	19,330**		326
Montana					
The University of Montana	BFA, MA, MFA	13,558	4977*		302
Nebraska					
University of Nebraska–Lincoln	BFA, MFA	22,106	6215**		303
New Hampshire					
New Hampshire Institute of Art	BFA	281	13,249*	Art	217
Plymouth State University	BA, BFA, BS, MAT	5,872	7766**		239
New Jersey					
The College of New Jersey	BA, BFA	6,934	10,553*		153
Rutgers, The State University of New Jersey, Mason Gross School of the Arts	BFA, MFA		NR		203
Seton Hall University	BA, BS, MA	9,637	24,720*	Art	267
New Mexico					
New Mexico Highlands University	BFA	3,750	2444*		218
New Mexico State University	BFA, MA, MFA	16,415	4230*		219
University of New Mexico	BAFA, BFA, MA, MFA, PhD	26,172	4571**		304
New York					
Alfred University	BFA, MFA	2,310	23,162**		115
Brooklyn College of the City University of New York	BFA, MA, MFA	15,947	4375*		140
Cazenovia College	BFA	1,006	21,500**		148
The College of New Rochelle	BFA, BS, MA, MS	2,341	23,700**	Art	154
Cooper Union for the Advancement of Science and Art	BFA	968	1550**		160

* Expenses for 2006–2007. ** Estimated expenses for 2007–2008. NR = Not reported.
For public institutions where tuition differs according to residence, the in-state tuition and fees are shown.

	Art	Enrollment	Tuition and Fees	Summer Programs	Page
New York—*continued*					
Cornell University	BFA, MFA	19,639	32,981*		162
Daemen College	BFA	2,414	18,750**		166
Fashion Institute of Technology	BFA, MA	10,010	4892**	Art	171
Ithaca College	BA, BFA, BFA	6,409	26,832*		182
Lehman College of the City University of New York	BA, BFA, MA, MFA	10,814	4290**		190
Long Island University, C.W. Post Campus	BFA, BS, MA, MFA, MS	8,494	25,770*		192
Manhattanville College	BFA, MAT	2,974	30,776**		198
New York Institute of Technology	BFA, MFA	11,404	20,358*	Art	220
New York School of Interior Design	BFA, MFA	736	20,750**		220
New York University	BFA, BFA, MA, MFA, PhD	40,870	35,290**	Art	223
Parsons The New School for Design	BBA, BFA, MA, MFA, MRCH	3,598	30,930**	Art	233
Pratt Institute	BA, BARC, BFA, BID, BPS, BS, MARC, MFA, MID, MPS, MS	4,673	31,080**	Art	241
Purchase College, State University of New York	BFA, MFA	3,901	5771**	Art	243
Russell Sage College	BA	800	25,990**		253
St. John's University	BFA	20,069	24,970*		254
School of Visual Arts	BFA, MAT, MFA, MPS	3,715	23,520**	Art	265
State University of New York at Plattsburgh	BFA	6,217	5416**		273
State University of New York at Fredonia	BFA	5,540	5542**		274
Syracuse University	BFA, BID, BS, MFA, MID	17,492	31,686**	Art	276
University at Buffalo, the State University of New York	BFA, MFA	27,220	6128*		281

* Expenses for 2006–2007.   ** Estimated expenses for 2007–2008.   NR = Not reported.
For public institutions where tuition differs according to residence, the in-state tuition and fees are shown.

	Art	Enrollment	Tuition and Fees	Summer Programs	Page
North Carolina					
Barton College	BFA, BS	1,136	17,654*	Art	135
Chowan University	BA, BS	800	16,040*		149
East Carolina University	BFA, MFA	24,351	4003*		169
Guilford College	BFA	2,687	24,470**		175
North Carolina School of the Arts	BFA	845	4891*	Art	224
The University of North Carolina at Charlotte	BFA	21,519	3895*		305
The University of North Carolina at Greensboro	BA, BFA, MFA	16,728	4029**		306
Western Carolina University	BFA, MAEd, MAT, MFA	8,861	4609*		328
North Dakota					
University of North Dakota	BFA, MFA	12,834	5792*		306
Ohio					
Art Academy of Cincinnati	BFA, MA		20,340**	Art	122
Capital University	BFA	3,825	26,360**		147
Central State University	BA, BS	1,766	5294*		149
The Cleveland Institute of Art	BFA, MFA	610	30,090**	Art	150
Columbus College of Art & Design	BFA	1,581	22,412**	Art	159
Kent State University	BFA, MFA	22,697	8430**		189
Miami University	BFA, BS, MA, MFA	16,329	11,925**	Art	207
Ohio Northern University	BFA	3,620	28,260*		227
The Ohio State University	BFA, MFA	51,818	8559*		228
The University of Akron	BA, BFA	21,882	8382*	Art	282
University of Cincinnati	BFA, MA, MFA	27,932	9399*		287
University of Dayton	BFA	10,503	23,970*		289
Wright State University	BFA	16,207	7278**		332
Youngstown State University	BA, BFA, BS	13,178	6721**		333

* Expenses for 2006–2007.   ** Estimated expenses for 2007–2008.   NR = Not reported.
For public institutions where tuition differs according to residence, the in-state tuition and fees are shown.

Visual

Arts

	Art	Enrollment	Tuition and Fees	Summer Programs	Page
Oklahoma					
Oklahoma Baptist University	BFA		14,666*		228
Oregon					
The Art Institute of Portland	BFA, BS	1,614	19,395**		131
Oregon College of Art & Craft	BFA		17,900*	Art	230
Southern Oregon University	BFA	4,675	4986*		272
University of Oregon	BFA, MFA	20,348	5838*		309
Pennsylvania					
Arcadia University	BA, BFA	3,595	25,990*	Art	120
Carnegie Mellon University	BFA, MFA	10,120	34,578*	Art	147
Drexel University	BARC, BS, MARC, MS	19,882	28,780**	Art	167
Edinboro University of Pennsylvania	BFA, BS, MA, MFA	7,579	6484*		169
Moore College of Art & Design	BFA	542	26,154**	Art	215
Pennsylvania Academy of the Fine Arts	BFA, MFA		NR	Art	235
Pennsylvania College of Art & Design	BFA	255	15,205**	Art	237
Point Park University	BA	3,546	18,990**	Art	240
Rosemont College	BFA	995	22,835**		252
Seton Hill University	BFA, MA	1,895	23,380*		267
Temple University	BARC, BFA, MA, MEd, MFA, PhD	33,865	10,802**	Art	281
The University of the Arts	BFA, BS, MA, MAT, MFA, MID	2,315	25,680*	Art	315
West Chester University of Pennsylvania	BA, BFA	12,882	6293*		327
Rhode Island					
Rhode Island School of Design	BFA, BGD, BID, MA, MARC, MAT, MFA, MIARC, MID, MLARC	2,259	33,118**	Art	246
Roger Williams University	BA	5,172	25,759**		252

* Expenses for 2006–2007.   ** Estimated expenses for 2007–2008.   NR = Not reported.
For public institutions where tuition differs according to residence, the in-state tuition and fees are shown.

	Art	Enrollment	Tuition and Fees	Summer Programs	Page
South Carolina					
The Art Institute of Charleston	BFA		20,064*		128
Tennessee					
The Art Institute of Tennessee–Nashville	BFA	32	$20,064		132
Austin Peay State University	BA, BFA	9,207	4837*		134
Belmont University	BFA	4,481	19,780**		135
Memphis College of Art	BFA, MA, MAT, MFA	308	20,660**	Art	204
Tennessee Technological University	BFA	9,733	4590*		119
The University of Tennessee	BFA, MFA	28,901	5864**		312
The University of Tennessee at Martin	BFA	6,893	4665*		312
Watkins College of Art and Design	BFA	393	12,960**	Art	325
Texas					
Abilene Christian University	BFA, BS	4,777	17,410**		111
The Art Institute of Dallas	BFA	1,354	20,600**		129
The Art Institute of Houston	BFA	1,619	26,420**	Art	130
Southern Methodist University	BFA, MFA	10,941	30,880**		272
Texas A&M University–Commerce	BA, BFA, BS, MFA	8,556	5190**		277
Texas A&M University–Corpus Christi	BFA, MFA	8,585	5148*		277
Texas Christian University	BFA, MA, MFA	8,865	24,868**		278
Texas Tech University	BFA, MFA, DA	27,996	6459*	Art	278
Texas Woman's University	BFA, MA, MFA	11,832	5832**		279
University of Houston	BFA, MFA	34,334	6909*		293
University of North Texas	BA, BFA, MA, MFA, PhD	33,443	6272**		307
The University of Texas at Arlington	BA, BFA, MFA	24,825	6400*	Art	313
The University of Texas at Austin	BFA, MFA	49,697	7630*		314

* Expenses for 2006–2007.   ** Estimated expenses for 2007–2008.   NR = Not reported.
For public institutions where tuition differs according to residence, the in-state tuition and fees are shown.

	Art	Enrollment	Tuition and Fees	Summer Programs	Page
Texas—*continued*					
The University of Texas at San Antonio	BFA, MA, MFA	28,380	6699**		314
West Texas A&M University	BFA, MA, MFA	7,412	4920**		330
Utah					
Brigham Young University	BA, BFA, MFA	34,185	7680**	Art	139
University of Utah	BFA, MFA	28,619	4986**		318
Vermont					
Green Mountain College	BFA	759	23,329*		175
Johnson State College	BFA, MFA	1,866	7625**		184
Virginia					
The Art Institute of Washington	BFA	1,400	19,968*		133
Old Dominion University	BFA, MFA	21,625	6107*		229
Radford University	BFA, MFA	9,220	6176**		245
Virginia Commonwealth University	BA, BFA, MA, MAE, MFA, PhD	30,381	4227*	Art	323
Washington					
The Art Institute of Seattle	BFA	2,352	19,968**		132
Cornish College of the Arts	BFA, BFA	768	22,750*	Art	163,165
University of Washington	BA, BFA, MA, MFA, PhD	39,524	5988*		318
Washington State University	BFA, MFA	23,655	6447*	Art	324
West Virginia					
Marshall University	BFA, MA	13,936	4560**		199
Shepherd University	BFA	4,091	4348*		268
West Virginia University	BFA, MA, MFA	27,115	4722**	Art	330

* Expenses for 2006–2007.   ** Estimated expenses for 2007–2008.   NR = Not reported.
For public institutions where tuition differs according to residence, the in-state tuition and fees are shown.

	Art	Enrollment	Tuition and Fees	Summer Programs	Page
Wisconsin					
Milwaukee Institute of Art and Design	BFA	645	23,400*	Art	209
University of Wisconsin–Madison	BFA, BS, MA, MFA, PhD	41,466	6726*		319
University of Wisconsin–Milwaukee	BFA, MA, MFA	28,309	7392*		320
University of Wisconsin–Oshkosh	BFA	11,080	5364*		321
University of Wisconsin–Stout	BFA, BS	8,327	6963**		321
CANADA					
Alberta					
Alberta College of Art & Design	BDes, BFA	1,169	Can$5170**		114
University of Calgary	BFA, MFA	27,928	NR		286
New Brunswick					
Mount Allison University	BFA	2,240	Can$6650*		216
Nova Scotia					
NSCAD University	BA, BD, BFA, MA, MFA	1,038	Can$5895*		227
Ontario					
Queen's University at Kingston	BFA	20,566	6167**		245
York University	BDes, BFA, MDes, MFA	50,691	Can$5065*		332

* Expenses for 2006–2007.   ** Estimated expenses for 2007–2008.   NR = Not reported.
For public institutions where tuition differs according to residence, the in-state tuition and fees are shown.

Profiles of Visual Arts Programs

Abilene Christian University

Abilene, Texas

Independent, coed. Urban campus. Total enrollment: 4,777. Art program established 1906.

Degrees Bachelor of Fine Arts in the areas of graphic design, 2-dimensional studies, 3-dimensional studies; Bachelor of Science in the area of interior design. Majors and concentrations: ceramic art and design, graphic design, illustration, interior design, jewelry and metalsmithing, painting/drawing, printmaking, sculpture. Cross-registration with Hardin-Simmons University, McMurry University.

Enrollment 190 total; all undergraduate.

Art Student Profile 60% females, 40% males, 10% minorities, 5% international.

Art Faculty 8 undergraduate (full-time), 2 undergraduate (part-time). 88% of full-time faculty have terminal degrees. Graduate students do not teach undergraduate courses. Undergraduate student–faculty ratio: 15:1.

Student Life Student groups/activities include Annual Student Competition.

Expenses for 2007–2008 Application fee: $25. Comprehensive fee: $23,760 includes full-time tuition ($16,710), mandatory fees ($700), and college room and board ($6350). College room only: $2950. Full-time tuition and fees vary according to course load. Room and board charges vary according to board plan and housing facility. Special program-related fees: $25–$125 per course for supplies.

Financial Aid Program-specific awards: 1 Juanita Tittle Pollard Scholarship for program majors ($125–$1000), Whitefield Scholarships for program majors ($500).

Application Procedures Students admitted directly into the professional program freshman year. Deadline for freshmen and transfers: continuous. Portfolio reviews held once on campus; the submission of slides may be substituted for portfolios.

Web Site http://www.acu.edu/academics/cas/art. html

Undergraduate Contact Beverly Rama, Administrative Coordinator, Department of Art and Design, Abilene Christian University, ACU Station, PO Box 27987, Abilene, Texas 76999-7987; 915-674-2085, fax: 915-674-2051.

Academy of Art University

San Francisco, California

Proprietary, coed. Urban campus. Total enrollment: 9,483. Art program established 1929.

Degrees Bachelor of Fine Arts in the areas of advertising, animation/visual effects, computer arts/new media, fashion, fine art, graphic design, illustration, industrial design, interior architecture and design, motion pictures & television, photography, digital arts and communication. Majors and concentrations: acting, advertising design, animation, computer art, digital arts and communication, fashion design and technology, film and video production, graphic design, illustration, industrial design, interior architecture, motion graphics, painting/drawing, photography, printmaking, sculpture, transportation design, visual effects. Graduate degrees offered: Master of Fine Arts in the areas of advertising, animation/visual effects, architecture, computer arts/new media, fashion, fine art, graphic design, illustration, industrial design, interior architecture and design, motion pictures & television, photography; Master of Architecture in the area of architecture. Program accredited by NASAD, CIDA, NAAB.

Enrollment 9,118 total; 7,073 undergraduate, 2,045 graduate.

Art Student Profile 52% females, 48% males, 23% minorities, 19% international.

Art Faculty 148 total (full-time), 899 total (part-time). 17% of full-time faculty have terminal degrees. Graduate students do not teach undergraduate courses. Undergraduate student–faculty ratio: 12:1.

Student Life Student groups/activities include American Society of Interior Designers, Western Art Directors Club, Society of Illustrators.

Expenses for 2007–2008 Application fee: $100. Comprehensive fee: $27,280 includes full-time tuition ($14,400), mandatory fees ($280), and college room and board ($12,600). Special program-related fees: $45–$400 per semester for lab fees; vary depending on major.

Financial Aid Program-specific awards available.

Application Procedures Students admitted directly into the professional program freshman year. Deadline for freshmen and transfers: continuous. Required: high school transcript,

Visual Arts

Academy of Art University (continued)

college transcript(s) for transfer students, high school diploma/GED. Recommended: interview.

Web Site http://www.academyart.edu

Undergraduate Contact Undergraduate Admissions, Academy of Art University, 79 New Montgomery Street, San Francisco, California 94105; 800-544-ARTS, fax: 415-618-6287, e-mail address: admissions@academyart.edu

Graduate Contact Graduate School Admissions, Academy of Art University, 79 New Montgomery Street, San Francisco, California 94105; 800-544-ARTS, fax: 415-618-6287, e-mail address: info@academyart.edu

More About the Academy

Founded in 1929, Academy of Art University (AAU) has steadily grown to become the largest private, accredited art and design school in the nation. The campus now encompasses more than twenty buildings in and around downtown San Francisco with more than 9,500 students from twenty-five countries. The Academy's mission is to provide aspiring artists and designers with career preparation, combined with academic excellence for the A.A., B.F.A., M.F.A. degrees and nondegree personal enrichment classes in the areas of art and design. Courses can be taken on campus and online.

Campus and Surroundings The city of San Francisco is one of the great cultural centers of the world—a melting pot of diversity and creativity that has spawned major museums and galleries, world-class performing arts, film production, and technological innovation. The climate is moderate and offers

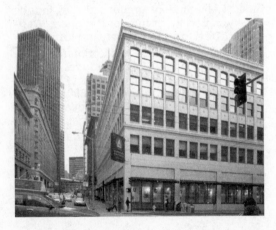

kaleidoscopic blends of sunshine and fog nine months of the year. The Academy's classrooms, studios, galleries, and dormitories are located in such areas as the world famous Fisherman's Wharf, historic Union Square, the Financial District, and the South of Market Area (SOMA). A private fleet of Academy buses, which are scheduled around classes and lab times, connect all campus facilities.

Program Facilities Academy of Art University is one of the leading schools in the country for providing students with the latest in technological advances, utilizing constantly updated, industry-professional equipment. AAU provides students with a number of facilities, including an eight-story Digital Arts Center with numerous computer workstations, software, and equipment that includes the Power Mac G5, G4, and G3; HP Desktops; and Silicon Graphics workstations, to name a few.

The Motion Picture and Television/Acting Department has multiple Final Cut Pro stations, Media 100, Avid Xpress, and Avid nonlinear editing stations and linear tape-to-tape suites, including a Bosch Telecine and several KEM flatbeds for celluloid linear editing; Arri cameras, fluid head tripods, magazines, changing bags/tents, and acrylic/timecode slates. Also available for student use are 16mm and 35mm film cameras, Beta SP, Sony 3-chip DV cameras, Canon 1-chip and 3-chip DV cameras, Panasonic SVHS video cameras, and an extensive inventory of lighting and sound grip equipment as well as a green screen studio and a newly constructed 150-seat theater.

The Fine Art Department houses three nonprofit galleries for students to display their work in San Francisco's downtown gallery district. The 50,000-square-foot Sculpture Center includes a 25-foot-high ceiling equipped with cranes that include scanners directly linked to the Computer Education Center.

Computer Arts/New Media, Animation & Visual Effects, and Digital Arts & Communications have an advanced facility, including a digital photography studio, G5, G4, and G3 Macintosh computers, Wacom Digitizing Tablets, CD/DVD burners complete with FireWire/USB connections, scanners (reflective and slide), Epson inkjet printers, Fiery printers, digital audio workstations, two flame and smoke suites, and industry software, such as Alias Maya, Illustrator, Flash, Fireworks, Dreamweaver, and DVD Studio Pro.

Academy of Art University also offers a very active schedule of events and activities throughout the year. Campus Affairs & Student Events (CASE) organizes a variety of student activities including mixers, San Francisco Bay boat tours, ski trips, camping trips, and more. Student groups and activities include the American Society of Interior Designers (ASID), Western Art Directors Club, Society of Illustrators, soccer, and rowing to name a few.

Student Performance/Exhibit Opportunities

More than eighty student shows are exhibited each year in the three main galleries. Each May, the Spring Show takes over five to eight floors of the Digital Arts Center for three weeks. The annual AAU Fashion Show highlights senior and M.F.A. collections in a runway show in which international designers such as Burberry and Oscar de la Renta have been guests of honor.

Faculty, Resident Artists, and Alumni

Students of the Academy have the rare opportunity to learn from professionals at the top of their field from the biggest art and design companies in the industry. This allows students to learn the most sought-after techniques, in addition to making the contacts they need to obtain positions with such companies as Warner Brothers, Pixar, LucasFilm, Electronic Arts, and Escada, who are known for recruiting AAU students. The Academy averages 450 instructors in the spring and fall semesters, 90 percent of whom are full-time art and design professionals and part-time teachers. The student to teacher ratio for undergraduate classes is about 18:1; for graduate students, it is 15:1. Internationally known artists also lecture and show their work in Academy galleries throughout the year.

Career Placement Services and Opportunities

Academy graduates embark upon successful careers in the art and design industry. Eighty percent of Academy of Art University's graduates are working in the art and design industry. Alumni have been hired by prestigious companies all over the world, including Walt Disney, Sega, Donna Karan, Apple, Industrial Light + Magic, Hewlett-Packard, and Electronic Arts.

The Academy does a great deal to give exposure to students' work, including job fairs and the Annual Spring show, which attracts recruiters for the industry's top professions. Students' work is also constantly shown in many publications and the Academy's three storefront art galleries located centrally in San Francisco. These galleries allow the students to showcase their fine art work and gain firsthand knowledge of how to become working artists.

Adrian College

Adrian, Michigan

Independent, coed. Small town campus. Total enrollment: 1,051. Art program established 1962.

Degrees Bachelor of Fine Arts in the areas of art, art education. Majors and concentrations: art education, art/fine arts, arts management, pre-architecture, pre-art therapy. Cross-registration with Siena Heights University, Fashion Institute of Technology, Center for Creative Studies-College of Art and Design, The American College, Chicago, Washington, and Philadelphia Centers, American Institute For Foreign Study, Central College.

Enrollment 75 total; all undergraduate.

Art Student Profile 69% females, 31% males, 7% minorities, 2% international.

Art Faculty 4 undergraduate (full-time), 12 undergraduate (part-time). 100% of full-time faculty have terminal degrees. Graduate students do not teach undergraduate courses. Undergraduate student–faculty ratio: 12:1.

Student Life Student groups/activities include Art Education Interest Group, Art Club, Pre-Art Therapy Interest Group.

Expenses for 2007–2008 Application fee: $0. Comprehensive fee: $28,770 includes full-time tuition ($21,350), mandatory fees ($270), and college room and board ($7150). College room only: $3200. Room and board charges vary according to board plan and housing facility. Special program-related fees: $15–$150 per course for supplies.

Financial Aid Program-specific awards: 55 studio art scholarships for program majors and minors ($2000), academic scholarships for students with high school GPA 3.3 and above ($7000–$20,000).

Application Procedures Students admitted directly into the professional program freshman year. Deadline for freshmen and transfers: August 15. Required: high school transcript, college transcript(s) for transfer students, minimum 2.0 high school GPA, SAT or ACT test scores (minimum composite ACT score of 18), portfolio for scholarship consideration. Recommended: essay, minimum 3.0 high school GPA, 2 letters of recommendation, portfolio. Portfolio reviews held numerous times on campus;

Visual *Arts*

Adrian College (continued)

the submission of slides may be substituted for portfolios when distance is prohibitive or scheduling is difficult.

Web Site http://art.adrian.edu/

Undergraduate Contact Ms. Caroline Quinlan, Director of Admissions, Adrian College, 110 South Madison Street, Adrian, Michigan 49221; 800-877-2246, fax: 517-264-3331, e-mail address: admissions@adrian.edu

Alberta College of Art & Design

Calgary, Alberta, Canada

Province-supported, coed. Urban campus. Total enrollment: 1,169.

Degrees Bachelor of Design in the area of visual communications design; Bachelor of Fine Arts in the areas of ceramics, drawing, glass, jewelry and metals, painting, print media, sculpture, fibre, photography, media arts and digital technologies. Majors and concentrations: ceramic art and design, fibers, glass, jewelry and metalsmithing, media arts and digital technology, multidisciplinary studies, painting/drawing, photography, printmaking, sculpture, visual communication design. Cross-registration with University of Calgary, Mount Royal College.

Enrollment 1,169 total; all undergraduate.

Art Student Profile 68% females, 32% males, 5% international.

Art Faculty 35 undergraduate (full-time), 81 undergraduate (part-time). 49% of full-time faculty have terminal degrees. Graduate students do not teach undergraduate courses. Undergraduate student–faculty ratio: 17:1.

Student Life Student groups/activities include gallery exhibitions, visiting artist talks, public design projects.

Expenses for 2007–2008 Application fee: $50 Canadian dollars. Tuition, fee, and room and board charges are reported in Canadian dollars. Province resident tuition: $4493 full-time. Mandatory fees: $677 full-time. College room and board: $8000. College room only: $4620. International student tuition: $13,832 full-time. Special program-related fees: $7–$25 per credit for supplemental materials.

Financial Aid Program-specific awards: 214 general scholarships for program students, 3 international entrance scholarships for international program students ($2000).

Application Procedures Students apply for admission into the professional program by junior year. Deadline for freshmen and transfers: April 1. Notification date for freshmen and transfers: June 1. Required: essay, high school transcript, college transcript(s) for transfer students, minimum 2.0 high school GPA, portfolio, 60% average GPA on 4 grade-12 subjects. Recommended: minimum 3.0 high school GPA. Portfolio reviews held twice on campus; the submission of slides may be substituted for portfolios for large works of art, three-dimensional pieces, or when distance is prohibitive.

Web Site http://www.acad.ca

Undergraduate Contact Joy Borman, Associate Director of Admissions, Student Services, Alberta College of Art & Design, 1407-14 Avenue NW, Calgary, Alberta T2N 4R3, Canada; 800-284-7689, fax: 403-284-7644, e-mail address: joy.borman@acad.ca

Albertus Magnus College

New Haven, Connecticut

Independent Roman Catholic, coed. Suburban campus. Total enrollment: 2,186. Art program established 1976.

Degrees Bachelor of Fine Arts in the area of art. Majors and concentrations: art history, graphic design, photography, studio art. Graduate degrees offered: Master of Arts in the area of art therapy.

Enrollment 48 total; 18 undergraduate, 30 graduate.

Art Student Profile 66% females, 34% males, 28% minorities.

Art Faculty 2 undergraduate (full-time), 4 undergraduate (part-time), 2 graduate (full-time), 6 graduate (part-time). 100% of full-time faculty have terminal degrees. Graduate students do not teach undergraduate courses. Undergraduate student–faculty ratio: 11:1.

Expenses for 2006–2007 Application fee: $35. Comprehensive fee: $27,793 includes full-time tuition ($18,672), mandatory fees ($718), and college room and board ($8403). Full-time tuition and fees vary according to class time and program. Special program-related fees: $40–$50 per course for expendable art supplies.

Financial Aid Program-specific awards available.

Application Procedures Students apply for admission into the professional program by freshman year. Deadline for freshmen and transfers: continuous. Required: high school transcript, college transcript(s) for transfer students, minimum 2.0 high school GPA, 2 letters of recommendation, SAT or ACT test scores. Recommended: essay, interview.

Web Site http://www.albertus.edu

Undergraduate Contact Mr. Richard Lolatte, Dean of Admissions, Albertus Magnus College, 700 Prospect Street, New Haven, Connecticut 06511; 203-773-8501, fax: 203-773-5248, e-mail address: admissions@albertus.edu

Graduate Contact Dr. Donna Kaiser, Director, Master of Arts in Art Therapy Program, Albertus Magnus College, 700 Prospect Street, New Haven, Connecticut 06511; 203-773-8903, e-mail address: kaiser@albertus.edu

Albion College

Albion, Michigan

Independent Methodist, coed. Small town campus. Total enrollment: 1,941. Art program established 1977.

Degrees Bachelor of Fine Arts. Majors and concentrations: art history, visual arts.

Enrollment 60 total; 10 undergraduate, 50 nonprofessional degree.

Art Student Profile 66% females, 34% males, 5% minorities, 1% international.

Art Faculty 7 undergraduate (full-time). 100% of full-time faculty have terminal degrees. Graduate students do not teach undergraduate courses. Undergraduate student–faculty ratio: 5:1.

Student Life Student groups/activities include Art Club, senior exhibition, New York Arts Program.

Expenses for 2006–2007 Application fee: $20. Comprehensive fee: $33,528 includes full-time tuition ($25,668), mandatory fees ($454), and college room and board ($7406). College room only: $3622. Room and board charges vary according to housing facility.

Financial Aid Program-specific awards: 25 Fine Arts Scholarships for freshmen ($500–$1000), 10 Janson Scholarships for program majors/minors ($200–$1000), 1 Taup Scholarship for program majors/minors ($5000), 1 Geoffrey Morris Scholarship for program majors/minors ($2500), 1 J. Gregory Scholarship for program majors/minors ($1200), 1 Harmon Scholarship for program majors/minors ($2000), 1 Cheek Scholarship for program majors/minors with ceramics emphasis ($1300).

Application Procedures Students apply for admission into the professional program by sophomore, junior year. Deadline for freshmen: May 1; transfers: continuous. Required: high school transcript, college transcript(s) for transfer students, SAT or ACT test scores, portfolio for scholarship consideration. Recommended: essay, minimum 2.0 high school GPA, interview. Portfolio reviews held on routine basis until March on campus; the submission of slides may be substituted for portfolios.

Web Site http://www.albion.edu

Undergraduate Contact Director of Admissions, Albion College, 616 East Michigan, Albion, Michigan 49224; 517-629-0321, fax: 517-629-0509.

Alfred University

Alfred, New York

Independent, coed. Rural campus. Total enrollment: 2,310. Art program established 1900.

Degrees Bachelor of Fine Arts in the areas of ceramics, graphic design, two-dimensional studies and electronic art, three-dimensional studies. Majors and concentrations: art education, art history, ceramics, glass, graphic design, metals, neon, painting/drawing, photography, pre-art therapy, print media, sculpture, video and sonic arts, wood design. Graduate degrees offered: Master of Fine Arts in the areas of ceramics, glass, sculpture, electronic integrated arts. Cross-registration with State University of New York College of Technology at Alfred, Houghton College, RAC Consortium (Rochester Area Colleges). Program accredited by NASAD.

Enrollment 557 total; 515 undergraduate, 35 graduate, 7 nonprofessional degree.

Art Student Profile 65% females, 35% males, 5% minorities, 4% international.

Alfred University (continued)

Art Faculty 41 total (full-time), 10 total (part-time). 99% of full-time faculty have terminal degrees. Graduate students do not teach undergraduate courses. Undergraduate student–faculty ratio: 12:1.

Student Life Student groups/activities include The Robert Turner Student Gallery exhibitions, Alternative Cinema/Alternative Space Festival, Annual Outdoor Light Exhibition. Special housing available for art students.

Expenses for 2007–2008 Application fee: $40. Comprehensive fee: $33,546 includes full-time tuition ($22,312), mandatory fees ($850), and college room and board ($10,384). College room only: $5384. Special program-related fees for material fees.

Financial Aid Program-specific awards: portfolio scholarships Art Portfolio Review Scholarship for students with an exceptional portfolio ($6500–$8500), art and design grants Alfred University Dean's Scholarship for students with exceptional high school grades/test scores ($5000–$7000), Scholastic Art Awards Alfred University Presidential Scholarship for students with exceptional high school grades/test scores ($6500–$8500), Jonathan Allen Leadership Award for demonstrated leaders with volunteer/service work experience ($3500–$5000).

Application Procedures Students admitted directly into the professional program freshman year. Deadline for freshmen: February 1; transfers: April 1. Notification date for freshmen: March 15; transfers: April 15. Required: essay, high school transcript, college transcript(s) for transfer students, minimum 2.0 high school GPA, letter of recommendation, portfolio, SAT or ACT test scores, slides of portfolio, application by freshman deadline for transfer students having completed fewer than 24 studio art credits. Recommended: minimum 3.0 high school GPA, interview. Portfolio reviews held numerous times depending on the number of applicants (all portfolios are reviewed by a committee of Art and Design Faculty) on campus; the submission of slides may be substituted for portfolios (only slides or CD/DVD's are accepted for portfolio submission).

Web Site http://art.alfred.edu

Undergraduate Contact Ms. Colleen Clarke, Art Recruitment Specialist, Admissions, Alfred University, 1 Saxon Drive, Alfred, New York 14802;

607-871-2115, fax: 607-871-2198, e-mail address: admissions@alfred.edu

Graduate Contact Ms. Valerie Stephens, Coordinator of Graduate Admissions, Admissions, Alfred University, 1 Saxon Drive, Alfred, New York 14802; 607-871-2141, fax: 607-871-2198, e-mail address: gradinquiry@alfred.edu

Allen R. Hite Art Institute
See University of Louisville

American Academy of Art
Chicago, Illinois
Proprietary, coed. Urban campus. Total enrollment: 410 (2006). Art program established 1923.

Web Site http://www.aaart.edu/

American InterContinental University
Los Angeles, California
Proprietary, coed. Urban campus. Art program established 1970.

Degrees Bachelor of Fine Arts in the areas of fashion design, fashion design & marketing, fashion marketing, interior design, media production, visual communication. Majors and concentrations: animation, computer animation, computer animation and interactive media, costume design, digital design, fashion design, fashion marketing, graphic design, interior design, media production, multimedia, post-production, visual communication, Web design. Program accredited by CIDA.

Enrollment 959 total; 531 undergraduate, 428 nonprofessional degree.

Art Student Profile 65% females, 35% males, 68% minorities, 12% international.

Art Faculty 17 undergraduate (full-time), 22 undergraduate (part-time). 37% of full-time faculty have terminal degrees. Graduate students do not teach undergraduate courses.

Student Life Student groups/activities include American Society of Interior Designers.

Financial Aid Program-specific awards: Travilla Scholarship for fashion design majors.

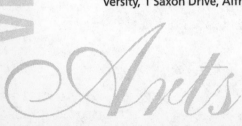

Application Procedures Students admitted directly into the professional program freshman year. Deadline for freshmen and transfers: continuous. Required: essay, high school transcript, college transcript(s) for transfer students, interview, proof of high school graduation.

Web Site http://www.aiula.com

Undergraduate Contact Admissions Advisor, American InterContinental University, 12655 West Jefferson Boulevard, Los Angeles, California 90066; 888-594-9888, fax: 310-302-2001.

American University
Washington, District of Columbia

Independent Methodist, coed. Suburban campus. Total enrollment: 11,279. Art program established 1942.

Degrees Bachelor of Fine Arts in the area of studio art. Majors and concentrations: art/fine arts, drawing, electronic media, graphic arts, installation art, painting, printmaking, sculpture, studio art. Graduate degrees offered: Master of Fine Arts in the area of studio art. Cross-registration with Consortium of Universities of the Washington Metropolitan Area.

Enrollment 335 total; 200 undergraduate, 35 graduate, 100 nonprofessional degree.

Art Student Profile 50% females, 50% males, 8% minorities, 20% international.

Art Faculty 14 total (full-time), 15 total (part-time). 100% of full-time faculty have terminal degrees. Graduate students do not teach undergraduate courses. Undergraduate student–faculty ratio: 12:1.

Student Life Student groups/activities include visiting artists programs.

Expenses for 2006–2007 Application fee: $45. Comprehensive fee: $41,243 includes full-time tuition ($29,206), mandatory fees ($467), and college room and board ($11,570). College room only: $7350. Full-time tuition and fees vary according to degree level. Room and board charges vary according to board plan and housing facility.

Financial Aid Program-specific awards available.

Application Procedures Students apply for admission into the professional program by sophomore year. Deadline for freshmen: Janu-

ary 15; transfers: March 1. Required: high school transcript, college transcript(s) for transfer students, minimum 2.0 high school GPA, 2 letters of recommendation, SAT test score only. Recommended: minimum 3.0 high school GPA, interview.

Web Site http://www.american.edu/academic.depts/cas/art

Contact Ms. Glenna Haynie, Administrator, Department of Art, American University, 4400 Massachusetts Avenue, NW, Washington, District of Columbia 20016; 202-885-1670, fax: 202-885-1132.

Anna Maria College
Paxton, Massachusetts

Independent Roman Catholic, coed. Rural campus. Total enrollment: 1,200. Art program established 1947.

Degrees Bachelor of Arts in the areas of art education, art therapy, art and business, graphic design, studio art. Majors and concentrations: art and business, art education, art therapy, graphic design, studio art. Cross-registration with Worcester Consortium.

Enrollment 42 total; 30 undergraduate, 12 graduate.

Art Student Profile 66% females, 34% males, 3% international.

Art Faculty 1 undergraduate (full-time), 10 undergraduate (part-time). 100% of full-time faculty have terminal degrees. Graduate students do not teach undergraduate courses. Undergraduate student–faculty ratio: 4:1.

Student Life Student groups/activities include senior art exhibit, student/teacher exhibit, gallery sitting.

Expenses for 2006–2007 Application fee: $40. Comprehensive fee: $31,644 includes full-time tuition ($21,094), mandatory fees ($2140), and college room and board ($8410). Room and board charges vary according to board plan. Special program-related fees: $25 per credit for model fee, $40 per 3-credit course for studio fee, $130 per 3-credit course for practicum/internship fee.

Application Procedures Students admitted directly into the professional program freshman year. Deadline for freshmen and transfers: continuous. Required: essay, high school transcript, college transcript(s) for transfer stu-

Anna Maria College (continued)

dents, minimum 2.0 high school GPA, 3 letters of recommendation, portfolio, SAT or ACT test scores. Recommended: interview. Portfolio reviews held by appointment on campus; the submission of slides may be substituted for portfolios when distance is prohibitive.

Web Site http://www.annamaria.edu

Undergraduate Contact Anna Maria College, Box U, Paxton, Massachusetts 01612-1198; 508-849-3365, fax: 508-849-3362.

More About the College

Anna Maria College (AMC), a private, comprehensive, four-year, coeducational Catholic college, was founded in 1946 by the Sisters of Saint Anne. AMC is a close-knit community. Small class sizes allow for mentor relationships to develop between faculty members and students. Freshman and sophomore classes generally have between 15 and 20 students; some upper-level classes have as few as 5 students. Faculty members teach and advise students based on their knowledge of each person as an individual, and classes are never taught by graduate assistants. The 600 full-time undergraduate students come from thirteen states and eleven other countries.

The College is located on a 190-acre wooded campus in Paxton, Massachusetts, 8 miles from downtown Worcester. The city offers numerous professional and cultural opportunities, and Boston, Providence, and Hartford are only an hour away. Local attractions include big-name entertainment and minor league hockey at the DCU Center; art, history, and science museums; classical music performances at Mechanics Hall; theater; and day and night skiing at Wachusett Mountain.

Art programs at AMC are offered through the Division of Fine Arts. The academic programs offered by the division provide students with a broad-based liberal arts education infused with the principles of the Catholic intellectual tradition. Students select a concentration in a specific art field: studio art, teacher of visual art (pre-K–8, 5–12, pre-K–12), art therapy, graphic design, or art and business.

The studio art major develops essential skills in several media through intensive studio courses, preparing students for a wide range of art-related career options or graduate study.

The Massachusetts Department of Education–approved program for initial license as a teacher of visual art provides students with the knowledge and skills required for a career in teaching in elementary, middle, or high schools.

The art therapy program prepares undergraduate students for the master's degree program in art therapy and art therapy licensing through the American Art Therapy Association. The curriculum is evenly balanced between art courses and human services courses.

Graphic design students develop problem-solving skills, critical-design thought, and language and technical skills. These skills integrate with the College's core curriculum, focused business courses, and the development of key communication skills to give the student the tools needed to enter the profession of graphic design. As this is a professional degree, students may wish to combine the program with a major or minor in business.

The art and business major is designed to provide an interdisciplinary course of study for art students who seek the opportunity to develop those talents in combination with a strong business background. The art courses cover the broad perspective of skills required of an artist, while the course work in business addresses areas of marketing, advertising, and management.

All students who major in art must possess a basic set of skills and knowledge, developed through the ten-course Art Core, including drawing and design skills, design and color theory, a knowledge of art history, and the completion of a senior seminar and senior art exhibit.

In the junior and senior years, advanced course work is designed to run concurrently with community field placements, so that students have the opportunity to observe and work alongside professionals in the community. Student talents and aptitudes are showcased in a senior capstone experience. During the capstone experience, studio art students prepare as professional artists for a senior art exhibit, art education students do student teaching, art therapy majors are placed in an internship experience that allows them a critical clinical experience under the direct supervision of professionals in their field, and graphic design and art and business majors are placed in supervised internships that allow them to gain practical experience and design and communication skills in their chosen field.

The Division of Fine Arts offers the possibility for students to engage in international studies. Students are encouraged to experience study abroad through programs ranging from summer study in the creative arts to a spring break in Berlin, Paris, or Vienna through the Urban Seminar Program. Students may also self-design a program in an area of interest.

Upon graduation, Anna Maria College alumni receive support and guidance from their Division V advisers and mentors for job placement.

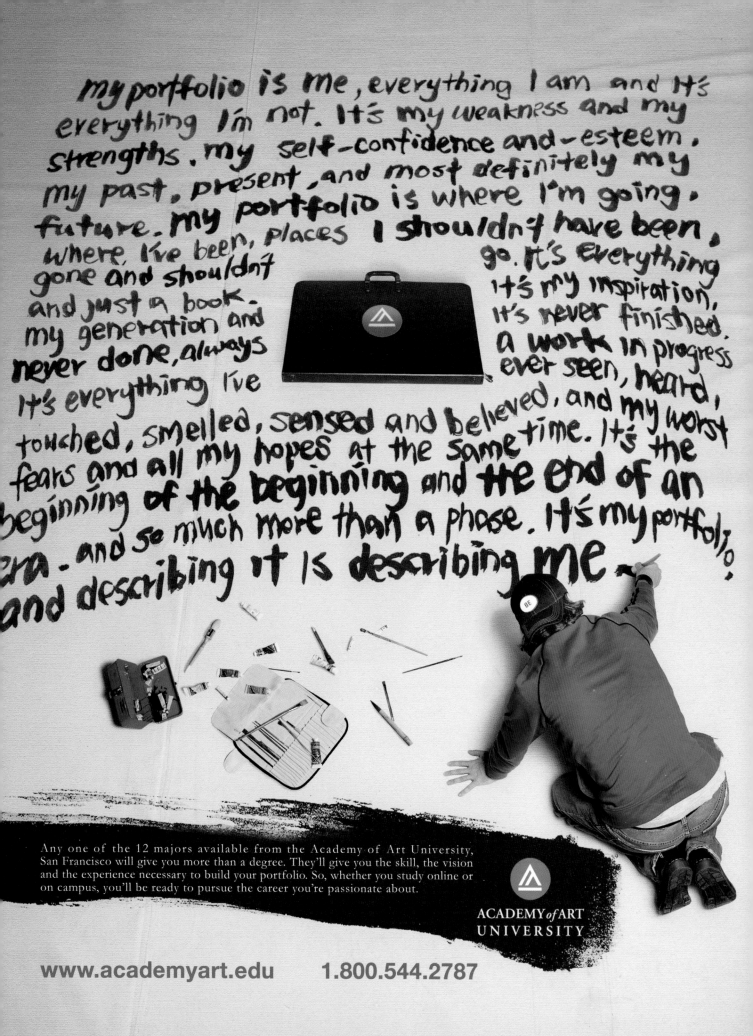

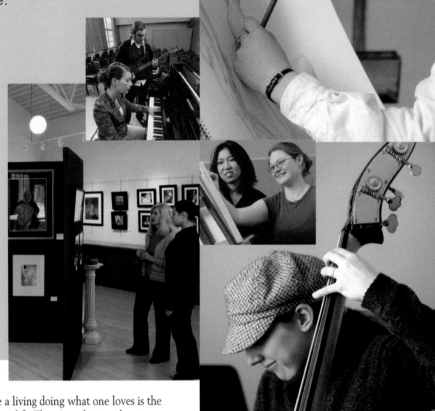

Tennessee Technological University
Appalachian Center for Craft

Cookeville, Tennessee

State-supported, coed. Small town campus. Total enrollment: 9,733. Art program established 1980.

Degrees Bachelor of Fine Arts in the areas of clay, fibers, glass, metals, wood, painting, art education. Majors and concentrations: art education, ceramics, clay, fibers, glass, jewelry and metalsmithing, metals, painting, surface design, textile arts, weaving and fibers, wood, woodworking design. Program accredited by NASAD.

Enrollment 130 total; all undergraduate.

Art Student Profile 50% females, 50% males, 7% minorities, 5% international.

Art Faculty 10 undergraduate (full-time). 100% of full-time faculty have terminal degrees. Graduate students do not teach undergraduate courses. Undergraduate student–faculty ratio: 12:1.

Student Life Student groups/activities include Visual Art Society, Annual Celebration of Craft. Special housing available for art students.

Expenses for 2006–2007 Application fee: $15. State resident tuition: $4590 full-time. Nonresident tuition: $14,284 full-time. Full-time tuition varies according to program. College room and board: $5964. College room only: $3020. Room and board charges vary according to board plan and housing facility. Special program-related fees: $60–$120 per credit hour for studio fees (in clay, fibers, glass, metals and wood).

Financial Aid Program-specific awards: 4 Bacchanal Scholarships for program majors ($1000).

Application Procedures Students admitted directly into the professional program freshman year. Deadline for freshmen and transfers: August 1. Required: high school transcript, college transcript(s) for transfer students, ACT test score only.

Web Site http://www.tntech.edu/craftcenter/

Undergraduate Contact Mr. Ward Doubet, Director, Appalachian Center for Craft, Tennessee Technological University, 1560 Craft Center Drive, Smithville, Tennessee 37166; 615-597-6801, fax: 615-597-6803, e-mail address: craftcenter@tntech.edu

More About the Craft Center and the University

The Appalachian Center for Craft, a satellite campus of Tennessee Tech University (TTU), promotes excellence in American craft by teaching tradition and innovation in technique, concept, and design. The Craft Center provides access to the highest quality craft education, professional artists, and career opportunities. The school offers students the option of five Bachelor of Fine Arts (B.F.A.) degree or nondegree Craft Certificate concentrations in fine craft: clay, fibers, glass, metals, and wood. The B.F.A. degree is accredited by the National Association of Schools of Art and Design and the Southern Association of Colleges and Schools.

The B.F.A. degree program features a contemporary approach to fine craft built on traditional techniques. Students become proficient in the materials, processes, and techniques used by professional craft artists and develop confidence in the use of tools and equipment in a studio environment. The measure of accomplishment is the B.F.A. senior thesis exhibition, requiring high standards of professionalism in preparation, design, and execution. The ultimate reflection of accomplishment is the students' consistent record of success beyond graduation. Craft Center students continue to raise the bar in contemporary craft innovation, winning national and regional awards, participating in prestigious shows and exhibitions, and receiving grants, scholarships, and artist residencies.

The nondegree Craft Certificate programs allow students to develop or enhance the professional skills necessary to embark on a career in craft. The certificate is conferred as a formal recognition by the

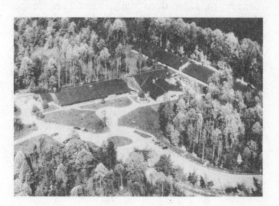

Visual Arts

Appalachian Center for Craft (continued)

Craft Center faculty of a level of studio knowledge and accomplishment at an emerging professional level.

Located on more than 500 wooded acres overlooking Center Hill Lake in Middle Tennessee, the Craft Center's facilities are among the finest in the nation. The facility exceeds 87,000 square feet, including 50,000 square feet of spacious studios, a library, a large conference room, two audiovisual/lecture rooms, more than 4,000 square feet of exhibition and gallery space, student housing, administrative offices, and a café.

In addition to the outstanding facilities and studio equipment, the Craft Center offers an experienced tenured faculty of nationally renowned craft artists; individual attention; and a private art school experience at a public school price. Students attend general education and art foundation courses on the main campus of Tennessee Tech University in Cookeville (approximately 25 minutes east of the Craft Center; free shuttle service is available).

The Craft Center's 5 full-time faculty members are nationally and internationally renowned and respected craft artists in the fields of clay (Vince Pitelka), fibers (Jeanne Brady), glass (Curtiss Brock), metals (Robert Coogan), and wood (Graham Campbell). All faculty members have Master of Fine Arts degrees in their respective fields and are extremely active in exhibitions, teaching workshops, publishing, and professional craft organizations, in addition to their teaching and studio work.

The Craft Center also offers an Artist-in-Residence program, which is a one- to three-year competitive program allowing emerging professional artists to work in the intensive studio environment of the Craft Center. Each studio has a resident artist with a B.F.A., M.F.A., or professional equivalent in his or her field. The residents come from all over the country and abroad to study, teach, and further develop their work at the Craft Center. They are invaluable to all programs of the Craft Center, providing additional expertise and experiences to the students.

The clay studio includes a variety of firing options from raku, bonfire, salt, soda, and wood to electric and gas kilns; tons of space for handbuilding and wheel work; and glaze and clay mixing rooms. The fibers studio, focused on surface design and weaving, has a large loom room, a dye kitchen, and fully equipped surface design facilities. The glass studio emphasizes the technical skills of glassblowing and has one of the best equipped hot- and cold-working shops in the nation. The metals department has studios for fine jewelry, large-scale sculptural work, and blacksmithing. The wood studio, focusing on studio furniture design and production, has bench rooms for work with hand and power tools, a large fully-equipped machine room, and a spray room.

The Craft Center is located approximately 60 miles east of Nashville and 120 miles west of Knoxville off Interstate-40, near the town of Smithville. The main campus of Tennessee Tech University is located in Cookeville, approximately 25 minutes east of the Craft Center, off I-40. The Craft Center offers free shuttle service from the Craft Center to TTU and return service in order to provide easy access to classes on the main campus and at the Craft Center. TTU also offers two other B.F.A. concentrations, art education and painting, on TTU's main campus. The studios of TTU's Bryan Fine Arts Building have been recently renovated to provide more work space for these programs as well as improved ventilation, lighting, and storage.

For more information about the Craft Center, students should call 615-597-6801, e-mail craftcenter@tntech.edu, or visit http://www.tntech.edu/craftcenter. For more general information about TTU and main campus art programs, students should visit http://www.tntech.edu.

Arcadia University
Glenside, Pennsylvania

Independent, coed. Suburban campus. Total enrollment: 3,595. Art program established 1925.

Degrees Bachelor of Arts in the areas of scientific illustration, art therapy, art history; Bachelor of Fine Arts in the areas of graphic design, interior design, painting, printmaking, ceramics, metals and jewelry, photography, art education. Majors and concentrations: art education, art history, art/fine arts, ceramic art and design, graphic design, interior design, jewelry and metalsmithing, painting/drawing, photography, pre-art therapy, printmaking, scientific illustration, studio art. Program accredited by NASAD.

Enrollment 238 total; all undergraduate.

Art Student Profile 79% females, 21% males, 9% minorities, 3% international.

Art Faculty 9 undergraduate (full-time), 22 undergraduate (part-time). 89% of full-time faculty have terminal degrees. Graduate students do not teach undergraduate courses. Undergraduate student–faculty ratio: 13:1.

Student Life Student groups/activities include Arcadia Association of Fine Arts, Arcadia University Art Gallery.

Expenses for 2006–2007 Application fee: $30. Comprehensive fee: $35,650 includes full-time tuition ($25,650), mandatory fees ($340), and college room and board ($9660). College room only: $6680. Full-time tuition and fees vary according to course load, degree level, and program. Room and board charges vary according to board plan. Special program-related fees: $25–$100 per course for lab supplies.

Financial Aid Program-specific awards: 15–20 achievement awards for program majors ($1000–$5000).

Application Procedures Students admitted directly into the professional program freshman year. Deadline for freshmen and transfers: continuous. Required: essay, high school transcript, college transcript(s) for transfer students, minimum 2.0 high school GPA, 2 letters of recommendation, portfolio, SAT or ACT test scores. Recommended: minimum 3.0 high school GPA, interview. Portfolio reviews held 11 times on campus and off campus in Philadelphia, PA; New York, NY; Boston, MA; Washington, DC; Baltimore, MD; the submission of slides may be substituted for portfolios if a campus visit is impossible.

Web Site http://www.arcadia.edu

Undergraduate Contact Office of Enrollment Management, Arcadia University, 450 South Easton Road, Glenside, Pennsylvania 19038-3295; 877-272-2342, fax: 215-572-4049, e-mail address: admiss@arcadia.edu

Arizona State University

Tempe, Arizona

State-supported, coed. Suburban campus. Total enrollment: 51,234. Art program established 1980.

Degrees Bachelor of Fine Arts in the area of art. Majors and concentrations: art education, ceramics, drawing, fibers, intermedia, metals, painting, photography, printmaking, sculpture. Graduate degrees offered: Master of Fine Arts in the area of art. Doctor of Philosophy in the area of art history.

Enrollment 1,469 total; 1,148 undergraduate, 132 graduate, 189 nonprofessional degree.

Art Student Profile 67% females, 33% males, 18% minorities, 2% international.

Art Faculty 50 total (full-time), 24 total (part-time). 100% of full-time faculty have terminal degrees. Graduate students teach a few undergraduate courses. Undergraduate student–faculty ratio: 17:1.

Student Life Student groups/activities include senior exhibition and portfolio, Step Gallery exhibitions, Northlight Gallery exhibitions.

Expenses for 2006–2007 Application fee: $25, $50 for nonresidents. State resident tuition: $4591 full-time. Nonresident tuition: $15,750 full-time. Mandatory fees: $97 full-time. Full-time tuition and fees vary according to location and program. College room and board: $6900. College room only: $4200. Room and board charges vary according to board plan, housing facility, and location. Special program-related fees: $15–$45 per class for expendable materials, $180 per class for software in computer-based courses.

Financial Aid Program-specific awards: 1 Markus/Scult Studio Art Scholarship for academically qualified studio students ($3000), 6 Herberger Scholarships/Fellowships for academically qualified students and studio students ($3000–$5000), 2 Martin Wong Scholarships for painting and ceramics students ($2000), 1 Ethel Larson Award for academically qualified students ($600), 1 Jack Breckenridge Award for art history seniors ($250), Herbert Smith Award, 2 Encinas Awards for watercolor and sculpture students ($500), 20–30 Art Special Talent Awards ($5000–$12,000), 2 J. Russell Nelson Undergraduate Scholarships for academically qualified studio seniors ($3000), 2 Windgate Awards for academically qualified studio students ($5000).

Application Procedures Students apply for admission into the professional program by sophomore year. Deadline for freshmen and transfers: continuous. Required: high school transcript, college transcript(s) for transfer students, minimum 3.0 high school GPA, SAT or ACT test scores, portfolio for studio art majors, minimum 2.7 GPA, minimum 2.5 college GPA for nonresident transfer students. Portfolio reviews held in fall and spring on campus; the submission of slides may be substituted for portfolios (or digital portfolio).

Web Site http://herbergercollege.asu.edu/art

Undergraduate Contact Office of Enrollment Management and Student Services, ASU

Arizona State University (continued)

Herberger College of the Arts, Arizona State University, Box 872102, Tempe, Arizona 85287-2102; 480-727-9810, fax: 480-727-6529.

Graduate Contact Vicki Kelley, Administrative Associate, School of Art, Arizona State University, Box 871505, Tempe, Arizona 85287-1505; 480-965-6303, fax: 480-965-8338, e-mail address: vicki.kelley@asu.edu

Arkansas State University

State University, Arkansas

State-supported, coed. Small town campus. Total enrollment: 10,727. Art program established 1936.

Degrees Bachelor of Fine Arts in the areas of studio art, art education, graphic design. Majors and concentrations: art education, ceramics, graphic design, painting/drawing, photography, printmaking, sculpture, studio art. Graduate degrees offered: Master of Arts in the areas of studio art, art education. Program accredited by NASAD.

Enrollment 180 total; 142 undergraduate, 38 nonprofessional degree.

Art Student Profile 48% females, 52% males, 8% minorities, 3% international.

Art Faculty 13 total (full-time). 100% of full-time faculty have terminal degrees. Graduate students do not teach undergraduate courses. Undergraduate student–faculty ratio: 12:1.

Student Life Student groups/activities include AIGA-American Institute of Graphic Arts, National Art Education Association (NAEA) Student Chapter.

Expenses for 2007–2008 Application fee: $15. State resident tuition: $4620 full-time. Nonresident tuition: $12,000 full-time. Mandatory fees: $1390 full-time. Full-time tuition and fees vary according to course load, location, and program. College room and board: $4710. Room and board charges vary according to board plan and housing facility.

Financial Aid Program-specific awards: 10 art scholarships for art majors ($1000–$3000).

Application Procedures Students apply for admission into the professional program by sophomore year. Deadline for freshmen and transfers: continuous. Required: high school

transcript, portfolio, SAT or ACT test scores, minimum 2.0 college GPA for transfer students. Portfolio reviews held 3 times on campus and off campus in Little Rock, AR; the submission of slides may be substituted for portfolios for three-dimensional work.

Web Site http://finearts.astate.edu/art/art.html

Undergraduate Contact Mr. Curtis Steele, Chair, Department of Art, Arkansas State University, PO Box 1920, State University, Arkansas 72467; 870-972-3050, fax: 870-972-3932, e-mail address: csteele@astate.edu

Graduate Contact Dean of the Graduate School, Graduate School, Arkansas State University, PO Box 60, State University, Arkansas 72467; 870-972-3029, fax: 870-972-3857, e-mail address: gradsch@astate.edu

Art Academy of Cincinnati

Cincinnati, Ohio

Independent, coed. Urban campus. Total enrollment: 164. Art program established 1869.

Degrees Bachelor of Fine Arts in the areas of fine art, communication arts, studio with an emphasis in art history/museum studies. Majors and concentrations: art history, digital design, digital media, drawing, graphic design, illustration, painting, photo design, photography, printmaking, sculpture. Graduate degrees offered: Master of Arts in the area of art education. Cross-registration with members of the Greater Cincinnati Consortium of Colleges and Universities. Program accredited by NASAD.

Enrollment 157 total; 156 undergraduate, 1 nonprofessional degree.

Art Student Profile 54% females, 46% males, 13% minorities, 2% international.

Art Faculty 15 total (full-time), 30 total (part-time). 98% of full-time faculty have terminal degrees. Graduate students do not teach undergraduate courses. Undergraduate student–faculty ratio: 10:1.

Expenses for 2007–2008 Application fee: $25. Tuition: $19,990 full-time. Mandatory fees: $350 full-time. Special program-related fees: $350 per year for student activities.

Financial Aid Program-specific awards: 60 entrance scholarships for incoming students ($1000–$16,000).

Visual

Arts

Application Procedures Students admitted directly into the professional program freshman year. Deadline for freshmen and transfers: continuous. Notification date for freshmen and transfers: August 1. Required: essay, high school transcript, college transcript(s) for transfer students, minimum 2.0 high school GPA, letter of recommendation, interview, portfolio, SAT or ACT test scores (minimum combined SAT score of 1200, minimum composite ACT score of 20). Recommended: minimum 3.0 high school GPA. Portfolio reviews held continuously on campus and off campus in 7 cities on National Portfolio Days; the submission of slides may be substituted for portfolios when distance is prohibitive.

Web Site http://www.artacademy.edu

Contact John J. Wadell, Director of Admissions, Art Academy of Cincinnati, 1212 Jackson Street, Cincinnati, Ohio 45202; 800-323-5692, fax: 513-562-8744, e-mail address: admissions@artacademy.edu

Art Center College of Design

Pasadena, California

Independent, coed. Suburban campus. Total enrollment: 1,631. Art program established 1930.

Degrees Bachelor of Fine Arts in the areas of advertising, illustration, graphic design, photography, fine arts, film; Bachelor of Science in the areas of environmental design, product and transportation design. Majors and concentrations: advertising design and communication, art/fine arts, environmental design, film studies, graphic design, illustration, industrial design, photography, product design, transportation design. Graduate degrees offered: Master of Arts in the area of art theory and criticism; Master of Fine Arts in the areas of media design, fine arts, broadcast cinema; Master of Science in the areas of product design, environmental design. Cross-registration with Occidental College, California Institute of Technology. Program accredited by NASAD.

Enrollment 1,631 total; 1,485 undergraduate, 146 graduate.

Art Student Profile 40% females, 60% males, 51% minorities, 23% international.

Art Faculty 66 undergraduate (full-time), 320 undergraduate (part-time), 4 graduate (full-time), 30 graduate (part-time). 99% of full-time faculty have terminal degrees. Graduate students do not teach undergraduate courses. Undergraduate student–faculty ratio: 9:1.

Student Life Student groups/activities include Contraste (Latino student group), Chroma (African-American student group), Industrial Design Society of America Student Chapter.

Expenses for 2007–2008 Application fee: $45. Tuition: $27,710 full-time. Mandatory fees: $200 full-time. Special program-related fees: $200 per semester for universal studio usage fee.

Financial Aid Program-specific awards: 300 Art Center Scholarships for program majors ($1000–$7000), 100 entering grants for program majors ($5000), 12 Art Center Outreach Grants for Latino, African-American, Native American students ($13,855), 1 Nike Grant for Latino, African-American graphics designers, female product designers ($3000), 1 Knapp Grant for Latino and African-American fine arts majors ($13,855).

Application Procedures Students admitted directly into the professional program freshman year. Deadline for freshmen and transfers: continuous. Notification date for freshmen and transfers: continuous. Required: essay, high school transcript, college transcript(s) for transfer students, portfolio, SAT or ACT test scores, minimum TOEFL score of 550 for international students. Recommended: minimum 3.0 high school GPA, interview. Portfolio reviews held continuously on campus.

Web Site http://www.artcenter.edu

Contact Ms. Kit Baron, Vice President, Admissions, Art Center College of Design, 1700 Lida Street, Pasadena, California 91103; 626-396-2373, fax: 626-795-0578.

More About the College

A rt Center College of Design was founded in 1930 in downtown Los Angeles with a single purpose—to educate students for careers of achievement in the visual arts professions. The founder, Tink Adams, vowed to work closely with the leaders of industry to prepare professionals for meaningful careers. This tradition of close industry relationships continues today at the Pasadena campus.

Art Center College of Design (continued)

Art Center attracts attention from firms throughout the world. Companies, such as Nike, Honda, Sony, The Gap, Nokia, and Universal Studios, have decided to sponsor special student research projects at the College. Students have the opportunity to work with real clients on futuristic and conceptual projects. Of special interest are projects concerning sustainability, the environment, and global and humanitarian issues.

In addition to visiting artists and representatives from industry, the College features a faculty of practicing professionals who reinforce this tradition of real-world influence. Most are part-time faculty members who maintain their own distinctive practices.

Fine arts students have an opportunity to work with some of the most provocative artists and painters working today, such as Mike Kelley, Liz Larner, and Jeremy Gilbert-Rolfe.

Art Center acknowledges and encourages the dissolution of boundaries between disciplines, and, although students apply to and study within specific majors, there are opportunities for new kinds of art making, based on digital and other technologies. The College's mission is to lead the way for the industry in exploring new roles for design, photography, and film.

The average freshman at Art Center is 23 years old. All students must declare a major before entering the College, and this has resulted in a mature and focused student body. Campus life, too, is influenced by the maturity of the students. There is currently no on-campus housing. Students choose from an abundance of housing within the Pasadena and Los Angeles area.

Art Center's graduates have made significant marks in the world of art and design, and alumni return to the campus to recruit for their own employment needs. The high demand for Art Center graduates is attributable to the degree of specialization and professionalism required of the students. In excess of 200 firms visit the College to interview graduating students each year, and job listings are printed regularly for the use of students and alumni. Some of the firms that have recruited on campus are Harcourt Brace & Co., Capitol Records, The Walt Disney Company, Ford Motor Company, Daimler Chrysler, Pentagram, Virgin Records, Landor Associates, Honda, Nike, MCA-Universal Studios, Neiman Marcus Direct, TBWA/Chiat/Day, Daimler-Chrysler, Industrial Light and Magic, DreamWorks SKG, and Mattel Toys.

With two campuses in suburban Pasadena, Art Center offers a physically beautiful environment

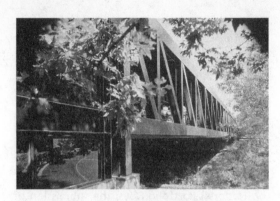

juxtaposed with the internationalism of Los Angeles and the Pacific Rim. Art Center encourages a diverse population of students and faculty members. The goal in bringing together a community of students from throughout the United States and the world is to develop new solutions to design issues and to promote the importance of design within the world communities. It is within this context that students receive highly individualized and rigorous programs of study. Critical thinking, as well as development of technical skills, is emphasized.

Facilities Art Center is an acknowledged leader in providing new technologies and state-of-the-art facilities to its students. Features include a distinctive contemporary campus in the hills overlooking Pasadena's Rose Bowl; a 215,000-square-foot glass and steel building designed by Craig Ellwood; an 11,000-square-foot computer graphics lab with 220 Macintosh stations, sixty-two Silicon Graphic workstations, thirty-one SGI/NT 320 workstations, and one of the world's largest computer-aided industrial design (CAID) networks as well as a vast array of software to introduce students to the newest digital technologies; a professional recording studio; photography areas with black-and-white labs with seventy-five enlargers, a color lab with a 20-inch fully automated E-6 processor, a 20-inch fully automated cibachrome processor, and a 20-inch RA4 fully automated processor; two 4,600-square-foot shooting stages that provide twenty-six shooting stages equipped with seamless background colors, including one 15 × 30 flying flat; and digital-imaging facilities, including Kodak XL 7700 thermal printer, RFS 2035 film scanners, H-P Paint Jet printer, 840 AV workstation, a Microtech 4 × 5 film scanner, and an Agfa flatbed transparency scanner. A second campus, also in Pasadena, houses graduate and public education programs.

Special Programs The College encourages a global and international approach to design education. Art

Center facilitates a wide variety of internship opportunities with major corporations and firms, such as Ford, Toyota Motor Corporation, Electronic Arts, Nike, and Wieden & Kennedy. Students may also accept paid mentorship positions or enroll in a mentorship class to assist local Pasadena high school students.

The Art Institute of Atlanta

Atlanta, Georgia

Proprietary, coed. Suburban campus. Total enrollment: 2,694. Art program established 1949.

Degrees Bachelor of Fine Arts in the areas of digital filmmaking and video production, game art and design, graphic design, illustration and design, interactive media design, interior design, media arts and animation, photographic imaging, visual effects and motion graphics. Majors and concentrations: digital film and video, game art and design, graphic design, illustration, interactive media, interior design, media arts/animation, photographic/electronic imaging, photography and imaging, visual effects and motion graphics. Program accredited by CIDA.

Enrollment 2,694 total.

Art Student Profile 43% females, 57% males.

Student Life Special housing available for art students.

Expenses for 2007–2008 Application fee: $50. Tuition: $20,064 full-time. College room only: $8250.

Financial Aid Program-specific awards available.

Application Procedures Students admitted directly into the professional program freshman year. Deadline for freshmen and transfers: continuous. Notification date for freshmen and transfers: continuous. Required: essay, high school transcript, college transcript(s) for transfer students, interview, SAT, ACT, ASSET, or COMPASS scores, portfolio (for high school seniors entering scholarship competition).

Web Site http://www.artinstitutes.edu/atlanta

Undergraduate Contact Director of Admissions, The Art Institute of Atlanta, 6600 Peachtree Dunwoody Road, 100 Embassy Row, Atlanta, Georgia 30328; 800-275-4242, fax: 770-394-0008, e-mail address: aiaadm@aii.edu

The Art Institute of Boston at Lesley University

Boston, Massachusetts

Independent, coed. Urban campus. Total enrollment: 6,539. Art program established 1912.

Degrees Bachelor of Fine Arts in the areas of fine arts, illustration, graphic design, fine arts/illustration, illustration/design, photography, illustration, animation, art history; Bachelor of Fine Arts/Master of Arts in the area of art/expressive therapies; Bachelor of Fine Arts/Master of Education in the area of art education. Majors and concentrations: advertising illustration, animation, art history, art/fine arts, book illustration, commercial photography, documentary photography, drawing, editorial illustration, graphic design, illustration, multimedia design, painting, photography, printmaking, sculpture, Web design. Graduate degrees offered: Bachelor of Fine Arts/Master of Arts in the area of art/expressive therapies; Master of Fine Arts in the area of visual arts; Bachelor of Fine Arts/Master of Education in the area of art education. Program accredited by NASAD.

Enrollment 553 total; 540 undergraduate, 13 graduate.

Art Student Profile 58% females, 42% males, 11% minorities, 12% international.

Art Faculty 25 total (full-time), 80 total (part-time). 90% of full-time faculty have terminal degrees. Graduate students do not teach undergraduate courses. Undergraduate student–faculty ratio: 10:1.

Student Life Student groups/activities include student exhibitions in galleries and sites around Boston, Graphic Artists Guild student membership (AIGA). Special housing available for art students.

Expenses for 2007–2008 Application fee: $40. Comprehensive fee: $35,550 includes full-time tuition ($23,200), mandatory fees ($250), and college room and board ($12,100). College room only: $6800. Special program-related fees: $475 per year for department fees.

The Art Institute of Boston at Lesley University (continued)

Financial Aid Program-specific awards: 50 AIB Scholarships for incoming students ($5000), 1 Presidential Scholarship for incoming students, 160 Art Institute of Boston Grants for those demonstrating need ($500–$3500), 10–20 Community College Transfer Scholarships for incoming students with AA degree ($4000), 1–2 ACCESS Scholarships for incoming African, Latino, Asian, or Native American students, 50 Deans Scholarships for incoming students ($7000).

Application Procedures Students admitted directly into the professional program freshman year. Deadline for freshmen and transfers: continuous. Required: essay, high school transcript, college transcript(s) for transfer students, interview, portfolio, SAT or ACT test scores, resumé/list of accomplishments, awards. Recommended: minimum 3.0 high school GPA, 2 letters of recommendation. Portfolio reviews held as needed on campus and off campus at National Portfolio Days; the submission of slides may be substituted for portfolios if a campus visit or National Portfolio Day review is not possible to arrange.

Web Site http://www.aiboston.edu

Undergraduate Contact Office of Admissions, The Art Institute of Boston at Lesley University, 700 Beacon Street, Boston, Massachusetts 02215; 617-585-6710, fax: 617-585-6720, e-mail address: admissions@aiboston.edu

Graduate Contact Graduate Office of Admissions, The Art Institute of Boston at Lesley University, 29 Everett Street, Cambridge, Massachusetts 02138; 617-349-8300, e-mail address: info@lesley.edu

More About the Institute

The Art Institute of Boston (AIB) at Lesley University is a professional college of art that was founded in 1912. Its programs are studio intensive, integrating liberal arts courses specifically designed to broaden students' intellectual and artistic perceptions. The Art Institute of Boston at Lesley University provides a supportive environment to enable students to succeed in their careers—the atmosphere is both challenging and nurturing, helping to maximize personal growth, intellectual growth, and artistic potential. The Art Institute of Boston at Lesley University is one of the four colleges within Lesley University. AIB's strengths as a professional college

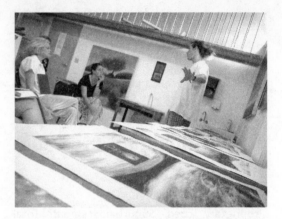

of the visual arts are combined with the resources of a university, providing expanded educational opportunities for students not usually found at most independent colleges of art yet preserving the character of a small private college of art.

The AIB community is small and close-knit, and most students and faculty members know each other by the end of the first semester. The Art Institute of Boston at Lesley University has an exceptional faculty, many of whom are well-known practicing artists, designers, illustrators, and photographers. Some of AIB's faculty members include Professor in the Foundation Department, Nathan Goldstein, a recognized authority on art education, lecturer and artist; Christopher James, Professor and Chair of the Photography Department, an internationally renowned photographer who has won numerous awards and fellowships and whose work is in museum collections around the world; Jane Tuckerman, Associate Professor of Photography, a widely-exhibited photographer and recipient of an NEA fellowship and other prestigious grants and fellowships; and Anthony Apesos, Professor of Visual Arts, who is an accomplished painter, lecturer, and art critic.

The faculty members at AIB serve as mentors to their students and are very accessible to them. Students at AIB benefit from lectures, exhibitions, and the visiting artists who contribute to the positive energy of studio critiques and workshops. Activities and opportunities for growth and learning at AIB include student on- and off-campus exhibitions, lectures, workshops, field trips to galleries in New York and New England, and a visiting artist program. Acclaimed artists, such as Chuck Close, Duane Michals, Edward Sorel, Milton Glaser, Roy DeCarava, Luis Gonzalez Palma, and Andres Serrano have recently been guest lecturers at the college.

Visual *Arts*

Education at AIB is not confined to the studios and galleries of the college. Students benefit from the talent and experience of the faculty members and the extensive connections to the Boston art and business communities that the college has nurtured. Boston is a thriving cultural and commercial center, home to countless museums and galleries, symphonies, and theaters and renowned for its medical centers, financial institutions, and universities. These communities provide venues for a wealth of internships and full-time employment. In addition to continuing exhibitions of student work throughout the University, students exhibit at numerous galleries around Boston. Students are encouraged to show their work long before graduation, gaining valuable life experiences outside the classroom.

The practical aspect of developing a career in art is part of the formal curriculum at AIB. By the time students graduate, they are well prepared for their professions through course work devoted to professional development, such as presentation and portfolio building, and learning to make contacts in their fields. AIB graduates cite the practical skills and the encouragement they received as key factors in building the confidence needed to succeed in their careers.

Program Facilities The Art Institute of Boston's facilities include five state-of-the-art Macintosh computer laboratories, an animation lab, an updated photography lab with color and black-and-white printers, a digital photography lab, a printmaking lab with etching and lithography presses, a wood shop, and a clay lab with kilns. Senior fine arts students have their own individual studios in which to create.

The Art Institute of Boston was selected to join the New Media Centers Program, a consortium of higher education institutions and digital technology companies dedicated to advancing learning through new media. AIB has newly expanded multimedia programs that use state-of-the-art technology and equipment.

The AIB library collection is devoted principally to the visual arts and contains more than 10,000 books, seventy-five serial titles, 45,000 slides, a video-viewing room, and more than 500 art-related videos, and it subscribes to AMICO, the image database. The library has the National Gallery of Art's American Art Collection on videodisc, a visual reference of more than 26,000 images spanning three centuries.

In addition, the Eleanor De Wolfe Ludcke Library at Lesley provides a state-of-the-art multimedia resource center and a collection of 100,000 books, 700 current periodicals, 2,200 computer software and CD-ROM titles, 650 film and video titles, media material, and circulating media equipment. Students have borrowing privileges at six additional libraries through the Fenway Library Online.

The Art Institute of Boston sponsors a full program of exhibitions and lectures by visiting artists. The gallery presents major exhibitions of contemporary and historical work by established and emerging artists, including the alumni of The Art Institute of Boston. Students have the opportunity to assist in mounting exhibitions and to personally meet visiting artists. A student gallery and reserved areas show student work year-round. Gallery South exhibits the work of student photographers throughout the year, including group and senior exhibitions.

Special Programs The duPont Lecture Series brings the work of accomplished artists of color to the college; frequent visits to the college by known artists; a collaboration with Maine Photographic Workshop; study-abroad programs in France and at the Art Institute of Florence, Lorenzo de Medici; internships at art galleries, design and animation studios, and advertising agencies; freelance and placement listings through artists' resources, counseling, guidance, and tutoring services. Master's degree programs in art education and expressive therapies are offered in conjunction with Lesley University. Precollege classes give high school students an opportunity to earn college credit and develop portfolios.

The Art Institute of California–San Diego

San Diego, California

Proprietary, coed. Urban campus. Total enrollment: 2,386.

Degrees Bachelor of Fine Arts in the area of fashion design. Majors and concentrations: fashion design.

Student Life Student groups/activities include Advertising Club, American Institute of Graphic Arts (AIGA), American Society of Interior Designers (ASID), International Interior Design Association, Concept Art Club. Special housing available for art students.

Expenses for 2007–2008 Application fee: $50. Tuition: $22,272 full-time. College room only: $9780.

The Art Institute of California–San Diego (continued)

Financial Aid Program-specific awards: 345 merit-based awards for current students, 20 general academic scholarships for incoming students.

Application Procedures Students admitted directly into the professional program freshman year. Deadline for freshmen and transfers: continuous. Notification date for freshmen and transfers: continuous. Required: essay, high school transcript, college transcript(s) for transfer students, minimum 2.0 high school GPA, interview, portfolio (for game art students only), 2 letters of recommendation if GPA is under 2.0 (4.0 scale). Recommended: SAT or ACT test scores. Portfolio reviews held 4 times (1 per quarter) on campus.

Web Site http://www.artinstitutes.edu/sandiego

Undergraduate Contact Admissions Director, The Art Institute of California–San Diego, 7650 Mission Valley Road, San Diego, California 92108; 866-275-2422, e-mail address: aicaadmin@aii.edu

The Art Institute of California–San Francisco

San Francisco, California

Proprietary, coed. Urban campus. Total enrollment: 1,624. Art program established 1939.

Degrees Bachelor of Fine Arts in the area of fashion design; Bachelor of Science in the areas of graphic design, media arts and animation, interactive media design, game art and design, visual and game programming, interior design, advertising, fashion marketing and management. Majors and concentrations: advertising, fashion design, fashion marketing and management, game art and design, graphic design, interactive media, interior design, media arts/animation, visual and game programming. Graduate degrees offered: Master of Fine Arts in the area of computer animation.

Art Faculty Graduate students do not teach undergraduate courses.

Student Life Student groups/activities include Game Art and Design Club, Animation Club, Anime Club, Graphic Design Club, Interior Design Club, Sculpture/VFX Props Club, SIGGRAPH Student Chapter, Student Photography Club, Society of Web Artists and Programmers (SWAP). Special housing available for art students.

Expenses for 2006–2007 Application fee: $50. Tuition: $20,640 full-time. College room only: $7851.

Financial Aid Program-specific awards available.

Application Procedures Students admitted directly into the professional program freshman year. Deadline for freshmen and transfers: continuous. Notification date for freshmen and transfers: continuous. Required: essay, high school transcript, college transcript(s) for transfer students, interview.

Web Site http://www.artinstitutes.edu/sanfrancisco

Contact Admissions Department, The Art Institute of California–San Francisco, 1170 Market Street, San Francisco, California 94102; 888-493-3261, fax: 415-863-6344.

The Art Institute of Charleston

Charleston, South Carolina

Proprietary, coed. Urban campus.

Degrees Bachelor of Fine Arts in the areas of graphic design, interior design, photographic imaging, interactive media design. Majors and concentrations: graphic design, interactive media, interior design, photographic/electronic imaging.

Expenses for 2006–2007 Application fee: $50. Tuition: $20,064 full-time. Special program-related fees: $100–$250 per month for supplies and books.

Financial Aid Program-specific awards available.

Application Procedures Students admitted directly into the professional program freshman year. Deadline for freshmen and transfers: continuous. Notification date for freshmen and transfers: continuous. Required: essay, high school transcript, college transcript(s) for transfer students, interview, SAT, ACT, ASSET, or COMPASS scores.

Web Site http://www.artinstitutes.edu/charleston

Undergraduate Contact Admissions Director, The Art Institute of Charleston, 24 North Market Street, Charleston, South Carolina 29401; 866-211-0107, fax: 843-727-3440.

The Art Institute of Colorado

Denver, Colorado

Proprietary, coed. Urban campus. Total enrollment: 2,765. Art program established 1952.

Degrees Bachelor of Arts. Majors and concentrations: digital film and video, fashion design and marketing, graphic design, industrial design, interactive media, interior design, media arts/animation, multimedia, photography, video production, visual effects and motion graphics, Web design.

Expenses for 2007–2008 Application fee: $50. Tuition: $20,928 full-time. Full-time tuition varies according to course load. College room only: $9000.

Application Procedures Students admitted directly into the professional program freshman year. Required: essay, high school transcript, college transcript(s) for transfer students, interview. Recommended: portfolio, SAT or ACT test scores. the submission of slides may be substituted for portfolios.

Web Site http://www.artinstitutes.edu/denver/

Undergraduate Contact Brian A. Parker, Director of Admissions, Admissions, The Art Institute of Colorado, 1200 Lincoln Street, Denver, Colorado 80203; 800-275-2420, e-mail address: aicadm@aii.edu

The Art Institute of Dallas

Dallas, Texas

Proprietary, coed. Urban campus. Art program established 1964.

Degrees Bachelor of Fine Arts in the areas of advertising design, digital media production, graphic design, interactive media design, interior design, media arts & animation. Majors and concentrations: advertising design, digital media production, graphic design, interactive media, interior design, media arts/animation.

Enrollment 1,417 total; all undergraduate.

Art Student Profile 53% females, 47% males, 35% minorities, 2% international.

Art Faculty 102 undergraduate (full-time), 48 graduate (full-time), 41 graduate (part-time). 45% of full-time faculty have terminal degrees. Graduate students do not teach undergraduate courses.

Student Life Student groups/activities include Student Council Association, Committee for Student Interests.

Expenses for 2007–2008 Application fee: $50. Tuition: $20,275 full-time. Mandatory fees: $325 full-time. College room only: $8504.

Financial Aid Program-specific awards: 400 merit awards for new students, 200 Varians Awards for continuing students.

Application Procedures Deadline for freshmen and transfers: continuous. Required: essay, high school transcript, college transcript(s) for transfer students, interview, portfolio for media arts and animation. Recommended: SAT or ACT test scores. Portfolio reviews held 4 times on campus; the submission of slides may be substituted for portfolios if unable to bring printed material.

Web Site http://www.artinstitutes.edu/dallas

Undergraduate Contact Mr. Chad Williams, Director of Admissions, Admissions, The Art Institute of Dallas, 8080 Park Lane, Suite 100, Dallas, Texas 75231-5993; 800-275-4243, fax: 214-696-4898, e-mail address: cwilliams@ aii.edu

The Art Institute of Fort Lauderdale

Fort Lauderdale, Florida

Proprietary, coed. Urban campus. Total enrollment: 3,058.

Degrees Bachelor of Science. Majors and concentrations: advertising, digital film and video, digital media production, fashion design, fashion merchandising, game art and design, graphic design, industrial design, interactive media, interior design, media arts/animation, visual effects and motion graphics.

Student Life Student groups/activities include Comic Book Club, Anime Club, American Society of Interior Designers (ASID) Student Chapter, American Institute of Graphic Arts

The Art Institute of Fort Lauderdale (continued)

(AIGA), Fashion Club, Photography Student Union. Special housing available for art students.

Expenses for 2007–2008 Application fee: $50. One-time mandatory fee: $50. Tuition: $19,890 full-time. Mandatory fees: $50 full-time. College room only: $5385.

Financial Aid Program-specific awards available.

Application Procedures Students admitted directly into the professional program freshman year. Deadline for freshmen and transfers: continuous. Notification date for freshmen and transfers: continuous. Required: essay, high school transcript, college transcript(s) for transfer students, interview.

Web Site http://www.artinstitutes.edu/ fortlauderdale/

Undergraduate Contact Director of Admissions, The Art Institute of Fort Lauderdale, 1799 South East 17th Street, Fort Lauderdale, Florida 33316-3000; 800-275-7603, fax: 954-728-8637.

The Art Institute of Houston

Houston, Texas

Proprietary, coed. Urban campus. Total enrollment: 1,619.

Degrees Bachelor of Fine Arts in the areas of graphic design, interactive media design, interior design, media arts & animation. Majors and concentrations: graphic design, interactive media, interior design, media arts/animation. Program accredited by CIDA.

Enrollment 1,601 undergraduate.

Art Student Profile 53% females, 47% males, 34% minorities, 1% international.

Art Faculty 34 undergraduate (full-time), 9 undergraduate (part-time). Graduate students do not teach undergraduate courses. Undergraduate student–faculty ratio: 20:1.

Student Life Student groups/activities include SIGGRAPH.

Expenses for 2007–2008 Application fee: $50. Comprehensive fee: $38,020 includes full-time tuition ($26,220), mandatory fees ($200), and college room and board ($11,600). College room only: $7608. Full-time tuition and fees

vary according to course load. Room and board charges vary according to housing facility.

Application Procedures Students admitted directly into the professional program freshman year. Deadline for freshmen and transfers: continuous. Required: high school transcript, interview. Portfolio reviews held 4 times on campus; the submission of slides may be substituted for portfolios for students living outside of the city.

Web Site http://www.artinstitutes.edu/houston

Undergraduate Contact Ms. Susanne Behrens, Director of Admissions, The Art Institute of Houston, 1900 Yorktown Street, Houston, Texas 77056; 800-275-4244.

The Art Institute of Jacksonville

Jacksonville, Florida

Proprietary, coed. Suburban campus. Art program established 2006.

Degrees Bachelor of Fine Arts in the areas of interior design, interactive media design, graphic design, digital film and video. Majors and concentrations: digital film and video, graphic design, interactive design, interior design.

Enrollment 53 total; all undergraduate.

Art Student Profile 70% females, 30% males, 13% minorities.

Art Faculty 1 undergraduate (full-time), 6 undergraduate (part-time). 100% of full-time faculty have terminal degrees. Graduate students do not teach undergraduate courses. Undergraduate student–faculty ratio: 12:1.

Expenses for 2007–2008 Application fee: $50. Tuition: $421 per credit hour.

Financial Aid Program-specific awards: National Art Honor Society Award, Presidents Scholarship for current students, 4 Scholastic Art and Writing Awards ($1000), Ai Jacksonville High School Scholarship, The Art Institute of Jacksonville Merit Award for new and continuing students.

Application Procedures Students admitted directly into the professional program freshman year. Deadline for freshmen and transfers: continuous. Required: essay, high school transcript, college transcript(s) for transfer students, interview. Recommended: minimum 2.0 high school GPA, minimum 3.0 high school GPA, letter of recommendation, portfolio, SAT or ACT test scores.

Web Site http://www.artinstitutes.edu/jacksonville/

Undergraduate Contact Admissions Department, The Art Institute of Jacksonville, 8775 Baypine Road, Jacksonville, Florida 32256; 904-732-9393, fax: 904-732-9473, e-mail address: scarlstrom@aii.edu

The Art Institute of Phoenix

Phoenix, Arizona

Proprietary, coed. Suburban campus. Total enrollment: 1,055. Art program established 1995.

Degrees Bachelor of Arts. Majors and concentrations: advertising, digital media production, fashion marketing, game art and design, graphic design, interactive media, interior design, media arts/animation, visual and game programming, visual effects and motion graphics.

Art Faculty Graduate students do not teach undergraduate courses.

Student Life Student groups/activities include International Interior Design Association (IIDA), SIGGRAPH Student Chapter, American Society of Interior Designers (ASID), Student Game Developers Association, Society of Student Filmmakers, Ani Motion (animation club). Special housing available for art students.

Expenses for 2006–2007 Application fee: $50. One-time mandatory fee: $100. Tuition: $18,576 full-time. Full-time tuition varies according to course load. College room only: $6028.

Financial Aid Program-specific awards available.

Application Procedures Students admitted directly into the professional program freshman year. Deadline for freshmen and transfers: continuous. Notification date for freshmen and transfers: continuous. Required: essay, high school transcript, college transcript(s) for transfer students, interview. Recommended: portfolio, SAT or ACT test scores.

Web Site http://www.artinstitutes.edu/phoenix

Undergraduate Contact Director of Admissions, The Art Institute of Phoenix, 2233 West Dunlap Avenue, Phoenix, Arizona 85021; 800-474-2479 ext. 7502, fax: 602-331-5301, e-mail address: aipxadm@aii.edu

The Art Institute of Portland

Portland, Oregon

Proprietary, coed. Urban campus. Total enrollment: 1,614. Art program established 1963.

Degrees Bachelor of Fine Arts in the areas of advertising, game art & design, graphic design, interior design, media arts & animation, visual effects & motion graphics, digital film & video, apparel design, design studies; Bachelor of Science. Majors and concentrations: advertising, apparel design, design, digital film and video, digital media production, game art and design, graphic design, interactive media, interior design, media arts/animation, visual and game programming, visual effects and motion graphics.

Student Life Student groups/activities include American Institute of Graphic Arts Student Chapter, American Society of Interior Designers (ASID) Student Chapter, International Interior Design Association (IIDA) Student Task Force. Special housing available for art students.

Expenses for 2007–2008 Application fee: $50. One-time mandatory fee: $50. Comprehensive fee: $27,645 includes full-time tuition ($19,395) and college room and board ($8250). College room only: $5215. Full-time tuition varies according to course load. Room and board charges vary according to housing facility. Special program-related fees: $100 per month for supplies.

Financial Aid Program-specific awards available.

Application Procedures Students admitted directly into the professional program freshman year. Deadline for freshmen and transfers: continuous. Notification date for freshmen and transfers: continuous. Required: essay, high school transcript, college transcript(s) for transfer students, interview. Recommended: portfolio, SAT or ACT test scores.

Visual Arts

The Art Institute of Portland (continued)

Web Site http://www.artinstitutes.edu/portland

Undergraduate Contact Director of Admissions, The Art Institute of Portland, 1122 NW Davis Street, Portland, Oregon 97209; 888-228-6528, fax: 503-227-1945, e-mail address: aipdadm@aii.edu

The Art Institute of Seattle

Seattle, Washington

Proprietary, coed. Urban campus. Total enrollment: 2,352.

Degrees Bachelor of Fine Arts in the areas of fashion design, game art & design, graphic design, interior design, media arts & animation, digital filmmaking and video production. Majors and concentrations: digital film and video, digital media production, fashion design, game art and design, graphic design, interior design, media arts/animation.

Student Life Special housing available for art students.

Expenses for 2007–2008 Application fee: $50. Tuition: $19,968 full-time. College room only: $9156.

Financial Aid Program-specific awards available.

Application Procedures Students admitted directly into the professional program freshman year. Deadline for freshmen and transfers: continuous. Notification date for freshmen and transfers: continuous. Required: essay, high school transcript, college transcript(s) for transfer students, interview, SAT, ACT, COMPASS, or ASSET scores.

Web Site http://www.artinstitutes.edu/seattle

Undergraduate Contact Director of Admissions, The Art Institute of Seattle, 2323 Elliott Avenue, Seattle, Washington 98121; 800-275-2471, e-mail address: aisadm@aii.edu

The Art Institute of Tampa

Tampa, Florida

Proprietary, coed. Suburban campus. Total enrollment: 685.

Degrees Bachelor of Fine Arts in the areas of digital filmmaking & video production, game art & design, graphic design, interactive media design, interior design, media arts & animation, visual effects and motion graphics. Majors and concentrations: digital film and video, digital media production, game art and design, graphic design, interactive media, interior design, media arts/animation, visual effects and motion graphics.

Student Life Special housing available for art students.

Expenses for 2006–2007 Application fee: $50. Tuition: $20,208 full-time. College room only: $4100.

Financial Aid Program-specific awards available.

Application Procedures Students admitted directly into the professional program freshman year. Deadline for freshmen and transfers: continuous. Notification date for freshmen and transfers: continuous. Required: essay, high school transcript, college transcript(s) for transfer students, interview, portfolio (for high school students entering scholarship competition).

Web Site http://www.artinstitutes.edu/tampa

Undergraduate Contact Director of Admissions, The Art Institute of Tampa, 4401 North Himes Avenue, Suite 150, Tampa, Florida 33614-7001; 866-703-3277, fax: 813-873-2171.

The Art Institute of Tennessee–Nashville

Nashville, Tennessee

Proprietary, coed. Urban campus. Total enrollment: 32.

Degrees Bachelor of Fine Arts in the areas of digital filmmaking and video production, graphic design, interactive media design, interior design. Majors and concentrations: digital film and video, graphic design, interactive design, interactive media.

Student Life Special housing available for art students.

Expenses for 2006–2007 Application fee: $50. Tuition: $20,064 full-time.

Financial Aid Program-specific awards available.

Application Procedures Students admitted directly into the professional program freshman year. Required: essay, high school transcript, interview.

Web Site http://www.artinstitutes.edu/nashville/

Undergraduate Contact Director of Admissions, The Art Institute of Tennessee–Nashville, 100 Centerview Drive, Suite 250, Nashville, Tennessee 37214; 866-747-5770.

The Art Institute of Washington

Arlington, Virginia

Proprietary, coed. Urban campus. Total enrollment: 1,400.

Degrees Bachelor of Fine Arts in the areas of digital filmmaking and video production, game art and design, graphic design, interactive media design, interior design, media arts and animation, visual effects and motion graphics. Majors and concentrations: digital film and video, digital media production, game art and design, graphic design, interactive media, interior design, media arts/animation, visual effects and motion graphics.

Art Faculty Undergraduate student–faculty ratio: 20:1.

Student Life Student groups/activities include Comic Book Club, American Society of Interior Designers. Special housing available for art students.

Expenses for 2006–2007 Application fee: $50. Tuition: $19,968 full-time. Special program-related fees: $125 per month for supplies.

Financial Aid Program-specific awards available.

Application Procedures Deadline for freshmen and transfers: continuous. Notification date for freshmen and transfers: continuous. Required: essay, high school transcript, college transcript(s) for transfer students, interview, SAT, ACT, ASSET, or COMPASS scores, portfolio (for high school seniors entering scholarship competition).

Web Site http://www.artinstitutes.edu/arlington

Undergraduate Contact Director of Admissions, The Art Institute of Washington, 1820 North

Fort Myer Drive, Arlington, Virginia 22209; 877-303-3771, fax: 703-358-9759, e-mail address: aiwadm@aii.edu

The Art Institutes International Minnesota

Minneapolis, Minnesota

Proprietary, coed. Urban campus. Art program established 1997.

Degrees Bachelor of Fine Arts in the area of photography; Bachelor of Science in the areas of media arts and animation, graphic design. Majors and concentrations: graphic design, interactive media, interior design, media arts/animation, photography, visual effects and motion graphics.

Enrollment 1,601 total; all undergraduate.

Art Student Profile 58% females, 42% males, 1% international.

Art Faculty 49 undergraduate (full-time), 62 undergraduate (part-time). 55% of full-time faculty have terminal degrees. Graduate students do not teach undergraduate courses. Undergraduate student–faculty ratio: 20:1.

Expenses for 2006–2007 Application fee: $50. Tuition: $18,336 full-time.

Application Procedures Students admitted directly into the professional program freshman year. Required: essay, high school transcript, college transcript(s) for transfer students, interview. Recommended: SAT or ACT test scores.

Web Site http://www.artinstitutes.edu/minneapolis

Undergraduate Contact Mary Strand, Director of Admissions, The Art Institutes International Minnesota, 15 South 9th Street, Minneapolis, Minnesota 55402; 800-777-3643, e-mail address: aimadm@aii.edu

Augusta State University

Augusta, Georgia

State-supported, coed. Urban campus. Total enrollment: 6,552. Art program established 1958.

Web Site http://www.aug.edu/

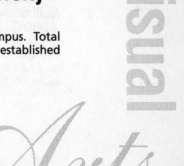

Austin Peay State University

Clarksville, Tennessee

State-supported, coed. Suburban campus. Total enrollment: 9,207.

Degrees Bachelor of Arts in the area of art education/licensure K-12; Bachelor of Fine Arts in the areas of studio arts, visual communication. Majors and concentrations: art education, ceramics, drawing, graphic design, illustration, painting, photography, printmaking, sculpture. Program accredited by NASAD.

Enrollment 280 total; all undergraduate.

Art Student Profile 60% females, 40% males, 15% minorities, 10% international.

Art Faculty 13 undergraduate (full-time), 8 undergraduate (part-time). 95% of full-time faculty have terminal degrees. Graduate students do not teach undergraduate courses. Undergraduate student–faculty ratio: 20:1.

Student Life Student groups/activities include Student Art League/ Student Art Show, Capsule Magazine, Student Chapter NAEA (art education).

Expenses for 2006–2007 Application fee: $15. State resident tuition: $3828 full-time. Nonresident tuition: $13,522 full-time. Mandatory fees: $1009 full-time. College room and board: $5190. College room only: $3200. Room and board charges vary according to board plan and housing facility.

Financial Aid Program-specific awards: 1 Tom Malone Scholarship for studio arts students ($1000), 1 Claudell Wootten Scholarship for art education students ($500), 2 Friends of Photography Scholarships for photography students ($250), 1 Jewel Birdsong Scholarship for art history/conservation students ($1000), 1 Art Alumni Scholarship for design/photography students ($500), 1 US Bank Scholarship for those with outstanding portfolios and demonstrating need ($1000), Friends of the Art Scholarship ($500), Helena Haskill Scholarship for typography students ($500).

Application Procedures Students apply for admission into the professional program by junior year. Required: high school transcript, college transcript(s) for transfer students, SAT or ACT test scores (minimum composite ACT score of 19). Recommended: letter of recommendation, interview. Portfolio reviews held once on campus; the submission of slides may be substituted for portfolios.

Web Site http://www.apsu.edu/art/

Undergraduate Contact Chair, Department of Art, Austin Peay State University, PO Box 4677, Clarksville, Tennessee 37044; 931-221-7333, fax: 931-221-7432.

Ball State University

Muncie, Indiana

State-supported, coed. Suburban campus. Total enrollment: 17,082.

Degrees Bachelor of Fine Arts in the area of art; Bachelor of Science in the area of art education. Majors and concentrations: animation, ceramics, drawing, electronic arts, jewelry and metalsmithing, painting, photography, printmaking, sculpture, visual communication. Graduate degrees offered: Master of Arts in the area of art. Program accredited by NASAD.

Enrollment 573 total; 447 undergraduate, 19 graduate, 107 nonprofessional degree.

Art Student Profile 55% females, 45% males, 3% minorities, 2% international.

Art Faculty 30 total (full-time), 4 total (part-time). 100% of full-time faculty have terminal degrees. Graduate students do not teach undergraduate courses. Undergraduate student–faculty ratio: 15:1.

Student Life Student groups/activities include National Art Education Association Student Chapter, Fine Arts League, Crafts Guild.

Expenses for 2006–2007 Application fee: $25. State resident tuition: $6360 full-time. Nonresident tuition: $16,736 full-time. Mandatory fees: $450 full-time. College room and board: $6898. Room and board charges vary according to board plan and housing facility.

Financial Aid Program-specific awards: 4–6 freshmen scholarship awards for outstanding freshmen program applicants ($1000), 8 Fine Art Scholarships for outstanding freshmen program applicants ($4000), 5 Ruth Swain Scholarships for outstanding sophomores, juniors, or seniors ($1000), 2 Roberta Law Scholarships for outstanding sophomores, juniors, seniors ($1000), 1 Dorotha Stock Scholarship for outstanding sophomores, juniors, or seniors ($500), 1 Alice Nichols Scholarship for outstanding art education students ($360), 1 Indiana Arts and Craftsman Scholarship for outstanding art majors ($250), 5 Presidential Scholar in the Arts Awards for outstanding freshmen.

Application Procedures Students admitted directly into the professional program freshman year. Deadline for freshmen: April 1; transfers: continuous. Notification date for freshmen: May 1. Required: high school transcript, college transcript(s) for transfer students, portfolio, SAT or ACT test scores. Recommended: minimum 2.0 high school GPA. Portfolio reviews held once on campus; the submission of slides may be substituted for portfolios if a campus visit is impossible.

Web Site http://www.bsu.edu/art/

Undergraduate Contact Ms. Barbara Giorgio-Booher, Primary Department Advisor, Department of Art, Ball State University, Muncie, Indiana 47306-0405; 765-285-5841, fax: 765-285-5838, e-mail address: bgiorgio@bsu.edu

Graduate Contact Prof. Kenton Hall, Graduate Director, Department of Art, Ball State University, Muncie, Indiana 47306-0405; 765-285-5838, fax: 765-285-5838, e-mail address: khall@bsu.edu

Barton College

Wilson, North Carolina

Independent, coed. Small town campus. Total enrollment: 1,136. Art program established 1902.

Degrees Bachelor of Fine Arts in the areas of art and design (emphasis in design, ceramics, painting, photography); Bachelor of Science in the area of art education K-12. Majors and concentrations: art education, ceramics, design, painting, photography.

Enrollment 70 total; 60 undergraduate, 10 nonprofessional degree.

Art Student Profile 50% females, 50% males, 15% minorities, 1% international.

Art Faculty 4 undergraduate (full-time), 3 undergraduate (part-time). 100% of full-time faculty have terminal degrees. Graduate students do not teach undergraduate courses. Undergraduate student–faculty ratio: 16:1.

Expenses for 2006–2007 Application fee: $25. Comprehensive fee: $23,918 includes full-time tuition ($16,352), mandatory fees ($1302), and college room and board ($6264). College room only: $3040. Full-time tuition and fees vary according to course load and program. Room and board charges vary according to housing facility. Special program-related fees: $43 per studio for supplies, $110 for photography supplies.

Financial Aid Program-specific awards: 1 Bessie Massengill Award for sophomores and juniors, 1 TEAM Award for sophomores and juniors ($1000), 1 National Scholastic Award for freshmen ($1000), 1 Art Faculty Scholarship for sophomores, juniors, seniors ($750), 1 Triangle East Advertising and Marketing Association Scholarship for sophomores, juniors, seniors ($1000), 1 Stuart Walston Scholarship for those with minimum 2.5 GPA ($500).

Application Procedures Students admitted directly into the professional program freshman year. Deadline for freshmen and transfers: continuous. Required: high school transcript, college transcript(s) for transfer students, letter of recommendation, SAT or ACT test scores. Recommended: minimum 2.0 high school GPA, interview, portfolio. Portfolio reviews held by appointment on campus; the submission of slides may be substituted for portfolios.

Web Site http://www.barton.edu/

Undergraduate Contact Ms. Susan B. Fecho, Chair, Art Department, Barton College, PO Box 5000, Wilson, North Carolina 27893-7000; 252-399-6480, fax: 252-399-6571.

Baylor University

Waco, Texas

Independent Baptist, coed. Urban campus. Total enrollment: 14,040.

Web Site http://www.baylor.edu/

Belmont University

Nashville, Tennessee

Independent Baptist, coed. Urban campus. Total enrollment: 4,481. Art program established 1984.

Degrees Bachelor of Fine Arts in the areas of studio, art education, design communications. Majors and concentrations: art education,

Belmont University (continued)

design communication, studio art. Cross-registration with O'More College. Program accredited by NASAD.

Enrollment 87 total; all undergraduate.

Art Student Profile 70% females, 30% males, 10% minorities, 1% international.

Art Faculty 5 undergraduate (full-time), 13 undergraduate (part-time). 100% of full-time faculty have terminal degrees. Graduate students do not teach undergraduate courses. Undergraduate student–faculty ratio: 14:1.

Student Life Student groups/activities include Art Association, Blvd Gallery and Design (student-run, on-campus business).

Expenses for 2007–2008 Application fee: $35. Comprehensive fee: $29,309 includes full-time tuition ($18,780), mandatory fees ($1000), and college room and board ($9529). College room only: $6000. Full-time tuition and fees vary according to class time and course load. Room and board charges vary according to board plan, housing facility, and location. Special program-related fees: $100 per semester for design communication courses, $100 per semester for photography lab fee, $100 per semester for model fees, materials fee for studio courses.

Financial Aid Program-specific awards: 4 Leu Art Scholarships for freshmen art majors ($2000), 4 art supply scholarships for those demonstrating need ($250), 1 rising senior award ($1000).

Application Procedures Students admitted directly into the professional program freshman year. Deadline for freshmen and transfers: continuous. Required: high school transcript, college transcript(s) for transfer students, minimum 2.0 high school GPA, letter of recommendation, portfolio, SAT or ACT test scores. Recommended: interview. Portfolio reviews held by arrangement on campus; the submission of slides may be substituted for portfolios whenever needed.

Web Site http://www.belmont.edu/art/

Undergraduate Contact David Ribar, Interim Chair, Department of Art, Belmont University, 1900 Belmont Boulevard, Nashville, Tennessee 37212-3537; 615-460-6773, fax: 615-460-6757, e-mail address: ribard@mail.belmont.edu

More About the University

The Department of Art is part of Belmont's College of Visual and Performing Arts and is located in the 40,000-square-foot Leu Center for the Visual Arts. This facility combines the latest technology with traditional studio space, including a Macintosh graphics lab and a student gallery. There are large studios specifically for drawing, painting, printmaking, photography, sculpture, and ceramics as well as a 118-seat audiovisual room for slide lectures and other multimedia presentations. In addition, the Leu Art Gallery in the Lila D. Bunch Library provides more than 1,000 square feet of exhibit space for traveling exhibits, regional art exhibitions, and regional and national artists.

Faculty Faculty members are practicing artists and designers who exhibit both regionally and nationally.

Exhibition Opportunities Each year, the Department of Art exhibits student work in a large art show. In addition, seniors exhibit their work during their last semester of study.

Special Programs International residencies in art are offered in France, Great Britain, Germany, Russia, and in Italy at the Lorenzo de Medici Art Institute of Florence. Course work in Florence may include photography, painting and drawing, textiles, fashion design, oil and fresco painting restoration, graphics, sculpture, jewelry, and art history. Internship programs allow students to gain valuable, practical work experience. In addition, the Belmont University Career Office offers assistance with career planning.

Birmingham-Southern College

Birmingham, Alabama

Independent Methodist, coed. Urban campus. Total enrollment: 1,256. Art program established 1946.

Degrees Bachelor of Fine Arts in the area of studio art. Majors and concentrations: art history, painting, photography, printmaking, sculpture. Cross-registration with University of Alabama at Birmingham, University of Montevallo, Samford University.

Enrollment 350 total; 190 undergraduate, 160 nonprofessional degree.

Art Student Profile 60% females, 40% males, 10% minorities, 5% international.

Art Faculty 7 undergraduate (full-time), 2 undergraduate (part-time). 100% of full-time faculty have terminal degrees. Graduate students do not teach undergraduate courses. Undergraduate student–faculty ratio: 15:1.

Student Life Student groups/activities include Art Students League.

Expenses for 2007–2008 Application fee: $25. Comprehensive fee: $32,362 includes full-time tuition ($23,600), mandatory fees ($700), and college room and board ($8062). College room only: $5000. Special program-related fees: $30–$80 per unit for materials.

Financial Aid Program-specific awards: 10–15 art scholarships for art majors ($1300–$8000).

Application Procedures Students admitted directly into the professional program freshman year. Notification date for freshmen and transfers: continuous. Required: essay, high school transcript, college transcript(s) for transfer students, minimum 2.0 high school GPA, SAT or ACT test scores (minimum composite ACT score of 21), interview for scholarship consideration. Recommended: 2 letters of recommendation, interview, portfolio. Portfolio reviews held once on campus; the submission of slides may be substituted for portfolios when distance is prohibitive, or work is too large to carry.

Web Site http://www.bsc.edu

Undergraduate Contact Ms. Sheri Salmon, Associate Vice President of Admissions, Birmingham-Southern College, 900 Arkadelphia Road, Box 549008, Birmingham, Alabama 35254; 205-226-4696, fax: 205-226-3074.

Boston University

Boston, Massachusetts

Independent, coed. Urban campus. Total enrollment: 31,574. Art program established 1954.

Degrees Bachelor of Fine Arts in the areas of painting, sculpture, graphic design, art education. Majors and concentrations: art education, graphic design, painting, sculpture. Graduate degrees offered: Master of Fine Arts in the areas of painting, sculpture, graphic design, art education, studio teaching. Cross-registration with Boston College, Brandeis University, Tufts University.

Enrollment 306 total; 230 undergraduate, 65 graduate, 11 nonprofessional degree.

Art Student Profile 60% females, 40% males, 10% minorities, 14% international.

Art Faculty 21 total (full-time), 10 total (part-time). 100% of full-time faculty have terminal degrees. Graduate students do not teach undergraduate courses. Undergraduate student–faculty ratio: 16:1.

Student Life Student groups/activities include American Institute of Graphic Arts, Copley Society, Boston University Art League. Special housing available for art students.

Expenses for 2006–2007 Application fee: $75. Comprehensive fee: $44,272 includes full-time tuition ($33,330), mandatory fees ($462), and college room and board ($10,480). College room only: $6760. Full-time tuition and fees vary according to class time and degree level. Room and board charges vary according to board plan and housing facility. Special program-related fees: $35–$50 for lab fee, $100 for studio fee for painting majors.

Financial Aid Program-specific awards: 160 grants-need/performance awards for enrolled program students ($17,000).

Application Procedures Students admitted directly into the professional program freshman year. Deadline for freshmen: January 1; transfers: April 1. Notification date for freshmen: April 15; transfers: May 30. Required: essay, high school transcript, college transcript(s) for transfer students, portfolio, SAT or ACT test scores. Recommended: minimum 3.0 high school GPA, 3 letters of recommendation. Portfolio reviews held continuously on campus; the submission of slides may be substituted for portfolios.

Web Site http://www.bu.edu/cfa/visual

Undergraduate Contact Jeannette Guillemin, Assistant Director/Director of Admissions and Student Affairs, School of Visual Arts, College of Fine Arts, Boston University, 855 Commonwealth Avenue, Boston, Massachusetts 02215; 617-353-3371, fax: 617-353-7217, e-mail address: visuarts@bu.edu

Graduate Contact Jeannette Guillemin, Assistant Director, School of Visual Arts, College of Fine Arts, Boston University, 855 Commonwealth Avenue, Boston, Massachusetts 02215; 617-353-3371, fax: 617-353-7217, e-mail address: visuarts@bu.edu

Visual

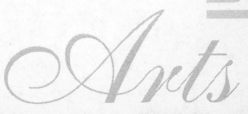

Arts

Boston University (continued)

More About the University

Boston University College of Fine Arts (CFA) is a small, conservatory-style school within a major university, offering outstanding professional training in music, the theater, and visual arts. The college was founded as the College of Music in 1873 and has a long and distinguished history of training artists. The Division of Applied Arts, now known as the School of Visual Arts, was added in 1919, and it currently enrolls approximately 250 students.

The student painters, sculptors, graphic designers, and art educators at the School of Visual Arts prepare for leading positions in the art world by engaging in its present and understanding its past. With a faculty composed of practicing professional artists, the school offers an intensive program of studio training combined with liberal arts studies leading to the Bachelor of Fine Arts (B.F.A.) and Master of Fine Arts (M.F.A.).

Campus Surroundings Boston University—independent, coeducational, nonsectarian—is an internationally recognized center of higher education and research. The University is located in the heart of Boston, along the banks of the Charles River and adjacent to the historic Back Bay district of Boston. Boston University is perfectly situated to enjoy both the charm and beauty of the city and its cultural and recreational attractions. School of Visual Arts students benefit from the many major museums and galleries as well as the theaters and musical organizations that make Boston a rich and varied environment for the art student.

Program Facilities The School of Visual Arts offers painting, drawing, and sculpture studios; a welding and wood shop; computer labs; photography and printmaking studios; a book and slide library; and exhibition spaces, including the Boston University Art Gallery, the 808 Showroom Gallery, the Sherman Gallery, and the Commonwealth Gallery.

Faculty, Resident Artists, and Alumni The faculty of dedicated teachers includes some of the finest painters, sculptors, graphic designers, and art educators in the country. Distinguished faculty members include John Walker, painter; Richard Raiselis, painter; Harold Reddicliffe, painter; Lynne Allen, printmaker; Judith Simpson, art educator; and Alston Purvis, graphic designer. Visiting artists include Vincent Desiderio, painter; Greg Amenoff, painter; William Tucker, sculptor; William Bailey, painter; Rackstraw Downes, printmaker; Mags Harries, sculptor, Jonathan Shahn, painter; Pat Steir, painter; Tim Rollins, educator; Al Leslie, painter; and

Suzanne Coffey, painter. Alumni include the distinguished American artists Pat Steir and Brice Martin; designer Ira Yoffe, Vice President and Creative Director for *Parade Magazine;* Penelope Zencks, sculptor; and Richard Heinrichs, sculpture and production/set designer, whose credits include *Planet of the Apes, Fargo,* and *Pirates of the Caribbean.*

Exhibition Opportunities Each year, the School of Visual Arts exhibits student work in its spring show. Additional exhibition opportunities exist throughout the year for students, faculty members, and alumni in the Boston University Art Gallery, the Sherman Gallery, the 808 Gallery, and the Commonwealth Gallery.

Special Programs Through the Boston University Collaborative Degree Program (BUCOP), students may obtain a dual degree in the College of Fine Arts and another of the University's schools or colleges. Students may minor in liberal arts, business, or communications. Painting and graphic design students are encouraged to study abroad at the Scuola Internazionale di Graphica in Venice, Italy, in their junior year. A five-year B.F.A./M.F.A. is available to students interested in majoring in a studio area along with art education.

Bowling Green State University

Bowling Green, Ohio

State-supported, coed. Small town campus. Total enrollment: 19,108.

Web Site http://www.bgsu.edu/

Bradley University

Peoria, Illinois

Independent, coed. Suburban campus. Total enrollment: 6,126.

Degrees Bachelor of Arts in the areas of studio art, art education, art history; Bachelor of Fine Arts in the area of studio art; Bachelor of Science in the areas of studio art, art education. Majors and concentrations: art education, art history, studio art. Graduate degrees offered: Master of Arts in the area of studio art; Master of Fine Arts in the area of studio art. Program accredited by NASAD.

Enrollment 153 total; all undergraduate.

Art Student Profile 54% females, 46% males, 11% minorities, 4% international.

Art Faculty 9 total (full-time), 8 total (part-time). 100% of full-time faculty have terminal degrees. Graduate students teach a few undergraduate courses. Undergraduate student–faculty ratio: 11:1.

Student Life Student groups/activities include Spectrum, American Institute of Graphic Arts (AIGA), Potters Guild, Art History Club, National Art Education Association Students (NAEAS).

Expenses for 2007–2008 Application fee: $35. Comprehensive fee: $28,410 includes full-time tuition ($21,200), mandatory fees ($160), and college room and board ($7050). College room only: $4100. Full-time tuition and fees vary according to student level. Room and board charges vary according to board plan. Special program-related fees: $25 per credit hour for supplies.

Financial Aid Program-specific awards: 33 art scholarships for art majors ($992).

Application Procedures Students apply for admission into the professional program by sophomore year. Deadline for freshmen and transfers: continuous. Required: high school transcript, college transcript(s) for transfer students, minimum 2.0 high school GPA, portfolio, SAT or ACT test scores. Recommended: 2 letters of recommendation. Portfolio reviews held 3 times on campus; the submission of slides may be substituted for portfolios (slides preferred for scholarship decisions).

Web Site http://art.bradley.edu

Undergraduate Contact Ms. Nickie Roberson, Director of Admissions, Office of Undergraduate Admissions, Bradley University, Swords Hall, Peoria, Illinois 61625; 800-447-6460, fax: 309-677-2797, e-mail address: admissions@bradley.edu

Graduate Contact Leslie Betz, Director of Graduate Enrollment Management, Graduate School, Bradley University, 1501 West Bradley Avenue, Peoria, Illinois 61625; 309-677-2375.

Brenau University
Gainesville, Georgia

Independent, Small town campus. Total enrollment: 846. Art program established 1973.

Web Site http://www.brenau.edu/

Brigham Young University
Provo, Utah

Independent, coed. Suburban campus. Total enrollment: 34,185. Art program established 1925.

Degrees Bachelor of Arts in the areas of art history, art education; Bachelor of Fine Arts in the areas of studio art, graphic design, photography, illustration, animation. Majors and concentrations: animation, art education, art history, graphic design, illustration, photography, studio art. Graduate degrees offered: Master of Fine Arts in the area of studio art. Program accredited by NASAD.

Enrollment 659 total; 625 undergraduate, 34 graduate.

Art Student Profile 70% females, 30% males.

Art Faculty 33 total (full-time), 30 total (part-time). 78% of full-time faculty have terminal degrees. Graduate students teach more than half of undergraduate courses.

Student Life Student groups/activities include Art History Student Association, National Art Education Association Student Chapter.

Expenses for 2007–2008 Application fee: $30. Comprehensive fee: $14,140 includes full-time tuition ($7680) and college room and board ($6460). Room and board charges vary according to board plan and housing facility. Latter Day Saints full-time student $3840 per year. Special program-related fees: $200 per semester for supplies.

Financial Aid Program-specific awards: 150 talent awards for program majors ($200–$1000), 1–5 J. Roman Andrus Printmaking Awards for printmaking majors ($200–$300), 5 Demery Scholarships for program majors ($200–$300), 5 Anna F. Sommers Scholarships for program majors ($200–$400), 25 Olena K. and George K. Lewis Scholarships for painting majors ($200–$400), 15 Betty M. and Paul J. Boshard Scholarships for program majors ($200–$300), 15 Cory Nathan Belleau Scholarships for program majors ($200–$700), 1–5 Max Dickson and Ruth Kimball Weaver Scholarships for ceramics majors ($200–$300).

Application Procedures Students apply for admission into the professional program by freshman, sophomore year. Deadline for freshmen: February 15; transfers: March 15. Notification date for freshmen: April 15; transfers:

Brigham Young University (continued)

May 1. Required: essay, high school transcript, college transcript(s) for transfer students, minimum 3.0 high school GPA, letter of recommendation, portfolio, ACT test score only (minimum composite ACT score of 25), 10 pieces of best work, creative exercise. Portfolio reviews held 3 times on campus.

Web Site http://cfac.byu.edu/

Undergraduate Contact Sonya Schiffman, Department Secretary, Department of Visual Arts, Brigham Young University, Provo, Utah 84602; 801-422-8773, fax: 801-422-0695, e-mail address: sonya_schiffman@byu.edu

Graduate Contact Ms. Sharon Heelis, Secretary to Chair, Department of Visual Arts, Brigham Young University, E-509 HFAC, Provo, Utah 84602; 801-422-4429, fax: 801-422-0695, e-mail address: sharon_heelis@byu.edu

Brooklyn College of the City University of New York

Brooklyn, New York

State and locally supported, coed. Urban campus. Total enrollment: 15,947. Art program established 1967.

Degrees Bachelor of Fine Arts in the area of art. Majors and concentrations: computer art, painting/drawing, photography, printmaking, sculpture. Graduate degrees offered: Master of Arts in the area of art education (K-12); Master of Fine Arts in the area of art. Cross-registration with City University of New York System.

Enrollment 84 total; 20 undergraduate, 34 graduate, 30 nonprofessional degree.

Art Student Profile 55% females, 45% males, 25% minorities, 15% international.

Art Faculty 17 total (full-time), 9 total (part-time). 100% of full-time faculty have terminal degrees. Graduate students teach a few undergraduate courses. Undergraduate student–faculty ratio: 16:1.

Student Life Student groups/activities include Art Group, Graduate Art Student Union.

Expenses for 2006–2007 Application fee: $65. State resident tuition: $4000 full-time. Nonresident tuition: $8640 full-time. Mandatory fees: $375 full-time. Special program-related fees: $15–$20 per course for supplies and model fees.

Financial Aid Program-specific awards: 10–20 Charles G. Shaw Memorial Awards for studio art majors ($400–$1000), 2–3 Bernard Horlick Awards for program majors ($500–$750), 1–2 Jerome J. Viola Memorial Scholarships for program majors ($350–$500), 1–2 Bernard Cole Memorial Scholarships for photography majors ($150–$250), 1 Thomas S. Buechner Award for program majors ($500), 2 Diana and Lewis Sills Memorial Scholarships for program majors ($500), 10–20 Walter Cerf Awards for program majors ($400–$1000).

Application Procedures Students apply for admission into the professional program by sophomore year. Deadline for freshmen and transfers: continuous. Notification date for freshmen and transfers: continuous. Required: high school transcript, college transcript(s) for transfer students, portfolio, minimum 2.8 high school GPA. Recommended: interview, SAT or ACT test scores. Portfolio reviews held once on campus; the submission of slides may be substituted for portfolios for large works of art.

Web Site http://depthome.brooklyn.cuny.edu/art/

Undergraduate Contact Prof. Michael Mallory, Chair, Department of Art, Brooklyn College of the City University of New York, 2900 Bedford Avenue, Brooklyn, New York 11210-2889; 718-951-5181, fax: 718-951-4728, e-mail address: mmallory@brooklyn.cuny.edu

Graduate Contact Prof. Janet Carlile, Deputy Chair, Department of Art, Brooklyn College of the City University of New York, 2900 Bedford Avenue, Brooklyn, New York 11210-2889; 718-951-5572, fax: 718-951-4728, e-mail address: artmfa@brooklyn.cuny.edu

California College of the Arts

San Francisco, California

Independent, coed. Urban campus. Total enrollment: 1,622. Art program established 1907.

Degrees Bachelor of Arts in the areas of writing and literature, visual studies; Bachelor of Architecture; Bachelor of Fine Arts in the areas of furniture, glass, ceramics, sculpture, painting, drawing, printmaking, photography, textiles, jewelry/metal arts, graphic design, illustration, industrial design, fashion design, media arts, community arts, interior design, animation. Majors and concentrations: animation, architecture, ceramic art and design, creative writing, fashion design, furniture design, glass, graphic design, illustration, industrial design, interior design, jewelry and metalsmithing, media arts, painting/drawing, photography, printmaking, public art studies, sculpture, textile arts, visual studies. Graduate degrees offered: Master of Arts in the areas of curatorial practice, visual and critical studies; Master of Architecture; Master of Fine Arts in the areas of design, writing, fine arts, film. Cross-registration with Mills College, Holy Names College. Program accredited by NAAB, NASAD, CIDA.

Enrollment 1,622 total; 1,310 undergraduate, 312 graduate.

Art Student Profile 60% females, 40% males, 25% minorities, 7% international.

Art Faculty 66 undergraduate (full-time), 413 undergraduate (part-time), 5 graduate (full-time), 65 graduate (part-time). 64% of full-time faculty have terminal degrees. Graduate students do not teach undergraduate courses. Undergraduate student–faculty ratio: 15:1.

Student Life Student groups/activities include American Institute of Graphic Arts, American Institute of Architects, American Society of Interior Designers. Special housing available for art students.

Expenses for 2006–2007 Application fee: $50. Comprehensive fee: $36,529 includes full-time tuition ($27,624), mandatory fees ($290), and college room and board ($8615). Full-time tuition and fees vary according to course load. Room and board charges vary according to housing facility. Special program-related fees: $50–$275 per year for lab fees, $60 for student activity fee, $230 per year for registration fee.

Financial Aid Program-specific awards: 114 Creative Achievement Awards for freshmen ($5833), 107 Faculty Honors Awards for transfer students ($5234), 1161 CCA Scholarships for students demonstrating need ($5918), 203 named scholarships for those demonstrating need ($3095), 36 diversity scholarships for under-represented populations ($6531).

Application Procedures Students admitted directly into the professional program freshman year. Deadline for freshmen and transfers: continuous. Required: essay, high school transcript, college transcript(s) for transfer students, minimum 2.0 high school GPA, 2 letters of recommendation, portfolio, minimum TOEFL score of 550 (paper-based) or 213 (computer-based) for international applicants. Recommended: interview, SAT or ACT test scores. Portfolio reviews held continuously on campus and off campus at National Portfolio Days; the submission of slides may be substituted for portfolios (digital portfolio preferred).

Web Site http://www.cca.edu

Undergraduate Contact Ms. Robynne Royster, Director of Undergraduate Admission, California College of the Arts, 1111 Eighth Street, San Francisco, California 94107; 415-703-9532, fax: 415-703-9539, e-mail address: enroll@cca.edu

Graduate Contact Ms. Kathryn Ward, Assistant Director of Graduate Admission, California College of the Arts, 1111 Eighth Street, San Francisco, California 94107; 415-703-9593, fax: 415-703-9539, e-mail address: graduateprograms@cca.edu

More About the College

Founded in 1907, California College of the Arts (CCA) is the largest regionally accredited, independent school of art and design in the western United States. CCA offers twenty undergraduate

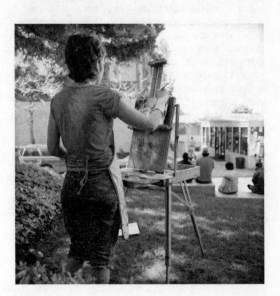

Visual *Arts*

California College of the Arts (continued)

majors in the areas of architecture, art, design, and writing. In 2007, the College will introduce a new Bachelor of Fine Arts (B.F.A.) program in animation.

At CCA, students make art that makes a difference. CCA programs emphasize creative expression, self-discipline, intellectual and artistic exploration, and technical mastery. Students are encouraged to collaborate within and across disciplines. This interdisciplinary approach to art-making provides fertile ground for emerging sensibilities. CCA undergraduates regularly win major recognition in their fields; in 2005, twelve graphic design students had work in the *Graphis New Talent Design Annual,* and in 2006, products by industrial design students were shown at the Milan Furniture Fair.

In CCA's intimate private-college environment, students have the opportunity to work closely in the studio with well-known faculty members, find support for personal goals, and prepare for professional achievement. CCA has strong connections to the arts community and helps students make the transition from school to career through internships.

CCA's Bay Area location offers exceptional access to world-class museums, galleries, theaters, film festivals, and diverse exhibition and performance spaces. Visiting artists and scholars bring fresh perspectives to the campus through stimulating lectures and studio visits. A wide range of approaches ensures a lively exchange of ideas in an environment where excellence is the standard.

Undergraduates begin in a Core program, emphasizing skill building, experimentation, problem solving, and critical skills through exposure to a variety of media, processes, principles, and imaginative strategies. After the first year, students move into their selected programs for in-depth exploration of a discipline, while grounding that work in a larger context. Studio course work includes traditional and technology-based art-making techniques. CCA encourages students to find their own voices, explore various media, and consider how theory and practice converge.

Program Facilities The Oakland campus is home to the B.A. programs and first-year and fine arts studios, including the spacious Treadwell Ceramic Arts Center; Simpson Sculpture Studio (featuring one of the largest working college foundries); Blattner Print Studio; silkscreen, papermaking, and drawing/painting studios; and facilities for glass, jewelry/metal arts, textiles, and media arts (film/video production and an innovative hybrid lab for interactive media). In San Francisco, CCA's light-filled main building houses the Boyce Fashion Design Studio

(facilities for cutting, draping, and sewing), Wornick Wood and Furniture Studios (bench room, machine room, spray booth, upholstery shop), and spacious architecture and design studios. Both campuses offer computer labs and individual studio spaces. Facilities are open to students from 16 to 24 hours daily.

San Francisco campus galleries include the CCA Wattis Institute for Contemporary Arts, presenting international exhibitions, and PlaySpace, which is run by an interdisciplinary group of graduate students. On the Oakland campus, faculty and alumni shows appear at the Oliver Art Center.

Faculty, Resident Artists, and Alumni Faculty members' work is in the Museum of Modern Art, Whitney Museum, Smithsonian, and other major collections. Architecture and design faculty members are recognized internationally. Noted alumni include painters Raymond Saunders and Squeak Carnwath; ceramicists Robert Arneson and Peter Voulkos; filmmaker Wayne Wang; and designers Lucille Tenazas and Michael Vanderbyl. The Wattis Institute's Capp Street Project residency program brings acclaimed artists to campus each year. Visiting artists also teach in selected programs.

Student Exhibitions The undergraduate exhibition program presents shows throughout the year in galleries dedicated to student work, including the Isabelle Percy West Gallery, Irwin Student Center Gallery, and North/South Galleries in Oakland and Bruce Galleries in San Francisco. The annual Baccalaureate Exhibition is held in Oakland; the Graduate Exhibition is held in San Francisco.

Special Programs CCA students may enrich their studies through the AICAD mobility program (allowing study at another art college) or by cross registration at Mills College and Holy Names College in Oakland. Through study abroad, students can experience different ways of seeing, making, and communicating about art at top art schools in Canada, Mexico, Europe, and Asia. CCA also offers its own summer study-abroad courses.

A teaching concentration, open to students in all majors, satisfies prerequisites for application to postgraduate art teacher credential programs. Through the College's Center for Art and Public Life, students serve as teaching assistants in public schools, mentor young artists, participate in Alternative Spring Break, and create their own community art projects. Through internships, students gain practical experience and make professional connections while earning academic credit. Internship sites include design and architecture firms, galleries, museums, nonprofit organizations, publishing houses, and others. Internships are required for architecture, community arts,

Visual

Arts

graphic design, and interior design students and are encouraged for all upper-division students.

California Design College

Los Angeles, California

Proprietary, coed. Urban campus.

Degrees Bachelor of Fine Arts in the area of fashion design. Majors and concentrations: fashion design.

Student Life Special housing available for art students.

Financial Aid Program-specific awards available.

Application Procedures Deadline for freshmen and transfers: continuous. Notification date for freshmen and transfers: continuous. Required: essay, high school transcript, interview.

Web Site http://www.artinstitutes.edu/cdc/

Undergraduate Contact Director of Admissions, California Design College, 3440 Wilshire Boulevard, 10th Floor, Los Angeles, California 90010; 877-468-6232, fax: 213-385-3545, e-mail address: aicdcadm@aii.edu

California Institute of the Arts

Valencia, California

Independent, coed. Suburban campus. Total enrollment: 1,349. Art program established 1961.

Degrees Bachelor of Fine Arts in the areas of character animation, experimental animation, film/video. Majors and concentrations: animation, film and video production. Graduate degrees offered: Master of Fine Arts in the areas of experimental animation, film/video, film directing.

Enrollment 372 total; 241 undergraduate, 131 graduate.

Art Student Profile 44% females, 56% males, 33% minorities, 24% international.

Art Faculty 31 total (full-time), 40 total (part-time). 80% of full-time faculty have terminal degrees. Graduate students do not teach undergraduate courses. Undergraduate student–faculty ratio: 6:1.

Student Life Student groups/activities include Community Arts Partnership, Integrated Media. Special housing available for art students.

Expenses for 2007–2008 Application fee: $70. Comprehensive fee: $39,865 includes full-time tuition ($31,290), mandatory fees ($575), and college room and board ($8000). College room only: $4530. Full-time tuition and fees vary according to course load. Room and board charges vary according to board plan, housing facility, and location. Special program-related fees: $475 per year for technology fee.

Financial Aid Program-specific awards: CalArts Scholarships for students demonstrating talent and need ($1000–$10,000).

Application Procedures Students admitted directly into the professional program freshman year. Deadline for freshmen and transfers: January 6. Required: essay, high school transcript, college transcript(s) for transfer students, 2 letters of recommendation, portfolio. Portfolio reviews held at National Portfolio Days.

Web Site http://www.calarts.edu

Contact Libby Hux, Admissions Counselor, California Institute of the Arts, 24700 McBean Parkway, Valencia, California 91355; 661-255-1050 ext. 7884, fax: 661-253-7710, e-mail address: lhux@calarts.edu

California Institute of the Arts

Valencia, California

Independent, coed. Suburban campus. Total enrollment: 1,349. Art program established 1961.

Degrees Bachelor of Fine Arts in the areas of art, graphic design, photography and media. Majors and concentrations: art/fine arts, graphic design, photography. Graduate degrees offered: Master of Fine Arts in the areas of art, graphic design, photography and media. Program accredited by NASAD.

Enrollment 285 total; 199 undergraduate, 86 graduate.

Art Student Profile 53% females, 47% males, 34% minorities, 6% international.

Art Faculty 30 total (full-time), 15 total (part-time). 90% of full-time faculty have terminal degrees. Graduate students do not

California Institute of the Arts (continued)

teach undergraduate courses. Undergraduate student–faculty ratio: 8:1.

Student Life Student groups/activities include Community Arts Partnership (CAP), Integrated Media Program, interdisciplinary project. Special housing available for art students.

Expenses for 2007–2008 Application fee: $70. Comprehensive fee: $39,865 includes full-time tuition ($31,290), mandatory fees ($575), and college room and board ($8000). College room only: $4530. Full-time tuition and fees vary according to course load. Room and board charges vary according to board plan, housing facility, and location. Special program-related fees: $475 per year for technology fee.

Financial Aid Program-specific awards: 120 CalArts Scholarships for those demonstrating merit ($4000–$8000), 6 CalArts Minority Scholarships for minority students ($4000–$8000).

Application Procedures Students admitted directly into the professional program freshman year. Deadline for freshmen and transfers: January 4. Notification date for freshmen and transfers: April 1. Required: essay, high school transcript, college transcript(s) for transfer students, portfolio, personal statement. Recommended: 2 letters of recommendation, video (if applicable). Portfolio reviews held continuously on campus and off campus at National Portfolio Days; the submission of slides may be substituted for portfolios (slides preferred).

Web Site http://www.calarts.edu

Contact Ms. Taryn Wolf, Assistant Director of Admissions, California Institute of the Arts, 24700 McBean Parkway, Valencia, California 91355; 661-255-1050, fax: 661-253-7710, e-mail address: twolf@calarts.edu

More About the Institute

The School of Art at California Institute of the Arts (CalArts) offers undergraduate and graduate programs in the areas of art, graphic design, and photography and media. The undergraduate programs lead to a Bachelor of Fine Arts (B.F.A.) degree and the graduate programs to a Master of Fine Arts (M.F.A.) degree.

Faculty, Resident Artists, and Alumni The School's faculty is made up of innovators and leaders in contemporary art practice. Since all faculty members are working artists with an abundance of real-world experience, they prepare students for the creative and professional demands of contemporary art and design.

A faculty mentor serves as each student's artistic adviser, guiding them through the program and assisting the student in customizing a curriculum to fit their personal interests and artistic goals. The School of Art regularly invites a wide range of visiting artists, designers, photographers, performers, writers, and theorists to share their experience and vision with students to supplement the expertise of the faculty members. The School of Art alumni are prominent in the art and design communities at the local, national, and international levels, and can often be found on faculty rosters of some of the most esteemed colleges.

Programs of Study Encompassing both studio practice and theory, The Program in Art offers instruction in a wide range of media, including but not limited to painting, drawing, printmaking, photography, digital imaging, sculpture, installation, video, film, writing, and performance. The program does not require students to concentrate on a particular medium; instead, it relies on a flexible structure of individualized instruction and mentoring to emphasize the articulation of ideas.

The four-year B.F.A. curriculum begins with a selection of foundation course options, along with critical studies, where students investigate various media, art-historical traditions, and theoretical positions. Additional course work includes a combination of seminars, group critique classes, technical workshops, and independent studies. By the third year in residence, undergraduates are expected to pursue independent projects.

The Program in Graphic Design prepares students for a wide range of professional options—from Web design and motion graphics to editorial design and environmental graphics, from film title and broadcast design to exhibitions and careers in education. The program emphasizes both practical and conceptual skills and enables each designer to integrate a command of visual language with imagination, theory, and new technology. The highly structured B.F.A. curriculum begins with courses covering basic design principles, imagemaking, typography, history, and theory.

The Program in Photography and Media is committed to educating independent artists in a world where photographic imagery and new media representations and strategies are omnipresent. The program encourages debate and experimentation, and students are encouraged to challenge conventions in a genre that includes many new practices.

The B.F.A. curriculum begins with a year of intensive photographic foundation work, followed by a mixture of courses that includes classes on specific issues in photography, video and Internet practice, the histories of photography and film, media theories and semiotics, as well as critique classes, technical workshops, and independent studies. Students are welcome to work in darkroom photography, digital imaging, time-based formats, and beyond.

Program Facilities The MacLab is used for creating digital and print-based work, including drawing, painting, photo manipulation, editorial design, type design, 3-D rendering, motion graphics, sound design and Web, and CD and DVD authoring.

The Photography and Media Lab includes high-capacity black-and-white and color processors, a 16-inch capacity Cibachrome color processor, black-and-white printing bays, and individual color darkrooms, including an 8-by-10 inch color mural enlarger. The digital photography and video lab is equipped with 4 Final Cut Pro Stations, digital imaging software, a negative scanner, and two large Epson digital photographic printers.

The Print and Media Lab is used for producing multiples through silk-screening, etching, lithography, or letterpress. It contains light tables, work tables, paper cutters, an exposure unit, various presses, and a digital imaging lab with a large output capacity printer and a vinyl cutter.

The Super Shop is the Institute's main sculpture studio and features work areas and equipment for woodworking, metalworking, machining, sandblasting, spraying, and mold making.

The Video Lab offers an assortment of high-quality equipment for time-based media production and post-production, as well as facilities for classroom instruction and student use. Digital video and Hi-8 cameras, tripods, microphones, lighting kits, mini-disc sound recorders, and other production equipment are available for checkout.

Beginning undergraduates in the Programs in Art and Photography and Media share studios, while most upper-level undergraduates work in individual studios. Graphic design students have individual workspace cubicles in larger studios that have adjoining critique rooms.

Student Performance/Exhibit Opportunities

School of Art students exhibit their work in seven on-campus galleries, and in various unconventional or informal settings around campus. First- and second-year undergraduates participate in several group shows, while upper-level undergraduates are required to mount solo exhibitions. Shows are often accompanied by opening receptions and parties,

which are organized by students and open to the public as well as the CalArts community.

California State University, Chico
Chico, California

State-supported, coed. Small town campus. Total enrollment: 16,250.

Degrees Bachelor of Fine Arts in the areas of studio art, interior design, electronic arts. Majors and concentrations: ceramic art and design, electronic arts, glass, interior design, painting/drawing, photography, printmaking, sculpture. Graduate degrees offered: Master of Fine Arts in the area of studio art. Cross-registration with California State University System. Program accredited by NASAD.

Enrollment 398 total; 25 undergraduate, 8 graduate, 365 nonprofessional degree.

Art Faculty 17 undergraduate (full-time), 15 undergraduate (part-time). 100% of full-time faculty have terminal degrees. Graduate students teach a few undergraduate courses. Undergraduate student–faculty ratio: 19:1.

Student Life Student groups/activities include General Student Art Club, Ceramics Student Art Club, Glass Art Club.

Expenses for 2007–2008 Application fee: $55. State resident tuition: $0 full-time. Nonresident tuition: $12,942 full-time. Mandatory fees: $3690 full-time. College room and board: $8466. College room only: $5860. Room and board charges vary according to board plan and housing facility. Special program-related fees: $10–$100 per course for materials fee.

Financial Aid Program-specific awards: academic and performance awards for incoming freshmen.

Application Procedures Students apply for admission into the professional program by junior year. Deadline for freshmen: November 30. Notification date for freshmen: continuous. Required: high school transcript, college transcript(s) for transfer students, minimum 3.0 high school GPA, 2 letters of recommendation, portfolio, SAT or ACT test scores, minimum 3.0 college GPA in art for entry into BFA program. Portfolio reviews held twice on campus; the submission of slides may be substituted for portfolios whenever necessary.

California State University, Chico (continued)

Web Site http://www.csuchico.edu

Undergraduate Contact Mr. Michael Bishop, Chairman, Department of Art and Art History, California State University, Chico, Chico, California 95929-0820; 530-898-5331, e-mail address: mbishop@csuchico.edu

Graduate Contact Cameron Crawford, Professor, Department of Art and Art History, California State University, Chico, Chico, California 95929-0820; 530-898-5331, e-mail address: ccrawford@csuchico.edu

California State University, Fullerton

Fullerton, California

State-supported, coed. Suburban campus. Total enrollment: 35,921. Art program established 1962.

Degrees Bachelor of Fine Arts in the areas of entertainment art/animation, drawing/painting, printmaking, sculpture, crafts, ceramics and glass, graphic design, illustration, creative photography. Majors and concentrations: ceramics, crafts, entertainment art/animation, glass, graphic design, illustration, jewelry and metalsmithing, painting/drawing, photography, printmaking, sculpture. Graduate degrees offered: Master of Arts in the areas of drawing/painting, printmaking, sculpture, ceramics and glass, graphic design, creative photography, illustration, jewelry and metalsmithing, exhibition design, art history, crafts; Master of Fine Arts in the areas of drawing/painting, printmaking, sculpture, ceramics and glass, crafts, graphic design, creative photography, illustration, jewelry and metalsmithing, exhibition design. Cross-registration with California State University System. Program accredited by NASAD.

Enrollment 1,559 total; 1,448 undergraduate, 111 graduate.

Art Student Profile 57% females, 43% males, 34% minorities, 5% international.

Art Faculty 32 total (full-time), 66 total (part-time). 76% of full-time faculty have terminal degrees. Graduate students teach a few undergraduate courses. Undergraduate student–faculty ratio: 19:1.

Student Life Student groups/activities include Pencil Mileage Club, The Art Network, Graphic Design Club. Special housing available for art students.

Expenses for 2006–2007 Application fee: $55. State resident tuition: $0 full-time. Nonresident tuition: $10,170 full-time. Mandatory fees: $3030 full-time. Full-time tuition and fees vary according to course load. College room only: $4408. Special program-related fees: $10 per course for ceramic glaze fee, $10–$16 per course for lab fees.

Financial Aid Program-specific awards: 2 Mert Purkiss Awards for incoming freshmen ($1000), 2–4 Florence Arnold Awards for continuing students ($500), 1–3 John Olson Awards for design/crafts majors ($700), 2–3 Tribute Fund Awards for transfer students ($750), 1 California China Painters Association Award for traditional/descriptive art majors ($1000), 2 Costa Mesa Art League Awards for juniors or seniors ($500), 1 Jeff and Rosalie Bacon Award for incoming students ($2000), 2 Orange County Fine Arts Awards for new and continuing students ($500), 2 Art Alliance Scholarships for transfer students from community colleges ($1000).

Application Procedures Students apply for admission into the professional program by sophomore year. Deadline for freshmen and transfers: continuous. Required: high school transcript, college transcript(s) for transfer students, minimum 2.0 high school GPA, SAT test score only.

Web Site http://www.art.fullerton.edu/

Undergraduate Contact Ms. Rachel Yunn, Undergraduate Secretary, Department of Visual Arts, California State University, Fullerton, PO Box 6850, Fullerton, California 92834-6850; 714-278-3471, fax: 714-278-2390.

Graduate Contact Ms. Jackie Reynolds, Graduate Secretary, Department of Visual Arts, California State University, Fullerton, PO Box 6850, Fullerton, California 92834-6850; 714-278-3471, fax: 714-278-2390, e-mail address: jreynolds@fullerton.edu

California State University, Long Beach

Long Beach, California

State-supported, coed. Suburban campus. Total enrollment: 35,574. Art program established 1949.
Web Site http://www.csulb.edu/

Capital University

Columbus, Ohio

Independent, coed. Suburban campus. Total enrollment: 3,825.

Degrees Bachelor of Fine Arts. Majors and concentrations: art education, art therapy. Cross-registration with Higher Education Council of Columbus.

Enrollment 30 total; all undergraduate.

Art Student Profile 92% females, 8% males, 11% minorities.

Art Faculty 3 undergraduate (full-time), 2 undergraduate (part-time). 67% of full-time faculty have terminal degrees. Graduate students do not teach undergraduate courses. Undergraduate student–faculty ratio: 9:1.

Student Life Student groups/activities include Capital University Student Art Therapy Association, Phi Beta.

Expenses for 2007–2008 Application fee: $25. Comprehensive fee: $33,180 includes full-time tuition ($26,360) and college room and board ($6820). Full-time tuition varies according to course load, degree level, program, and student level. Room and board charges vary according to board plan and housing facility.

Financial Aid Program-specific awards available.

Application Procedures Students admitted directly into the professional program freshman year. Deadline for freshmen and transfers: continuous. Required: high school transcript, college transcript(s) for transfer students, SAT or ACT test scores (minimum composite ACT score of 18), minimum 2.6 high school GPA, minimum 2.5 cumulative college GPA for transfer students, high school counselor form, 880 reading/math only, application end of freshman year (art education only). Recommended: interview, portfolio. Portfolio re-

views held as needed on campus; the submission of slides may be substituted for portfolios for large works of art.
Web Site http://www.capital.edu
Undergraduate Contact Ms. Lisa McKitrick, Associate Director of Admission, Capital University, 1 College and Main, Columbus, Ohio 43209; 614-236-6101, fax: 614-236-6926, e-mail address: admissions@capital.edu

Carnegie Mellon University

Pittsburgh, Pennsylvania

Independent, coed. Urban campus. Total enrollment: 10,120. Art program established 1910.

Degrees Bachelor of Fine Arts. Majors and concentrations: art. Graduate degrees offered: Master of Fine Arts in the area of art. Cross-registration with Chatham College, University of Pittsburgh, Duquesne University, Point Park College, Community College of Allegheny County, Pittsburgh Theological Seminary, LaRoche College, Robert Morris University, Carlow University. Program accredited by NASAD.

Enrollment 169 total; 151 undergraduate, 18 graduate.

Art Student Profile 60% females, 40% males, 34% minorities, 9% international.

Art Faculty 5 undergraduate (part-time), 1 graduate (part-time), 24 total (full-time). 100% of full-time faculty have terminal degrees. Graduate students do not teach undergraduate courses. Undergraduate student–faculty ratio: 6:1.

Student Life Student groups/activities include weekly exhibitions, student-managed gallery exhibitions, Surg (undergraduate research grant projects).

Expenses for 2006–2007 Application fee: $65. Comprehensive fee: $43,858 includes full-time tuition ($34,180), mandatory fees ($398), and college room and board ($9280). College room only: $5440. Special program-related fees: $20–$215 per 10 units for materials fees for various courses.

Financial Aid Program-specific awards: Jacques and Natasha Gelman Scholarships, Scholastic

Carnegie Mellon University (continued)

Art Awards, Ethel Murdock Kirk Awards, Eleanor Zygler Awards for junior and senior painting majors.

Application Procedures Students admitted directly into the professional program freshman year. Deadline for freshmen: October 1; transfers: December 1. Notification date for freshmen: continuous; transfers: April 15. Required: essay, high school transcript, college transcript(s) for transfer students, 3 letters of recommendation, portfolio, SAT or ACT test scores. Recommended: minimum 3.0 high school GPA, interview. Portfolio reviews held 11 times on campus and off campus at National Portfolio Day Associations locations; the submission of slides may be substituted for portfolios.

Web Site http://artserver.cfa.cmu.edu

Undergraduate Contact Michael Steidel, Director of Admission, Carnegie Mellon University, 5000 Forbes Avenue, Warner Hall 212, Pittsburgh, Pennsylvania 15213-3890; 412-268-2082.

Graduate Contact Ms. Cynthia Lammert, Facilities and Project Manager, School of Art, Carnegie Mellon University, College of Fine Arts Building, Room 300, 5000 Forbes Avenue, Pittsburgh, Pennsylvania 15213-3890; 412-268-6707, fax: 412-268-7817, e-mail address: cl2w@andrew.cmu.edu

Cazenovia College

Cazenovia, New York

Independent, coed. Small town campus. Total enrollment: 1,006. Art program established 1982.

Degrees Bachelor of Fine Arts in the areas of interior design, studio art, visual communications, fashion design. Majors and concentrations: advertising graphic design, fashion design, interior design, photography, studio art, visual communication, Web design.

Art Faculty 13 undergraduate (full-time), 20 undergraduate (part-time). 79% of full-time faculty have terminal degrees. Graduate students do not teach undergraduate courses. Undergraduate student–faculty ratio: 13:1.

Student Life Student groups/activities include Art Club, Fashion Design Club, New York State Eleven Albany Conference (Interior Design).

Expenses for 2007–2008 Application fee: $30. Comprehensive fee: $30,440 includes full-time tuition ($21,280), mandatory fees ($220), and college room and board ($8940). Full-time tuition and fees vary according to class time and course load. Room and board charges vary according to board plan and housing facility. Special program-related fees: $78 per semester for required fee.

Financial Aid Program-specific awards available.

Application Procedures Students admitted directly into the professional program freshman year. Deadline for freshmen and transfers: continuous. Required: essay, high school transcript, college transcript(s) for transfer students, letter of recommendation. Recommended: minimum 2.0 high school GPA, minimum 3.0 high school GPA, interview, portfolio, SAT or ACT test scores. Portfolio reviews held as needed on campus; the submission of slides may be substituted for portfolios when distance is prohibitive or if scheduling is difficult.

Web Site http://www.cazenovia.edu

Undergraduate Contact Robert Croot, Dean for Enrollment Management, Admissions and Financial Aid, Cazenovia College, 3 Sullivan Street, Cazenovia, New York 13035; 315-655-7208, fax: 315-655-4486, e-mail address: admission@cazenovia.edu

Centenary College

Hackettstown, New Jersey

Independent, coed. Suburban campus. Total enrollment: 2,662.

Web Site http://www.centenarycollege.edu/

Central Michigan University

Mount Pleasant, Michigan

State-supported, coed. Small town campus. Total enrollment: 26,710. Art program established 1971.

Web Site http://www.cmich.edu/

Central State University

Wilberforce, Ohio

State-supported, coed. Rural campus. Total enrollment: 1,766.

Degrees Bachelor of Arts in the area of art; Bachelor of Science in the area of art education. Majors and concentrations: advertising graphic design, art education, drawing, painting. Cross-registration with Consortium of Ohio State Universities.

Enrollment 40 total; all undergraduate.

Art Student Profile 60% females, 40% males, 90% minorities.

Art Faculty 4 total (full-time), 5 total (part-time). 100% of full-time faculty have terminal degrees. Graduate students do not teach undergraduate courses. Undergraduate student–faculty ratio: 6:1.

Student Life Student groups/activities include Art Club.

Expenses for 2006–2007 Application fee: $20. State resident tuition: $5294 full-time. Nonresident tuition: $11,462 full-time. Full-time tuition varies according to course load. College room and board: $7402. College room only: $3978. Room and board charges vary according to board plan.

Financial Aid Program-specific awards: 15 Fine and Performing Arts Scholarships ($400–$1200).

Application Procedures Students admitted directly into the professional program freshman year. Deadline for freshmen and transfers: continuous. Required: high school transcript, SAT or ACT test scores, minimum 2.0 high school GPA for in-state students, minimum 2.5 high school GPA for out-of-state students, minimum ACT score of 15 for in-state students, minimum ACT score of 18 for out-of-state students. Recommended: portfolio. Portfolio reviews held by appointment on campus; the submission of slides may be substituted for portfolios.

Web Site http://www.centralstate.edu

Undergraduate Contact Admissions Department, Central State University, Wilberforce, Ohio 45384; 937-376-6348.

Chowan University

Murfreesboro, North Carolina

Independent Baptist, coed. Rural campus. Total enrollment: 800 (2005). Art program established 1978.

Degrees Bachelor of Arts in the area of studio art; Bachelor of Science in the areas of studio art, graphic design.

Enrollment 55 total; 8 undergraduate.

Art Student Profile 50% females, 50% males, 50% minorities.

Art Faculty 3 undergraduate (full-time), 3 undergraduate (part-time). 67% of full-time faculty have terminal degrees. Graduate students do not teach undergraduate courses. Undergraduate student–faculty ratio: 12:1.

Student Life Student groups/activities include "Artisus" Art Club, trips to Smithsonian (Washington, DC), Europe, Chrysler Museum, Gallery Exhibitions in Green Hall Galleries.

Expenses for 2006–2007 Application fee: $20. Comprehensive fee: $22,840 includes full-time tuition ($15,800), mandatory fees ($240), and college room and board ($6800). College room only: $3200. Room and board charges vary according to board plan.

Financial Aid Program-specific awards available.

Application Procedures Students admitted directly into the professional program freshman year. Required: essay, high school transcript, college transcript(s) for transfer students, letter of recommendation, interview, audition, portfolio, SAT or ACT test scores. Portfolio reviews held on campus.

Web Site http://www.chowan.edu/academics/school-arts-sciences-visual-art.htm

Undergraduate Contact Christina Rupsch, MS, Chair, Department of Visual Art, Department of Visual Art, Chowan University, 1 University Place, Murfreesboro, North Carolina 27855; 252-398-6306, e-mail address: rupscc@chowan.edu

Clarke College

Dubuque, Iowa

Independent Roman Catholic, coed. Urban campus. Total enrollment: 1,201. Art program established 1843.

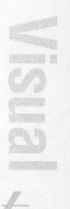

Clarke College (continued)

Degrees Bachelor of Fine Arts in the areas of studio art, graphic design. Majors and concentrations: art history, ceramics, drawing, graphic design, painting, printmaking, sculpture. Cross-registration with Loras College, University of Dubuque.

Enrollment 60 total; 35 undergraduate, 25 nonprofessional degree.

Art Student Profile 65% females, 35% males, 3% minorities, 3% international.

Art Faculty 5 undergraduate (full-time), 2 undergraduate (part-time). 80% of full-time faculty have terminal degrees. Graduate students do not teach undergraduate courses. Undergraduate student–faculty ratio: 12:1.

Student Life Student groups/activities include gallery exhibits, visiting artists workshops.

Expenses for 2006–2007 Application fee: $25. Comprehensive fee: $26,871 includes full-time tuition ($19,682), mandatory fees ($615), and college room and board ($6574). College room only: $3198. Room and board charges vary according to board plan and housing facility. Special program-related fees: $20–$50 per course for lab fees.

Financial Aid Program-specific awards: 12–15 art scholarships for art students (renewable) ($1000–$3000).

Application Procedures Students apply for admission into the professional program by sophomore year. Deadline for freshmen and transfers: continuous. Required: high school transcript, college transcript(s) for transfer students, minimum 2.0 high school GPA, letter of recommendation, portfolio, SAT or ACT test scores (minimum composite ACT score of 21), portfolio review for scholarship consideration. Recommended: essay, interview. Portfolio reviews held by appointment from January to April on campus and off campus in Chicago, IL; St. Louis, MO; Minneapolis, MN; the submission of slides may be substituted for portfolios when distance is prohibitive.

Web Site http://www.clarke.edu

Undergraduate Contact Andy Schroeder, Director, Office of Admissions, Clarke College, 1550 Clarke Avenue, Dubuque, Iowa 52001; 563-588-6366, fax: 563-588-6789, e-mail address: andy.schroeder@clarke.edu

The Cleveland Institute of Art

Cleveland, Ohio

Independent, coed. Urban campus. Total enrollment: 610. Art program established 1882.

Degrees Bachelor of Fine Arts. Majors and concentrations: ceramics, digital art, drawing, enameling, fibers, glass, graphic design, illustration, industrial design, interior design, medical illustration, metals, painting, photography, printmaking, sculpture. Graduate degrees offered: Master of Fine Arts in the area of medical illustration and digital arts. Cross-registration with members of the Northeast Ohio Council on Higher Education. Program accredited by NASAD.

Enrollment 500 total; 489 undergraduate, 10 graduate, 1 nonprofessional degree.

Art Student Profile 54% females, 46% males, 13% minorities, 3% international.

Art Faculty 45 undergraduate (full-time), 55 undergraduate (part-time). 80% of full-time faculty have terminal degrees. Graduate students do not teach undergraduate courses. Undergraduate student–faculty ratio: 8:1.

Student Life Student groups/activities include Industrial Design Society of America. Special housing available for art students.

Expenses for 2007–2008 Application fee: $30. Comprehensive fee: $38,859 includes full-time tuition ($28,100), mandatory fees ($1990), and college room and board ($8769). Full-time tuition and fees vary according to program. Room and board charges vary according to board plan. Special program-related fees: $40 per credit hour for lab fees (under 12 credit hours), $50 per credit hour for technology fee (under 12 credit hours), $275–$525 per semester for technology fee (depending on major), $275 per semester for lab fees (12-15 credit hours).

Financial Aid Program-specific awards: portfolio scholarships and grants for freshmen ($4000–$19,745), 100 portfolio grants ($2000–$5000), 18 transfer portfolio grants for transfer students ($2000–$5000).

Application Procedures Students admitted directly into the professional program freshman year. Deadline for freshmen and transfers: continuous. Required: essay, high school transcript, college transcript(s) for transfer students, minimum 2.0 high school GPA, 2 letters of recommendation, SAT or ACT test scores, slides or CD of portfolio. Recommended: interview. Portfolio reviews held bi-monthly on campus.

Web Site http://www.cia.edu

Undergraduate Contact Ms. Corey Thrush, Director of Admissions, The Cleveland Institute of Art, 11141 East Boulevard, Cleveland, Ohio 44106; 216-421-7422, fax: 216-754-3634, e-mail address: cthrush@cia.edu

Graduate Contact Dr. Gary Sampson, Director of Graduate Studies, The Cleveland Institute of Art, 11141 East Boulevard, Cleveland, Ohio 44106; 216-421-7369, fax: 216-421-7438, e-mail address: gsampson@cia.edu

More About the Institute

The Cleveland Institute of Art (CIA) offers one of America's most comprehensive educational programs in the visual arts.

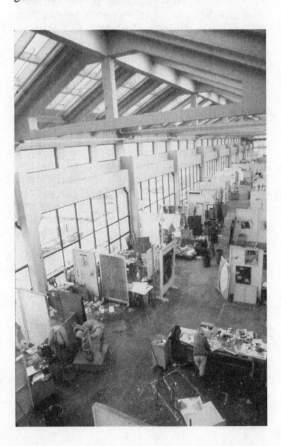

Drawing, color, design, art history, literature, and digital art classes make up the core curriculum of the Foundation. Both traditional and conceptual approaches to drawing and painting are emphasized. Composition, design theory, and the organization of 2-D and 3-D space are the focus of design classes. Art history includes the Paleolithic era through contemporary works of the late twentieth to early twenty-first centuries, which are discussed in the last semester of study. The contemporary writings of each era are studied in the literature classes, which encompass composition and critical analysis of those works. Digital art courses are required and serve as an introduction to both the Macintosh platform and the use of graphics software as a tool for art and design. Foundation students take an open environmental elective, which helps students make informed decisions, based on experience, regarding which major they wish to study during the later years of their education.

Each major at CIA is categorized into one of four environments—visual art and technology, design culture, craft material studies, or integrated media. Cross-discipline study is an integral part of the curriculum. Regardless of their major, all students take courses outside their discipline, and everyone graduates with a Bachelor of Fine Arts (B.F.A.) degree.

Liberal arts electives continue to play an important role in a student's development as a professional artist during the later years of study. An array of subjects in the humanities and social sciences are offered each term. The structure of the program ensures a broad distribution by requiring students to pursue advanced studies across six areas.

The culmination point of the program is the B.F.A. thesis exhibition and review. During this requirement for graduation, the candidates present their work throughout the school and receive formal critique by peers and faculty members. Much of the final year is spent independently preparing for this review, much the same way that one would prepare work for an agency or develop a body of work for a gallery show.

Program Facilities Individual studio spaces are provided for all majors. The facilities at the Cleveland Institute of Art include big, bright, professional art and design studios. Available to students are high-output printers; woodshops; darkrooms; a foundry; Macintosh, Silicon Graphics, and IBM computer labs; printmaking equipment; glass furnaces; metal lathes; milling machines; kilns; critique spaces; and the Jessica Gund Memorial Library.

Faculty, Resident Artists, and Alumni Studio faculty members are practicing artists and designers.

Visual

Arts

The Cleveland Institute of Art (continued)

Their work can be found in national and international, public and private collections, including the Hirshhorn Museum; the Corcoran Gallery; the Library of Congress; the Smithsonian Institution of Washington, D.C.; the Metropolitan Museum of Art; the Museum of Modern Photography in New York City; the Cleveland Museum of Art; and the Victoria and Albert Museum in London. Liberal arts faculty members are historians, poets, and researchers. The Visiting Artist program offers learning through the firsthand experiences of prominent artists. Alumni work in a variety of art fields at distinguished institutions and industry leaders, including Fisher Price, General Electric, Disney, Yale University, Rubbermaid, Mattel, the Metropolitan Museum of Art, General Motors, and American Greetings.

Student Performance and Exhibit Opportunities The Cleveland Institute of Art offers generous student gallery space, library gallery space, the annual Student Independent Exhibition, and various local restaurants, coffeehouses, and galleries.

Special Programs Students attending the Cleveland Institute of Art have the opportunity to participate in the New York Studio program, extensive internship opportunities, cross-registration with other colleges and universities, intensive summer workshops, and liberal arts tutoring. Biomedical art students work with the medical and dental schools of Case Western Reserve University, University Hospitals, and the Cleveland Clinic Foundation. A wide range of study-abroad opportunities are available.

College for Creative Studies

Detroit, Michigan

Independent, coed. Urban campus. Total enrollment: 1,302. Art program established 1906.

Degrees Bachelor of Fine Arts in the areas of fine arts, crafts, photography, communication design/illustration, transportation design, interior design, animation/digital media, advertising design, product design. Majors and concentrations: advertising design, animation, art/fine arts, ceramic art and design, crafts, furniture design, glass, graphic design, illustration, industrial design, interior design, jewelry and metalsmithing, painting/drawing, photography, printmaking, product design, sculpture, studio art, textile arts, transportation design.

Cross-registration with Association of Independent Colleges of Art and Design. Program accredited by NASAD.

Enrollment 1,302 total; all undergraduate.

Art Student Profile 41% females, 59% males, 10% minorities, 5% international.

Art Faculty 46 undergraduate (full-time), 200 undergraduate (part-time). Graduate students do not teach undergraduate courses. Undergraduate student–faculty ratio: 10:1.

Student Life Student groups/activities include Student Government, Black Artists Researching Trends, Industrial Design Society of America. Special housing available for art students.

Expenses for 2007–2008 Application fee: $35. Tuition: $25,230 full-time. Mandatory fees: $1145 full-time. College room only: $3900. Special program-related fees: $400–$900 per year for lab/material fees.

Financial Aid Program-specific awards: 1 Award of Excellence for entering students ($25,291), 12 Walter B. Ford Scholarships for entering students ($12,000), 15 President's Scholarships for entering students ($10,000), CCS Scholarships for entering students ($3500–$6000).

Application Procedures Students admitted directly into the professional program freshman year. Deadline for freshmen and transfers: continuous. Notification date for freshmen and transfers: August 15. Required: high school transcript, college transcript(s) for transfer students, portfolio, SAT or ACT test scores, minimum 2.5 high school GPA, minimum 2.0 college GPA for transfer students. Recommended: essay, 2 letters of recommendation. Portfolio reviews held throughout the year on campus and off campus in during National Portfolio Days and during high school visits; the submission of slides may be substituted for portfolios.

Web Site http://www.ccscad.edu

Undergraduate Contact Julie Hingelberg, Dean of Enrollment Services, Admissions Office, College for Creative Studies, 201 East Kirby Street, Detroit, Michigan 48202; 800-952-ARTS, fax: 313-872-2739, e-mail address: admissions@ccscad.edu

More About the College

The College for Creative Studies (CCS) is among the nation's leading colleges of art and design. Students can pursue a Bachelor of Fine Arts degree in the following majors: advertising design, animation and digital media, art education, crafts, fine arts, graphic design, illustration, interior design, photography, product design, and transportation design.

At the College for Creative Studies, first-year students can enter their chosen department and concentrate their studies in one area or spend their first semester "undeclared" and take an orientation class to learn about the eleven studio majors. While students are immersed in their chosen area of study immediately upon entering CCS, they are also encouraged to take classes outside of their major to broaden their skills.

Each department emphasizes four distinct components of a visual arts education: technical skill, aesthetic sensibility, conceptual ability, and practical experience, combining studio and academic classes with more individualized instruction. Upper-level students have the opportunity to begin working independently in private and semiprivate studio settings. While these students have the freedom to cultivate their own personal vision and style, they are regularly visited by faculty members for critiques and guidance. Internships give students an opportunity to work side-by-side with art and design professionals.

CCS' faculty consists of professional artists and designers who are also working and exhibiting in their fields of expertise. They provide students with an immediate connection to the real world by bringing new trends, practical insights, and networking opportunities to the College, shedding a realistic light on theoretical classroom exercises. Students are assigned a faculty academic adviser in their department upon entering the school.

Studies at CCS are also fully supported by state-of-the-art facilities. The College has woodworking, metalsmithing, and hot glass studios; a foundry; a clay modeling studio; a Thermwood 5-axis CNC milling machine; a rapid prototyping studio for creating 3-D color models from computer-generated designs; an AutoCad lab for interior design; a digital photography lab; advanced audio-video editing suites; and a film production studio. There is also a visual arts library with a large collection of art and design publications. An on-site imaging center offers color and wide-format printing and a campuswide network provides Internet access in all dorm rooms and e-mail for all students and faculty members.

Computer facilities are constantly updated to adapt to rapidly changing technology. Currently, there are approximately 400 Macintosh and Windows 2000 computer workstations running 3D Studio Max; Alias/Wavefront Studio Tools; AutoCad; After Effects; Final Cut Pro; Illustrator; Macromedia Dreamweaver, Flash, Fireworks, and Director; Maya;

Photoshop; Premiere; and InDesign software. Students can take computer-based courses in animation, interactive media, Web page design, publishing, graphic design, illustration, and digital imaging, among others.

The Academic Advising Center helps with general advising questions regarding scheduling, transfer credits, and the College's mobility program. Students in need of academic assistance have access to the Student Success Center (SSC), where trained professionals help students develop study and time management skills. The SSC also helps students improve their language, reading, and writing abilities. A career counselor is available to assist current students with internships and summer jobs as well as to help graduating seniors or CCS alumni secure jobs.

CCS students have many opportunities to exhibit their work publicly. Work is displayed in the U245 Student Gallery and at such events as the Detroit Festival of the Arts and numerous gallery exhibitions. The annual Student Exhibition, held in conjunction with commencement, is a major public event that draws thousands of people to view and purchase student artwork.

CCS' location is a valuable resource in itself. The campus is situated in Detroit's Cultural Center. It is within walking distance of a number of educational institutions and museums, including the Detroit Institute of Arts (the nation's fifth-largest museum), the Charles H. Wright Museum of African-American History, the Detroit Public Library, and Wayne State University. The surrounding metropolitan area is also inspiring to art students, with theaters and cafés, eclectic neighborhoods, and galleries displaying the work of emerging and established artists.

Professional opportunities abound in the Detroit area. Automotive manufacturing and supply industries have a constant need for creative industrial designers, and because Detroit is the fourth-largest producer of advertising in the U.S., creative professionals are in constant demand.

For a visual arts education that stresses the personal development of style and vision and the practical experience needed to succeed in the real world, the College for Creative Studies is an excellent educational option.

The College of New Jersey

Ewing, New Jersey

State-supported, coed. Suburban campus. Total enrollment: 6,934.

The College of New Jersey (continued)

Degrees Bachelor of Arts in the area of art education; Bachelor of Fine Arts in the areas of fine arts, graphic design, digital arts. Majors and concentrations: art education, art history, art/fine arts, digital art, graphic design.

Enrollment 228 undergraduate.

Art Faculty 14 undergraduate (full-time), 15 undergraduate (part-time). 100% of full-time faculty have terminal degrees. Graduate students do not teach undergraduate courses.

Student Life Student groups/activities include Art Directors Club of New Jersey, National Art Education Association Student Chapter, International Sculpture Center, AIGA-American Institute of Graphic Arts.

Expenses for 2006–2007 Application fee: $60. State resident tuition: $7615 full-time. Nonresident tuition: $14,161 full-time. Mandatory fees: $2938 full-time. College room and board: $8843. College room only: $6380. Room and board charges vary according to board plan. Special program-related fees: $10–$25 per semester for supplemental materials.

Application Procedures Students admitted directly into the professional program freshman year. Deadline for freshmen and transfers: March 1. Notification date for freshmen and transfers: April 1. Required: essay, high school transcript, college transcript(s) for transfer students, portfolio, SAT test score only. Recommended: minimum 3.0 high school GPA, letter of recommendation. Portfolio reviews held continuously (slide/CD submissions) on campus; the submission of slides may be substituted for portfolios (slides preferred).

Web Site http://www.tcnj.edu/~artmain/

Undergraduate Contact Office of Admissions, The College of New Jersey, PO Box 7718, Ewing, New Jersey 08628; 609-771-2131.

The College of New Rochelle

New Rochelle, New York

Independent, coed, primarily women. Suburban campus. Total enrollment: 2,341. Art program established 1929.

Degrees Bachelor of Fine Arts in the areas of studio art, art therapy, art education; Bachelor of Science in the areas of art therapy, art education. Majors and concentrations: art education, art therapy, art/fine arts, computer art, graphic design, painting, printmaking, sculpture, studio art. Graduate degrees offered: Master of Arts in the area of art education; Master of Science in the area of art therapy.

Enrollment 55 total; 50 undergraduate, 5 nonprofessional degree.

Art Student Profile 100% females, 20% minorities, 3% international.

Art Faculty 5 undergraduate (full-time), 4 undergraduate (part-time), 2 graduate (full-time), 13 graduate (part-time). 100% of full-time faculty have terminal degrees. Graduate students do not teach undergraduate courses. Undergraduate student–faculty ratio: 10:1.

Student Life Student groups/activities include Artists Anonymous, Phoenix Literary & Art Magazine, Student Theater Ensemble. Special housing available for art students.

Expenses for 2007–2008 Application fee: $20. Comprehensive fee: $32,400 includes full-time tuition ($23,200), mandatory fees ($500), and college room and board ($8700). Full-time tuition and fees vary according to course load and program. Room and board charges vary according to housing facility.

Financial Aid Program-specific awards: 7–10 art scholarships for program majors ($2000–$5000).

Application Procedures Students admitted directly into the professional program freshman year. Deadline for freshmen and transfers: continuous. Required: high school transcript, college transcript(s) for transfer students, SAT or ACT test scores, minimum 2.5 high school GPA, portfolio for BFA applicants. Recommended: essay, minimum 3.0 high school GPA, letter of recommendation, interview, portfolio. Portfolio reviews held continuously on campus; the submission of slides may be substituted for portfolios if a campus visit is impossible.

Web Site http://www.cnr.edu

Undergraduate Contact Ms. Cristina de Gennaro, Chair, Art Department, School of Arts and Sciences, The College of New Rochelle, 29 Castle Place, New Rochelle, New York 10805; 914-654-5856, fax: 914-654-5290, e-mail address: cdegennaro@cnr.edu

The College of Saint Rose

Albany, New York

Independent, coed. Urban campus. Total enrollment: 5,062. Art program established 1995.

Web Site http://www.strose.edu/

College of Santa Fe

Santa Fe, New Mexico

Independent, coed. Suburban campus. Total enrollment: 2,004. Art program established 1984.

Web Site http://www.csf.edu

College of Visual Arts

St. Paul, Minnesota

Independent, coed. Urban campus. Total enrollment: 172. Art program established 1924.

Degrees Bachelor of Fine Arts in the areas of visual communication, fine arts, visual studies. Majors and concentrations: communication design, drawing, illustration, interdisciplinary art and design, painting, photography, sculpture.

Enrollment 172 total; all undergraduate.

Art Student Profile 58% females, 42% males, 9% minorities, 3% international.

Art Faculty 7 undergraduate (full-time), 39 undergraduate (part-time). 71% of full-time faculty have terminal degrees. Graduate students do not teach undergraduate courses. Undergraduate student–faculty ratio: 8:1.

Student Life Student groups/activities include College of Visual Arts Design Group-AIGA Student Chapter, The Sculpture Posse, Chasing the Sublime: A Journal of the College of Visual Arts.

Expenses for 2007–2008 Application fee: $40. Tuition: $21,184 full-time. Mandatory fees: $500 full-time. Special program-related fees: $53 per course for lab fees.

Financial Aid Program-specific awards: 59 merit scholarships for continuing and incoming students ($1580), 96 College of Visual Arts Grants for those demonstrating need ($1025).

Application Procedures Students admitted directly into the professional program freshman year. Deadline for freshmen and transfers: continuous. Notification date for freshmen and transfers: continuous. Required: essay, high school transcript, college transcript(s) for transfer students, minimum 2.0 high school GPA, interview, portfolio, SAT or ACT test scores, portfolio home exam as explained in the college catalog. Recommended: minimum 3.0 high school GPA, 2 letters of recommendation. Portfolio reviews held continuously on campus; the submission of slides may be substituted for portfolios for large works of art, three-dimensional pieces, or when distance is prohibitive.

Web Site http://www.cva.edu

Undergraduate Contact Ms. Jane Nordhorn, Director of Admissions, College of Visual Arts, 344 Summit Avenue, St. Paul, Minnesota 55102-2124; 800-224-1536, fax: 651-224-8854, e-mail address: jnordhorn@cva.edu

Collins College: A School of Design and Technology

Tempe, Arizona

Proprietary, coed. Urban campus. Total enrollment: 1,690. Art program established 1978.

Degrees Bachelor of Arts in the areas of visual communication, animation, media arts, visual arts-game art, game design. Majors and concentrations: animation, film and television, game art and design, graphic design, interior design, motion graphics, visual effects.

Enrollment 1,497 total; all undergraduate.

Art Student Profile 40% females, 60% males, 40% minorities, 4% international.

Art Faculty 86 undergraduate (full-time), 5 undergraduate (part-time). 5% of full-time faculty have terminal degrees. Graduate students do not teach undergraduate courses. Undergraduate student–faculty ratio: 15:1.

Student Life Student groups/activities include IIDA-International Interior Design Association, AIGA-American Institute of Graphic Arts, IGDA-International Game Designers Association.

Expenses for 2006–2007 Application fee: $50. Tuition: $24,250 full-time. Full-time tuition varies according to class time, course level, course load, degree level, location, program,

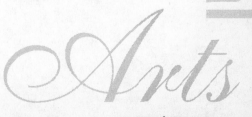

Collins College: A School of Design and Technology (continued)

reciprocity agreements, and student level. College room only: $4600.

Financial Aid Program-specific awards: 40 scholarships for enrolled students ($1000), 50–75 institutional grants for enrolled students ($1500).

Application Procedures Students admitted directly into the professional program freshman year. Deadline for freshmen and transfers: continuous. Required: essay, high school transcript, college transcript(s) for transfer students, interview. Recommended: portfolio. Portfolio reviews held continuously by appointment on campus.

Web Site http://www.collinscollege.edu

Undergraduate Contact Toby Craver, Senior Director of Admissions, Collins College: A School of Design and Technology, 1140 South Priest Drive, Tempe, Arizona 85281; 480-946-1204, fax: 480-829-0183, e-mail address: tcraver@collinscollege.edu

Colorado State University

Fort Collins, Colorado

State-supported, coed. Urban campus. Total enrollment: 26,723.

Degrees Bachelor of Fine Arts in the area of art. Majors and concentrations: drawing, fibers, graphic design, metals, painting, photography, pottery, printmaking, sculpture. Graduate degrees offered: Master of Fine Arts in the areas of metalsmithing, fibers, sculpture, printmaking, graphic design, drawing, painting.

Enrollment 580 total; 550 undergraduate, 30 graduate.

Art Student Profile 59% females, 41% males, 10% minorities, 1% international.

Art Faculty 23 total (full-time), 15 total (part-time). 96% of full-time faculty have terminal degrees. Graduate students teach a few undergraduate courses. Undergraduate student–faculty ratio: 20:1.

Student Life Student groups/activities include Student Organization for the Visual Arts. Special housing available for art students.

Expenses for 2006–2007 Application fee: $50. State resident tuition: $3466 full-time. Nonresi-

dent tuition: $14,994 full-time. Mandatory fees: $1251 full-time. Full-time tuition and fees vary according to course load. College room and board: $6602. College room only: $2980. Room and board charges vary according to board plan and housing facility. Special program-related fees: $50 per semester for technology fee.

Financial Aid Program-specific awards: 40 Creative and Performing Arts Awards for program students ($1000), 4 Founding Faculty Awards for program students ($1000), 2 Anna Lawton Printmaking Awards for printmakers ($1000), 1 Tracie Noah Memorial Scholarship for painters ($1000), 1 Bob Coonts Scholarship for graphic designers ($350), 1 Northern Colorado Artists Association Award for studio majors ($750), 1 Melanie Metz Memorial Scholarship for graphic designers ($500), 1 Evalyn Prouty Hickman Scholarship for program students ($1000).

Application Procedures Students admitted directly into the professional program freshman year. Deadline for freshmen and transfers: continuous. Notification date for freshmen and transfers: continuous. Required: high school transcript, college transcript(s) for transfer students, minimum 3.0 high school GPA, 3 letters of recommendation, SAT or ACT test scores, portfolio for transfer students. Portfolio reviews held as needed on campus.

Web Site http://www.colostate.edu/Depts/Art/

Undergraduate Contact Ms. Julia Morrigan, Administrative Assistant II, Art Department, Colorado State University, Fort Collins, Colorado 80523-1770; 970-491-6774, fax: 970-491-0505, e-mail address: julia.morrigan-mcdonough@colostate.edu

Graduate Contact Kathy Chynoweth, Graduate Coordinator, Art Department, Colorado State University, Fort Collins, Colorado 80523-1770; 970-491-6775, fax: 970-491-0505, e-mail address: kathleen.chynoweth@colostate.edu

Columbia College

Columbia, Missouri

Independent, coed. Small town campus. Total enrollment: 1,186. Art program established 1858.

Degrees Bachelor of Fine Arts in the area of art. Majors and concentrations: ceramics,

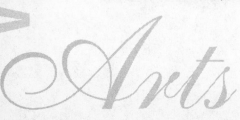

graphic design, illustration, painting/drawing, photography, printmaking. Cross-registration with University of Missouri, Stephens College, William Woods University, Lincoln University, Westminster College.

Enrollment 84 total; 23 undergraduate, 61 nonprofessional degree.

Art Student Profile 60% females, 40% males, 18% minorities, 7% international.

Art Faculty 5 undergraduate (full-time), 1 undergraduate (part-time). 100% of full-time faculty have terminal degrees. Graduate students do not teach undergraduate courses. Undergraduate student–faculty ratio: 5:1.

Student Life Student groups/activities include C.A.L.M. Club.

Expenses for 2006–2007 Application fee: $25. Comprehensive fee: $17,578 includes full-time tuition ($12,414) and college room and board ($5164). College room only: $3248. Full-time tuition varies according to class time and course load. Room and board charges vary according to board plan. Special program-related fees: $20 per course for model fees, lab fees.

Financial Aid Program-specific awards: 24 talent awards for program majors ($695), 3 Louis Blosser Scholarships for program majors ($570), 2 Vivian Sloan Fiske Scholarships for program majors ($1125), 1 Elizabeth Estes Gentry Scholarship for program majors ($1250), 4 Lucinda Van Meter Haynie Awards for art students ($500), 4 Mary Robinson Art Scholarships for program majors ($100), 1 Hurst John Scholarship for art students ($500), 1 Margaret Courter Memorial Scholarship for program majors ($125), 1 Sidney Larson Student Art Award for program majors ($750).

Application Procedures Students apply for admission into the professional program by sophomore year. Deadline for freshmen and transfers: continuous. Required: high school transcript, college transcript(s) for transfer students, minimum 2.0 high school GPA, SAT or ACT test scores, portfolio for scholarship consideration. Portfolio reviews held as needed on campus; the submission of slides may be substituted for portfolios when distance is prohibitive.

Web Site http://www.ccis.edu/departments/arts/

Undergraduate Contact Ms. Regina Morin, Director of Admissions, Columbia College, 1001 Rogers Street, Columbia, Missouri 65216; 573-875-7352, fax: 573-875-8765, e-mail address: admissions@ccis.edu

Art and Design Department
Columbia College Chicago
Chicago, Illinois

Independent, coed. Urban campus. Total enrollment: 11,499. Art program established 1970.

Degrees Bachelor of Arts in the area of art and design; Bachelor of Fine Arts in the areas of advertising art direction, product design, fashion design, interior design, graphic design, illustration. Majors and concentrations: advertising art direction, art and design, art/fine arts, fashion design, graphic design, illustration, interior architecture and design, product design. Graduate degrees offered: Master of Fine Arts in the areas of architectural studies, interior design.

Enrollment 1,644 total; 1,619 undergraduate, 25 graduate.

Art Student Profile 68% females, 32% males, 28% minorities, 2% international.

Art Faculty 35 undergraduate (full-time), 128 undergraduate (part-time), 1 graduate (part-time). Graduate students do not teach undergraduate courses. Undergraduate student–faculty ratio: 10:1.

Student Life Student groups/activities include Arts Community, Columbia College Fashion Association, International Interior Design Association.

Expenses for 2006–2007 Application fee: $35. Comprehensive fee: $26,553 includes full-time tuition ($16,328), mandatory fees ($460), and college room and board ($9765). College room only: $8265. Special program-related fees: $5–$415 per course for class fees.

Financial Aid Program-specific awards: 1 Pougialis Fine Arts Award for continuing fine arts majors ($2500).

Application Procedures Students admitted directly into the professional program freshman year. Deadline for freshmen and transfers: continuous. Notification date for freshmen and transfers: continuous. Required: essay, high school transcript, college transcript(s) for

Columbia College Chicago (continued)

transfer students, letter of recommendation, meeting with admissions counselor for a personal interview and possible remediation program attendance for students with less than a 2.0 GPA, portfolio for transfer students. Recommended: minimum 2.0 high school GPA, interview, SAT or ACT test scores. Portfolio reviews held continuously on campus.

Web Site http://www.colum.edu

Undergraduate Contact Mr. Murphy Monroe, Director, Office of Admissions, Columbia College Chicago, 600 South Michigan Avenue, Chicago, Illinois 60605; 312-344-7133, fax: 312-344-8024, e-mail address: admissions@ colum.edu

Graduate Contact Mr. Robert Garcia, Director of Graduate Admission, Graduate School Admissions, Columbia College Chicago, 600 South Michigan Avenue, Chicago, Illinois 60605; 312-344-7262, fax: 312-344-8047, e-mail address: rgarcia@colum.edu

Photography Department
Columbia College Chicago

Chicago, Illinois

Independent, coed. Urban campus. Total enrollment: 11,499. Art program established 1968.

Degrees Bachelor of Arts in the area of photography; Bachelor of Fine Arts in the area of photography. Majors and concentrations: fine art photography, photojournalism, professional photography. Graduate degrees offered: Master of Fine Arts in the area of photography.

Enrollment 733 total; 709 undergraduate, 24 graduate.

Art Student Profile 65% females, 35% males, 16% minorities, 1% international.

Art Faculty 16 total (full-time), 63 total (part-time). Undergraduate student–faculty ratio: 9:1.

Expenses for 2006–2007 Application fee: $35. Comprehensive fee: $26,553 includes full-time tuition ($16,328), mandatory fees ($460), and college room and board ($9765). College room

only: $8265. Special program-related fees: $5–$415 per course for class fees.

Financial Aid Program-specific awards: Kodak Scholarship for photography majors ($2000).

Application Procedures Students admitted directly into the professional program freshman year. Deadline for freshmen and transfers: continuous. Notification date for freshmen and transfers: continuous. Required: essay, high school transcript, college transcript(s) for transfer students, letter of recommendation, meeting with admissions counselor for a personal interview and possible remediation program attendance for students with less than a 2.0 GPA, portfolio for transfer students. Recommended: minimum 2.0 high school GPA, interview, SAT or ACT test scores. Portfolio reviews held continuously on campus.

Web Site http://www.colum.edu

Undergraduate Contact Mr. Murphy Monroe, Director, Office of Admissions, Columbia College Chicago, 600 South Michigan Avenue, Chicago, Illinois 606050; 312-344-7133, fax: 312-344-8024, e-mail address: admissions@ colum.edu

Graduate Contact Robert Garcia, Director of Graduate Studies, Graduate School Admissions, Columbia College Chicago, 600 South Michigan Avenue, Chicago, Illinois 60605; 312-344-7262, fax: 312-344-8047, e-mail address: rgarcia@colum.edu

Film and Video Department
Columbia College Chicago

Chicago, Illinois

Independent, coed. Urban campus. Total enrollment: 11,499. Art program established 1967.

Degrees Bachelor of Arts in the area of film/video. Majors and concentrations: alternative forms, audio for visual media, cinematography, computer animation, critical studies, directing, documentary, editing, post-production, producing, screenwriting, traditional animation. Graduate degrees offered: Master of Fine Arts in the area of film/video.

Enrollment 2,284 total; 2,223 undergraduate, 61 graduate.

Visual *Arts*

Art Student Profile 26% females, 74% males, 23% minorities, 2% international.

Art Faculty 34 total (full-time), 154 total (part-time). Graduate students do not teach undergraduate courses. Undergraduate student–faculty ratio: 12:1.

Student Life Student groups/activities include Documentary Film Group, Japanese Animation Club, Sunrayz Film Society.

Expenses for 2006–2007 Application fee: $35. Comprehensive fee: $26,553 includes full-time tuition ($16,328), mandatory fees ($460), and college room and board ($9765). College room only: $8265. Special program-related fees: $5–$415 per course for class fee (varies by class and class-related activities).

Application Procedures Students admitted directly into the professional program freshman year. Deadline for freshmen and transfers: continuous. Notification date for freshmen and transfers: continuous. Required: essay, high school transcript, college transcript(s) for transfer students, letter of recommendation, meeting with admissions counselor for a personal interview and possible remediation program attendance for students with less than a 2.0 GPA, portfolio for transfer students. Recommended: minimum 2.0 high school GPA, interview, SAT or ACT test scores. Portfolio reviews held continuously on campus.

Web Site http://www.colum.edu

Undergraduate Contact Mr. Murphy Monroe, Director, Office of Admissions, Columbia College Chicago, 600 South Michigan Avenue, Chicago, Illinois 60605; 312-344-7133, fax: 312-344-8024, e-mail address: admissions@colum.edu

Graduate Contact Robert Garcia, Director of Graduate Admission, Graduate School Admissions, Columbia College Chicago, 600 South Michigan Avenue, Chicago, Illinois 60605; 312-344-7262, fax: 312-344-8047, e-mail address: rgarcia@colum.edu

Columbus College of Art & Design

Columbus, Ohio

Independent, coed. Urban campus. Total enrollment: 1,581. Art program established 1879.

Degrees Bachelor of Fine Arts in the areas of fine art, visual communication, interior design, industrial design, media studies, illustration, fashion design. Majors and concentrations: art/fine arts, fashion design, graphic design, illustration, industrial design, interior design, media studies, visual communication. Cross-registration with Higher Education Council of Columbus. Program accredited by NASAD.

Enrollment 1,374 total; all undergraduate.

Art Student Profile 57% females, 43% males, 18% minorities.

Art Faculty 80 undergraduate (full-time), 100 undergraduate (part-time). 41% of full-time faculty have terminal degrees. Graduate students do not teach undergraduate courses. Undergraduate student–faculty ratio: 12:1.

Student Life Special housing available for art students.

Expenses for 2007–2008 Application fee: $25. Comprehensive fee: $29,062 includes full-time tuition ($21,768), mandatory fees ($644), and college room and board ($6650). Room and board charges vary according to housing facility and student level. Special program-related fees: $25–$160 for lab/studio fees.

Financial Aid Program-specific awards: 300 International Scholarship Competition Awards for incoming freshmen ($4500–$11,000), 150 Art Competition Awards for members of National Art Honor Society ($2000).

Application Procedures Students admitted directly into the professional program freshman year. Deadline for freshmen and transfers: continuous. Required: essay, high school transcript, college transcript(s) for transfer students, minimum 2.0 high school GPA, letter of recommendation, portfolio, SAT or ACT test scores. Recommended: interview. Portfolio reviews held continuously by appointment on campus and off campus; the submission of slides may be substituted for portfolios if a campus visit is impossible.

Web Site http://www.ccad.edu

Undergraduate Contact Thomas E. Green, Director of Admissions, Columbus College of Art & Design, 107 North Ninth Street, Columbus, Ohio 43215; 614-224-9101, fax: 877-869-5897, e-mail address: admissions@ccad.edu

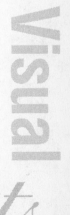

Visual *Arts*

Concordia University

Seward, Nebraska

Independent, coed. Small town campus. Total enrollment: 1,251. Art program established 1963.

Web Site http://www.cune.edu/

Concordia University

Montreal, Quebec, Canada

Province-supported, coed. Urban campus. Total enrollment: 32,033. Art program established 1975.

Web Site http://www.concordia.ca/

The Cooper Union School of Art

Cooper Union for the Advancement of Science and Art

New York, New York

Independent, coed. Urban campus. Total enrollment: 968. Art program established 1859.

Degrees Bachelor of Fine Arts in the area of fine arts. Majors and concentrations: art/fine arts. Cross-registration with Parsons School of Design-New School University. Program accredited by NASAD.

Enrollment 291 total; all undergraduate.

Art Student Profile 54% females, 46% males, 30% minorities, 9% international.

Art Faculty 9 undergraduate (full-time), 49 undergraduate (part-time). 90% of full-time faculty have terminal degrees. Graduate students do not teach undergraduate courses. Undergraduate student–faculty ratio: 7:1.

Student Life Student groups/activities include End of the Year Show, Cultural Show, open mike nights.

Expenses for 2007–2008 Application fee: $65. Comprehensive fee: $15,050 includes full-time tuition ($0), mandatory fees ($1550), and college room and board ($13,500). College room only: $9500. All students are awarded full-tuition scholarships. Living expenses are subsidized by college-administered financial aid.

Financial Aid Program-specific awards: full-tuition scholarships for all admitted students ($31,500).

Application Procedures Students admitted directly into the professional program freshman year. Deadline for freshmen and transfers: January 10. Notification date for freshmen and transfers: April 1. Required: essay, high school transcript, college transcript(s) for transfer students, minimum 2.0 high school GPA, portfolio, SAT or ACT test scores, home test. Recommended: 2 letters of recommendation, portfolio review. Portfolio reviews held 4 times during fall semester on campus and off campus at National Portfolio Days (about 20/year); the submission of slides may be substituted for portfolios for large works of art.

Web Site http://www.cooper.edu

Undergraduate Contact Mr. Mitchell L. Lipton, Dean of Admissions and Records and Registrar, Cooper Union for the Advancement of Science and Art, 30 Cooper Square, Suite 300, New York, New York 10003; 212-353-4120, fax: 212-353-4342, e-mail address: admissions@cooper.edu

The Cooper Union School of Art

See Cooper Union for the Advancement of Science and Art

Corcoran College of Art and Design

Washington, District of Columbia

Independent, coed. Urban campus. Total enrollment: 592. Art program established 1890.

Degrees Bachelor of Fine Arts in the areas of fine art, graphic design, photography, photojournalism, digital media design; Bachelor of Fine Arts/Master of Arts in Teaching in the area of fine art/teaching. Majors and concentrations: art education, art/fine arts, ceramics, digital art, digital media, drawing, graphic design, painting, photography, photojournal-

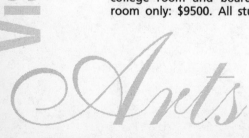

ism, printmaking, sculpture. Graduate degrees offered: Bachelor of Fine Arts/Master of Arts in Teaching in the area of fine art/teaching; Master of Arts in the areas of interior design, history of decorative arts, art education. Program accredited by NASAD.

Enrollment 590 total; 520 undergraduate, 70 graduate.

Art Student Profile 69% females, 31% males, 22% minorities, 7% international.

Art Faculty 32 undergraduate (full-time), 223 undergraduate (part-time), 32 graduate (part-time). 30% of full-time faculty have terminal degrees. Graduate students do not teach undergraduate courses. Undergraduate student–faculty ratio: 4:1.

Student Life Student groups/activities include Student Government, Off The Walls Art Sale, student exhibitions, WPA/C. Special housing available for art students.

Expenses for 2006–2007 Application fee: $40. Comprehensive fee: $35,284 includes full-time tuition ($24,289), mandatory fees ($200), and college room and board ($10,795). College room only: $8476. Full-time tuition and fees vary according to degree level.

Financial Aid Program-specific awards: 66 Dean's Scholarships for freshmen and transfers ($1000–$5000), 20 departmental scholarships for continuing students ($1000–$2500), 3 Academic Achievement Awards for entering freshmen ($2000–$9000), 19 President's Awards for freshmen and transfers ($2000–$9000), 8 Delaware College of Art and Design Grants for transfer students from DCAD ($2000–$5500), 8 Faculty Chairs' Grants for entering freshmen ($11,350–$22,700).

Application Procedures Students admitted directly into the professional program freshman year. Deadline for freshmen and transfers: continuous. Required: high school transcript, college transcript(s) for transfer students, minimum 2.0 high school GPA, interview, portfolio, SAT or ACT test scores. Recommended: essay, minimum 3.0 high school GPA, 3 letters of recommendation. Portfolio reviews held continuously by appointment on campus and off campus in various cities in the U.S.; the submission of slides may be substituted for portfolios for applicants living beyond 200-mile radius.

Web Site http://www.corcoran.edu

Contact Office of Admissions, Corcoran College of Art and Design, 500 17th Street, NW, Washington, District of Columbia 20006-4804; 202-639-1814, fax: 202-639-1830, e-mail address: admissions@corcoran.org

More About the College

The Corcoran College of Art and Design is one of the oldest art schools in the United States and upholds a long tradition of partnership between art schools and museums. Studying at one of the few museum-schools in the country, Corcoran students are surrounded by great art and frequently by the contemporary masters whose work is regularly exhibited. The Corcoran Museum of Art has one of the finest collections of American art in the world, which is supplemented by holdings in European painting and sculpture, classical antiquities, and the decorative arts. As Washington's first museum of art, the Corcoran has played a central role in the development of American culture for more than 125 years. The aspiring young professionals who study today at the Corcoran College of Art and Design join

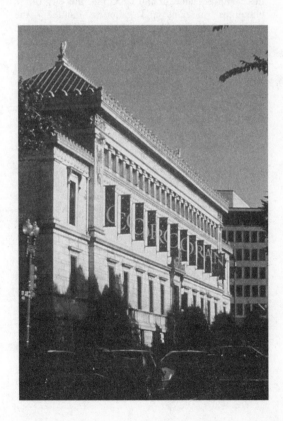

Corcoran College of Art and Design (continued)

a great and long tradition of quality and impact on the development of American and international art and design.

Corcoran undergraduate students take the integrated first-year Foundation program, which includes an introduction to the many art collections of Washington. After their first year, students select a major field of study in art education, fine art, digital media design, graphic design, photography, or photojournalism. Fine Art majors may choose to concentrate in ceramics, digital art, drawing, painting, printmaking, or sculpture. At the graduate studies level, a master's degree is offered in art education, interior design, and the history of decorative arts.

Location Washington is a city of monuments and museums set off by the neoclassical architecture of government buildings, parks, trees, and greenery. With dozens of major colleges and universities in the metropolitan area, there exists a feeling of a giant "campus" in which restaurants, coffee shops, movie theaters, and night spots are intermingled with bookstores, clothing boutiques, and academic facilities. Within a mile of the Corcoran, the city offers numerous museums and galleries, including the National Gallery of Art, the Phillips Collection, the Hirshhorn Museum and Sculpture Garden, and the Smithsonian National Museum of Natural History. Also a short walk from Corcoran are the world-famous Mall and performing arts institutions such as the Kennedy Center, Ford's Theater, and the National Theater. Rock Creek Park, a 1,700-acre public park that has a golf course, bicycle path, picnic area, nature center, playgrounds, tennis center, and Horse Center, is nearby as well.

Program Facilities The Downtown Campus of the Corcoran College of Art and Design is located in the same building as the Corcoran Gallery of Art, one block from the White House, with additional facilities in proximity. The building is one of America's finest examples of Beaux-Arts architecture, with wings designed by Ernest Flagg and Charles Platt.

Freshmen students spend their class time in the downtown and Georgetown buildings. Juniors and seniors in Fine Art have designated studio space as well as generous studio hours.

The Corcoran's nearby Georgetown Campus is home to the design and printmaking departments, papermaking and silkscreen facilities, jewelry studio, and state-of-the-art computer laboratories.

As an appealing alternative to crowded traditional dormitory housing, the College provides new students with attractive, spacious supervised apartments.

These furnished apartments are subway accessible, close to downtown and Georgetown, and have 24-hour security.

Student and Alumni Exhibit Opportunities
Students of all levels have several opportunities to exhibit their work. In the College/Museum space, there are several exhibition areas, including the White Walls Gallery and the Corcoran Gallery for the annual student sale of art work.

The Corcoran is the only college of art and design that incorporates an exhibition in a prominent museum into its curriculum. For three months of every year, graduating seniors showcase their thesis projects in the Corcoran Museum in a series of weeklong rotating exhibitions. The students are responsible for all aspects of these shows, from exhibition design to installation. These exhibitions culminate in a final exhibition featuring at least one work by every graduating senior. Through the formal presentation of their work in the museum, students make the transition to professional artists and designers and are introduced to the public as emerging talents.

The Corcoran Museum is also the site of the annual juried Corcoran Alumni Association exhibition, presenting works by some of the College's most accomplished alumni, all with extensive lists of exhibitions to their credit and many with gallery affiliations. The Visiting Artists Program also holds its exhibitions in the museum, allowing renowned contemporary artists, scholars, and critics to visit the Corcoran's campus each semester.

The Alumni Gallery, located off the main atrium of the Corcoran Gallery of Art, is dedicated to works by artists and designers who have received their degree from the Corcoran College of Art and Design.

Cornell University

Ithaca, New York

Independent, coed. Small town campus. Total enrollment: 19,639. Art program established 1921.

Degrees Bachelor of Fine Arts. Majors and concentrations: combined media, electronic imaging, painting/drawing, photography, printmaking, sculpture. Graduate degrees offered: Master of Fine Arts.

Enrollment 130 total; 120 undergraduate, 10 graduate.

Art Student Profile 70% females, 30% males, 30% minorities, 8% international.

Art Faculty 10 total (full-time), 6 total (part-time). 100% of full-time faculty have terminal degrees. Graduate students do not teach undergraduate courses. Undergraduate student–faculty ratio: 8:1.

Student Life Student groups/activities include Minority Organization of Architecture, Art, and Planning, Art Majors Organization (AMO). Special housing available for art students.

Expenses for 2006–2007 Application fee: $65. Comprehensive fee: $43,757 includes full-time tuition ($32,800), mandatory fees ($181), and college room and board ($10,776). College room only: $6390. Room and board charges vary according to board plan and housing facility. Special program-related fees: $50–$150 for departmental fees.

Application Procedures Students admitted directly into the professional program freshman year. Deadline for freshmen: January 1; transfers: March 15. Notification date for freshmen: April 1; transfers: May 1. Required: essay, high school transcript, college transcript(s) for transfer students, minimum 3.0 high school GPA, 2 letters of recommendation, SAT or ACT test scores, portfolio containing 15-20 slides. Recommended: interview. Portfolio reviews held by appointment on campus.

Web Site http://www.aap.cornell.edu

Undergraduate Contact Ms. Deborah Durnam, Director of Admissions, College of Architecture, Art and Planning, Cornell University, B-1 West Sibley Hall, Ithaca, New York 14853; 607-255-4376, fax: 607-254-2848, e-mail address: aap_admissions@cornell.edu

Graduate Contact Mr. Buzz Spector, Chair, Department of Art, Cornell University, 224 Olive Tjaden Hall, Ithaca, New York 14853; 607-255-3558, fax: 607-255-3462.

Art Department
Cornish College of the Arts

Seattle, Washington

Independent, coed. Urban campus. Total enrollment: 768 (2006). Art program established 1914.

Degrees Bachelor of Fine Arts in the area of art. Majors and concentrations: art/fine arts, painting/drawing, photography, printmaking, sculpture, video art. Program accredited by NASAD.

Enrollment 170 total; all undergraduate.

Art Student Profile 65% females, 35% males, 14% minorities, 3% international.

Art Faculty 11 undergraduate (full-time), 5 undergraduate (part-time). 58% of full-time faculty have terminal degrees. Graduate students do not teach undergraduate courses. Undergraduate student–faculty ratio: 9:1.

Student Life Student groups/activities include Film Society.

Expenses for 2006–2007 Application fee: $35. Tuition: $22,350 full-time. Mandatory fees: $400 full-time. Special program-related fees: $250 per semester for lab fees.

Financial Aid Program-specific awards: Nellie Scholarships for new students ($2000–$5000), departmental scholarships for new and continuing students ($500–$7500), Presidential Scholarships for continuing students ($2000–$5000).

Application Procedures Students admitted directly into the professional program freshman year. Deadline for freshmen and transfers: August 15. Notification date for freshmen and transfers: August 30. Required: essay, high school transcript, college transcript(s) for transfer students, minimum 2.0 high school GPA, portfolio. Recommended: 2 letters of recommendation, interview, SAT or ACT test scores. Portfolio reviews held 20 times and by appointment on campus and off campus in Denver, CO; Portland, OR; Phoenix, AZ; San Francisco, CA; Los Angeles, CA; San Diego, CA; the submission of slides may be substituted for portfolios when distance is prohibitive.

Web Site http://www.cornish.edu

Undergraduate Contact Eric Pedersen, Director of Admission, Cornish College of the Arts, 1000 Lenora, Seattle, Washington 98121; 800-726-ARTS, fax: 206-720-1011, e-mail address: epedersen@cornish.edu

More About the College

For more than ninety years, Cornish College of the Arts has educated students and nurtured artists who, as professionals, have consistently contributed to the culture of society. The Cornish School was founded in 1914 when Nellie Cornish, a woman of profound vision and unlimited energy, realized her

Cornish College of the Arts (continued)

vision of a school that offered arts training based on inspirational encouragement and guidance of student self-expression. While Cornish's mission is to "provide students aspiring to become practicing artists with an educational program of the highest quality," its role is far broader. Cornish students, alumni, and faculty members are working artists—theater directors, visual artists, set and lighting designers, dancers, and musicians—making art in and for the community. They are also innovative designers, business leaders, teachers, passionate and supportive audience members, and torchbearers for the arts.

Cornish College of the Arts, one of only three private, nonprofit performing and visual arts colleges in the nation, offers a Bachelor of Music degree and Bachelor of Fine Arts degrees in art, dance, design, music, theater, and performance production. The academic programs are a distinctive blend of visual and performing arts grounded in a core curriculum of humanities and sciences. With more than 145 faculty members and an enrollment of over 775, Cornish has the lowest student-faculty ratio (8:1) in the country for an institution of its kind. Individualized attention and mentoring for every student are emphasized, and students thrive in their chosen artistic disciplines. They are encouraged to exchange ideas, to experiment and find their unique artistic voices, and to share them in both innovative and traditional projects. Cornish challenges artists to broaden their artistic perspectives and engage in creative collaboration by encouraging students to select from a wide range of elective studio courses outside their majors. The

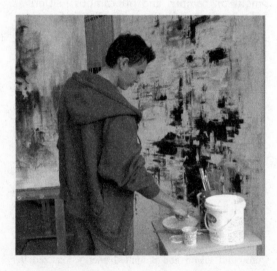

educational programs are of the highest possible quality, and the environment at Cornish nurtures creativity and intellectual curiosity and also prepares students to contribute to society as artists, citizens, and innovators.

The Art Department is devoted to realizing the individuality and full potential of each student. The faculty members support artistic play and risk, rigor, and a strong work ethic. Students are challenged to be involved in cross-disciplinary creation and collaboration and to engage with their peers in rich, critical discourse; studio projects; and exhibitions. They become adept at both traditional and contemporary technical approaches to art-making, develop fluency in various visual languages, and learn to understand their work in the context of history and culture and within the larger world of contemporary artistic endeavor.

Campus and Surroundings Seattle has more cultural construction projects in the works than any other urban area in the U.S., with more than $1.2 billion in cultural infrastructure for concert halls, museums, and theaters. The city has 190 galleries, five cultural heritage museums, five art museums, a dance company, a symphony, and twenty-nine professional theater companies and fifty-six fringe theater companies as well as more than eighty clubs with live music. Cornish serves as a focal point for public presentation, artistic criticism, participation, and discussion of the arts in this artistically rich community.

Faculty, Resident Artists, and Alumni The faculty at Cornish represents the largest concentration of practicing artists in the Northwest. They are nationally renowned in their fields and are dedicated to instruction of the arts. Their art can be found in major galleries, theaters, dance troupes, and other prestigious art organizations around the nation. Dedication to Cornish College and the stability of its programs is demonstrated by a faculty retention rate of more than 90 percent.

Since its earliest days, the College has fostered influential artists, arts movements, and arts organizations in the local community and beyond. Prominent members of the Northwest School of Artists, including Mark Tobey, Morris Graves, Guy Anderson, and William Cumming, taught at Cornish College, as did Martha Graham, an inventor of modern dance. Merce Cunningham, the legendary contemporary dancer/choreographer, and broadcast pioneer Chet Huntley were Cornish students. Revolutionary composer John Cage worked and invented the prepared piano at Cornish. In more recent years, the

Visual

Arts

College has nurtured the talents of Heart's Nancy Wilson, Brendan Fraser, and award-winning composer Wendell Yuponce.

Cornish has hosted elite members of the artistic community as artists-in-residence, including Meredith Monk (performance), Mark Morris (dance), Bill Frisell (music), Rinde Eckert (theater), Syvilla Fort (dance), Imogen Cunningham (photography), and Lou Harrison (music). These acclaimed artists provide Cornish students with unique and invaluable educational experiences.

Design Department
Cornish College of the Arts

Seattle, Washington

Independent, coed. Urban campus. Total enrollment: 768 (2006). Art program established 1914.

Degrees Bachelor of Fine Arts in the area of design. Majors and concentrations: advertising design, animation, computer animation and interactive media, interior design, visual communication. Program accredited by NASAD.

Enrollment 164 total; all undergraduate.

Art Student Profile 65% females, 35% males, 14% minorities, 3% international.

Art Faculty 10 undergraduate (full-time), 21 undergraduate (part-time). 58% of full-time faculty have terminal degrees. Graduate students do not teach undergraduate courses. Undergraduate student–faculty ratio: 9:1.

Student Life Student groups/activities include American Society of Interior Designers, American Institute of Graphic Arts.

Expenses for 2006–2007 Application fee: $35. Tuition: $22,350 full-time. Mandatory fees: $400 full-time.

Financial Aid Program-specific awards: Nellie Scholarships for new students, departmental scholarships for new and continuing students, Presidential Scholarships for continuing students.

Application Procedures Students admitted directly into the professional program freshman year. Deadline for freshmen and transfers: August 15. Notification date for freshmen and transfers: August 30. Required: essay, high school transcript, college transcript(s) for trans-fer students, portfolio. Recommended: 2 letters of recommendation, interview, SAT or ACT test scores. Portfolio reviews held 12 times on campus and off campus at National Portfolio Days (California, Colorado, Oregon, Washington, Illinois, Minnesota, Hawaii); the submission of slides may be substituted for portfolios when distance is prohibitive.

Web Site http://www.cornish.edu

Undergraduate Contact Eric Pederson, Director of Admission, Cornish College of the Arts, 1000 Lenora, Seattle, Washington 98121; 800-726-ARTS, fax: 206-720-1011, e-mail address: epedersen@cornish.edu

Culver-Stockton College

Canton, Missouri

Independent, coed. Rural campus. Total enrollment: 869. Art program established 1900.

Degrees Bachelor of Fine Arts in the area of art. Majors and concentrations: graphic design, studio art.

Enrollment 42 total; 30 undergraduate, 12 nonprofessional degree.

Art Student Profile 60% females, 40% males, 8% minorities, 4% international.

Art Faculty 2 undergraduate (full-time), 3 undergraduate (part-time). 100% of full-time faculty have terminal degrees. Graduate students do not teach undergraduate courses. Undergraduate student–faculty ratio: 12:1.

Student Life Student groups/activities include Images Unlimited (art club).

Expenses for 2007–2008 Application fee: $25. Comprehensive fee: $23,450 includes full-time tuition ($16,600) and college room and board ($6850). College room only: $3100. Room and board charges vary according to board plan.

Financial Aid Program-specific awards: scholarship awards for program majors ($500–$1750).

Application Procedures Students admitted directly into the professional program freshman year. Deadline for freshmen and transfers: August 31. Required: high school transcript, portfolio, SAT or ACT test scores. Portfolio reviews held once in November (formally), and as needed on campus; the submission of slides may be substituted for portfolios.

Web Site http://www.culver.edu

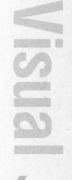

Visual Arts

Culver-Stockton College (continued)

Undergraduate Contact Mr. Joseph E. Jorgensen, Head, Art Department, Culver-Stockton College, Herrick Center, 1 College Hill, Canton, Missouri 63435-1299; 217-231-6368, fax: 217-231-6611, e-mail address: jjorgensen@culver.edu

Daemen College

Amherst, New York

Independent, coed. Suburban campus. Total enrollment: 2,414. Art program established 1948.

Degrees Bachelor of Fine Arts in the areas of applied design, graphic design, fine art. Majors and concentrations: applied design, drawing, graphic design, illustration, painting, printmaking, sculpture. Cross-registration with 17 institutions in the Western New York Consortium of Higher Education.

Enrollment 109 total; 68 undergraduate, 41 nonprofessional degree.

Art Student Profile 68% females, 32% males, 55% minorities.

Art Faculty 5 undergraduate (full-time), 6 undergraduate (part-time). 60% of full-time faculty have terminal degrees. Graduate students do not teach undergraduate courses. Undergraduate student–faculty ratio: 6:1.

Student Life Student groups/activities include Art Club, Academic Festival, art exhibits.

Expenses for 2007–2008 Application fee: $25. Comprehensive fee: $27,360 includes full-time tuition ($18,300), mandatory fees ($450), and college room and board ($8610). Room and board charges vary according to board plan and housing facility.

Financial Aid Program-specific awards: 6 Visual Art Scholars Awards for freshmen enrolling in fine arts curriculum ($5000), 7 high school art show scholarships for entering first year students (award becomes available upon enrollment) ($1357).

Application Procedures Students admitted directly into the professional program freshman year. Deadline for freshmen and transfers: continuous. Notification date for freshmen and transfers: continuous. Required: high school transcript, college transcript(s) for transfer students, portfolio, SAT or ACT test scores (minimum composite ACT score of 16), "C"

average in prior college work for transfer students. Recommended: 3 letters of recommendation, interview. Portfolio reviews held continuously on campus; the submission of slides may be substituted for portfolios when distance is prohibitive.

Web Site http://www.daemen.edu/academics/visual_performing_arts/

Undergraduate Contact Admissions Counselor, Admissions Office, Daemen College, 4380 Main Street, Amherst, New York 14226; 716-839-8225, fax: 716-839-8229, e-mail address: admissions@daemen.edu

Dorothy F. Schmidt College of Arts and Letters

See Florida Atlantic University

Drake University

Des Moines, Iowa

Independent, coed. Suburban campus. Total enrollment: 5,366. Art program established 1881.

Degrees Bachelor of Arts in the areas of art history, graphic design, studio art; Bachelor of Fine Arts in the areas of studio art, graphic design. Majors and concentrations: art history, drawing, graphic arts, painting, printmaking, sculpture. Cross-registration with The Institute of Italian Studies (Italy). Program accredited by NASAD.

Enrollment 140 total; all undergraduate.

Art Student Profile 75% females, 25% males, 5% minorities, 5% international.

Art Faculty 9 undergraduate (full-time), 5 undergraduate (part-time). 100% of full-time faculty have terminal degrees. Graduate students do not teach undergraduate courses. Undergraduate student–faculty ratio: 12:1.

Student Life Student groups/activities include Art Student Club, American Institute of Graphic Arts (AIGA), Art Directors Association of Iowa.

Expenses for 2006–2007 Application fee: $25. Comprehensive fee: $29,182 includes full-time tuition ($22,270), mandatory fees ($412), and college room and board ($6500). College room only: $3190. Full-time tuition and fees vary according to class time, course load, and student level. Room and board charges vary according to board plan.

Financial Aid Program-specific awards: 25–30 art scholarships for entering freshmen and transfers ($500–$6000).

Application Procedures Students admitted directly into the professional program freshman year. Deadline for freshmen and transfers: continuous. Required: essay, high school transcript, college transcript(s) for transfer students, SAT or ACT test scores, portfolio for scholarship consideration. Portfolio reviews held as needed on campus; the submission of slides may be substituted for portfolios.

Web Site http://www.drake.edu

Undergraduate Contact Robert Craig, Chair, Department of Art and Design, Drake University, 25th and University Avenue, Des Moines, Iowa 50311; 515-271-2863, fax: 515-271-2558, e-mail address: robert.craig@drake.edu

Drexel University

Philadelphia, Pennsylvania

Independent, coed. Urban campus. Total enrollment: 19,882. Art program established 1963.

Degrees Bachelor of Architecture; Bachelor of Science. Majors and concentrations: architecture, digital media, fashion design, fashion design and merchandising, film and video production, graphic design, interior design, music industry, photography, playwriting, screenwriting. Graduate degrees offered: Master of Architecture in the area of architecture; Master of Science in the areas of fashion and interior design, arts administration, digital media, television management. Program accredited by NAAB, CIDA, NASAD.

Enrollment 1,765 total; 1,598 undergraduate, 167 graduate.

Art Student Profile 58% females, 42% males, 3% international.

Art Faculty 70 total (full-time), 170 total (part-time). 90% of full-time faculty have terminal degrees. Graduate students do not teach undergraduate courses. Undergraduate student–faculty ratio: 15:1.

Student Life Student groups/activities include Graphics Group (graphic design students only).

Expenses for 2007–2008 Application fee: $50. Comprehensive fee: $40,390 includes full-time tuition ($27,200), mandatory fees ($1580), and college room and board ($11,610). College room only: $6960. Full-time tuition and fees vary according to course load, program, and student level. Room and board charges vary according to board plan and housing facility. Special program-related fees: $500 per term for music lessons (private).

Financial Aid Program-specific awards: 2 Suzanne Roberts Awards for graphic and fashion design students with financial need ($15,000).

Application Procedures Students admitted directly into the professional program freshman year. Deadline for freshmen: March 1; transfers: May 1. Notification date for freshmen and transfers: continuous. Required: high school transcript, college transcript(s) for transfer students, minimum 2.0 high school GPA, 2 letters of recommendation, portfolio, SAT or ACT test scores, essay for architecture applicants, portfolio for fashion design applicants, graphic design, photo, essay for screenwriting, film and video, interior design, design and merchandising. Recommended: minimum 3.0 high school GPA. Portfolio reviews held by appointment on campus; the submission of slides may be substituted for portfolios.

Web Site http://www.drexel.edu/comad

Undergraduate Contact David Miller, Director of Recruitment, Office of the Dean, College of Media Arts and Design, Drexel University, 33rd and Market Streets, Philadelphia, Pennsylvania 19104; 215-895-1675, fax: 215-895-4917, e-mail address: ddm22@drexel.edu

Graduate Contact David Miller, Director of Recruitment, Office of the Dean, Drexel University, Co MAD-33rd and Market Streets, Philadelphia, Pennsylvania 19104; 215-895-1675, fax: 215-895-4917, e-mail address: ddm22@drexel.edu

More About the University

Drexel University, founded in 1891, is a private university comprising thirteen colleges and schools. The Antoinette Westphal College of Media Arts & Design is the third-largest college in the system, with approximately 1,700 students. There are eleven undergraduate and five graduate programs in a variety of design, media, and performing arts disciplines. Students work closely with faculty

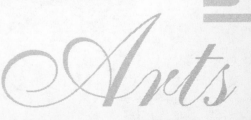

Drexel University (continued)

members, who are accomplished designers, filmmakers, photographers, animators, artists, and performers, as they study the process and products of their disciplines.

The undergraduate curricula include a liberal arts and science foundation with broad electives; an arts foundation; and professional courses in studio, lab, and classroom formats—providing a thorough understanding of principles and a hands-on approach to learning. Development of the individual student is a fundamental goal of the curricula, and it is achieved through extensive one-to-one interaction between student and teacher.

Program Facilities The facilities are housed in five buildings and include a gallery, two auditoriums, exhibition spaces, drawing and painting studios, a woodshop, and open computer labs. Program-specific facilities and equipment include the following: Architecture (dedicated space for each student, with drafting tables, storage, and a computer lab); Fashion Design (three studios with cutting tables, dress-forms, industrial sewing equipment, a resource library, storage space, computer facilities for pattern/textile design, and an historic costume collection); Design and Merchandising (dedicated classrooms with TeamBoard and a computer lab with Powerbook G4s, Adobe products, and various merchandising software programs); Interior Design (two studios with drafting tables, a resource library, two PC computer labs, AutoCAD, FormZ, and Microstation); Digital Media (two composite stations, two computer labs with Pentium 4/dual processors, a green screen, digital photography and digital audio stations, a gaming lab, a variety of animation software; 3D Studio, Combustion, Maya, Flash, Director, and Adobe products); Screenwriting and Playwriting (classrooms with video, DVD, and film projection); Film and Video (a television station, a video production studio, two screening rooms, professional-quality Sony and Panasonic digital cameras, Arri lights, 16mm cameras, DAT recorders, microphones, dollies, c-stands, field monitors, nonlinear editing stations, video, and film projectors); Graphic Design (four digital studios with Macintosh G4s, Quark Express, and Adobe products); Photography (a large shooting studio, two digital photography labs, two large wet labs, six individual senior darkrooms, Nikon digital cameras, Hasselblads, and large format cameras); and Music Industry (three fully equipped digital recording studios; the College's record label, Mad Dragon Records; and two computer labs with mixing boards, electronic keyboards, and practice facilities).

Student Performance/Exhibit Opportunities

Graduating seniors from each discipline in the College of Media Arts and Design are required to exhibit thesis projects. Photography, Interior Design, Graphic Design, Architecture, and Digital Media programs all hold annual exhibitions. Screenwriting and Playwriting majors have the option to have their plays produced. Fashion Design seniors and graduate students showcase their collections in a professionally produced and juried fashion show. Five of Drexel's fashion students also competed in the top international student fashion design competition held in Paris last December, and senior Megan Stein became the first American to win the grand prize. All Film and Video students compete in the Mad Dragon Film and Video Festival. The Photography senior exhibition takes place at a commercial gallery and has received critical acclaim. A photography student won a *New York Times* photography contest, and a student filmmaker was a finalist in a recent MTV student competition. Music Industry students cultivate talent and produce CDs for the College's record label, Mad Dragon Records.

The College's annual AnnX Exhibit is open to all students and faculty and staff members, allowing them to showcase works of painting, drawing, sculpture, film and video, digital media, photography, fashion, interiors, architecture, music, and performance.

Drexel University's Annual Research Day offers all students the opportunity to showcase and exhibit their work while competing for cash prizes.

Career Placement Opportunities Drexel University is a leader in career preparation and has long been recognized for its co-operative education programs, through which students alternate periods of full-time professional employment in their fields of interest with classroom studies. Drexel Co-op employers have included Liz Claiborne, NBC Television, Disney Studios, Urban Outfitters, Macy's Northeast, Unisys, Cubist Post & Effects, the University of Pennsylvania, G4 Media, Comcast, Mary Ellen Mark, Andrew Smith Gallery, and National Geographic.

Special Programs The London Program is open to all majors with at least sophomore standing, allowing students to take advantage of London as an international center for fashion, interiors, business, culture, and design and merchandising. Because of its broad focus, students from all majors are encouraged to apply.

The Fashion in London program is open to second-year fashion design students and, by special arrangement, transfer students. The program is offered during the winter term.

The NENE Graphic Design Exchange program in Northampton, United Kingdom, is open to graphic design majors during the fall of their senior year.

Western Landscape is a unique offering that takes students to the canyons of Southern Utah for an intensive landscape photography class.

East Carolina University

Greenville, North Carolina

State-supported, coed. Urban campus. Total enrollment: 24,351. Art program established 1909.

Degrees Bachelor of Fine Arts in the areas of art, art education. Majors and concentrations: art education, ceramic art and design, graphic design, illustration, jewelry and metalsmithing, painting/drawing, photography, printmaking, sculpture, surface design, textile arts, weaving, woodworking design. Graduate degrees offered: Master of Fine Arts in the area of art. Program accredited by NASAD.

Enrollment 550 undergraduate, 45 graduate, 25 nonprofessional degree.

Art Student Profile 60% females, 40% males, 20% minorities, 1% international.

Art Faculty 48 total (full-time), 10 total (part-time). 98% of full-time faculty have terminal degrees. Graduate students teach a few undergraduate courses. Undergraduate student–faculty ratio: 16:1.

Student Life Student groups/activities include Visual Art Forum, North Carolina Art Education Association Student Chapter.

Expenses for 2006–2007 Application fee: $60. State resident tuition: $2335 full-time. Nonresident tuition: $12,849 full-time. Mandatory fees: $1668 full-time. College room and board: $6940. College room only: $3790. Room and board charges vary according to board plan and housing facility. Special program-related fees: $25–$75 per course for supplies in selected classes.

Financial Aid Program-specific awards: 2 University Book Exchange Scholarships for program majors ($500), 1 Art Enthusiasts Scholarship for freshmen ($500), 1 K Eastern Carolina Advertising Federation Scholarship for communication art majors, 40 out-of-state special talent awards for out-of-state freshmen ($950).

Application Procedures Students admitted directly into the professional program freshman year. Deadline for freshmen: May 15; transfers: April 15. Required: high school transcript, SAT or ACT test scores, minimum 2.5 high school GPA.

Web Site http://www.ecu.edu/art/

Undergraduate Contact Ms. Ann Melanie, Academic Advisor, School of Art and Design, East Carolina University, Jenkins Fine Arts Center, East Fifth Street, Greenville, North Carolina 27858-4353; 252-328-6665, fax: 252-328-6441, e-mail address: melaniea@ecu.edu

Graduate Contact Mr. Scott Eagle, Director of Graduate Studies, School of Art and Design, East Carolina University, Jenkins Fine Arts Center, East Fifth Street, Greenville, North Carolina 27858-4353; 252-328-6665, fax: 252-328-6441, e-mail address: eagles@ecu.edu

Edinboro University of Pennsylvania

Edinboro, Pennsylvania

State-supported, coed. Small town campus. Total enrollment: 7,579. Art program established 1920.

Degrees Bachelor of Fine Arts in the areas of applied media arts, studio arts; Bachelor of Science in the area of art education. Majors and concentrations: art education, art history, ceramics, drawing, film/animation/video, furniture design, graphic design, jewelry and metalsmithing, painting, photography, printmaking, sculpture, weaving and fibers. Graduate degrees offered: Master of Arts in the area of art; Master of Fine Arts in the area of art. Program accredited by NASAD.

Enrollment 960 total; 950 undergraduate, 10 graduate.

Art Faculty 42 total (full-time), 7 total (part-time). Graduate students do not teach undergraduate courses. Undergraduate student–faculty ratio: 18:1.

Student Life Student groups/activities include Student Art League, clubs in every studio area.

Expenses for 2006–2007 Application fee: $30. State resident tuition: $5038 full-time. Nonresident tuition: $7558 full-time. Mandatory fees: $1446 full-time. College room and board: $5718. College room only: $3600. Room and

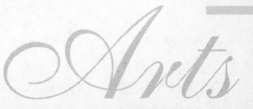

Edinboro University of Pennsylvania (continued)

board charges vary according to board plan. Special program-related fees for lab fees for art studio courses.

Financial Aid Program-specific awards: 1 alumni departmental award for general art majors ($500–$1000), 1 Ralph and Mildred Bruce Award for art education majors ($500–$1000), 1 Hank Katzwinkle Award for jewelry or art majors ($500–$1000), 1 George Nicholas Award for animation majors ($500–$1000).

Application Procedures Students admitted directly into the professional program freshman year. Deadline for freshmen and transfers: continuous. Required: high school transcript, college transcript(s) for transfer students, SAT or ACT test scores. Recommended: interview, personal statement.

Web Site http://www.edinboro.edu

Undergraduate Contact William Mathie, Chair, Department of Art, Edinboro University of Pennsylvania, DH 113, Edinboro, Pennsylvania 16444; 814-732-2406.

Graduate Contact Dr. Scott Baldwin, Graduate Dean, School of Graduate Studies, Edinboro University of Pennsylvania, Edinboro, Pennsylvania 16444; 814-732-2856.

Emerson College

Boston, Massachusetts

Independent, coed. Urban campus. Total enrollment: 4,324.

Web Site http://www.emerson.edu/

Emmanuel College

Boston, Massachusetts

Independent Roman Catholic, coed. Urban campus. Total enrollment: 2,340. Art program established 1957.

Degrees Bachelor of Fine Arts in the areas of painting and printmaking, graphic design. Majors and concentrations: graphic arts, studio art. Cross-registration with Simmons College, Wheelock College, Wentworth Institute of Technology, Massachusetts College of Pharmacy and Allied Health Sciences, Massachusetts College of Art.

Enrollment 121 total.

Art Student Profile 70% females, 30% males, 5% international.

Art Faculty 4 undergraduate (full-time), 5 undergraduate (part-time). 100% of full-time faculty have terminal degrees. Graduate students do not teach undergraduate courses. Undergraduate student–faculty ratio: 15:1.

Student Life Student groups/activities include professional gallery on campus, membership in Boston Museum of Fine Arts.

Expenses for 2006–2007 Application fee: $40. Comprehensive fee: $34,600 includes full-time tuition ($23,800), mandatory fees ($400), and college room and board ($10,400). Full-time tuition and fees vary according to course load, degree level, and program. Room and board charges vary according to housing facility. Special program-related fees: $35–$75 per course for materials fee for studio classes.

Financial Aid Program-specific awards available.

Application Procedures Students admitted directly into the professional program freshman year. Deadline for freshmen and transfers: September 1. Notification date for freshmen and transfers: September 16. Required: essay, high school transcript, college transcript(s) for transfer students, minimum 2.0 high school GPA, 2 letters of recommendation, interview, SAT test score only. Recommended: portfolio. Portfolio reviews held twice on campus; the submission of slides may be substituted for portfolios when time constraints exist (digital media also acceptable).

Web Site http://www.emmanuel.edu

Undergraduate Contact Director of Admissions, Emmanuel College, 400 The Fenway, Boston, Massachusetts 02115; 617-735-9715, fax: 617-735-9877.

Emporia State University

Emporia, Kansas

State-supported, coed. Small town campus. Total enrollment: 6,473. Art program established 1863.

Degrees Bachelor of Fine Arts in the areas of ceramics, painting, photography, printmaking, sculpture and glassforming, graphic design, engraving arts, metals; Bachelor of Science in Education in the area of art. Majors and concentrations: art education, art therapy, ceramics, engraving arts, glassworking, graphic design, painting/drawing, photography, printmaking, sculpture. Program accredited by NASAD.

Enrollment 175 total; 95 undergraduate, 80 nonprofessional degree.

Art Student Profile 60% females, 40% males, 5% minorities, 3% international.

Art Faculty 13 undergraduate (full-time), 6 undergraduate (part-time). 100% of full-time faculty have terminal degrees. Graduate students do not teach undergraduate courses. Undergraduate student–faculty ratio: 15:1.

Student Life Student groups/activities include Alpha Rho Theta, Glass Guild, Kansas Art Education Association Student Chapter.

Expenses for 2006–2007 Application fee: $30. State resident tuition: $2862 full-time. Nonresident tuition: $10,214 full-time. Mandatory fees: $724 full-time. Full-time tuition and fees vary according to degree level. College room and board: $5170. College room only: $2552. Room and board charges vary according to board plan and housing facility. Special program-related fees: $10–$120 per class for expendable supplies.

Financial Aid Program-specific awards: 1 Timothy Sharp Memorial Scholarship for art majors ($250), 2 Jerry Ely Awards for art majors ($1000), 1 Hazelrigg Memorial Award for art majors ($250), 3 Art Faculty Awards for art majors ($250), 4 Beulah Holton Memorial Awards for art education majors ($1700), 1 Linda Ball Memorial Award for art majors ($250), 1 Cremer Family Memorial Award for art majors ($500), 1 Jean Hesenbart Memorial Award for art majors ($500), 1 Art 96 Award for art majors ($2000), 4 Ames Family Memorial Awards for art majors ($225).

Application Procedures Students admitted directly into the professional program freshman year. Deadline for freshmen and transfers: continuous. Required: high school transcript, college transcript(s) for transfer students, minimum 3.0 high school GPA, ACT test score only (minimum composite ACT score of 21), portfolio for scholarship consideration. Portfolio reviews held once on campus; the submission of slides may be substituted for portfolios (slides preferred; digital media also accepted).

Web Site http://www.emporia.edu/art/

Undergraduate Contact Elaine O. Henry, Chair, Department of Art, Emporia State University, Campus Box 4015, 1200 Commercial, Emporia, Kansas 66801-5087; 620-341-5246, fax: 620-341-6246, e-mail address: ehenry@emporia.edu

Fashion Institute of Technology

New York, New York

State and locally supported, coed, primarily women. Urban campus. Total enrollment: 10,010. Art program established 1976.

Degrees Bachelor of Fine Arts. Majors and concentrations: accessories design and fabrication, advertising design, art/fine arts, computer animation and interactive media, fabric styling, fashion design, graphic design, illustration, interior design, packaging design, photography, textile/surface design, toy design. Graduate degrees offered: Master of Arts in the areas of exhibition design, art market: principles and practice, fashion and textile studies, illustration. Cross-registration with State University of New York System. Program accredited by NASAD, CIDA.

Enrollment 3,072 total; 1,323 undergraduate, 75 graduate, 1,674 nonprofessional degree.

Art Student Profile 85% females, 15% males, 33% minorities, 10% international.

Art Faculty 100 undergraduate (full-time), 437 undergraduate (part-time), 4 graduate (full-time), 21 graduate (part-time). Graduate students do not teach undergraduate courses. Undergraduate student–faculty ratio: 13:1.

Student Life Student groups/activities include literary publications, professional clubs and societies.

Expenses for 2007–2008 Application fee: $40. State resident tuition: $4567 full-time. Nonresident tuition: $11,140 full-time. Mandatory fees: $325 full-time. College room and board: varies.

Application Procedures Students apply for admission into the professional program by junior year. Deadline for freshmen and transfers: continuous. Required: essay, high school transcript, college transcript(s) for transfer students, minimum 2.0 high school GPA, portfolio. Portfolio reviews held several times on campus; the submission of slides may be substituted for portfolios with permission of the chair.

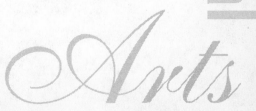

Fashion Institute of Technology (continued)

Web Site http://www.fitnyc.edu

Undergraduate Contact Ms. Dolores Lombardi, Director of Admissions, Fashion Institute of Technology, 7th Avenue at 27th Street, New York, New York 10001-5992; 212-217-7675, fax: 212-217-7481, e-mail address: dolores_lombardi@fitnyc.edu

Graduate Contact Dr. Steven Zucker, Dean, School of Graduate Studies, Fashion Institute of Technology, 7th Avenue at 27th Street, New York, New York 10001-5992; 212-217-5714, fax: 212-217-5156.

More About the Institute

The Fashion Institute of Technology (FIT) is a selective, State University of New York (SUNY) college of art and design, business, and technology offering more than forty programs of study leading to the A.A.S., B.F.A., B.S., M.A., and M.P.S. degrees. Known worldwide as the premier educational institution for fashion and related design fields, FIT provides students an unmatched combination of specialized curricula, an in-depth liberal arts education, affordable tuition, and an extraordinary location in the center of New York City, world capital of art and media. The college is an accredited institutional member of the Middle States Association of Colleges and Schools, the National Association of Schools of Art and Design, and the Council for Interior Design Accreditation.

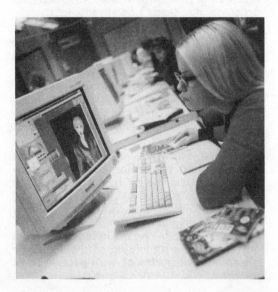

All undergraduate students at FIT first complete a two-year A.A.S. program in their major area of study and the liberal arts and may then choose to go on to a related, two-year B.F.A. or B.S. program. Alternatively, they may begin their careers with the A.A.S. degree, which qualifies them for positions in a wide range of fields. All Master of Arts graduate students complete a capstone/thesis project that serves as the culmination of their studies and a professional-level addition to their portfolio or resume.

Campus and Surroundings FIT's campus comprises an entire city block in Manhattan's Chelsea neighborhood. Its location permits an exceptional two-way flow between college and city, offering students unparalleled creative and professional opportunities. World-class art galleries, museums, and theaters are within walking distance of campus, and there is easy access to subways, buses, and the city's major transportation hubs.

Program Facilities FIT's classrooms, laboratories, and studios reflect the most advanced educational and professional practices. Facilities include drawing, painting, photography, printmaking, and sculpture studios; a broadcasting studio; cutting and sewing laboratories; a design/research lighting laboratory; display and exhibit design rooms; a knitting lab; a model-making workshop; a multimedia foreign languages laboratory; and a graphics printing service bureau. Computer-aided design and communications facilities provide the latest advancements in technology and their integration in the fields of animation, design, and photography. Twenty-three computer labs contain nearly 700 Mac and PC workstations, and several additional labs offer computers reserved for students in specific programs.

The Museum at FIT is the repository for one of the most important collections of fashion and textiles in the world, and it is used year-round by students, historians, and designers for research and inspiration. The Gladys Marcus Library contains more than 300,000 volumes, 90 searchable databases, and specialized resources like clipping and sketch files and trend forecasting services.

Four residence halls house 2,300 students in fully furnished single, double, triple, and quad rooms. Students have the option of either traditional (meal plan included) or apartment-style accommodations. All full-time, degree-seeking students are eligible for housing.

Faculty and Alumni FIT's faculty members—made up of the city's art, design, and business elite—provide a hands-on teaching approach and professional acumen. Their classes, limited to 25 students each, are designed to encourage participation, independent thinking, and self-expression. Well-known alumni include Calvin Klein, Nanette Lepore, and Chris Madden, and there are thousands more—from creative directors to designers of toys, packaging, and interiors; from animators and illustrators to graphic and fine artists. Alumni often serve on FIT advisory boards, as guest lecturers, and as project critics.

Student Exhibit Opportunities Exhibitions of student work are held throughout the year. Every spring, the college hosts its Art and Design Graduating Student Exhibition and the Fashion Design BFA show, a runway show whose attendees and judges include leading names in the industry and media. Graduate students in Art Market: Principles and Practices curate an annual exhibition at a New York City gallery, and graduate students in Fashion and Textile Studies: History, Theory, Museum Practice curate an annual exhibition at The Museum at FIT. Sponsored competitions promote student work to prospective employers and in prominent trade publications, and clubs like Urban Studio provide public art opportunities in venues throughout the city.

Special Programs FIT's International Programs provide students the option of studying abroad for a year, a semester, or in summer or winter sessions in countries from Australia to China, Italy to Mexico.

The Presidential Scholars Program, available to academically exceptional students in all disciplines, offers special liberal arts courses and extracurricular activities designed to broaden horizons and stimulate discourse. Presidential Scholars are awarded priority course registration and an annual merit stipend.

Precollege Programs are available to high school students during the fall, spring, and summer. More than forty-five courses help students develop their portfolios, explore a range of creative careers, and discover talents and abilities. Courses for middle school students are available in the summer.

The School of Continuing Education and Professional Studies provides evening/weekend classes to students and working professionals. Four art and design degrees are available through evening/weekend programs: Communication Design A.A.S., Fashion Design A.A.S., Graphic Design B.F.A., and Illustration B.F.A.

Cooperative Agreements Since its inception, FIT has maintained close ties with the professional world. Academic departments maintain their own advisory boards of noted experts, who ensure that the curriculum adapts apace with real-world practices. Field trips, guest lectures, internships, and sponsored competitions introduce students to the opportunities and challenges of their disciplines. Internships are a required element of most programs and are available

to all students. Sponsor organizations have included Calvin Klein, Fairchild Publications, MTV, and Saatchi & Saatchi.

Career Placement Services and Opportunities FIT's Career Services offers lifetime placement and career-building workshops to all of its alumni, with a graduation employment rate of nearly 90 percent. Approximately one third of student internships result in job offers by the sponsoring organization.

Dorothy F. Schmidt College of Arts and Letters
Florida Atlantic University
Boca Raton, Florida

State-supported, coed. Suburban campus. Total enrollment: 25,385. Art program established 1961.
Web Site http://www.fau.edu/

Florida International University
Miami, Florida

State-supported, coed. Urban campus. Total enrollment: 37,997. Art program established 1972.
Web Site http://www.fiu.edu/

Florida State University
Tallahassee, Florida

State-supported, coed. Suburban campus. Total enrollment: 39,973. Art program established 1973.

Degrees Bachelor of Fine Arts in the areas of studio art, graphic design. Majors and concentrations: graphic design, studio art. Graduate degrees offered: Master of Fine Arts in the area of studio art. Program accredited by NASAD.

Enrollment 632 total; 48 undergraduate, 24 graduate, 560 nonprofessional degree.

Art Student Profile 63% females, 37% males, 25% minorities, 5% international.

Art Faculty 25 total (full-time), 15 total (part-time). 100% of full-time faculty have

Visual Arts

Florida State University (continued)

terminal degrees. Graduate students teach a few undergraduate courses.

Student Life Student groups/activities include Art Student League.

Expenses for 2006–2007 Application fee: $30. State resident tuition: $3307 full-time. Nonresident tuition: $16,439 full-time. Full-time tuition varies according to location. College room and board: $7078. College room only: $3780. Room and board charges vary according to board plan and housing facility. Special program-related fees: $25–$50 per course for lab fee.

Financial Aid Program-specific awards: 2 Andy McLachlin Memorial Endowment Awards for sculpture students ($1000), 5 Ann Kirn Scholarships for graphic design students ($800).

Application Procedures Students apply for admission into the professional program by sophomore year. Deadline for freshmen and transfers: continuous. Required: essay, high school transcript, college transcript(s) for transfer students, minimum 2.0 high school GPA, portfolio, SAT or ACT test scores, portfolio review at end of second year for admission into BFA program. Recommended: minimum 3.0 high school GPA, letter of recommendation. Portfolio reviews held 3 times on campus; the submission of slides may be substituted for portfolios whenever necessary.

Web Site http://www.fsu.edu/~art

Undergraduate Contact Ms. Phyllis Straus, Undergraduate Admissions Coordinator, College of Visual Arts, Theatre and Dance, Florida State University, 220 FAB, Tallahassee, Florida 32306-1150; 850-644-6474, fax: 850-644-8977.

Graduate Contact Bunnie Hunter, Program Assistant, Department of Art, Florida State University, 220 FAB, Tallahassee, Florida 32306-1150; 850-644-6474, fax: 850-644-8977.

Fontbonne University

St. Louis, Missouri

Independent Roman Catholic, coed. Suburban campus. Total enrollment: 2,924.

Web Site http://www.fontbonne.edu/

Frostic School of Art

See Western Michigan University

Grand Valley State University

Allendale, Michigan

State-supported, coed. Small town campus. Total enrollment: 23,295. Art program established 1961.

Degrees Bachelor of Fine Arts. Majors and concentrations: ceramic art and design, graphic design, illustration, jewelry and metalsmithing, painting/drawing, printmaking, sculpture. Program accredited by NASAD.

Enrollment 271 total; 204 undergraduate, 67 nonprofessional degree.

Art Student Profile 73% females, 27% males, 5% minorities, 1% international.

Art Faculty 25 undergraduate (full-time), 5 undergraduate (part-time). 100% of full-time faculty have terminal degrees. Graduate students do not teach undergraduate courses. Undergraduate student–faculty ratio: 12:1.

Student Life Special housing available for art students.

Expenses for 2006–2007 Application fee: $30. State resident tuition: $6588 full-time. Nonresident tuition: $12,510 full-time. Full-time tuition varies according to program and student level. College room and board: $6600. College room only: $4700. Room and board charges vary according to board plan, housing facility, and location. Special program-related fees: $5–$15 per credit for studio maintenance.

Financial Aid Program-specific awards: 6 recruitment awards for freshmen ($1000), 1 Branstrom Award for program majors ($2000), 1 Calder Award for program majors ($1000–$1500), 1 Ox Bow Summer Program Award for program majors ($2000), 1 Margaret Warol Award for art education students ($500), 1 Nedra Otis Smith Award for program majors ($1200), 1 Koeze Award for program majors ($1000).

Application Procedures Students admitted directly into the professional program freshman year. Deadline for freshmen and transfers: August 1. Notification date for freshmen and transfers: continuous. Required: essay, high school transcript, minimum 3.0 high school

GPA, portfolio, ACT test score only (minimum composite ACT score of 21). Portfolio reviews held 8 times on campus and off campus in various cities in Michigan and contiguous states; the submission of slides may be substituted for portfolios.

Web Site http://www.gvsu.edu/art/

Undergraduate Contact Dr. Patricia Clark, Interim Chair, Art and Design Department, Grand Valley State University, 1105 CAC, Allendale, Michigan 49401; 616-331-2575, fax: 616-331-3240, e-mail address: clarkp@gvsu.edu

Green Mountain College

Poultney, Vermont

Independent, coed. Small town campus. Total enrollment: 759. Art program established 1990.

Degrees Bachelor of Fine Arts. Majors and concentrations: studio art. Cross-registration with Castleton State College.

Art Faculty 4 undergraduate (full-time), 2 undergraduate (part-time). 100% of full-time faculty have terminal degrees. Graduate students do not teach undergraduate courses.

Student Life Student groups/activities include exhibitions.

Expenses for 2006–2007 Application fee: $30. Comprehensive fee: $31,755 includes full-time tuition ($22,662), mandatory fees ($667), and college room and board ($8426). College room only: $5076. Full-time tuition and fees vary according to course load. Room and board charges vary according to housing facility. Special program-related fees: $10–$60 per semester for studio fees.

Financial Aid Program-specific awards: program scholarships for freshmen/sophomore/junior art majors, Peyser Painting Prize.

Application Procedures Students admitted directly into the professional program freshman year. Deadline for freshmen and transfers: continuous. Required: essay, high school transcript, college transcript(s) for transfer students, minimum 2.0 high school GPA. Recommended: letter of recommendation, interview, video, portfolio, SAT or ACT test scores. Portfolio reviews held once on campus; the submission of slides may be substituted for portfolios (slides preferred).

Web Site http://www.greenmtn.edu

Undergraduate Contact Dean of Admissions, Green Mountain College, 1 College Circle, Poultney, Vermont 05764-1199; 802-287-8208, fax: 802-287-8099, e-mail address: admiss@greenmtn.edu

Guilford College

Greensboro, North Carolina

Independent, coed. Suburban campus. Total enrollment: 2,687. Art program established 1960.

Degrees Bachelor of Fine Arts in the area of studio art. Majors and concentrations: ceramics, painting/drawing, photography, printmaking, sculpture. Cross-registration with University of North Carolina at Greensboro.

Enrollment 60 total.

Art Student Profile 60% females, 40% males, 3% minorities, 2% international.

Art Faculty 3 undergraduate (full-time), 4 undergraduate (part-time). 100% of full-time faculty have terminal degrees. Graduate students do not teach undergraduate courses. Undergraduate student–faculty ratio: 13:1.

Student Life Student groups/activities include Annual Student Art Exhibition, senior thesis exhibition.

Expenses for 2007–2008 Application fee: $25. Comprehensive fee: $31,330 includes full-time tuition ($24,140), mandatory fees ($330), and college room and board ($6860). Room and board charges vary according to board plan and housing facility.

Financial Aid Program-specific awards: 1–2 J. S. Laing Art Awards for sophomore and junior program majors ($800), 2 Merry Moore Winette Scholarships for photography majors ($800).

Application Procedures Students apply for admission into the professional program by junior year. Deadline for freshmen: February 1; transfers: May 1. Notification date for freshmen: March 15; transfers: June 1. Required: essay, high school transcript, minimum 2.0 high school GPA, SAT or ACT test scores. Recommended: letter of recommendation, interview, portfolio. Portfolio reviews held once at end of junior year or by appointment on campus; the submission of slides may be substituted for portfolios whenever necessary.

Web Site http://www.guilford.edu

Guilford College (continued)

Undergraduate Contact Roy Nydorf, Chair, Art Department, Guilford College, 5800 West Friendly Avenue, Greensboro, North Carolina 27410; 336-316-2249, fax: 336-316-2467.

Harding University

Searcy, Arkansas

Independent, coed. Small town campus. Total enrollment: 6,085. Art program established 1936.

Degrees Bachelor of Fine Arts in the areas of graphic design, painting, three-dimensional design; Bachelor of Science in the areas of art therapy, interior design, art (teacher certification). Majors and concentrations: art education, art therapy, graphic design, interior design, painting, three-dimensional studies. Program accredited by NCATE.

Enrollment 186 total; 150 undergraduate, 36 nonprofessional degree.

Art Faculty 9 undergraduate (full-time), 4 undergraduate (part-time). 75% of full-time faculty have terminal degrees. Graduate students do not teach undergraduate courses. Undergraduate student–faculty ratio: 18:1.

Student Life Student groups/activities include Kappa Pi (international honorary art fraternity), Red Brick Studio (graphic design club), American Society of Interior Designers.

Expenses for 2007–2008 Application fee: $35. Comprehensive fee: $17,939 includes full-time tuition ($11,940), mandatory fees ($420), and college room and board ($5579). College room only: $2811. Full-time tuition and fees vary according to course load. Room and board charges vary according to board plan and housing facility. Special program-related fees: $10–$200 per course for supplies.

Financial Aid Program-specific awards: 15 art scholarships for program majors ($350–$700).

Application Procedures Students apply for admission into the professional program by sophomore year. Deadline for freshmen and transfers: continuous. Required: high school transcript, college transcript(s) for transfer students, 2 letters of recommendation, SAT or ACT test scores (minimum composite ACT score of 19), portfolio for scholarship consideration. Recommended: interview, portfolio.

Portfolio reviews held once on campus; the submission of slides may be substituted for portfolios.

Web Site http://www.harding.edu/

Undergraduate Contact Dr. John E. Keller, Chairman, Department of Art and Design, Harding University, Box 12253, Searcy, Arkansas 72149-0001; 501-279-4426, fax: 501-279-4717, e-mail address: art@harding.edu

Harrington College of Design

Chicago, Illinois

Proprietary, coed, primarily women. Urban campus. Total enrollment: 1,563. Art program established 1931.

Degrees Bachelor of Fine Arts in the areas of interior design, communication design. Majors and concentrations: communication design, interior design. Program accredited by NASAD, CIDA.

Enrollment 1,490 total; all undergraduate.

Art Student Profile 85% females, 15% males, 43% minorities, 2% international.

Art Faculty 19 undergraduate (full-time), 131 undergraduate (part-time). 43% of full-time faculty have terminal degrees. Graduate students do not teach undergraduate courses. Undergraduate student–faculty ratio: 16:1.

Student Life Student groups/activities include American Society of Interior Designers (ASID) Student Chapter, International Interior Design Association, American Institute of Graphic Arts (AIGA) Student Chapter.

Expenses for 2007–2008 Application fee: $60. Tuition: $18,000 full-time. Mandatory fees: $2520 full-time. College room only: $2600. Special program-related fees: $380 per semester for technology, library and resource, and CTA U-Pass fees for interior design program, $630 per semester for technology, graphic/photography, library and resource, and CTA U-Pass fees for communication design program.

Application Procedures Students admitted directly into the professional program freshman year. Deadline for freshmen and transfers: continuous. Required: high school transcript, college transcript(s) for transfer students, interview. Recommended: essay, minimum 2.0 high school GPA, SAT or ACT test scores.

Web Site http://www.harringtoncollege.com

Undergraduate Contact Wendi Franczyk, Vice President of Admissions, Admissions, Harrington College of Design, 200 West Madison, Chicago, Illinois 60606; 877-939-4975 ext. 1188, fax: 312-697-8032, e-mail address: wfranczyk@harringtoncollege.com

Hartford Art School

See University of Hartford

Henry Radford Hope School of Fine Arts

See Indiana University Bloomington

Herron School of Art and Design

See Indiana University–Purdue University Indianapolis

Hope College

Holland, Michigan

Independent, coed. Suburban campus. Total enrollment: 3,203. Art program established 1949.

Degrees Bachelor of Arts in the area of fine arts. Majors and concentrations: art education, art history, studio art. Program accredited by NASAD.

Enrollment 51 total; all undergraduate.

Art Student Profile 78% females, 22% males, 10% minorities, 2% international.

Art Faculty 7 undergraduate (full-time), 4 undergraduate (part-time). 85% of full-time faculty have terminal degrees. Graduate students do not teach undergraduate courses. Undergraduate student–faculty ratio: 6:1.

Student Life Student groups/activities include GLCA New York Arts Program, DePree Gallery exhibition program, NYCAMS.

Expenses for 2007–2008 Application fee: $35. Comprehensive fee: $31,100 includes full-time tuition ($23,660), mandatory fees ($140), and college room and board ($7300). College room only: $3330. Full-time tuition and fees vary according to course load. Room and board charges vary according to board plan.

Financial Aid Program-specific awards: 9 Distinguished Artist Awards for freshman/transfer art students ($2500).

Application Procedures Students admitted directly into the professional program freshman year. Deadline for freshmen and transfers: continuous. Required: high school transcript, college transcript(s) for transfer students, SAT or ACT test scores. Recommended: portfolio. Portfolio reviews held once on campus; the submission of slides may be substituted for portfolios.

Web Site http://www.hope.edu/academic/art

Undergraduate Contact Steve Nelson, Chair, Department of Art and Art History, Hope College, PO Box 9000, Depree Art Center, Holland, Michigan 49424; 616-395-7503, fax: 616-395-7499, e-mail address: nelson@hope.edu

Idaho State University

Pocatello, Idaho

State-supported, coed. Small town campus. Total enrollment: 12,679. Art program established 1960.

Web Site http://www.isu.edu/

The Illinois Institute of Art–Chicago

Chicago, Illinois

Proprietary, coed. Urban campus. Total enrollment: 2,680.

Degrees Bachelor of Arts in the area of fashion marketing and management; Bachelor of Fine Arts in the areas of fashion design, interior design, visual communications, media arts and animation, digital filmmaking and video production, game art and design, interactive media design, visual effects and motion graphics. Majors and concentrations: digital film and video, digital media production, fashion design, fashion marketing and management, game art and design, interactive media,

The Illinois Institute of Art–Chicago (continued)

interior design, media arts/animation, visual communication, visual effects and motion graphics.

Art Faculty Graduate students do not teach undergraduate courses.

Student Life Student groups/activities include American Society of Interior Designers, Fashion Group Student Chapter, Center for Design Student Chapter. Special housing available for art students.

Expenses for 2007–2008 Application fee: $50. Tuition: $19,968 full-time. Mandatory fees: $316 full-time. College room only: $11,512. Special program-related fees for art supplies.

Financial Aid Program-specific awards available.

Application Procedures Students admitted directly into the professional program freshman year. Deadline for freshmen and transfers: continuous. Notification date for freshmen and transfers: continuous. Required: essay, high school transcript, college transcript(s) for transfer students, interview. Recommended: minimum 2.0 high school GPA, SAT or ACT test scores.

Web Site http://www.artinstitutes.edu/chicago

Undergraduate Contact Director of Admissions, The Illinois Institute of Art–Chicago, 350 North Orleans Street, Chicago, Illinois 60654; 800-351-3450, fax: 312-280-8562.

The Illinois Institute of Art–Schaumburg

Schaumburg, Illinois

Proprietary, coed. Suburban campus. Total enrollment: 1,213. Art program established 1995.

Degrees Bachelor of Fine Arts in the areas of digital media production, digital photography, game art and design, graphic design, interactive media, design, interior design, media arts and animation, visual effects and motion graphics. Majors and concentrations: digital media production, digital photography, game art and design, graphic design, interactive media, interior design, media arts/animation, visual effects and motion graphics. Program accredited by CIDA.

Art Faculty Graduate students do not teach undergraduate courses.

Student Life Student groups/activities include American Society of Interior Designers, Center for Design Student Chapter, American Institute of Graphic Arts. Special housing available for art students.

Expenses for 2006–2007 Application fee: $0. Tuition: $18,675 full-time.

Financial Aid Program-specific awards available.

Application Procedures Students admitted directly into the professional program freshman year. Deadline for freshmen and transfers: continuous. Notification date for freshmen and transfers: continuous. Required: essay, high school transcript, college transcript(s) for transfer students, interview. Recommended: minimum 2.0 high school GPA, SAT or ACT test scores.

Web Site http://www.artinstitutes.edu/schaumburg

Undergraduate Contact Ron McKinney, Director of Admissions, The Illinois Institute of Art–Schaumburg, 1000 Plaza Drive, Schaumburg, Illinois 60173; 800-314-3450, fax: 847-619-3064.

Illinois State University

Normal, Illinois

State-supported, coed. Urban campus. Total enrollment: 20,521. Art program established 1965.

Web Site http://www.ilstu.edu/

Illinois Wesleyan University

Bloomington, Illinois

Independent, coed. Suburban campus. Total enrollment: 2,144. Art program established 1850.

Degrees Bachelor of Fine Arts in the area of art and design. Majors and concentrations: art/fine arts, ceramic art and design, computer graphics, drawing, graphic arts, painting, photography, printmaking, sculpture, studio art. Cross-registration with Institute for European and Asian Studies.

Enrollment 80 total; 65 undergraduate, 15 nonprofessional degree.

Art Student Profile 52% females, 48% males, 8% minorities, 5% international.

Art Faculty 5 undergraduate (full-time), 2 undergraduate (part-time). 100% of full-time faculty have terminal degrees. Graduate students do not teach undergraduate courses. Undergraduate student–faculty ratio: 10:1.

Student Life Student groups/activities include Students in Design, Kappa Pi (international honorary art fraternity). Special housing available for art students.

Expenses for 2007–2008 Application fee: $0. Comprehensive fee: $37,780 includes full-time tuition ($30,580), mandatory fees ($170), and college room and board ($7030). College room only: $4330. Room and board charges vary according to board plan and housing facility. Special program-related fees: $100 for departmental fee.

Financial Aid Program-specific awards: 60 art talent awards for freshmen ($3000–$8500).

Application Procedures Students admitted directly into the professional program freshman year. Deadline for freshmen and transfers: continuous. Required: essay, high school transcript, college transcript(s) for transfer students, minimum 3.0 high school GPA, portfolio, SAT or ACT test scores. Recommended: interview. Portfolio reviews held by appointment on campus; the submission of slides may be substituted for portfolios for large works of art, three-dimensional pieces, or when distance is prohibitive.

Web Site http://titan.iwu.edu/~art/

Undergraduate Contact Tony Bankston, Director of Admissions, Illinois Wesleyan University, PO Box 2900, Bloomington, Illinois 61702-2900; 309-556-3031, fax: 309-556-3411, e-mail address: bankston@iwu.edu

Indiana State University

Terre Haute, Indiana

State-supported, coed. Small town campus. Total enrollment: 10,568. Art program established 1870.

Degrees Bachelor of Fine Arts in the area of studio art and design; Bachelor of Science in the area of art education. Majors and concentrations: art education, ceramic art and design, graphic design, painting/drawing, photography, printmaking, sculpture, studio art. Graduate degrees offered: Master of Fine Arts in the area of studio art and design. Program accredited by NASAD.

Enrollment 195 total; 173 undergraduate, 22 graduate.

Art Student Profile 65% females, 35% males, 26% minorities, 8% international.

Art Faculty 10 total (full-time), 1 total (part-time). 90% of full-time faculty have terminal degrees. Graduate students teach a few undergraduate courses. Undergraduate student–faculty ratio: 15:1.

Student Life Student groups/activities include Student Gallery Program, Design Club, Art Club. Special housing available for art students.

Expenses for 2006–2007 Application fee: $25. State resident tuition: $6102 full-time. Nonresident tuition: $13,518 full-time. Mandatory fees: $334 full-time. Full-time tuition and fees vary according to course load. College room and board: $6294. College room only: $3339. Room and board charges vary according to board plan, housing facility, and student level. Special program-related fees: $24 per course for studio lab fee.

Financial Aid Program-specific awards: 1 Hildegard Ping Art and Anthropology Scholarship for program majors ($400), 1 ISU Friends of Art Scholarship for program majors ($500), 10–12 Creative and Performing Arts Scholarships for freshmen ($2000), 1 Indiana Artist-Craftsmen/Talbot Street Art Fair Scholarship for program majors ($350), 1 Violet Helen Rich Scholarship for painting majors ($1500), 1 Elmer J. Porter Scholarship for program majors ($675), 1 Mark Hannig Scholarship for program majors ($1000), 3 Marian J. Frutiger Awards for art majors ($1000).

Application Procedures Students admitted directly into the professional program freshman year. Deadline for freshmen and transfers: August 15. Notification date for freshmen and transfers: continuous. Required: high school transcript, college transcript(s) for transfer students, minimum 2.0 high school GPA, SAT or ACT test scores, portfolio for scholarship consideration. Portfolio reviews held 6 times on campus and off campus in Vincennes, IN; Fort Wayne, IN; Louisville, KY; Indianapolis, IN; St. Louis, MO; Chicago, IL; the submission of slides may be substituted for portfolios when distance is prohibitive, if original work is unavailable, or for large works of art.

Visual Arts

Indiana State University (continued)

Web Site http://www.indstate.edu/art-dept/

Undergraduate Contact Fran Lattanzio, Undergraduate Advisor, Department of Art, Indiana State University, Fine Arts 108, Terre Haute, Indiana 47809; 812-237-8528, fax: 812-237-4369, e-mail address: artdept@isugw.indstate.edu

Graduate Contact Charles Mayer, Interim Chair, Department of Art, Indiana State University, Fine Arts 108, Terre Haute, Indiana 47809; 812-237-3697, fax: 812-237-4369, e-mail address: artdept@isugw.indstate.edu

Henry Radford Hope School of Fine Arts
Indiana University Bloomington
Bloomington, Indiana

State-supported, coed. Small town campus. Total enrollment: 38,247. Art program established 1896.

Degrees Bachelor of Fine Arts in the areas of ceramics, graphic design, jewelry and metalsmithing, painting, photography, printmaking, sculpture, textiles, digital art. Majors and concentrations: ceramic art and design, digital art, graphic design, jewelry and metalsmithing, painting/drawing, photography, printmaking, sculpture, textile arts. Graduate degrees offered: Master of Arts in the area of art history; Master of Arts in Teaching in the area of art education; Master of Fine Arts in the areas of ceramics, graphic design, jewelry and metalsmithing, painting, photography, printmaking, sculpture, textiles, digital art. Doctor of Philosophy in the area of art history. Program accredited by NASAD.

Enrollment 645 total; 74 undergraduate, 135 graduate, 436 nonprofessional degree.

Art Student Profile 70% females, 30% males, 8% minorities, 3% international.

Art Faculty 40 undergraduate (full-time), 8 undergraduate (part-time). 100% of full-time faculty have terminal degrees. Graduate students teach about a quarter of undergraduate courses. Undergraduate student–faculty ratio: 15:1.

Student Life Student groups/activities include Art History Association, Fine Arts Student Association, Graphic Design Student Association.

Expenses for 2006–2007 Application fee: $50. State resident tuition: $6657 full-time. Nonresident tuition: $19,669 full-time. Mandatory fees: $803 full-time. Full-time tuition and fees vary according to location and program. College room and board: $6352. College room only: $3872. Room and board charges vary according to board plan and housing facility. Special program-related fees: $23–$100 per course for material fees.

Financial Aid Program-specific awards: 10–15 Hope School of Fine Arts Student Awards for program majors ($150–$2500).

Application Procedures Students apply for admission into the professional program by sophomore, junior year. Deadline for freshmen and transfers: continuous. Notification date for freshmen and transfers: August 29. Required: high school transcript, college transcript(s) for transfer students, SAT or ACT test scores.

Web Site http://www.fa.indiana.edu/

Undergraduate Contact Nell Weatherwax, Undergraduate Advisor, Henry Radford Hope School of Fine Arts, Indiana University Bloomington, 1201 East 7th Street, Room 123, Bloomington, Indiana 47405; 812-855-1693, fax: 812-855-7498, e-mail address: nweather@indiana.edu

Graduate Contact Brad Wicklund, Graduate Services Coordinator, Henry Radford Hope School of Fine Arts, Indiana University Bloomington, 1201 East 7th Street, Room 123, Bloomington, Indiana 47405; 812-855-0188, fax: 812-855-7498, e-mail address: faoffice@indiana.edu

Herron School of Art and Design
Indiana University–Purdue University Indianapolis
Indianapolis, Indiana

State-supported, coed. Urban campus. Total enrollment: 29,764. Art program established 1902.

Web Site http://www.iupui.edu/

International Academy of Design & Technology

Tampa, Florida

Proprietary, coed. Urban campus. Total enrollment: 2,405 (2006). Art program established 1984.

Degrees Bachelor of Fine Arts. Majors and concentrations: computer animation, digital media production, digital photography, digital production, fashion design and marketing, graphic design, interior design, Web design. Graduate degrees offered: Master of Fine Arts in the areas of media design, management, animation, game and virtual space studies. Program accredited by CIDA.

Enrollment 2,000 total.

Art Faculty 27 undergraduate (full-time), 127 undergraduate (part-time). Graduate students do not teach undergraduate courses. Undergraduate student–faculty ratio: 17:1.

Student Life Student groups/activities include American Society of Interior Designers Student Chapter, Fashion Design Club, SIGGRAPH (graphics and animation).

Expenses for 2006–2007 Application fee: $50.

Financial Aid Program-specific awards: Florida High School Partnership Scholarships for entering freshmen ($1000), merit award scholarships for incoming freshmen ($1000–$10,000), Portfolio Review Scholarships for incoming freshmen ($150–$500), International Academy Scholarship for international students ($500–$2500), President's Institutional Scholarship for continuing students ($250–$1000), National Academy Scholarship for incoming freshmen ($500–$2500), Academy Local Applicant Award for incoming freshmen ($2000), Future Artist Scholarship for incoming freshmen ($250), Designers Scholarship for new or continuing students ($500–$7200), Florida Resident Scholarship for Interior or Graphic Design for incoming freshmen ($2000).

Application Procedures Students admitted directly into the professional program freshman year. Deadline for freshmen and transfers: continuous. Required: college transcript(s) for transfer students, interview, high school transcript or GED attestation. Recommended: essay, minimum 2.0 high school GPA, portfolio. Portfolio reviews held on campus.

Web Site http://www.academy.edu

Undergraduate Contact Heidi Demello, Associate Vice President, Admissions and Marketing, International Academy of Design & Technology, 5104 Eisenhower Boulevard, Tampa, Florida 33634; 800-ACADEMY ext. 8092, fax: 813-881-0008.

International Academy of Design & Technology

Chicago, Illinois

Proprietary, coed. Urban campus. Art program established 1977.

Web Site http://www.iadtchicago.edu/

Iowa State University of Science and Technology

Ames, Iowa

State-supported, coed. Suburban campus. Total enrollment: 25,462. Art program established 1920.

Degrees Bachelor of Fine Arts in the areas of graphic design, interior design, integrated studio arts. Majors and concentrations: graphic design, integrated studio arts, interior design. Graduate degrees offered: Master of Fine Arts in the areas of graphic design, interior design, integrated visual arts. Program accredited by CIDA.

Enrollment 999 total; 550 undergraduate, 50 graduate, 399 nonprofessional degree.

Art Student Profile 60% females, 40% males, 6% minorities, 4% international.

Art Faculty 38 total (full-time), 12 total (part-time). 95% of full-time faculty have terminal degrees. Graduate students teach a few undergraduate courses. Undergraduate student–faculty ratio: 18:1.

Student Life Student groups/activities include Interior Design Student Association, American Institute of Graphic Arts Student Chapter, College of Design Art Club. Special housing available for art students.

Expenses for 2007–2008 Application fee: $30. State resident tuition: $5352 full-time. Nonresident tuition: $16,110 full-time. Mandatory fees: $809 full-time. Full-time tuition and fees

Iowa State University of Science and Technology (continued)

vary according to class time, degree level, and program. College room and board: $6715. College room only: $3561. Room and board charges vary according to board plan and housing facility. Special program-related fees: $5–$100 per course for in-studio expenses.

Financial Aid Program-specific awards: 10–12 art and design excellence awards for program majors ($500–$1500), 2 Garfield/Boody Awards for fine arts majors ($1600), 3 Kiser/Beard Awards for interior design majors ($1500), 2–4 art and design minority awards for program majors ($500–$1000), 1–2 graphic design sophomore scholarships for program majors ($500).

Application Procedures Students apply for admission into the professional program by freshman year. Deadline for freshmen and transfers: continuous. Required: high school transcript, college transcript(s) for transfer students, SAT or ACT test scores, minimum TOEFL score of 550 for international applicants, portfolio for graphic, interior design, and integrated studio arts. Recommended: minimum 2.0 high school GPA, standing in top half of graduating class. Portfolio reviews held once in spring on campus.

Web Site http://www.design.iastate.edu/

Undergraduate Contact Director of Admissions, Iowa State University of Science and Technology, 100 Alumni Hall, Ames, Iowa 50011-2010; 515-294-5836, fax: 515-294-2592, e-mail address: admissions@iastate.edu

Graduate Contact Mona Pett, Secretary, Department of Art and Design, Iowa State University of Science and Technology, 158 College of Design, Ames, Iowa 50011-2010; 515-294-6725, fax: 515-294-2725, e-mail address: grad_admissions@iastate.edu

Roy H. Park School of Communications
Ithaca College
Ithaca, New York

Independent, coed. Small town campus. Total enrollment: 6,409. Art program established 1986.

Degrees Bachelor of Fine Arts in the areas of film, photography, visual arts. Majors and concentrations: film/photography/visual arts. Cross-registration with Cornell University, Wells College.

Enrollment 79 total; all undergraduate.

Art Student Profile 41% females, 59% males, 9% minorities, 5% international.

Art Faculty 12 undergraduate (full-time), 6 undergraduate (part-time). 100% of full-time faculty have terminal degrees. Graduate students do not teach undergraduate courses. Undergraduate student–faculty ratio: 5:1.

Student Life Student groups/activities include television station, radio station, Production Unit.

Expenses for 2006–2007 Application fee: $60. Comprehensive fee: $37,146 includes full-time tuition ($26,832) and college room and board ($10,314). College room only: $5388.

Financial Aid Program-specific awards: 1 Kristen Landen Film Scholarship for cinema majors ($2305), 2 Mark Mazura Video Production Scholarships for video production students ($1530), 1 James B. Pendleton Filmmaking Award for film majors ($1000), 18 James B. Pendleton Scholarships for cinema and photography majors ($5000–$15,000), 1 Rod Serling Scholarship for video production students ($4845), 1 Mark Wilder Memorial Scholarship for video production students ($1420).

Application Procedures Students admitted directly into the professional program freshman year. Deadline for freshmen: February 1; transfers: March 1. Notification date for freshmen: April 15. Required: essay, high school transcript, college transcript(s) for transfer students, letter of recommendation, SAT or ACT test scores. Recommended: minimum 3.0 high school GPA, interview.

Web Site http://www.ithaca.edu/rhp.php

Undergraduate Contact Mr. Gerard Turbide, Director, Admission, Ithaca College, 100 Job Hall, Ithaca, New York 14850-7020; 607-274-3124, fax: 607-274-1900, e-mail address: admission@ithaca.edu

School of Humanities and Sciences
Ithaca College
Ithaca, New York

Independent, coed. Small town campus. Total enrollment: 6,409. Art program established 1960.

Degrees Bachelor of Arts in the area of art education; Bachelor of Fine Arts in the area of art. Majors and concentrations: art, art education. Cross-registration with Cornell University, Wells College.

Enrollment 40 total; 13 undergraduate, 27 nonprofessional degree.

Art Student Profile 73% females, 27% males, 15% minorities, 8% international.

Art Faculty 7 undergraduate (full-time), 3 undergraduate (part-time). 100% of full-time faculty have terminal degrees. Graduate students do not teach undergraduate courses. Undergraduate student–faculty ratio: 5:1.

Student Life Student groups/activities include Ithaca College Art Club.

Expenses for 2006–2007 Application fee: $60. Comprehensive fee: $37,146 includes full-time tuition ($26,832) and college room and board ($10,314). College room only: $5388. Special program-related fees: $25–$60 per semester for supplies.

Financial Aid Program-specific awards: 1 Donald and Martha Negus Scholarship for program majors ($875).

Application Procedures Students admitted directly into the professional program freshman year. Deadline for freshmen: February 1; transfers: March 1. Notification date for freshmen: April 15. Required: essay, high school transcript, college transcript(s) for transfer students, letter of recommendation, SAT or ACT test scores. Recommended: minimum 3.0 high school GPA, interview, portfolio. Portfolio reviews held continuously by appointment on campus; the submission of slides may be substituted for portfolios.

Web Site http://www.ithaca.edu/hs.php

Undergraduate Contact Mr. Gerard Turbide, Director, Admission, Ithaca College, 100 Job Hall, Ithaca, New York 14850-7020; 607-274-3124, fax: 607-274-1900, e-mail address: admission@ithaca.edu

Jacksonville State University

Jacksonville, Alabama

State-supported, coed. Small town campus. Total enrollment: 8,957.

Degrees Bachelor of Fine Arts in the area of studio art. Majors and concentrations: ceramics, graphic design, painting/drawing, photography, printmaking. Program accredited by NASAD.

Enrollment 169 total; 102 undergraduate, 67 nonprofessional degree.

Art Student Profile 63% females, 37% males, 12% minorities, 2% international.

Art Faculty 8 undergraduate (full-time), 3 undergraduate (part-time). 100% of full-time faculty have terminal degrees. Graduate students do not teach undergraduate courses. Undergraduate student–faculty ratio: 14:1.

Student Life Student groups/activities include Student Art Alliance, The Potter's Guild.

Expenses for 2007–2008 Application fee: $20. State resident tuition: $5070 full-time. Nonresident tuition: $10,140 full-time. College room and board: $3763. Room and board charges vary according to board plan and housing facility.

Financial Aid Program-specific awards: 1 Art Department Award for incoming freshmen ($1000), 2 Art Department Awards for upperclassmen ($1000), 1 Lee Manners Scholarship for junior art majors with 3.0 minimum GPA ($150), 2 Visual Art Society/JSU Scholarships for upperclassmen ($2000).

Application Procedures Students apply for admission into the professional program by sophomore year. Deadline for freshmen and transfers: continuous. Required: high school transcript, portfolio, SAT or ACT test scores. Recommended: minimum 2.0 high school GPA. Portfolio reviews held twice on campus.

Web Site http://art.jsu.edu

Undergraduate Contact Mr. Charles Groover, Head, Department of Art, Jacksonville State University, 700 Pelham Road North, Jacksonville, Alabama 36265; 256-782-5625, fax: 256-782-5419.

Jacksonville University

Jacksonville, Florida

Independent, coed. Suburban campus. Total enrollment: 3,093. Art program established 1961.

Degrees Bachelor of Fine Arts in the areas of studio art, computer art and design, art

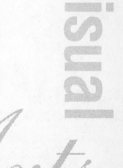

Jacksonville University (continued)

history. Majors and concentrations: art history, computer art, studio art.

Enrollment 72 total; all undergraduate.

Art Student Profile 58% females, 42% males, 27% minorities, 3% international.

Art Faculty 10 undergraduate (full-time). 90% of full-time faculty have terminal degrees. Graduate students do not teach undergraduate courses. Undergraduate student–faculty ratio: 7:1.

Student Life Student groups/activities include Fine Art Society, volunteer city-wide art projects, student group shows.

Expenses for 2006–2007 Application fee: $30. Comprehensive fee: $27,980 includes full-time tuition ($21,200) and college room and board ($6780). College room only: $3180.

Financial Aid Program-specific awards: 2 Phillips Scholarships for those demonstrating exceptional talent ($1500–$6000), 2 Sheldon Bryan Scholarships for those demonstrating exceptional talent ($1000–$6000).

Application Procedures Students admitted directly into the professional program freshman year. Deadline for freshmen and transfers: continuous. Notification date for freshmen and transfers: continuous. Required: high school transcript, college transcript(s) for transfer students, minimum 2.0 high school GPA, portfolio, SAT or ACT test scores. Recommended: essay, letter of recommendation. Portfolio reviews held 5 times and by appointment on campus and off campus in various high schools in Duval County; the submission of slides may be substituted for portfolios if a campus visit is impossible.

Web Site http://www.ju.edu

Undergraduate Contact Ms. Miriam King, Vice President of Enrollment Management, Jacksonville University, 2800 University Boulevard North, Jacksonville, Florida 32211; 904-256-7000, fax: 904-256-7012, e-mail address: admissions@ju.edu

Johnson State College

Johnson, Vermont

State-supported, coed. Rural campus. Total enrollment: 1,866. Art program established 1982.

Degrees Bachelor of Fine Arts in the area of studio art. Majors and concentrations: ceramics, drawing, painting, sculpture. Graduate degrees offered: Master of Fine Arts in the areas of painting, sculpture, drawing, mixed media. Cross-registration with members of National Student Exchange Program, schools within the Vermont State College System.

Enrollment 116 total; 18 undergraduate, 24 graduate, 74 nonprofessional degree.

Art Student Profile 58% females, 42% males, 5% minorities, 4% international.

Art Faculty 5 total (full-time), 30 total (part-time). 100% of full-time faculty have terminal degrees. Graduate students do not teach undergraduate courses. Undergraduate student–faculty ratio: 4:1.

Student Life Student groups/activities include Student Art Coalition, gallery displays.

Expenses for 2007–2008 Application fee: $35. State resident tuition: $7100 full-time. Nonresident tuition: $15,168 full-time. Mandatory fees: $525 full-time. College room and board: $7745. College room only: $4300. Special program-related fees: $15–$35 per course for studio material fees.

Financial Aid Program-specific awards: 13 Dibden Talent Scholarships for talented artists ($250–$500).

Application Procedures Students apply for admission into the professional program by sophomore year. Deadline for freshmen and transfers: continuous. Notification date for freshmen and transfers: continuous. Required: essay, high school transcript, college transcript(s) for transfer students, minimum 2.0 high school GPA, 2 letters of recommendation, SAT or ACT test scores (minimum combined SAT score of 1350, minimum composite ACT score of 18), portfolio for entry into BFA program. Recommended: interview, portfolio. Portfolio reviews held twice on campus.

Web Site http://www.johnsonstatecollege.com

Undergraduate Contact Penny P. Howrigan, Associate Dean for Enrollment Services, Johnson State College, 337 College Hill, Johnson, Vermont 05656; 800-635-2356, fax: 802-635-1230, e-mail address: jscapply@badger.jsc.vsc.edu

Graduate Contact Ms. Cathy Higley, Administrative Assistant, Graduate Studies, Johnson State

College, 337 College Hill, Johnson, Vermont 05656; 802-635-1244, e-mail address: higleyc@badger.jsc.vsc.edu

J. William Fulbright College of Arts and Sciences

See University of Arkansas

Kansas City Art Institute

Kansas City, Missouri

Independent, coed. Urban campus. Total enrollment: 674. Art program established 1885.

Degrees Bachelor of Fine Arts in the areas of ceramics, fiber, painting, printmaking, photography/new media, sculpture, art history, creative writing, animation, graphic design, interdisciplinary arts. Majors and concentrations: animation, art history, ceramics, creative writing, fibers, graphic design, interdisciplinary studies, painting/drawing, photography/new media, printmaking, sculpture. Cross-registration with Kansas City Area Student Exchange. Program accredited by NASAD.

Enrollment 674 total; all undergraduate.

Art Student Profile 56% females, 44% males, 14% minorities, 2% international.

Art Faculty 50 undergraduate (full-time), 62 undergraduate (part-time). 80% of full-time faculty have terminal degrees. Graduate students do not teach undergraduate courses. Undergraduate student–faculty ratio: 12:1.

Student Life Student groups/activities include Student Gallery Committee, Ethnic Student Association, Student Film Series Committee. Special housing available for art students.

Expenses for 2007–2008 Application fee: $35. Comprehensive fee: $33,554 includes full-time tuition ($25,680) and college room and board ($7874). Full-time tuition varies according to program. Room and board charges vary according to board plan and housing facility. Special program-related fees: $45 per course for sculpture fee, $50 per course for painting fee, $60 per course for design fee, $70 per course for fiber fee, $75 per course for print fee, $100 per course for printmaking fee, $160 per course for photo and new media fee, $390 per course for ceramics materials.

Financial Aid Program-specific awards: 300–350 need-based scholarships for program majors ($2000–$8000), 100–125 merit-based scholarships for program majors ($2000–$8000).

Application Procedures Students apply for admission into the professional program by sophomore year. Deadline for freshmen and transfers: continuous. Required: essay, high school transcript, college transcript(s) for transfer students, 2 letters of recommendation, portfolio, SAT or ACT test scores (minimum composite ACT score of 20), minimum 2.5 high school GPA. Recommended: interview. Portfolio reviews held continuously on campus and off campus in various locations on National Portfolio Days; the submission of slides may be substituted for portfolios (slides, CD-DVD preferred).

Web Site http://www.kcai.edu

Undergraduate Contact Mr. Larry E. Stone, Vice President for Enrollment Management, Kansas City Art Institute, 4415 Warwick Boulevard, Kansas City, Missouri 64111; 800-522-5224, fax: 816-802-3309, e-mail address: admiss@kcai.edu

More About the Institute

Kansas City Art Institute (KCAI), founded in 1885, is a private and fully accredited distinguished four-year college of art and design. Kansas City Art Institute is accredited by the National Association of Schools of Art and Design (NASAD) and the North Central Association of Colleges and Secondary Schools. KCAI's 600 students are from thirty-seven states and sixteen nations. Kansas City Art Institute combines intensive time in the classroom, extensive experience in the studio, a broad liberal arts background, focused learning opportunities, and a dynamic campus community. It is this rich combination that develops the "whole" student as an artist and a person.

Kansas City Art Institute is located in the heart of the cultural community of Kansas City. Across the street to the east is the Nelson-Atkins Museum of Art, consistently ranked in the top fifteen general art museums. The Kemper Museum of Contemporary Art is across the street to the west. Galleries and studios, restaurants and cafés, the Country Club Plaza, and other entertainment spots are only a short distance from the campus.

Kansas City Art Institute provides an ideal environment to bring the students' art to life. A scenic

Kansas City Art Institute (continued)

15-acre campus is complete with individual studio space as early as freshman year, cutting-edge technology, wide open spaces, and first-rate facilities that foster creative spirit. The commitment to high-quality resources provides materials that enhance a finished product. The Living Center is a hub of student life and very much the students' space, from the Foundation artwork displayed in the cafeteria to the places, indoors and outdoors, where students gather and talk about their work.

KCAI, consistently recognized for the rigor and diversity of its curriculum, provides quality academic programs that are strengthened by first-rate support services such as the Academic Resource Center, the Computer Graphics Center, the Media Center, the Central Shop, the Career Services Office, and the Library.

KCAI makes it possible for students to study at other schools in the United States and Canada as well as schools in Australia, Ecuador, England, Germany, Hungary, Ireland, Israel, Japan, New Zealand, the Netherlands, and Spain. It is also possible for students to take part in internships at places such as Hallmark Cards, Industrial Light and Magic, Warner Bros., and Bernstein-Rein.

All serious students with a passion for art are encouraged to apply. While it is not mandatory that applicants follow a college preparatory program in high school and take courses in studio and art history, it is highly recommended to assure competitiveness with other applicants. Students are advised to follow a college preparatory curriculum based on the following: four years of English, three years of social sciences, and art courses if possible. Considerable emphasis is placed on abilities in the areas of drawing, color, and design. The criteria for admission requires evaluation of the student's portfolio, academic transcripts, standardized test scores, statement of purpose, letters of recommendation, and other indicators of potential success as a professional artist. Applicants must have successfully completed a recognized secondary school program (high school) or its equivalent, with a good academic record to be eligible for admission to KCAI. KCAI students' backgrounds are diverse, but they share a desire to pursue an education in the arts. The Admissions Committee looks for serious and motivated students who are willing to work hard and take risks. The committee evaluates each application with a great deal of sensitivity and open-mindedness before reaching an admission decision because the Committee knows each student's level of imagination, innovation, and academic achievement is highly individual.

KCAI makes every effort to help students who need financial aid. More than 90 percent of the students attending KCAI receive assistance from one or more financial aid sources. When awarding need-based assistance, KCAI first looks to the financial contribution of the parents and/or student. Students are expected to take an active part in the financing of their education through working, saving, and pursuing scholarships from outside sources. Grants, loans, employment, and monthly payment plans are available. KCAI offers a competitive scholarship competition and KCAI merit awards. The state of Missouri also provides the Charles Gallagher Grant for in-state residents, the A+ Program, and the Bright Flight Program. Applications from students seeking the full range of financial aid opportunities must include the Free Application for Federal Student Aid (FAFSA). For more information, students should contact the admissions office or the financial aid office.

Visual

Arts

For more information about The Kansas City Art Institute in general, students should call 800-522-5224 (toll-free) or visit KCAI's Web site at http://www.kcai.edu.

Faculty The approximately 75 faculty members at KCAI are a distinguished group. They are recognized scholars, sought-after consultants, talented artists, and professional mentors. They bring impressive degrees from Cranbrook Academy of Art, Pratt Institute, Alfred University, Yale University, and other prestigious programs. Their work has been exhibited all around the world, and it resides in the permanent collections of places such as the Metropolitan Museum of Art, MoMA, The National Museum of Wales, The Nelson-Atkins Museum of Art, and the Smithsonian. They have professional experience through employment and consulting with companies such as Atlantic Records; Hallmark Cards, Inc.; Perry Ellis; and Time/Life Books.

Program Facilities KCAI's ceramics department contains a clay-mixing room, a plaster room, potter's wheels, kilns, and a pitfiring space. There are also various low, mid-range, and high-temperature gas and electric kilns. Students in the painting program have individual studio space as well as studio facilities and resources for a range of painting media and techniques, including oil, acrylic, watercolor, collage, and mixed-media construction as well as art-making innovations in computer technology. Students in the printmaking program work in a well-equipped facility with access at all times to etching, lithography, monoprinting, screen and relief printing, photography, letterpress, digital imaging, and multimedia software. Students in the sculpture program work in both indoor and outdoor areas containing hoists, a forklift, loft studios, and video and slide projection equipment. It is also possible to access ceramic kilns, clay mixing facilities, a complete foundry, and metal fabrication facilities. In all programs, computer hardware and software are available in networked, multiplatform surroundings.

Special Programs In pursuit of the Bachelor of Fine Arts degree, students may complete a comprehensive liberal arts program that complements an emphasis in one of the following majors: animation, art history, ceramics, creative writing, fiber, graphic design, painting, printmaking, photo and new media, sculpture, and interdisciplinary arts.

The School of the Foundation Year provides KCAI's first year studio program. Foundation provides an ideal groundwork for upper-level studies and combines discovery, discipline, and dedication. Studio space is reserved solely for freshmen, giving them an ideal place in which to create.

The School of Liberal Arts offers a curriculum that adds a dimension to a B.F.A. degree that makes a vital difference in the student's education. The liberal arts enhance education by fostering critical-thinking skills and by opening the doors to new subjects in the arts and sciences. At KCAI, it is possible to pursue a major in art history or studio art with an emphasis in creative writing.

The School of Design prepares students to grow with the rapidly developing professional design and animation fields. These programs explore how graphic design and animation create rich communications and tell important stories, emphasizing visual form, process, and "the architecture of experience."

The School of Fine Arts offers majors in the following areas: ceramics, fiber, photo and new media, painting, printmaking, sculpture, and interdisciplinary arts.

The ceramics program at KCAI provides a technical, visual, and conceptual basis for the education of artists. Traditions in ceramic history, pottery, the figure, architecture, and new forms in contemporary sculpture and installation are all explored in the curriculum.

The fiber program at KCAI encompasses not only textile processes, but also experimental techniques and the investigation of materials, issues, ideas, and forms of presentation. Students discover the vast potential of fiber, its history, and its place in contemporary art and design. Internationally prominent faculty members direct an integrated program involving surface design, weaving, papermaking, felting, basketry, clothing and costume construction, and sculptural form-making.

The photography and new media department is divided into three tracks: photography, digital filmmaking, and new media. Students produce innovative forms of contemporary image-making in a 20,000-square-foot facility with well-designed networked production and post-production equipment. Students are actively engaged in critical, historical, and theoretical discussions examining the interaction of media, art, and society. The program stresses experimentation, collaboration, self-motivation, research, mentoring, and professionalism through curating, exhibitions, and internships.

The painting program at KCAI covers painting's past and present and introduces students to an unusually broad foundation in drawing, painting, and printmaking. The program balances formal and technical experience with intellectual activity, perceptual acumen with conceptual skills, and an awareness of space with attention to effect.

The printmaking program provides a blend of basic studio practice—drawing, painting, collage—

Kansas City Art Institute (continued)

with a core of technologies specific to print, such as intaglio, wood block, lithography, letterpress, silkscreen, and book-making. Simultaneously, students learn to utilize digital and Web possibilities, including iMovie, Photoshop, Illustrator, InDesign, Dreamweaver, Flash, and FinalCut Pro.

The sculpture program at KCAI is known among undergraduate programs for providing a strong background in materials, techniques, aesthetics, and ideas. Students learn to carve stone, cast metal, choreograph performance, shoot video, program electronic media, and manipulate sound and light.

The interdisciplinary arts major establishes a dialogue between students and faculty members who are grounded in an established discipline yet are simultaneously investigating ideas and processes that are not easily categorized or defined. Audience, public art, community, ecology, and technology are all explored in order to discover new avenues for art to influence culture and to affect social and political change.

Kansas State University

Manhattan, Kansas

State-supported, coed. Suburban campus. Total enrollment: 23,141. Art program established 1964.

Degrees Bachelor of Arts in the area of art history; Bachelor of Fine Arts. Majors and concentrations: art education, art history, ceramic art and design, digital art, drawing, graphic design, illustration, jewelry and metalsmithing, painting, pre-art therapy, printmaking, sculpture. Graduate degrees offered: Master of Fine Arts. Cross-registration with Norwich School of Art and Design (England), Glasgow School of Art (Scotland), Trier School of Applied Arts and Sciences (Germany). Program accredited by NASAD.

Enrollment 456 total; 423 undergraduate, 28 graduate, 5 nonprofessional degree.

Art Student Profile 50% females, 50% males, 12% minorities, 8% international.

Art Faculty 16 total (full-time), 6 total (part-time). 100% of full-time faculty have terminal degrees. Graduate students teach about a quarter of undergraduate courses. Undergraduate student–faculty ratio: 15:1.

Student Life Student groups/activities include exhibitions, visiting artists, workshops.

Expenses for 2006–2007 Application fee: $30. State resident tuition: $4830 full-time. Nonresident tuition: $13,916 full-time. Mandatory fees: $604 full-time. College room and board: $5912. Room and board charges vary according to board plan. Special program-related fees: $2–$147 per semester for lab fees (materials).

Financial Aid Program-specific awards: 18 art scholarships for art majors ($150–$1000).

Application Procedures Students apply for admission into the professional program by sophomore year. Deadline for freshmen and transfers: continuous. Required: high school transcript, college transcript(s) for transfer students, ACT test score only, portfolio for scholarship consideration. Recommended: interview. Portfolio reviews held twice on campus; the submission of slides may be substituted for portfolios when distance is prohibitive.

Web Site http://www.ksu.edu/art

Undergraduate Contact Art Advisor, Department of Art, Kansas State University, Willard Hall 322, Manhattan, Kansas 66506; 785-532-1757, fax: 785-532-0334.

Graduate Contact Prof. Elliott Pujol, Director of Graduate Studies, Department of Art, Kansas State University, Willard Hall 322, Manhattan, Kansas 66506; 785-532-6605, fax: 785-532-0334, e-mail address: hepujol@ksu.edu

Kendall College of Art and Design of Ferris State University

Grand Rapids, Michigan

State-supported, coed. Urban campus. Art program established 1928.

Degrees Bachelor of Fine Arts in the areas of furniture design, industrial design, interior design, illustration, fine arts, metals/jewelry design, art with K-12 art education certificate; Bachelor of Science in the areas of art history-studio, art history-academics. Majors and concentrations: art education, art history, art/fine arts, digital media, furniture design, graphic design, illustration, industrial design, interior design, metals and jewelry, painting, photography, sculpture. Graduate degrees offered: Master of Fine Arts. Program accredited by NASAD, CIDA.

Enrollment 1,082 total; 953 undergraduate, 39 graduate, 90 nonprofessional degree.

Art Student Profile 50% females, 50% males, 10% minorities, 1% international.

Art Faculty 45 total (full-time), 129 total (part-time). 56% of full-time faculty have terminal degrees. Graduate students do not teach undergraduate courses.

Student Life Student groups/activities include Industrial Design Society of America, American Society of Interior Designers, Grand Rapids Area Furniture Designers, Society of Illustrators, American Center for Design.

Expenses for 2006–2007 Special program-related fees: $140 per semester for studio lab fee, $205 per semester for technology fee.

Financial Aid Program-specific awards: 250 Kendall Scholarships of Merit for program students ($4000).

Application Procedures Students admitted directly into the professional program freshman year. Deadline for freshmen and transfers: continuous. Required: essay, high school transcript, college transcript(s) for transfer students, minimum 2.0 high school GPA, portfolio, ACT test score only (minimum composite ACT score of 17). Recommended: letter of recommendation. Portfolio reviews held continuously on campus and off campus in various high schools, National Portfolio Days; the submission of slides may be substituted for portfolios.

Web Site http://www.kcad.edu

Contact Sandra Britton, Director of Enrollment Services, Kendall College of Art and Design of Ferris State University, 17 Fountain NW, Grand Rapids, Michigan 49503-2003; 616-451-2787, fax: 616-831-9689.

Kent State University

Kent, Ohio

State-supported, coed. Suburban campus. Total enrollment: 22,697. Art program established 1940.

Degrees Bachelor of Fine Arts in the areas of fine arts (drawing, painting, printmaking, sculpture), crafts (ceramics, glass, jewelry/

metals, textile arts). Majors and concentrations: ceramics, drawing, glass, jewelry and metalsmithing, painting, printmaking, sculpture, textile arts. Graduate degrees offered: Master of Fine Arts in the areas of ceramics, drawing, glass, jewelry/metals, painting, printmaking, sculpture, textile arts. Program accredited by NASAD.

Enrollment 600 total; 207 undergraduate, 18 graduate, 375 nonprofessional degree.

Art Student Profile 73% females, 27% males, 7% minorities, 1% international.

Art Faculty 21 total (full-time), 43 total (part-time). 86% of full-time faculty have terminal degrees. Graduate students teach a few undergraduate courses. Undergraduate student–faculty ratio: 25:1.

Student Life Student groups/activities include Art Education Club, Fine Arts Clubs, Art History Club. Special housing available for art students.

Expenses for 2007–2008 Application fee: $30. State resident tuition: $8430 full-time. Nonresident tuition: $15,862 full-time. Full-time tuition varies according to course load, program, and reciprocity agreements. College room and board: $7200. College room only: $4410. Room and board charges vary according to board plan and housing facility. Special program-related fees: $10–$240 per semester for art materials and project supplies.

Financial Aid Program-specific awards: 12–14 School of Art Scholarships for program majors ($550–$1000), 12 Creative Arts Awards for program majors ($500–$2000).

Application Procedures Students admitted directly into the professional program freshman year. Deadline for freshmen and transfers: continuous. Required: high school transcript, college transcript(s) for transfer students, minimum 2.0 high school GPA, SAT or ACT test scores (minimum composite ACT score of 21), completion of college preparatory courses. Recommended: minimum 3.0 high school GPA. Portfolio reviews held 5-7 times on campus; the submission of slides may be substituted for portfolios when distance is prohibitive.

Web Site http://dept.kent.edu/art

Undergraduate Contact Dr. Christine Havice, Director, School of Art, Kent State University, PO Box 5190, Kent, Ohio 44242-0001; 330-672-2192, fax: 330-672-4729, e-mail address: chavice@kent.edu

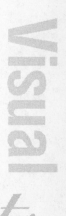

Visual Arts

Kent State University (continued)

Graduate Contact Prof. Janice Lessman-Moss, Graduate Coordinator, School of Art, Kent State University, PO Box 5190, Kent, Ohio 44242-0001; 330-672-2192, fax: 330-672-4729.

Kutztown University of Pennsylvania

Kutztown, Pennsylvania

State-supported, coed. Rural campus. Total enrollment: 10,193. Art program established 1924.
Web Site http://www.kutztown.edu/

Lamar Dodd School of Art

See University of Georgia

La Roche College

Pittsburgh, Pennsylvania

Independent, coed. Suburban campus. Total enrollment: 1,533.
Web Site http://www.laroche.edu/

La Sierra University

Riverside, California

Independent Seventh-day Adventist, coed. Suburban campus. Total enrollment: 1,896. Art program established 1923.
Web Site http://www.lasierra.edu/

Lawrence Technological University

Southfield, Michigan

Independent, coed. Suburban campus. Total enrollment: 4,049. Art program established 1991.

Degrees Bachelor of Fine Arts in the area of imaging; Bachelor of Interior Architecture; Bachelor of Science in the area of transportation design. Majors and concentrations: digital imaging, graphic design, interior architecture, transportation design. Graduate degrees offered: Master of Interior Design. Program accredited by CIDA, NASAD.

Enrollment 150 total; 130 undergraduate, 20 graduate.

Art Student Profile 50% females, 50% males, 10% minorities, 10% international.

Art Faculty 4 undergraduate (full-time), 22 undergraduate (part-time), 2 graduate (full-time). 67% of full-time faculty have terminal degrees. Graduate students do not teach undergraduate courses. Undergraduate student–faculty ratio: 16:1.

Student Life Student groups/activities include International Interior Design Association, American Society of Interior Designers, Illuminating Engineering Society Student Group, American Institute of Graphic Arts.

Expenses for 2006–2007 Application fee: $30. Comprehensive fee: $26,709 includes full-time tuition ($19,073), mandatory fees ($370), and college room and board ($7266). College room only: $5286. Special program-related fees: $100 per studio for studio maintenance.

Financial Aid Program-specific awards: 6–7 LTU Scholarships for incoming freshmen ($8000–$8500), 6–7 Trustee Scholarships for incoming freshmen ($1600–$2000).

Application Procedures Students admitted directly into the professional program freshman year. Deadline for freshmen and transfers: continuous. Required: high school transcript, college transcript(s) for transfer students, minimum 2.5 high school GPA. Recommended: essay, 2 letters of recommendation, interview.

Web Site http://www.ltu.edu

Contact Virginia North, Chair, Department of Art and Design, Lawrence Technological University, 21000 West Ten Mile Road, Southfield, Michigan 48075; 248-204-2848, fax: 248-204-2900, e-mail address: north@ltu.edu

Lehman College of the City University of New York

Bronx, New York

State and locally supported, coed. Urban campus. Total enrollment: 10,814. Art program established 1968.

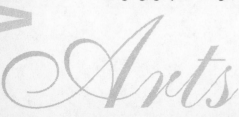

Degrees Bachelor of Arts; Bachelor of Fine Arts in the areas of printmaking, painting, sculpture, ceramics, photography, computer imaging. Majors and concentrations: art/fine arts, ceramic art and design, computer imaging, painting/drawing, photography, printmaking, sculpture. Graduate degrees offered: Master of Arts in the areas of painting, graphics, sculpture (for secondary school teachers of art); Master of Fine Arts in the areas of painting, graphics, sculpture, computer imaging. Cross-registration with City University of New York System.

Enrollment 115 total; 3 undergraduate, 30 graduate, 82 nonprofessional degree.

Art Student Profile 60% females, 40% males, 75% minorities, 15% international.

Art Faculty 13 total (full-time), 13 total (part-time). 100% of full-time faculty have terminal degrees. Graduate students do not teach undergraduate courses. Undergraduate student–faculty ratio: 8:1.

Student Life Student groups/activities include Meridian (student newspaper), internships in galleries and museums.

Expenses for 2007–2008 Application fee: $65. State resident tuition: $4000 full-time. Nonresident tuition: $10,800 full-time. Mandatory fees: $290 full-time.

Application Procedures Students apply for admission into the professional program by sophomore year. Deadline for freshmen and transfers: continuous. Required: high school transcript, college transcript(s) for transfer students, minimum 3.0 high school GPA, portfolio, SAT or ACT test scores, standing in top third of high school graduating class.

Web Site http://www.lehman.cuny.edu

Undergraduate Contact Mr. Clarence Wilkes, Director of Admissions, 155 Shuster Hall, Lehman College of the City University of New York, 250 Bedford Park Boulevard West, Bronx, New York 10468; 718-960-8706.

Graduate Contact Marilyn Hauser, Coordinator of Graduate Admissions, 155 Shuster Hall, Lehman College of the City University of New York, 250 Bedford Park Boulevard West, Bronx, New York 10468; 718-960-8702.

Leigh Gerdine College of Fine Arts

See Webster University

Lindenwood University

St. Charles, Missouri

Independent Presbyterian, coed. Suburban campus. Total enrollment: 9,525.

Degrees Bachelor of Arts in the areas of arts administration, art education, fashion design, studio art, art history; Bachelor of Fine Arts in the areas of art, fashion design, graphic design, computer art, multimedia. Majors and concentrations: art education, art history, arts administration, ceramics, computer graphics, design, fashion design, graphic design, multimedia, painting/drawing, photography, printmaking, studio art. Graduate degrees offered: Master of Arts in the area of studio art; Master of Fine Arts in the area of studio art. Cross-registration with Maryville University of Saint Louis, Fontbonne University, Missouri Baptist College, Webster University.

Art Faculty 6 undergraduate (full-time), 3 undergraduate (part-time), 6 graduate (full-time), 3 graduate (part-time). 90% of full-time faculty have terminal degrees. Graduate students do not teach undergraduate courses.

Student Life Student groups/activities include juried art shows, The Pride (Lindenwood magazine), scenic painting.

Expenses for 2007–2008 Application fee: $30. Comprehensive fee: $18,900 includes full-time tuition ($12,400), mandatory fees ($300), and college room and board ($6200). College room only: $3100. Special program-related fees: $25–$80 per class for studio lab fees.

Financial Aid Program-specific awards: art scholarships, talent awards for undergraduates and transfers, talent awards and scholarships for high school students.

Application Procedures Students admitted directly into the professional program freshman year. Deadline for freshmen and transfers: continuous. Required: essay, high school transcript, college transcript(s) for transfer students, minimum 2.0 high school GPA, interview, portfolio, ACT test score only. Recommended: letter of recommendation. Portfolio reviews held continuously on campus and off campus in area high schools; community colleges; art exhibitions; the submission of slides may be substituted for portfolios.

Web Site http://www.lindenwood.edu/

Undergraduate Contact Mr. John Troy, Director, Art Department, Lindenwood University, 209

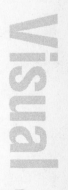

Visual

Arts

Lindenwood University (continued)

South Kings Highway, St. Charles, Missouri 63301; 636-949-4856, e-mail address: jtroy@lindenwood.edu

Graduate Contact Dr. Elaine C. Tillinger, Chair, Department of Art, Lindenwood University, 209 South Kings Highway, St. Charles, Missouri 63301; 636-949-4862, fax: 636-949-4910, e-mail address: etillinger@lindenwood.edu

Long Island University, C.W. Post Campus

Brookville, New York

Independent, coed. Suburban campus. Total enrollment: 8,494. Art program established 1954.

Degrees Bachelor of Fine Arts in the areas of art education, digital art and design, fine art, photography; Bachelor of Science in the area of art therapy. Majors and concentrations: art education, art therapy, art/fine arts, ceramics, digital art and design, photography. Graduate degrees offered: Master of Arts in the areas of clinical art therapy, art, interactive multimedia; Master of Fine Arts in the area of fine arts and design; Master of Science in the area of art education.

Enrollment 551 total; 364 undergraduate, 174 graduate, 13 nonprofessional degree.

Art Student Profile 65% females, 35% males, 20% minorities, 12% international.

Art Faculty 20 total (full-time), 50 total (part-time). 99% of full-time faculty have terminal degrees. Graduate students do not teach undergraduate courses. Undergraduate student–faculty ratio: 15:1.

Student Life Student groups/activities include American Association for Art Therapists, Art Students League.

Expenses for 2006–2007 Application fee: $30. Comprehensive fee: $35,200 includes full-time tuition ($24,570), mandatory fees ($1200), and college room and board ($9430). College room only: $6020. Special program-related fees: $75 per course for supplies.

Financial Aid Program-specific awards: 6–8 art scholarships for Art Portfolio Day for freshmen and transfer students ($1000–$5000), 15 O'Malley Scholarship Fund and Posner Awards

for continuing program majors ($500–$1000), 1 Harry Siegal Memorial Award for sophomore or junior art majors ($500).

Application Procedures Students admitted directly into the professional program freshman year. Deadline for freshmen and transfers: continuous. Required: high school transcript, college transcript(s) for transfer students, SAT or ACT test scores, minimum verbal SAT score of 430, portfolio for transfer applicants and for scholarship consideration. Recommended: essay, minimum 3.0 high school GPA, 2 letters of recommendation, interview. Portfolio reviews held as needed for transfer applicants on campus; the submission of slides may be substituted for portfolios for large works of art; CD-ROMs also accepted.

Web Site http://www.liu.edu/svpa

Undergraduate Contact Mr. Gary Bergman, Associate Provost for Enrollment Services, Long Island University, C.W. Post Campus, 720 Northern Boulevard, Brookville, New York 11548-1300; 516-299-2900, fax: 516-299-2137, e-mail address: enroll@cwpost.liu.edu

Graduate Contact Ms. Beth Carson, Associate Director of Graduate Admissions, Long Island University, C.W. Post Campus, 720 Northern Boulevard, Brookville, New York 11548-1300; 516-299-2719, fax: 516-299-2137, e-mail address: beth.carson@liu.edu

Longwood University

Farmville, Virginia

State-supported, coed. Total enrollment: 4,479. Art program established 1920.

Web Site http://www.longwood.edu/

Louisiana State University and Agricultural and Mechanical College

Baton Rouge, Louisiana

State-supported, coed. Urban campus. Total enrollment: 29,925. Art program established 1930.

Web Site http://www.lsu.edu/

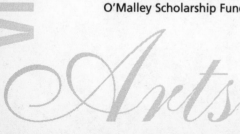

Louisiana Tech University

Ruston, Louisiana

State-supported, coed. Small town campus. Total enrollment: 11,203. Art program established 1894.

Degrees Bachelor of Fine Arts in the areas of studio art, photography, communication design. Majors and concentrations: art/fine arts, ceramic art and design, commercial art, computer graphics, painting/drawing, photography, printmaking, sculpture. Graduate degrees offered: Master of Fine Arts in the areas of studio art, photography, interior design, communication design. Cross-registration with Grambling State University. Program accredited by NASAD.

Enrollment 394 total; 386 undergraduate, 8 graduate.

Art Student Profile 55% females, 45% males, 5% minorities, 2% international.

Art Faculty 16 total (full-time), 3 total (part-time). 100% of full-time faculty have terminal degrees. Graduate students teach a few undergraduate courses. Undergraduate student–faculty ratio: 24:1.

Student Life Student groups/activities include Art and Architecture Student Association.

Expenses for 2006–2007 Application fee: $20. State resident tuition: $4502 full-time. Nonresident tuition: $9407 full-time. Full-time tuition varies according to course load, location, and program. College room and board: $4365. College room only: $2310. Room and board charges vary according to board plan and housing facility. Special program-related fees: $30 per quarter for art and architecture fee and enhancement fee for lecturers, special equipment, and workshops.

Financial Aid Program-specific awards: 8–10 incoming freshmen scholarships for regional high school students ($1000–$2500).

Application Procedures Students admitted directly into the professional program freshman year. Deadline for freshmen and transfers: continuous. Required: high school transcript, college transcript(s) for transfer students, minimum 2.0 high school GPA, SAT or ACT test scores (minimum composite ACT score of 22). Recommended: interview.

Web Site http://www.art.latech.edu

Undergraduate Contact Ms. Katie Wells, Assistant to the Director, School of Art, Louisiana Tech University, PO Box 3175, Ruston, Louisiana 71272; 318-257-3909, fax: 318-257-4890, e-mail address: kwells@latech.edu

Graduate Contact Ms. Marie Bukowski, Graduate Coordinator, School of Art, Louisiana Tech University, PO Box 3175, Ruston, Louisiana 71272; 318-257-3909, fax: 318-257-4890, e-mail address: bukowski@latech.edu

Loyola University New Orleans

New Orleans, Louisiana

Independent Roman Catholic (Jesuit), coed. Urban campus. Total enrollment: 4,604. Art program established 1976.

Degrees Bachelor of Arts in the areas of graphic design, studio art; Bachelor of Fine Arts in the area of studio art. Majors and concentrations: graphic design, studio art.

Enrollment 114 total; all undergraduate.

Art Faculty 10 undergraduate (full-time), 7 undergraduate (part-time). 100% of full-time faculty have terminal degrees. Graduate students do not teach undergraduate courses.

Student Life Student groups/activities include Untitled (art organization), American Institute of Graphic Arts Student Chapter.

Expenses for 2007–2008 Application fee: $20. Comprehensive fee: $35,658 includes full-time tuition ($25,632), mandatory fees ($876), and college room and board ($9150). College room only: $5488. Special program-related fees: $75 per class for lab fee (selected studio courses).

Financial Aid Program-specific awards: 1 Scully Scholarship for upperclassmen ($500–$1000), 1 Visual Arts Scholarship for entering studio art majors, 1 Visual Arts Scholarship for entering graphic design majors ($1000–$3000).

Application Procedures Students admitted directly into the professional program freshman year. Deadline for freshmen: February 15; transfers: continuous. Notification date for freshmen and transfers: March 15. Required: essay, high school transcript, college transcript(s) for transfer students, minimum 2.0 high school GPA, letter of recommendation, portfolio, portfolio for scholarship consideration. Portfolio reviews held twice on campus;

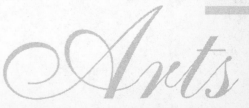

Loyola University New Orleans (continued)

the submission of slides may be substituted for portfolios (33mm slide, or Mac compatible c; DVD required).

Web Site http://www.loyno.edu/visualarts/

Undergraduate Contact Georgia McBride, Department of Visual Arts, Loyola University New Orleans, 6363 Saint Charles Avenue, PO Box 008 or 18, New Orleans, Louisiana 70118.

Lyme Academy College of Fine Arts

Old Lyme, Connecticut

Independent, coed. Small town campus. Art program established 1976.

Degrees Bachelor of Fine Arts. Majors and concentrations: painting, sculpture. Program accredited by NASAD.

Enrollment 164 total; 160 undergraduate, 4 graduate.

Art Student Profile 60% females, 40% males, 14% minorities, 2% international.

Art Faculty 11 undergraduate (full-time), 10 undergraduate (part-time). 45% of full-time faculty have terminal degrees. Graduate students do not teach undergraduate courses.

Student Life Student groups/activities include Student Forum, Student Government.

Expenses for 2006–2007 Special program-related fees: $50 per semester for student activities fee, $95–$330 per semester for model/materials fees.

Financial Aid Program-specific awards: 28 Institutional Awards for program majors ($6000).

Application Procedures Students admitted directly into the professional program freshman year. Deadline for freshmen and transfers: continuous. Required: essay, high school transcript, college transcript(s) for transfer students, minimum 2.0 high school GPA, 2 letters of recommendation, portfolio. Recommended: interview, SAT or ACT test scores. Portfolio reviews held as needed on campus and off campus at National Portfolio Day Conferences; the submission of slides may be substituted for portfolios if a campus visit is impossible.

Web Site http://www.lymeacademy.edu

Undergraduate Contact Debra A. Sigmon, Director of Admissions, Lyme Academy College of Fine Arts, 84 Lyme Street, Old Lyme, Connecticut 06371; 860-434-5232 ext. 119, fax: 860-434-8725.

More About the Academy

The Lyme Academy College of Fine Art has the unique mission of supporting a contemporary dialogue with classical sources providing an education in the principles, history, techniques, and critical thought processes that have shaped society from the Renaissance to the present.

The College was founded in 1976 by sculptor Elisabeth Gordon Chandler and others dedicated to the belief that serious artists must study the figurative traditions of painting and sculpture, studies that produced the great master artists from Michelangelo to Picasso. The College embraces these disciplines in a rigorous curriculum that places emphasis on life drawing as the foundation for aesthetic development.

Students from across the country seek the College for the education offered, recognizing that their

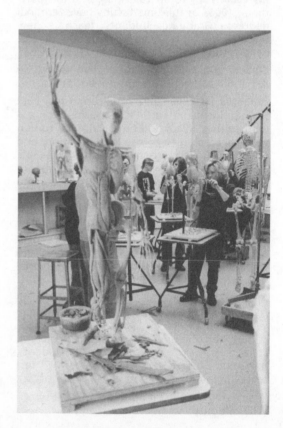

professional future depends on learning the fundamental and basic skills of drawing, painting, and sculpture.

Students and alumni from the College receive honors annually at the Copley Society of Boston, the oldest art association in America. Several have earned the prestigious Robert Brooks Memorial Scholarship. For the past five years, Academy students have earned the four highest awards in the National Arts Club Juried Student Exhibition in New York City. Graduates in the B.F.A. Painting program are eligible to apply for a $5000 Stobart Foundation Fellowship supporting their first year as an emerging artist.

The College offers opportunities for assistantships in area schools and volunteer work for arts groups. The eight-week summer program includes intensive workshops and an eight-week session with a variety of traditional painting, drawing, printmaking, and sculpture courses.

The College's cultural campus extends from New York City to Boston, each just 100 miles away. Additional cultural venues can be found in Connecticut and Rhode Island as well. The College attracts outstanding contemporary, representational, and figurative master teacher/artists to its faculty.

The College encourages its student artists to bring intelligence, passion, and creativity to bear upon each drawing, painting, and sculpture. Emphasizing studio work, the College seeks to create an environment that encourages individual creation and personal responsibility through the profoundly difficult act of making the not-yet-seen and the not-yet-known.

Program Facilities The Lyme Academy College of Fine Art's studios are located adjacent to the Historic Sill House and feature nine spacious well-lit studios and an art supply/book store. The Art History/seminar room and a classroom are located in the Academic Center. Sill House has a professional gallery, administrative offices, and a student kitchen. Campus facilities doubled in 2003 when the Academic Center was completed, bringing individual senior studios on campus along with additional studios, classrooms, galleries, cafe food service, and administrative offices.

Five drawing and painting studios feature north light, air exchange systems, easels, and large storage racks for oversize paintings. Sculpture facilities include two spacious studios with modeling stands, abundant storage shelves, separate storage rooms for works in progress, a carving studio, and a casting room. Student lockers are in the hallways connecting all studios. The Student Commons provides space for exhibitions and student activities. The Academic Center lecture hall hosts visiting artist's lectures,

presentations by art dealers and gallery owners, and additional programming. Conversation and counseling is available in the comfortable Student Services office in the Academic Center.

The Krieble Library features Mission Style chairs, study tables, and large windows overlooking the Lieutenant River. The library has over 13,000 volumes for Fine Arts and Liberal Arts and Sciences and more than 19,000 slides for research and special projects, fifty-six regular periodical subscriptions, and six computer workstations. The library doubles its size to 46,000 square feet with expansion.

The Art supply/book store has all materials and books necessary for studio and academic programs. Material lists for classes are in the store for reference, which is conveniently open before every class.

Student Exhibit Opportunities Students participate in a Senior Thesis Exhibition before graduation, an annual "All Student Exhibition," and "Faculty Selects Exhibition," and "Student Exhibit" during the holiday season. Freshman-, sophomore-, and junior-level exhibitions are displayed in the Commons and works in progress are shown in the studio hallways. Faculty members recommend students for the National Arts Club Annual Student Exhibition in New York and the Copley Society in Boston. The Academy supports an "Award of Excellence" exhibition fourteen months after graduation.

Special Programs Students may apply for mobility to attend a different college for the first semester of their junior year with an Association of Independent Colleges of Art and Design member school. Frequent trips to New York and Boston take advantage of other cultural opportunities in the area. Precollege life-drawing classes help with portfolio development. The Academy sponsors a Visiting Artist's Lecture series.

Maharishi University of Management

Fairfield, Iowa

Independent, coed. Small town campus. Total enrollment: 931. Art program established 1983.

Degrees Bachelor of Fine Arts in the area of visual arts. Majors and concentrations: ceramics, digital media, painting/drawing, photography, sculpture, video art.

Enrollment 32 total; 25 undergraduate, 7 nonprofessional degree.

Maharishi University of Management (continued)

Art Student Profile 50% females, 50% males, 15% minorities, 30% international.

Art Faculty 5 total (full-time), 4 total (part-time). 65% of full-time faculty have terminal degrees. Graduate students do not teach undergraduate courses. Undergraduate student–faculty ratio: 5:1.

Student Life Student groups/activities include Iowa-wide exhibits.

Expenses for 2006–2007 Application fee: $15. Comprehensive fee: $30,430 includes full-time tuition ($24,000), mandatory fees ($430), and college room and board ($6000). Special program-related fees: $10–$100 per course for lab fees, $150 per course for field trips in Art History courses.

Application Procedures Students apply for admission into the professional program by sophomore, junior year. Deadline for freshmen: continuous. Notification date for freshmen: September 15. Required: essay, high school transcript, college transcript(s) for transfer students, 2 letters of recommendation, SAT or ACT test scores, minimum 2.5 high school GPA. Recommended: portfolio. Portfolio reviews held twice on campus; the submission of slides may be substituted for portfolios for transfer applicants.

Web Site http://mum.edu/arts

Undergraduate Contact Barbara Rainbow, Director, Office of Admissions, Maharishi University of Management, 1000 North 4th Street, Fairfield, Iowa 52557; 641-472-1110, fax: 641-472-1179, e-mail address: rainbow@mum.edu

Maine College of Art

Portland, Maine

Independent, coed. Urban campus. Total enrollment: 409. Art program established 1882.

Degrees Bachelor of Fine Arts in the areas of ceramics, graphic design, painting, printmaking, photography, sculpture, metalsmithing and jewelry, self-designed studies, illustration, woodworking and furniture design, new media. Majors and concentrations: ceramics, graphic design, illustration, individualized major, metals and jewelry, new media, painting, photography, printmaking, sculpture, woodworking and furniture design. Graduate degrees offered: Master of Fine Arts in the area of self-designed studio concentrations. Cross-registration with Bowdoin College, Greater Portland Alliance of Colleges and Universities. Program accredited by NASAD.

Enrollment 405 total; 377 undergraduate, 28 graduate.

Art Student Profile 63% females, 37% males, 6% minorities, 1% international.

Art Faculty 30 undergraduate (full-time), 40 undergraduate (part-time), 2 graduate (full-time). 12% of full-time faculty have terminal degrees. Graduate students do not teach undergraduate courses. Undergraduate student–faculty ratio: 8:1.

Student Life Student groups/activities include Creative Community Partnerships, Student Representative Association (SRA). Special housing available for art students.

Expenses for 2007–2008 Application fee: $40. Comprehensive fee: $35,885 includes full-time tuition ($25,410), mandatory fees ($1205), and college room and board ($9270). College room only: $5600. Full-time tuition and fees vary according to course load. Room and board charges vary according to board plan and housing facility. Required fees include $525 health insurance. Special program-related fees: $10–$90 per course for studio fees, $150 per year for technology fee.

Financial Aid Program-specific awards: 2 full-tuition scholarships ($25,410), partial-tuition scholarships ($4000–$10,000).

Application Procedures Students admitted directly into the professional program freshman year. Deadline for freshmen and transfers: continuous. Notification date for freshmen and transfers: continuous. Required: essay, high school transcript, college transcript(s) for transfer students, minimum 2.0 high school GPA, 2 letters of recommendation, portfolio, SAT or ACT test scores. Recommended: interview. Portfolio reviews held continuously on campus and off campus at National Portfolio Days; the submission of slides may be substituted for portfolios when distance is prohibitive.

Web Site http://www.meca.edu

Undergraduate Contact Karen Townsend, Director of Admissions, Maine College of Art, 97 Spring Street, Portland, Maine 04101; 207-775-

5157 ext. 254, fax: 207-772-5069, e-mail address: ktownsend@meca.edu

Graduate Contact Ms. Katarina Weslien, Director, MFA in Studio Art, Maine College of Art, 97 Spring Street, Portland, Maine 04101; 207-775-5154 ext. 57, fax: 207-772-5069, e-mail address: kweslien@meca.edu

More About the College

Maine College of Art (MECA) is a dynamic college of art and design where a vibrant student community, world-class faculty, innovative interdisciplinary programs, and expansive facilities come together to give fresh vision to Maine's extraordinary legacy in the visual arts. MECA educates artists at all stages of their creative careers, offering both the Bachelor of Fine Arts (B.F.A.) and Master of Fine Arts (M.F.A.) degrees and a wide range of professional institutes and continuing studies classes for individuals of all ages, including a new postbaccalaureate certificate in art education. Founded in 1882, MECA is a fully accredited, independent college with 450 students who come from across the United States and throughout the world. The College offers eleven studio majors and three minors, including art history. In addition to their studio courses, MECA students take a concurrent stream of liberal arts courses, complementing their studio work and offering the broad cultural context critical to an artist's education. Faculty members at Maine College of Art are accomplished, professional artists and dedicated teachers who work closely with their students throughout all four years and beyond. MECA graduates enter the professional world with one of the finest visual arts educations available.

Maine College of Art offers the Bachelor of Fine Arts degree in eleven majors: ceramics, graphic design, illustration, metalsmithing and jewelry, new media, painting, photography, printmaking, sculpture, self-designed, and woodworking and furniture design. Students may also minor in art history, drawing, and illustration. Art education is important to many MECA students, and a postbaccalaureate program in art education offers B.F.A. degree-holders a one-year course of study, as well as hands-on experience in classrooms, museums, and community settings, that leads to certification as K–12 art educators. There is an innovative, low-residency Master of Fine Arts in studio arts program as well.

Located in the heart of Portland's Art's District, amidst galleries, studios, and designer boutiques, MECA's campus consists of two studio and classroom buildings, two residence halls, and a building for administration. First-year students enjoy multiple housing options from traditional dormitories to apartment and family styles. MECA recently added a sixty-bed dormitory and an eighty-bed apartment house to its campus. The beautiful beaux arts Porteous Building, students' primary studio building, is an architectural landmark and one of the finest facilities for art making in the country. Porteous boasts breathtaking views of the Casco Bay Islands to the south and the White Mountains to the north. The Baxter Building also houses classrooms and studios and is a fine example of Romanesque Revival architecture. Clapp House is the original site of the College and is listed on the National Register of Historic Places. All studios are open to students 24 hours a day, seven days a week.

Portland is a great attraction for students and artists from around the world. MECA is only blocks from the Portland Museum of Art, Portland Symphony Orchestra, Portland Stage Company, and a wealth of other cultural resources. The historic Old Port is home to a wide and eclectic array of restaurants, music venues, and independent retail stores. With a bustling, buzzing city scene, Portland draws artists from across the United States and around the world. Over the past two centuries, Maine has played an important and unique role in shaping American art. Renowned artists such as Winslow Homer, Marsden Hartley, Berenice Abbott, Edward Hopper, and Andrew Wyeth have all drawn inspiration from the Maine landscape and people. Currently, MECA students and faculty members are a vital voice in Portland and influence emerging contemporary movements in the visual arts. Hip and comfortable, Portland offers all the advantages of a small city, with easy access to beaches, ski resorts, and Boston.

Student life is busy, and extracurricular activities include exhibition openings, visiting artist workshops and lectures, film series, music and cultural events, hiking, outings to the ocean, day trips to Boston galleries, and parties and other celebrations. Students and staff members gather weekly for "Soup and Bread," a popular free lunch held Tuesdays in the College's Student Center. Student life at MECA begins with a weeklong orientation, and peer mentors provide yearlong support for new students. Career services include both individual career counseling sessions and small-group workshops and curatorial and professional internships that prepare students for work in their chosen fields.

Faculty and Visiting Artists Maine College of Art has 38 full-time and 35 part-time faculty members teaching in the B.F.A. program. Faculty members are professional artists, designers, writers, and scholars who are devoted to teaching undergraduate students

Maine College of Art (continued)

at all levels of the curriculum. They have been honored by many notable foundations and organizations, including the National Endowment of the Arts, the Getty Foundation, the Mellon Foundation, the New England Foundation of the Arts, and the Haystack Mountain School of Crafts. Their works are featured in galleries and museums throughout the world and in magazines and newspapers like the *New York Times,* the *New Yorker,* and the *Boston Globe.* Faculty members also serve as academic advisers and engage their students in close relationships, actively assisting them in formulating and carrying out their career plans.

Each year, MECA hosts well-known artists, designers, writers, and other scholars who lecture on their work and contemporary issues in the arts. These artists visit classes and work with individual students, providing another rich resource in the creative learning process.

Program Facilities Each department at MECA offers expansive, well-equipped studios that are open to students 24 hours a day. Individual studio space is provided for all students who have declared a major.

The College hosts exhibitions in two of its gallery spaces: the Friedman Student Gallery and the Institute of Contemporary Art (ICA) at Maine College of Art. Works by MECA students as well as regional, national, and international artists are shown in these professional gallery spaces. In addition, students have opportunities to exhibit work in galleries and businesses throughout the city. The College's Joanne Waxman Library is the largest library collection in northern New England that supports teaching and research in the visual arts. The collection consists of approximately 30,000 volumes, ninety current periodical subscriptions, and 52,000 slides. Ideally situated in the Porteous Building, the library's handsome quarters feature tin ceilings and large, Chicago-style windows that overlook historic Congress Street and bathe the reference, study, and reading areas in natural light.

Three computer labs offer more than fifty computers with complete Web, print, and design software; a selection of slide and flatbed scanners; and video production systems. Output capabilities include color laser printing. MECA is committed to incorporating technology across its broad curriculum, from digital life drawing to sound installation, from graphic animation to furniture design, and beyond. MECA graduates are well prepared to thrive in today's artistic world.

Special Programs MECA students take advantage of off-campus study through the Association of Independent Colleges of Art and Design (AICAD) Mobility Program, which provides students with the chance to study for a semester at thirty-five of the member institutions throughout the U.S. and Canada (a complete listing of AICAD schools is included later in this publication). In addition, recent student foreign exchanges have included study in Vietnam, Australia, Ireland, Italy, and South Africa. MECA students also take summer courses at such institutions as the renowned Provincetown Fine Arts Work Center in Massachusetts. The College has a cross-registration program with Bowdoin College and belongs to a consortium with the University of New England, the University of Southern Maine, Saint Joseph's College, and the Southern Maine Technical Center, allowing cross-registration among the five schools to enrich and expand educational opportunities for all their students.

MECA internships provide ample opportunities for students to apply their expertise while furthering their knowledge of dynamic fields, such as graphic design, animation, and curatorial work. Through MECA's Creative Community Partnerships program, students use art to serve the Greater Portland community, engaging in many social service and education settings that include working with at-risk youth in alternative programs and assisting special-needs children in the local schools. Students are enriched by their active commitment to the community and deeply appreciate the lasting, close-knit relationships with faculty members and peers. This experience of community—engaged, supportive, inspiring, and creative—makes MECA unique.

Manhattanville College

Purchase, New York

Independent, coed. Suburban campus. Total enrollment: 2,974. Art program established 1957.

Degrees Bachelor of Fine Arts in the areas of studio art, fine arts, visual arts education, arts and education. Majors and concentrations: ceramics, computer graphics, digital media/graphic design, graphic communication, illustration, painting, photography, printmaking, sculpture, three-dimensional studies, two-dimensional studies. Graduate degrees offered: Master of Arts in Teaching in the area of visual arts education. Cross-registration with Purchase College-State University of New York.

Enrollment 110 total; 75 undergraduate, 35 nonprofessional degree.

Art Student Profile 68% females, 32% males, 22% minorities, 8% international.

Art Faculty 5 undergraduate (full-time), 27 undergraduate (part-time). 100% of full-time faculty have terminal degrees. Graduate students do not teach undergraduate courses. Undergraduate student–faculty ratio: 5:1.

Student Life Student groups/activities include Art Club, Shakespeare in the Castle, Quad Jam.

Expenses for 2007–2008 Application fee: $55. Comprehensive fee: $43,016 includes full-time tuition ($29,636), mandatory fees ($1140), and college room and board ($12,240). College room only: $7270.

Financial Aid Program-specific awards: merit awards for art for program majors ($5000–$10,000).

Application Procedures Students admitted directly into the professional program freshman year. Deadline for freshmen and transfers: continuous. Required: high school transcript, college transcript(s) for transfer students, minimum 2.0 high school GPA, portfolio, SAT or ACT test scores, high school transcript for transfer applicants with fewer than 45 credits. Recommended: minimum 3.0 high school GPA, 2 letters of recommendation, interview. Portfolio reviews held continuously as needed on campus; the submission of slides may be substituted for portfolios.

Web Site http://www.manhattanville.edu

Undergraduate Contact Mr. Jose Flores, Director of Admissions, Manhattanville College, 2900 Purchase Street, Purchase, New York 10577; 800-328-4553, fax: 914-694-1732, e-mail address: jflores@mville.edu

Marshall University

Huntington, West Virginia

State-supported, coed. Urban campus. Total enrollment: 13,936. Art program established 1984.

Degrees Bachelor of Fine Arts in the area of art studio. Majors and concentrations: ceramics, new media, painting, photography, print media, printmaking, sculpture, weaving. Graduate degrees offered: Master of Arts in the areas of art education, art studio. Program accredited by NCATE.

Enrollment 220 total; 200 undergraduate, 20 graduate.

Art Student Profile 52% females, 48% males, 5% minorities, 1% international.

Art Faculty 15 total (full-time), 15 total (part-time). 100% of full-time faculty have terminal degrees. Graduate students teach a few undergraduate courses. Undergraduate student–faculty ratio: 17:1.

Student Life Student groups/activities include Sculpture Club, Keramos (Ceramics Club), Graphic Design Club-AIGA.

Expenses for 2007–2008 Application fee: $30. State resident tuition: $4360 full-time. Nonresident tuition: $11,264 full-time. Mandatory fees: $200 full-time. Full-time tuition and fees vary according to degree level, location, program, and reciprocity agreements. College room and board: $6818. College room only: $3944. Room and board charges vary according to board plan and housing facility. Special program-related fees: $60 per studio course for art supplies.

Financial Aid Program-specific awards: 4–5 art scholarships for program majors ($500), 10 tuition waivers for program majors ($1000), 1 Garth Brown Memorial Scholarship for program majors ($500), 15 Donald Harper Scholarships for program majors ($4000), 1 College of Fine Arts Gala Scholarship for program majors ($2000), 1 John Q. Hill Memorial Scholarship for minority program majors ($1000), 1 Stewart Smith Scholarship for program majors ($800).

Application Procedures Students admitted directly into the professional program freshman year. Deadline for freshmen and transfers: August 15. Notification date for freshmen and transfers: continuous. Required: high school transcript, college transcript(s) for transfer students, minimum 2.0 high school GPA, SAT or ACT test scores. Recommended: essay, 3 letters of recommendation, interview, portfolio. Portfolio reviews held twice on campus; the submission of slides may be substituted for portfolios if a campus visit is impossible.

Web Site http://www.marshall.edu/cofa

Undergraduate Contact Byron D. Clercx, Chair, Department of Art, Marshall University, 1 John Marshall Drive, Huntington, West Virginia 25755; 304-696-5451, fax: 304-696-6505.

Graduate Contact Peter Massing, Graduate Coordinator, Department of Art and Design,

Marshall University (continued)

Marshall University, One John Marshall Drive, Huntington, West Virginia 25755; 304-696-5451, fax: 304-696-6505.

Maryland Institute College of Art

Baltimore, Maryland

Independent, coed. Urban campus. Total enrollment: 1,866. Art program established 1826.

Degrees Bachelor of Fine Arts in the areas of drawing, painting, printmaking, general fine arts, ceramics, fibers, photography, illustration, graphic design, environmental design, experimental animation, video, interactive media, art history, interdisciplinary sculpture; Bachelor of Fine Arts/Master of Arts in the area of digital arts; Bachelor of Fine Arts/Master of Arts in Teaching in the area of art education. Majors and concentrations: animation, art history, art/fine arts, ceramic art and design, drawing, environmental design, fibers, graphic arts, illustration, interactive media, interdisciplinary sculpture, painting, photography, printmaking, video art. Graduate degrees offered: Bachelor of Fine Arts/Master of Arts in the area of digital arts; Bachelor of Fine Arts/Master of Arts in Teaching in the area of art education; Master of Arts in the areas of digital arts, art education, community arts; Master of Fine Arts in the areas of painting, sculpture, art education, photography, mixed media, graphic design. Cross-registration with Johns Hopkins University, University of Baltimore, Goucher College, Loyola College, Peabody Conservatory of Music, Notre Dame College, Association of Independent Colleges of Art and Design, Institute for American Universities (France), Baltimore Collegetown Network. Program accredited by NASAD.

Enrollment 1,863 total; 1,637 undergraduate, 226 graduate.

Art Student Profile 66% females, 34% males, 20% minorities, 6% international.

Art Faculty 101 undergraduate (full-time), 152 undergraduate (part-time), 21 graduate (full-time), 20 graduate (part-time). 81% of full-time faculty have terminal degrees. Graduate students do not teach undergraduate courses. Undergraduate student–faculty ratio: 10:1.

Student Life Student groups/activities include student-run forum group, National Art Education Association, American Institute of Graphic Arts. Special housing available for art students.

Expenses for 2007–2008 Application fee: $50. Comprehensive fee: $36,580 includes full-time tuition ($27,840), mandatory fees ($830), and college room and board ($7910). College room only: $5850. Room and board charges vary according to board plan and housing facility.

Financial Aid Program-specific awards: 30 Thalheimer Scholarships for incoming freshmen ($3000–$7500), 15 Academic Excellence Scholarships for incoming freshmen ($5000), 20 C.V. Starr Scholarships for incoming international freshmen or transfers ($2500), 40 Competitive Scholarships for incoming transfers ($1000–$12,000), 150 Competitive Scholarships for incoming freshmen ($1000–$12,000).

Application Procedures Students admitted directly into the professional program freshman year. Deadline for freshmen: February 15; transfers: March 1. Notification date for freshmen: March 15; transfers: April 17. Required: essay, high school transcript, college transcript(s) for transfer students, 3 letters of recommendation, portfolio, SAT or ACT test scores, minimum TOEFL score of 550 for international applicants. Recommended: minimum 3.0 high school GPA, interview, honors and advanced placement level coursework in English and other humanities subjects. Portfolio reviews held continuously on campus and off campus in various cities; the submission of slides may be substituted for portfolios (slides preferred).

Web Site http://www.mica.edu

Undergraduate Contact Ms. Theresa Lynch Bedoya, Vice President and Dean, Admission and Financial Aid, Maryland Institute College of Art, 1300 Mt. Royal Avenue, Baltimore, Maryland 21217; 410-225-2222, fax: 410-225-2337, e-mail address: admissions@mica.edu

Graduate Contact Scott Kelly, Associate Dean of Graduate Admission, Graduate Studies, Maryland Institute College of Art, 1300 Mt. Royal Avenue, Baltimore, Maryland 21217; 410-225-2256, fax: 410-225-2408, e-mail address: graduate@mica.edu

More About the College

For 180 years the top-rated Maryland Institute College of Art (MICA) has assembled some of the most talented and committed students and faculty members from across the nation and around the world in a creatively energized, intellectually stimulating environment. A diverse, 1,800-strong student body comes to this highly selective program from forty-seven states and forty-eight other countries.

Art in the twenty-first century can take the form of object, energy, or expendable materials. The definition of art is expanding. The boundaries among disciplines and mediums are dissolving. MICA's curriculum has been designed to prepare students for these contemporary approaches to art-making and thinking through a wide choice of studio majors. Students can focus on traditional discipline-based processes or they can create art that is interactive, uses multiple mediums, or relies on collaboration with other artists—or scientists, writers, or musicians—for its execution.

MICA has also taken the position that the quality and rigor of its liberal arts program should equal that of its nationally recognized studio program. This commitment is evident in MICA's course offerings and faculty appointments. Each year students can choose from nearly 200 courses offered in art history, literature, writing, humanities, and sciences taught by an exceptional faculty of scholars who have earned advanced degrees from such institutions as Columbia, Harvard, Oxford, Princeton, and the University of Chicago.

Baltimore, located at the heart of the New York-Washington arts corridor, offers an array of cultural, social, and creative opportunities. MICA's campus of twenty-five buildings is nestled in a charming historic neighborhood in the midst of the city's cultural center. Nearby are world-class museums and galleries, the symphony hall and opera house, experimental and community theaters, cafés, bookstores, shops, and art cinemas. The MICA campus shuttle system provides transportation throughout the city, and weekly trips to New York City and Washington, D.C., are also available.

A highly successful Career Development Center is staffed by dedicated professionals who specialize in developing art and art-related career opportunities. The center provides career counseling and workshops, facilitates connections with the Institute's alumni network, lists 1,000 internship opportunities and 1,130 art-related jobs, hosts dozens of corporate recruiters, and offers reality-based programs and courses in topics ranging from promoting oneself as an artist to developing business skills.

Facilities The twenty-seven buildings on the MICA campus include 430,700 square feet of outstanding instructional facilities dedicated to departments of painting, ceramics, drawing, sculpture, photography, printmaking, fibers, environmental design, graphic design, illustration, interactive media, video, animation, art education, and liberal arts. There is specialized equipment for work in both traditional and new media in each of these areas. In addition, MICA offers intimately sized liberal arts classrooms; a 550-seat auditorium for film, performance art, theater, poetry readings, and lectures; 24-hour access to studios; independent studio space for seniors; and seven art galleries. The arts-oriented library houses 50,000 volumes, 300 periodicals/media resources, and 250,000 examples of contemporary and historical art in slide, video, CD-ROM, and DVD format. Digital classrooms, labs, printing studios, sound recording studios, video editing labs, and specialized digital equipment such as looms and sewing machines permeate every corner of MICA's campus. Computers are available in all buildings and departments including the new Art/Tech Center. The wireless network provides campuswide Internet and e-mail access.

Faculty, Resident Artists, and Alumni The faculty of 267 professional artists, designers, and scholars are widely published and represented in public and private collections—from MOMA to the Stedelijk. Faculty members' honors include the Fulbright, Guggenheim, and MacArthur Awards. There are also more than 175 visiting artists, designers, critics, poets, art historians, and filmmakers for residencies or lectures each year. Recent visitors included David Hickey, Manthia Diawara, Joan Fontcuberta, Roberta Smith, William Wegman, Chipp Kidd, Peter Halley, Eric Fischl, and Leslie Dill.

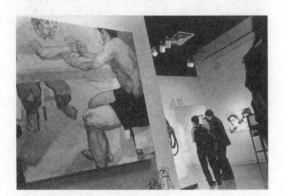

Visual

Arts

Maryland Institute College of Art (continued)

Student Performance/Exhibit Opportunities
MICA has one of the best exhibition programs of art schools in the U.S., with ninety exhibitions per year, many of which are devoted to student work. Students write, produce and act in plays, stage an annual fashion show, and present showings of their videos and films bi-monthly.

Special Programs MICA offers a five-year, dual-degree Bachelor of Fine Arts/Master of Arts in Teaching (B.F.A./M.A.T.) program that combines an undergraduate degree in studio art with teaching certification at the master's level. This dual-degree program boasts a 100 percent placement rate. There are study-abroad opportunities in Canada, England, France, Greece, Ireland, Italy, Japan, Jamaica, the Netherlands, Scotland, South Korea, and Turkey, and students can also participate in MICA's New York studio program, MICA in TRIBECA. Cross-enrollment is possible with The Johns Hopkins University and the Peabody Conservatory of Music.

Marylhurst University

Marylhurst, Oregon

Independent Roman Catholic, coed. Suburban campus. Total enrollment: 1,249. Art program established 1982.

Web Site http://www.marylhurst.edu/

Maryville University of Saint Louis

St. Louis, Missouri

Independent, coed. Suburban campus. Total enrollment: 3,333. Art program established 1970.

Degrees Bachelor of Arts in the area of art education K-12; Bachelor of Fine Arts in the areas of studio art, graphic design, interior design. Majors and concentrations: art education, graphic design, interior design, studio art. Cross-registration with Webster University, Fontbonne University, Missouri Baptist University, Lindenwood University. Program accredited by NASAD, NCATE, CIDA.

Enrollment 176 total; 148 undergraduate, 28 nonprofessional degree.

Art Student Profile 86% females, 14% males, 9% minorities, 1% international.

Art Faculty 10 undergraduate (full-time), 22 undergraduate (part-time). 90% of full-time faculty have terminal degrees. Graduate students do not teach undergraduate courses. Undergraduate student–faculty ratio: 11:1.

Student Life Student groups/activities include American Institute of Graphic Arts (AIGA) Student Chapter, Maryville Chapter of American Society of Interior Design/International Designers
Association, Student Life Art Club.

Expenses for 2006–2007 Application fee: $25. Comprehensive fee: $25,840 includes full-time tuition ($17,800), mandatory fees ($320), and college room and board ($7720). College room only: $6800. Full-time tuition and fees vary according to course load. Room and board charges vary according to housing facility. Special program-related fees: $10 per course for audiovisual teaching resources in art history courses, $10–$110 per course for expendable supplies in studio courses.

Financial Aid Program-specific awards: 5–8 art and design scholarships for undergraduates, first time freshmen, and outstanding transfer students ($2500–$4000), 1 The Fine Arts Scholarship for those demonstrating outstanding creative ability in art and design ($1000), 1 The Newman Scholarship for art and design students ($1000).

Application Procedures Deadline for freshmen and transfers: continuous. Required: high school transcript, college transcript(s) for transfer students, minimum 2.0 high school GPA, portfolio, SAT or ACT test scores (minimum composite ACT score of 20). Recommended: letter of recommendation, interview. Portfolio reviews held continuously on campus and off campus in St. Louis, MO; on National Portfolio Days; the submission of slides may be substituted for portfolios if original work is not available, for large works of art, or for three-dimensional pieces.

Web Site http://www.maryville.edu/

Undergraduate Contact Ms. Shani Lenord, Director, Office of Admissions, Maryville University of Saint Louis, 650 Maryville University Drive, St. Louis, Missouri 63141-7299; 314-529-9350, fax: 314-529-9927, e-mail address: admissions@maryville.edu

Rutgers, The State University of New Jersey
Mason Gross School of the Arts

New Brunswick, New Jersey

State-supported, coed. Small town campus. Art program established 1976.

Degrees Bachelor of Fine Arts in the area of visual arts. Majors and concentrations: ceramics, graphic design, painting/drawing, photography, printmaking, sculpture, video production. Graduate degrees offered: Master of Fine Arts in the area of visual arts.

Enrollment 424 total; 300 undergraduate, 44 graduate, 80 nonprofessional degree.

Art Student Profile 57% females, 43% males, 11% minorities, 5% international.

Art Faculty 20 total (full-time), 11 total (part-time). 98% of full-time faculty have terminal degrees. Graduate students teach a few undergraduate courses. Undergraduate student–faculty ratio: 11:1.

Expenses for 2006–2007 Special program-related fees: $20–$50 per class for supplies/materials.

Financial Aid Program-specific awards: 1 James O. Dumont Award for upperclassmen ($2300), 2–3 Betts Scholarships for upperclassmen ($500).

Application Procedures Students admitted directly into the professional program freshman year. Deadline for freshmen: January 15; transfers: March 15. Notification date for freshmen: June 1; transfers: July 1. Required: high school transcript, college transcript(s) for transfer students, minimum 2.0 high school GPA, portfolio, SAT or ACT test scores. Recommended: essay. Portfolio reviews held twice on campus and off campus in various cities at College Art Recruitment Fairs; the submission of slides may be substituted for portfolios for out-of-state applicants.

Web Site http://www.masongross.rutgers.edu

Undergraduate Contact Ms. Diane W. Harris, Associate Director, Undergraduate Admissions, Rutgers, The State University of New Jersey, Mason Gross School of the Arts, 65 Davidson Road, Piscataway, New Jersey 08854-8097; 732-932-INFO, fax: 732-445-0237, e-mail address: admissions@asb-ugadm.rutgers.edu

Graduate Contact Linda Costa, Associate Director, Graduate and Professional Admissions, Rutgers, The State University of New Jersey, Mason Gross School of the Arts, 18 Bishop Place, New Brunswick, New Jersey 08901; 732-932-7711, fax: 732-932-8231, e-mail address: smeds@rci.rutgers.edu

Massachusetts College of Art

Boston, Massachusetts

State-supported, coed. Urban campus. Total enrollment: 2,286. Art program established 1873.

Degrees Bachelor of Fine Arts in the areas of art education, art history, fine arts, design, media and performing arts. Majors and concentrations: animation, architectural design, art education, art history, art/fine arts, ceramic art and design, fashion design and technology, film studies, glass, graphic arts, illustration, industrial design, interrelated media, jewelry and metalsmithing, painting/drawing, photography, printmaking, sculpture, studio art, textile arts. Graduate degrees offered: Master of Fine Arts in the areas of design, fine arts, media and performing arts; Master of Science in the area of art education. Cross-registration with ProArts Consortium, College Academic Program Sharing, Public College Exchange Program, Colleges of the Fenway.

Enrollment 1,682 total; 1,571 undergraduate, 111 graduate.

Art Student Profile 66% females, 34% males, 14% minorities, 3% international.

Art Faculty 85 total (full-time), 134 total (part-time). 78% of full-time faculty have terminal degrees. Graduate students teach a few undergraduate courses. Undergraduate student–faculty ratio: 13:1.

Student Life Student groups/activities include All School Show, visiting artists and professional exhibitions, Holiday Art Sale and Spring Art Sale.

Expenses for 2007–2008 Application fee: $65. State resident tuition: $7450 full-time. Nonresident tuition: $21,900 full-time. College room and board: $10,900. Room and board charges

Massachusetts College of Art (continued)

vary according to housing facility. Special program-related fees: $25–$250 per course for course lab fees.

Financial Aid Program-specific awards: 44 Presidential Awards for outstanding non-Massachusetts residents ($4000–$20,000), 12 Tsongas Scholarships for outstanding Massachusetts residents ($7200).

Application Procedures Students admitted directly into the professional program freshman year. Deadline for freshmen: February 15; transfers: March 15. Notification date for freshmen: April 15; transfers: May 15. Required: essay, high school transcript, college transcript(s) for transfer students, minimum 3.0 high school GPA, 2 letters of recommendation, portfolio, SAT or ACT test scores. Portfolio reviews held continuously on campus.

Web Site http://www.massart.edu/

Undergraduate Contact Ms. Lydia Polanco-Pena, Associate Director of Admissions, Massachusetts College of Art, 621 Huntington Avenue, Boston, Massachusetts 02115-5882; 617-879-7222, fax: 617-879-7250, e-mail address: admissions@massart.edu

Graduate Contact Ms. Nadia Savage, Admissions Assistant, Graduate Programs, Massachusetts College of Art, 621 Huntington Avenue, Boston, Massachusetts 02115-5882; 617-879-7162.

Meadows School of the Arts

See Southern Methodist University

Memphis College of Art

Memphis, Tennessee

Independent, coed. Urban campus. Total enrollment: 308. Art program established 1936.

Degrees Bachelor of Fine Arts in the areas of fine arts, design arts. Majors and concentrations: applied art, ceramic art and design, commercial art, computer graphics, graphic arts, illustration, jewelry and metalsmithing, painting/drawing, photography, printmaking, sculpture, studio art. Graduate degrees offered: Master of Arts in the area of art education; Master of Arts in Teaching in the area of art education with licensure; Master of Fine Arts in the areas of studio art, computer arts. Cross-registration with Rhodes College, Christian Brothers University, Le Moyne-Owen College. Program accredited by NASAD.

Enrollment 308 total; 289 undergraduate, 19 graduate.

Art Student Profile 50% females, 50% males, 23% minorities, 2% international.

Art Faculty 20 undergraduate (full-time), 25 undergraduate (part-time). 85% of full-time faculty have terminal degrees. Graduate students teach a few undergraduate courses. Undergraduate student–faculty ratio: 10:1.

Student Life Student groups/activities include Student Government, Arteli (Arts in the Schools), children's community art classes. Special housing available for art students.

Expenses for 2007–2008 Application fee: $25. Tuition: $20,100 full-time. Mandatory fees: $560 full-time. College room only: $5760. Special program-related fees: $560 per year for studio/activity.

Financial Aid Program-specific awards: 300 admissions scholarships for program majors ($3500–$20,100), 200 work-study awards for program majors ($1000).

Application Procedures Students admitted directly into the professional program freshman year. Deadline for freshmen and transfers: continuous. Required: high school transcript, college transcript(s) for transfer students, portfolio, SAT or ACT test scores (minimum composite ACT score of 17). Recommended: minimum 2.0 high school GPA, letter of recommendation, interview. Portfolio reviews held weekly on campus and off campus at National Portfolio Days; the submission of slides may be substituted for portfolios whenever needed.

Web Site http://www.mca.edu

Contact Ms. Annette James Moore, Director of Admissions, Memphis College of Art, 1930 Poplar Avenue, Overton Park, Memphis, Tennessee 38104; 800-727-1088, fax: 901-272-5158, e-mail address: info@mca.edu

More About the College

Since 1936, Memphis College of Art (MCA) has been a small, distinctive community of artists. The MCA experience is organized around small classes, independent work, and one-on-one attention and guidance not usually found at a larger institution. Currently students from thirty states and seven countries attend MCA, providing a diversity that is often associated with larger schools.

MCA is located in a 342-acre park in midtown Memphis adjacent to the Memphis Brooks Museum of Art and the Memphis Zoo. Nearby student residences provide living space for new and returning students. Suite-style apartments provide each resident a private room with shared kitchen, laundry, and living room areas. Studio spaces are provided. Other residential options include shared apartments or efficiencies. Two roommates share a furnished apartment with hardwood floors, a sun porch, a kitchen, and studio space. A large variety of affordable housing is also available off-campus to suit all lifestyles and budgets.

Memphis is a great place for an aspiring artist. Known for blues, barbecue, and Elvis, Memphis is also home to Fortune 500 companies, the Grizzlies NBA team, a symphony, an opera, a theater, other colleges and universities, museums, galleries, and almost 1 million residents. Annual festivals on Beale Street and the Mississippi River are popular with students.

MCA is a close-knit community where it's easy to make friends. There are plenty of organized activities to keep students busy, such as Friday night movies, exhibition receptions, community dinners, and an annual ski trip, rafting trip, and Halloween Costume Ball.

Tobey Exhibition Hall hosts numerous shows that expose students to a wide range of contemporary art; the Brode Gallery is a large space dedicated to student art. Students also have the opportunity to learn from visiting artists who provide a constant flow of new creative and intellectual energy. MCA organizes study trips to cities around the world renowned for their culture. In early May, a weeklong workshop is held on Horn Island off the Mississippi coast.

The Career Center offers career assistance for graduating students and part-time job placement for current students. Informative sessions are held to prepare students for career choices and for the job search/interview process. The Job Fair brings regional and national companies to MCA each spring for interviews. Internships and the student-run design agency provide students with professional experience while in school.

Faculty members have been selected for their understanding of the relationship between art and teaching. MCA's Fine Arts faculty members are professional artists who exhibit frequently and regularly execute commissions. The Design Arts faculty members stay on top of the industry through continuing professional design projects. With their knowledge of the job market and galleries at the regional and national levels, faculty members are well qualified to guide students on their career paths. Liberal Studies faculty members are chosen for their impressive credentials and their understanding of the unique nature of MCA students.

MCA is concerned about students whose financial resources are limited. More than 90 percent of the College's students receive some type of financial assistance. Financial aid programs include scholarships, loans, grants, and work-study awards. More than $1 million is awarded by MCA in scholarship and grants each year.

Program Facilities Three fully equipped computer labs feature Macintosh LCD flat-panel desktop computers with high-speed Internet access, laser printers, large-format color ink jet printers, DVD burners, color scanners, and other high-end multimedia peripherals. All stations have the latest graphic design, video, and multimedia software. MCA's shop has 4,400 square feet, with machines for woodworking, metalworking, plastic molding, glass cutting, shrink wrapping, and stretcher and frame construction. The library has more than 16,000 volumes, 120 art journals and periodicals, 36,000 slides, an extensive reproduction collection, audiovisual equipment, a computer writing lab, and an image file. Students have studio spaces provided in their area of study. Conference rooms allow for slide viewing, critiques, and lectures. Sculpture, small metals, and clay have studios with foundry/welding areas for casting and metal work. Clay has wheels, handbuilding, and glazing space as well as a semi-enclosed firing room. Fiber/surface design has three studios, a dye room, manual and computerized looms, washer/dryer, range tops, refrigerators, and sewing machines. Printmaking, papermaking, and book arts studios provide interaction between these media. Printmaking has facilities for lithography, etching, serigraphy, and other processes. Book arts include letter presses and bindery. Papermaking has beaters, hydraulic press, and pulper. Photography has beginning and advanced black and white darkrooms to print 35mm through 4*5 formats. A color lab with a 20-inch color processor and facilities for non-silver and alternative processes and a fully-equipped lighting studio are also available.

Special Programs The New York Studio Program offers students an exciting semester in New York City with artists and students from across the country. The Mobility Program can place a student at another art

Memphis College of Art (continued)

college for a semester of study. Internships offer experience in fine and design arts fields, such as museum work, art therapy, set design, and advertising. Consortiums with local colleges provide a greater variety of course selection.

Metropolitan State College of Denver

Denver, Colorado

State-supported, coed. Urban campus. Total enrollment: 20,761 (2005). Art program established 1965.

Degrees Bachelor of Fine Arts in the area of art. Majors and concentrations: art education, art history, ceramics, communication design, computer imaging, digital art, jewelry and metalsmithing, painting/drawing, photography, printmaking, sculpture. Cross-registration with University of Colorado at Denver, Colorado community colleges. Program accredited by NASAD.

Enrollment 856 total; 837 undergraduate, 19 nonprofessional degree.

Art Student Profile 66% females, 34% males, 27% minorities, 1% international.

Art Faculty 24 undergraduate (full-time), 55 undergraduate (part-time). 96% of full-time faculty have terminal degrees. Graduate students do not teach undergraduate courses. Undergraduate student–faculty ratio: 15:1.

Student Life Student groups/activities include Art Guild and other clubs, Center for Visual Art, Emmanuel Gallery student show.

Expenses for 2006–2007 Application fee: $25. State resident tuition: $2,839 full-time. Nonresident tuition: $10,249 full-time. Mandatory fees: $592 full-time. Full-time tuition and fees vary according to course load and location. Special program-related fees: $6 per credit hour for expendable materials and modeling fees.

Application Procedures Students admitted directly into the professional program freshman year. Deadline for freshmen and transfers: continuous. Notification date for freshmen and transfers: continuous. Required: high school transcript, college transcript(s) for trans-

fer students, SAT or ACT test scores, minimum college GPA of 2.0 for transfer students.

Web Site http://clem.mscd.edu/~art_cs/

Undergraduate Contact Ms. Patricia Yarrow, Program Assistant, Art Department, Metropolitan State College of Denver, Campus Box 59, PO Box 173362, Denver, Colorado 80217-3362; 303-556-3090, fax: 303-556-4094, e-mail address: yarrowp@mscd.edu

Miami International University of Art & Design

Miami, Florida

Proprietary, coed. Urban campus. Total enrollment: 1,406. Art program established 1965.

Degrees Bachelor of Fine Arts in the areas of computer animation, visual effects and motion graphics, interactive media design, film and digital production, graphic design, advertising, visual and entertainment arts, photography, fashion design, fashion merchandising, interior design. Majors and concentrations: advertising, computer animation, digital photography, fashion design, fashion merchandising, film and digital production, graphic design, interactive media, interior design, visual and entertainment arts, visual effects and motion graphics. Graduate degrees offered: Master of Fine Arts in the areas of computer animation, graphic design, visual arts, film, interior design, film and digital production, visual and entertainment arts.

Enrollment 1,380 undergraduate, 78 graduate.

Art Student Profile 54% females, 46% males, 65% minorities, 11% international.

Art Faculty 46 total (full-time), 85 total (part-time). 95% of full-time faculty have terminal degrees. Graduate students do not teach undergraduate courses. Undergraduate student–faculty ratio: 18:1.

Student Life Student groups/activities include SIGGRAPH, American Institute of Graphic Arts, American Society of Interior Designers. Special housing available for art students.

Expenses for 2006–2007 Application fee: $50. Tuition: $18,960 full-time. College room only: $6150.

visual

Arts

Financial Aid Program-specific awards: 4 President's Scholarships for students in final year of study ($5000), merit scholarships for undergraduates with financial need ($1000).

Application Procedures Students admitted directly into the professional program freshman year. Deadline for freshmen and transfers: continuous. Notification date for freshmen and transfers: continuous. Required: essay, high school transcript, college transcript(s) for transfer students, minimum 2.0 high school GPA, interview, minimum TOEFL score of 500. Recommended: minimum 3.0 high school GPA, 2 letters of recommendation, SAT or ACT test scores. Portfolio reviews held 4 times on campus and off campus in locations in south Florida; the submission of slides may be substituted for portfolios.

Web Site http://www.artinstitutes.edu/miami

Contact Kevin Ryan, Director of Admission, Admissions, Miami International University of Art & Design, 1501 Biscayne Boulevard, Miami, Florida 33132; 305-428-5600, fax: 305-374-5933, e-mail address: kryan@aii.edu

Miami University

Oxford, Ohio

State-related, coed. Small town campus. Total enrollment: 16,329. Art program established 1929.

Degrees Bachelor of Fine Arts in the areas of painting/drawing, jewelry and metalsmithing, printmaking, sculpture, ceramic art and design, graphic arts, photography; Bachelor of Science in the area of art education. Majors and concentrations: art education, art history, ceramic art and design, computer graphics, jewelry and metalsmithing, painting/drawing, photography, printmaking, sculpture. Graduate degrees offered: Master of Arts in the area of art education; Master of Fine Arts in the areas of painting, ceramics, sculpture, jewelry and metalsmithing, printmaking. Cross-registration with John E. Dolibois European Center (Luxembourg). Program accredited by NASAD.

Enrollment 399 total; 380 undergraduate, 19 graduate.

Art Student Profile 68% females, 32% males, 3% minorities.

Art Faculty 12 undergraduate (full-time), 9 undergraduate (part-time), 10 graduate (full-time). 81% of full-time faculty have terminal degrees. Graduate students teach a few undergraduate courses. Undergraduate student–faculty ratio: 15:1.

Student Life Student groups/activities include Art History Association, National Art Education Association Student Chapter, Visual Arts Club. Special housing available for art students.

Expenses for 2007–2008 Application fee: $45. State resident tuition: $9910 full-time. Nonresident tuition: $22,362 full-time. Mandatory fees: $2015 full-time. College room and board: $8600. College room only: $4410. Room and board charges vary according to board plan and housing facility. Special program-related fees: $20–$100 per course for studio supplies.

Financial Aid Program-specific awards: 1 Miami University Scholarship for program majors ($4300), 1 Arthur Damon Art Award for program majors ($1500), 1 School of Fine Arts Award for program majors ($2000), 1 Marston D. Hodgin Award for program majors ($1000), 1 George R. and Galen Glasgow Hoxie Award ($890), 2 Fred and Molly Pye Awards for sophomores and juniors ($475), 1 Barbara Hershey Photo Award for female junior photography majors ($1000), 1 National Woodcarvers Award for upperclass sculpture majors ($1000), 1 Robert Wolfe Printmakers Award for junior and senior printmaking majors ($400).

Application Procedures Students admitted directly into the professional program freshman year. Deadline for freshmen: January 30; transfers: March 1. Notification date for freshmen: March 15. Required: high school transcript, college transcript(s) for transfer students, portfolio, SAT or ACT test scores, essay (art history majors only). Portfolio reviews held twice on campus.

Web Site http://www.fna.muohio.edu/artweb/

Undergraduate Contact Mr. Dennis Tobin, Professor, Department of Art, Miami University, Art Building, Oxford, Ohio 45056; 513-529-1505, fax: 513-529-1532, e-mail address: tobinde@muohio.edu

Graduate Contact Prof. Susan Ewing, Department of Art, Miami University, Art Building, Oxford, Ohio 45056; 513-529-5627, fax: 513-529-1532, e-mail address: ewingsr@muohio.edu

Michigan State University

East Lansing, Michigan

State-supported, coed. Suburban campus. Total enrollment: 45,520. Art program established 1931.

Degrees Bachelor of Fine Arts in the areas of studio art, art education. Majors and concentrations: art education, ceramics, graphic design, painting/drawing, photography, printmaking, sculpture. Graduate degrees offered: Master of Fine Arts in the area of studio art.

Enrollment 340 total; 175 undergraduate, 15 graduate, 150 nonprofessional degree.

Art Faculty 17 total (full-time), 2 total (part-time). 100% of full-time faculty have terminal degrees. Graduate students teach a few undergraduate courses. Undergraduate student–faculty ratio: 13:1.

Student Life Student groups/activities include Saturday Art Program, undergraduate exhibit at Kresge Art Museum, Gallery 114 (student exhibition space).

Expenses for 2007–2008 Application fee: $35. State resident tuition: $8400 full-time. Nonresident tuition: $22,260 full-time. Mandatory fees: $1240 full-time. Full-time tuition and fees vary according to course load, degree level, program, and student level. College room and board: $6676. College room only: $2756. Room and board charges vary according to board plan, housing facility, and student level.

Financial Aid Program-specific awards: 1–4 Creative Arts Scholarships for Michigan resident studio art majors ($500–$3000).

Application Procedures Students admitted directly into the professional program freshman year. Deadline for freshmen and transfers: continuous. Required: high school transcript, college transcript(s) for transfer students, minimum 2.0 high school GPA, SAT or ACT test scores. Recommended: minimum 3.0 high school GPA.

Web Site http://www.art.msu.edu

Undergraduate Contact Cindy Walter, Academic Advisor, Studio Art Undergraduate Program, Michigan State University, 113 Kresge Art Center, East Lansing, Michigan 48824-1119; 517-432-7033, fax: 517-432-3938, e-mail address: walterc2@msu.edu

Graduate Contact Michelle Word, Academic Specialist, Studio Art Graduate Program, Michigan State University, 113 Kresge Art Center, East Lansing, Michigan 48824-1119; 517-355-7610, fax: 517-432-3938, e-mail address: wordmich@msu.edu

Midge Karr Fine Art Department

See New York Institute of Technology

Midwestern State University

Wichita Falls, Texas

State-supported, coed. Urban campus. Total enrollment: 6,042.

Web Site http://www.mwsu.edu/

Millikin University

Decatur, Illinois

Independent, coed. Suburban campus. Total enrollment: 2,488. Art program established 1903.

Degrees Bachelor of Fine Arts. Majors and concentrations: art education, art therapy, art/fine arts, commercial art, computer graphics, studio art.

Enrollment 100 total; all undergraduate.

Art Student Profile 50% females, 50% males, 4% minorities.

Art Faculty 5 undergraduate (full-time), 1 undergraduate (part-time). 100% of full-time faculty have terminal degrees. Graduate students do not teach undergraduate courses. Undergraduate student–faculty ratio: 16:1.

Student Life Student groups/activities include Art Club, AIGA-American Institute of Graphic Arts. Special housing available for art students.

Expenses for 2007–2008 Application fee: $0. Comprehensive fee: $31,055 includes full-time tuition ($23,250), mandatory fees ($595), and college room and board ($7210). College room only: $4010. Special program-related fees: $10–$50 per semester for lab fees.

Financial Aid Program-specific awards: 20–30 talent awards for incoming students ($500–$3000).

Application Procedures Students apply for admission into the professional program by sophomore year. Deadline for freshmen and transfers: continuous. Required: high school transcript, college transcript(s) for transfer students, letter of recommendation, interview, portfolio, SAT or ACT test scores. Portfolio reviews held by appointment on campus and off campus in St. Louis, MO; Indianapolis, IN; the submission of slides may be substituted for portfolios for large works of art.

Web Site http://www.millikin.edu

Undergraduate Contact Mr. Ed Walker, Chairman, Art Department, Millikin University, 1184 West Main Street, Decatur, Illinois 62522; 217-424-6228, fax: 217-424-3993, e-mail address: ewalker@mail.millikin.edu

Milwaukee Institute of Art and Design

Milwaukee, Wisconsin

Independent, coed. Art program established 1974.

Degrees Bachelor of Fine Arts. Majors and concentrations: communication design, computer animation and interactive media, drawing, fine art studio, illustration, industrial design, interior architecture and design, painting, photography, printmaking, sculpture. Cross-registration with Marquette University. Program accredited by NASAD.

Enrollment 646 total; all undergraduate.

Art Student Profile 53% females, 47% males, 16% minorities, 4% international.

Art Faculty 33 undergraduate (full-time), 86 undergraduate (part-time). 70% of full-time faculty have terminal degrees. Graduate students do not teach undergraduate courses. Undergraduate student–faculty ratio: 9:1.

Student Life Student groups/activities include student exhibitions, Student Government, student publication. Special housing available for art students.

Expenses for 2006–2007 Application fee: $25. Comprehensive fee: $30,400 includes full-time tuition ($23,100), mandatory fees ($300), and college room and board ($7000). Special program-related fees: $5–$95 per course for supplies/models.

Financial Aid Program-specific awards: 22–35 MIAD Scholarships for continuing students ($2000–$2200), 125 MIAD Admissions Scholarships for incoming students ($5775–$23,100).

Application Procedures Students admitted directly into the professional program freshman year. Deadline for freshmen and transfers: continuous. Required: essay, high school transcript, college transcript(s) for transfer students, minimum 2.0 high school GPA, interview, portfolio. Recommended: minimum 3.0 high school GPA, 2 letters of recommendation, SAT or ACT test scores, minimum 3.0 GPA in high school art classes. Portfolio reviews held continuously on campus and off campus; the submission of slides may be substituted for portfolios when distance is prohibitive.

Web Site http://www.miad.edu

Undergraduate Contact Mr. Mark Fetherston, Director of Admissions, Milwaukee Institute of Art and Design, 273 East Erie Street, Milwaukee, Wisconsin 53202; 414-291-8070, fax: 414-291-8077, e-mail address: miadadm@miad.edu

More About the Institute

The Milwaukee Institute of Art and Design (MIAD) is Wisconsin's only four-year independent professional art and design college. Founded in 1974 as a successor to the Layton School of Art, MIAD offers a Bachelor of Fine Arts (B.F.A.) degree in eleven majors: communication design, drawing, illustration, industrial design, integrated fine-arts studio, interior architecture and design, painting, photography, printmaking, sculpture, and time-based media. Minors can be earned in all eleven disciplines as well as in advertising, animation, art history, business, video, and writing. The curricula reflect the latest in professional needs, techniques, trends, and innovations. The ongoing emphasis is on problem solving within a rapidly changing world. MIAD is a place where students learn to achieve their goals and do not merely replicate the theories and processes of others.

All MIAD faculty members are practicing professionals recognized in their field of instruction. They share their knowledge and experience with talented, motivated students. Attention to individual students and their work is ensured through a small student-faculty ratio.

MIAD studios and classrooms are in a state-of-the-art, multiwindowed, renovated, five-story building. It

Milwaukee Institute of Art and Design (continued)

has the light necessary to artists and wide-open spaces for creating oversized paintings and sculptures and full-size industrial prototypes. The ventilation system provides a safe environment, and the studio space per student is one of the largest in the country.

Computer labs offer the most current software and hardware for animation; graphic, industrial, and interior/architectural design; and video editing as well as fine-art imaging. A fully equipped sculpture department, a 3-D lab, extensive printmaking facilities, and digital photography facilities offer artists wide choices and venues for expressing themselves.

The college is located in Milwaukee's historic Third Ward near Lake Michigan. This safe neighborhood of turn-of-the-century buildings is home to artists' lofts, galleries, specialty shops, restaurants, and a live theater complex. Student housing and a Student Center are in historic buildings that offer comfort, security, and convenience in unique, artistic settings.

MIAD students have a wide range of exhibition and internship opportunities each year. These include an ongoing series of shows in the MIAD Student Gallery, as well as the annual Graduate Exhibition and internships with many of the area's most prestigious design, architectural, and photographic studios and several of the city's professional performing art troupes. Also, MIAD students are regularly invited by local galleries to submit work for local and regional exhibitions.

Alumni own or are affiliated with local and national advertising agencies, design studios, and publishers, and many design for industries throughout the world. Their fine art is in private and corporate collections; they operate their own galleries; and, thanks to their education, they pursue myriad other satisfying and rewarding careers.

Special Programs Extended academic opportunities are available to students through an affiliation with nearby Marquette University. MIAD students can choose from a wide variety of liberal studies courses, plus, they may use that school's excellent Recreation Center and access its full range of health services.

A mobility program allows MIAD students to study at more than thirty affiliated U.S. art and design schools, including an internship/study program in New York City. MIAD offers a unique blend of international-study experiences. These include trips to major European cities as part of course offerings in liberal studies. MIAD maintains exchange opportunities for students to study with other notable art and design colleges in France, Germany, Japan, Korea, and Poland.

Minneapolis College of Art and Design

Minneapolis, Minnesota

Independent, coed. Urban campus. Art program established 1886.

Degrees Bachelor of Fine Arts in the areas of design, fine arts, media arts; Bachelor of Science in the area of visualization. Majors and concentrations: advertising, animation, comic art, drawing, filmmaking, furniture design, graphic design, illustration, multimedia, painting, photography, printmaking, sculpture, visualization. Graduate degrees offered: Master of Fine Arts in the area of visual studies. Cross-registration with Macalester College. Program accredited by NASAD.

Enrollment 766 total; 722 undergraduate, 44 graduate.

Art Student Profile 57% females, 43% males, 5% minorities, 3% international.

Art Faculty 41 total (full-time), 81 total (part-time). 75% of full-time faculty have terminal degrees. Graduate students do not teach undergraduate courses. Undergraduate student–faculty ratio: 11:1.

Student Life Student groups/activities include Comic Heads-Comic Book Club, International Association of Graphic Arts Student Chapter (IAGA), Lingo Club. Special housing available for art students.

Expenses for 2007–2008 Application fee: $35. Tuition: $27,000 full-time. Mandatory fees: $200 full-time. College room only: $4160. Special program-related fees: $100 per semester for student activity fee.

Financial Aid Program-specific awards: BFA Trustee Scholarship for new BS/BFA freshmen/BS/BFA transfers ($12,000), BFA Presidential Scholarship for new BS/BFA freshmen/BS/BFA transfers ($10,000), BFA Visual Scholarship for new BS/BFA freshmen/BS/BFA transfers ($8000), BFA Friends of MCAD Award for new BS/BFA freshmen/BS/BFA transfers ($6000), BS Trustee Scholarship for new BS/BFA freshmen/BS/BFA transfers ($12,000), BS Presidential Scholarship for new BS/BFA freshman/BS/BFA transfer

($10,000), BS Emerging Leader Scholarship for new BS/BFA freshmen/BS/BFA transfers ($8000).

Application Procedures Students admitted directly into the professional program freshman year. Deadline for freshmen and transfers: February 15. Required: essay, high school transcript, college transcript(s) for transfer students, minimum 2.0 high school GPA, letter of recommendation, portfolio, SAT or ACT test scores (minimum combined SAT score of 1100, minimum composite ACT score of 21), statement of interest (BFA and BS applicants), essay for visualization majors (BS applicants only). Recommended: minimum 3.0 high school GPA, interview. Portfolio reviews held as needed by appointment or event on campus and off campus at National Portfolio Days; high school portfolio days; the submission of slides may be substituted for portfolios for large works of art or when distance is prohibitive.

Web Site http://www.mcad.edu/

Contact Mr. William Mullen, Vice President of Enrollment Management, Admissions, Minneapolis College of Art and Design, 2501 Stevens Avenue, Minneapolis, Minnesota 55404; 612-874-3762, fax: 612-874-3701, e-mail address: william_mullen@mcad.edu

Minnesota State University Mankato

Mankato, Minnesota

State-supported, coed. Small town campus. Total enrollment: 14,148.

Degrees Bachelor of Fine Arts in the area of art. Majors and concentrations: ceramics, drawing, fibers, graphic arts, painting, photography, printmaking, sculpture. Graduate degrees offered: Master of Arts in the area of studio art. Cross-registration with Gustavus Adolphus College. Program accredited by NASAD.

Enrollment 312 total; 243 undergraduate, 12 graduate, 57 nonprofessional degree.

Art Student Profile 55% females, 45% males, 2% minorities, 5% international.

Art Faculty 14 undergraduate (full-time), 7 undergraduate (part-time), 14 graduate (full-time). 100% of full-time faculty have terminal degrees. Graduate students teach a few undergraduate courses. Undergraduate student–faculty ratio: 20:1.

Student Life Student groups/activities include Art League, Photography Club, Mudworks Ceramics Student Organization, AIGA-American Institute of Graphic Arts Student Chapter.

Expenses for 2007–2008 Application fee: $20. State resident tuition: $5308 full-time. Nonresident tuition: $11,370 full-time. Mandatory fees: $742 full-time. Full-time tuition and fees vary according to course load and reciprocity agreements. College room and board: $5354. Room and board charges vary according to board plan. Special program-related fees: $15–$90 per semester for art supplies.

Financial Aid Program-specific awards: 6–8 Faculty Nominated Awards for program majors ($500).

Application Procedures Students apply for admission into the professional program by sophomore, junior year. Deadline for freshmen: March 15; transfers: continuous. Notification date for freshmen and transfers: continuous. Required: high school transcript, college transcript(s) for transfer students, SAT or ACT test scores.

Web Site http://www.mnsu.edu/dept/artdept

Contact Mr. James Johnson, Chair, Art Department, Minnesota State University Mankato, Nelson Hall 136, Mankato, Minnesota 56001; 507-389-6412, fax: 507-389-2816, e-mail address: james.johnson@mnsu.edu

Mississippi State University

Mississippi State, Mississippi

State-supported, coed. Total enrollment: 16,206. Art program established 1968.

Degrees Bachelor of Fine Arts in the areas of fine arts, graphic design. Majors and concentrations: ceramics, drawing, graphic design, painting, photography, printmaking, sculpture. Program accredited by NASAD.

Enrollment 1,195 total; 264 undergraduate, 931 nonprofessional degree.

Art Student Profile 41% females, 59% males, 8% minorities, 1% international.

Art Faculty 21 undergraduate (full-time), 1 undergraduate (part-time). 94% of full-time faculty have terminal degrees. Graduate students do not teach undergraduate courses. Undergraduate student–faculty ratio: 13:1.

Mississippi State University (continued)

Student Life Student groups/activities include exhibitions, American Advertising Federation Chapter.

Expenses for 2006–2007 Application fee: $25. State resident tuition: $4596 full-time. Nonresident tuition: $10,552 full-time. College room and board: $6331. College room only: $3296. Room and board charges vary according to board plan, housing facility, and student level. Special program-related fees: $50–$100 per semester for lab fee per class/computer resource access.

Financial Aid Program-specific awards: 10 Gulmon Scholarships for freshmen ($1000), 1 Ferretti/Karnstedt Award for sophomores ($1000), 1 DuBoise Scholarship in Photography for juniors and seniors ($750), 1 Del Rendon Scholarship for freshmen through seniors ($2000), 3 John Richard Scholarships for freshmen through juniors ($1000).

Application Procedures Students admitted directly into the professional program freshman year. Deadline for freshmen and transfers: July 26. Notification date for freshmen and transfers: continuous. Required: high school transcript, college transcript(s) for transfer students, minimum 2.0 high school GPA, SAT or ACT test scores (minimum composite ACT score of 17), portfolio for transfers. Portfolio reviews held twice on campus.

Web Site http://www.msstate.edu/dept/art/index.html

Undergraduate Contact Ms. Kay De Marsche, Head, Department of Art, Mississippi State University, PO Box 5182, Mississippi State, Mississippi 39762; 662-325-3850, fax: 662-325-3850, e-mail address: kdemarsche@caad.msstate.edu

Mississippi University for Women

Columbus, Mississippi

State-supported, coed, primarily women. Small town campus. Total enrollment: 2,328 (2005). Art program established 1941.

Web Site http://www.muw.edu/

Missouri State University

Springfield, Missouri

State-supported, coed. Suburban campus. Total enrollment: 19,218. Art program established 1945.

Degrees Bachelor of Fine Arts in the areas of design, art, digital animation; Bachelor of Science in the area of electronic art; Bachelor of Science in Education. Majors and concentrations: art education, ceramics, computer animation, digital art, drawing, electronic arts, graphic design, illustration, jewelry and metalsmithing, painting, photography, printmaking, sculpture. Graduate degrees offered: Master of Science in the area of art education.

Enrollment 572 total; 490 undergraduate, 12 graduate, 70 nonprofessional degree.

Art Faculty 27 total (full-time), 14 total (part-time). 100% of full-time faculty have terminal degrees. Graduate students do not teach undergraduate courses. Undergraduate student–faculty ratio: 15:1.

Student Life Student groups/activities include Design Student Club, Student Artist Association, clubs in various areas of emphasis.

Expenses for 2007–2008 Application fee: $30. State resident tuition: $5988 full-time. Nonresident tuition: $11,088 full-time. Mandatory fees: $618 full-time. Full-time tuition and fees vary according to course load, degree level, location, and program. College room and board: $5416. Room and board charges vary according to board plan and housing facility.

Financial Aid Program-specific awards: 10 departmental awards for program majors ($500–$800).

Application Procedures Students apply for admission into the professional program by sophomore year. Deadline for freshmen and transfers: July 30. Notification date for freshmen and transfers: continuous. Required: high school transcript, college transcript(s) for transfer students, minimum 2.0 high school GPA, portfolio, SAT or ACT test scores. Portfolio reviews held twice on campus; the submission of slides may be substituted for portfolios.

Web Site http://art.missouristate.edu/

Undergraduate Contact Prof. Wade S. Thompson, Department Head, Art and Design Department, Missouri State University, 901 South

National, Springfield, Missouri 65804; 417-836-5110, fax: 417-836-6055, e-mail address: wadethompson@missouristate.edu

Graduate Contact Dr. Steve Willis, Coordinator, Art Education Department, Missouri State University, 901 South National, Springfield, Missouri 65804; 417-836-6693, fax: 417-836-6055, e-mail address: stevewillis@missouristate.edu

Montserrat College of Art

Beverly, Massachusetts

Independent, coed. Suburban campus. Total enrollment: 308 (2006). Art program established 1970.

Degrees Bachelor of Fine Arts. Majors and concentrations: art/fine arts, graphic design, illustration, painting/drawing, photography, printmaking, sculpture. Cross-registration with Northeast Consortium of Colleges and Universities in Massachusetts, Association of Independent Colleges of Art and Design. Program accredited by NASAD.

Enrollment 299 total; all undergraduate.

Art Student Profile 64% females, 36% males, 5% minorities.

Art Faculty 24 undergraduate (full-time), 38 undergraduate (part-time). 67% of full-time faculty have terminal degrees. Graduate students do not teach undergraduate courses. Undergraduate student–faculty ratio: 7:1.

Student Life Student groups/activities include Student Government, Meals-on-the-Cheap Committee, Coffee House Organization. Special housing available for art students.

Expenses for 2007–2008 Application fee: $40. Tuition: $21,500 full-time. Mandatory fees: $800 full-time. Full-time tuition and fees vary according to course load and reciprocity agreements. College room only: $5800. Room charges vary according to housing facility.

Financial Aid Program-specific awards: 185 Montserrat Grants for those demonstrating need ($2477), 2 Presidential Awards for program majors ($15,250), 178 talent awards for those demonstrating merit ($2498), 2 Beverly Scholarships for residents of Beverly demonstrating need ($5625).

Application Procedures Students admitted directly into the professional program freshman year. Deadline for freshmen and transfers: August 1. Notification date for freshmen and transfers: August 15. Required: essay, high school transcript, college transcript(s) for transfer students, minimum 2.0 high school GPA, 2 letters of recommendation, portfolio, SAT or ACT test scores, minimum TOEFL score of 550 for international students. Recommended: minimum 3.0 high school GPA, interview. Portfolio reviews held continuously on campus and off campus in various locations across the country; the submission of slides may be substituted for portfolios if a campus visit is impossible.

Web Site http://www.montserrat.edu

Undergraduate Contact Ms. Jessica Sarin-Perry, Dean of Admissions and Enrollment Management, Admissions, Montserrat College of Art, 23 Essex Street, Box 26, Beverly, Massachusetts 01915; 800-836-0487, fax: 978-921-4241, e-mail address: admiss@montserrat.edu

More About the College

Montserrat College of Art takes a highly personal approach to teaching, valuing above all else the combination of strong individual support and challenging creative instruction. Located on Boston's North Shore, it is a place where students feel inspired, encouraged, and at home.

Students come to Montserrat to gain professional competence, to develop their own unique abilities, and to engage in new areas of experience in pursuit of their Bachelor of Fine Arts (B.F.A.) degree. With an enrollment of approximately 275 students of diverse cultural and artistic backgrounds, the College is large enough to offer the wide array of courses and concentrations that compose a strong visual arts curriculum, yet small enough to provide the personal attention that is often difficult to find in larger educational environments. Small classes encourage intensive, individualized instruction by a faculty of professional artists and designers and accomplished scholars.

The first year of foundation studies is a carefully crafted sequence of complementary courses emphasizing the visual, technical, written, and verbal skills essential to a successful art college experience. After foundation, a student may choose to major in graphic design, illustration, painting and drawing, photography and video, printmaking, or sculpture or do a self-directed study combining elements from different disciplines. Students may also combine any one of the studio concentrations with art education for a dual concentration. The Montserrat curriculum allows students to explore a wide range of studio electives

Montserrat College of Art (continued)

not necessarily related to their concentration, encouraging the development of a truly unique, artistic voice.

Experiential learning provides a unique opportunity for students to gain professional practice. During the junior year, required internships and apprenticeships provide students with opportunities to experience the world of work and to integrate classroom learning with the realities of the workplace.

Entry into the Senior Seminar is determined by a faculty panel. Here, students have the opportunity to delve independently into a significant, coherent body of work and exhibit seminar work. This revelatory experience helps the artist and designer to mature and ultimately make the transition into professional life.

Montserrat is a residential college with apartment-style housing nestled among the homes of downtown Beverly, located on Boston's North Shore. Boston and Cambridge are easily accessible by car or commuter train. World-class museums, such as the Boston Museum of Fine Arts; galleries; libraries; shopping; sports; and a variety of entertainment

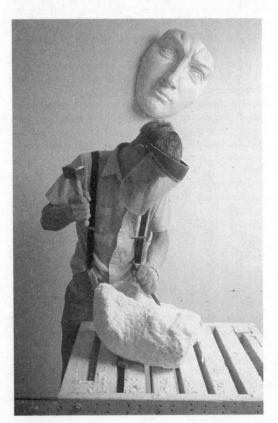

options provide a stimulating intellectual, cultural, and social environment in which to live and learn.

Program Facilities The Montserrat campus has three galleries that feature exciting exhibitions by professional artists of national and international note and artists within the College community. The Visiting Artist and Lectures Series programs expose students to a wide range of viewpoints and aesthetics.

Montserrat's main building, the historic Hardie Building, houses four floors of studios, classrooms, exhibition spaces, and the Paul Scott Library. Specially equipped studios for printmaking, photography, painting, illustration, and graphic design as well as video and computer labs are located here. The library contains a collection of more than 14,000 books, numerous art and related periodicals, videos, CD-ROMs, and other resources. The library offers Internet access and houses a comprehensive slide collection with more than 60,000 images. The 301 Cabot Studio Building offers facilities for sculpture and semiprivate studios for seniors.

All students are entitled to free admission to Boston's Museum of Fine Arts, which has one of the finest collections of art in the world. The museum houses permanent exhibits of art and artifacts representing virtually all periods and civilizations as well as changing exhibitions of art.

Special Programs Montserrat offers students a variety of opportunities to broaden their horizons and earn credit towards their degree through local, national, and international study. The College is a member of the Northeast Consortium of Colleges and Universities in Massachusetts; students may take classes and use the library facilities of member colleges. Through Montserrat's membership in the Association of Independent Colleges of Art and Design (AICAD), students may spend a semester or year in comparable studies at a member institution. The AICAD New York Studio Program offers third-year students the opportunity to spend a summer in New York City.

Students may spend a month in the walled, papal city of Viterbo in Italy while attending Montserrat's summer, residential program. Intensive courses in painting, drawing, photography, art history, and writing are offered. A two-week trip to Mali, Africa, is also offered during the winter break.

High school students can experience life at Montserrat through the summer Pre-College program, which takes place in July on the College's campus. This four-week program is primarily for students entering their sophomore, junior, or senior year of high school and is designed to help young artists evaluate a career in the arts and develop a portfolio suitable for college admission. Students participate in assignments and critiques led by top instructors from Montserrat and other Boston-area colleges and, upon completion of the program, earn 3 college credits.

Moore College of Art & Design

Philadelphia, Pennsylvania

Independent, women only. Urban campus. Art program established 1848.

Degrees Bachelor of Fine Arts in the areas of art education, art history, fine arts, fashion design, illustration, interior design, graphic design, textile design, curatorial studies, photography, digital arts. Majors and concentrations: art education, art history, curatorial studies, fashion design, graphic design, illustration, interior design, photography/digital arts, textile arts, three-dimensional studies, two-dimensional studies. Program accredited by NASAD, CIDA.

Enrollment 546 total; 507 undergraduate, 39 graduate.

Art Student Profile 99% females, 1% males, 26% minorities, 2% international.

Art Faculty 32 undergraduate (full-time), 77 undergraduate (part-time). 66% of full-time faculty have terminal degrees. Graduate students do not teach undergraduate courses. Undergraduate student–faculty ratio: 8:1.

Student Life Student groups/activities include senior show/student show, fashion show, Moore Magazine. Special housing available for art students.

Expenses for 2007–2008 Application fee: $40. Comprehensive fee: $36,060 includes full-time tuition ($25,290), mandatory fees ($864), and college room and board ($9906). College room only: $5964. Full-time tuition and fees vary according to student level. Room and board charges vary according to board plan and housing facility.

Financial Aid Program-specific awards: 1 Evelyn A. Whittaker Award for those demonstrating need and talent ($15,000), 100 Moore College of Art and Design Presidential and Merit Awards for academically and artistically talented students ($500–$4000), 10 W. W. Smith Awards for those demonstrating talent and academic achievement ($2000), 1 Moore Col-

lege of Art and Design Partnership Award for Philadelphia public school applicants demonstrating need ($15,000), 8 Sarah Peters Awards for talented freshmen ($500), 2–4 Appleman Awards for adult students demonstrating need/talent ($10,000–$12,500), 8 Fred and Naomi Hazell Awards for oil painters demonstrating need/talent ($16,000), 1 Charming Shops Scholarship for fashion/textile design juniors and seniors ($2000), 1 Kristen McCabe Memorial Award for talented junior or senior graphic design majors ($500).

Application Procedures Students apply for admission into the professional program by sophomore year. Deadline for freshmen and transfers: continuous. Notification date for freshmen and transfers: August 15. Required: high school transcript, college transcript(s) for transfer students, minimum 2.0 high school GPA, letter of recommendation, portfolio, SAT or ACT test scores (minimum composite ACT score of 17). Recommended: essay, interview. Portfolio reviews held continuously on campus and off campus at National Portfolio Days; the submission of slides may be substituted for portfolios when distance is prohibitive.

Web Site http://www.moore.edu

Undergraduate Contact Ms. Heeseung Lee, Director of Admissions, Admissions, Moore College of Art & Design, 20th and The Parkway, Philadelphia, Pennsylvania 19103-1179; 215-568-4515 ext. 1107, fax: 215-568-3547, e-mail address: admiss@moore.edu

More About the College

Moore College of Art & Design sets the standard of excellence in educating women for careers in art and design. As the first and only women's college of the visual arts in the nation, founded in 1848, Moore students enjoy an accessible, supportive small college community and learn from a dedicated faculty of award-winning artists, designers, and scholars.

With an average of 500 students and a 9:1 student-to-faculty member ratio, Moore offers ten Bachelor of Fine Arts majors in art education, art history, curatorial studies, fashion design, fine arts (with 2-D and/or 3-D emphasis), graphic design, illustration, interior design, photography and digital arts, and textile design. Career and leadership skills are emphasized throughout the academic programs, with each major providing extensive career preparation for their respective fields.

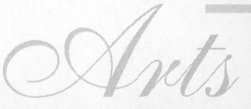

Moore College of Art & Design (continued)

The Locks Career Center for Women in the Arts facilitates internships for students to gain practical professional experience. The Locks Career Center also provides a broad range of career resources for students and alumnae, such as one-on-one career counseling, mentoring, job bulletins, and workshops on topics from networking to resume writing.

On-campus leadership organizations provide the chance to learn about and utilize leadership skills, and to develop self-confidence. Leadership fellowship opportunities provide financial support for students to work, either with an individual leader in the arts community or within an innovative organization. Other experiences are available through community service or study abroad.

Moore's size creates a community experience where students live and learn in a comfortable, supportive environment—one where students from different majors, backgrounds, cultures, and lifestyles can learn from each other. The campus includes Sarah Peter Hall, Wilson Hall, Stahl Residence Hall, and Sartain Hall. The main campus includes expansive studios and classrooms, technology centers, two auditoriums, Fox Commons, MAC and PC computer labs, a professional woodshop, ferrous and nonferrous metal workshops, ceramic studios with indoor and outdoor kilns, abundant student exhibition space, two contemporary art galleries, several outdoor courtyards, and the dining café. The Connolly Library's holdings feature 40,000 monographs, Internet access, 185 art journals, a slide collection of more than 123,000 images, and picture files of 300,000 images.

The support system and friendships formed by living in college housing often help ease first-year students' transition into the college setting. Approximately 70 percent of first-year students live in College housing, which includes Stahl Residence Hall and Sartain Hall. Other students choose to live off campus. There are numerous apartments in Philadelphia's neighboring residential areas.

Moore graduates become part of and have access to a broad network of fellow alumnae of accomplished artists, designers, and creative leaders in a wide variety of industries. Among Moore's notable graduates are fashion designer and business icon Adrienne Vittadini; renowned twentieth-century portraitist Alice Neel; award-winning interior designer Karon Daroff; and Pulitzer Prize-winning photojournalist Sharon J. Wohlmuth.

Moore College of Art & Design is accredited by the Commission on Higher Education of the Middle States Association of Colleges and Schools, 3624 Market Street, Philadelphia, Pennsylvania 19104-2680, 215-662-5606. The Commission on Higher Education is an institutional accrediting agency recognized by the U.S. Secretary of Education and the Commission on Recognition of Postsecondary Accreditation; by the National Association of Schools of Art and Design, 11250 Roger Bacon Drive, Suite 21, Reston, Virginia 20190, 703-437-0700; by the Commonwealth of Pennsylvania, Department of Education, 333 Market Street, Harrisburg, Pennsylvania 17126-0333, 717-787-5820; and by the Foundation for Interior Design Education Research, 146 Monroe Center NW, #1318, Grand Rapids, Michigan 49503-2822, 616-458-0400.

Mount Allison University
Sackville, New Brunswick, Canada

Province-supported, coed. Small town campus. Total enrollment: 2,240. Art program established 1941.

Degrees Bachelor of Fine Arts. Majors and concentrations: open media, painting/drawing, photography, printmaking, sculpture. Cross-registration with Université de Strasbourg (France), Universitöt Tubingen (Germany).

Enrollment 127 total; all undergraduate.

Art Student Profile 95% females, 5% males, 16% international.

Art Faculty 7 undergraduate (full-time), 3 undergraduate (part-time). 86% of full-time faculty have terminal degrees. Graduate students do not teach undergraduate courses. Undergraduate student–faculty ratio: 18:1.

Student Life Student groups/activities include Fine Arts Society.

Expenses for 2006–2007 Application fee: $50 Canadian dollars. Tuition, fee, and room and board charges are reported in Canadian dollars. Province resident tuition: $6405 full-time. Mandatory fees: $245 full-time. Full-time tuition and fees vary according to course load. College room and board: $6795. College room only: $3530. Room and board charges vary according to board plan. International student tuition: $12,810 full-time.

Financial Aid Program-specific awards: 1 Pulford Award for freshmen program majors ($1000), 1–2 Chang Awards for senior program majors ($500–$1000), 1 Crake Award for graduating students ($500), 2 Gairdner Awards for top program majors ($1000), University Scholarships for those in top 10% of program ($750).

Application Procedures Students admitted directly into the professional program freshman year. Deadline for freshmen: April 1; transfers: July 5. Notification date for freshmen and transfers: continuous. Required: high school transcript, college transcript(s) for transfer students, minimum 3.0 high school GPA, 2 letters of recommendation, portfolio. Portfolio reviews held once on campus; the submission of slides may be substituted for portfolios at student's discretion, (CD/DVD also accepted).

Web Site http://www.mta.ca/faculty/arts-letters/finearts/

Undergraduate Contact Mr. Matt Sheridan-Jonah, Manager of Admissions, Scholarships and Financial Aid, Student Services, Mount Allison University, 65 York Street, Sackville, New Brunswick E4L 1E4, Canada; 506-364-3294, fax: 506-364-2272, e-mail address: mjonah@mta.ca

Murray State University

Murray, Kentucky

State-supported, coed. Small town campus. Total enrollment: 10,298. Art program established 1926.

Degrees Bachelor of Fine Arts in the areas of studio art, art education. Majors and concentrations: art education, ceramics, graphic design, jewelry and metalsmithing, painting/drawing, photography, printmaking, sculpture, wood. Program accredited by NASAD, NCATE.

Enrollment 178 total; 89 undergraduate, 89 nonprofessional degree.

Art Student Profile 65% females, 35% males, 8% minorities, 3% international.

Art Faculty 14 undergraduate (full-time), 2 undergraduate (part-time). 100% of full-time faculty have terminal degrees. Graduate students do not teach undergraduate courses. Undergraduate student–faculty ratio: 14:1.

Student Life Student groups/activities include Organization of Murray Art Students.

Expenses for 2007–2008 Application fee: $30. State resident tuition: $4650 full-time. Nonresident tuition: $6728 full-time. Mandatory fees: $768 full-time. Full-time tuition and fees vary according to reciprocity agreements. College room and board: $5670. College room only: $3036. Room and board charges vary according to board plan. Special program-related fees: $14 per credit hour for supplies and equipment.

Financial Aid Program-specific awards: 15–20 Department of Art Scholarships for program majors ($500–$2500).

Application Procedures Students admitted directly into the professional program freshman year. Deadline for freshmen and transfers: continuous. Required: high school transcript, college transcript(s) for transfer students, ACT test score only.

Web Site http://www.murraystate.edu

Undergraduate Contact Mr. Dick Dougherty, Chair, Department of Art, Murray State University, 604 Fine Arts Building, Murray, Kentucky 42071-3342; 270-809-3784, fax: 270-809-3920, e-mail address: dick.dougherty@murraystate.edu

Myers School of Art

See The University of Akron

The New England School of Art & Design

See Suffolk University

New Hampshire Institute of Art

Manchester, New Hampshire

Proprietary, coed. Urban campus. Art program established 1997.

Degrees Bachelor of Fine Arts. Majors and concentrations: ceramics, illustration, interdisciplinary studies, painting, photography. Program accredited by NASAD.

Enrollment 286 undergraduate.

Art Student Profile 70% females, 30% males, 3% minorities, 1% international.

Art Faculty 16 undergraduate (full-time), 42 undergraduate (part-time). 85% of full-time faculty have terminal degrees. Graduate students do not teach undergraduate courses. Undergraduate student–faculty ratio: 10:1.

Visual Arts

New Hampshire Institute of Art (continued)

Student Life Student groups/activities include Gallery Committee, Student Council, student reviews/exhibition. Special housing available for art students.

Expenses for 2006–2007 Application fee: $25. Tuition: $11,950 full-time. Mandatory fees: $1290 full-time. College room only: $6000. Room charges vary according to housing facility. Special program-related fees: $30 per semester for registration fee, $40 per semester for student activity fee, $50 per semester for technology fee, $175 per semester for supplemental lab fee, $600 per semester for studio fee.

Financial Aid Program-specific awards: Founders Award for outstanding applicants, Fuller Merit Award for students with outstanding portfolios, Gakidis Award for current, non-traditional students, Housing Award for students with financial need, NHIA Scholastic Art Awards Top Portfolio, Presidential Award for students with outstanding portfolio and GPA, Transfer Award for students with a minimum of 24 college credits, Paul and Anne Harvey Award for nominated current students, John Hubenthal Award for nominated junior/senior students.

Application Procedures Students admitted directly into the professional program freshman year. Deadline for freshmen and transfers: continuous. Required: essay, high school transcript, college transcript(s) for transfer students, 2 letters of recommendation, interview, portfolio. Recommended: minimum 2.0 high school GPA, SAT or ACT test scores. Portfolio reviews held ongoing on campus and off campus in several locations; the submission of slides may be substituted for portfolios applicant is unable to visit campus for a portfolio review.

Web Site http://www.nhia.edu

Undergraduate Contact Amanda Abbott, Admissions Administrator, Admissions, New Hampshire Institute of Art, 148 Concord Street, Manchester, New Hampshire 03104; 603-836-2576, fax: 603-647-0658, e-mail address: aabbott@nhia.edu

New Mexico Highlands University

Las Vegas, New Mexico

State-supported, coed. Small town campus. Total enrollment: 3,750.

Degrees Bachelor of Fine Arts. Majors and concentrations: ceramics, drawing, foundry, jewelry, metals, painting, photography, printmaking, sculpture, studio art, visual communication.

Art Faculty 2 undergraduate (full-time), 5 undergraduate (part-time). 100% of full-time faculty have terminal degrees. Graduate students do not teach undergraduate courses.

Student Life Student groups/activities include Crossroads Art Club.

Expenses for 2006–2007 Application fee: $15. State resident tuition: $2424 full-time. Nonresident tuition: $3636 full-time. Mandatory fees: $20 full-time. Full-time tuition and fees vary according to course load and location. College room and board: $4476. College room only: $2056. Room and board charges vary according to board plan and housing facility. Special program-related fees: $25–$45 per course for specific studio courses.

Financial Aid Program-specific awards: Lorraine Schula Outstanding Art Student Award for junior/senior program majors.

Application Procedures Students admitted directly into the professional program freshman year. Deadline for freshmen and transfers: May 15. Notification date for freshmen and transfers: continuous. Required: high school transcript, college transcript(s) for transfer students, minimum 2.0 high school GPA, portfolio, SAT or ACT test scores. Portfolio reviews held twice on campus.

Web Site http://www.nmhu.edu

Undergraduate Contact Ms. Melissa A. Williamson, Administrative Secretary, Department of Communication and Fine Arts, New Mexico Highlands University, Burris Hall, Las Vegas, New Mexico 87701; 505-454-3024, fax: 505-454-3241, e-mail address: mawilliamson@nmhu.edu

Visual *Arts*

New Mexico State University

Las Cruces, New Mexico

State-supported, coed. Suburban campus. Total enrollment: 16,415. Art program established 1948.

Degrees Bachelor of Fine Arts in the area of studio art. Majors and concentrations: ceramic art and design, graphic design, jewelry and metalsmithing, painting/drawing, photography, printmaking, sculpture. Graduate degrees offered: Master of Arts in the areas of studio art, art history; Master of Fine Arts in the area of studio art.

Enrollment 302 total; 272 undergraduate, 30 graduate.

Art Student Profile 55% females, 45% males, 30% minorities.

Art Faculty 12 total (full-time), 4 total (part-time). 100% of full-time faculty have terminal degrees. Graduate students teach a few undergraduate courses. Undergraduate student–faculty ratio: 15:1.

Student Life Special housing available for art students.

Expenses for 2006–2007 Application fee: $15. State resident tuition: $3164 full-time. Nonresident tuition: $12,738 full-time. Mandatory fees: $1066 full-time. College room and board: $5576. College room only: $3226. Room and board charges vary according to board plan and gender.

Financial Aid Program-specific awards: 1 Jose Cisneros Student Travel Award for art students ($400), 2 Mary Lawbaugh Awards for art students ($400), 10 Janet Swenson Memorial Awards for art students ($500), 6 Dodier Awards for art students ($2000).

Application Procedures Students admitted directly into the professional program freshman year. Deadline for freshmen and transfers: August 14. Required: high school transcript, college transcript(s) for transfer students, minimum 2.0 high school GPA, SAT or ACT test scores.

Web Site http://www.nmsu.edu/~artdept

Contact Mr. Spencer Fidler, Head, Art Department, New Mexico State University, Box 30001, Department 3572, Las Cruces, New Mexico 88003-0001; 505-646-1705, fax: 505-646-8036, e-mail address: artdept@nmsu.edu

The New School: A University

See Parsons The New School for Design

New World School of the Arts

Miami, Florida

State-supported, coed. Urban campus. Total enrollment: 400. Art program established 1988.

Degrees Bachelor of Fine Arts in the area of visual art. Majors and concentrations: drawing, electronic intermedia, graphic design, painting, photography, printmaking, sculpture. Mandatory cross-registration with University of Florida, Miami Dade College. Program accredited by NASAD.

Enrollment 174 total; all undergraduate.

Art Student Profile 54% females, 46% males, 76% minorities, 2% international.

Art Faculty 5 undergraduate (full-time), 13 undergraduate (part-time). 100% of full-time faculty have terminal degrees. Graduate students do not teach undergraduate courses. Undergraduate student–faculty ratio: 11:1.

Student Life Student groups/activities include juried art shows.

Expenses for 2007–2008 Application fee: $0. State resident tuition: $3000 full-time. Nonresident tuition: $10,000 full-time.

Financial Aid Program-specific awards: 4 Nation's Bank Merit Scholarships for program majors ($2000), 6 Ronnie Bogaev Merit Scholarships for female in-state program majors ($2000), 18 Frances Wolfson Merit Scholarships for program majors ($2000), 15 Miami-Dade College Scholarships for program majors ($1000).

Application Procedures Students admitted directly into the professional program freshman year. Deadline for freshmen and transfers: continuous. Notification date for freshmen and transfers: continuous. Required: essay, high school transcript, college transcript(s) for

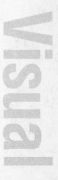

Visual *Arts*

New World School of the Arts (continued)

transfer students, 2 letters of recommendation, portfolio. Recommended: minimum 2.0 high school GPA, interview, SAT or ACT test scores. Portfolio reviews held continuously on campus and off campus in various locations in Florida; the submission of slides may be substituted for portfolios when distance is prohibitive.

Web Site http://www.mdc.edu/nwsa

Undergraduate Contact Pamela Neumann, Recruitment and Admissions Coordinator, Student Services, New World School of the Arts, 300 NE 2nd Avenue, Miami, Florida 33132; 305-237-7007, fax: 305-237-3794, e-mail address: nwsaadm@mdc.edu

Midge Karr Fine Art Department
New York Institute of Technology
Old Westbury, New York

Independent, coed. Suburban campus. Total enrollment: 11,404. Art program established 1960.

Degrees Bachelor of Fine Arts in the areas of computer graphics, graphic design, art education. Majors and concentrations: art education, computer graphics, graphic design. Graduate degrees offered: Master of Fine Arts in the areas of computer graphics, fine art, graphic design.

Enrollment 250 undergraduate, 30 graduate.

Art Student Profile 55% females, 45% males, 25% minorities, 20% international.

Art Faculty 8 undergraduate (full-time), 30 undergraduate (part-time). 100% of full-time faculty have terminal degrees. Graduate students do not teach undergraduate courses. Undergraduate student–faculty ratio: 7:1.

Student Life Student groups/activities include American Society of Interior Designers, Digital Sculpture Club, Computer Graphics Club.

Expenses for 2006–2007 Application fee: $50. Comprehensive fee: $31,810 includes full-time tuition ($19,818), mandatory fees ($540), and college room and board ($11,452). Full-time tuition and fees vary according to course load and program. Room and board charges vary according to board plan, housing facility, and location. Special program-related fees: $10–$40 per course for studio supplies.

Financial Aid Program-specific awards: Presidential Awards for academically qualified applicants ($2200–$2600), Academic Achievement Awards for academically qualified applicants ($1200–$1800), Academic Incentive Awards for academically qualified applicants ($600).

Application Procedures Students admitted directly into the professional program freshman year. Deadline for freshmen and transfers: continuous. Required: essay, high school transcript, college transcript(s) for transfer students, minimum 2.0 high school GPA, interview, portfolio, SAT or ACT test scores. Recommended: 2 letters of recommendation. Portfolio reviews held continuously on campus and off campus in New York, NY; the submission of slides may be substituted for portfolios for out-of-state applicants.

Web Site http://www.nyit.edu

Undergraduate Contact Mr. Emanuel Saladino, Administrative Assistant, Midge Karr Fine Art Department, New York Institute of Technology, PO Box 8000, Old Westbury, New York 11568-8000; 516-686-7542, fax: 516-686-7428, e-mail address: esaladin@nyit.edu

New York School of Interior Design
New York, New York

Independent, coed, primarily women. Urban campus. Total enrollment: 736. Art program established 1916.

Degrees Bachelor of Fine Arts in the area of interior design. Majors and concentrations: interior design. Graduate degrees offered: Master of Fine Arts in the area of interior design. Program accredited by NASAD, CIDA.

Enrollment 719 total; 161 undergraduate, 19 graduate, 539 nonprofessional degree.

Art Student Profile 82% females, 18% males, 22% minorities, 10% international.

Art Faculty 4 total (full-time), 71 total (part-time). 35% of full-time faculty have terminal degrees. Graduate students do not teach undergraduate courses. Undergraduate student–faculty ratio: 10:1.

Student Life Student groups/activities include American Society of Interior Designers Student Chapter.

Expenses for 2007–2008 Application fee: $50. Tuition: $20,460 full-time. Mandatory fees: $290 full-time. Full-time tuition and fees vary according to course load.

Financial Aid Program-specific awards: 50 Institutional and Endowed Scholarships for program majors ($1000–$10,000).

Application Procedures Students admitted directly into the professional program freshman year. Deadline for freshmen and transfers: continuous. Required: essay, high school transcript, college transcript(s) for transfer students, minimum 2.0 high school GPA, 2 letters of recommendation, portfolio, SAT or ACT test scores (minimum combined SAT score of 1500, minimum composite ACT score of 20). Recommended: minimum 3.0 high school GPA, interview. Portfolio reviews held continuously on campus and off campus in various college fairs; the submission of slides may be substituted for portfolios when distance is prohibitive.

Web Site http://www.nysid.edu

Contact Mr. David T. Sprouls, Director of Admissions, New York School of Interior Design, 170 East 70th Street, New York, New York 10021; 212-472-1500 ext. 202, fax: 212-472-1867, e-mail address: admissions@nysid.edu

More About the School

Throughout its history, the New York School of Interior Design (NYSID) has devoted all of its resources to a single field of study—interior design. NYSID is specifically designed for those who wish to pursue a career in one or more of the various fields of interior design and wish to do so under the guidance of a faculty consisting of practicing designers, architects, and art and architectural historians. The various academic programs comprise an integrated curriculum covering architecture, design problem solving, history of art, interior design concepts, interiors and furniture, materials and methods, philosophy and theory, professional design procedures, and technical and communication skills.

Because of its select faculty and established reputation, the School continues to maintain a close relationship with the interior design industry. This provides an excellent means for students to develop associations that offer opportunities to move into the profession after completing their degree program at NYSID.

Many of the world's most important museums, galleries, and showrooms are within walking distance. The city is world-renowned for its cultural activities, architecture, historic districts, and cosmopolitan urban experience.

NYSID is located on a quiet, tree-lined street in Manhattan's landmark Upper East Side Historic District. The School has two auditorium spaces, light-filled studios and classrooms, a CAD lab, and a lighting design lab. NYSID also has a library containing a comprehensive collection of books, journals, periodicals, and trade and auction catalogs specifically devoted to the interior design field and related fine arts; a materials library; an atelier; two galleries; a rooftop terrace; and a café, bookstore, and student lounge.

NYSID has an active student chapter of the American Society of Interior Designers (ASID). ASID organizes lectures, tours, workshops, and other events throughout the school year, providing an inside view of the interior design industry.

One of the strengths of NYSID is its gallery exhibitions relating to architecture and design. Open to both students and the public, the gallery has mounted such acclaimed shows as *Designers Salute Edith Wharton and The Mount; Albert Hadley: Drawings and the Design Process;* and *Bob the Roman: Heroic Antiquity and the Architecture of Robert Adam.* The School also sponsors lectures and symposia. Guest lecturers have included Mario Buatta, Charlotte Moss, Albert Hadley, Eric Cohler, John Saladino, Clodagh, and David Garrard Lowe. Students are encouraged to attend the lecture series.

The School maintains an active placement service for graduates and current students. Many students find work while still at NYSID. Because of its reputation in the design field, many NYSID graduates are employed in the best design, architectural, and industry-related firms in New York City, across the United States, and around the world.

Steinhardt School of Culture, Education, and Human Development, Department of Art and Art Professions
New York University
New York, New York

Independent, coed. Urban campus. Total enrollment: 40,870.

Degrees Bachelor of Fine Arts in the area of studio art. Majors and concentrations: studio

New York University (continued)

art. Graduate degrees offered: Master of Arts in the areas of studio art (3-summer program), visual culture: theory, visual culture: costume studies, art education, visual arts administration, art therapy; Master of Fine Arts in the area of studio art. Doctor of Philosophy in the area of visual culture and education.

Enrollment 469 total; 212 undergraduate, 257 graduate.

Art Student Profile 80% females, 20% males, 26% minorities, 13% international.

Art Faculty 16 total (full-time), 89 total (part-time). 81% of full-time faculty have terminal degrees. Graduate students teach a few undergraduate courses. Undergraduate student–faculty ratio: 2:1.

Student Life Student groups/activities include gallery exhibitions, lectures, performances, panels, symposia with visiting artists and scholars, courses in partnership with Costume Institute of the Metropolitan Museum of Art and others.

Expenses for 2007–2008 Application fee: $65. Comprehensive fee: $47,490 includes full-time tuition ($33,268), mandatory fees ($2022), and college room and board ($12,200). Full-time tuition and fees vary according to course load and program. Room and board charges vary according to board plan and housing facility. Special program-related fees: $250 per semester for lab fees.

Financial Aid Program-specific awards: Art Talent Scholarships for BFA candidates.

Application Procedures Students admitted directly into the professional program freshman year. Deadline for freshmen: January 15; transfers: April 1. Notification date for freshmen: April 1; transfers: September 1. Required: essay, high school transcript, college transcript(s) for transfer students, 3 letters of recommendation, portfolio, SAT or ACT test scores, TOEFL score for non-native English speakers, strong high school GPA. Portfolio reviews held on campus and off campus in venues in New York State; the submission of slides may be substituted for portfolios.

Web Site http://www.steinhardt.nyu.edu/

Undergraduate Contact Ms. Candice MacLusky, Assistant Director of Undergraduate Admissions, New York University, 22 Washington Square North, New York, New York 10011-9191; 212-998-4500, fax: 212-995-4902.

Graduate Contact Mr. John Myers, Director of Enrollment Services, Office of Graduate Admissions, New York University, 82 Washington Square East, New York, New York 10003-6680; 212-998-5030, fax: 212-995-4328, e-mail address: steinhardt.gradadmissions@nyu.edu

More About the University

NYU's Steinhardt School of Culture, Education, and Human Development offers a diverse range of undergraduate and graduate programs in applied psychology, art, communication, education, health, and music. Our School has a long history of connecting theory to applied learning experiences through dozens of affiliations and partnerships with urban institutions, building communities within and beyond our classrooms, and nurturing the human spirit. Our faculty members are intellectually adventurous and socially conscious. Our students study in the expansive environment of a great research university, and use the urban neighborhoods of New York City and countries around the world as their laboratories. Now in our 117th year of educating professionals, scholars, and researchers, we are applying our creativity and knowledge where it is needed most.

Located in the heart of downtown New York, NYU Steinhardt's Department of Art and Art Professions is shaped by the intensity and innovation of the international art world. A home for artists who are celebrated for their dedication, creativity, and skill in exploring unconventional ideas, New York City has long been a place where art truly matters. The city's galleries, museums, schools, studios, and performance spaces are an integral part of our department, as are the University's vast intellectual and academic resources.

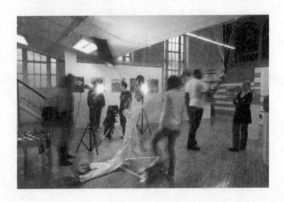

The Department's Barney Building, a six-story complex of studios, classrooms, and exhibition spaces—as well as facilities for painting, drawing, sculpture, craft media, printmaking, photography, video, and digital art—pays homage to the visionary and iconoclastic artists of its legendary East Village neighborhood. Enriched by this legacy, the Department's interdisciplinary approach to art, with its commitment to individual insight and experimentation as well as collaboration and community practice, underscores the central role of contemporary art in translating social and historical change into human experience. We seek to nurture and empower our students and artists to find a visual language through which they can respond to current culture on their own terms.

The B.F.A. combines an ambitious series of interdisciplinary studio courses with art history, seminar, and liberal arts classes to expose students to a wide range of ideas and practices. Many participate in internships during the junior and senior years, and one semester of study abroad is encouraged. In the senior year, students take the course Art, Culture, and Society, which culminates in a written thesis. With special permission, students may also enroll in a senior honors section of the Undergraduate Projects course. In addition to participating in group critiques, students meet independently in their studio workspace with two senior mentors and visiting artists. Over the course of the year, students develop a cohesive body of work as well as a written thesis outlining the ideas and contexts that drive their creative process. In the spring, students participate in a formal exhibition in the Rosenberg Gallery.

The M.F.A. and M.A. programs bring exceptional students together with artists, educators, therapists, administrators, and visual culture innovators who influence the visual arts at local, national, and international levels. The Department offers top graduate-level internship and field placement experiences with unparalleled networking potential. Recent internships have included the Metropolitan Museum of Art, the Museum of Modern Art, the Whitney Museum of American Art, the New Museum, P.S. 1, Art in General, Percent for Art, Creative Time, Christie's, Sotheby's, and prominent galleries and artists' studios.

The Department is a work in progress, bringing exceptional students together with internationally renowned artists, critics, educators, and art professionals in a shared exploration of the issues, forms, and ideas that continually redefine contemporary art.

Faculty, Resident Artists, and Alumni Faculty members are artists, educators, and professionals who are recognized nationally and internationally for their expertise and accomplishments. Faculty artists show extensively worldwide and represent broadly diverse approaches to content and media. Faculty arts professionals influence arts policy and practice.

Student Exhibition Opportunities Undergraduate and graduate students have many exhibition opportunities throughout the department and can submit proposals to participate as curators and exhibitors in the Rosenberg Gallery and the Commons. Barney Building open houses and open studios are organized twice a year, and all students are encouraged to participate. The Department's 80 Washington Square East Galleries provide excellent professional exhibition space in the heart of the campus.

Special Programs Undergraduates are encouraged to enroll in one of several excellent University-based study-abroad programs in Berlin, Florence, Ghana, London, Madrid, Paris, Prague, and Shanghai. Graduate summer-study-abroad programs include studio art in Venice; photography in China; visual arts culture in Cape Town and Pretoria, South Africa; and arts administration in the Netherlands and Berlin. A high school residential summer art intensive allows young artists ages 16 to 18 the opportunity to explore their ideas in the heart of the international art world.

Tisch School of the Arts - Department of Photography and Imaging
New York University
New York, New York

Independent, coed. Urban campus. Total enrollment: 40,870. Art program established 1965.

Degrees Bachelor of Fine Arts. Majors and concentrations: photography and imaging.

Enrollment 130 total; all undergraduate.

Art Student Profile 63% females, 37% males, 20% minorities, 5% international.

Art Faculty 10 undergraduate (full-time), 20 undergraduate (part-time). 50% of full-time faculty have terminal degrees. Graduate students do not teach undergraduate courses. Undergraduate student–faculty ratio: 4:1.

Student Life Student groups/activities include Community Connections, The Collective, Tisch Talent Guild.

New York University (continued)

Expenses for 2007–2008 Application fee: $65. Comprehensive fee: $47,490 includes full-time tuition ($33,268), mandatory fees ($2022), and college room and board ($12,200). Full-time tuition and fees vary according to course load and program. Room and board charges vary according to board plan and housing facility. Special program-related fees: $255 per course for photo lab fee.

Application Procedures Students admitted directly into the professional program freshman year. Deadline for freshmen: January 15; transfers: April 1. Notification date for freshmen: April 1; transfers: May 15. Required: essay, high school transcript, college transcript(s) for transfer students, 2 letters of recommendation, portfolio, SAT or ACT test scores, resumé, department questionnaire. Recommended: minimum 3.0 high school GPA.

Web Site http://photo.tisch.nyu.edu

Undergraduate Contact Ms. Patricia A. Decker, Director of Recruitment, Tisch School of the Arts, New York University, 721 Broadway, 8th Floor, New York, New York 10003-6807; 212-998-1900, fax: 212-995-4060.

North Carolina School of the Arts

Winston-Salem, North Carolina

State-supported, coed. Urban campus. Total enrollment: 845. Art program established 1990.

Degrees Bachelor of Fine Arts in the area of filmmaking. Majors and concentrations: cinematography, directing, editing and sound, production, production/design, screenwriting.

Enrollment 243 total; 204 undergraduate, 39 nonprofessional degree.

Art Student Profile 29% females, 71% males, 17% minorities, 2% international.

Art Faculty 25 undergraduate (full-time), 2 undergraduate (part-time), 2 graduate (full-time). 14% of full-time faculty have terminal degrees. Graduate students do not teach undergraduate courses. Undergraduate student–faculty ratio: 10:1.

Student Life Special housing available for art students.

Expenses for 2006–2007 Application fee: $50. State resident tuition: $3074 full-time. Nonresident tuition: $14,354 full-time. Mandatory fees: $1817 full-time. Full-time tuition and fees vary according to program. College room and board: $6139. College room only: $3189. Room and board charges vary according to board plan and housing facility. Special program-related fees: $750 per year for supplies.

Financial Aid Program-specific awards: 100 talent/need scholarships ($1879).

Application Procedures Students admitted directly into the professional program freshman year. Deadline for freshmen and transfers: March 1. Required: essay, high school transcript, college transcript(s) for transfer students, 2 letters of recommendation, interview, audition, on-site writing exercise. Recommended: SAT or ACT test scores.

Web Site http://www.ncarts.edu

Undergraduate Contact Ms. Sheeler Lawson, Director of Admissions, North Carolina School of the Arts, 1533 South Main Street, Winston-Salem, North Carolina 27117; 336-770-3291, fax: 336-770-3370, e-mail address: admissions@ncarts.edu

Northern Illinois University

De Kalb, Illinois

State-supported, coed. Small town campus. Total enrollment: 25,313.

Degrees Bachelor of Arts in the areas of art history, art; Bachelor of Fine Arts in the area of studio and design; Bachelor of Science in the area of art education. Majors and concentrations: art education, art history, art/fine arts, ceramics, fibers, illustration, metals and jewelry, painting/drawing, photography, printmaking, sculpture, time arts, visual communication. Graduate degrees offered: Master of Arts in the area of studio art and design; Master of Fine Arts in the area of studio and design; Master of Science in Education in the area of art education. Cross-registration with twelve Illinois community colleges. Program accredited by NASAD.

Enrollment 690 undergraduate, 124 graduate, 109 nonprofessional degree.

Art Student Profile 59% females, 41% males, 6% minorities, 1% international.

Art Faculty 41 total (full-time), 21 total (part-time). 90% of full-time faculty have terminal degrees. Graduate students teach a few undergraduate courses. Undergraduate student–faculty ratio: 16:1.

Student Life Student groups/activities include National Art Education Association Student Chapter, American Institute of Graphic Arts Student Chapter, Ars Nova Student Group. Special housing available for art students.

Expenses for 2007–2008 State resident tuition: $5940 full-time. Nonresident tuition: $12,500 full-time. Mandatory fees: $1515 full-time. College room and board: $7568. Room and board charges vary according to board plan and housing facility. Special program-related fees: $5–$126 per course for lab/materials fees/visiting artists and scholars/technology.

Financial Aid Program-specific awards: 6–12 tuition scholarships for entering first year students ($2362–$3148).

Application Procedures Students admitted directly into the professional program freshman year. Deadline for freshmen and transfers: continuous. Notification date for freshmen and transfers: continuous. Required: high school transcript, college transcript(s) for transfer students, minimum 2.0 high school GPA, SAT or ACT test scores (minimum composite ACT score of 19), standing in top half of graduating class, completion of college preparatory courses.

Web Site http://www.vpa.niu.edu/art/

Undergraduate Contact Office of Admissions, Northern Illinois University, Williston Hall Room 101, De Kalb, Illinois 60115; 815-753-0446, fax: 815-753-1783, e-mail address: admissions-info@niu.edu

Graduate Contact Yale Factor, Coordinator of Graduate Program, School of Art, Northern Illinois University, De Kalb, Illinois 60115-2883; 815-753-0292.

Northern Kentucky University

Highland Heights, Kentucky

State-supported, coed. Suburban campus. Total enrollment: 14,617. Art program established 1968.

Degrees Bachelor of Fine Arts in the areas of graphic design, intermedia, art history with studio. Majors and concentrations: applied photography, art education, art history, ceramics, graphic design, intermedia, painting/drawing, photography, printmaking, sculpture. Cross-registration with Northern Kentucky/Greater Cincinnati Consortium of Colleges and Universities.

Enrollment 410 total; 60 undergraduate, 350 nonprofessional degree.

Art Student Profile 60% females, 40% males, 2% minorities, 1% international.

Art Faculty 19 undergraduate (full-time), 7 undergraduate (part-time). 90% of full-time faculty have terminal degrees. Graduate students do not teach undergraduate courses. Undergraduate student–faculty ratio: 17:1.

Student Life Student groups/activities include Students in Design, Mudd Club, Photography Club.

Expenses for 2006–2007 Application fee: $40. State resident tuition: $5448 full-time. Nonresident tuition: $10,200 full-time. Full-time tuition varies according to course load, location, program, and reciprocity agreements. College room and board: $5690. College room only: $3450. Room and board charges vary according to board plan, housing facility, and location. Special program-related fees: $20–$200 per semester for incidental fee, technology fee, and support of learning surcharge.

Financial Aid Program-specific awards: 1–2 Friends of Fine Arts Awards for continuing students ($2500), 6 University Art Awards for continuing students ($2500), 1 Schiff Scholarship for continuing students ($2500).

Application Procedures Students apply for admission into the professional program by sophomore, junior year. Deadline for freshmen and transfers: August 1. Required: high school transcript, college transcript(s) for transfer students, minimum 2.0 high school GPA, ACT test score only, minimum 2.5 college GPA with a 3.0 art major GPA.

Web Site http://www.nku.edu/~art

Undergraduate Contact Thomas McGovern, Office of Admissions, Northern Kentucky University, Lucas Administrative Center, Highland Heights, Kentucky 41099; 859-572-5220, fax: 859-572-6665, e-mail address: admitnku@nku.edu

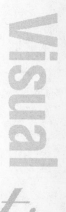

Visual Arts

Northwestern State University of Louisiana

Natchitoches, Louisiana

State-supported, coed. Small town campus. Total enrollment: 9,431.

Degrees Bachelor of Fine Arts in the area of fine and graphic arts. Majors and concentrations: graphic communication, studio art. Program accredited by NASAD.

Enrollment 112 total; all undergraduate.

Art Student Profile 60% females, 40% males, 20% minorities, 5% international.

Art Faculty 7 total (full-time), 1 total (part-time). 83% of full-time faculty have terminal degrees. Graduate students teach a few undergraduate courses. Undergraduate student–faculty ratio: 16:1.

Student Life Student groups/activities include Kappa Pi International Art Fraternity (Gamma Mu Chapter), Student Art Show. Special housing available for art students.

Expenses for 2006–2007 Application fee: $20. State resident tuition: $2240 full-time. Nonresident tuition: $8318 full-time. Mandatory fees: $1313 full-time. Full-time tuition and fees vary according to course load. College room and board: $4686. College room only: $2816. Room and board charges vary according to board plan, housing facility, and location. Special program-related fees: $25–$50 for supplies, models.

Financial Aid Program-specific awards: 10 art scholarships ($500).

Application Procedures Students admitted directly into the professional program freshman year. Deadline for freshmen and transfers: continuous. Required: high school transcript, college transcript(s) for transfer students, minimum 2.0 high school GPA, SAT or ACT test scores (minimum composite ACT score of 20), 16.5 units of Regents' High School core curriculum (T.O.P.S.). Recommended: minimum 3.0 high school GPA, letter of recommendation, portfolio. Portfolio reviews held continuously on campus; the submission of slides may be substituted for portfolios.

Web Site http://www.nsula.edu/capa

Undergraduate Contact Dr. Roger A. Chandler, Associate Professor/Coordinator of Fine and Graphic Art, Fine and Graphic Arts, Northwestern State University of Louisiana, NSU College Avenue, Natchitoches, Louisiana 71497; 318-357-6176, fax: 318-357-5906, e-mail address: chandlerr@nsula.edu

Notre Dame de Namur University

Belmont, California

Independent Roman Catholic, coed. Suburban campus. Total enrollment: 1,583. Art program established 1851.

Degrees Bachelor of Arts; Bachelor of Fine Arts. Majors and concentrations: art, art history, graphic design, painting/drawing, printmaking, studio art. Cross-registration with Trinity College, Emmanuel College.

Enrollment 35 total; all undergraduate.

Art Student Profile 70% females, 30% males, 40% minorities, 10% international.

Art Faculty 2 undergraduate (full-time), 7 undergraduate (part-time). 100% of full-time faculty have terminal degrees. Graduate students do not teach undergraduate courses. Undergraduate student–faculty ratio: 7:1.

Student Life Student groups/activities include College Art Association, American Institute of Graphic Arts.

Expenses for 2007–2008 Application fee: $40. Comprehensive fee: $35,230 includes full-time tuition ($24,450), mandatory fees ($200), and college room and board ($10,580). College room only: $7000. Room and board charges vary according to board plan and housing facility.

Financial Aid Program-specific awards: 8 Emerging Artist Talent Scholarships for program students ($7500–$9500).

Application Procedures Students admitted directly into the professional program freshman year. Deadline for freshmen and transfers: continuous. Notification date for freshmen and transfers: continuous. Required: essay, high school transcript, college transcript(s) for transfer students, letter of recommendation, SAT or ACT test scores, minimum 2.0 college GPA for transfers. Recommended: portfolio. Portfolio reviews held 24 times on campus; the submission of slides may be substituted for portfolios.

Web Site http://www.ndnu.edu

Undergraduate Contact Betty Friedman, Chair, Department of Art, Notre Dame de Namur University, 1500 Ralston Avenue, Belmont, California 94002-1997; 650-508-3631, fax: 650-508-3488, e-mail address: bfriedman@ndnu.edu

NSCAD University

Halifax, Nova Scotia, Canada

Province-supported, coed. Urban campus. Art program established 1887.

Degrees Bachelor of Arts in the area of art history; Bachelor of Design; Bachelor of Fine Arts in the area of fine arts. Majors and concentrations: art history, art/fine arts, ceramics, film, interdisciplinary design, jewelry and metalsmithing, media arts, photography, textiles. Graduate degrees offered: Master of Arts in the area of art education; Master of Fine Arts in the areas of fine arts, design, craft. Cross-registration with Dalhousie University, St. Mary's University, Mount St. Vincent University, University of King's College.

Enrollment 1,106 total; 1,088 undergraduate, 18 graduate.

Art Student Profile 70% females, 30% males, 6% international.

Art Faculty 42 total (full-time), 38 total (part-time). 95% of full-time faculty have terminal degrees. Graduate students teach a few undergraduate courses. Undergraduate student–faculty ratio: 12:1.

Student Life Student groups/activities include "SOTA" (college publication), Women's Collective, Mosaic (minority ethnic group).

Expenses for 2006–2007 Application fee: $35 Canadian dollars. Tuition and fee charges are reported in Canadian dollars. Province resident tuition: $5895 full-time. Canadian resident tuition: $5895 full-time. International student tuition: $12,125 full-time.

Financial Aid Program-specific awards: 85 merit scholarships for those demonstrating talent and academic achievement ($800), 6 Joseph Beuys Memorial Scholarships for those demonstrating talent and academic achievement ($1500), 5 Harrison McCain Scholarships for those demonstrating talent and academic achievement ($13,500).

Application Procedures Students admitted directly into the professional program freshman year. Deadline for freshmen: March 15; trans-fers: February 15. Notification date for freshmen and transfers: June 20. Required: essay, high school transcript, college transcript(s) for transfer students, portfolio, minimum TOEFL score of 577 for non-English speaking applicants, 2 letters of recommendation for mature applicants. Recommended: interview. Portfolio reviews held twice on campus; the submission of slides may be substituted for portfolios for all portfolio submissions.

Web Site http://www.nscad.ns.ca

Contact Mr. Terrence Bailey, Director of Admissions and Enrollment Services, Office of Student and Academic Services, NSCAD University, 5163 Duke Street, Halifax, Nova Scotia B3J 3J6, Canada; 902-494-8129, fax: 902-425-2987, e-mail address: admissions@nscad.ca

Ohio Northern University

Ada, Ohio

Independent, coed. Small town campus. Total enrollment: 3,620. Art program established 1961.

Degrees Bachelor of Fine Arts. Majors and concentrations: advertising design, graphic design, studio art. Cross-registration with University of Ulster (UK), Burren College of Art (Ireland), Studio Art Centers International (Italy).

Enrollment 30 total; all undergraduate.

Art Student Profile 50% females, 50% males, 3% minorities, 1% international.

Art Faculty 4 undergraduate (full-time), 5 undergraduate (part-time). 100% of full-time faculty have terminal degrees. Graduate students do not teach undergraduate courses. Undergraduate student–faculty ratio: 5:1.

Student Life Student groups/activities include Kappa Pi/Alpha Epsilon Rho, Theta Alpha Phi, American Institute of Graphic Arts.

Expenses for 2006–2007 Application fee: $30. Comprehensive fee: $35,340 includes full-time tuition ($28,050), mandatory fees ($210), and college room and board ($7080). College room only: $3540.

Financial Aid Program-specific awards: art talent awards for art majors ($2500–$8000).

Application Procedures Students admitted directly into the professional program freshman year. Deadline for freshmen and transfers:

Ohio Northern University (continued)

continuous. Notification date for freshmen and transfers: August 15. Required: high school transcript, college transcript(s) for transfer students, minimum 2.0 high school GPA, SAT or ACT test scores, minimum 2.5 high school GPA, portfolio for scholarship consideration. Recommended: essay, minimum 3.0 high school GPA, interview, portfolio. Portfolio reviews held by request on campus; the submission of slides may be substituted for portfolios with approval from the department.

Web Site http://www.onu.edu

Undergraduate Contact Ms. Karen Condeni, Vice President and Dean of Admissions, Ohio Northern University, 525 South Main Street, Ada, Ohio 45810; 419-772-2260, fax: 419-772-2313, e-mail address: admissions-ug@onu.edu

The Ohio State University

Columbus, Ohio

State-supported, coed. Total enrollment: 51,818.

Degrees Bachelor of Fine Arts. Majors and concentrations: art and technology, ceramics, glass, painting/drawing, photography, printmaking, sculpture. Graduate degrees offered: Master of Fine Arts in the areas of ceramics, glass, sculpture, painting/drawing, printmaking, photography, art and technology. Program accredited by NASAD.

Enrollment 345 total; 158 undergraduate, 54 graduate, 133 nonprofessional degree.

Art Student Profile 60% females, 40% males, 3% minorities, 20% international.

Art Faculty 22 total (full-time), 15 total (part-time). 100% of full-time faculty have terminal degrees. Graduate students teach more than half of undergraduate courses. Undergraduate student–faculty ratio: 7:1.

Student Life Student groups/activities include Student League of Independent Potters, Student Printmakers Association, Undergraduate Student Art League. Special housing available for art students.

Expenses for 2006–2007 Application fee: $40. State resident tuition: $8298 full-time. Nonresident tuition: $20,193 full-time. Mandatory fees: $261 full-time. Full-time tuition and fees vary according to course load, program,

reciprocity agreements, and student level. College room and board: $6720. Room and board charges vary according to board plan and housing facility. Special program-related fees: $50 per quarter for technology fee.

Financial Aid Program-specific awards: 1 Hoylt L. Sherman Scholarship for art majors ($1500), 2–5 Arthur E. Baggs Memorial Scholarships for ceramic majors ($750), 1–3 Robert and Marion Gatrell Scholarships for art majors ($900), 1–5 Edith Fergus Gilmore Awards for art majors ($400).

Application Procedures Students apply for admission into the professional program by sophomore, junior year. Deadline for freshmen and transfers: continuous. Required: high school transcript, college transcript(s) for transfer students, SAT or ACT test scores, portfolio upon completion of foundation courses. Portfolio reviews held twice a year on campus; the submission of slides may be substituted for portfolios for transfer applicants when original work is no longer available or for large works of art and three-dimensional pieces.

Web Site http://art.osu.edu

Undergraduate Contact University Admissions, The Ohio State University, 1800 Cannon Drive, 3rd Floor Lincoln Tower, Columbus, Ohio 43210; 614-292-3980, fax: 614-292-4818.

Graduate Contact Ms. Stephanie Hall, Assistant to Chair, Department of Art, The Ohio State University, 146 Hopkins Hall, 128 North Oval Mall, Columbus, Ohio 43210; 614-292-5072, fax: 614-292-1674, e-mail address: hall.1084@osu.edu

Oklahoma Baptist University

Shawnee, Oklahoma

Independent Southern Baptist, coed. Art program established 1980.

Degrees Bachelor of Fine Arts.

Enrollment 40 total; 6 undergraduate, 34 nonprofessional degree.

Art Student Profile 75% females, 25% males, 13% minorities.

Art Faculty 3 undergraduate (full-time), 3 undergraduate (part-time). 33% of full-time faculty have terminal degrees. Graduate students do not teach undergraduate courses. Undergraduate student–faculty ratio: 13:1.

Student Life Student groups/activities include Art Club.

Expenses for 2006–2007 Application fee: $25. Comprehensive fee: $18,996 includes full-time tuition ($13,654), mandatory fees ($1012), and college room and board ($4330). College room only: $1930. Full-time tuition and fees vary according to course load. Room and board charges vary according to board plan and housing facility. Special program-related fees: $25 per course for material fees.

Financial Aid Program-specific awards: 24 art scholarships for program majors ($1117).

Application Procedures Students admitted directly into the professional program freshman year. Deadline for freshmen and transfers: continuous. Required: high school transcript, college transcript(s) for transfer students, minimum 2.0 high school GPA, SAT or ACT test scores. Recommended: portfolio. Portfolio reviews held continuously on campus; the submission of slides may be substituted for portfolios when distance is prohibitive.

Web Site http://www.okbu.edu

Undergraduate Contact Mr. Bruce Perkins, Director of Admissions, Oklahoma Baptist University, Box 61174, 500 West University, Shawnee, Oklahoma 74804; 800-654-3285, fax: 405-878-2046, e-mail address: bruce.perkins@okbu.edu

Oklahoma State University

Stillwater, Oklahoma

State-supported, coed. Small town campus. Total enrollment: 23,307. Art program established 1924.

Web Site http://osu.okstate.edu/

Old Dominion University

Norfolk, Virginia

State-supported, coed. Urban campus. Total enrollment: 21,625. Art program established 1963.

Degrees Bachelor of Fine Arts in the area of studio art. Majors and concentrations: art education, drawing, fibers, graphic design, jewelry and metalsmithing, painting, photography, printmaking, sculpture, studio art. Graduate degrees offered: Master of Fine Arts in the area of visual studies. Cross-registration with Tidewater Community College, Norfolk State University. Program accredited by NASAD.

Enrollment 340 total; 300 undergraduate, 15 graduate, 25 nonprofessional degree.

Art Student Profile 52% females, 48% males, 15% minorities, 10% international.

Art Faculty 14 undergraduate (full-time), 27 undergraduate (part-time), 12 graduate (full-time), 6 graduate (part-time). 92% of full-time faculty have terminal degrees. Graduate students teach a few undergraduate courses. Undergraduate student–faculty ratio: 18:1.

Student Life Student groups/activities include Student Art League, Art Education Club.

Expenses for 2006–2007 Application fee: $40. State resident tuition: $5910 full-time. Nonresident tuition: $16,470 full-time. Mandatory fees: $197 full-time. Full-time tuition and fees vary according to course level, course load, and location. College room and board: $6640. College room only: $3640. Room and board charges vary according to board plan and housing facility. Special program-related fees: $20–$30 per course for lab fees.

Financial Aid Program-specific awards: 3 Sibley Scholarships for enrolled program students by portfolio competition ($1000), 2 Margolious Scholarships for enrolled program students by portfolio competition ($700), 1–2 Gorlinsky Scholarships for enrolled program students by portfolio competition ($300–$500).

Application Procedures Students admitted directly into the professional program freshman year. Deadline for freshmen: March 15; transfers: July 1. Required: high school transcript, college transcript(s) for transfer students, minimum 2.0 high school GPA, SAT or ACT test scores, portfolio for transfer students. Recommended: interview, portfolio. Portfolio reviews held on a case-by-case basis on campus; the submission of slides may be substituted for portfolios at student's discretion.

Web Site http://www.odu.edu/al/art

Undergraduate Contact Mr. Ken Daley, Chief Departmental Advisor, Art Department, Old Dominion University, Visual Arts Building, 49th Street, Norfolk, Virginia 23529; 757-683-4047, fax: 757-683-5923, e-mail address: kdaley@odu.edu

Visual

Arts

Old Dominion University (continued)

Graduate Contact Mr. Elliott Jones, Graduate Program Director, Visual Studies Department, Old Dominion University, Visual Arts Building, 49th Street, Norfolk, Virginia 23529; 757-683-4047, fax: 757-683-5923, e-mail address: ejones@odu.edu

O'More College of Design

Franklin, Tennessee

Independent, coed, primarily women. Small town campus. Total enrollment: 194. Art program established 1970.

Web Site http://www.omorecollege.edu/

Oregon College of Art & Craft

Portland, Oregon

Independent, coed. Urban campus. Total enrollment: 153. Art program established 1994.

Degrees Bachelor of Fine Arts in the area of crafts. Majors and concentrations: book arts, ceramics, fibers, metals, painting/drawing, photography, wood. Cross-registration with All Oregon Independent Colleges. Program accredited by NASAD.

Enrollment 139 total; 134 undergraduate, 5 nonprofessional degree.

Art Student Profile 65% females, 35% males, 8% minorities, 2% international.

Art Faculty 10 undergraduate (full-time), 15 undergraduate (part-time). 90% of full-time faculty have terminal degrees. Graduate students do not teach undergraduate courses. Undergraduate student–faculty ratio: 9:1.

Student Life Student groups/activities include teaching summer children's classes, Annual Juried Student Show, Student Lecture Series. Special housing available for art students.

Expenses for 2006–2007 Application fee: $35. Tuition: $16,900 full-time. Mandatory fees: $1000 full-time. College room only: $3600. Special program-related fees: $1000 per year for studio fees.

Financial Aid Program-specific awards: 85 tuition grants for those demonstrating need ($1500), 52 tuition work-study awards for those demonstrating need ($2300), 5 merit scholarships for talented incoming students ($5000), 2 May Georges Fibers Scholarships for first, second, and third-year students ($500–$3000), 1 Jean Vollum Metals Scholarship for first, second, and third-year students ($500–$1000), 2 Oregon Guild of Woodworkers Scholarships for first, second, and third-year students ($250).

Application Procedures Students admitted directly into the professional program freshman year. Deadline for freshmen and transfers: continuous. Required: essay, high school transcript, college transcript(s) for transfer students, 2 letters of recommendation, interview, portfolio, minimum 2.5 high school GPA for applicants direct from high school, minimum 2.0 college GPA for transfer students. Recommended: minimum 3.0 high school GPA, SAT or ACT test scores. Portfolio reviews held as needed on campus and off campus at National Portfolio Days; the submission of slides may be substituted for portfolios (slides preferred).

Web Site http://www.ocac.edu

Undergraduate Contact Debrah J. Spencer, Interim Director of Admissions, Oregon College of Art & Craft, 8245 Southwest Barnes Road, Portland, Oregon 97225; 800-390-0632 ext. 129, fax: 503-297-9651, e-mail address: admissions@ocac.edu

Otis College of Art and Design

Los Angeles, California

Independent, coed. Urban campus. Total enrollment: 1,125. Art program established 1918.

Degrees Bachelor of Fine Arts in the areas of fine arts, architecture/landscape/interiors, communication arts, digital media, fashion design, interactive product design, toy design. Majors and concentrations: advertising design, architecture, art/fine arts, digital multi-media, drawing, fashion design and technology, graphic design, illustration, interior design, landscape architecture, new genres, painting, photography, printmaking, product design, sculpture, toy design, video art. Graduate degrees offered: Master of Fine Arts in the areas of painting, photography, sculpture, new media, writing, public practice. Program accredited by NASAD.

Enrollment 1,125 total; 1,073 undergraduate, 52 graduate.

Art Student Profile 66% females, 34% males, 55% minorities, 12% international.

Art Faculty 58 undergraduate (full-time), 199 undergraduate (part-time), 2 graduate (full-time), 12 graduate (part-time). 71% of full-time faculty have terminal degrees. Graduate students teach a few undergraduate courses. Undergraduate student–faculty ratio: 8:1.

Student Life Student groups/activities include Wash Magazine, SIGGRAPH, Cultural and Social Network Groups. Special housing available for art students.

Expenses for 2007–2008 Application fee: $50. Tuition: $27,796 full-time. Mandatory fees: $550 full-time. Special program-related fees: $25 per semester for general college materials fee, $75 per semester for technology fee, $200 per semester for registration fee.

Financial Aid Program-specific awards: 783 Otis Institutional Grants for program students ($6306), 16 international student scholarships for international students ($5100), 124 transfer student scholarships for transfer students ($2719).

Application Procedures Students admitted directly into the professional program freshman year. Deadline for freshmen and transfers: continuous. Notification date for freshmen and transfers: continuous. Required: essay, high school transcript, college transcript(s) for transfer students, portfolio, SAT or ACT test scores, minimum TOEFL score of 550 (paper-based), 79 (internet), 213 (computer-based) for international applicants 79/internet, minimum 2.5 high school GPA/college GPA. Recommended: minimum 3.0 high school GPA, 2 letters of recommendation, interview. Portfolio reviews held continuously on campus and off campus at National Portfolio Days; the submission of slides may be substituted for portfolios (slides or CDs/DVDs preferred).

Web Site http://www.otis.edu

Undergraduate Contact Mr. Marc D. Meredith, Dean of Admissions, Admissions Office, Otis College of Art and Design, 9045 Lincoln Boulevard, Los Angeles, California 90045; 310-665-6820, fax: 310-665-6821, e-mail address: admissions@otis.edu

Graduate Contact Graduate Studies, Otis College of Art and Design, 9045 Lincoln Boulevard, Los Angeles, California 90045; 310-665-6892, fax: 310-665-6890, e-mail address: grads@otis.edu

More About the School

Otis prepares diverse students of art and design to enrich the world through their creativity, their skills, and their vision.

A four-year education at Otis begins with Foundation year, during which students from all majors take core studio classes: drawing and composition, figure-drawing, and two- and three-dimensional design. The philosophy is that all artists and designers need well-developed hand-eye skills and sophisticated creative-thinking skills in order to succeed. As they move into the second year, students begin to make their skills more specialized according to their intended major. Top-level studio training in all disciplines is enhanced by a liberal arts and sciences curriculum (LAS) that emphasizes cultural curiosity and intellectual rigor. The LAS classes are intended to complement and expand students' critical thinking as they prepare for the workplaces of the future.

Faculty members who are working professionals, along with visiting artists, designers, lecturers, and writers, share a wealth of expertise and new perspectives with the diverse student population. Lectures, hands-on instruction, studio visits, and personal critiques facilitate dynamic teacher/student and student/student interactions. As part of the commitment to giving students every opportunity to succeed, Otis offers a new Learning Resource Center. Otis also offers an Honors program in liberal studies and art history.

A network of alumni includes individuals who have created such cultural icons as the first Walt Disney animated cartoons; the Academy Award–

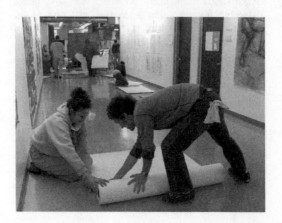

Otis College of Art and Design (continued)

winning special effects for *Lord of the Rings;* products and promotional materials for Columbia, A&M, and Virgin Records; editorial illustrations and cover art for the *Los Angeles Times, Time, Omni, The New Yorker, Buzz,* and *American Film*; costumes for the *Titanic,* Bram Stoker's *Dracula,* and *Harry Potter* and numerous Academy Award–winning films costumed by alumna Edith Head; production design for Spike Lee; and the fashion-forward imagery of such industry leaders as NIKE, Guess?, Richard Tyler, Isaac Mizrahi, Mossimo, and Anne Cole. Otis alumni are featured in major museums, such as the Whitney Museum of American Art; Museum of Modern Art, New York; Guggenheim Museum; Art Institute of Chicago; Corcoran Gallery of Art; Los Angeles County Museum of Art; and Museum of Contemporary Art, Los Angeles, and in galleries around the world.

Otis College of Art and Design, founded in 1918, stands as one of LA's oldest and most important cultural institutions. Otis is proud of its long traditions. Its growth and dynamic character demonstrate the long-term commitment of the College, its faculty members, and its administration as well as the solid support of the art, design, and philanthropic communities. Today's Otis students are artists and designers dedicated to developing technical, critical, and creative skills that can lead them into the future.

Program Facilities The new Galef Center for Fine Arts houses painting and sculpture studios, photo/video studios, and individual student spaces. Other facilities include wood/metal/plastic shops; expanded industry-standard Mac/Windows lab and scanning, large-scale output, and 3-D laser modeling; video/sound editing; lithography/etching presses; the city's oldest, most renowned college fine arts press; extensive library holdings in fine art, design, art history, humanities, critical studies, and periodicals; visual resources center; and Graduate Studios.

Faculty and Visiting Artists Professional faculty members include fashion, toy, digital, and product designers; architects; photographers; and fine artists, among them Roy Dowell, Annette Kapon, Suzanne Lacy, Linda Pollari, Harry Mott, Martin Caveza, Steve McAdam, Ave Pildas, Rosemary Brantley, Scott Grieger, Holly Tempo, Carole Caroompas, Linda Burnham, Judie Bamber, Meg Cranston, Dana Duff, Linda Hudson, Larry Johnson, Debra Ballard, Parme Giutini, Heather Joseph-Witham, and Paul Vangelisti. Guest lecturers and visiting artists/designers include Dave Hickey, Alexis Smith, Barbara Kruger, Dan Graham, Rod Beatty, Bob Mackie, Jeremy Scott, Eduardo Lucero, and Isabel Toldeo.

Student Exhibit Opportunities Students have the opportunity to exhibit their work at numerous locations and functions, such as the Abe and Helen Bolsky Gallery, extensive informal exhibit space in the Galef Center, the annual senior show in all departments, the MFA exhibition, local and national competitions, juried fashion shows, the annual literary magazine, and the Otis Design and Illustration Groups.

Special Programs Special Programs include the Summer of Art precollege program; summer study in Pont-Aven, France; the Spring Paris trip for Foundation students; internship opportunities in all departments; OTIS-LA, an intensive language and acculturation program designed for incoming international students; and community outreach through Otis Evening College. A new fine arts program, ACT (Artists, Community, and Teaching), gives students an introduction to teaching art as a social practice and as a career path.

Housing The College recently added Otis Housing, which is based in a nearby luxury apartment complex and overseen by the Student Affairs Office. Geared toward first-year students, the apartments are two-bedroom/two-bath units that are shared by 4 students. Paid utilities, secure parking, T1 access, and full kitchens, along with a pool, spa, and recreation facilities, make Otis Housing attractive and comfortable. Residence Life staff members live in the complex.

Campuses Otis College of Art and Design's Goldsmith Campus consists of the Galef Center for Fine Arts (housing the School of Fine Arts) and Kathleen Ahmanson Hall (housing Architecture/Landscape/Interiors, Communication Arts, Digital Media, Interactive Product Design, and Toy Design). The campus is located on Los Angeles' Westside. Nearby are the communities of Venice and Santa Monica, home to many prominent fine arts studios and galleries. The location of the Goldsmith campus and the nearby Graduate Studios places students in the center of the vital, international artistic/design community that fuels the Los Angeles fine arts, toy, digital media, and product design worlds.

Otis School of Fashion is located in LA's downtown fashion district within the California Mart Center that is headquarters for many fashion collections and vendors. This places students' day-to-day activities in a unique relationship to an industry that is in need of talented and well-educated designers. The program's structure brings in top designers to work as mentors with junior and senior students on projects from children's sports and swimwear categories to finely tailored men's and glamorous women's evening wear. The annual Otis Scholarship Benefit Fashion Show is an important fashion industry and celebrity event that showcases the best work created by students.

Pacific Northwest College of Art

Portland, Oregon

Independent, coed. Urban campus. Art program established 1909.

Web Site http://www.pnca.edu/

Paier College of Art, Inc.

Hamden, Connecticut

Proprietary, coed. Suburban campus. Total enrollment: 248. Art program established 1946.

Degrees Bachelor of Fine Arts. Majors and concentrations: art/fine arts, graphic design, illustration, interior design, photography.

Enrollment 226 total; all undergraduate.

Art Student Profile 71% females, 29% males, 1% minorities, 1% international.

Art Faculty 10 undergraduate (full-time), 36 undergraduate (part-time). 79% of full-time faculty have terminal degrees. Graduate students do not teach undergraduate courses. Undergraduate student–faculty ratio: 7:1.

Expenses for 2006–2007 Application fee: $25. Tuition: $12,000 full-time. Mandatory fees: $380 full-time. Special program-related fees: $100–$250 per course for lab and model fees.

Financial Aid Program-specific awards: Paier Minority Scholarship for minority students, PCA tuition reductions for those demonstrating need.

Application Procedures Students admitted directly into the professional program freshman year. Deadline for freshmen and transfers: continuous. Required: high school transcript, college transcript(s) for transfer students, 2 letters of recommendation, interview, portfolio, SAT or ACT test scores. Portfolio reviews held twice and by appointment on campus;

the submission of slides may be substituted for portfolios for large works of art.

Web Site http://www.paiercollegeofart.edu

Undergraduate Contact Ms. Lynn Pascale, Secretary, Admissions Department, Paier College of Art, Inc., 20 Gorham Avenue, Hamden, Connecticut 06514-3902; 203-287-3031, fax: 203-287-3021, e-mail address: paier.admin@ snet.net

The New School: A University
Parsons The New School for Design

New York, New York

Independent, coed. Urban campus. Total enrollment: 3,598. Art program established 1896.

Degrees Bachelor of Fine Arts in the areas of fine art, illustration, communication design, fashion design, product design, architectural design, interior design, photography, integrated design curriculum, design and technology; Bachelor of Business Administration in the area of design and management. Majors and concentrations: architectural design, architecture, art/fine arts, communication design, design and management, design technology, fashion design, fashion merchandising, graphic arts, history of decorative arts, illustration, integrated design curriculum, interior design, lighting design, photography, product design. Graduate degrees offered: Master of Arts in the area of history of decorative arts; Master of Fine Arts in the areas of design and technology, fine arts, lighting design, photography; Master of Architecture. Cross-registration with Eugene Lang College-New School University. Program accredited by NASAD.

Enrollment 2,775 total; 1,946 undergraduate, 334 graduate, 495 nonprofessional degree.

Art Student Profile 75% females, 25% males, 30% minorities, 31% international.

Art Faculty 72 total (full-time), 879 total (part-time). Graduate students do not teach undergraduate courses. Undergraduate student–faculty ratio: 12:1.

Student Life Student groups/activities include Student Gallery, Student Government.

Expenses for 2007–2008 Application fee: $50. Comprehensive fee: $42,680 includes full-time

Parsons The New School for Design (continued)

tuition ($30,270), mandatory fees ($660), and college room and board ($11,750). College room only: $8750.

Financial Aid Program-specific awards: Parsons Scholarships for those demonstrating need, University Scholars Scholarships for African-American and Latino students demonstrating need, Parsons Restricted Scholarships for those demonstrating need and academic achievement.

Application Procedures Students admitted directly into the professional program freshman year. Deadline for freshmen and transfers: continuous. Notification date for freshmen and transfers: July 1. Required: high school transcript, college transcript(s) for transfer students, minimum 2.0 high school GPA, portfolio, SAT or ACT test scores, home examination, minimum TOEFL score of 550 (paper-based) for all non-native speakers of English. Recommended: minimum 3.0 high school GPA, interview. Portfolio reviews held continuously by appointment on campus; the submission of slides may be substituted for portfolios when distance is prohibitive.

Web Site http://www.parsons.edu

Contact Terence Peavy, Assistant Vice President for Admissions, Parsons The New School for Design, 66 Fifth Avenue, New York, New York 10011-8878; 212-229-5150, fax: 212-229-8975, e-mail address: parsadm@newschool.edu

More About the School

At Parsons The New School for Design, students not only learn about art and design—they redefine it. Successful alumni have paved the way for future graduates for a century, and both current students and recent graduates find that a Parsons education resonates in this competitive industry. From the latest in technology design to fashion, product design, and architecture, the School takes pride in staying on the cutting edge and emphasizes the need to design innovative solutions to real-world issues. Students explore new ways to use art and design to help meet society's evolving needs, including using green technology in architecture projects, developing educational video games, and building portable, low-cost dwellings. The faculty members, many of whom are working artists and designers in New York City, bring their professional expertise into the classroom and challenge and encourage students to realize their artistic and professional goals.

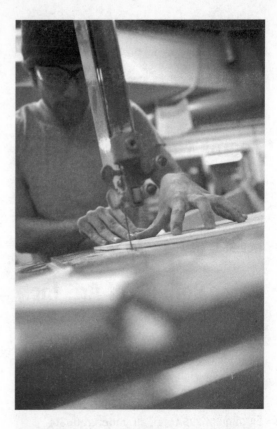

Campus and Surroundings Parsons' New York City location provides students with perhaps their most important resource. An international center for art, entertainment, and commerce, the city is an exceptional place to live and study design. The School's main campus is located in Greenwich Village, and the Fashion Design Department is located in midtown, in the heart of the Fashion District. For Parsons' students, the city becomes their home away from home as well as the source of their ideas. Parsons' faculty members use New York City as an urban design laboratory, visiting institutions such as the Metropolitan Museum of Art, Cooper-Hewitt National Design Museum, the Museum of Modern Art, and about eighty other museums. Although every art school organizes student exhibitions, Parsons students have the opportunity to show their work in some of the major galleries and design fairs in New York and internationally. In the past, student work has appeared in Chelsea galleries and museums, the International Contemporary Furniture Fair, the Art Director's Club, and Saks Fifth Avenue.

Program Facilities Since 1970, Parsons The New School for Design has been part of The New School,

Arts

one of the most diverse educational establishments in the nation, and students benefit from being part of a university community. Campuswide liberal arts programs give Parsons students the opportunity to study with other New School faculty members and share classes with students in liberal studies, social and political science, and performing arts programs. To take full advantage of the university setting, Parsons and Eugene Lang College The New School for Liberal Arts have structured a five-year curriculum in which students simultaneously complete two degrees, the fine arts or design B.F.A. and the liberal arts B.A. The New School offers students access to more than 1,000 computer workstations and several libraries. The Adam & Sophie Gimbel Design Library includes new and rare books and special collections books on art and design as well as mounted plates, slide collections, and periodicals. The Gimbel Library also stores a digital image collection with online access and is home to the world-renowned Anna-Maria and Stephen Kellen Archives Center. A citywide consortium links the libraries of Parsons, The New School, New York University, and Cooper Union, providing unparalleled access to information. The new Angelo Donghia Materials Library and Study Center houses a computer lab, gallery, lecture hall, and library that put state-of-the-art materials at students' fingertips.

Parsons plans to unveil the sprawling 25,000-square-foot Shelia C. Johnson Design Center at Fifth Avenue and 13th Street in late 2008. It will feature an innovative urban quad, state-of-the-art galleries, generous lecture and meeting spaces, a design store, and a new home for the Anna-Maria and Stephen Kellen Archives Center, a significant collection of drawings, photographs, letters, and objects documenting twentieth-century design.

Faculty, Resident Artists, and Alumni Alumni are an important part of the Parsons community and make up an unparalleled network of designers and artists. Notable graduates include Mark Badgley and James Mischka, fashion designers; Sheila Bridges, interior designer; Bridget de Socio, graphic designer; Peter de Seve, illustrator; Sue de Beer, artist; Angelo Donghia, interior designer; Jamie Drake, interior designer; Bea Feitler, graphic designer; Tom Ford, fashion designer; Albert Hadley, interior designer; Edward Hopper, artist; Marc Jacobs, fashion designer; Jasper Johns, artist; Donna Karan, fashion designer; Reed Krakoff, CEO of Coach; Alex Lee, product designer and president of OXO; Ryan McGinley, photographer; Lazaro Hernandez and Jack McCollough, fashion designers (Proenza Schouler); Norman Rockwell, illustrator; Joel Schumacher,

filmmaker; Richard Silverstein, graphic designer; Anna Sui, fashion designer; and Brian Tolle, artist.

Student Performance Opportunities The School has also worked hard to create relationships with New York's impressive art and design community. It organizes its own public exhibitions and programs, which gives students access to top professionals. Panels and lectures with leading artists and designers, such as Donna Karen, Chuck Close, and Frank Gehry supplement studio and class work. There are also a number of internships and job opportunities available to through the School's office of career services. In fact, many of the alumni who interned as students with businesses, such as galleries, private studios, design houses, and e-commerce and technology start-ups, have gone on to have successful careers in those industries.

Special Programs Parsons has been a forerunner in the field of art and design since the school's founding in 1896. By locating visual beauty in the ordinary things of middle-class American life, Parsons virtually invented the modern concept of design in America. In 2006, Parsons celebrated the centennial of its Fashion Design, Interior Design, and Communication Design programs, which were the first of their kind in the nation. Internationalism has also always been an essential ingredient of Parsons' success. In 1920, Parsons was the first art and design school in America to found a campus abroad. Today, Parsons has affiliate schools in Paris; Kanazawa, Japan; Seoul, South Korea; and Altos de Chavon in the Dominican Republic. Parsons' rigorous programs and distinguished faculty members embrace curricular innovation, pioneer new uses of technology, and instill in students a global perspective in design.

Peck School of the Arts

See University of Wisconsin–Milwaukee

Pennsylvania Academy of the Fine Arts

Philadelphia, Pennsylvania

Independent, coed. Urban campus. Art program established 1805.

Degrees Bachelor of Fine Arts in the areas of painting, printmaking, sculpture, drawing. Majors and concentrations: drawing, painting, printmaking, sculpture. Graduate degrees offered: Master of Fine Arts in the areas of

Pennsylvania Academy of the Fine Arts (continued)

painting, sculpture, printmaking, drawing. Cross-registration with University of Pennsylvania. Program accredited by NASAD.

Enrollment 306 total; 213 undergraduate, 93 graduate.

Art Student Profile 50% females, 50% males, 16% minorities, 5% international.

Art Faculty 31 total (full-time), 32 total (part-time). 40% of full-time faculty have terminal degrees. Graduate students do not teach undergraduate courses. Undergraduate student–faculty ratio: 6:1.

Student Life Student groups/activities include visiting artists lectures, sculpture competitions, drawing marathon. Special housing available for art students.

Expenses for 2006–2007 Special program-related fees: $20 for locker fee, $20 for technology fee, $40 for student activity fee, $175 for general fee, $200 for studio deposit (3rd and 4th year).

Financial Aid Program-specific awards: travel scholarships for juniors and seniors, Institutional Scholarships for those demonstrating need and merit.

Application Procedures Students admitted directly into the professional program freshman year. Deadline for freshmen and transfers: March 1. Required: essay, high school transcript, college transcript(s) for transfer students, 2 letters of recommendation, portfolio, TOEFL score and affidavit of support for international applicants. Recommended: minimum 3.0 high school GPA, interview. Portfolio reviews held as needed on campus; the submission of slides may be substituted for portfolios for large works of art or when distance is prohibitive.

Web Site http://www.pafa.edu

Contact Stan Greidus, Vice President of Admissions and Financial Aid, Pennsylvania Academy of the Fine Arts, 128 North Broad Street, Philadelphia, Pennsylvania 19102; 215-972-7625, fax: 215-569-0153, e-mail address: admissions@pafa.edu

More About the Academy

The Pennsylvania Academy has been training America's best artists for more than 200 years. Steeped in history, the Academy has a long list of

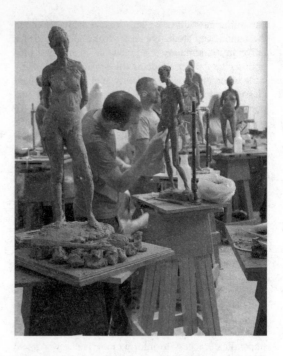

famous alumni and a current faculty of working professional artists who form a continuous tradition of excellence in the studio arts of painting, drawing, sculpture, and printmaking. Students at the Academy are passionate about their craft and their future as artists. The Academy teaches technique and imparts knowledge and skills to enable students to become the artists they want to be. The Academy is a unique community of working artists combined with a world-class collection of American art, located in one of the largest and liveliest art communities in the country.

The Academy offers a two-year Master of Fine Arts (M.F.A.) Program, a one-year Post-Baccalaureate Program, a four-year Certificate Program, and a coordinated Bachelor of Fine Arts (B.F.A.) program with the University of Pennsylvania, with studio-based majors in painting, drawing, printmaking, and sculpture. Students work closely with a large faculty of resident and visiting artist-critics. The range of styles and approaches represented by both students and faculty members is diverse and supportive of the many directions in contemporary art making. Students at the Academy come from all walks of life, age groups, and widely varying backgrounds. This creates a high-energy community, bound together by a passion for making art and being artists.

The four-year Certificate Program is the most historic of the academic programs at the Pennsylvania

Visual

Arts

Academy. In the first two years, students receive a thorough training in traditional and contemporary techniques of painting, drawing, sculpture, and printmaking. Under the mentorship of master artists, students take classes in cast drawing, life drawing and painting, anatomy, color, still life, figure modeling, perspective, etching, woodcut, and art history. In their second year, students choose to focus their study in the majors of drawing, painting, sculpture, or printmaking. Third- and fourth-year students receive private studios while continuing an intensive mentoring relationship with critics chosen from a large faculty of professional working artists who represent a wide range of aesthetic viewpoints.

The Certificate program emphasizes excellence in studio art–making skills and abilities, and drawing is emphasized at all levels of the curriculum. All students attend critiques and lectures given by visiting artists and critics and are in daily contact with the Academy's outstanding collection of American art. At the conclusion of their studies, students mount a thesis exhibition within the galleries of the Samuel M.V. Hamilton Building.

Academy students can also obtain a Bachelor of Fine Arts (B.F.A.) degree through the coordinated program with the University of Pennsylvania. For more than seventy years, Pennsylvania Academy of the Fine Arts and the University of Pennsylvania have cooperatively offered a unique educational combination of nationally renowned studio art training and Ivy League academics.

Students admitted to the B.F.A. program may begin studies at Penn after completing their first year of study at the Academy. This self-paced program offers students maximum flexibility in their academic pursuits.

The Master of Fine Arts (M.F.A.) program is an intensive, two-year studio art–making experience that involves daily interaction with an outstanding faculty of resident and visiting artists, regular private and group critiques, seminars in critical readings, a written thesis component, exposure to an outstanding visiting-artist program, and participation in graduate drawing and painting—reflecting the Pennsylvania Academy's emphasis on achieving a high degree of skill in drawing and studio art–making practice. Students are expected to possess an unusually strong work ethic and to be highly productive and able to work independently.

The master's degree program is centered in the studio arts of painting, drawing, printmaking, and sculpture, but within these disciplines, it displays considerable diversity in its approach. All students are provided a private studio in the new Samuel M.V.

Hamilton Building, with proper ventilation and 24-hour secure access to facilities.

During both years of study, every M.F.A. student must enroll in drawing and seminar classes that meet once a week at scheduled times. Students may also elect to take classes within the Academy's Certificate Program, with its emphasis on working from life and the acquisition of traditional art-making skills. This, in conjunction with extensive access to the private studio, provides an open schedule that allows flexibility within the program. The Studio Critique system allows the student to choose three faculty critics from a large faculty representing a wide range of studio practice.

The Post-Baccalaureate Program is designed to address the needs of a wide range of students: those with an undergraduate degree who have substantial studio experience but need an additional year of studio work to develop a strong, cohesive, and competitive body of work; students requiring a year of intensive studio work prior to beginning a graduate-level program, or individuals with a degree in art who wish to pursue work in a different medium. It combines an advanced academic program of foundation and techniques with an upper-level, independent studio/critique system and seminars designed to develop personal vision through exposure to trends in contemporary art issues.

Pennsylvania College of Art & Design

Lancaster, Pennsylvania

Independent, coed. Urban campus. Total enrollment: 255. Art program established 1982.

Degrees Bachelor of Fine Arts in the areas of communication arts, fine art, photography. Majors and concentrations: art/fine arts, graphic design, illustration, photography. Program accredited by NASAD.

Enrollment 225 total; all undergraduate.

Art Student Profile 61% females, 39% males, 14% minorities.

Art Faculty 11 undergraduate (full-time), 40 undergraduate (part-time). 70% of full-time faculty have terminal degrees. Graduate students do not teach undergraduate courses. Undergraduate student–faculty ratio: 9:1.

Student Life Student groups/activities include Society of Illustrators Student Competition, Lancaster Museum of Art Annual Open Art

Pennsylvania College of Art & Design (continued)

Award Exhibition, client-based projects resulting in printed work (for designers and illustrators).

Expenses for 2007–2008 Application fee: $40. Tuition: $14,425 full-time. Mandatory fees: $780 full-time.

Financial Aid Program-specific awards: 3 PSA&D Foundation Scholarships for incoming foundation students demonstrating artistic merit and academic achievement ($3500), 1 Brenda Swain Memorial Scholarship for juniors demonstrating academic and artistic achievement ($500), 1 UPS Scholarship for current students demonstrating academic achievement ($1375), 1 UPS Minority Scholarship for current students of Hispanic or African-American descent demonstrating academic achievement ($1375), 1 Susquehanna Pfaltzgraff Scholarship for incoming foundation students from York County, PA demonstrating academic achievement ($1000).

Application Procedures Students admitted directly into the professional program freshman year. Deadline for freshmen and transfers: continuous. Required: essay, high school transcript, college transcript(s) for transfer students, interview, portfolio. Recommended: minimum 2.0 high school GPA, 2 letters of recommendation. Portfolio reviews held on campus and off campus in Baltimore, MD; Philadelphia, PA; the submission of slides may be substituted for portfolios when distance is prohibitive.

Web Site http://www.pcad.edu

Undergraduate Contact Susan P. Matson, Director of Enrollment Management and Marketing, Pennsylvania College of Art & Design, 204 North Prince Street, Lancaster, Pennsylvania 17608-0059; 717-396-7833, fax: 717-396-1339, e-mail address: admissions@pcad.edu

More About the College

Pennsylvania College of Art and Design (PCA&D) began as the dream of a handful of dedicated artists and their supporters in the spring of 1982. Two decades later, PCA&D has grown into a professional art college recognized as a leader in Central Pennsylvania's visual arts community. While the school has grown and the curriculum has been enhanced, PCA&D's mission has remained the same—to provide a professional education in the visual arts that allows students to pursue art as a life's

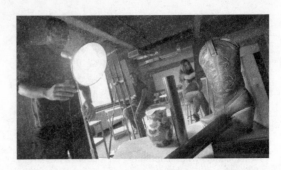

work and gives them the breadth of knowledge needed to live a life that is personally meaningful and contributes to the cultural and economic aspects of the community.

Accredited by the National Association of Schools of Art and Design, and a candidate for accreditation by the Middle States Association of Colleges and Schools, PCA&D offers four-year Bachelor of Fine Arts (B.F.A.) degree programs in fine arts, graphic design, illustration, and photography. The College also offers continuing education opportunities with certificate programs in print design, Web design, home interiors, and mural painting. In addition, a wide variety of credit and noncredit studio and computer courses for adults and youths are available.

Providing a complementary balance to the program's studio work, the College has carefully developed specific liberal arts requirements and electives with a relevance to the education and life of an artist. Another feature of the curriculum is the internship program for all B.F.A. students, which provides them with professional experiences and opportunities. PCA&D students have produced work for or interned at numerous companies on the East Coast, including advertising agencies, design studios, art galleries, publishing companies, and museums.

PCA&D prides itself on maintaining a professionally relevant curriculum and providing students with a good educational value. The College is pleased to offer its program at a tuition that is considerably less expensive than other professional art colleges. Coupling that with the fact that PCA&D is located in historic downtown Lancaster, Pennsylvania, a city where living expenses are much lower than its metropolitan counterparts, further alleviates the impact of financing a college education.

Another attribute of PCA&D's programs is the low teacher-student ratio (1:10). With individualized attention from faculty members, who are all working artists and designers, PCA&D students have a first-hand view of an artist's lifestyle, challenges, and rewards. Gaining such insight is critical to sustaining a career in the visual arts.

PCA&D salutes its alumni who are making their mark in the field of art and design. Whether they are exhibiting fine artists, creative directors in advertising agencies, designers for international corporations, or illustrators for national publications, the College's graduates are sharing their talents with industry giants. These successes are evidence of the high-quality education and invaluable real-life experiences the College provides its students.

The College facility has more than 62,000 square feet of well-maintained and highly-functional work and study space, with numerous art and design studios, computer imaging labs, printmaking studios, darkrooms, woodshop, photo labs, plug-n-play labs, and galleries. The College also houses its own library on-site, with Access Pennsylvania (AccessPA) privileges.

Pennsylvania College of Art & Design's Lancaster, Pennsylvania, location offers both the advantages of a city and the comfort and safety of a small town. The city's tree-lined streets provide a beautiful setting for many galleries, shops, restaurants, and clubs. In addition, Lancaster is centrally located and only a few hours from some of the East Coast's most important cultural centers—Baltimore, New York City, Philadelphia, and Washington, D.C.

PCA&D is proud of the quality and strength of its programs, curriculum, and faculty, and encourages prospective students to visit the College and learn more about the PCA&D experience.

For more information, students should contact: Pennsylvania College of Art and Design, 204 N. Prince Street, P.O. Box 59, Lancaster, Pennsylvania 17608-0059; Phone: (717) 396-7833; E-mail: admissions@pcad.edu; Web site: http://www.pcad.edu.

Penn State University Park

University Park, Pennsylvania

State-related, coed. Small town campus. Total enrollment: 42,914. Art program established 1964.

Web Site http://www.psu.edu/

Pittsburg State University

Pittsburg, Kansas

State-supported, coed. Small town campus. Total enrollment: 6,859.

Web Site http://www.pittstate.edu/

Plymouth State University

Plymouth, New Hampshire

State-supported, coed. Total enrollment: 5,872. Art program established 1960.

Degrees Bachelor of Arts in the areas of fine arts, studio art, graphic design, art history; Bachelor of Fine Arts in the area of studio and graphic design; Bachelor of Science in the area of art education. Majors and concentrations: art education, art history, ceramics, drawing, graphic design, interdisciplinary studies, painting, printmaking, sculpture. Graduate degrees offered: Master of Arts in Teaching in the area of art education. Program accredited by NCATE.

Enrollment 372 undergraduate, 15 graduate.

Art Student Profile 50% females, 50% males, 2% minorities, 5% international.

Art Faculty 12 undergraduate (full-time), 17 undergraduate (part-time), 2 graduate (full-time), 2 graduate (part-time). 100% of full-time faculty have terminal degrees. Graduate students do not teach undergraduate courses. Undergraduate student–faculty ratio: 15:1.

Student Life Student groups/activities include exhibition program, Art Education Mentor Network, Art and Art History Club.

Expenses for 2007–2008 Application fee: $35. State resident tuition: $6040 full-time. Nonresident tuition: $13,640 full-time. Mandatory fees: $1726 full-time. College room and board: $7893.

Financial Aid Program-specific awards: 1 Karl Drerup Scholarship for program students ($500), 2 Art Department Scholarships for program students ($700).

Application Procedures Students admitted directly into the professional program freshman year. Deadline for freshmen: May 30. Required: high school transcript, 2 letters of recommendation, portfolio, SAT or ACT test scores, extracurricular activities. Portfolio reviews held 8-10 times on campus; the submission of slides may be substituted for portfolios.

Web Site http://www.plymouth.edu/psc/artdept

Undergraduate Contact Deb Stalnaker, Administrative Assistant, Art Department, Plymouth State University, 17 High Street, Plymouth,

Plymouth State University (continued)

New Hampshire 03264-1595; 603-535-2201, fax: 603-535-2938, e-mail address: dstalnaker@plymouth.edu

Graduate Contact Dennise Maslakowski, Associate Vice President, College of Graduate Studies, Plymouth State University, MSC 11, 23 Avery Street, Plymouth, New Hampshire 03264; 603-535-2286, fax: 603-535-2648, e-mail address: dmmaslakowski@plymouth.edu

Point Park University

Pittsburgh, Pennsylvania

Independent, coed. Urban campus. Total enrollment: 3,546. Art program established 2003.

Degrees Bachelor of Arts in the area of cinema and digital arts. Majors and concentrations: cinema and digital arts. Cross-registration with Carnegie Mellon University, University of Pittsburgh, Chatham College, Robert Morris University, Duquesne University, Carlow University.

Enrollment 169 total; all undergraduate.

Art Student Profile 26% females, 74% males, 5% minorities, 3% international.

Art Faculty 4 undergraduate (full-time), 10 undergraduate (part-time). 90% of full-time faculty have terminal degrees. Graduate students do not teach undergraduate courses. Undergraduate student–faculty ratio: 18:1.

Student Life Student groups/activities include John P. Harris Film Club.

Expenses for 2007–2008 Application fee: $40. Comprehensive fee: $27,430 includes full-time tuition ($18,460), mandatory fees ($530), and college room and board ($8440). College room only: $3980. Full-time tuition and fees vary according to program. Room and board charges vary according to board plan and housing facility.

Financial Aid Program-specific awards: Cinema Scholarship for those demonstrating talent and academic achievement ($1500–$5000), Cinema Apprenticeship for those demonstrating talent ($1500–$5000), Academic Scholarship for those demonstrating talent and academic achievement ($1000–$5000).

Application Procedures Students admitted directly into the professional program freshman year. Deadline for freshmen and transfers: May 1. Required: essay, high school transcript, minimum 2.0 high school GPA, 2 letters of recommendation, interview, portfolio, SAT or ACT test scores. Portfolio reviews held 10 times on campus and off campus in by telephone.

Web Site http://www.pointpark.edu

Undergraduate Contact Bonnie Sampson, Administrative Assistant, Cinema & Digital Arts, Conservatory of Performing Arts, Point Park University, 201 Wood Street, Pittsburgh, Pennsylvania 15222-1988; 412-392-3450.

More About the University

Point Park University offers students real-world experiences in an exciting campus environment, the chance to meet and learn with students from thirty-five states and fifty countries, and the excitement and culture of the vibrant city surrounding the University.

The Cinema and Digital Arts Program is offered through the Media Production Program, which is part of the Conservatory of Performing Arts. As one of the top programs of its kind in the nation, the Conservatory of Performing Arts combines hands-on experience and rigorous training with internationally recognized master teachers, so students develop their craft working with professional artists who are involved in their professions outside of the University as well as in the classroom.

Cinema and Digital Arts is an innovatively designed program, with an emphasis on professional education and liberal arts, both in theory and in practice. Exploring the integration of media and the arts in society as well as the impact of technology on culture, the curriculum provides practical, professional training while developing a sound foundation in the arts and humanities. Theory and aesthetics are taught as an integral part of developing communication and production skills. The degree offered is a four-year, 120-credit Bachelor of Arts (B.A.).

The program consists of a combination of courses, workshops, productions, and crew assignments, and students have opportunities to earn credit for real-world experience through the internship program. There is a strong emphasis on collaboration. While the teachers demand professionalism and discipline, they go out of their way to mentor and evaluate the students as they develop as artists.

During the first two years, students are trained in all the fundamental crafts of cinema production. Then, in the junior and senior years, students select a concentration in producing, directing, editing, screenwriting, or cinematography for advanced study and practice. Each year, students make films using

Visual

Arts

professional digital video cameras and nonlinear editing systems. This approach allows each student to develop a specific set of skills and to produce a reel that showcases their talents in their specializations. Furthermore, by shooting primarily on digital formats, students do not have the extra expense of film, processing, and video transfers. So, instead of worrying about the budget, they can focus on the creative challenges of bringing their stories to the screen. Students graduate with several great pieces and all the technical skills they need to take the world by storm.

The University's downtown location provides convenient access to numerous theaters, restaurants, parks, sports venues, museums, and movie theaters. Through the philanthropic efforts of such financial entrepreneurs as Carnegie and Frick, Pittsburgh has had a long tradition as a cultural center. The city has an excellent symphony and ballet company, and the Pittsburgh Opera gives performances regularly. Theaters, ethnic festivals, and club attractions fill out the entertainment spectrum. In addition, the nation's first educational television station, WQED, provides a wealth of stimulating offerings. PNC Park, Heinz Field, and Mellon Arena are homes of Pittsburgh's professional sports teams, which also host concerts and other special events and are within walking distance of the University. A short bus ride away is the Oakland section of Pittsburgh, the location of several renowned museums.

Program Facilities The Cinema and Digital Arts Program has new, state-of-the-art facilities, including ten nonlinear editing suites, a sound mixing studio, a Foley/audio recording studio, and a professionally equipped soundstage. With Western Pennsylvania as its back lot, the creative possibilities are limitless.

The recent construction of the television studio in the University Center marks the start of a two-year period of exciting capital projects. The state-of-the-art television studio and editing suites, together with the GRW Theater that is already there, will provide cutting-edge experiences for students in the Cinema and Digital Arts Program.

Exhibit Opportunities The campus offers a student-run cinema society, the Sprocket Guild, and frequent movie screenings that include open showings of student work. The Cinema and Digital Arts Program culminates with the annual Point Park Digital Film Festival, which is presented to showcase graduating senior thesis production projects.

Special Programs Characterized by a willingness to innovate, the University has been active since its inception in establishing internship possibilities with the many resources for career preparation in Pittsburgh, including internship programs with local broadcasting stations.

Pratt Institute

Brooklyn, New York

Independent, coed. Urban campus. Art program established 1887.

Degrees Bachelor of Arts in the areas of critical and visual studies, art history; Bachelor of Architecture; Bachelor of Fine Arts in the areas of communications design, fine arts, fashion design, interior design, art and design education, computer graphics, criticism and history of art, media arts, writing for publication, performance and media; Bachelor of Industrial Design; Bachelor of Science in the area of construction management; Bachelor of Professional Studies. Majors and concentrations: animation, architecture, art direction, art education, art history, ceramic art and design, computer graphics, construction management, fashion design, film, graphic design, illustration, industrial design, interior design, jewelry and metalsmithing, painting/drawing, photography, printmaking, sculpture, visual and critical studies, visual studies, writing for publication/performance/media. Graduate degrees offered: Master of Architecture; Master of Fine Arts in the areas of fine arts, digital arts, art history; Master of Industrial Design; Master of Professional Studies in the areas of art therapy, design management, arts and cultural management, art therapy-special education; Master of Science in the areas of interior design, art and design education, art history and criticism, urban design, library science, industrial design, architecture, historic preservation, city/regional planning, environmental systems management, facilities. Program accredited by NASAD, CIDA.

Enrollment 4,763 total; 2,958 undergraduate, 1,606 graduate, 199 nonprofessional degree.

Art Student Profile 63% females, 37% males, 40% minorities, 15% international.

Art Faculty 119 total (full-time), 795 total (part-time). Graduate students do not teach undergraduate courses. Undergraduate student–faculty ratio: 12:1.

Student Life Student groups/activities include Industrial Design Society of America, American

Pratt Institute (continued)

Society of Interior Designers, American Institute of Graphic Arts. Special housing available for art students.

Expenses for 2007–2008 Application fee: $40. Comprehensive fee: $39,998 includes full-time tuition ($29,900), mandatory fees ($1180), and college room and board ($8918). College room only: $5718. Special program-related fees: $106 per year for student activities fee, $400 per year for technology fee, $600 per year for academic facilities fee.

Financial Aid Program-specific awards: Presidential Pratt Merit Awards for freshmen and transfer students ($1000–$15,000).

Application Procedures Students admitted directly into the professional program freshman year. Deadline for freshmen and transfers: February 1. Notification date for freshmen and transfers: April 1. Required: essay, high school transcript, college transcript(s) for transfer students, letter of recommendation, portfolio, SAT or ACT test scores, writing sample for some majors. Recommended: minimum 3.0 high school GPA, interview. Portfolio reviews held continuously on campus and off campus in various locations on National Portfolio Days; the submission of slides may be substituted for portfolios when distance is prohibitive (beyond a 100-mile radius).

Web Site http://www.pratt.edu/

Undergraduate Contact Ms. Judith Aaron, Vice President for Enrollment, Admissions Department, Pratt Institute, 200 Willoughby Avenue, Brooklyn, New York 11205; 718-636-3669 ext. 3743, fax: 718-399-4242, e-mail address: jaaron@pratt.edu

Graduate Contact Ms. Young Hah, Director of Graduate and International Admissions, Admissions Department, Pratt Institute, 200 Willoughby Avenue, Brooklyn, New York 11205; 718-636-3669, fax: 718-399-4242, e-mail address: yhah@pratt.edu

More About the Institute

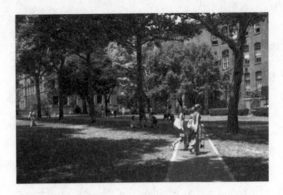

Pratt Institute is located on a 25-acre tree-lined campus, with twenty-seven buildings, including landmarked Romanesque- and Renaissance Revival–style structures, in Brooklyn's historic Clinton Hill section. Approximately 84 percent of freshmen live in one of Pratt's six residence halls. On-campus parking is available for residents and commuters. Pratt's proximity to New York City, which offers a vast array of professional, cultural, and recreational opportunities, is a distinct advantage to students. Through Pratt's optional internship program, qualified students are offered challenging on-the-job experience in Manhattan's top galleries and design firms, giving them firsthand work experience as well as credit toward their professional degree. This extension of the classroom into the professional world adds a practical dimension to their education.

Pratt is one of the largest undergraduate and graduate schools for art, design, and architecture in the United States, offering a wide range of cross-disciplinary study options, dual degrees, and major concentrations. Pratt offers undergraduate degrees in architecture, art history and criticism, art and design education, communication design (advertising art direction, graphic design, and illustration), computer graphics/digital arts, construction management, critical and visual studies, fine arts (ceramics, jewelry design, painting/drawing, printmaking, and sculpture), fashion design, industrial design, interior design, media arts (animation, film/video and photography), and writing for publication, performance, and media. Graduate degrees are offered in architecture, art history and criticism, art and design education, art therapy, dance therapy, city and regional planning, computer graphics/digital arts, communication design (graphic and packaging design), design management, facilities management, fine art (painting/drawing, printmaking, photography, sculpture, and new forms), arts and cultural management, design management, environmental systems management, industrial design, interior design, historic preservation, library science, and urban design.

Student services include academic advisement, career planning and placement, counseling, and academic skills development. There are more than sixty student-run organizations, including fraternities, sororities, professional societies, and clubs. Pratt participates in NCAA and ECAA men's and women's varsity competitions and has intramural sports teams as well.

Pratt Institute has educated professionals for productive careers in artistic and technical fields since its founding in 1887. By employing seasoned professionals as instructors; supporting its innovative programming with an extensive array of art- and design-related studios, workshops, computer labs, and galleries; and providing a rigorous liberal arts core curriculum (mandatory for all students), Pratt Institute offers students an outstanding professional as well as an academically well-rounded education. The fact that Pratt has one of the highest student retention rates in the country among schools of its kind confirms the satisfaction students and their families report about the quality of the education they receive here.

Pratt's faculty members, all practicing professionals, bring to the classroom a "real-world" expertise, a strong theoretical base, and the high standards of their professional work. Pratt faculty members enjoy overwhelming success and critical acclaim in their prospective fields. They have garnered prestigious academic and professional awards, including Tiffany, Fulbright, and Guggenheim grants, and have been provided with publishing contracts, travel and research scholarships, and exhibition opportunities. This intimate acquaintance with "real-world" success and high critical standards has a significant impact on Pratt students, leading them to rewarding and lucrative careers in the fields of art and design.

For more than 100 years, the Institute has produced great artists and designers. The following are just a few of Pratt's alumni and their outstanding accomplishments: Bob Giraldi, director of award-winning TV commercials, including the Michael Jackson Pepsi commercials; Morris Cousins, industrial designer and founder of Tupperware; Betsey Johnson, fashion designer; Ellsworth Kelly, painter; Robert Wilson, performance artist; Bruce Hannah, Knoll furniture designer; Paul Rand, graphic designer of IBM, Westinghouse, and NEXT computer logos; William Boyer, automobile designer of the classic Thunderbird; Peter Blake, prominent architecture author and editor; Harvey Fierstein, playwright of *Torch Song Trilogy*; Robert Mapplethorpe, photographer; Robert Redford, actor and director; Jeremy Scott, fashion designer; Tomie DePaola, author and illustrator of the children's classic, *Strega Nona*; Patti Smith, rock star and poet; and Peter Max, pop artist.

Pratt is the only school for art and design in New York that has a traditional college campus containing spacious lawns and tree-lined plazas. Its numerous buildings offer an abundance of light, air, and open space—highly conducive to focused, serious studio work—and house a wealth of art and design support facilities that include exhibition galleries; printmaking, woodworking, and metalworking shops; casting forges; sculpture and ceramic studios; photo printing darkrooms; film studios; projection and editing rooms; animation stands; and computer labs.

The educational goal of the School of Art and Design is to educate whole artists, writers, and designers. A Pratt education focuses primarily on two objectives: professional training—emphasizing the learning of skills, techniques, and the methodology necessary for students to perform in the professional community as productive artists, writers, or designers—and building students' critical awareness through exposure to a strong liberal arts curriculum. Pratt students are encouraged to enroll in courses outside their major and explore the interconnectedness of art, design, writing, technology, and human need.

At Pratt, future art teachers discover themselves by teaching classes in the Department of Art and Design Education's Saturday Art School. For almost a century, this laboratory school has provided New York City children, adolescents, and, more recently, adults and senior citizens with a high-quality art program.

By educating more than four generations of students to be creative, technically skilled, and adaptable professionals, Pratt has earned an international reputation that attracts more than 4,700 undergraduate and graduate students annually from more than forty-seven states and forty countries.

Purchase College, State University of New York
Purchase, New York

State-supported, coed. Small town campus. Total enrollment: 3,901. Art program established 1972.

Degrees Bachelor of Fine Arts in the areas of painting/drawing, printmaking, photography, design, sculpture, art of the book. Majors and concentrations: art/fine arts, book arts, graphic design, painting/drawing, photography, printmaking, sculpture, studio art. Graduate degrees offered: Master of Fine Arts in the areas of painting/drawing, printmaking, sculpture, art of the book. Program accredited by NASAD.

Enrollment 419 total; 406 undergraduate, 13 graduate.

Purchase College, State University of New York (continued)

Art Student Profile 58% females, 42% males, 16% minorities, 8% international.

Art Faculty 19 total (full-time), 23 total (part-time). 88% of full-time faculty have terminal degrees. Graduate students teach a few undergraduate courses. Undergraduate student–faculty ratio: 16:1.

Student Life Student groups/activities include Visual Artists for Visual Arts, Sonodanza (interdisciplinary performing arts/visual arts group), senior show.

Expenses for 2007–2008 Application fee: $40. State resident tuition: $4350 full-time. Nonresident tuition: $10,610 full-time. Mandatory fees: $1421 full-time. Full-time tuition and fees vary according to program. College room and board: $9444. College room only: $5886. Room and board charges vary according to board plan and housing facility. Special program-related fees: $35–$165 per course for materials fee for studio courses.

Financial Aid Program-specific awards: 70 art and design scholarships/awards ($1500).

Application Procedures Students admitted directly into the professional program freshman year. Deadline for freshmen and transfers: March 15. Notification date for freshmen and transfers: April 15. Required: essay, high school transcript, college transcript(s) for transfer students, minimum 2.0 high school GPA, 2 letters of recommendation, portfolio, SAT or ACT test scores, minimum TOEFL score of 550 for international applicants. Recommended: minimum 3.0 high school GPA, interview. Portfolio reviews held twice on campus and off campus at National Portfolio Day Association events; the submission of slides may be substituted for portfolios whenever needed.

Web Site http://www.purchase.edu

Undergraduate Contact Ms. Simone Varadian, Counselor, Admissions Department, Purchase College, State University of New York, 735 Anderson Hill Road, Purchase, New York 10577-1400; 914-251-6307, fax: 914-251-6314, e-mail address: simone.varadian@purchase.edu

Graduate Contact Ms. Sabrina Johnston, Counselor, Admissions Department, Purchase College, State University of New York, 735 Anderson Hill Road, Purchase, New York 10577-1400; 914-251-6479, fax: 914-251-6314.

More About the College

Purchase College is fulfilling its mission that "artists and scholars are indispensable both to each other and to an enlightened society." Unique in the history of postsecondary education, professional and conservatory programs in visual and performing arts coexist and interact with a small and selective liberal arts college. Philosophically as well as pragmatically, the purpose of the Visual Arts program is to provide an educational atmosphere in which students and artists work together, engage in critical dialogue, experiment, test their ideas, and learn. The School of Art+Design at Purchase College offers professional programs that prepare students for careers in the visual arts by honoring tradition, encouraging experimentation, and embracing new concepts, materials, and technologies. A faculty of working artists and designers is committed to creating a supportive climate in which students are passionate about learning to see, to think, to create, and to reflect. The internationally renowned Neuberger Museum, located next door to the Art+Design Building, enhances learning through its collections and exhibitions and access to curators, artists, designers, and educators.

The School of Art+Design offers a four-year curriculum, which culminates in the Bachelor of Fine Arts (B.F.A.) degree.

Each student works closely with a faculty adviser to establish a program of study that allows the student to develop particular areas of interest and to prepare for professional status in art and design. In the professional art school program, the student investigates introductory courses in different visual arts disciplines and, in the course of four years, specializes in one area of study, including graphic design, painting and drawing, photography, printmaking/art of the book, video and time-based media, and sculpture/3-D media. Some students may wish to pursue an interdisciplinary course of study where several media areas are investigated with an emphasis on synthesis and juxtaposition.

Performing arts students and faculty members from the three other conservatories on campus: Dance, Music, and Theater Arts and Film, as well as the Performing Arts Center, add to the scope of the critical and aesthetic discourse at the College. Study in the visual and performing arts is enhanced by a strong liberal arts curriculum, which informs the work and expands the interests of art students to better prepare them to not only make art, but to excel and to contribute to the field in significant ways.

This ability is evidenced in the professional achievement of recent alumni in exhibiting in such venues as the Museum of Modern Art, the Los Angeles County Museum of Art, and the Whitney Museum of American Art and a wide range of noted galleries nationally and in other countries. Alumni of the School hold a variety of positions in the design field, including those of art director at Rolling Stone magazine, Atlantic Records, and Coach, Inc. Accolades for the School's alumni/ae include selection as the United States' representative to the prestigious Venice Biennale, a coveted honor, and such significant and highly regarded fellowships and grants as the Fulbright, Guggenheim, MacArthur, Prix de Rome, and New York Foundation for the Arts.

The interaction of artists in conservatory programs and scholars in the liberal arts and sciences creates a cross-fertilization that is mutually beneficial. This, then, is the premise and promise of Purchase College, and the culture of the campus reflects it. On any given day, one can attend a lecture on music, a dance rehearsal, a gallery opening, and more. This environment is stimulating and a springboard for the individual imagination.

Queen's University at Kingston

Kingston, Ontario, Canada

Province-supported, coed. Urban campus. Total enrollment: 20,566. Art program established 1969.

Degrees Bachelor of Fine Arts in the area of studio art with an art history component (general and honours). Majors and concentrations: media arts, painting, printmaking, sculpture.

Enrollment 120 total; all undergraduate.

Art Student Profile 80% females, 20% males, 20% minorities, 1% international.

Art Faculty 3 undergraduate (full-time), 4 undergraduate (part-time). 50% of full-time faculty have terminal degrees. Graduate students do not teach undergraduate courses. Undergraduate student–faculty ratio: 20:1.

Student Life Student groups/activities include Docents of Agnes Etherington Art Centre, shows at student-run Union Gallery, shows at local galleries.

Expenses for 2007–2008 Application fee: $165 Canadian dollars. Province resident tuition: $5373 full-time. Canadian resident tuition: $5373 full-time. Mandatory fees: $794 full-time. International student tuition: $15,880 full-time. Special program-related fees: $75 per trip for Montreal, Toronto, Ottawa trips, $300 per trip for gallery tour to New York City, $500–$1000 per year for materials (fine art students).

Financial Aid Program-specific awards: 1 Robert Shotton Memorial Entrance Scholarship for freshmen art students demonstrating talent ($500), 1 The Alfred Bader Scholarship for art history students ($600), 1 The Janet Braicle Book Prize for art history students ($70), 1 The Harold and Helen Cave Scholarship for art history students ($2500), 1 The Milada Svaton Neumann Award for art history students ($800), 1 The Wallace Near Prize for art history students ($3200), 1 The Margaret Craig Scholarship in Fine Art for 4th year studio students, 1 The Helen Nininger Memorial Scholarship in Fine Art for full-time 2nd, 3rd or 4th year painter.

Application Procedures Students admitted directly into the professional program freshman year. Deadline for freshmen and transfers: March 30. Required: high school transcript, college transcript(s) for transfer students, minimum 3.0 high school GPA, portfolio. Portfolio reviews held in the spring on campus; the submission of slides may be substituted for portfolios (preferred).

Web Site http://www.queensu.ca/art

Undergraduate Contact Jan Winton, BFA Coordinator, Department of Art, Queen's University at Kingston, Ontario Hall, Kingston, Ontario K7L 3N6, Canada; 613-533-6000 ext. 77353, fax: 613-533-6891, e-mail address: jw5@queensu.ca

Quincy University

Quincy, Illinois

Independent Roman Catholic, coed. Small town campus. Total enrollment: 1,250.

Web Site http://www.quincy.edu/

Radford University

Radford, Virginia

State-supported, coed. Small town campus. Total enrollment: 9,220.

Radford University (continued)

Degrees Bachelor of Fine Arts in the areas of art, graphic design. Majors and concentrations: animation, art history and museum studies, art/fine arts, ceramics, drawing, graphic design, jewelry and metalsmithing, painting, photography, printmaking, sculpture, watercolors. Graduate degrees offered: Master of Fine Arts in the area of art.

Enrollment 236 total; 49 undergraduate, 27 graduate, 160 nonprofessional degree.

Art Student Profile 65% females, 35% males, 7% minorities, 1% international.

Art Faculty 14 total (full-time), 6 total (part-time). 87% of full-time faculty have terminal degrees. Graduate students teach a few undergraduate courses. Undergraduate student–faculty ratio: 14:1.

Student Life Student groups/activities include Student Art Guild, Jewelry Guild, Ceramic Guild. Special housing available for art students.

Expenses for 2007–2008 Application fee: $50. State resident tuition: $4026 full-time. Nonresident tuition: $12,360 full-time. Mandatory fees: $2150 full-time. College room and board: $6490. College room only: $3452. Room and board charges vary according to board plan and housing facility.

Financial Aid Program-specific awards: 5 Arts Society Scholarships for program students ($600–$1100), 2 De la Burdé Scholarships for program students ($600–$1100), 1 Fran Carson Scholarship for program students ($600–$1100), 1 Zheng Liang Feng Scholarship for international art program students ($750).

Application Procedures Students apply for admission into the professional program by freshman, sophomore, junior year. Deadline for freshmen: April 1; transfers: June 1. Notification date for freshmen and transfers: continuous. Required: high school transcript, college transcript(s) for transfer students, minimum 2.0 high school GPA, SAT or ACT test scores, minimum 2.0 college GPA for transfer students. Portfolio reviews held once on campus.

Web Site http://www.radford.edu/~art-web/

Undergraduate Contact Admissions, Radford University, Box 6903, Radford, Virginia 24142; 540-831-5371, fax: 540-831-5038, e-mail address: ruadmiss@radford.edu

Graduate Contact College of Graduate and Extended Education, Radford University, Box 6928, Radford, Virginia 24142; 540-831-5724, e-mail address: gradcoll@radford.edu

Rhode Island College

Providence, Rhode Island

State-supported, coed. Suburban campus. Total enrollment: 8,939.

Web Site http://www.ric.edu/

Rhode Island School of Design

Providence, Rhode Island

Independent, coed. Urban campus. Total enrollment: 2,259. Art program established 1877.

Degrees Bachelor of Fine Arts; Bachelor of Graphic Design; Bachelor of Industrial Design. Majors and concentrations: apparel design, architecture, ceramics, film/animation/video, furniture design, glass, graphic design, illustration, industrial design, interior architecture, jewelry and metalsmithing, painting, photography, printmaking, sculpture, textiles. Graduate degrees offered: Master of Arts in the area of art education; Master of Architecture; Master of Arts in Teaching in the area of art education; Master of Fine Arts in the areas of ceramics, furniture design, graphic design, glass, jewelry and metals, painting, printmaking, photography, sculpture, textiles, digital media; Master of Interior Architecture; Master of Industrial Design; Master of Landscape Architecture. Cross-registration with Brown University. Program accredited by NASAD, ASLA, NAAB.

Enrollment 2,258 total; 1,878 undergraduate, 380 graduate.

Art Student Profile 70% females, 30% males, 23% minorities, 16% international.

Art Faculty 139 total (full-time), 355 total (part-time). 73% of full-time faculty have terminal degrees. Graduate students teach a few undergraduate courses. Undergraduate student–faculty ratio: 9:1.

Student Life Student groups/activities include Film Society, Performance Club. Special housing available for art students.

Visual *Arts*

Expenses for 2007–2008 Application fee: $50. Comprehensive fee: $42,978 includes full-time tuition ($32,858), mandatory fees ($260), and college room and board ($9860). College room only: $5630. Special program-related fees: $10–$100 per course for lab fees for certain courses.

Financial Aid Program-specific awards: 600 RISD Scholarships for those demonstrating financial need ($12,141), 5–7 Trustees Scholarships for above-average students with exceptional artistic ability ($5000).

Application Procedures Students admitted directly into the professional program freshman year. Deadline for freshmen: February 15; transfers: March 31. Notification date for freshmen: April 1; transfers: May 1. Required: essay, high school transcript, college transcript(s) for transfer students, portfolio, SAT or ACT test scores, 3 original drawings. Recommended: minimum 3.0 high school GPA, 3 letters of recommendation. the submission of slides may be substituted for portfolios (slides or prints required).

Web Site http://www.risd.edu

Contact Admissions Office, Rhode Island School of Design, 2 College Street, Providence, Rhode Island 02903; 401-454-6300, fax: 401-454-6309, e-mail address: admissions@risd.edu

More About the School

Students who come to Rhode Island School of Design (RISD, pronounced riz-dee) join an intense creative artists' community that has been internationally respected for its excellent education for more than 130 years. This dynamic atmosphere—created among people with similar interests, talents, and focus—is frequently noted by many sources as a distinguishing feature of RISD, which has been cited consistently as a leading visual arts college in numerous college guides and surveys.

RISD's 2,260 students, coming from more than forty-five nations around the world, find an extensive range of sixteen majors in areas of architecture, design, and the fine arts. This diverse choice of disciplines creates an enriched environment of ideas and personal directions. Students find balance in the curriculum between focus on their major interest, experimentation in related studios, and innovative cross-disciplinary study. It is a frequent happening at RISD for a student in one studio major to work jointly with a classmate from another department on a single project, broadening understanding of the creative opportunities between disciplines. Digital technology continues to expand the range of tools available to artists and designers, and RISD now has more than 400 computer systems and related equipment available in twenty departmental and specialized labs. A number of departments now assign each student a powerful laptop computer with specialized software, running on a wireless campus network. There are a number of real-world connections to industry at RISD, involving research design studios sponsored by NASA, Sikorsky, Rubbermaid, and Nissan and innovative courses taught jointly with other colleges, such as the product development collaboration between RISD's Industrial Design Department and M.B.A. students from MIT.

The environment of the college is greatly enhanced by the advanced projects and research undertaken by 400 graduate students in seventeen graduate programs. RISD's graduate programs are widely respected and frequently cited in surveys as leaders in their visual disciplines.

RISD's 400 studio faculty members are among the leaders in the visual arts, passionate about the fulfillment that the arts bring to the individual and the role of the arts and design in society. They include designers of products found in most homes, award-winning authors and illustrators, painters and sculptors whose work can be seen in major museums and galleries, and acclaimed architects, filmmakers, and textile artists.

Liberal arts form an important component of each student's study as well, and RISD invests notably in the quality of its academic course offerings. There are 28 full-time faculty members in liberal arts departments, all holding the highest degree in their discipline, and 55 part-time faculty members who specialize in certain areas; this number and quality of academic faculty members is unusual for a visual arts college and results in a varied selection of more than 210 courses yearly. Students may choose to enrich the basic liberal arts requirements by pursuing a concentration in art history; English; or history, philosophy, and social sciences. RISD students may also enroll for courses at our neighbor, Brown University.

RISD is located in Providence, described in numerous media stories as a "Renaissance City" and chronicled recently in *Money* magazine as "the best place to live in the eastern United States." Home to students from a number of colleges, Providence offers numerous social and cultural opportunities and an active visual and performing arts community.

Comprehensive career planning support is available to all students and alumni in the Alumni and Career Services Office. Seminars on a wide array of

Rhode Island School of Design (continued)

topics that are critical to artists and their career development, individual career counseling, on-campus recruiting, and online listings of available jobs, internships, and fellowships are among the services available. Students are encouraged to participate in professional internships and, on average, more than 60 percent of graduates have experienced at least one internship opportunity. Students have interned recently at WGBE, Cannondale, Walt Disney, Pixar, and Pentagram. RISD surveys all graduates one year after the completion of their studies and, consistently, about 91 percent are employed in their discipline or a related art or design field.

RISD alumni consistently win major competitions, prestigious awards, and recognition for their works in the arts, industry, and education. David Weisner and Chris van Allsburg have won the nationally acclaimed Caldecott Medal for their children's books. Designer Nicole Miller is noted for her collections of women's apparel and men's accessories. Roz Chast's books of her own cartoons (featured often in *The New Yorker*) and Henry Horenstein's photography books have won numerous awards. Seth MacFarlane is the creator of the animated sitcom, *Family Guy*. Architect Deborah Berke is recognized for her work in a variety of residential and commercial settings. Glass artists Toots Zynsky and Howard Ben Tre, painter Kara Walker, and filmmakers Martha Coolidge and Gus van Sant are but a few of the successes among RISD's 16,000 alumni. In 2007, four RISD alums were awarded a MacArthur Fellowship, bringing the total to eight RISE recipients of this prestigious award over the last ten years. Profiles of many others are available on RISD's Web site at http://www.risd.edu.

Program Facilities RISD's facilities consist of forty buildings with more than 1,000,000 square feet of space, including specialized studio spaces and equipment; access to studio spaces, with upperclass students often having a private studio space; sixteen residence halls offering a variety of living environments; the Museum of Art, with more than 85,000 objects frequently used for study purposes by faculty members and students; a library with more than 130,000 volumes, including artist's and rare books, an image research collection of 470,000 clippings and photographs and 160,000 slides; and the Nature Lab with 80,000 objects available for study and research.

Faculty and Resident Artists RISD has 480 faculty members, 145 of them full-time and readily available to students on campus. More than 200 artists and guest critics visit the campus on average

each year. Among recent visitors were Janine Antoni, sculptor; Philip Glass, composer/musician; Pat Olezko, performance artist; David Byrne, musician; Todd Oldham, designer; David Hickey, art critic; James Rosenquist, painter; Gore Vidal, author; and Dale Chihuly, glass artist.

Student Exhibit Opportunities Exhibition opportunities for students include two college-wide galleries and eight departmental exhibition spaces on campus, with an average of 125 shows staged each year.

Special Programs The European Honors Program allows students to study in Rome for their junior or senior year. Study-abroad exchange agreements are in place with fifty other art and design colleges around the world. Wintersession term provides unique study opportunities each year, including travel-abroad courses (recently to Italy, Switzerland, Paris, Cuba, Ghana, New Zealand, and Mexico). Mobility program are available with thirty-two other arts colleges. RISD also offers a Summer Studies Program, with courses designed to meet the needs of beginning to advanced students. These courses run from two to six weeks, many offer college credit, and all are taught by distinguished teachers drawn from the School's regular faculty members or visiting experts. Summer Studies also offers a study-abroad option.

Ringling College of Art and Design

Sarasota, Florida

Independent, coed. Small town campus. Total enrollment: 1,090. Art program established 1931.

Degrees Bachelor of Fine Arts. Majors and concentrations: art/fine arts, business of art and design, computer animation, digital film and video, game art and design, graphic and interactive communication, illustration, interior design, photography and digital imaging. Cross-registration with members of Association of Independent Colleges of Art and Design. Program accredited by NASAD, CIDA.

Enrollment 1,090 total; all undergraduate.

Art Student Profile 51% females, 49% males, 19% minorities, 5% international.

Art Faculty 63 undergraduate (full-time), 61 undergraduate (part-time). 52% of full-time faculty have terminal degrees. Graduate students do not teach undergraduate courses. Undergraduate student–faculty ratio: 13:1.

Student Life Student groups/activities include Campus Activities Board, Phi Delta Theta/ Sigma Sigma Sigma, preprofessional organizations. Special housing available for art students.

Expenses for 2007–2008 Application fee: $35. Comprehensive fee: $34,725 includes full-time tuition ($24,100), mandatory fees ($625), and college room and board ($10,000). College room only: $5500. Full-time tuition and fees vary according to course load, program, and student level. Room and board charges vary according to board plan and housing facility. Special program-related fees: $800 per year for fine arts technology fee, $1200 per year for photography and digital imaging technology fee, $1200 per year for illustration technology fee, $1200 per year for core studio program technology fee, $1400 per year for interior design technology fee, $1700 per year for graphic and interactive communication technology fee, $2500 per year for computer animation technology fee.

Financial Aid Program-specific awards: 5 Presidential Scholarships for incoming students ($7000), 103 need/merit scholarships for incoming students ($2619).

Application Procedures Students admitted directly into the professional program freshman year. Deadline for freshmen and transfers: continuous. Notification date for freshmen and transfers: continuous. Required: essay, high school transcript, college transcript(s) for transfer students, minimum 2.0 high school GPA, 2 letters of recommendation, portfolio. Recommended: interview, SAT or ACT test scores. Portfolio reviews held continuously on campus and off campus at National Portfolio Days; the submission of slides may be substituted for portfolios.

Web Site http://www.ringling.edu

Undergraduate Contact Mr. James H. Dean, Dean of Admissions, Admissions, Ringling College of Art and Design, 2700 North Tamiami Trail, Sarasota, Florida 34234; 941-351-5100 ext. 7523, fax: 941-359-7517, e-mail address: admissions@ringling.edu

More About the College

For nearly 75 years, Ringling College of Art and Design has cultivated the creative spirit in art and design students from around the globe . . .

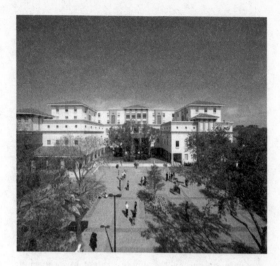

transforming our visual world. Founded in 1931 by noted art collector, real estate magnate, and circus impresario John Ringling, the private, not-for-profit college is fully accredited by the National Association of Schools of Art and Design (NASAD; http://nasad. arts-accredit.org) and the Southern Association of Colleges and Schools (SACS; http://www.sacscoc.org).

Located on the Gulf Coast of Florida, the picturesque 35-acre campus today includes ninety buildings and enrolls more than 1,100 students from forty-three states and twenty-eight other countries—more than half of whom reside on the pedestrian-friendly residential campus. The College's 130 faculty members are all professional artists, designers, and scholars who actively pursue their own work outside the classroom.

The College's rigorous curriculum engages innovation and tradition through a strong, well-rounded first-year Core Studio Program and a deep focus on the liberal arts. Students pursue one of fourteen majors leading to their B.F.A. degrees: advertising design, broadcast design/motion graphics, business of art and design, computer animation, digital film, fine arts, game art and design, graphic and interactive communication, illustration, interior design, painting, photography and digital imaging, printmaking, or sculpture.

The academic emphasis on professional portfolio development and career preparation provides students with a well-rounded education. This is backed up by the extensive career-related services available during a student's time at the College and throughout their professional life.

The Center for Career Services lists nearly 1,000 employment opportunities and internships each year,

Visual Arts

Ringling College of Art and Design (continued)

available 24 hours a day at http://www.collegecentral.com/ringling. The center offers workshops and seminars on professional skills, such as portfolio preparation, resume writing, and interviewing, and can assist students in researching opportunities for additional training and graduate education. Nearly four dozen nationally recognized recruiters visit Ringling College's campus each year to interview students and to make employment and internship offers. Among the most outstanding organizations recruiting at Ringling College are Hallmark Cards, CNN, Target, Headline News, Sony Pictures ImageWorks, DreamWorks Animation SKG, Disney, Electronic Arts (EA), American Greetings, and even the Central Intelligence Agency (CIA).

The College believes passionately in the development and support of the whole student by preparing each graduate to be successful in their chosen careers as well as socially responsible artist-citizens. As a testament to the educational principles instilled in them, students donate hours upon hours of their personal time to volunteering on myriad local community public service projects and participating in student organizations. Clubs on campus provide a well-balanced calendar of cocurricular events, leadership opportunities, and social activities. Organizations include the Student Government Association and many diverse clubs focusing on artistic development, recreation, special interests, theater and dance, social and community service, Greek and spiritual life, and more. Students are recognized for their contributions through awards and honors and a comprehensive cocurricular transcript reflecting their participation in these areas.

Ringling College traditions include Family Weekend, Latino Heritage Month, National Collegiate Alcohol Awareness Week, National Coming Out Day, Black History Month, and Women's History Month. Other celebrations include beach parties, holiday parties, and a President's reception for graduates and their families.

More than half of Ringling College students live on campus in one of ten different, modern, and well-equipped residence halls and apartments. In addition to the convenience of campus living, residents benefit from a variety of programs, residence hall support staff, and campus food service. To enhance the campus experience and create a hub for student activities, a dynamic, 80,000-square-foot five-story Student Center opened in fall 2006. The building includes a fitness center and exercise studio,

student activity center and meeting spaces, Outtakes Café, classrooms, an exhibition hall, and two floors of student residences.

To begin the school year, a New Student Orientation program is held for all new students and their parents during the week prior to the start of the fall semester. Orientation includes opportunities to meet other students, hear from key faculty members and administrators, attend presentations on academic expectations and campus resources, and to enjoy a number of relaxing, social activities with family members and classmates.

Ringling College of Art and Design welcomes applications from students with a serious commitment to the visual arts. Admission is based on a review of the student's portfolio, academic record, essay, and teacher recommendations. All applicants are reviewed individually, with special consideration given to creative ability and potential for success in college-level studies.

Program/Academic Facilities At Ringling College, facilities include the Verman Kimbrough Memorial Library, with 55,000 volumes, including more than 6,100 videos, CDs, and DVDs, 350 periodical subscriptions, hand-made artist's books, and a separate collection of more than 127,000 slides; Selby Gallery, with international and nationally recognized shows, annual juried student and faculty exhibitions; specialized studios for painting, printmaking, sculpture, wood, graphic design, computer animation, illustration, figure drawing, interior design, and CAD; and the Deborah M. Cooley Photography Center, with studios, darkrooms, and digital labs.

The computer-student ratio is greater than 1:2. Computer facilities include four high-end visual 3-D workstation laboratories, twelve high-end Macintosh workstation laboratories, three Intel-Xeon-based class workstation laboratories, three audio and video editing laboratories, and several digital photography labs. Labs are equipped with high-end workstations, peripherals (scanners, printers, etc.), and numerous general-purpose software packages and tools, including desktop publishing, editors, file-transfer tools, spreadsheets, Web tools, imaging tools, utility applications, and graphics-generation equipment. All personal computers, workstations, and printers are connected to the campus network.

A rich collection of discipline-specific software packages is also available in the computer labs, including Alias Maya; 2d3 Boujou; Shake; Pixar Rendering Tools; Apple Computer: Compressor, Cinema Tools, FinalCut Pro, DVD Studio Pro, iDVD, iPhoto, iMovie, iTunes, LiveType, Safari, Soundtrack,

Pro Kit, and Ableton; Crater: CTP; Reel Smart: Motion Blur and Stop Motion Pro; Maxon: Body Paint 3D, Auto*des*sys, and FormZ; AutoDesk: Architectural Desktop, AutoCAD, and Autodesk VIZ; Adobe Creative Suite; Acrobat Pro; After Effects; Audition; GoLive; Encore; ImageReady; FontFolio; Premiere; Dreamweaver and Flash; Microsoft: Office, Front Page, Access, Project, and Implementation Tools; and Corel: Painter, BareBones, and BBEdit.

All on-campus residence halls allow students direct access to on-campus computing resources and the Internet with a blazing DS3 speed from the comfort and convenience of their own rooms.

Rockford College

Rockford, Illinois

Independent, coed. Suburban campus. Total enrollment: 1,426.

Degrees Bachelor of Fine Arts in the area of art. Majors and concentrations: ceramics, drawing, painting, photography, printmaking, sculpture.

Art Student Profile 60% females, 40% males, 16% minorities, 1% international.

Art Faculty 4 undergraduate (full-time), 1 undergraduate (part-time). 100% of full-time faculty have terminal degrees. Graduate students do not teach undergraduate courses. Undergraduate student–faculty ratio: 10:1.

Student Life Student groups/activities include Art Club, SOAP (Society of Artsy People).

Expenses for 2007–2008 Application fee: $35. Comprehensive fee: $29,700 includes full-time tuition ($22,950) and college room and board ($6750). College room only: $3850.

Financial Aid Program-specific awards: Margaret Schuh Des Pland Scholarship for senior women art students.

Application Procedures Students apply for admission into the professional program by sophomore year. Deadline for freshmen and transfers: continuous. Required: high school transcript, college transcript(s) for transfer students, portfolio, SAT or ACT test scores (minimum composite ACT score of 19), minimum 2.65 high school GPA, minimum 2.3 cumulative college GPA for transfer students, top 1/2 of graduating class for first-years. Recommended: 2 letters of recommendation, interview. Portfolio reviews held once each semester on campus.

Web Site http://www.rockford.edu

Undergraduate Contact Cassie Swanson, Assistant Director of Admission, Rockford College, Burpee Center, 5050 East State Street, Rockford, Illinois 61108-2393; 800-892-2984, fax: 815-226-2822, e-mail address: rcadmissions@rockford.edu

Rocky Mountain College of Art & Design

Denver, Colorado

Proprietary, coed. Suburban campus. Art program established 1963.

Degrees Bachelor of Fine Arts. Majors and concentrations: animation, art education, art/fine arts, graphic design and interactive media, illustration, interior design. Program accredited by NASAD, CIDA.

Enrollment 455 total; all undergraduate.

Art Student Profile 58% females, 42% males, 5% minorities, 4% international.

Art Faculty 24 undergraduate (full-time), 48 undergraduate (part-time). 80% of full-time faculty have terminal degrees. Graduate students do not teach undergraduate courses. Undergraduate student–faculty ratio: 19:1.

Student Life Student groups/activities include ASIFA (International Animated Film Association), American Society of Interior Designers, American Institute of Graphic Arts.

Expenses for 2006–2007 Application fee: $35. Tuition: $18,984 full-time.

Financial Aid Program-specific awards: admissions merit award for incoming students ($15,000), RMCAD Portfolio Merit Award for incoming students ($12,000).

Application Procedures Students admitted directly into the professional program freshman year. Deadline for freshmen and transfers: continuous. Notification date for freshmen and transfers: continuous. Required: essay, high school transcript, college transcript(s) for transfer students, minimum 2.0 high school GPA, interview, portfolio, SAT or ACT test scores. Portfolio reviews held continuously on campus; the submission of slides may be substituted for portfolios.

Web Site http://www.rmcad.edu

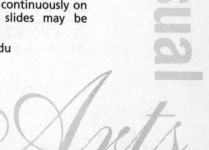

Visual Arts

Rocky Mountain College of Art & Design (continued)

Undergraduate Contact Ms. Angela Carlson, Director of Admissions, Rocky Mountain College of Art & Design, 1600 Pierce Street, Denver, Colorado 80214; 800-888-2787, fax: 303-759-4970, e-mail address: admissions@rmcad.edu

Roger Williams University

Bristol, Rhode Island

Independent, coed. Total enrollment: 5,172. Art program established 1972.

Degrees Bachelor of Arts in the area of visual art studies. Majors and concentrations: art, ceramics, drawing, painting, photography.

Enrollment 37 total; all undergraduate.

Art Student Profile 51% females, 49% males, 6% minorities, 2% international.

Art Faculty 4 undergraduate (full-time), 14 undergraduate (part-time). Graduate students do not teach undergraduate courses. Undergraduate student–faculty ratio: 3:1.

Student Life Student groups/activities include Art Society.

Expenses for 2007–2008 Application fee: $50. Comprehensive fee: $36,702 includes full-time tuition ($24,192), mandatory fees ($1567), and college room and board ($10,943). College room only: $5819.

Application Procedures Students admitted directly into the professional program freshman year. Deadline for freshmen and transfers: continuous. Required: essay, high school transcript, college transcript(s) for transfer students, 2 letters of recommendation, portfolio, SAT or ACT test scores. Portfolio reviews held on campus; the submission of slides may be substituted for portfolios.

Web Site http://www.rwu.edu

Undergraduate Contact Michelle L. Beauregard, Director of Freshman Admissions, Roger Williams University, 1 Old Ferry Road, Bristol, Rhode Island 02809; 401-254-3500, fax: 401-254-3557, e-mail address: admit@rwu.edu

Rosemont College

Rosemont, Pennsylvania

Independent Roman Catholic, Suburban campus. Total enrollment: 995. Art program established 1969.

Degrees Bachelor of Fine Arts. Majors and concentrations: art education, art therapy, art/fine arts, fashion design, graphic design, interior design. Cross-registration with Cabrini College, Villanova University, Eastern College, Arcadia University.

Enrollment 50 undergraduate.

Art Student Profile 100% females.

Art Faculty 4 undergraduate (full-time), 10 undergraduate (part-time). 100% of full-time faculty have terminal degrees. Graduate students do not teach undergraduate courses. Undergraduate student–faculty ratio: 10:1.

Student Life Student groups/activities include Studio Art Club.

Expenses for 2007–2008 Application fee: $35. Comprehensive fee: $32,035 includes full-time tuition ($21,630), mandatory fees ($1205), and college room and board ($9200). Special program-related fees: $50 per course for supply fees.

Financial Aid Program-specific awards: 1 Sister Stella Kelly Scholarship for high school senior art students ($13,480).

Application Procedures Deadline for freshmen and transfers: continuous. Required: essay, high school transcript, college transcript(s) for transfer students, letter of recommendation, interview, portfolio, SAT or ACT test scores. Portfolio reviews held twice on campus; the submission of slides may be substituted for portfolios when distance is prohibitive.

Web Site http://www.rosemont.edu/

Undergraduate Contact Amy Orr, Department Chair, Arts Division, Rosemont College, 1400 Montgomery Avenue, Rosemont, Pennsylvania 19010-1699; 610-527-0200 ext. 2311, fax: 610-527-0341, e-mail address: a.orr@rosemont.edu

Roski School of Fine Arts

See University of Southern California

Roy H. Park School of Communications

See Ithaca College

Russell Sage College

Troy, New York

Independent, Urban campus. Total enrollment: 800. Art program established 1916.

Degrees Bachelor of Arts. Majors and concentrations: creative arts and therapy. Program accredited by NASAD.

Enrollment 29 total; all undergraduate.

Art Student Profile 100% females, 10% minorities.

Art Faculty 4 undergraduate (full-time), 2 undergraduate (part-time). 81% of full-time faculty have terminal degrees. Graduate students do not teach undergraduate courses. Undergraduate student–faculty ratio: 11:1.

Expenses for 2007–2008 Application fee: $30. Comprehensive fee: $34,790 includes full-time tuition ($25,000), mandatory fees ($990), and college room and board ($8800). College room only: $4500.

Application Procedures Students admitted directly into the professional program freshman year. Deadline for freshmen: August 1; transfers: continuous. Required: essay, high school transcript, college transcript(s) for transfer students, minimum 2.0 high school GPA, 2 letters of recommendation, SAT or ACT test scores. Recommended: interview, portfolio. Portfolio reviews held on an individual basis on campus; the submission of slides may be substituted for portfolios.

Web Site http://www.sage.edu

Undergraduate Contact Kathy Rusch, Director of Admissions, Admissions, Russell Sage College, 45 Ferry Street, Troy, New York 12180; 518-244-2217, fax: 518-244-6880, e-mail address: ruschk@sage.edu

Rutgers, The State University of New Jersey

See Mason Gross School of the Arts

St. Cloud State University

St. Cloud, Minnesota

State-supported, coed. Suburban campus. Total enrollment: 15,964. Art program established 1973.

Degrees Bachelor of Fine Arts in the areas of studio art, graphic design. Majors and concentrations: ceramics, drawing, graphic design, painting, photography, printmaking, sculpture. Program accredited by NASAD.

Enrollment 365 total; 175 undergraduate, 190 nonprofessional degree.

Art Student Profile 50% females, 50% males, 1% minorities, 10% international.

Art Faculty 16 undergraduate (full-time), 7 undergraduate (part-time). 100% of full-time faculty have terminal degrees. Graduate students do not teach undergraduate courses. Undergraduate student–faculty ratio: 20:1.

Student Life Student groups/activities include Art Student Union, Graphic Design Association, Future Art Educators.

Expenses for 2006–2007 Application fee: $20. State resident tuition: $5045 full-time. Nonresident tuition: $10,952 full-time. Mandatory fees: $673 full-time. Full-time tuition and fees vary according to course load and reciprocity agreements. College room and board: $5194. Room and board charges vary according to board plan and housing facility. Special program-related fees for course supplies.

Financial Aid Program-specific awards: 2–3 Bill Ellingson Awards for program majors ($300), 1 May Bowle Award for program majors ($300).

Application Procedures Students apply for admission into the professional program by sophomore year. Deadline for freshmen and transfers: June 1. Required: high school transcript, college transcript(s) for transfer students, minimum 2.0 high school GPA, ACT test score only, portfolio for scholarship consideration, portfolio for admission to majors upon completion of foundation classes. Portfolio reviews held twice on campus; the submission of slides may be substituted for portfolios whenever needed.

Web Site http://www.stcloudstate.edu/~art

Undergraduate Contact Dr. David Sebberson, Chair, Art Department, St. Cloud State University, Kiehle Visual Arts Building, St. Cloud, Minnesota 56301; 320-255-4283, fax: 320-255-2232.

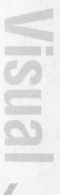

Visual Arts

St. John's University

Jamaica, New York

Independent, coed. Urban campus. Total enrollment: 20,069.

Degrees Bachelor of Fine Arts in the areas of fine arts, graphic design, photography, illustration. Majors and concentrations: graphic design, illustration, painting, photography, printmaking. Mandatory cross-registration with International Center of Photography (for photography majors). Program accredited by NASAD.

Enrollment 100 total; all undergraduate.

Art Student Profile 40% females, 60% males, 30% minorities, 10% international.

Art Faculty 13 undergraduate (full-time), 17 undergraduate (part-time). 100% of full-time faculty have terminal degrees. Graduate students do not teach undergraduate courses. Undergraduate student–faculty ratio: 15:1.

Student Life Student groups/activities include New Vision Art Society, art exhibits in University Gallery, Torch/University Newspaper, Sequoya/University Literary Magazine. Special housing available for art students.

Expenses for 2006–2007 Application fee: $30. Comprehensive fee: $36,440 includes full-time tuition ($24,400), mandatory fees ($570), and college room and board ($11,470). College room only: $7200. Full-time tuition and fees vary according to class time, course load, program, and student level. Room and board charges vary according to board plan and housing facility. Special program-related fees: $30 per course per semester for studio lab fee.

Financial Aid Program-specific awards: 2 Fine Arts Scholarships for incoming freshmen ($13,000), 1 Fine Arts Scholarship for incoming freshmen ($26,000), 3 Visual Arts Awards for incoming freshmen ($1000).

Application Procedures Students admitted directly into the professional program freshman year. Deadline for freshmen and transfers: continuous. Required: high school transcript, college transcript(s) for transfer students, 2 letters of recommendation, portfolio, SAT test score only (minimum combined SAT score of 1050). Recommended: essay, minimum 3.0 high school GPA, interview. Portfolio reviews held continuously by appointment on campus; the submission of slides may be substituted for portfolios for international students and U.S. students from a great distance.

Web Site http://www.stjohns.edu/

Undergraduate Contact Mr. Andrew Ippolito, Director, Admissions, St. John's University, 8000 Utopia Parkway, Jamaica, New York 11439; 718-990-5579, fax: 718-990-1677, e-mail address: ippolita@stjohns.edu

Saint Mary's College

Notre Dame, Indiana

Independent Roman Catholic, women only. Suburban campus. Total enrollment: 1,527.

Degrees Bachelor of Arts in the area of art; Bachelor of Fine Arts in the area of art. Majors and concentrations: art history, art/fine arts, ceramic art and design, fibers, painting/drawing, photography, printmaking, sculpture, studio art. Cross-registration with University of Notre Dame, Indiana Technical College, Indiana University South Bend, Goshen College, Bethel College. Program accredited by NASAD.

Enrollment 58 total; all undergraduate.

Art Student Profile 100% females, 10% minorities, 10% international.

Art Faculty 6 undergraduate (full-time), 3 undergraduate (part-time). 100% of full-time faculty have terminal degrees. Graduate students do not teach undergraduate courses. Undergraduate student–faculty ratio: 10:1.

Student Life Student groups/activities include Art Club, National Association of Schools of Art and Design.

Expenses for 2007–2008 Application fee: $30. Comprehensive fee: $35,550 includes full-time tuition ($26,282), mandatory fees ($590), and college room and board ($8678). College room only: $5346.

Financial Aid Program-specific awards: art talent awards for art majors demonstrating need ($500), 5 Theresa McLaughlin Awards for freshmen art majors demonstrating need ($1000).

Application Procedures Students admitted directly into the professional program freshman year. Deadline for freshmen: March 1; transfers: April 15. Notification date for freshmen and transfers: continuous. Required: essay, high school transcript, college transcript(s) for transfer students, minimum 3.0 high school GPA, letter of recommendation, SAT or ACT test scores. Recommended: interview, portfolio. Portfolio reviews held twice on campus; the submission of slides may be substituted for portfolios for large works of art and three-dimensional pieces.

Web Site http://www.saintmarys.edu

Undergraduate Contact Admissions Office, Saint Mary's College, Notre Dame, Indiana 46556; 574-284-4587, fax: 219-284-4716.

Salisbury University

Salisbury, Maryland

State-supported, coed. Small town campus. Total enrollment: 7,383.

Degrees Bachelor of Fine Arts in the area of art. Majors and concentrations: art/fine arts, ceramics, glass, graphic design, new media, painting/drawing, photography, sculpture, three-dimensional studies, two-dimensional studies. Cross-registration with University of Maryland System, The Art Institute of Philadelphia, Art Institute of Atlanta.

Enrollment 250 total; all undergraduate.

Art Student Profile 60% females, 40% males, 10% minorities, 2% international.

Art Faculty 15 undergraduate (full-time), 12 undergraduate (part-time). 93% of full-time faculty have terminal degrees. Graduate students do not teach undergraduate courses. Undergraduate student–faculty ratio: 15:1.

Student Life Student groups/activities include Glass Club, Art Club. Special housing available for art students.

Expenses for 2007–2008 Application fee: $45. State resident tuition: $4814 full-time. Nonresident tuition: $12,902 full-time. Mandatory fees: $1598 full-time. College room and board: $7601. College room only: $3880. Room and board charges vary according to board plan and housing facility. Special program-related fees: $60 per year for supplies for studio courses.

Financial Aid Program-specific awards: 1 3-D Scholarship for 3-D majors in sculpture, glass, or ceramics ($500), 3 art scholarships for program majors ($500), 2–4 Art Department Meritorious Awards for program students ($50), 1 Photography Award for photography

majors ($500), 1 Student Assistantship Award for program majors ($250).

Application Procedures Students admitted directly into the professional program freshman year. Deadline for freshmen: February 1; transfers: March 1. Required: high school transcript, college transcript(s) for transfer students, minimum 2.0 high school GPA, SAT or ACT test scores, portfolio for scholarship consideration. Recommended: essay. Portfolio reviews held once and as needed on campus; the submission of slides may be substituted for portfolios when distance is prohibitive (may submit CD digital images).

Web Site http://www.salisbury.edu/ArtDept/

Undergraduate Contact Admissions Department, Salisbury University, 1101 Camden Avenue, Salisbury, Maryland 21801; 410-543-6000, fax: 410-546-6016.

San Francisco Art Institute

San Francisco, California

Independent, coed. Urban campus. Total enrollment: 652. Art program established 1871.

Degrees Bachelor of Arts in the areas of history and theory of contemporary art, urban studies; Bachelor of Fine Arts in the areas of design and technology, film, new genres, painting, photography, printmaking, sculpture. Majors and concentrations: design and technology, film, history and theory of contemporary art, new genres, painting, photography, printmaking, sculpture, urban studies. Graduate degrees offered: Master of Arts in the areas of exhibition and museum studies, history and theory of contemporary art, urban studies; Master of Fine Arts in the areas of design and technology, film, new genres, painting, photography, printmaking, sculpture. Cross-registration with International exchange program with 15+ institutions. Program accredited by NASAD.

Enrollment 639 total; 388 undergraduate, 251 graduate.

Art Student Profile 55% females, 45% males, 31% minorities, 9% international.

Art Faculty 145 total. 95% of full-time faculty have terminal degrees. Graduate students do

San Francisco Art Institute (continued)

not teach undergraduate courses. Undergraduate student–faculty ratio: 4:1.

Student Life Student groups/activities include student-run galleries, exhibitions, and lectures, Student Union events, internships. Special housing available for art students.

Expenses for 2006–2007 Application fee: $65. Tuition: $27,200 full-time. Mandatory fees: $35 full-time. College room only: $7200. Room charges vary according to housing facility.

Financial Aid Program-specific awards: 35 Community College Scholarships for outstanding transfer students from community colleges ($5979), 153 merit-based scholarships for all undergraduate students ($6515), 307 Competitive Scholarships for all undergraduate students ($5717).

Application Procedures Students admitted directly into the professional program freshman year. Deadline for freshmen and transfers: continuous. Required: essay, high school transcript, college transcript(s) for transfer students, 2 letters of recommendation, portfolio, SAT or ACT test scores, TOEFL score of 580 for international students, English translation of transcripts for international students, WES evaluation for international students. Recommended: minimum 2.0 high school GPA, interview. Portfolio reviews held continuously on campus and off campus in locations nationwide, see www.npda.org; the submission of slides may be substituted for portfolios for out-of-state or international applicants.

Web Site http://www.sfai.edu

Contact Director of Admissions, San Francisco Art Institute, 800 Chestnut Street, San Francisco, California 94133; 415-749-4500, fax: 415-749-4592, e-mail address: admissions@sfai.edu

More About the College

San Francisco Art Institute (SFAI) consists of two schools: the School of Studio Practice and the School of Interdisciplinary Studies. The School of Studio Practice offers B.F.A., M.F.A., and Low-residency Summer M.F.A. degree programs and postbaccalaureate certificates in design+technology, film, new genres, painting, photography, printmaking, and sculpture. The School of Interdisciplinary Studies offers degree programs in exhibition and museum studies (M.A.), history and theory of contemporary art (B.A., M.A.), and urban studies (B.A., M.A.).

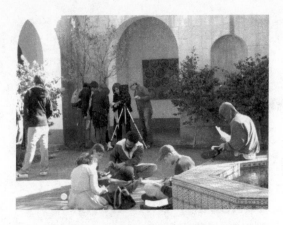

Students at SFAI receive a broad education that informs and enhances their primary area of study, choosing electives and fulfilling curriculum requirements from both schools. The high percentage of electives in the curriculum allows for an individualized education that is as well-rounded as it is focused. SFAI prepares students to be creative leaders in whatever professions they pursue.

Students at SFAI build on a rich legacy of the kind of questioning that encourages the experimentation necessary for independent and collaborative invention. Students work closely with peers and faculty members from a wide variety of backgrounds and fields; studio courses and seminars have a maximum of fifteen students. Students also participate in projects that allow them to move beyond the classroom and into the world. These programs combine SFAI's historical ways of teaching—through critique seminars, studio courses, and tutorials—with forms of research that emphasize the independent and collaborative nature of both teaching and learning. Internships, independent study, travel courses, and international exchange programs give students practical and professional experience.

Program Facilities SFAI's main campus is located at 800 Chestnut Street in San Francisco's Russian Hill neighborhood, overlooking the bay. The campus provides 24-hour access to light-filled painting, drawing, sculpture, photography, and printmaking studios; black-box studios for film, video, and performance; galleries; and lecture hall/theater and seminar rooms. Postproduction facilities include darkrooms, mural printing, and large-scale digital photo output; Super 8 and 16mm film processing and editing; digital video and Final Cut Pro editing; an HDcam- and DVCam-equipped video finishing suite; and sound studios. SFAI's Anne Bremer Memorial Library holds over 30,000 volumes, subscriptions to

Visual

Arts

more than 200 periodicals, and collections of slides, audiotapes, videotapes, films, and DVDs.

The Graduate Center is a large industrial loft building along the San Francisco Bay. The facility provides individual and group studios, digital lab, film and sound studios, darkrooms, a wood shop, seminar classrooms, a gallery, and installation critique rooms; 24-hour access, and convenience to public transportation. Graduate students also have access to all of the facilities on the main campus.

Faculty, Resident Artists, and Alumni With a faculty of more than 130, SFAI enjoys an extraordinary student-faculty ratio of 5:1. Students work closely with faculty members and develop important and lasting relationships that continue beyond graduation.

SFAI's faculty includes artists, curators, writers, historians, theorists, activists, critics, urbanists, architects, designers, performers, philosophers, musicians, and scientists. Okwui Enwezor, Dean of Academic Affairs, is a curator and writer, and was the Artistic Director of the 2006 Bienal Internacional de Arte Contemporaneo, in Seville, Spain. Renée Green is Dean of Graduate Studies at SFAI, and her work has been seen throughout the world in museums, galleries, biennials, and festivals. Hou Hanru, Chair of SFAI's graduate program in exhibitions and museum studies, is the curator of the Chinese pavilion at the 2007 Venice Biennale and director of the 2007 Istanbul Biennial. Trisha Donnelly's work was included in the 2004 and 2006 Whitney Biennials. Caitlin Mitchell-Dayton's paintings were used in the film "Art School Confidential." Henry Wessel's photographs were recently published as a five-volume boxed set by Steidl. Jon Phillips is an open-source programmer for Creative Commons. Mark Van Proyen is one of the editors of *AfterBurn: Reflections on Burning Man.* Amy Franceschini is the founder of FutureFarmers and has been involved in numerous projects aimed at raising public awareness of critical ecological issues. Thomas Humphrey is a nuclear physicist and director of exhibitions at the Exploratorium.

In addition to working with SFAI's esteemed full- and part-time faculty, students are introduced to a spectrum of visiting artists and scholars. SFAI provides students direct access to an exhibition program showcasing the work of regional and international artists as well as SFAI students; an extensive roster of lectures that brings over 60 artists, designers, curators, and writers to campus every year; and film screenings, symposia, and panel discussions that engage in contemporary issues and ideas.

The accomplishments of SFAI's alumni can be found in museums and galleries around the world, in libraries and bookstores, in movie theaters, on the Web, on television, on the streets, and elsewhere. A partial list includes Annie Leibovitz, who began photographing for Rolling Stone while a student; Molly Katzen's vegetarian *Moosewood Cookbook,* which she wrote and illustrated; Don Ed Hardy's over 20 books on the art of tattooing; Karen Finley, whose performances challenge notions of femininity and political power; the music of the Tubes, Romeo Void, Mutants, and Avengers, all pioneers of Punk; the work of Lance Acord, cinematographer for *Adaptation, Lost in Translation,* and *Marie Antoinette;* Peter Strietmann and Christopher Seguine, editors and cinematographers for Mathew Barney's *Cremaster"* cycle; painter Kehinde Wiley's commissioned portraits of VH1's 2005 honorees; environmental activist Roxanne Quimby's Burt's Bees products; Robert Gamblin's eco-friendly oil paint; Devendra Banhart's music and drawings; Rob Reger's Emily the Strange; and many more.

Exhibition Opportunities Two large student-run galleries show weekly exhibitions of student work; each department has its own exhibition space; the lecture hall is open for student film and video screenings, as well as performances; large exterior walls are designated for mural projects; outdoor terraces and the meadow are used for large sculpture and installation work; weekly noon concerts by student musicians and DJs are held in the Quad. The annual Winter Sale is both an exhibition and opportunity to sell work open to all students. The M.F.A. Graduate exhibition, attracting over 5,000 visitors each year, occupies 4,000 square feet at Fort Mason. The B.F.A. exhibition takes over the entire Chestnut Street campus each May.

San Jose State University
San Jose, California

State-supported, coed. Urban campus. Total enrollment: 29,604. Art program established 1911.
Web Site http://www.sjsu.edu/

Savannah College of Art and Design
Savannah, Georgia

Independent, coed. Urban campus. Total enrollment: 8,236. Art program established 1978.

Savannah College of Art and Design (continued)

Degrees Bachelor of Fine Arts. Majors and concentrations: advertising design, animation, architectural history, architecture, art history, broadcast design, fashion design, fibers, film and television, furniture design, graphic design, historical preservation, illustration, industrial design, interactive design and game development, interior design, metals and jewelry, painting, performing arts, photography, printmaking, production/design, sculpture, sequential art, sound design, visual communication, visual effects. Graduate degrees offered: Master of Arts; Master of Fine Arts; Master of Architecture in the area of architecture. Program accredited by NAAB.

Enrollment 8,236 total; 6,913 undergraduate, 1,323 graduate.

Art Student Profile 53% females, 47% males, 12% minorities, 9% international.

Art Faculty 169 undergraduate (full-time), 45 undergraduate (part-time), 240 graduate (full-time), 54 graduate (part-time). 80% of full-time faculty have terminal degrees. Graduate students do not teach undergraduate courses. Undergraduate student–faculty ratio: 18:1.

Student Life Student groups/activities include Industrial Design Society of America, American Institute of Graphic Arts, American Institute of Architecture Students.

Expenses for 2007–2008 Application fee: $50. Comprehensive fee: $34,905 includes full-time tuition ($24,390), mandatory fees ($500), and college room and board ($10,015). College room only: $6460. Room and board charges vary according to board plan and housing facility.

Financial Aid Program-specific awards: May and Paul Poetter Scholarships (full tuition) for National Merit Finalists and high school valedictorians/salutatorians (minimum 1450 SAT/minimum 33 ACT) or perfect score on SAT or ACT, Academic Honors Scholarships for those with minimum SAT/ACT of 1110/24 or 3.3 GPA with minimum SAT/ACT 1030/22 or International Baccalaureate Diploma (4 levels with amount awarded based on test scores and/or GPA) ($5000–$20,000), Frances Larkin McCommon Scholarship for those with superior portfolio, Artistic Honors Scholarship for Congressional Art Competition first-place recipients and Governor's Honors Scholars

($15,000–$18,000), Combined Honors Scholarships for undergraduate students who have demonstrated outstanding ability in both academic and artistic endeavors ($6000–$18,000), SCAD Scholars Awards for those with minimum 3.5 high school GPA and minimum SAT/ACT 1220/27 demonstrating superior leadership ($15,000), Transfer Scholars Awards for those with 45 quarter or 27 semester hours with 3.50 GPA and outstanding talent in visual or performing arts ($15,000), Atlanta College of Art Scholars Award for those with minimum SAT/ACT of 1220/27 or International Baccalaureate Diploma, minimum GPA of 3.5 ($15,000).

Application Procedures Students admitted directly into the professional program freshman year. Deadline for freshmen and transfers: continuous. Notification date for freshmen and transfers: continuous. Required: high school transcript, college transcript(s) for transfer students, 3 letters of recommendation, SAT or ACT test scores, portfolio for some studio majors and audition for performing arts majors (for scholarship consideration). Recommended: interview, portfolio. Portfolio reviews held monthly on campus and off campus in various cities; the submission of slides may be substituted for portfolios when distance is prohibitive and for international applicants.

Web Site http://www.scad.edu

Undergraduate Contact Ginger Hansen, Executive Director of Recruitment, Admission, Savannah College of Art and Design, PO Box 2072, Savannah, Georgia 31402-3146; 912-525-5964, fax: 912-525-5983, e-mail address: ghunt@scad.edu

Graduate Contact Darrell Tutchton, Director of Graduate Enrollment, Admission, Savannah College of Art and Design, PO Box 2072, Savannah, Georgia 31402-3146; 912-525-5961, fax: 912-525-5985, e-mail address: dtutchto@scad.edu

More About the College

The Savannah College of Art and Design (SCAD) was founded in 1978 and is a private, accredited, coeducational college, preparing students for careers in the visual and performing arts, design, the building arts, and the history of art and architecture. The College emphasizes learning through individual attention in a positively oriented environment and is open to both resident and nonresident students. A balanced fine arts and liberal arts curriculum has attracted students from every state and more than 80 countries, making SCAD one of the largest art and design colleges in the United States; current enrollment is approximately 7,350 students. SCAD has locations in Savannah and Atlanta, Georgia, and in Lacoste, France.

The College awards Bachelor of Fine Arts (B.F.A.), Master of Fine Arts (M.F.A.), Master of Arts (M.A.), Master of Architecture (M.Arch.), and Master of Urban Design (M.U.D.) degrees. A postprofessional M.Arch. degree is also offered. Some programs are available online through SCAD E-learning.

Degrees are offered in advertising design, animation, architectural history, architecture, art history, broadcast design and motion graphics, cinema studies, commercial photography, digital photography, documentary photography, fashion, fibers, film and television, furniture design, graphic design, historic preservation, illustration, illustration design, industrial design, interactive design and game development, interior design, media and performing arts, metals and jewelry, painting, photography, production design, sequential art, sound design, urban design, and visual effects.

SCAD has locations in Atlanta and Savannah, Georgia, and in Lacoste, France. The Savannah campus offers a full university experience in one of the largest National Historic Landmark districts in the United States. The state-of-the-art Atlanta facility is situated in a major metropolitan hub for business, the arts, and transportation. The Lacoste campus is nestled in a picturesque hillside village in Provence.

Attractive residence hall accommodations, with meal plans, are provided for on a first-come, first-served basis. Furnishings include drafting tables, and the housing fee covers utilities.

SCAD competes in the National Association of Intercollegiate Athletics in men's and women's basketball, cross-country, golf, soccer, swimming, and tennis; women's softball, rowing and volleyball; and men's baseball.

Campus events such as concerts, lectures, plays, film screenings, and other entertainment, as well as cultural, recreational, and social programs, are planned and produced by the Student Activities Council.

Program Facilities Architecture, interior design, and historic preservation facilities include an intranet of PCs configured with electronic design software including AutoCAD, Bentley Microstation V8, Adobe Photoshop, form-Z, 3D Studio VIZ, SURFCAM, and Alias/Wavefront Maya. A video microscope, as well

as architectural conservation, metals conservation, and paint analysis labs, also are available in the School of Building Arts.

Animation, broadcast design, interactive design and game development, and visual effects facilities offer ready access to high-end industry standard equipment and software, including an intranet of Macintosh G4, Pentium IV, and SGI workstations configured with a diverse range of graphics software; high-end 2-D, 3-D, interactive, and compositing tools, including the Adobe product line; Alias/ Wavefront Maya; Side Effects' Houdini products; Pixar's Renderman; Avid Softimage XSI, Symphony, and Xpress DV; Discreet 3ds max, flame, flint, combustion, and smoke; Animo; the Unreal game engine; the Quake game engine; and Apple Final Cut Pro, ZBrush and Shake. Other tools include Lightwave and Macromedia products.

Fashion and fibers students use computer-aided design workstations and scanners; Juki industrial sewing machines and sergers; a heat transfer press; customized dress forms; weaving facilities, including a variety of four- and eight-shaft floor looms, two AVL CompuDobby looms, and an AVL electronic Jacquard loom; a dye lab; and a screenprinting studio.

Furniture design and industrial design facilities include a woodworking and metals and plastics fabrication lab, bench rooms and design studios, a plastic working area, a welding facility, CNC milling, spray booths and a finishing room, and state-of-the-art electronic design studios configured with the latest versions of design and visualization software, such as Alias Studio, Rhino 3-D, SolidWorks, and Vellum Cobalt. The computer lab has two 3-D printers with capabilities to print polycarbonate or ABS 3-D models of computer-generated designs.

Advertising design, graphic design, and illustration facilities include Macintosh computers with CD and DVD burners, scanners, black-and-white laser printers, light tables, and digital cameras. The Adobe product line; Macromedia Director, Dreamweaver, Flash, and FreeHand; Quark XPress; and other graphics packages are available.

Photography students have access to Macintosh digital imaging labs with extensive peripherals, two Imacon scanners, professional color print processing machines for both negative and reversal papers, E-6 and C-41 color film processing machines, an alternative processes lab, studios, lighting equipment, view camera systems, medium-format camera systems, and digital backs.

Metals and jewelry studios include equipment for precision casting, finishing, enameling, lapidary, anodizing, CAD/CAM modeling, forming, and stone setting processes. Students may incorporate 3-D

Visual

Arts

Savannah College of Art and Design (continued)

computer modeling and Computer Numeric Controlled programming and milling skills into their portfolios. Using the Stratasys FDM 3000 rapid prototyping system, students can print wax or ABS models of their CAD prototypes.

Film and television facilities include the Steadicam EFP and Super Panther Dolly, a chroma key/green screen studio, and a sound stage. Students have access to a Pro Tools surround sound lab and an audio production studio featuring a Digidesign Control/24 control surface for Pro Tools. The department houses Avid Media Composer, Symphony, and Xpress DV workstations; MiniDV and DVCPRO cameras; a Sony Digital High Definition Television camera; 16 mm, Super 16 mm and 35 mm cameras; and an all-digital studio. Sound design equipment and software includes more than fifty Digidesign Pro Tools audio workstations, a 500-gigabyte searchable sound-effects server, an extensive collection of studio microphones, and a professionally equipped location sound cart for film production.

College galleries exhibit student and faculty work as well as that of renowned professional artists. The College library contains approximately 335,000 slides, 113,000 volumes, 950 periodicals, 6,200 microform units, and 3,400 audiovisual materials. College facilities include a restored 1946 theater and a 150-seat black box theater.

Student Performance/Exhibit Opportunities

The College is enlivened by a full calendar of gallery exhibitions, lectures, festivals, workshops, performances, and conferences each year. The College holds exhibitions of a variety of work (including student work) in several on-campus galleries, and hosts an internationally renowned film festival, a spring fashion show, and features year-round student theater performances on campus. The College also hosts exhibitions in New York City, Paris, and elsewhere.

Faculty, Visiting Artists, and Alumni

During the academic year, each major field of study may sponsor lectures and workshops, providing students the opportunity to meet and talk with working artists, architects, and designers. Special on-campus programming has included exhibits of work by renowned artists such as Robert Rauschenberg, Jasper Johns, Helen Frankenthaler, Romare Bearden, Andy Warhol, and Miriam Schapiro. Recently, Christo and Jeanne-Claude, Audrey Flack, Betye Saar, Benny Andrews, Sandy Skoglund, Judy Pfaff, Maya Lin, Danny Glover, Robert Redford, and Gregory Hines have lectured at SCAD.

Special Programs

The College offers professional and faculty academic counseling, with special programs for first-year students and tutors available at no charge. SCAD also provides an English as a Second Language program for students whose native language is not English. Writing assistance, drawing assistance, and other learning assistance is provided for students as needed.

Internships are available and highly recommended for undergraduate and graduate students in a wide variety of programs. The federal work-study program is also available.

Study trips to major centers of artistic activity provide further opportunities for enrichment. SCAD faculty members direct off-campus studies in locations throughout the world, including the College's campus in Lacoste, France.

Career Planning and Placement

The office of career planning and placement provides career development and professional job search assistance to students and alumni through individual career counseling and exploration of career opportunities in art and design. The office also provides instruction in writing résumés and cover letters, making portfolio presentations, self- promotion, honing interviewing skills, and developing networking techniques to prepare students for the job market. The College routinely attracts major art and design corporate recruiters from companies such as Industrial Light and Magic, Pixar, Sony Pictures Imageworks, Nike, Michelin, Hallmark, and many others.

School of the Art Institute of Chicago

Chicago, Illinois

Independent, coed. Urban campus. Total enrollment: 2,873. Art program established 1866.

Degrees Bachelor of Arts in the area of visual and critical studies; Bachelor of Fine Arts in the areas of studio with emphasis in art history, theory and criticism, with emphasis in art education, or emphasis in writing; Bachelor of Interior Architecture. Majors and concentrations: architecture, art and technology, art education, art history, ceramic art and design, designed objects, fashion design and technology, fiber arts, film/video/new media, graphic arts/visual communication, interior architecture, painting/drawing, performance art, photography, print media, sculpture, sound design, textile arts, theory and criticism, video art, visual and critical studies, writing. Graduate degrees offered: Master of Arts in the areas of art education, modern art history and criticism, art therapy, teaching, visual and critical studies, arts administration and policy; Master of Fine Arts in the areas of studio, writing; Master of Science in the area of historic preservation; Master of Architecture; Master of Design in Designed Objects; Master of Interior Architecture. Cross-registration with Roosevelt University, member schools of Association of Independent Colleges of Art and Design. Program accredited by NASAD.

Enrollment 2,873 total; 2,194 undergraduate, 599 graduate, 80 nonprofessional degree.

Art Student Profile 65% females, 35% males, 21% minorities, 18% international.

Art Faculty 132 total (full-time), 400 total (part-time). 88% of full-time faculty have terminal degrees. Graduate students teach a few undergraduate courses. Undergraduate student–faculty ratio: 11:1.

Student Life Student groups/activities include Student Government, "F" Student Newspaper, Student Union Galleries. Special housing available for art students.

Expenses for 2007–2008 Application fee: $65. One-time mandatory fee: $2,175.00. Tuition: $30,750 full-time. Mandatory fees: $270 full-time. College room only: $8900.

Financial Aid Program-specific awards: 70 Academic Incentive Awards for qualified applicants ($2000), 6 Chairman's Awards for qualified applicants, 100 Distinguished Scholar Grants for qualified applicants ($8000), 39 New Arts Society Presidential Awards for qualified applicants ($15,000), 259 Recognition Scholarships for qualified applicants ($6000), 479 Incentive Awards for qualified applicants ($4000), 74 Enrichment Awards for qualified applicants ($2000), 338 Enrichment Scholar Grants for qualified applicants ($2000).

Application Procedures Students admitted directly into the professional program freshman year. Deadline for freshmen: March 15; transfers: continuous. Required: essay, high school transcript, college transcript(s) for transfer students, letter of recommendation, portfolio, SAT or ACT test scores. Recommended: minimum 3.0 high school GPA, interview. Portfolio reviews held continuously on campus and off campus; the submission of slides may be substituted for portfolios required for transfer credit evaluation.

Web Site http://www.saic.edu

Undergraduate Contact Scott Ramon, Director, Undergraduate Admissions, School of the Art Institute of Chicago, 36 South Wabash Avenue, Chicago, Illinois 60603; 312-629-6100, fax: 312-629-6101, e-mail address: admiss@saic.edu

Graduate Contact Andre Van De Putte, Associate Director, Graduate Admissions, School of the Art Institute of Chicago, 36 South Wabash Avenue, Suite 1201, Chicago, Illinois 60603; 312-629-6100, fax: 312-629-6101, e-mail address: admiss@saic.edu

More About the School

Since its founding in 1866, the School of the Art Institute of Chicago (SAIC) has been providing a leading global vision for the education of artists, designers, and others who shape contemporary art practice. SAIC's primary purpose is to foster the conceptual and technical education of artists, designers, and scholars in a highly professional, studio-oriented, and academically rigorous environment, encouraging excellence, critical inquiry, and experimentation. In 2002, the School was recognized as "the most influential art school in the nation" by a poll conducted by Columbia University and a panel of national art critics. *U.S. News & World Report* has consistently ranked SAIC's Master of Fine Arts program as number one in the nation.

More than 2,000 undergraduates, 580 graduate students, and a faculty consisting of artists, designers, and scholars work in an environment that facilitates the exchange of ideas, the sharing of resources, and the critiquing and refining of technical abilities and conceptual issues.

SAIC is distinguished from other art and design schools in the breadth and depth of its curriculum, with more than 900 courses offered each semester. SAIC is committed to interdisciplinary exploration and the awareness that the boundaries between artistic fields are not always easily defined. Students do not declare a major but are free to design a path of study that best suits their creative development. A student may choose to do all their course work in one area of study or amongst multiple department areas. SAIC's credit/no-credit grading system encourages students to think creatively and to develop the self-motivation necessary for life as a practicing artist, designer, and scholar. SAIC enriches its strong studio program with a first-rate, nationally and regionally accredited liberal arts education, and it has one of the largest art history departments in the nation. SAIC is the only college in the country that

School of the Art Institute of Chicago (continued)

offers a systematic series of courses on the history, theory, and philosophical bases of art criticism.

SAIC is located in the heart of downtown Chicago, home to the nation's second-largest art scene that includes world-class museums, galleries, alternative spaces, and arts organizations. Chicago itself is a vital part of SAIC, as a source of social and cultural activities and the stimulus for ideas and attitudes ultimately expressed through art. Peter Frank, art critic and curator says, "Of all American cities, Chicago has contributed the most solid and distinctive artwork and art thinking. The School of the Art Institute of Chicago is at the nucleus of this longstanding distinction."

Millennium Park, located across the street from SAIC, is a twenty-first-century marvel, and SAIC, its faculty members, and its students played a key role in its realization. One of the signature pieces of public art in the park, the Crown Fountain by Spanish artist Jaume Plensa, was created with the assistance of both SAIC students and faculty members, who collaborated with Plensa in producing the 1,000 video portraits that are screened continuously on the fountain's twin video towers. The park, with its unique mix of art, architecture, and nature, has become an urban oasis for SAIC students.

SAIC maintains two distinctive residence halls with loft-style rooms—each with their own bathroom, kitchen, voicemail, and Internet access. The residence halls offer 24-hour security and controlled access as well as spacious, well-lit studios; lounge rooms with big screen TVs; computer labs; and laundry facilities. Students can immerse themselves in a community of fellow artists, live in the heart of Chicago's loop, and enjoy conveniences unavailable in most student apartments.

SAIC offers a wide variety of unique resources, beginning with the collection of its sister institution, the Art Institute of Chicago, and its Ryerson Library and Burnham Library of Architecture, the largest art and architecture research libraries in the country. The Gene Siskel Film Center presents significant programs of world cinema and presentations by an international array of film and video artists. SAIC's Video Data Bank houses more than 1,800 titles and is the leading resource in the country for videotapes by and about contemporary artists. The Poetry Center brings renowned poets and writers to Chicago to share their work with the public.

Additional services include an international student office, a multicultural affairs office, health and counseling services, a learning center (offering support services for students with learning disabilities), and an extensive program for academic advising. SAIC is home to the largest and most successful arts-related Cooperative Education program in the country, providing employment opportunities worldwide. The Career Development Center assists in researching job and grant opportunities, preparing portfolios and artist statements, exploring exhibition possibilities, and understanding the legal aspects of entrepreneurship. The center maintains an online database that lists local and national positions, including freelance, part-time, and full-time employment.

Program Facilities SAIC's campus encompasses six buildings in downtown Chicago, including a 40,000-square-foot permanent exhibition space. There are fully equipped studios for each area of concentration, and the School's policy allows 24-hour access to facilities.

The Painting and Drawing department has many well-lit studio classrooms, individual space for select undergraduate and graduate students, and space for critiques. Facilities in the sculpture department include a complete woodshop, a welding shop, a bronze and aluminum foundry, a plaster room, and both indoor and outdoor exhibition spaces. A well-equipped metals shop allows for forging, forming, joining, and casting of nonferrous metals. The Printmedia department has etching presses, stone lithography presses, a screen-printing studio, a Heidelberg Kord and Chief offset press, a process camera, a large-format camera, a professional photomechanical darkroom, artists' books studio, a computer lab, and a Novajet printer.

The Art and Technology department supports several computer labs, including Macintosh-based labs equipped with Maya and Shake animation software. The department also maintains a multimedia authoring suite, an electronics construction shop, a microcontroller development and programming area, a kinetics shop, neon and holography studios, installation space, and MIDI and digital sound systems. The Film, Video, and New Media department has equipment ranging from a unique hand-built image processor to the latest prosumer, professional, and industrial video equipment. Digital editing systems support current digital, tape, and disk output. Equipment available to students includes digital cameras, projectors, switchers, light kits, and microphones. Film equipment includes sync and nonsync film cameras, sound equipment, optical printers, a wet lab for image processing, and animation stands, cameras, and editing software. In addition, the department facilities also include a sixty-seat theater, a 25-foot shooting set, work studios for 3-D and 2-D animation, and a professional interlock sound suite.

The Photography department has large printing labs, an alternative process darkroom, individual color-exposing rooms, mural printing rooms, 30-inch by 50-inch processors for color negative and positive printing, a shooting studio, a computer classroom with multiple stations, a computer peripheral area with a flatbed and a variety of film scanners, a 4-by-5 film recorder, various printers, Durst-Lambda digital laser, and large format capability. The Sound department offers studios and workstations equipped with digital editing systems, multitracks and digital recorders, and several digital and rare vintage analog synthesizers and samplers. A larger configurable space is equipped with a multichannel sound system and ceiling grid that makes it suitable for performances and installations.

The Ceramics department's facilities include clay mixers, an extruder, a slab roller, complete moldmaking and casting facilities, and several styles of wheels. Diverse firing options in various kiln styles include high- and low-fire oxidation and reduction, soda, and raku. The Visual Communication department's facilities include state-of-the-art computer labs with color scanners, a copy stand, and spacious studios. Students in the Fashion Design department study design and construction in a spacious facility with industrial-grade equipment. The department houses a Fashion Resource Center, with a collection of worldwide designer garments and a research library with rare books, videotapes, and international publications. The Fiber and Material Studies department has AVL computer looms, more than thirty traditional looms, a large area for hand construction, full facilities for screenprinting on fabric that includes a darkroom for photo-screeners, a computer lab, and a kitchen with industrial washers and dryers used for the setting of dyes.

Architecture, interior architecture, and designed objects equipment and facilities include an advanced output center with ABS plastic rapid prototyper, laser cutter, and large format printers; complete wood and plastic shop with heavy machine tools and a CNC router; separate highly ventilated mold-making room with paint hood, wax and fume hood, and vacuformer; graduate and undergraduate studios with desks, pin up areas, and complete built-in digital audio visual support; the GFRY display studio funded by Motorola Corporation; several critique and exhibition spaces; a materials library; 2-D/slide scanner and projectors; digital copy stand; small model tools; and lecture room. In the new AIADO Design Shop, students can work with both analog fabrication/modeling equipment and digitally con-

trolled (CNC) tools. DesOb Core Design Studios and Lab courses are specifically structured to provide students with instruction on all of these technologies. Field trips to local design offices and manufacturing facilities introduce students to an extended range of contemporary design and production processes.

Three general-access Media Centers lend thousands of pieces of audiovisual equipment to students. General-access computer labs are equipped with Macintosh workstations that have the latest versions of digital video, desktop publishing, 3-D rendering, Web-site authoring, animation, multimedia, graphic, and audio software applications. The workstations are equipped with various flatbed, negative and slide scanners, film recorders, CD/DVD authoring, and editing peripherals. The lab offers 24-hour access and weekly instructional workshops on specialized equipment. SAIC also has a full-service color digital output Service Bureau, which specializes in laser printing and large-format ink-jet printing.

The John M. Flaxman Library collections include 60,000 volumes on art and the liberal arts and sciences, 360 periodical subscriptions, films, videos, audiotapes, CDs, microforms, and picture files. The Joan Flasch Artists' Book Collection contains more than 3,000 artists' books, along with a research collection of exhibition catalogs and other related material. The MacLean Visual Resource Center maintains a noncirculating collection of more than 500,000 slides.

Faculty, Resident Artists, and Alumni Faculty members are selected for their skills, insight, and dedication as teachers and for their professional accomplishments as artists, designers, and scholars. There are currently 470 full- and part-time faculty members, among them 70 NEA grant recipients, 11 Louis Comfort Tiffany Foundation Fellowship recipients, and 9 Rockefeller Foundation grant recipients. SAIC faculty members have their work exhibited in museums, galleries, and festivals nationally and internationally. They publish books, plays, poetry, and criticism; organize and curate exhibitions; and design, build, and preserve buildings throughout the world. Each year, 100 or more well-known visiting artists, including poets, political activists, designers, and visual artists, present workshops and provide individual student critiques through the Visiting Artists Program. Notable alumni include Claes Oldenburg, Ivan Albright, Georgia O'Keefe, David Sedaris, Cynthia Rowley, and Vincente Minnelli.

Student Performance/Exhibit Opportunities

The School's exhibition spaces include the Betty Rymer Gallery, which highlights work from departments and presents special exhibitions, and Gallery 2,

School of the Art Institute of Chicago (continued)

with exhibition space, a performance space, and a space designed for site-specific installations. In addition, Gallery X and the Lounge Gallery, sponsored by the Student Union Galleries, provide exhibition space for currently enrolled students. The Fashion department hosts a fashion show in late spring for students in their second, third, and fourth year. The First-Year Program sponsors ArtBash in the spring of each year, highlighting the work produced in its program.

Off-Campus Arrangements SAIC's Mobility Program allows students to attend partner schools within the United States and Canada and includes the New York Studio semester. The School also maintains semester exchange agreements with more than twenty schools in Europe, Asia, and South America, and students may develop their own individual programs. SAIC faculty members also lead study trips during each summer and winter interim to such destinations as Cuba, Czech Republic, Italy, Japan, Los Angeles, Puerto Rico, and Vietnam.

School of the Museum of Fine Arts, Boston

Boston, Massachusetts

Independent, coed. Urban campus. Total enrollment: 733. Art program established 1876.

Degrees Bachelor of Arts/Bachelor of Fine Arts. Majors and concentrations: animation, art education, art/fine arts, ceramics, drawing, film, graphic design, illustration, interdisciplinary studies, jewelry and metalsmithing, painting, papermaking, performance, photography, printmaking, screenprinting, sculpture, self-designed art, sound art, stained glass, studio art, text and image art, textile arts, video art. Graduate degrees offered: Master of Arts in Teaching; Master of Fine Arts. Cross-registration with ProArts Consortium, Association of Independent Colleges of Art and Design, Wheaton College, Tufts University, Massachusetts Institute of Technology. Program accredited by NASAD.

Enrollment 733 total; 634 undergraduate, 99 graduate.

Art Student Profile 66% females, 34% males, 12% minorities, 6% international.

Art Faculty 51 total (full-time), 129 total (part-time). 65% of full-time faculty have terminal degrees. Graduate students teach a few undergraduate courses. Undergraduate student–faculty ratio: 9:1.

Student Life Student groups/activities include Film Club, Infra Sculpture, Gay/Lesbian/Transgender and Supporters (Outloud!). Special housing available for art students.

Expenses for 2007–2008 Application fee: $65. One-time mandatory fee: $125. Tuition: $26,950 full-time. Mandatory fees: $1020 full-time. Full-time tuition and fees vary according to course load, degree level, and program. College room only: $11,600. Special program-related fees: $482 per semester for comprehensive fee, $1895 per year for health insurance.

Financial Aid Program-specific awards: 50 art merit scholarships, 418 School of the Museum of Fine Arts Grants for those demonstrating need ($14,000).

Application Procedures Students admitted directly into the professional program freshman year. Deadline for freshmen: February 1; transfers: March 1. Notification date for freshmen and transfers: continuous. Required: essay, high school transcript, college transcript(s) for transfer students, 2 letters of recommendation, portfolio, SAT or ACT test scores. Recommended: interview. Portfolio reviews held weekly on campus and off campus at National Portfolio Days; the submission of slides may be substituted for portfolios.

Web Site http://www.smfa.edu

Undergraduate Contact Susan Clain, Dean of Admissions, School of the Museum of Fine Arts, Boston, 230 The Fenway, Boston, Massachusetts 02115; 617-369-3626, fax: 617-369-4264, e-mail address: admissions@smfa.edu

Graduate Contact David Murray, Associate Dean of Admissions, School of the Museum of Fine Arts, Boston, 230 The Fenway, Boston, Massachusetts 02115; 617-369-3626, fax: 617-369-4264, e-mail address: admissions@smfa.edu

More About the School

The School of the Museum of Fine Arts, Boston (SMFA), is a unique institution dedicated to educating artists and focused on fostering creative investigation, risk-taking, and individual vision. Everyone at the SMFA recognizes that disciplines converge and influence each other and that contemporary art is truly interdisciplinary. The School does not have a mandatory foundations program nor does it have majors. Instead, all students are encouraged to build solid foundations and acquire skill sets in numerous disciplines in order to create new possibilities and forms of artmaking. Students are given the freedom to design a program of study that best suits their needs and goals. This freedom comes with strong support and guidance from faculty advisers.

In partnership with Tufts University, the School offers the following degree programs: the Bachelor of Fine Arts (B.F.A.), the Bachelor of Fine Arts in art education, the five-year combined-degree program (B.A./B.F.A. or B.S./B.F.A.), the Master of Fine Arts (M.F.A.), and the Master of Arts in Teaching (M.A.T.) in art education. In partnership with Northeastern, the School offers a Bachelor of Fine Arts and a Master of Fine Arts in studio art. All students in degree programs are fully enrolled at the School of the Museum of Fine Arts and Tufts or Northeastern University and graduate with a Tufts or Northeastern degree. The School also offers the all-studio Diploma program, the one-year Fifth Year Certificate program, and the Post-Baccalaureate Certificate program. The School is a division of the Museum of Fine Arts, Boston, which is located across the street from the School.

The diversity of the faculty members and the range of facilities allow the student to develop a very personal and individual means of expression. Course teaching methods range from structured classes, with regular attendance, to individual instruction for work done independently outside the School. Class sizes are generally small, and every area of study is supported by accomplished, professional faculty members; extensive programs with visiting artists; and an energetic schedule of exhibitions. At the end of each semester, the student presents a body of art work to a review board consisting of faculty members and students. There is a discussion of the total semester experience, and suggestions are made for future study. A block of credits is awarded, appropriate to the term's accomplishments, and a written evaluation is made.

Boston is home to many educational and cultural institutions. The Museum School is a vital member of the art community, presenting a dynamic schedule of exhibitions, lectures, and panel discussions throughout the academic year. As a division of the Museum of Fine Arts, students also have special access to the educational resources, collections, curatorial departments, and special programs of one of the most comprehensive and outstanding collections of art in the world.

Program Facilities The SMFA campus features several buildings with 24-hour security and extensive access for students. The two main buildings house classrooms, studios, state-of-the-art equipment, exhibition spaces, computer and video labs, the Writing Center, the W. Van Alan Clark Jr. Library, and Café des Arts, which serves breakfast, lunch, and dinner.

The School provides a limited number of individual studio spaces for undergraduate degree students and diploma students. Students have 24-hour access to most studio spaces and facilities. Students may apply for studio space in the summer months.

There is a limited amount of residential housing in the Artists' Residence Hall at Massachusetts College of Art. The majority of students choose to live in nearby off-campus apartments, and the SMFA Student Affairs Office can help find the right location and the right roommate.

Faculty, Visiting Artists, and Alumni All studio faculty members are practicing professional artists with regional, national, and international reputations. The Visiting Artists and Curators program encourages students to interact with prominent artists.

Exhibition Opportunities The Museum School provides students with more than 8,000 square feet of exhibition space in six galleries. These excellent sites are in addition to contemporary gallery space at the Museum of Fine Arts, Boston, where winners of the prestigious Traveling Scholarship awards exhibit every year. Student-curated exhibitions are also on view at the Museum throughout the year. The School also sponsors a number of special prize funds, offering students the chance to win travel grants, cash awards, and exhibition opportunities.

Special Programs The School is a member of the Pro Arts Consortium in Boston, which allows students to take classes on a space-available basis at Berklee College of Music, the Boston Architectural Center, Emerson College, the Boston Conservatory, and Massachusetts College of Art. The School also offers selective cross-registration with MIT. As a member of the Association of Independent Colleges of Art and Design (AICAD), students also have the opportunity to study at colleges throughout the United States and abroad.

School of Visual Arts
New York, New York

Proprietary, coed. Urban campus. Total enrollment: 3,715. Art program established 1947.

Degrees Bachelor of Fine Arts in the areas of advertising, animation, cartooning, computer

School of Visual Arts (continued)

art, film and video, fine arts, graphic design, illustration, interior design, photography, visual and critical studies. Majors and concentrations: advertising design, animation, art/fine arts, cartooning, computer art, film and video production, graphic design, illustration, interior design, painting/drawing, photography, printmaking, sculpture, studio art, visual studies. Graduate degrees offered: Master of Arts in Teaching in the area of art education; Master of Fine Arts in the areas of computer art, design, fine arts, illustration as visual essay, art criticism and writing, photography, video and related media; Master of Professional Studies in the areas of art therapy, digital photography. Program accredited by NASAD.

Enrollment 3,500 total; 3,093 undergraduate, 407 graduate.

Art Student Profile 54% females, 46% males, 13% minorities, 15% international.

Art Faculty 800 total (part-time). Graduate students do not teach undergraduate courses. Undergraduate student–faculty ratio: 4:1.

Student Life Student groups/activities include Visual Arts Students Association, Visual Opinion (campus literary magazine), WSVA campus radio station.

Expenses for 2007–2008 Application fee: $50. Tuition: $23,520 full-time. Full-time tuition varies according to program. College room only: $10,950. Room charges vary according to gender, housing facility, and location. Special program-related fees: $200–$1200 per semester for departmental fee.

Financial Aid Program-specific awards: Silas H. Rhodes Scholarship ($10,000).

Application Procedures Students admitted directly into the professional program freshman year. Deadline for freshmen and transfers: continuous. Required: essay, high school transcript, college transcript(s) for transfer students, portfolio, SAT or ACT test scores, 2-part essay for film applicants, TOEFL score for applicants whose primary language is not English. Recommended: minimum 2.5 high school GPA. Portfolio reviews held by appointment year-round on campus and off campus in various locations throughout the U.S. on National Portfolio Days; the submission of slides may be substituted for portfolios (required for transfers, scholarship applicants, and students not attending an in-person portfolio review).

Web Site http://www.sva.edu

Contact Adam Rogers, Director of Admissions, School of Visual Arts, 209 East 23rd Street, New York, New York 10010; 212-592-2100, fax: 212-592-2116, e-mail address: admissions@sva.edu

More About the School

The School of Visual Arts (SVA) in New York City is an established leader and innovator in the education of artists. From its inception in 1947, the faculty has consisted of professionals working in the arts and art-related fields. SVA provides an environment that nurtures creativity, inventiveness, and experimentation—enabling students to develop a strong sense of identity and a clear direction of purpose.

The four-year curriculum remains responsive to the needs and demands of the industry and is designed to allow students a greater freedom of choice in electives and requirements with each succeeding year. The first year of each program, a foundation year, ensures the mastery of basic skills in each chosen discipline as well as in writing and art history. After the first year, students focus on specific areas of concentration and, under the guidance of academic advisers and faculty members, pursue their own individual goals.

In addition, SVA's Internship for Credit Program gives students the chance to work alongside top art directors, photographers, painters, and illustrators as well as in film and animation studios. SVA has a very high job placement rate—approximately 89 percent of SVA's students are employed within a year of graduation.

Program Facilities SVA provides students with studios that continually mirror the standards of the professional art world. Studio space and equipment are offered in different departments, varying in availability depending on such factors as the student's class seniority and major of study. The SVA library's holdings include distinctive multimedia collections, over 65,000 books, more than 260 periodicals subscriptions, and special collections of pictures, color slides, film scripts, comics, videotapes, exhibition catalogs, CD-ROMs, and recordings.

Faculty, Resident Artists, and Alumni The School of Visual Arts is proud of its illustrious faculty of more than 700 professional artists and designers who represent an array of fields in the fine and applied arts. Each faculty member has chosen to commit to the professional art world as well as to teaching the next generation of artists. The SVA community is enthusiastic about the faculty's ability to balance the life of a dynamic artist with the vivaciousness that only a dedicated teacher can provide to his or her students. SVA has some of the world's greatest artists among its alumni. Many of them live and work in New York City; others can be found throughout the United States and in more than thirty countries around the world. They work at advertising agencies, television networks, publishing houses, film studios, recording companies, design firms, art galleries, and major museums. Others do freelance work or run their own start-up companies.

Exhibit Opportunities The College operates two campus galleries as well as a Chelsea gallery space, affording SVA students the opportunity to exhibit their work twelve months a year. Students are encouraged to show their work outside of SVA by participating in exhibits and competitions held in New York City and throughout the United States.

Special Programs SVA students have the opportunity to participate in art programs abroad during the summer semester. SVA offers Painting in Barcelona; Painting in Florence; Digital Photography in Florence; the Art, Myths, and History of Ancient Greece; and Cinema in Toulouse. Third-year students in film and video, fine arts, graphic design, illustration, interior design, and photography have the opportunity to study abroad for one semester at an AIAS (Association of Independent Art Schools) affiliate in Europe.

Seton Hall University

South Orange, New Jersey

Independent Roman Catholic, coed. Suburban campus. Total enrollment: 9,637 (2006). Art program established 1968.

Degrees Bachelor of Arts in the areas of art history, fine arts, graphic interactive and advertising design; Bachelor of Science in the area of art education. Majors and concentrations: advertising, art education, art history, art/fine arts, graphic design, interactive design. Graduate degrees offered: Master of Arts in the area of museum professions.

Enrollment 130 total; 60 undergraduate, 70 graduate.

Art Student Profile 60% females, 40% males, 15% minorities, 5% international.

Art Faculty 9 undergraduate (full-time), 8 undergraduate (part-time), 3 graduate (full-time), 4 graduate (part-time). 100% of full-time faculty have terminal degrees. Graduate students do not teach undergraduate courses. Undergraduate student–faculty ratio: 15:1.

Student Life Student groups/activities include student exhibitions, gallery exhibitions.

Expenses for 2006–2007 Application fee: $55. Comprehensive fee: $35,186 includes full-time tuition ($22,770), mandatory fees ($1950), and college room and board ($10,466). College room only: $6664. Special program-related fees: $50 per graphic design for computer fees.

Financial Aid Program-specific awards: 1 Henry Gasser Scholarship for art majors demonstrating talent and/or academic achievement ($1800).

Application Procedures Students admitted directly into the professional program freshman year. Deadline for freshmen and transfers: continuous. Required: essay, high school transcript, college transcript(s) for transfer students, minimum 2.0 high school GPA, 3 letters of recommendation, SAT or ACT test scores. Recommended: minimum 3.0 high school GPA, interview, portfolio. Portfolio reviews held as needed on campus; the submission of slides may be substituted for portfolios for large works of art.

Web Site http://www.shu.edu

Undergraduate Contact Admissions Office, Seton Hall University, 400 South Orange Avenue, South Orange, New Jersey 07079-2696; 973-761-9000 ext. 9332.

Graduate Contact Dr. Petra Chu, Director, MA Program in Museum Professions, Department of Art and Music, Seton Hall University, 400 South Orange Avenue, South Orange, New Jersey 07079-2696; 973-761-7966, fax: 973-275-2368, e-mail address: chupetra@shu.edu

Seton Hill University

Greensburg, Pennsylvania

Independent Roman Catholic, coed. Small town campus. Total enrollment: 1,895. Art program established 1955.

Degrees Bachelor of Fine Arts in the areas of graphic design, 2-D media, 3-D media, art and technology. Majors and concentrations: art

Visual Arts

Seton Hill University (continued)

and technology, graphic design, three-dimensional studies, two-dimensional studies. Graduate degrees offered: Master of Arts in the area of art therapy. Cross-registration with Pittsburgh Filmmakers, St. Vincent College, University of Pittsburgh at Greensburg, Westmoreland County Community College.

Enrollment 141 total; 53 undergraduate, 27 graduate, 61 nonprofessional degree.

Art Student Profile 80% females, 20% males, 10% minorities, 10% international.

Art Faculty 6 undergraduate (full-time), 5 undergraduate (part-time), 1 graduate (full-time), 2 graduate (part-time). 85% of full-time faculty have terminal degrees. Graduate students do not teach undergraduate courses. Undergraduate student–faculty ratio: 8:1.

Student Life Student groups/activities include Student In The Arts (SITA), Graphic Design Club, Student Art Therapy Association.

Expenses for 2006–2007 Application fee: $35. Comprehensive fee: $30,610 includes full-time tuition ($23,180), mandatory fees ($200), and college room and board ($7230). Room and board charges vary according to board plan and housing facility. Special program-related fees: $120 per course for supplies.

Financial Aid Program-specific awards: Division of Visual and Performing Arts Scholarships for incoming freshmen ($3000), 1 Josefa Filkosky Scholarship for juniors ($700).

Application Procedures Students admitted directly into the professional program freshman year. Deadline for freshmen and transfers: August 15. Notification date for freshmen and transfers: continuous. Required: essay, high school transcript, college transcript(s) for transfer students, minimum 2.0 high school GPA, 3 letters of recommendation, portfolio, SAT or ACT test scores. Recommended: minimum 3.0 high school GPA, interview. Portfolio reviews held continuously on campus; the submission of slides may be substituted for portfolios when distance is prohibitive.

Web Site http://www.setonhill.edu

Undergraduate Contact Sherri Bett, Director, Admissions Office, Seton Hill University, 1 Seton Hill Drive, Greensburg, Pennsylvania 15601; 724-838-4255, fax: 724-830-4611, e-mail address: bett@setonhill.edu

Graduate Contact Ms. Nina Denninger, Director, Graduate Program in Art Therapy, Seton Hill University, Seton Hill Drive, Greensburg, Pennsylvania 15601; 724-830-1047, fax: 724-830-4611, e-mail address: denninger@setonhill.edu

Shepherd University
Shepherdstown, West Virginia

State-supported, coed. Small town campus. Total enrollment: 4,091. Art program established 1950.

Degrees Bachelor of Fine Arts in the areas of graphic design, photography/computer digital imagery, painting, printmaking, sculpture. Majors and concentrations: art/fine arts, digital imaging, graphic design, illustration, painting/drawing, photography, printmaking, sculpture.

Enrollment 275 total; 225 undergraduate, 50 nonprofessional degree.

Art Student Profile 55% females, 45% males, 9% minorities, 5% international.

Art Faculty 10 undergraduate (full-time), 10 undergraduate (part-time). 100% of full-time faculty have terminal degrees. Graduate students do not teach undergraduate courses. Undergraduate student–faculty ratio: 15:1.

Student Life Student groups/activities include Art Alliance Exhibits, Performing and Visual Arts Series, American Institute of Graphic Arts.

Expenses for 2006–2007 Application fee: $35. State resident tuition: $4348 full-time. Nonresident tuition: $11,464 full-time. Full-time tuition varies according to degree level, program, and reciprocity agreements. College room and board: $6456. Room and board charges vary according to board plan and housing facility. Special program-related fees: $30 per course for studio fee.

Financial Aid Program-specific awards: 12 art scholarships for West Virginia resident program majors ($2000), 2 Blundell Awards for first-year students ($700), 2 Bridgeforth Awards for photography/computer imaging students ($500–$1000), 2 Hendricks Scholarships for art majors ($600), 1 Jeffrey Miller Scholarship for non-traditional design majors ($500).

Application Procedures Students admitted directly into the professional program freshman year. Deadline for freshmen and transfers: February 1. Notification date for freshmen and transfers: April 1. Required: high school transcript, college transcript(s) for transfer students, minimum 2.0 high school GPA, interview, portfolio, SAT or ACT test scores. Portfolio reviews held 6 times on campus; the submission of slides may be substituted for portfolios (slides/CD preferred).

Web Site http://www.shepherd.edu

Undergraduate Contact Ms. Kimberly Scranage, Director of Admissions, Shepherd University, PO Box 3210, Shepherdstown, West Virginia 25443; 304-876-5212, fax: 304-876-3101, e-mail address: kscranag@shepherd.edu

Shorter College

Rome, Georgia

Independent Baptist, coed. Small town campus. Total enrollment: 1,044. Art program established 1994.

Degrees Bachelor of Fine Arts in the area of art. Majors and concentrations: ceramics, painting/drawing, sculpture. Cross-registration with Berry College.

Enrollment 46 total; 40 undergraduate, 6 nonprofessional degree.

Art Student Profile 60% females, 40% males, 2% minorities, 5% international.

Art Faculty 2 undergraduate (full-time), 2 undergraduate (part-time). 100% of full-time faculty have terminal degrees. Graduate students do not teach undergraduate courses. Undergraduate student–faculty ratio: 15:1.

Student Life Student groups/activities include Art Student League.

Expenses for 2006–2007 Application fee: $25. Comprehensive fee: $20,900 includes full-time tuition ($14,000), mandatory fees ($300), and college room and board ($6600). College room only: $3600. Full-time tuition and fees vary according to course load. Room and board charges vary according to board plan and housing facility.

Financial Aid Program-specific awards: 10 art scholarships for art majors ($500–$3000).

Application Procedures Students admitted directly into the professional program freshman year. Deadline for freshmen and transfers: continuous. Required: essay, high school transcript, college transcript(s) for transfer students, minimum 2.0 high school GPA, letter of recommendation, interview, portfolio, SAT or ACT test scores. Portfolio reviews held 4 times on campus.

Web Site http://www.shorter.edu

Undergraduate Contact Dr. Alan B. Wingard, Dean, School of the Arts, Shorter College, 315 Shorter Avenue, Rome, Georgia 30165; 706-233-7248, fax: 706-236-1517, e-mail address: awingard@shorter.edu

Simon Fraser University

Burnaby, British Columbia, Canada

Province-supported, coed. Suburban campus. Total enrollment: 24,842. Art program established 1992.

Web Site http://www.sfu.ca/

Sonoma State University

Rohnert Park, California

State-supported, coed. Small town campus. Total enrollment: 7,749. Art program established 1967.

Degrees Bachelor of Fine Arts in the areas of painting, printmaking, sculpture, photography. Majors and concentrations: art history, art/fine arts, painting, photography, printmaking, sculpture, works on paper. Cross-registration with San Francisco State University. Program accredited by NASAD.

Enrollment 198 total; 18 undergraduate, 180 nonprofessional degree.

Art Student Profile 60% females, 40% males, 30% minorities.

Art Faculty 6 undergraduate (full-time), 3 undergraduate (part-time). 100% of full-time faculty have terminal degrees. Graduate students do not teach undergraduate courses. Undergraduate student–faculty ratio: 15:1.

Student Life Student groups/activities include BFA Student Exhibition, Student Art Exhibition, Ceramics Guild.

Expenses for 2006–2007 Application fee: $55. State resident tuition: $0 full-time. Nonresident tuition: $10,170 full-time. Mandatory fees: $3648 full-time. Special program-related fees: $10–$68 per course for supplies.

Financial Aid Program-specific awards: 1 William Smith Award for ceramics majors ($500), 1

Sonoma State University (continued)

William Smith Award for studio art majors ($500), 1 Brooks Award for art history majors ($400), 1 John Bolles Scholarship for program majors ($750), 2 Art Department Scholarships for program majors ($300), 2 Edward Boyle Scholarships for program majors ($250), 1 Hendrickson Family Scholarship for painting majors ($750).

Application Procedures Students apply for admission into the professional program by sophomore, junior year. Deadline for freshmen and transfers: May 31. Required: essay, college transcript(s) for transfer students, minimum 3.0 high school GPA, 2 letters of recommendation, portfolio, completion of lower division studio requirements. Portfolio reviews held twice on campus; the submission of slides may be substituted for portfolios (slides preferred).

Web Site http://www.sonoma.edu/art/

Undergraduate Contact Mr. Stephen Galloway, Department of Art and Art History, Sonoma State University, 1801 East Cotati Avenue, Rohnert Park, California 94928; 707-664-2364, fax: 707-664-4333, e-mail address: stephen.galloway@sonoma.edu

Southern California Institute of Architecture

Los Angeles, California

Independent, coed. Urban campus. Total enrollment: 438.

Degrees Bachelor of Architecture in the area of architecture. Majors and concentrations: architecture. Graduate degrees offered: Master of Architecture in the area of architecture. Program accredited by NAAB.

Enrollment 422 total; 201 undergraduate, 221 graduate.

Art Student Profile 35% females, 65% males, 35% minorities, 23% international.

Art Faculty 28 total (full-time), 50 total (part-time). Graduate students do not teach undergraduate courses. Undergraduate student–faculty ratio: 15:1.

Student Life Student groups/activities include Sci-Arc Public Programs (Lecture Series) and Gallery Installations and Exhibits, Student Union and Academic Council.

Expenses for 2007–2008 Application fee: $60. Tuition: $10,636 full-time. Mandatory fees: $60 full-time.

Financial Aid Program-specific awards: 28 Undergraduate Admissions Awards for undergraduate students ($3260), 14 Undergrad Financial Aid awards for undergraduate F.A. students ($2692).

Application Procedures Students admitted directly into the professional program freshman year. Deadline for freshmen: February 1; transfers: May 1. Notification date for freshmen and transfers: August 1. Required: essay, high school transcript, college transcript(s) for transfer students, minimum 2.0 high school GPA, 3 letters of recommendation, portfolio, SAT or ACT test scores, TOEFL scores for international applicants, $60 processing fee. Recommended: minimum 3.0 high school GPA, interview. Portfolio reviews held continuously March-July on campus.

Web Site http://www.sciarc.edu/

Contact Mr. J. J. Jackman, Director, Admissions, Southern California Institute of Architecture, 960 East 3rd Street, Los Angeles, California 90013; 213-356-5321, fax: 213-613-2260, e-mail address: jj@sciarc.edu

Southern Illinois University Carbondale

Carbondale, Illinois

State-supported, coed. Rural campus. Total enrollment: 21,003. Art program established 1931.

Degrees Bachelor of Fine Arts in the area of art. Majors and concentrations: art education, ceramic art and design, communication design, glass, industrial design, jewelry and metalsmithing, painting/drawing, printmaking, sculpture. Graduate degrees offered: Master of Fine Arts in the area of art. Program accredited by NASAD.

Enrollment 509 total; 159 undergraduate, 55 graduate, 295 nonprofessional degree.

Art Student Profile 46% females, 54% males, 17% minorities, 4% international.

Art Faculty 20 total (full-time), 9 total (part-time). 100% of full-time faculty have terminal degrees. Graduate students teach about a quarter of undergraduate courses. Undergraduate student–faculty ratio: 5:1.

Student Life Student groups/activities include League of Art and Design, Industrial Design Society of America Student Chapter, American Center for Design. Special housing available for art students.

Expenses for 2007–2008 Application fee: $30. State resident tuition: $5808 full-time. Nonresident tuition: $14,520 full-time. Mandatory fees: $2263 full-time. College room and board: $6666. College room only: $3650. Special program-related fees: $3–$75 per course for studio materials, $70 per course for model fees.

Financial Aid Program-specific awards: 5–7 talent scholarships for incoming students ($1000), 2 Mitchell Scholarships for incoming students from southern Illinois ($1000), 2–4 Celine A. Chu Memorial Scholarships for junior and senior painting, drawing, printmaking majors ($500), 2–10 Rickert Ziebold Trust Awards for graduating seniors ($2000–$10,000).

Application Procedures Students apply for admission into the professional program by sophomore year. Deadline for freshmen and transfers: continuous. Notification date for freshmen and transfers: continuous. Required: high school transcript, college transcript(s) for transfer students, portfolio, SAT or ACT test scores (minimum composite ACT score of 20), minimum 2.0 college GPA for transfer students. Portfolio reviews held twice on campus.

Web Site http://www.artanddesign.siu.edu

Undergraduate Contact Ms. Valerie L. Brooks, Academic Advisor, School of Art and Design, Southern Illinois University Carbondale, 1100 South Normal Avenue, MC 4301, Carbondale, Illinois 62901; 618-453-4313, fax: 618-453-7710, e-mail address: vlbrooks@siu.edu

Graduate Contact Mr. Chris Wildrick, Graduate Program Head, School of Art and Design, Southern Illinois University Carbondale, 1100 South Normal Avenue, MC 4301, Carbondale, Illinois 62901; 618-453-7760, fax: 618-453-7710, e-mail address: wildrick@siu.edu

Southern Illinois University Edwardsville

Edwardsville, Illinois

State-supported, coed. Suburban campus. Total enrollment: 13,449. Art program established 1958.

Degrees Bachelor of Fine Arts in the area of art studio; Bachelor of Science in the area of art education. Majors and concentrations: art education, art history, ceramic art and design, computer graphics, jewelry and metalsmithing, painting/drawing, photography, printmaking, sculpture, textile arts. Graduate degrees offered: Master of Arts in the area of art therapy; Master of Fine Arts in the area of art studio.

Enrollment 310 total; 238 undergraduate, 52 graduate, 20 nonprofessional degree.

Art Student Profile 55% females, 45% males, 20% minorities, 10% international.

Art Faculty 16 undergraduate (full-time), 10 undergraduate (part-time), 3 graduate (full-time), 2 graduate (part-time). 100% of full-time faculty have terminal degrees. Graduate students teach a few undergraduate courses. Undergraduate student–faculty ratio: 16:1.

Student Life Student groups/activities include Student Sculpture on Campus Program, Mexico Foreign Study Program, New York and Washington D.C. study program. Special housing available for art students.

Expenses for 2007–2008 Application fee: $30. State resident tuition: $5938 full-time. Nonresident tuition: $13,075 full-time. Mandatory fees: $1180 full-time. College room and board: $6500. College room only: $3970. Special program-related fees: $12–$75 per course for studio fee.

Financial Aid Program-specific awards: 10 Chancellor's Scholarships for art majors ($3000).

Application Procedures Students apply for admission into the professional program by sophomore, junior year. Deadline for freshmen and transfers: continuous. Notification date for freshmen and transfers: continuous. Required: essay, high school transcript, college transcript(s) for transfer students, minimum 3.0 high school GPA, SAT or ACT test scores (minimum combined SAT score of 810, minimum composite ACT score of 17). Portfolio

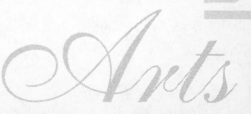

Southern Illinois University Edwardsville (continued)

reviews held twice on campus; the submission of slides may be substituted for portfolios (slides preferred).

Web Site http://www.siue.edu/ART/

Undergraduate Contact Dr. Todd Burrell, Director of Admission, Southern Illinois University Edwardsville, Campus Box 1047, Edwardsville, Illinois 62026; 618-650-2937, fax: 618-650-5013, e-mail address: tburrel@siue.edu

Graduate Contact Paul A. Dresang, Graduate Advisor, Art and Design Department, Southern Illinois University Edwardsville, Campus Box 1774, Edwardsville, Illinois 62026; 618-650-3071, fax: 618-650-3096.

Meadows School of the Arts
Southern Methodist University
Dallas, Texas

Independent, coed. Suburban campus. Total enrollment: 10,941. Art program established 1939.

Degrees Bachelor of Fine Arts in the area of art. Majors and concentrations: ceramics, drawing, painting, photography, printmaking, sculpture. Graduate degrees offered: Master of Fine Arts in the area of art. Program accredited by NASAD.

Enrollment 87 total; 75 undergraduate, 12 graduate.

Art Student Profile 59% females, 41% males, 22% minorities, 5% international.

Art Faculty 12 total (full-time), 4 total (part-time). 90% of full-time faculty have terminal degrees. Graduate students do not teach undergraduate courses. Undergraduate student–faculty ratio: 6:1.

Student Life Student groups/activities include Student Art Association, Meadows Graduate Council, Pollock Gallery. Special housing available for art students.

Expenses for 2007–2008 Application fee: $60. Comprehensive fee: $41,705 includes full-time tuition ($27,400), mandatory fees ($3480), and college room and board ($10,825). College

room only: $6730. Special program-related fees: $30 per credit hour for model and supply fees.

Financial Aid Program-specific awards: 10–15 Meadows Artistic Scholarships for talented program majors ($1000–$6000).

Application Procedures Students apply for admission into the professional program by sophomore year. Deadline for freshmen and transfers: continuous. Required: essay, high school transcript, college transcript(s) for transfer students, letter of recommendation, SAT or ACT test scores. Recommended: interview, portfolio. Portfolio reviews held once on campus and off campus in digital format by uploading to Web site: smu.slideshow.com.

Web Site http://smu.edu/meadows/art/

Undergraduate Contact Tommy Newton, Director of Recruitment, Meadows School of the Arts, Southern Methodist University, PO Box 750356, Dallas, Texas 75275-0356; 214-768-4067, fax: 214-768-3272, e-mail address: tnewton@smu.edu

Graduate Contact Ms. Jean Cherry, Director of Graduate Admissions, Meadows School of the Arts, Southern Methodist University, PO Box 750356, Dallas, Texas 75275-0356; 214-768-3765, fax: 214-768-3272, e-mail address: jcherry@smu.edu

Southern Oregon University
Ashland, Oregon

State-supported, coed. Small town campus. Total enrollment: 4,675. Art program established 1983.

Degrees Bachelor of Fine Arts. Majors and concentrations: ceramics, digital art and design, painting/drawing, photography, printmaking, sculpture. Cross-registration with members of the National Student Exchange Program, Rogue Community College.

Enrollment 271 total; 21 undergraduate, 250 nonprofessional degree.

Art Student Profile 50% females, 50% males, 10% minorities, 10% international.

Art Faculty 10 undergraduate (full-time). 90% of full-time faculty have terminal degrees.

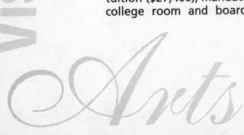

Graduate students do not teach undergraduate courses. Undergraduate student–faculty ratio: 2:1.

Student Life Student groups/activities include Schneider Museum of Art, student gallery management programs, Southern Oregon Fine Art Students.

Expenses for 2006–2007 Application fee: $50. State resident tuition: $4986 full-time. Nonresident tuition: $14,691 full-time. College room and board: $6468. Special program-related fees: $5–$100 per course for lab/materials fees, $50 per quarter for resource fee.

Financial Aid Program-specific awards: 1 Mulling Award in Art for art majors demonstrating artistic ability ($500), 1 Schneider Merit Award in Art for art majors demonstrating artistic ability ($1000), 1–4 John Humbird Dickey Memorial Scholarships for art majors demonstrating artistic ability and financial need ($1000), 1 Sam and Helen Bernstein Award for artistically talented students ($200), 4 Leon Mulling Awards for art majors demonstrating academic excellence ($3000).

Application Procedures Students apply for admission into the professional program by sophomore year. Deadline for freshmen and transfers: continuous. Notification date for freshmen and transfers: continuous. Required: high school transcript, college transcript(s) for transfer students, minimum 3.0 high school GPA, portfolio, SAT or ACT test scores, artist statement. Portfolio reviews held twice on campus; the submission of slides may be substituted for portfolios for transfer applicants.

Web Site http://www.sou.edu/art/

Undergraduate Contact Mara Affre, Director, Admissions and Records Department, Southern Oregon University, 1250 Siskiyou Boulevard, Ashland, Oregon 97520; 541-552-6411, fax: 541-552-6614.

State University of New York at Plattsburgh

Plattsburgh, New York

State-supported, coed. Small town campus. Total enrollment: 6,217.

Degrees Bachelor of Fine Arts in the area of art. Majors and concentrations: studio art.

Cross-registration with Clinton Community College, State University of New York Empire State College.

Enrollment 242 total; all undergraduate.

Art Student Profile 66% females, 34% males, 7% minorities, 7% international.

Art Faculty 10 undergraduate (full-time), 5 undergraduate (part-time). 100% of full-time faculty have terminal degrees. Graduate students do not teach undergraduate courses. Undergraduate student–faculty ratio: 20:1.

Student Life Student groups/activities include campus student exhibits, on-campus workshops presented by renowned artists, critics, and historians, off-campus field trips.

Expenses for 2007–2008 Application fee: $40. State resident tuition: $4350 full-time. Nonresident tuition: $10,610 full-time. Mandatory fees: $1066 full-time. College room and board: $7970. Room and board charges vary according to board plan. Special program-related fees: $15–$35 per studio course for specialized lab/equipment fees.

Financial Aid Program-specific awards: 15 Winkel Awards for art students ($200–$1000), 1 Glauhinger Award for sculpture students ($3400), 1 Parnass Award for photography students ($2000).

Application Procedures Students admitted directly into the professional program freshman year. Deadline for freshmen and transfers: continuous. Required: high school transcript, college transcript(s) for transfer students, minimum 3.0 high school GPA, portfolio, SAT or ACT test scores (minimum composite ACT score of 19). Recommended: essay, interview, 2-3 letters of recommendation. Portfolio reviews held continuously on campus; the submission of slides may be substituted for portfolios.

Web Site http://www.plattsburgh.edu/art

Undergraduate Contact Richard J. Higgins, Director, Admissions, State University of New York at Plattsburgh, 101 Broad Street, Kehoe Administration Building, Plattsburgh, New York 12901; 518-564-2040, e-mail address: higginrj@plattsburgh.edu

State University of New York at Fredonia

Fredonia, New York

State-supported, coed. Small town campus. Total enrollment: 5,540. Art program established 1968.

Degrees Bachelor of Fine Arts in the areas of drawing and painting, sculpture, ceramics, animation and illustration, photography, graphic design, media arts. Majors and concentrations: animation and illustration, ceramics, graphic design, media arts, painting, painting/drawing, photography, sculpture.

Enrollment 240 total; 30 undergraduate, 210 nonprofessional degree.

Art Student Profile 55% females, 45% males, 1% minorities, 2% international.

Art Faculty 14 undergraduate (full-time), 6 undergraduate (part-time). 100% of full-time faculty have terminal degrees. Graduate students do not teach undergraduate courses. Undergraduate student–faculty ratio: 14:1.

Student Life Student groups/activities include Art Forum, AIGA-American Institute of Graphic Arts, Media Arts.

Expenses for 2007–2008 Application fee: $40. State resident tuition: $4350 full-time. Nonresident tuition: $10,610 full-time. Mandatory fees: $1192 full-time. College room and board: $8380. College room only: $5050. Room and board charges vary according to board plan and housing facility. Special program-related fees: $10–$75 per course for lab fees.

Financial Aid Program-specific awards: 6 departmental scholarships for talented students ($500), 1 George W. Booth Award for incoming freshmen ($2000).

Application Procedures Students apply for admission into the professional program by junior year. Deadline for freshmen and transfers: continuous. Required: essay, high school transcript, college transcript(s) for transfer students, portfolio, SAT or ACT test scores (minimum combined SAT score of 1000). Recommended: minimum 3.0 high school GPA, 3 letters of recommendation, interview. Portfolio reviews held by appointment on campus; the submission of slides may be substituted for portfolios (slides or CD/DVD preferred).

Web Site http://www.fredonia.edu/department/art/

Undergraduate Contact Ms. Elizabeth Lee, Chair, Department of Visual Arts and New Media, State University of New York at Fredonia, Rockefeller Center, Fredonia, New York 14063; 716-673-3537, fax: 716-673-4990, e-mail address: elizabeth.lee@fredonia.edu

Steinhardt School of Culture, Education, and Human Development, Department of Art and Art Professions

See New York University

Stephen F. Austin State University

Nacogdoches, Texas

State-supported, coed. Small town campus. Total enrollment: 11,756. Art program established 1923.

Web Site http://www.sfasu.edu/

Stephens College

Columbia, Missouri

Independent, Urban campus. Total enrollment: 964. Art program established 1954.

Degrees Bachelor of Fine Arts in the areas of graphic design, fashion design, interior design. Majors and concentrations: fashion design, graphic design, interior design. Cross-registration with Mid-Missouri Associated Colleges and Universities.

Enrollment 155 total; all undergraduate.

Art Student Profile 100% females, 17% minorities.

Art Faculty 8 undergraduate (full-time), 19 undergraduate (part-time). 80% of full-time faculty have terminal degrees. Graduate students do not teach undergraduate courses. Undergraduate student–faculty ratio: 12:1.

Student Life Student groups/activities include Pi Phi Rho (fashion honorary society), Innovative Fashion Association (all fashion majors), Interior Design Club.

Expenses for 2006–2007 Application fee: $25. Comprehensive fee: $28,475 includes full-time tuition ($20,500) and college room and board ($7975). College room only: $4760. Room and board charges vary according to board plan, gender, and housing facility. Special program-related fees: $20–$150 per course for lab fee.

Financial Aid Program-specific awards: 1–3 Gardner Nettleton Endowed Scholarships for outstanding art and graphic students ($3500), 1–2 Carolyn Jill Kasten Scholarships for outstanding fashion design students ($3000).

Application Procedures Students admitted directly into the professional program freshman year. Deadline for freshmen and transfers: July 31. Notification date for freshmen and transfers: continuous. Required: essay, high school transcript, college transcript(s) for transfer students, minimum 2.0 high school GPA, letter of recommendation, SAT or ACT test scores (minimum composite ACT score of 21). Recommended: minimum 3.0 high school GPA, interview, portfolio. Portfolio reviews held as needed for advanced placement on campus; the submission of slides may be substituted for portfolios if original work is not available.

Web Site http://www.stephens.edu

Undergraduate Contact Office of Admission, Stephens College, Campus Box 2121, Columbia, Missouri 65215; 800-876-7207, fax: 573-876-7237, e-mail address: apply@stephens.edu

The New England School of Art & Design
Suffolk University

Boston, Massachusetts

Independent, coed. Urban campus. Total enrollment: 8,863. Art program established 1923.

Degrees Bachelor of Fine Arts in the areas of fine arts, graphic design, interior design. Majors and concentrations: art/fine arts, graphic design, interior design. Graduate degrees offered: Master of Arts in the areas of interior design, graphic design. Program accredited by NASAD, CIDA.

Enrollment 344 total; 214 undergraduate, 118 graduate, 12 nonprofessional degree.

Art Student Profile 72% females, 28% males, 5% minorities, 18% international.

Art Faculty 17 undergraduate (full-time), 48 undergraduate (part-time), 3 graduate (full-time), 6 graduate (part-time). 91% of full-time faculty have terminal degrees. Graduate students do not teach undergraduate courses. Undergraduate student–faculty ratio: 8:1.

Student Life Student groups/activities include American Society of Interior Designers Student Chapter, International Interior Design Association Student Chapter, American Institute of Graphic Arts (AIGA).

Expenses for 2007–2008 Application fee: $50. Comprehensive fee: $37,550 includes full-time tuition ($24,170), mandatory fees ($80), and college room and board ($13,300). College room only: $11,120. Room and board charges vary according to board plan and housing facility. Special program-related fees: $140 per course for studio fee.

Financial Aid Program-specific awards: 2–4 J.W.S. Cox Scholarships for those demonstrating talent ($1000–$2000), 1–2 Peter and Gretchen Paige Scholarships for those demonstrating talent ($4000–$5000), 2–4 Schrafft Scholarships Program for Boston residents ($2000–$3000).

Application Procedures Students admitted directly into the professional program freshman year. Deadline for freshmen and transfers: continuous. Required: essay, high school transcript, college transcript(s) for transfer students, minimum 2.0 high school GPA, 2 letters of recommendation, portfolio, SAT or ACT test scores. Recommended: interview. Portfolio reviews held continuously on campus and off campus at National Portfolio Days; the submission of slides may be substituted for portfolios whenever needed.

Web Site http://www.suffolk.edu/nesad

Undergraduate Contact Ms. Kristen Cahalane, Admissions Counselor, Undergraduate Admission, Suffolk University, 8 Ashburton Place, Boston, Massachusetts 02108; 617-573-8460, fax: 617-742-4291, e-mail address: kcahalan@suffolk.edu

Graduate Contact Ms. Terry Bishop, Director of Admission, Graduate Admission, Suffolk University, 8 Ashburton Place, Boston, Massachu-

Visual

Arts

Suffolk University (continued)

setts 02108; 617-573-8302, fax: 617-523-0116, e-mail address: tbishop@suffolk.edu

Sul Ross State University

Alpine, Texas

State-supported, coed. Small town campus. Total enrollment: 1,954. Art program established 1923.

Web Site http://www.sulross.edu/

Syracuse University

Syracuse, New York

Independent, coed. Urban campus. Total enrollment: 17,492. Art program established 1873.

Degrees Bachelor of Fine Arts in the areas of advertising design, art education, art video, ceramics, computer art, communication design, fashion design, fiber art/material studies, history of art, interior design, jewelry/ metalsmithing, painting, photography, printmaking, sculpture, surface pattern design, illustration, film; Bachelor of Industrial Design in the area of industrial and interaction design; Bachelor of Science in the area of environmental design. Majors and concentrations: advertising design, art education, art history, ceramics, communication design, computer art, environmental design, fashion design, fibers, film, illustration, industrial design, interior design, jewelry and metalsmithing, painting/drawing, photography, printmaking, sculpture, surface design, textile design, video art. Graduate degrees offered: Master of Fine Arts in the areas of art education, ceramics, computer arts, fiber arts/material studies, film, illustration, jewelry and metalsmithing, museum studies, painting, photography, printmaking, sculpture, surface pattern design, video; Master of Industrial Design. Program accredited by NASAD, CIDA.

Enrollment 1,403 total; 1,259 undergraduate, 144 graduate.

Art Student Profile 66% females, 34% males, 13% minorities.

Art Faculty 67 total (full-time), 43 total (part-time). 88% of full-time faculty have terminal degrees. Graduate students teach a few undergraduate courses. Undergraduate student–faculty ratio: 18:1.

Student Life Student groups/activities include American Society of Interior Designers, Industrial Design Society of America, New York Society of Illustrators.

Expenses for 2007–2008 Application fee: $70. Comprehensive fee: $42,626 includes full-time tuition ($30,470), mandatory fees ($1216), and college room and board ($10,940). College room only: $5660. Room and board charges vary according to board plan and housing facility. Special program-related fees: $10–$150 per semester for lab fees to cover costs of models and special supplies.

Financial Aid Program-specific awards: art merit scholarships for incoming freshmen ($4000), 1 National Scholastic Award for Art National Scholarship winners ($2000).

Application Procedures Students admitted directly into the professional program freshman year. Deadline for freshmen and transfers: January 1. Notification date for freshmen: March 1; transfers: August 15. Required: essay, high school transcript, college transcript(s) for transfer students, minimum 3.0 high school GPA, 2 letters of recommendation, portfolio, SAT or ACT test scores, high school counselor evaluation. Recommended: interview. Portfolio reviews held continuously on campus and off campus in New York, NY; Boston, MA; Philadelphia, PA; Baltimore, MD; Hartford, CT; Chicago, IL; the submission of slides may be substituted for portfolios when distance is prohibitive.

Web Site http://vpa.syr.edu/

Undergraduate Contact Director, CVPA Recruitment and Admissions, College of Visual and Performing Arts, Syracuse University, 202 Crouse College, Syracuse, New York 13244-1010; 315-443-2769, fax: 315-443-1935, e-mail address: admissu@syr.edu

Graduate Contact Graduate School, Syracuse University, Suite 303 Bowne Hall, Syracuse, New York 13244; 315-443-3028, fax: 315-443-3423, e-mail address: gradschl@syr.edu

Temple University, Tyler School of Art

See Tyler School of Art of Temple University

Tennessee Technological University

See Appalachian Center for Craft

Texas A&M University–Commerce

Commerce, Texas

State-supported, coed. Small town campus. Total enrollment: 8,556.

Degrees Bachelor of Arts in the area of photography; Bachelor of Fine Arts in the areas of design communications, new media, art direction, studio art; Bachelor of Science in the area of photography. Majors and concentrations: art, art direction, art education, ceramics, design communication, experimental studies, illustration, new media, painting, photography, sculpture. Graduate degrees offered: Master of Fine Arts in the areas of sculpture, painting, ceramics, illustration, experimental studies, photography, design communication. Cross-registration with University of North Texas, Texas Woman's University.

Enrollment 280 total; 261 undergraduate, 19 graduate.

Art Student Profile 51% females, 49% males, 21% minorities, 3% international.

Art Faculty 18 undergraduate (part-time), 9 graduate (full-time). 100% of full-time faculty have terminal degrees. Graduate students do not teach undergraduate courses. Undergraduate student–faculty ratio: 14:1.

Student Life Student groups/activities include Student Art Association, Photo Society, Clay Club.

Expenses for 2007–2008 Application fee: $25. State resident tuition: $5190 full-time. Nonresident tuition: $13,440 full-time. College room and board: $6340. College room only: $3500. Special program-related fees: $5–$50 per semester for instruction and curriculum fee.

Financial Aid Program-specific awards: 7–12 endowed scholarships for program majors ($200–$1000).

Application Procedures Students apply for admission into the professional program by sophomore year. Deadline for freshmen: August 15; transfers: August 19. Required: high school transcript, college transcript(s) for transfer students, SAT or ACT test scores, portfolio for transfer students in communication arts and photography. Portfolio reviews held by request on campus; the submission of slides may be substituted for portfolios if of good quality.

Web Site http://www.tamu-commerce.edu/art

Undergraduate Contact Michael Odom, Head, Department of Art, Texas A&M University–Commerce, PO Box 3011, Commerce, Texas 75429-3011; 903-886-5234, fax: 903-886-5987, e-mail address: michael-odom@tamu-commerce.edu

Graduate Contact Mr. Michael Miller, Graduate Coordinator, Department of Art, Texas A&M University–Commerce, PO Box 3011, Commerce, Texas 75429-3011; 903-886-5208, fax: 903-886-5987, e-mail address: michael_miller@tamu-commerce.edu

Texas A&M University–Corpus Christi

Corpus Christi, Texas

State-supported, coed. Suburban campus. Total enrollment: 8,585.

Degrees Bachelor of Fine Arts. Majors and concentrations: art education, studio art. Graduate degrees offered: Master of Fine Arts in the area of studio art.

Enrollment 163 total; 26 undergraduate, 8 graduate, 129 nonprofessional degree.

Art Student Profile 67% females, 33% males, 31% minorities, 2% international.

Art Faculty 9 total (full-time), 1 total (part-time). 90% of full-time faculty have terminal degrees. Graduate students do not teach undergraduate courses.

Student Life Student groups/activities include Student Art Association.

Expenses for 2006–2007 Application fee: $30. State resident tuition: $3720 full-time. Nonresident tuition: $10,392 full-time. Mandatory fees: $1428 full-time. Special program-related fees: $25–$65 per course for art material fees.

Financial Aid Program-specific awards: Fine Arts Studio Scholarships for program majors ($500–$2000).

Texas A&M University–Corpus Christi (continued)

Application Procedures Students apply for admission into the professional program by junior year. Required: essay, high school transcript, college transcript(s) for transfer students, minimum 2.0 high school GPA, portfolio, SAT or ACT test scores, completion of college preparatory courses. Recommended: minimum 3.0 high school GPA, letter of recommendation. Portfolio reviews held twice on campus; the submission of slides may be substituted for portfolios if accompanied by a slide list and descriptions.

Web Site http://www.tamucc.edu

Undergraduate Contact Prof. Jack Gron, Chair, Department of Art, Texas A&M University–Corpus Christi, 6300 Ocean Drive, Unit 5721, Corpus Christi, Texas 78412-5721; 361-825-3473, fax: 361-825-6097, e-mail address: jack.gron@tamucc.edu

Graduate Contact Prof. Jack Gron, Graduate Program Coordinator, Professor, Department of Art, Texas A&M University–Corpus Christi, 6300 Ocean Drive, Unit 5721, Corpus Christi, Texas 78412-5721; 361-825-3473, fax: 361-825-6097, e-mail address: jack.gron@tamucc.edu

Texas Christian University

Fort Worth, Texas

Independent, coed. Suburban campus. Total enrollment: 8,865. Art program established 1884.

Degrees Bachelor of Fine Arts in the areas of art education, graphic design, studio art. Majors and concentrations: art education, ceramics, graphic design, painting/drawing, photography, printmaking, sculpture. Graduate degrees offered: Master of Arts in the area of art history; Master of Fine Arts in the areas of painting, printmaking, sculpture. Cross-registration with Universidad de las Américas (Mexico).

Enrollment 165 total; 126 undergraduate, 12 graduate, 27 nonprofessional degree.

Art Student Profile 72% females, 28% males, 14% minorities, 2% international.

Art Faculty 16 total (full-time), 14 total (part-time). 100% of full-time faculty have terminal degrees. Graduate students do not teach undergraduate courses. Undergraduate student–faculty ratio: 10:1.

Student Life Student groups/activities include Visual Arts Committee of the Student Programming Council, Design Focus.

Expenses for 2007–2008 Application fee: $40. Comprehensive fee: $33,068 includes full-time tuition ($24,820), mandatory fees ($48), and college room and board ($8200). College room only: $5000. Room and board charges vary according to board plan and housing facility.

Financial Aid Program-specific awards: 2 Nordan Scholarships for freshmen ($7000).

Application Procedures Students admitted directly into the professional program freshman year. Deadline for freshmen and transfers: April 15. Required: essay, high school transcript, college transcript(s) for transfer students, minimum 3.0 high school GPA, 3 letters of recommendation, SAT or ACT test scores. Recommended: interview.

Web Site http://www.artandarthistory.tcu.edu

Contact Mr. Ronald Watson, Chairman, Department of Art and Art History, Texas Christian University, 2805 S. University, TCU Box 298000, Fort Worth, Texas 76129; 817-257-7643, fax: 817-257-7399, e-mail address: r.watson@tcu.edu

Texas State University–San Marcos

San Marcos, Texas

State-supported, coed. Suburban campus. Total enrollment: 27,485. Art program established 1940.

Web Site http://www.txstate.edu/

Texas Tech University

Lubbock, Texas

State-supported, coed. Urban campus. Total enrollment: 27,996. Art program established 1967.

Degrees Bachelor of Fine Arts in the areas of studio art, design communication, visual studies. Majors and concentrations: ceramics, communication design, jewelry and metalsmithing, painting/drawing, photography, printmaking, sculpture, visual studies. Graduate degrees

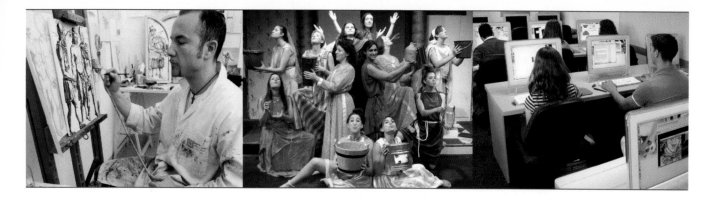

Our world can be your stage.

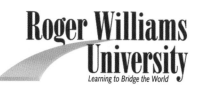
Creativity flourishes at Roger Williams University, a leading liberal arts university in New England.

Refine your writing, visual arts skills and performance techniques, energized by our beautiful 140-acre waterfront campus in historic Bristol, Rhode Island, easily accessible from Boston and New York.

Accredited by the New England Association of Schools and Colleges, Roger Williams University draws 3,775 full-time undergraduates who benefit from a dedicated faculty and an ideal academic setting with excellent facilities, recreation, athletics, and social opportunities. The Roger Williams education produces well-rounded students who successfully bridge transitions to a rewarding career and gratifying life.

The Theatre Program
The Roger Williams Theatre Program is unique in the range and breadth of its areas of study, offering you the opportunity to major in Theatre, leading to a Bachelor of Arts degree.

Creative Writing Program
Roger Williams University is one of the few colleges and universities in the United States to offer an undergraduate major in Creative Writing, leading to a Bachelor of Fine Arts degree.

Dance Performance Studies
The University offers courses in technique, choreography, history, pedagogy, movement analysis, performance techniques, and movement theatre (we are the only dance-based university program in the country to offer this training).

Graphic Design Communications
This program consists of a contemporary blend of a liberal arts education and applied technology. Students draw on their complete educational experience to create images and visual messages that are thought-provoking, well-researched, and technically excellent.

Visual Arts Studies
Our School of Architecture, Art and Historic Preservation offers the Bachelor of Arts degree in Visual Arts Studies. You can develop your talents in one of the following disciplines: Painting/Drawing/Printmaking, Sculpture, or Photography/Digital Media.

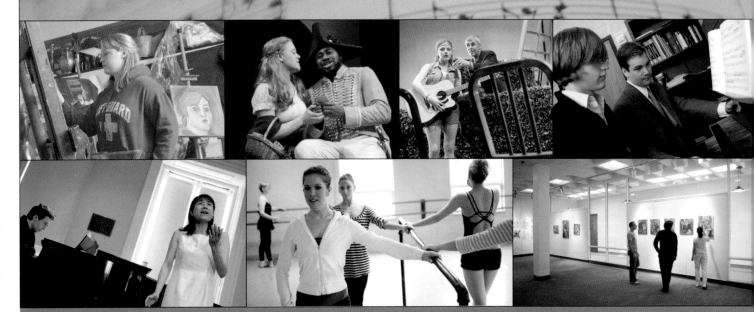
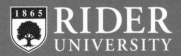

offered: Master of Fine Arts in the area of art. Doctor of Arts in the area of fine arts. Program accredited by NASAD.

Enrollment 452 total; 400 undergraduate, 32 graduate, 20 nonprofessional degree.

Art Student Profile 54% females, 46% males, 18% minorities, 1% international.

Art Faculty 29 total (full-time), 14 total (part-time). 93% of full-time faculty have terminal degrees. Graduate students teach a few undergraduate courses. Undergraduate student–faculty ratio: 11:1.

Student Life Student groups/activities include National Art Education Association Student Chapter, Design Communication Association, Metalsmithing Club.

Expenses for 2006–2007 Application fee: $50. State resident tuition: $4050 full-time. Nonresident tuition: $12,300 full-time. Mandatory fees: $2409 full-time. Full-time tuition and fees vary according to course load, program, and reciprocity agreements. College room and board: $7288. College room only: $3883. Room and board charges vary according to board plan and housing facility. Special program-related fees: $8–$150 per course for art supplies.

Financial Aid Program-specific awards: 20–25 art scholarships for program students ($200–$500), 3–5 H.Y. Price Scholarships for program students ($3000).

Application Procedures Students admitted directly into the professional program freshman year. Deadline for freshmen and transfers: continuous. Notification date for freshmen and transfers: continuous. Required: essay, high school transcript, minimum 2.0 high school GPA, SAT or ACT test scores, minimum TOEFL score of 550 for international applicants, slides or videotape of portfolio. Portfolio reviews held 4 times on campus and off campus in Junction, TX.

Web Site http://www.art.ttu.edu

Undergraduate Contact Djuana Young, Director, Undergraduate Admissions, Texas Tech University, Box 45005, Lubbock, Texas 79409-5005; 806-742-1482.

Graduate Contact Ann McGlynn, Assistant Dean, Graduate Admissions, Texas Tech University, Box 41030, Lubbock, Texas 79409-1030; 806-742-2787, fax: 806-742-4038.

Texas Woman's University

Denton, Texas

State-supported, coed, primarily women. Suburban campus. Total enrollment: 11,832. Art program established 1903.

Degrees Bachelor of Fine Arts in the areas of painting, photography, ceramics, sculpture, graphic design. Majors and concentrations: art history, clay, graphic design, painting/drawing, photography, sculpture. Graduate degrees offered: Master of Arts in the areas of art education, graphic design, art history; Master of Fine Arts in the areas of painting, photography, ceramics, sculpture. Cross-registration with University of North Texas, Texas A&M University-Commerce.

Enrollment 230 total; 150 undergraduate, 50 graduate, 30 nonprofessional degree.

Art Student Profile 90% females, 10% males, 25% minorities, 10% international.

Art Faculty 9 total (full-time), 4 total (part-time). 100% of full-time faculty have terminal degrees. Graduate students teach a few undergraduate courses. Undergraduate student–faculty ratio: 13:1.

Student Life Student groups/activities include Delta Phi Delta, Clay Underground, Art Teachers Network, Sculpture-No Boundaries, Photographic Artists Coalition, Painters At Large, Pioneers in Design, Homecoming, Open House Studios, Denton Arts and Jazz Festival. Special housing available for art students.

Expenses for 2007–2008 Application fee: $30. State resident tuition: $4290 full-time. Nonresident tuition: $12,540 full-time. Mandatory fees: $1542 full-time. College room and board: $5846. College room only: $3825. Room and board charges vary according to board plan and housing facility. Special program-related fees: $12–$90 per semester for studio courses.

Financial Aid Program-specific awards: 2–5 Marie Delleney Awards for art majors ($200–$500), 2 Helen Thomas Perry Awards for junior or senior art majors ($1000), 1–3 Hazel Snodgrass Awards for art majors ($200–$300), 1–2 Ludie Clark Thompson Awards for art majors ($200–$300), 2–4 Noreen Kitsinger Awards for art education majors ($200–$300), 2–5 Sue Comer Awards for art majors ($200–$300), 1–3 Dorothy Laselle Awards for fresh-

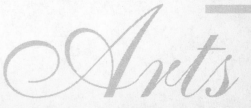

Texas Woman's University (continued)

men or sophomore art majors ($300–$400), 6–12 Coreen Spellman Awards for Delta Phi Delta members ($100–$200), 1 J. Brough Miller Scholarship for art majors ($400), 1–2 Rowena Caldwell Elkin Scholarships for art majors ($500–$1000), 6 Delta Phi Delta Awards for art majors ($200–$300).

Application Procedures Students admitted directly into the professional program freshman year. Deadline for freshmen and transfers: July 15. Required: high school transcript, college transcript(s) for transfer students, minimum 2.0 high school GPA, SAT or ACT test scores. Recommended: 3 letters of recommendation, interview, portfolio. Portfolio reviews held twice on campus; the submission of slides may be substituted for portfolios (or electronic disk portfolio).

Web Site http://www.twu.edu/as/va

Contact Mr. John Weinkein, Chair, Department of Visual Arts, Texas Woman's University, PO Box 425469, TWU Station, Denton, Texas 76204; 940-898-2530, fax: 940-898-2496, e-mail address: visualarts@twu.edu

Tisch School of the Arts - Department of Photography and Imaging

See New York University

Truman State University

Kirksville, Missouri

State-supported, coed. Small town campus. Total enrollment: 5,762. Art program established 1985.

Degrees Bachelor of Fine Arts in the areas of studio art, visual communications. Majors and concentrations: ceramic art and design, fibers, painting, printmaking, sculpture, visual communication. Graduate degrees offered: Master of Art Education.

Enrollment 205 total; 173 undergraduate, 5 graduate, 27 nonprofessional degree.

Art Student Profile 70% females, 30% males, 1% minorities.

Art Faculty 13 total (full-time). 100% of full-time faculty have terminal degrees. Graduate students do not teach undergraduate courses. Undergraduate student–faculty ratio: 14:1.

Student Life Student groups/activities include Student Art History Society, Missouri Art Education Association, American Institute of Graphic Arts.

Expenses for 2006–2007 Application fee: $0. State resident tuition: $5970 full-time. Nonresident tuition: $10,400 full-time. Mandatory fees: $372 full-time. College room and board: $5570. Room and board charges vary according to housing facility. Special program-related fees: $10–$30 per semester for art supplies.

Financial Aid Program-specific awards: 8 endowed scholarships for outstanding program majors ($500–$1500), 14 service scholarships for program majors ($400–$700).

Application Procedures Students admitted directly into the professional program freshman year. Deadline for freshmen and transfers: May 1. Notification date for freshmen: December 15. Required: essay, high school transcript, college transcript(s) for transfer students, minimum 3.0 high school GPA, portfolio, SAT or ACT test scores. Portfolio reviews held twice on campus; the submission of slides may be substituted for portfolios when distance is prohibitive.

Web Site http://www.truman.edu

Undergraduate Contact Mr. Russell Nelson, Chair, Art, Truman State University, 100 East Normal, Ophelia Parrish 1101, Kirksville, Missouri 63501; 660-785-4417, fax: 660-785-7463, e-mail address: art@truman.edu

Graduate Contact Prof. Wynne Wilbur, MAE Program Coordinator, Art, Truman State University, 100 East Normal, Ophelia Parrish 1101, Kirksville, Missouri 63501; 660-785-4417, fax: 660-785-7463, e-mail address: wwilbur@truman.edu

Temple University, Tyler School of Art

Tyler School of Art of Temple University

Philadelphia, Pennsylvania

State-related, coed. Urban campus. Total enrollment: 33,865. Art program established 1935.

Degrees Bachelor of Architecture in the area of architecture; Bachelor of Fine Arts in the areas of ceramics/glass, fibers, graphic and interactive design, painting/drawing, photography, printmaking, sculpture, art education, metals/jewelry/CAD-CAM. Majors and concentrations: architecture, art education, art history, CAD/CAM, ceramic art and design, commercial art, computer graphics, digital imaging, fibers, glass, graphic arts, graphic design, illustration, jewelry and metalsmithing, painting/drawing, photography, printmaking, sculpture, visual studies. Graduate degrees offered: Master of Arts in the area of art history; Master of Education in the area of art education; Master of Fine Arts in the areas of ceramics/glass, fibers, jewelry/metals, painting/drawing, photography, printmaking, sculpture, graphic and interactive design. Doctor of Philosophy in the area of art history. Program accredited by NASAD, NAAB.

Enrollment 1,449 total; 760 undergraduate, 81 graduate, 608 nonprofessional degree.

Art Student Profile 60% females, 40% males, 14% minorities, 4% international.

Art Faculty 70 total (full-time), 32 total (part-time). 95% of full-time faculty have terminal degrees. Graduate students teach a few undergraduate courses. Undergraduate student–faculty ratio: 11:1.

Student Life Student groups/activities include Student Alliance, Intellectual Heritage Society, Art Honor Society. Special housing available for art students.

Expenses for 2007–2008 Application fee: $50. State resident tuition: $10,252 full-time. Nonresident tuition: $18,770 full-time. Mandatory fees: $550 full-time. Full-time tuition and fees vary according to course load, program, and reciprocity agreements. College room and board: $8518. College room only: $5604. Room and board charges vary according to board

plan and housing facility. Special program-related fees: $25–$300 per course for lab fees.

Financial Aid Program-specific awards: 10–25 merit scholarships for program students ($1000–$12,500), academic scholarships for program students ($1000–$12,500).

Application Procedures Students admitted directly into the professional program freshman year. Deadline for freshmen: April 1; transfers: June 1. Notification date for freshmen and transfers: continuous. Required: essay, high school transcript, college transcript(s) for transfer students, portfolio, SAT or ACT test scores (minimum composite ACT score of 23), slides for transfer applicants (or CD ROM), self-portrait. Recommended: minimum 3.0 high school GPA, interview. Portfolio reviews held 27 times on campus and off campus at National Portfolio Day Association venues and selected high schools; the submission of slides may be substituted for portfolios for freshmen applicants, for large works of art, or if distance is prohibitive.

Web Site http://www.temple.edu/tyler

Undergraduate Contact Ms. Carmina Cianciulli, Assistant Dean for Admissions, Tyler School of Art, Temple University, 7725 Penrose Avenue, Elkins Park, Pennsylvania 19027; 215-782-2875, fax: 215-782-2711, e-mail address: tylerart@temple.edu

Graduate Contact Ms. Carmina Cianciulli, Assistant Dean for Admissions, Tyler School of Art of Temple University, Temple University, 7725 Penrose Avenue, Elkins Park, Pennsylvania 19027; 215-782-2875, fax: 215-782-2711, e-mail address: tylerart@temple.edu

University at Buffalo, the State University of New York

Buffalo, New York

State-supported, coed. Total enrollment: 27,220. Art program established 1954.

Degrees Bachelor of Fine Arts in the area of fine art. Majors and concentrations: communication design, painting/drawing, photography, printmaking, sculpture, studio art/emerging practices, visual studies. Graduate degrees offered: Master of Fine Arts in the

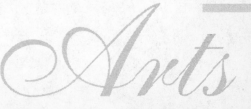

University at Buffalo, the State University of New York (continued)

area of fine art. Cross-registration with State University of New York College at Buffalo. Program accredited by NASAD.

Enrollment 273 total; 171 undergraduate, 22 graduate, 80 nonprofessional degree.

Art Student Profile 61% females, 39% males, 18% minorities, 6% international.

Art Faculty 15 total (full-time), 14 total (part-time). 93% of full-time faculty have terminal degrees. Graduate students teach a few undergraduate courses. Undergraduate student–faculty ratio: 12:1.

Student Life Student groups/activities include university gallery exhibits, Student Visual Art Organization, Visual Studies Department Gallery exhibits.

Expenses for 2006–2007 Application fee: $40. State resident tuition: $4350 full-time. Nonresident tuition: $10,610 full-time. Mandatory fees: $1778 full-time. College room and board: $8108. College room only: $5008. Room and board charges vary according to board plan and housing facility. Special program-related fees: $20–$100 per course for lab fees, supplies, models.

Financial Aid Program-specific awards: 1 Julius Bloom Memorial Scholarship for graphic arts or graphic design students ($350), 1 Dennis Domkowski Memorial Scholarship for communication design program students ($350), 1 Rumsey Summer Scholarship for junior art majors ($2000), 8 Morrison Scholarships for art majors demonstrating financial need ($1500), 1 Elliott Painting Scholarship for painting juniors ($500–$600), 1 Sentz Award for art majors ($450), 2 Eugene L. Gaier Excellence in Printmaking Awards for students in printmaking ($250), 1 Eugene L. Gaier Excellence in Drawing Award for drawing students ($500), 1 Sentz Award for art majors ($450), 1 Cober Award for drawing students ($500), 1 Townsend Award for photo students ($500).

Application Procedures Students admitted directly into the professional program freshman year. Deadline for freshmen: April 15; transfers: October 30. Notification date for freshmen: May 1; transfers: November 15. Required: high school transcript, college transcript(s) for transfer students, SAT or ACT test scores, portfolio review after freshman year for admission to department. Recom-

mended: essay, portfolio. Portfolio reviews held 5 times on campus and off campus at National Portfolio Days; Rochester or Syracuse NY; Toronto, CAN; Cleveland, OH; Sarasota, FL; the submission of slides may be substituted for portfolios if a campus visit is impossible.

Web Site http://www.visualstudies.buffalo.edu

Undergraduate Contact Mr. Kim James Yarwood, Academic Advisor, Department of Visual Studies, University at Buffalo, the State University of New York, 202 Center for the Arts, Buffalo, New York 14260-6010; 716-645-6000 ext. 1351, fax: 716-645-6970, e-mail address: yarwood@buffalo.edu

Graduate Contact Ms. Adele Henderson, Director of Graduate Studies, Department of Visual Studies, University at Buffalo, the State University of New York, 202 Center for the Arts, Buffalo, New York 14260-6010; 716-645-6878 ext. 1353, fax: 716-645-6970, e-mail address: adeleh@buffalo.edu

Myers School of Art
The University of Akron
Akron, Ohio

State-supported, coed. Urban campus. Total enrollment: 21,882. Art program established 1970.

Degrees Bachelor of Arts in the areas of art studio, art history, art education; Bachelor of Fine Arts in the areas of photography, printmaking, metalsmithing, graphics, sculpture, ceramics, painting and drawing. Majors and concentrations: art education, art history, ceramic art and design, graphic design, jewelry and metalsmithing, painting/drawing, photography, printmaking, sculpture, studio art. Program accredited by NASAD.

Enrollment 852 total; 490 undergraduate, 362 nonprofessional degree.

Art Student Profile 50% females, 50% males, 8% minorities, 1% international.

Art Faculty 23 undergraduate (full-time), 23 undergraduate (part-time). 100% of full-time faculty have terminal degrees. Graduate students do not teach undergraduate courses. Undergraduate student–faculty ratio: 14:1.

Student Life Student groups/activities include Student Art League.

Expenses for 2006–2007 Application fee: $30. State resident tuition: $7218 full-time. Nonresident tuition: $16,467 full-time. Mandatory fees: $1164 full-time. Full-time tuition and fees vary according to course load, degree level, and location. College room and board: $7640. College room only: $4764. Room and board charges vary according to board plan and housing facility. Special program-related fees: $35 per semester for metalsmithing materials, $35 per semester for printmaking materials, $35 per semester for photography supplies, $50 per semester for computer materials, $65 per semester for ceramics supplies.

Financial Aid Program-specific awards: 1–4 Scholastics Art and Writing Awards for incoming freshmen program majors ($2000), 1–4 Governor's Art Youth Awards for Ohio resident program majors ($1000), 3–7 incoming freshmen awards for incoming freshmen program majors ($1200), 13–20 School of Art Scholarships for continuing program majors based on portfolio and GPA ($2000), 25 funded travel awards for current students ($1000), 10 tools and materials awards for current students ($500).

Application Procedures Required: high school transcript, college transcript(s) for transfer students, minimum 2.0 high school GPA, SAT or ACT test scores, portfolio for transfer students, minimum 3.0 college GPA in art courses for transfer students, letters of recommendation and portfolio for scholarship consideration. Recommended: minimum 3.0 high school GPA, letter of recommendation, interview, portfolio.

Web Site http://www.uakron.edu/art/

Undergraduate Contact Office of Admissions, The University of Akron, 381 Buchtel Common, Akron, Ohio 44325-2001; 330-972-7100, fax: 330-972-7022, e-mail address: admissions@uakron.edu

The University of Alabama

Tuscaloosa, Alabama

State-supported, coed. Suburban campus. Total enrollment: 23,838. Art program established 1946.

Degrees Bachelor of Fine Arts in the area of studio art. Majors and concentrations: art/fine arts, ceramic art and design, digital media, painting/drawing, photography, printmaking, sculpture. Graduate degrees offered: Master of Arts in the areas of studio art, art history; Master of Fine Arts in the areas of painting, printmaking, ceramics, sculpture, photography, studio art. Program accredited by NASAD.

Enrollment 270 total; 42 undergraduate, 25 graduate, 203 nonprofessional degree.

Art Student Profile 63% females, 37% males, 13% minorities, 2% international.

Art Faculty 14 total (full-time), 4 total (part-time). 93% of full-time faculty have terminal degrees. Graduate students teach a few undergraduate courses. Undergraduate student–faculty ratio: 2:1.

Student Life Student groups/activities include Art Student League, Crimson Ceramics Society, College of Arts and Sciences Undergraduate Research Competition.

Expenses for 2006–2007 Application fee: $35. State resident tuition: $5278 full-time. Nonresident tuition: $15,294 full-time. Full-time tuition varies according to course load. College room and board: $5380. College room only: $3400. Room and board charges vary according to board plan and housing facility. Special program-related fees: $25–$55 per semester for studio fees for classes.

Financial Aid Program-specific awards: 3 Mary M. Morgan Scholarships for program students ($9000), 3 Bradley Endowed Scholarships for program students ($4330), 1 Ruth K. Larcom Society for the Fine Arts Scholarship for students based on competition ($4400), 5 Julie Peake Holaday Memorial Scholarships for program students ($7228), 2 Art Students Endowed Scholarships for program students ($1462), 1 Richard Zollner Scholarship for program students ($1542), 2 Alvin C. Sella and Joseph Sella Endowed Scholarships for program students ($1338).

Application Procedures Students admitted directly into the professional program freshman year. Deadline for freshmen and transfers: continuous. Required: high school transcript, college transcript(s) for transfer students, minimum 2.0 high school GPA, SAT or ACT test scores (minimum composite ACT score of 22), high school transcript for transfer applicants with fewer than 24 semester hours. Portfolio

The University of Alabama (continued)

reviews held twice on campus; the submission of slides may be substituted for portfolios contact department for details.

Web Site http://www.as.ua.edu/art

Undergraduate Contact Ms. Mary K. Spiegel, Director, Undergraduate Admissions, The University of Alabama, Box 870132, Tuscaloosa, Alabama 35487; 205-348-8197, fax: 205-348-9046, e-mail address: mary.spiegel@ua.edu

Graduate Contact Dr. Carl F. Williams, Director, Graduate Admissions and Recruitment, The University of Alabama, PO Box 870118, Tuscaloosa, Alabama 35487; 205-348-5921, fax: 205-348-0400, e-mail address: cwilliam@aalan.ua.edu

The University of Arizona

Tucson, Arizona

State-supported, coed. Urban campus. Total enrollment: 36,805.

Degrees Bachelor of Fine Arts in the areas of art education, studio art. Majors and concentrations: art education, art history, ceramic art and design, computer graphics, painting/drawing, photography, printmaking, sculpture, studio art, textile arts, visual communication. Graduate degrees offered: Master of Arts in the areas of art education, art history; Master of Fine Arts in the area of studio art. Doctor of Philosophy in the area of history and theory of art. Program accredited by NASAD.

Enrollment 831 total; 274 undergraduate, 54 graduate, 503 nonprofessional degree.

Art Student Profile 67% females, 33% males, 17% minorities.

Art Faculty 39 total (full-time), 6 total (part-time). 97% of full-time faculty have terminal degrees. Graduate students teach about a quarter of undergraduate courses. Undergraduate student–faculty ratio: 17:1.

Student Life Student groups/activities include AHGSA-Art History Graduate Student Association, Art Club/Photo Club, SAGA-School of Art Graduate Association, American Institute of Graphic Arts Student Chapter, Clay Club, National Art Education Association Student Chapter.

Expenses for 2006–2007 Application fee: $25. State resident tuition: $4594 full-time. Nonresi-

dent tuition: $14,800 full-time. Mandatory fees: $172 full-time. Full-time tuition and fees vary according to course load. College room and board: $7850. College room only: $4350. Room and board charges vary according to board plan and housing facility. Special program-related fees: $10–$50 per semester for supplies for some studio courses.

Financial Aid Program-specific awards: 1 Robert C. Brown Memorial Scholarship for program majors ($750), Edward Francis Dunn Scholarships for program majors ($4600), Albert and Kathryn Haldeman Scholarships for program majors ($3600), 1 Hudson Foundation Scholarship for program majors ($1200), Samuel Latta Kingan Scholarships for program majors ($2300), 1 Stephen Langmade Scholarship for program majors ($950), 8 Regents In-State Registration Scholarships for state resident program majors ($1700), 5 Regents In-State Registration Scholarships for state resident program majors demonstrating need ($1700), 36 Regents Non-Resident Tuition Scholarships for out-of-state program majors ($4000), 1 Sandy Truett Memorial Scholarship for program majors ($1050).

Application Procedures Students admitted directly into the professional program freshman year. Deadline for freshmen and transfers: May 1. Required: high school transcript, college transcript(s) for transfer students, 2 letters of recommendation, portfolio, SAT or ACT test scores (minimum composite ACT score of 22), minimum 2.0 high school GPA for state residents, minimum 2.5 high school GPA for out-of-state residents. Portfolio reviews held twice on campus; the submission of slides may be substituted for portfolios.

Web Site http://www.arts.arizona.edu/art

Undergraduate Contact Martina Shenal, Assistant Director, School of Art, The University of Arizona, Art Building, Room 101D, PO Box 210002, Tucson, Arizona 85721-0002; 520-621-7570, fax: 520-621-2353, e-mail address: mshenal@email.arizona.edu

Graduate Contact Brooke Grucella, Graduate Program Coordinator, School of Art, The University of Arizona, Art Building, Room 101D, PO Box 210002, Tucson, Arizona 85721-0002; 520-621-8518, fax: 520-621-2955, e-mail address: brookeg@email.arizona.edu

J. William Fulbright College of Arts and Sciences

University of Arkansas

Fayetteville, Arkansas

State-supported, coed. Suburban campus. Total enrollment: 17,926. Art program established 1874.

Degrees Bachelor of Fine Arts in the areas of studio art, art education. Majors and concentrations: art education, ceramics, graphic design, painting, photography, printmaking, sculpture, visual design. Graduate degrees offered: Master of Fine Arts in the area of art.

Enrollment 212 total; 40 undergraduate, 12 graduate, 160 nonprofessional degree.

Art Faculty 12 total (full-time), 4 total (part-time). 98% of full-time faculty have terminal degrees. Graduate students do not teach undergraduate courses.

Student Life Student groups/activities include Fine Arts League, University Union Programs Fine Arts Committee.

Expenses for 2007–2008 Application fee: $40. State resident tuition: $4772 full-time. Nonresident tuition: $13,226 full-time. Mandatory fees: $1266 full-time. Full-time tuition and fees vary according to program. College room and board: $7017. College room only: $4387. Room and board charges vary according to board plan and housing facility. Special program-related fees: $4 per credit hour for teaching equipment.

Financial Aid Program-specific awards: David Durst Award for program students, Blanche Elliot Awards for sophomores, juniors, and seniors, Tom Turpin Award for freshmen, Neppie Conner Award for sophomores, Collier Photo Award for juniors and seniors, Bedford Camera Award for juniors and seniors, Charles Okerbloom Scholarships for program majors, Mountain Lake Estates Photography Award for program majors, Nina Erikson Awards for program majors.

Application Procedures Students apply for admission into the professional program by sophomore year. Deadline for freshmen: February 15. Notification date for freshmen and transfers: August 15. Required: essay, high school transcript, college transcript(s) for transfer students, SAT or ACT test scores (minimum composite ACT score of 30), minimum 2.0 college GPA for transfers.

Web Site http://www.uark.edu/~artinfo/art.html

Undergraduate Contact Chair, Art Department, University of Arkansas, 116 Fine Arts Center, Fayetteville, Arkansas 72701; 479-575-5202, fax: 479-575-2062.

Graduate Contact Prof. Michael Peven, MFA Coordinator, Art Department, University of Arkansas, 116 Fine Arts Center, Fayetteville, Arkansas 72701; 479-575-5202, fax: 479-575-2062, e-mail address: mpeven@uark.edu

University of Bridgeport

Bridgeport, Connecticut

Independent, coed. Urban campus. Total enrollment: 4,018.

Degrees Bachelor of Arts in the areas of graphic design, illustration; Bachelor of Fine Arts in the areas of graphic design, illustration; Bachelor of Science in the areas of interior design, industrial design, graphic design, illustration. Majors and concentrations: graphic design, illustration, industrial design, interior design. Program accredited by NASAD.

Enrollment 123 total; all undergraduate.

Art Student Profile 51% females, 49% males, 35% minorities, 15% international.

Art Faculty 5 undergraduate (full-time), 14 undergraduate (part-time). 100% of full-time faculty have terminal degrees. Graduate students do not teach undergraduate courses. Undergraduate student–faculty ratio: 10:1.

Student Life Student groups/activities include art shows.

Expenses for 2007–2008 Application fee: $25. Comprehensive fee: $32,860 includes full-time tuition ($21,150), mandatory fees ($1710), and college room and board ($10,000). College room only: $5200. Full-time tuition and fees vary according to program. Room and board charges vary according to board plan and student level.

Application Procedures Students admitted directly into the professional program freshman year. Deadline for freshmen and transfers: continuous. Required: essay, high school transcript, college transcript(s) for transfer stu-

University of Bridgeport (continued)

dents, portfolio, SAT or ACT test scores. Recommended: minimum 2.0 high school GPA, 2 letters of recommendation, interview. Portfolio reviews held as needed on campus; the submission of slides may be substituted for portfolios for international applicants.

Web Site http://www.bridgeport.edu

Undergraduate Contact Ms. Audrey Ashton Savage, Vice President Enrollment Management, University of Bridgeport, 126 Park Avenue, Bridgeport, Connecticut 06604; 800-EXCEL-UB, fax: 203-576-4941, e-mail address: admit@bridgeport.edu

The University of British Columbia

Vancouver, British Columbia, Canada

Province-supported, coed. Urban campus. Total enrollment: 43,301. Art program established 1955.

Web Site http://www.ubc.ca/

University of Calgary

Calgary, Alberta, Canada

Province-supported, coed. Urban campus. Total enrollment: 27,928 (2005). Art program established 1967.

Degrees Bachelor of Fine Arts in the area of visual studies (studio concentration and developmental art concentration). Majors and concentrations: developmental art, painting/drawing, photography, printmaking, sculpture. Graduate degrees offered: Master of Fine Arts in the area of art.

Enrollment 249 total; 162 undergraduate, 12 graduate, 75 nonprofessional degree.

Art Student Profile 66% females, 34% males, 4% international.

Art Faculty 12 total (full-time), 9 total (part-time). 100% of full-time faculty have terminal degrees. Graduate students teach a few undergraduate courses. Undergraduate student–faculty ratio: 14:1.

Student Life Student groups/activities include on-campus exhibitions in two venues, BFA and MFA shows, Art Students Society.

Financial Aid Program-specific awards: 1 Alberta Printmakers Society Award for printmakers ($100), 1 Continuing Arts Association Travel Scholarship for those demonstrating academic achievement ($900), 1 Bow Fort Chapter I.O.D.E. Bursary for those demonstrating academic achievement ($250), 2 Heinz Jordan Memorial Scholarships for those demonstrating academic achievement ($500), 2 Santo Mignosa Awards for printmakers ($500), 1 Sadie M. Nelson Bursary in Art for those demonstrating need and academic merit ($500), 1 Western Silk Screen Prize for silk screen majors ($300), 1 BFA Graduation Committee Prize for those entering final year in visual arts program ($250), 1 Jack Wise Award for Excellence in Painting for continuing students who have completed Art 451 and 453 ($300), 2 25th Anniversary Scholarships for those demonstrating academic merit ($1000), 1 Stadelbauer Award for developmental art students ($1250).

Application Procedures Students admitted directly into the professional program freshman year. Deadline for freshmen and transfers: April 1. Required: high school transcript, portfolio, standing in top 75% of graduating class. Recommended: SAT test score only. Portfolio reviews held once on campus; the submission of slides may be substituted for portfolios (CD or DVD only).

Web Site http://www.ucalgary.ca

Contact Ms. Karen Lyons, Student Advisor, Faculty of Fine Arts Student Success Team (FASST), University of Calgary, 2500 University Drive, NW, Calgary, Alberta T2N 1N4, Canada; 403-220-5384, fax: 403-282-6925, e-mail address: lyons@ucalgary.ca

University of Central Arkansas

Conway, Arkansas

State-supported, coed. Small town campus. Total enrollment: 12,330. Art program established 1927.

Degrees Bachelor of Fine Arts. Majors and concentrations: studio art. Program accredited by NASAD.

Enrollment 220 total; 19 undergraduate, 201 nonprofessional degree.

Art Student Profile 66% females, 34% males, 15% minorities, 3% international.

Art Faculty 13 undergraduate (full-time), 6 undergraduate (part-time). 100% of full-time faculty have terminal degrees. Graduate students do not teach undergraduate courses. Undergraduate student–faculty ratio: 15:1.

Student Life Student groups/activities include American Institute of Graphic Arts Student Chapter, National Art Education Association Student Chapter, Student Art History Association, Clay Club.

Expenses for 2007–2008 Application fee: $0. State resident tuition: $4830 full-time. Nonresident tuition: $9660 full-time. Mandatory fees: $1375 full-time. College room and board: $4600. College room only: $2680. Room and board charges vary according to board plan and housing facility.

Financial Aid Program-specific awards: 1 Windgate Scholarship for art majors ($10,000), 15 Performance in Art Scholarships for art majors ($1000–$2000), 1 Disterheft Scholarship for art majors ($1200), 1 Curtis Scholarship for art majors ($600).

Application Procedures Students apply for admission into the professional program by sophomore year. Deadline for freshmen and transfers: continuous. Required: high school transcript, college transcript(s) for transfer students, ACT test score only, portfolio review for transfer students. Recommended: minimum 3.0 high school GPA.

Web Site http://www.uca.edu/cfac/art

Undergraduate Contact Dr. Jeffry R. Young, Chair, Department of Art, University of Central Arkansas, Conway, Arkansas 72035; 501-450-3113, fax: 501-450-5788, e-mail address: jyoung@uca.edu

University of Central Florida

Orlando, Florida

State-supported, coed. Suburban campus. Total enrollment: 46,719.

Web Site http://www.ucf.edu/

University of Central Missouri

Warrensburg, Missouri

State-supported, coed. Small town campus. Total enrollment: 10,711. Art program established 1871.

Web Site http://www.ucmo.edu/

University of Cincinnati

Cincinnati, Ohio

State-supported, coed. Urban campus. Total enrollment: 27,932. Art program established 1967.

Degrees Bachelor of Fine Arts in the area of fine arts. Majors and concentrations: media arts, three-dimensional studies, two-dimensional studies. Graduate degrees offered: Master of Arts in the areas of art history, art education; Master of Fine Arts in the area of fine arts. Cross-registration with The Ohio Valley Consortium of Colleges and Universities. Program accredited by NASAD.

Enrollment 500 total; 380 undergraduate, 120 graduate.

Art Student Profile 55% females, 45% males, 2% minorities, 5% international.

Art Faculty 26 total (full-time), 9 total (part-time). 100% of full-time faculty have terminal degrees. Graduate students teach a few undergraduate courses. Undergraduate student–faculty ratio: 13:1.

Student Life Student groups/activities include Fine Arts Association, National Art Education Association Student Chapter, Graduate Student Association-Fine Arts Chapter.

Expenses for 2006–2007 Application fee: $40. State resident tuition: $7896 full-time. Nonresident tuition: $22,419 full-time. Mandatory fees: $1503 full-time. Full-time tuition and fees vary according to course load, degree level, location, program, and reciprocity agreements. College room and board: $9246. College room only: $5874. Room and board charges vary according to board plan and housing facility. Special program-related fees: $45 per course for lab fee-art supplies.

Financial Aid Program-specific awards: 3–7 Wolf Stein Travel Fellowships for upper-level

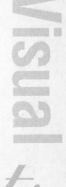

Visual *Arts*

University of Cincinnati (continued)

undergraduates ($1500–$2500), 1 Rockwood Production Grant for electronic art majors ($1000), 1 Dean Tatgenhorst Conrad Scholarship for art/art history majors ($1000), 6 art scholarships for art majors ($1500).

Application Procedures Students admitted directly into the professional program freshman year. Deadline for freshmen and transfers: continuous. Notification date for freshmen: September 20. Required: essay, high school transcript, college transcript(s) for transfer students, minimum 3.0 high school GPA, portfolio, SAT or ACT test scores (minimum combined SAT score of 1020, minimum composite ACT score of 22), minimum 2.5 college GPA for transfer students. Recommended: interview. Portfolio reviews held 6 times on campus and off campus in Cincinnati, OH; Louisville, KY; the submission of slides may be substituted for portfolios if the applicant cannot come personally.

Web Site http://daap.uc.edu/art

Undergraduate Contact Prof. Denise Burge, Undergraduate Advisor, School of Art, University of Cincinnati, Mail Location 0016, Cincinnati, Ohio 45221; 513-556-2426, fax: 513-556-2887, e-mail address: dburge@cinci.rr.com

Graduate Contact Ms. Kimberly Burleigh, Director of Graduate Studies in Fine Arts, School of Art, University of Cincinnati, Mail Location 0016, Cincinnati, Ohio 45221; 513-556-2075, fax: 513-556-2887, e-mail address: kimberly.burleigh@uc.edu

University of Colorado at Boulder

Boulder, Colorado

State-supported, coed. Suburban campus. Total enrollment: 31,399. Art program established 1932.

Degrees Bachelor of Arts in the area of art history; Bachelor of Fine Arts in the area of studio art; Bachelor of Arts in Studio Arts. Majors and concentrations: art history, studio art. Graduate degrees offered: Master of Arts in the area of art history; Master of Fine Arts in the area of studio art.

Enrollment 1,157 total; 1,100 undergraduate, 57 graduate.

Art Student Profile 69% females, 31% males, 7% minorities, 4% international.

Art Faculty 31 total (full-time), 10 total (part-time). 100% of full-time faculty have terminal degrees. Graduate students teach about a quarter of undergraduate courses. Undergraduate student–faculty ratio: 35:1.

Student Life Student groups/activities include Art Student League.

Expenses for 2006–2007 Application fee: $50. State resident tuition: $4554 full-time. Nonresident tuition: $22,450 full-time. Mandatory fees: $1089 full-time. Full-time tuition and fees vary according to program. College room and board: $8300. Room and board charges vary according to board plan, location, and student level. Special program-related fees: $50 per course for non-studio course, $50 per credit hour for studio course.

Financial Aid Program-specific awards: 20 scholarships for program majors ($500–$2000).

Application Procedures Deadline for freshmen and transfers: continuous. Required: high school transcript, college transcript(s) for transfer students, minimum 2.0 high school GPA, SAT or ACT test scores, portfolio upon completion of foundation courses (slides permissible) for BFA. Portfolio reviews held once on campus; the submission of slides may be substituted for portfolios.

Web Site http://www.colorado.edu/arts

Undergraduate Contact Admissions, University of Colorado at Boulder, Campus Box 552, Boulder, Colorado 80309; 303-492-6301.

Graduate Contact Alexei Bogdanov, Graduate Coordinator, Department of Fine Arts, University of Colorado at Boulder, Campus Box 318, Boulder, Colorado 80309-0318; 303-492-2419, fax: 303-492-4886, e-mail address: alexei.bogdanov@colorado.edu

University of Connecticut

Storrs, Connecticut

State-supported, coed. Rural campus. Total enrollment: 23,557.

Degrees Bachelor of Fine Arts in the area of art. Majors and concentrations: art history, art/fine arts, communication design, illustration, painting/drawing, photography, printmaking, sculpture. Graduate degrees offered: Master of Fine Arts in the area of art. Program accredited by NASAD.

Enrollment 260 total; 240 undergraduate, 20 graduate.

Art Student Profile 58% females, 42% males, 7% minorities, 3% international.

Art Faculty 24 total (full-time), 14 total (part-time). 100% of full-time faculty have terminal degrees. Graduate students teach a few undergraduate courses. Undergraduate student–faculty ratio: 14:1.

Student Life Special housing available for art students.

Expenses for 2007–2008 Application fee: $70. State resident tuition: $6816 full-time. Nonresident tuition: $20,760 full-time. Mandatory fees: $2026 full-time. College room and board: $8850. College room only: $4698. Special program-related fees: $15–$75 per course for expendable supplies in studio courses.

Financial Aid Program-specific awards: 1 Victor Borge Scholarship for incoming freshmen ($1000), 8 Fine Arts Talent Scholarships for program students ($3000), 1 Anniversary Scholarship for program students ($1400), 1 Alaimo Scholarship for program students ($1000), 2 Fine Arts Talent Scholarships for incoming freshmen ($3000), 1 Fine Arts Talent Scholarship for incoming freshmen ($1000).

Application Procedures Students admitted directly into the professional program freshman year. Deadline for freshmen: April 1; transfers: May 1. Required: essay, high school transcript, college transcript(s) for transfer students, minimum 2.0 high school GPA, portfolio, SAT or ACT test scores. Recommended: minimum 3.0 high school GPA, 3 letters of recommendation, interview. Portfolio reviews held 3 times on campus and off campus in Boston, MA; Hartford, CT; the submission of slides may be substituted for portfolios at student's discretion.

Web Site http://www.art.uconn.edu

Undergraduate Contact Ray DiCapua, Associate Head and Associate Professor, Department of Art and Art History, University of Connecticut, 830 Bolton Road, U-1099, Storrs, Connecticut 06269-1099; 860-486-3930, fax: 860-486-3869, e-mail address: ralph.dicapua@uconn.edu

Graduate Contact Monica Bock, Graduate Program Coordinator and Associate Professor, Department of Art and Art History, University of Connecticut, 830 Bolton Road, U-1099, Storrs, Connecticut 06269-1099; 860-486-3930, fax: 860-486-3869.

University of Dayton

Dayton, Ohio

Independent Roman Catholic, coed. Suburban campus. Total enrollment: 10,503. Art program established 1960.

Degrees Bachelor of Fine Arts in the areas of art education, studio art, visual communication design, photography. Majors and concentrations: art education, art/fine arts, computer graphics, graphic arts, illustration, photography, studio art. Cross-registration with Miami Valley Consortium. Program accredited by NASAD.

Enrollment 209 total; 149 undergraduate, 60 nonprofessional degree.

Art Student Profile 73% females, 27% males, 5% minorities, 1% international.

Art Faculty 13 undergraduate (full-time), 19 undergraduate (part-time). 100% of full-time faculty have terminal degrees. Graduate students do not teach undergraduate courses. Undergraduate student–faculty ratio: 6:1.

Student Life Student groups/activities include Horvath Student Art Show, Stander Symposium, student organization in design, fine art, and photography.

Expenses for 2006–2007 Application fee: $0. Comprehensive fee: $31,160 includes full-time tuition ($23,000), mandatory fees ($970), and college room and board ($7190). College room only: $4300. Full-time tuition and fees vary according to program. Room and board charges vary according to board plan, housing facility, and student level. Special program-related fees: $20–$75 per semester for studio/lab fees.

Financial Aid Program-specific awards: 5–10 Visual Arts Scholarships for freshmen ($4000), 1 Gordon Richardson Scholarship for juniors ($2000), 3 Horvath Scholarships for sophomores ($1000), 1 Anne Perman Scholarship for upperclassmen ($2000).

Application Procedures Required: essay, high school transcript, college transcript(s) for transfer students, minimum 2.0 high school GPA, letter of recommendation, SAT or ACT test

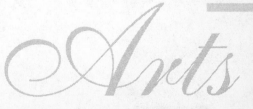

University of Dayton (continued)

scores, record of leadership and service. Recommended: interview, portfolio.

Web Site http://www.as.udayton.edu/visualarts/

Undergraduate Contact Office of Admission, University of Dayton, 300 College Park, Dayton, Ohio 45469-1611; 937-229-4411.

University of Denver

Denver, Colorado

Independent, coed. Total enrollment: 10,374. Art program established 1929.

Degrees Bachelor of Fine Arts in the areas of electronic media arts design, art education, studio art, pre-art-conservation. Majors and concentrations: ceramics, painting/drawing, photography, printmaking, sculpture. Graduate degrees offered: Master of Arts in the area of art history/museum studies; Master of Fine Arts in the area of electronic media arts design. Program accredited by NASAD.

Enrollment 192 total; 27 undergraduate, 46 graduate, 119 nonprofessional degree.

Art Student Profile 77% females, 23% males, 15% minorities, 10% international.

Art Faculty 17 total (full-time), 5 total (part-time). 100% of full-time faculty have terminal degrees. Graduate students teach a few undergraduate courses. Undergraduate student–faculty ratio: 12:1.

Student Life Student groups/activities include ...isms (student art organization), Gallery 023 (student run exhibition space), American Institute of Graphic Arts (AIGA) Student Chapter.

Expenses for 2007–2008 Application fee: $50. Comprehensive fee: $41,910 includes full-time tuition ($31,428), mandatory fees ($804), and college room and board ($9678). College room only: $6015. Full-time tuition and fees vary according to class time, course load, and program. Room and board charges vary according to board plan and housing facility. Special program-related fees: $10–$80 per course for lab fees, course materials.

Financial Aid Program-specific awards: 5 Harrison Scholarships for those demonstrating talent and need ($5000–$20,000), 20 art scholarships for those demonstrating talent and academic achievement ($4000–$20,000).

Application Procedures Students admitted directly into the professional program freshman year. Deadline for freshmen: February 1; transfers: continuous. Notification date for freshmen and transfers: continuous. Required: essay, high school transcript, college transcript(s) for transfer students, 2 letters of recommendation, interview, portfolio, SAT or ACT test scores. Portfolio reviews held as needed on campus; the submission of slides may be substituted for portfolios (slides or URL or CD-ROM preferred).

Web Site http://www.du.edu/art/

Undergraduate Contact Ms. Margret Korzus, Associate Dean, Office of Admissions, University of Denver, University Hall, 2197 South University Boulevard, Denver, Colorado 80208; 303-871-2794, fax: 303-871-3301, e-mail address: mkorzus@du.edu

Graduate Contact Dr. Elizabeth Owen, School of Art and Art History, University of Denver, 2121 East Asbury Avenue, Denver, Colorado 80208; 303-871-2846, fax: 303-871-4112, e-mail address: eowen@du.edu

University of Evansville

Evansville, Indiana

Independent, coed. Urban campus. Total enrollment: 2,879. Art program established 1960.

Degrees Bachelor of Fine Arts. Majors and concentrations: ceramics, painting, sculpture.

Enrollment 80 total; all undergraduate.

Art Student Profile 62% females, 38% males, 1% minorities, 15% international.

Art Faculty 3 undergraduate (full-time), 6 undergraduate (part-time). 100% of full-time faculty have terminal degrees. Graduate students do not teach undergraduate courses. Undergraduate student–faculty ratio: 11:1.

Student Life Student groups/activities include Clay Club, Kappa Pi.

Expenses for 2006–2007 Application fee: $35. Comprehensive fee: $30,100 includes full-time tuition ($22,370), mandatory fees ($610), and college room and board ($7120). College room only: $3540. Room and board charges vary according to board plan and housing facility. Special program-related fees: $25–$50 per semester for ceramics, photography, printmaking, metals, sculpture.

Financial Aid Program-specific awards: 25 art and academic scholarships for freshmen program majors ($500–$10,000), art and academic scholarships for transfer program majors.

Application Procedures Students apply for admission into the professional program by sophomore, junior year. Deadline for freshmen: May 1; transfers: June 1. Notification date for freshmen and transfers: continuous. Required: essay, high school transcript, college transcript(s) for transfer students, minimum 2.0 high school GPA, SAT or ACT test scores (minimum composite ACT score of 19). Recommended: minimum 3.0 high school GPA, 2 letters of recommendation, interview, portfolio. Portfolio reviews held continuously on campus and off campus in Louisville, KY; the submission of slides may be substituted for portfolios whenever needed.

Web Site http://www.evansville.edu

Undergraduate Contact Mr. William F. Brown, Chairman, Department of Art, University of Evansville, 1800 Lincoln Avenue, Evansville, Indiana 47722; 812-479-2043, fax: 812-479-2320, e-mail address: bb32@evansville.edu

University of Florida

Gainesville, Florida

State-supported, coed. Suburban campus. Total enrollment: 50,822. Art program established 1929.

Degrees Bachelor of Arts in the areas of art history, art education, general visual art studies; Bachelor of Fine Arts in the areas of ceramics, drawing, graphic design, painting, creative photography, printmaking, sculpture, digital media. Majors and concentrations: art education, art history, ceramics, digital media, general visual arts studies, graphic design, painting/drawing, photography, printmaking, sculpture. Graduate degrees offered: Master of Arts in the areas of museum studies, art education, art history; Master of Fine Arts in the areas of ceramics, drawing, graphic design, painting, creative photography, printmaking, sculpture, digital media. Doctor of Philosophy in the area of art history. Cross-registration with Penland School of Crafts, New World School for the Arts. Program accredited by NASAD, NCATE.

Enrollment 552 total; 450 undergraduate, 102 graduate.

Art Student Profile 68% females, 32% males, 30% minorities, 2% international.

Art Faculty 27 total (full-time), 2 total (part-time). 97% of full-time faculty have terminal degrees. Graduate students teach about a quarter of undergraduate courses. Undergraduate student–faculty ratio: 17:1.

Student Life Student groups/activities include Departure: GNV publication, Fine Arts College Council, Annual Juried Student Exhibition. Special housing available for art students.

Expenses for 2006–2007 Application fee: $30. State resident tuition: $3206 full-time. Nonresident tuition: $17,790 full-time. College room and board: $6590. College room only: $4170. Room and board charges vary according to board plan and student level. Special program-related fees: $8–$65 per course for lab fee for studio courses.

Financial Aid Program-specific awards: 2 Amy DeGrove Scholarships for freshmen and juniors ($2500), 2 James J. Rizzi Scholarships for studio majors ($3000).

Application Procedures Students apply for admission into the professional program by sophomore year. Deadline for freshmen: January 30; transfers: February 15. Notification date for freshmen: continuous; transfers: March 29. Required: essay, high school transcript, college transcript(s) for transfer students, minimum 3.0 high school GPA, letter of recommendation, SAT or ACT test scores (minimum composite ACT score of 20), completion of pre-professional courses Drawing I and II, Design I and II, Survey Art History I and II, portfolio for transfers. Portfolio reviews held twice on campus; the submission of slides may be substituted for portfolios.

Web Site http://www.arts.ufl.edu/art

Undergraduate Contact Dana Myers, Undergraduate Coordinator/Academic Advisor, School of Art and Art History, University of Florida, FAC 101, PO Box 115801, Gainesville, Florida 32611-5801; 352-392-0201, fax: 352-392-8453, e-mail address: dmyers@arts.ufl.edu

Graduate Contact Kristin Flierl, Graduate Program Assistant, School of Art and Art History, University of Florida, FAC 101, PO Box 115801, Gainesville, Florida 32611-5801; 352-392-0201 ext. 201, fax: 352-392-8453, e-mail address: kflierl@ufl.edu

Lamar Dodd School of Art
University of Georgia
Athens, Georgia

State-supported, coed. Suburban campus. Total enrollment: 33,959. Art program established 1937.

Degrees Bachelor of Fine Arts in the area of art. Majors and concentrations: art education, art history, ceramics, digital media, fabric design, graphic design, interior design, jewelry and metalsmithing, painting/drawing, photography, printmaking, scientific illustration, sculpture. Graduate degrees offered: Master of Arts in the areas of art history, art education; Master of Fine Arts in the area of art. Doctor of Education in the area of art education; Doctor of Philosophy in the areas of art history, art education. Cross-registration with 19 area institutions. Program accredited by NASAD, CIDA.

Enrollment 1,072 total; 296 undergraduate, 96 graduate, 680 nonprofessional degree.

Art Student Profile 68% females, 32% males, 12% minorities, 4% international.

Art Faculty 57 total (full-time), 20 total (part-time). 98% of full-time faculty have terminal degrees. Graduate students teach a few undergraduate courses. Undergraduate student–faculty ratio: 15:1.

Student Life Student groups/activities include American Society of Interior Designers Student Chapter, National Art Education Association Student Chapter.

Expenses for 2007–2008 Application fee: $50. State resident tuition: $4496 full-time. Nonresident tuition: $19,600 full-time. Mandatory fees: $1126 full-time. Full-time tuition and fees vary according to course load, location, program, and student level. College room and board: $7292. College room only: $4010. Room and board charges vary according to board plan and housing facility. Special program-related fees: $10–$100 per course for supplies.

Financial Aid Program-specific awards: 30 art awards for program students ($500–$1000).

Application Procedures Students apply for admission into the professional program by freshman year. Deadline for freshmen: March 1; transfers: July 1. Notification date for freshmen: March 31. Required: high school transcript, minimum 3.0 high school GPA, SAT or ACT test scores, portfolio after the first semester.

Web Site http://www.art.uga.edu

Undergraduate Contact Dr. Nancy G. McDuff, Director of Admissions, University of Georgia, 114 Academic Building, Athens, Georgia 30602; 706-542-8776, fax: 706-542-1466.

Graduate Contact Ms. Kate Gearity, Degree Program Specialist, Lamar Dodd School of Art, University of Georgia, Visual Arts Building, Athens, Georgia 30602; 706-542-1636, fax: 706-542-0226.

Hartford Art School
University of Hartford
West Hartford, Connecticut

Independent, coed. Suburban campus. Total enrollment: 7,308. Art program established 1877.

Degrees Bachelor of Fine Arts in the area of art. Majors and concentrations: ceramics, drawing, illustration, media arts, painting, photography, printmaking, sculpture, visual communication design. Graduate degrees offered: Master of Fine Arts in the area of art. Cross-registration with Trinity College, Saint Joseph College, Hartford Seminary, Central Connecticut University, University of Connecticut-Hartford, Capital Community College. Program accredited by NASAD.

Enrollment 387 total; 340 undergraduate, 47 graduate.

Art Student Profile 55% females, 45% males, 5% minorities, 2% international.

Art Faculty 20 undergraduate (full-time), 22 undergraduate (part-time), 1 graduate (full-time), 9 graduate (part-time). 86% of full-time faculty have terminal degrees. Graduate students do not teach undergraduate courses. Undergraduate student–faculty ratio: 14:1.

Student Life Student groups/activities include Student Association, student newspaper and yearbook staff, professional fraternities and sororities. Special housing available for art students.

Expenses for 2007–2008 Application fee: $35. Comprehensive fee: $37,414 includes full-time tuition ($25,806), mandatory fees ($1190), and

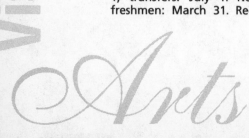

college room and board ($10,418). College room only: $6424. Full-time tuition and fees vary according to program. Room and board charges vary according to board plan and housing facility.

Financial Aid Program-specific awards: 45 endowed scholarships for those demonstrating need ($2500), 15–20 artistic merit awards for artistically talented students ($5000–$17,000), 15–25 academic talent awards for those with high SAT scores, high GPA, in top 10% of class ($9000–$15,000).

Application Procedures Students admitted directly into the professional program freshman year. Deadline for freshmen and transfers: continuous. Notification date for freshmen and transfers: continuous. Required: high school transcript, college transcript(s) for transfer students, minimum 2.0 high school GPA, 2 letters of recommendation, portfolio, SAT or ACT test scores. Recommended: essay, interview. Portfolio reviews held by appointment on campus and off campus in Hartford, CT; Philadelphia, PA; Miami, FL; New York, NY; Boston, MA; Syracuse, NY; Baltimore, MD; the submission of slides may be substituted for portfolios when distance is prohibitive.

Web Site http://www.hartfordartschool.org

Undergraduate Contact Mr. Robert Calafiore, Assistant Dean, Hartford Art School, University of Hartford, 200 Bloomfield Avenue, West Hartford, Connecticut 06117; 860-768-4827, fax: 860-768-5296.

Graduate Contact Ms. Mary Frey, Professor, Graduate Director, Hartford Art School, University of Hartford, 200 Bloomfield Avenue, West Hartford, Connecticut 06117; 860-768-4393, fax: 860-768-5296.

University of Houston

Houston, Texas

State-supported, coed. Urban campus. Total enrollment: 34,334. Art program established 1962.

Degrees Bachelor of Fine Arts in the areas of graphic communication, photography/digital media, sculpture, painting. Majors and concentrations: graphic design, painting/drawing, photography/digital media, sculpture. Graduate degrees offered: Master of Fine Arts in the areas of graphic communication, photography/digital media, painting, sculpture.

Enrollment 1,151 total; 830 undergraduate, 39 graduate, 282 nonprofessional degree.

Art Student Profile 68% females, 32% males, 50% minorities, 3% international.

Art Faculty 22 total (full-time), 11 total (part-time). 100% of full-time faculty have terminal degrees. Graduate students teach a few undergraduate courses. Undergraduate student–faculty ratio: 25:1.

Student Life Student groups/activities include Graphic Communication Student Association, Clayworks (ceramics student association).

Expenses for 2006–2007 Application fee: $50. State resident tuition: $4260 full-time. Nonresident tuition: $12,510 full-time. Mandatory fees: $2649 full-time. Full-time tuition and fees vary according to course level, course load, degree level, location, program, reciprocity agreements, and student level. College room and board: $6418. College room only: $3632. Room and board charges vary according to board plan and housing facility. Special program-related fees: $20–$100 per course for equipment maintenance and supplies fee.

Financial Aid Program-specific awards: 10–25 Flaxman Scholarships for seniors ($500–$1500), 2–4 George Bunker Scholarships for program majors ($1500–$2000), 1–4 Choate/Palmer Scholarships for program majors demonstrating need ($700–$1000), 1 Swails Fine ARts Scholarship for program majors with financial need ($500).

Application Procedures Students admitted directly into the professional program freshman year. Deadline for freshmen: April 1; transfers: May 1. Notification date for freshmen and transfers: continuous. Required: high school transcript, college transcript(s) for transfer students, SAT or ACT test scores, GPA (minimum varies according to test scores and class rank).

Web Site http://www.art.uh.edu/

Undergraduate Contact Admission Office, University of Houston, 129 Ezekiel Cullen Building, Houston, Texas 77204-2023; 713-743-1010.

Graduate Contact Cathy Hunt, Graduate Advisor, School of Art, University of Houston, Fine Arts Building, Room 100, Houston, Texas 77204-4019; 713-743-2830, fax: 713-743-2823, e-mail address: chunt@uh.edu

University of Illinois at Chicago

Chicago, Illinois

State-supported, coed. Total enrollment: 24,654. Art program established 1966.

Degrees Bachelor of Fine Arts in the areas of studio arts, graphic design, industrial design, photo/film/electronic media, art education. Majors and concentrations: art education, electronic arts, film, graphic arts, industrial design, painting/drawing, photography, sculpture, studio art, video art. Graduate degrees offered: Master of Fine Arts in the areas of studio arts, photography, graphic design, industrial design, film/animation/video, electronic visualization. Program accredited by NASAD.

Enrollment 697 total; 607 undergraduate, 90 graduate.

Art Student Profile 60% females, 40% males, 20% minorities, 10% international.

Art Faculty 27 total (full-time), 9 total (part-time). 100% of full-time faculty have terminal degrees. Graduate students teach a few undergraduate courses. Undergraduate student–faculty ratio: 25:1.

Student Life Student groups/activities include American Center for Design Student Chapter, Industrial Design Society of America Student Chapter.

Expenses for 2006–2007 Application fee: $40. State resident tuition: $6780 full-time. Nonresident tuition: $19,170 full-time. Mandatory fees: $2962 full-time. Full-time tuition and fees vary according to program. College room and board: $7446. Room and board charges vary according to board plan and housing facility. Special program-related fees: $15–$150 per class for models, equipment, darkroom facilities.

Financial Aid Program-specific awards: 10–12 talent/tuition waivers for academically qualified program majors ($2722–$6052).

Application Procedures Students apply for admission into the professional program by sophomore year. Deadline for freshmen: May 1; transfers: June 1. Notification date for freshmen and transfers: continuous. Required: high school transcript, college transcript(s) for transfer students, minimum 2.0 high school GPA, SAT or ACT test scores (minimum composite ACT score of 21), minimum TOEFL score of 520 for international applicants, minimum 2.5 (4.0 scale) or 3.75 (5.0 scale) college GPA for transfer students, portfolio for graphic design and art education majors and transfers in certain areas, standing in upper 50% of graduating class. Recommended: essay, letter of recommendation, interview. Portfolio reviews held by arrangement on campus; the submission of slides may be substituted for portfolios (slides preferred).

Web Site http://www.uic.edu/aa/artd/

Undergraduate Contact Erin Brady, Academic Advisor, Undergraduate, School of Art and Design, University of Illinois at Chicago, 929 West Harrison Street, 106 Jefferson Hall, M/C 036, Chicago, Illinois 60607-7038; 312-996-3337, fax: 312-413-2333, e-mail address: ebrady@uic.edu

Graduate Contact Mara Kruger, Academic Advisor, Graduate, School of Art and Design, University of Illinois at Chicago, 929 West Harrison Street, 106 Jefferson Hall M/C 036, Chicago, Illinois 60607-7038; 312-996-3337, fax: 312-413-2333, e-mail address: marak@uic.edu

University of Illinois at Urbana–Champaign

Champaign, Illinois

State-supported, coed. Urban campus. Total enrollment: 42,728. Art program established 1877.

Degrees Bachelor of Fine Arts in the areas of ceramics, GD, ID, metals, painting, photography, art history, art education, sculpture, new media. Majors and concentrations: art education, art history, ceramics, graphic design, industrial design, metals, new media, painting, photography, sculpture. Graduate degrees offered: Master of Arts in the areas of art education, art history; Master of Fine Arts in the areas of ceramics, graphic design, industrial design, metals, painting, photography, sculpture, new media. Doctor of Education; Doctor of Philosophy in the areas of art history, art education. Program accredited by NASAD.

Enrollment 620 total; 520 undergraduate, 100 graduate.

Art Student Profile 64% females, 36% males, 1% minorities, 2% international.

Art Faculty 7 undergraduate (part-time), 49 graduate (full-time). 98% of full-time faculty have terminal degrees. Graduate students teach a few undergraduate courses. Undergraduate student–faculty ratio: 10:1.

Student Life Student groups/activities include organizations for all major areas, Industrial Design Society of America, National Art Education Association Student Chapter.

Expenses for 2007–2008 Application fee: $40. State resident tuition: $8440 full-time. Nonresident tuition: $22,526 full-time. Mandatory fees: $2690 full-time. Full-time tuition and fees vary according to course load, program, and student level. College room and board: $8196. Room and board charges vary according to board plan and housing facility. Entering degree-seeking students are guaranteed the same tuition rates for 4 years. Special program-related fees: $200–$300 per semester for equipment and materials fees.

Financial Aid Program-specific awards: 60–70 tuition support awards for program majors ($3000–$4000).

Application Procedures Students apply for admission into the professional program by freshman year. Deadline for freshmen: January 1; transfers: March 1. Notification date for freshmen: March 15. Required: essay, high school transcript, college transcript(s) for transfer students, SAT or ACT test scores, CD or slide portfolio for all studio programs, writing sample for art history transfers, ITBS for transfer into art education. Recommended: minimum 3.0 high school GPA. Portfolio reviews held on campus by committee only, off campus at National Portfolio days on campus and off campus in Chicago, IL; St. Louis, MO; and Indianapolis, IN; the submission of slides may be substituted for portfolios (CD or slides also permissible).

Web Site http://www.art.uiuc.edu

Undergraduate Contact Mark Avery, Undergraduate Specialist in Academic Affairs, School of Art and Design, University of Illinois at Urbana–Champaign, 408 East Peabody Drive, Champaign, Illinois 61820; 217-333-6632, fax: 217-244-7688.

Graduate Contact Ms. Marsha Biddle, Graduate Specialist in Academic Affairs, School of Art and Design, University of Illinois at Urbana–Champaign, 408 East Peabody Drive, Champaign, Illinois 61820; 217-333-0642, fax: 217-244-7688.

University of Indianapolis

Indianapolis, Indiana

Independent, coed. Urban campus. Total enrollment: 4,389. Art program established 1904.

Degrees Bachelor of Fine Arts in the areas of studio art, visual communication design. Majors and concentrations: ceramics, painting/drawing, visual communication design, works on paper. Cross-registration with Consortium for Urban Education. Program accredited by NASAD.

Enrollment 107 total; 13 undergraduate, 94 nonprofessional degree.

Art Student Profile 60% females, 40% males, 5% minorities, 15% international.

Art Faculty 6 undergraduate (full-time), 6 total (part-time). 100% of full-time faculty have terminal degrees. Graduate students do not teach undergraduate courses. Undergraduate student–faculty ratio: 6:1.

Student Life Student groups/activities include Indianapolis Student Art Association.

Expenses for 2007–2008 Application fee: $20. Comprehensive fee: $27,290 includes full-time tuition ($19,540), mandatory fees ($190), and college room and board ($7560). College room only: $3590. Room and board charges vary according to board plan and housing facility.

Financial Aid Program-specific awards: 1 Gerald Boyce Scholarship for art majors ($3000), 6–8 departmental scholarships for incoming freshmen ($3000), 1 A. E. Gott Award for art majors ($1000), 1 M. E. Gott Award for art majors ($600).

Application Procedures Students apply for admission into the professional program by sophomore year. Deadline for freshmen and transfers: continuous. Required: essay, high school transcript, college transcript(s) for transfer students, minimum 2.0 high school GPA, SAT or ACT test scores, interview and portfolio for scholarship consideration. Portfolio reviews held once in January, February, and June

Visual

Arts

University of Indianapolis (continued)

on campus; the submission of slides may be substituted for portfolios when distance in prohibitive.

Web Site http://art.uindy.edu

Undergraduate Contact Ronald Wilks, Director of Admissions, University of Indianapolis, 1400 East Hanna Avenue, Indianapolis, Indiana 46227-3697; 317-788-3216, fax: 317-788-6105, e-mail address: cambridge@uindy.edu

The University of Iowa

Iowa City, Iowa

State-supported, coed. Small town campus. Total enrollment: 28,816. Art program established 1936.

Degrees Bachelor of Fine Arts in the area of studio arts. Majors and concentrations: art education, art history, ceramics, design, intermedia, jewelry and metalsmithing, painting/drawing, photography, printmaking, sculpture, studio art. Graduate degrees offered: Master of Arts in the areas of art history, studio arts; Master of Fine Arts in the area of studio arts. Doctor of Philosophy in the area of art history.

Enrollment 753 undergraduate, 124 graduate.

Art Student Profile 60% females, 40% males, 8% minorities, 4% international.

Art Faculty 31 total (full-time), 13 total (part-time). 100% of full-time faculty have terminal degrees. Graduate students teach a few undergraduate courses. Undergraduate student–faculty ratio: 17:1.

Student Life Student groups/activities include Art History Society, College Art Association, art exhibitions.

Expenses for 2007–2008 Application fee: $40. State resident tuition: $5376 full-time. Nonresident tuition: $18,548 full-time. Mandatory fees: $917 full-time. Special program-related fees: $10–$200 per course for model/lab fees/materials.

Financial Aid Program-specific awards: 1 Iowa Center for Art Scholarship for freshmen program majors, 1–2 Mary Sue Miller Memorial Awards for freshmen program majors ($600–$1000), 1–2 Emma McAllister Novel Awards for minority program majors ($1000), 1–3 Schumacher Awards for program majors ($1600–$1800), 1–3 Paula Patton Grahame

Award for upperclass students in sculpture, studio art, 1 Glenn C. Nelson Scholarship for upperclass students in ceramics ($1000), 1–3 Louise Losten Scholarships for upperclass students in metals and jewelry, 1 Luanda Mendenhalle Wilde Scholarship for upperclass undergraduates ($600), 1 Orton and Eugenia Hamby Scholarship for studio art majors.

Application Procedures Students admitted directly into the professional program freshman year. Deadline for freshmen and transfers: continuous. Required: high school transcript, college transcript(s) for transfer students, SAT or ACT test scores, minimum 2.25 high school GPA. Recommended: interview, portfolio for transfer students. Portfolio reviews held twice on campus; the submission of slides may be substituted for portfolios for three-dimensional works of art.

Web Site http://www.uiowa.edu/~art/

Undergraduate Contact Evelyn Acosta-Weirich, Undergraduate Advisor, School of Art and Art History, The University of Iowa, 120 Art Building West, Iowa City, Iowa 52242; 319-335-1779, fax: 319-335-1774, e-mail address: evelyn-weirich@uiowa.edu

Graduate Contact Ms. Laura Jorgensen, Graduate Secretary, School of Art and Art History, The University of Iowa, 122 Art Building West, Iowa City, Iowa 52242; 319-335-1758, fax: 319-335-1774, e-mail address: laura-jorgensen@uiowa.edu

University of Kansas

Lawrence, Kansas

State-supported, coed. Suburban campus. Total enrollment: 28,924.

Degrees Bachelor of Fine Arts in the areas of painting, sculpture, printmaking, expanded media. Majors and concentrations: expanded media, painting, printmaking, sculpture. Graduate degrees offered: Master of Fine Arts in the areas of painting, sculpture, printmaking, expanded media. Program accredited by NASAD.

Enrollment 174 total; 156 undergraduate, 17 graduate, 1 nonprofessional degree.

Art Faculty 15 total (full-time), 5 total (part-time). 100% of full-time faculty have terminal degrees. Graduate students teach a few undergraduate courses. Undergraduate student–faculty ratio: 9:1.

Student Life Special housing available for art students.

Expenses for 2006–2007 Application fee: $30. State resident tuition: $5513 full-time. Nonresident tuition: $14,483 full-time. Mandatory fees: $640 full-time. Full-time tuition and fees vary according to program and reciprocity agreements. College room and board: $5747. College room only: $2997. Room and board charges vary according to board plan and housing facility.

Financial Aid Program-specific awards: 7 Creative and Performing Arts Scholarships for incoming freshmen ($4100), 6 Foundations Scholarships for sophomores ($1500), 50 departmental scholarships and awards for program majors ($3100), 13 Hollander Foundation Scholarships and Awards for program majors ($2700).

Application Procedures Students apply for admission into the professional program by freshman year. Deadline for freshmen: April 1; transfers: June 1. Notification date for freshmen and transfers: January 19. Required: high school transcript, SAT or ACT test scores. Recommended: portfolio for transfer applicants. Portfolio reviews held 3 times in Chicago, IL; St. Louis, MO; Kansas City, MO; the submission of slides may be substituted for portfolios for large works of art.

Web Site http://www.ku.edu/~sfa/

Undergraduate Contact Ms. Dawn Marie Guernsey, Chair, Department of Art, University of Kansas, 1467 Jayhawk Boulevard, Lawrence, Kansas 66045-7531; 785-864-4401, fax: 785-864-4404, e-mail address: guernsey@ku.edu

Graduate Contact Gina Westergard, Graduate Director, Department of Art, University of Kansas, 1467 Jayhawk Boulevard, Lawrence, Kansas 66045-7531; 785-864-4401, fax: 785-864-4404, e-mail address: ginaw@ku.edu

University of Louisiana at Lafayette

Lafayette, Louisiana

State-supported, coed. Urban campus. Total enrollment: 16,302. Art program established 1957.

Web Site http://www.louisiana.edu/

Allen R. Hite Art Institute
University of Louisville
Louisville, Kentucky

State-supported, coed. Urban campus. Total enrollment: 20,804. Art program established 1936.

Degrees Bachelor of Fine Arts in the areas of interior architecture, communication arts and design, 2-D studios, 3-D studios. Majors and concentrations: graphic arts, interior design, three-dimensional studies, two-dimensional studies. Graduate degrees offered: Master of Arts in the areas of art, art history, critical and curatorial studies; Master of Arts in Teaching in the area of art education. Doctor of Philosophy in the area of art history. Cross-registration with Metroversity/University Exchange Consortium. Program accredited by CIDA.

Enrollment 557 total; 149 undergraduate, 67 graduate, 341 nonprofessional degree.

Art Student Profile 69% females, 31% males, 9% minorities, 2% international.

Art Faculty 23 total (full-time), 12 total (part-time). 100% of full-time faculty have terminal degrees. Graduate students do not teach undergraduate courses. Undergraduate student–faculty ratio: 7:1.

Student Life Student groups/activities include Student Art League, American Society of Interior Designers, Louisville Graphic Design Association.

Expenses for 2006–2007 Application fee: $30. State resident tuition: $6252 full-time. Nonresident tuition: $16,072 full-time. Full-time tuition varies according to reciprocity agreements. College room and board: $5096. College room only: $3396. Room and board charges vary according to board plan and housing facility. Special program-related fees: $13–$25 per course for supplies.

Financial Aid Program-specific awards: 24 Hite Scholarships for enrolled students ($1000–$5500), 4 Hendershot Scholarships for incoming freshmen ($6000), 1 Nay Scholarship for incoming freshmen ($5500), 1 Kaden Scholarship for enrolled students ($1000–$3000).

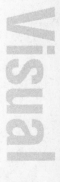

Visual Arts

University of Louisville (continued)

Application Procedures Students apply for admission into the professional program by sophomore year. Deadline for freshmen and transfers: continuous. Required: essay, high school transcript, college transcript(s) for transfer students, minimum 2.0 high school GPA, portfolio, SAT or ACT test scores (minimum composite ACT score of 21). Recommended: interview, minimum 3.0 high school GPA in major area. Portfolio reviews held as needed on campus; the submission of slides may be substituted for portfolios (slides or digital images preferred).

Web Site http://art.louisville.edu

Undergraduate Contact Theresa Berbet, Administrative Assistant, Fine Arts Department, University of Louisville, 104 Schneider Hall, Louisville, Kentucky 40292; 502-852-6794, fax: 502-852-6791.

Graduate Contact Ms. Janice Blair, Program Assistant, Fine Arts Department, University of Louisville, Lutz Hall, Louisville, Kentucky 40292; 502-852-5914, fax: 502-852-6791, e-mail address: janice.blair@louisville.edu

University of Massachusetts Amherst

Amherst, Massachusetts

State-supported, coed. Total enrollment: 25,593. Art program established 1958.

Web Site http://www.umass.edu/

University of Massachusetts Dartmouth

North Dartmouth, Massachusetts

State-supported, coed. Suburban campus. Total enrollment: 8,756. Art program established 1964.

Degrees Bachelor of Arts in the area of art history; Bachelor of Fine Arts in the areas of visual design, painting, sculpture, artisanry, art education. Majors and concentrations: art education, art history, ceramics, electronic imaging, fiber arts, graphic design/letterform, illustration, jewelry and metalsmithing, painting, photography, sculpture, textile design/ fiber arts. Graduate degrees offered: Master of Art Education in the area of art education; Master of Fine Arts in the areas of visual design, artisanry, fine arts. Cross-registration with University of Massachusetts System, Southeastern Association for Cooperation in Higher Education in Massachusetts. Program accredited by NASAD.

Enrollment 688 total; 590 undergraduate, 98 graduate.

Art Student Profile 65% females, 35% males, 9% minorities, 1% international.

Art Faculty 42 total (full-time), 18 total (part-time). 88% of full-time faculty have terminal degrees. Graduate students teach a few undergraduate courses. Undergraduate student–faculty ratio: 12:1.

Student Life Student groups/activities include Metals Guild, Sculpture Club, Communicatus.

Expenses for 2006–2007 Application fee: $40, $55 for nonresidents. State resident tuition: $1417 full-time. Nonresident tuition: $8099 full-time. Mandatory fees: $6892 full-time. Full-time tuition and fees vary according to reciprocity agreements. College room and board: $8162. College room only: $5400. Room and board charges vary according to board plan and housing facility. Special program-related fees: $342 per semester for CVPA fee.

Financial Aid Program-specific awards: Clement Yeager Scholarships for visual or performing art students ($700–$2500), 1 Barbara Eckhardt Memorial Scholarship for fiber arts students ($1500–$2000), 1 Emil "Smokey" Ameen Endowment Scholarship for CVPA students ($200), 1 David and Alfrede Myerson Scholarship for CVPA students ($600), 1 Alda Alves and Bruce Yenawine Scholarship for CVPA students ($1000), 4 Ayuko Ito Scholarships for CVPA students ($1000), 1 Lillian Telles Jenkins Scholarship for CVPA students ($400), 1 Samuel Gamburd Memorial Art Scholarship for design or fine arts students ($750).

Application Procedures Students admitted directly into the professional program freshman year. Deadline for freshmen and transfers: continuous. Notification date for freshmen and transfers: continuous. Required: high school transcript, college transcript(s) for transfer students, minimum 2.0 high school GPA, portfolio, SAT or ACT test scores, slides of portfolio. Recommended: essay, minimum 3.0 high school GPA, 3 letters of recommendation.

Portfolio reviews held continuously on campus; the submission of slides may be substituted for portfolios (required).

Web Site http://www.umassd.edu/CVPA

Undergraduate Contact Mr. Steven T. Briggs, Director of Admissions, University of Massachusetts Dartmouth, 285 Old Westport Road, North Dartmouth, Massachusetts 02747-2300; 508-999-8606, fax: 508-999-8755, e-mail address: admissions@umassd.edu

Graduate Contact Ms. Carol Novo, Staff Assistant, Graduate Admissions, University of Massachusetts Dartmouth, 285 Old Westport Road, North Dartmouth, Massachusetts 02747-2300; 508-999-8604, fax: 508-999-8183, e-mail address: graduate@umassd.edu

More About the College

The College of Visual and Performing Arts (CVPA) is a fully accredited, comprehensive arts college, with bachelor's and master's degree programs that prepare students for careers in the arts. Unlike most professional art schools, which are independent, CVPA is an active component of a comprehensive university, with all of the educational resources that implies.

CVPA offers a breadth of high-level programs. Students can study art education, art history, illustration, graphic design/letterform, photographic/electronic imaging, ceramics, jewelry/metals, textile design, fiber arts, painting/2-D studies, sculpture/3-D studies, and music—which includes classical music, world music, technology, jazz studies, music education, and composition. The visual arts Foundation Program introduces students to visual concepts and practices and is required of all first-year studio majors.

The Campus Noted architect Paul Rudolf created a dramatic design for UMass Dartmouth's 710-acre main campus. CVPA's studios and classrooms are located there and in the exciting new Star Store campus. Formerly a department store in nearby downtown New Bedford, the Star Store has been converted into a modern urban arts complex with spacious studios, galleries, and state-of-the-art equipment. CVPA is located just minutes from the Atlantic Ocean; about 30 minutes from Cape Cod or Providence, Rhode Island; and 1 hour from Boston.

Facilities Located on both the North Dartmouth and New Bedford campuses of the University, the facilities and equipment available to students in the College of Visual and Performing Arts are among the finest in New England. CVPA encourages applicants to attend its Open House or to schedule a campus visit to tour the College's artist studios, ample classroom spaces, state-of-the-art computer labs, artisanry workshops, photography and printmaking studios, music practice rooms, recital hall, and the many additional features the University has to offer.

Faculty CVPA faculty members are artists, musicians, composers, and educators—each distinguished in his or her field. Many are recipients of such prestigious awards as the National Endowment for the Arts, Massachusetts Cultural Council grants, Fulbright fellows, and national and international arts fellowships. Faculty members exhibit in galleries and museums regionally and nationally and perform on concert stages and smaller venues both in the United States and abroad.

Exhibition Opportunities CVPA's significant contribution to the regional arts scene is evident in its dynamic presence within the southcoast communities. The College is active in downtown New Bedford, participating in the monthly AHA! Night venues and exhibiting work in local storefronts. The College's galleries maintain a high caliber of exhibitions on the Dartmouth campus in the Campus Gallery and Gallery One and in New Bedford at the University Art Gallery and Gallery 244.

The University Art Gallery is devoted to showing the work of international and national artists. The CVPA Campus Gallery and Gallery One feature frequently changing exhibitions of CVPA student and faculty work that is curated by college faculty members. Gallery 244 is a student-run gallery, featuring work by graduate students—emerging artists in their own right.

Special Programs Study abroad is encouraged; current programs in Scotland, Portugal, and Sicily offer excellent opportunities to expand a student's experience. Internships and experiential learning are also encouraged; recent placements have included Graphics Express; WGBH; the Museum of Fine Arts, Boston; the Smithsonian; Guilford of Maine; and the Walt Disney Studios.

University of Massachusetts Lowell

Lowell, Massachusetts

State-supported, coed. Urban campus. Total enrollment: 11,208. Art program established 1982.

Web Site http://www.uml.edu/

University of Michigan

Ann Arbor, Michigan

State-supported, coed. Suburban campus. Total enrollment: 40,025. Art program established 1954.

Degrees Bachelor of Fine Arts in the area of art and design. Majors and concentrations: art, art and design, ceramics, electronic media, fibers, graphic design, industrial design, installation art, jewelry and metalsmithing, painting/drawing, photography, printmaking, scientific illustration, sculpture, sound art. Graduate degrees offered: Master of Fine Arts in the area of art and design. Program accredited by NASAD.

Enrollment 496 total; 470 undergraduate, 26 graduate.

Art Student Profile 65% females, 35% males, 14% minorities, 3% international.

Art Faculty 34 total (full-time), 40 total (part-time). 95% of full-time faculty have terminal degrees. Graduate students do not teach undergraduate courses. Undergraduate student–faculty ratio: 18:1.

Student Life Student groups/activities include Society of Art Students, Industrial Design Society of America Student Chapter, American Institute of Graphic Arts. Special housing available for art students.

Expenses for 2006–2007 Application fee: $40. State resident tuition: $9609 full-time. Nonresident tuition: $28,381 full-time. Mandatory fees: $189 full-time. Full-time tuition and fees vary according to course load, degree level, location, program, and student level. College room and board: $7838. Room and board charges vary according to board plan and housing facility. Special program-related fees: $250–$500 per semester for materials fee.

Financial Aid Program-specific awards: 1 Shipman Scholarship for those demonstrating academic achievement and artistic ability.

Application Procedures Students admitted directly into the professional program freshman year. Deadline for freshmen and transfers: February 1. Notification date for freshmen and transfers: May 1. Required: essay, high school transcript, college transcript(s) for transfer students, minimum 3.0 high school GPA, portfolio, SAT or ACT test scores (minimum composite ACT score of 25). Recommended: interview. Portfolio reviews held 10 times plus ad hoc on campus; the submission of slides may be substituted for portfolios if accompanied by an index sheet detailing each piece and sufficient return postage.

Web Site http://www.art-design.umich.edu

Undergraduate Contact Joann McDaniel, Director of Undergraduate Academic Services, School of Art and Design, University of Michigan, 2000 Bonisteel Boulevard, Ann Arbor, Michigan 48109-2069; 734-764-0397, fax: 734-936-0469, e-mail address: a&d@umich.edu

Graduate Contact Wendy Dignan, Director of Graduate Academic Services, School of Art and Design, University of Michigan, 2000 Bonisteel Boulevard, Ann Arbor, Michigan 48109-2069; 734-764-0397, fax: 734-936-0469, e-mail address: a&dgradinfo@umich.edu

University of Minnesota, Duluth

Duluth, Minnesota

State-supported, coed. Suburban campus. Total enrollment: 11,090. Art program established 1947.

Web Site http://www.d.umn.edu/

University of Minnesota, Twin Cities Campus

Minneapolis, Minnesota

State-supported, coed. Urban campus. Total enrollment: 50,402. Art program established 1950.

Degrees Bachelor of Fine Arts in the area of art. Majors and concentrations: ceramics, painting/drawing, photography, printmaking, sculpture, time and interactivity. Graduate degrees offered: Master of Fine Arts in the area of art.

Enrollment 490 total; 50 undergraduate, 40 graduate, 400 nonprofessional degree.

Art Student Profile 52% females, 48% males, 18% minorities, 6% international.

Art Faculty 22 undergraduate (full-time), 20 undergraduate (part-time), 22 graduate (full-time). 95% of full-time faculty have terminal degrees. Graduate students teach a few undergraduate courses.

Visual *Arts*

Student Life Student groups/activities include Arts Collective. Special housing available for art students.

Expenses for 2006–2007 Application fee: $45. State resident tuition: $7588 full-time. Nonresident tuition: $19,218 full-time. Mandatory fees: $1585 full-time. Full-time tuition and fees vary according to program and reciprocity agreements. College room and board: $6996. College room only: $4042. Room and board charges vary according to board plan, housing facility, and location. Special program-related fees: $15–$250 per class for materials fees.

Application Procedures Students apply for admission into the professional program by junior year. Deadline for freshmen: December 15; transfers: June 1. Notification date for freshmen: January 15; transfers: July 15. Required: high school transcript, college transcript(s) for transfer students, SAT or ACT test scores, minimum 2.8 high school GPA.

Web Site http://art.umn.edu

Undergraduate Contact Office of Admissions, University of Minnesota, Twin Cities Campus, 240 Williamson, 231 Pillsbury Avenue SE, Minneapolis, Minnesota 55455; 800-752-1000.

Graduate Contact Director of Graduate Studies, Department of Art, University of Minnesota, Twin Cities Campus, 405 21st Avenue South, Minneapolis, Minnesota 55455; 612-625-8096, fax: 612-625-7881, e-mail address: artdept@umn.edu

University of Mississippi

University, Mississippi

State-supported, coed. Small town campus. Total enrollment: 15,220. Art program established 1948.

Degrees Bachelor of Fine Arts in the area of art. Majors and concentrations: studio art. Graduate degrees offered: Master of Fine Arts in the area of art. Program accredited by NASAD.

Enrollment 263 total; 35 undergraduate, 13 graduate, 215 nonprofessional degree.

Art Student Profile 29% females, 71% males, 9% minorities, 1% international.

Art Faculty 11 total (full-time), 13 total (part-time). 100% of full-time faculty have terminal degrees. Graduate students teach a few undergraduate courses. Undergraduate student–faculty ratio: 3:1.

Student Life Student groups/activities include Student Art Association, Mud Daubers, American Institute of Graphic Arts, Vasari Society (art history student organization), Kappa Pi.

Expenses for 2006–2007 Application fee: $25, $40 for nonresidents. State resident tuition: $4602 full-time. Nonresident tuition: $10,548 full-time. College room and board: $5892. College room only: $3000. Room and board charges vary according to board plan and housing facility. Special program-related fees: $20 per credit hour for materials fees.

Financial Aid Program-specific awards: 10–15 art merit scholarships for portfolio students ($200–$800).

Application Procedures Students apply for admission into the professional program by sophomore, junior year. Deadline for freshmen and transfers: July 25. Notification date for freshmen and transfers: continuous. Required: high school transcript, college transcript(s) for transfer students, minimum 2.0 high school GPA, ACT test score only (minimum composite ACT score of 18), portfolio for transfer applicants and for acceptance into the BFA program upon completion of 18 semester hours in studio art. Portfolio reviews held once on campus; the submission of slides may be substituted for portfolios.

Web Site http://www.olemiss.edu/depts/art

Undergraduate Contact Dr. Nancy L. Wicker, Chair, Art Department, University of Mississippi, 116 Meek Hall, University, Mississippi 38677; 662-915-7193, fax: 662-915-5013, e-mail address: art@olemiss.edu

Graduate Contact Dr. Nancy L. Wicker, Graduate Coordinator, Art Department, University of Mississippi, 116 Meek Hall, University, Mississippi 38677; 662-915-7193, fax: 662-915-5013, e-mail address: art@olemiss.edu

University of Missouri–Columbia

Columbia, Missouri

State-supported, coed. Suburban campus. Total enrollment: 28,253. Art program established 1979.

University of Missouri–Columbia (continued)

Degrees Bachelor of Fine Arts in the area of art. Majors and concentrations: ceramics, drawing, fibers, graphic design, painting, photography, printmaking, sculpture, watercolors. Graduate degrees offered: Master of Fine Arts in the area of art. Cross-registration with Mid-Missouri Associated Colleges and Universities.

Enrollment 249 total; 85 undergraduate, 18 graduate, 146 nonprofessional degree.

Art Student Profile 60% females, 40% males, 5% minorities, 3% international.

Art Faculty 19 total (full-time), 11 total (part-time). 90% of full-time faculty have terminal degrees. Graduate students teach about a quarter of undergraduate courses. Undergraduate student–faculty ratio: 10:1.

Student Life Student groups/activities include Imprint (graphics club), Muck (ceramics club), Student Art Community. Special housing available for art students.

Expenses for 2006–2007 Application fee: $45. State resident tuition: $6364 full-time. Nonresident tuition: $15,946 full-time. Mandatory fees: $944 full-time. Full-time tuition and fees vary according to course load, program, and reciprocity agreements. College room and board: $6977. College room only: $3837. Room and board charges vary according to board plan and housing facility. Special program-related fees: $40–$100 per course for lab fees.

Financial Aid Program-specific awards: 1 Hennessey Scholarship for program majors demonstrating financial need ($2500), 1 William Ittner Award for program majors ($500), 1 Cox Scholarship for ceramics students ($500), 1 McNair Fellowship for program majors demonstrating financial need, 1 Radford Michael Perrine Scholarship for program majors, 1 Hazel (Pat) Steele Burney Endowment for program majors-undergraduate and graduate.

Application Procedures Students admitted directly into the professional program freshman year. Deadline for freshmen: May 1; transfers: July 1. Notification date for freshmen and transfers: continuous. Required: high school transcript, college transcript(s) for transfer students, SAT or ACT test scores, minimum 3.0 high school GPA in studio art courses.

Web Site http://art.missouri.edu

Undergraduate Contact Deborah Huelsbergen, Director of Undergraduate Studies, Department of Art, University of Missouri–Columbia, A 126 Fine Arts, Columbia, Missouri 65211-6090; 573-882-9444, fax: 573-884-6807, e-mail address: huelsbergend@missouri.edu

Graduate Contact James H. Calvin, Director of Graduate Studies, Department of Art, University of Missouri–Columbia, A 126 Fine Arts, Columbia, Missouri 65211-6090; 573-882-9440, fax: 573-884-6807, e-mail address: calvinjh@missouri.edu

The University of Montana

Missoula, Montana

State-supported, coed. Total enrollment: 13,558. Art program established 1957.

Degrees Bachelor of Fine Arts in the area of art. Majors and concentrations: art education, art/fine arts, ceramics, painting/drawing, photography, printmaking, sculpture. Graduate degrees offered: Master of Arts in the area of art history; Master of Fine Arts in the area of art. Program accredited by NASAD.

Enrollment 424 total; 306 undergraduate, 14 graduate, 104 nonprofessional degree.

Art Student Profile 53% females, 47% males, 1% minorities, 1% international.

Art Faculty 13 total (full-time), 11 total (part-time). 100% of full-time faculty have terminal degrees. Graduate students teach a few undergraduate courses. Undergraduate student–faculty ratio: 20:1.

Student Life Student groups/activities include Artists' Collective, Gallery of Visual Arts, Montana Museum of Arts and Culture.

Expenses for 2006–2007 Application fee: $30. State resident tuition: $3686 full-time. Nonresident tuition: $13,193 full-time. Mandatory fees: $1291 full-time. Full-time tuition and fees vary according to degree level, location, program, reciprocity agreements, and student level. College room and board: $5860. College room only: $2660. Room and board charges vary according to board plan and housing facility. Special program-related fees: $18–$65 per course for materials and supplies.

Financial Aid Program-specific awards: 2 Wallace Awards for sophomore or junior program majors ($1000), 1 Pat Williams Scholarship for sophomore or junior program majors ($500), 1 Walter Hook Scholarship for sophomore or junior program majors ($1000), 1 Diggs Scholarship for sophomore or junior program majors ($500), 1 Thomas Wickes Award for sophomore or junior art majors ($2500).

Application Procedures Students apply for admission into the professional program by sophomore year. Deadline for freshmen and transfers: continuous. Required: high school transcript, SAT or ACT test scores, minimum 2.5 high school GPA. Recommended: portfolio. Portfolio reviews held twice on campus; the submission of slides may be substituted for portfolios.

Web Site http://www.sfa.umt.edu

Undergraduate Contact New Student Services, The University of Montana, Lommasson Center #103, Missoula, Montana 59812; 406-243-6266, fax: 406-243-4087.

Graduate Contact Graduate School, The University of Montana, Lommasson Center, Missoula, Montana 59812; 406-243-2572, fax: 406-243-4593, e-mail address: gradschl@mso.umt.edu

University of Montevallo

Montevallo, Alabama

State-supported, coed. Small town campus. Total enrollment: 2,895.

Degrees Bachelor of Fine Arts in the area of studio art. Majors and concentrations: ceramic art and design, graphic design, new media, painting/drawing, photography, printmaking, sculpture. Cross-registration with Birmingham Area Consortium for Higher Education (BACHE). Program accredited by NASAD.

Enrollment 300 total; 208 undergraduate, 92 nonprofessional degree.

Art Student Profile 61% females, 39% males, 12% minorities, 2% international.

Art Faculty 11 undergraduate (full-time), 3 undergraduate (part-time). 100% of full-time faculty have terminal degrees. Graduate students do not teach undergraduate courses. Undergraduate student–faculty ratio: 17:1.

Student Life Student groups/activities include Kappa Pi, "College Night" Performance.

Expenses for 2006–2007 Application fee: $25. State resident tuition: $5460 full-time. Nonresident tuition: $10,920 full-time. Mandatory fees: $204 full-time. Full-time tuition and fees vary according to course load. College room and board: $4084. Room and board charges vary according to board plan and housing facility.

Financial Aid Program-specific awards: 1–2 Dean's Fine Arts Awards for freshmen and transfers ($2000), 2 endowed scholarships for juniors and seniors ($600), 1 Jefferson County Alumni Scholarship for freshmen ($2500), 1 Joan Gregory Art Scholarship for freshmen and transfer students ($800), 1–2 Southern Progress/Graphic Design Awards for freshmen and transfer students ($500).

Application Procedures Students admitted directly into the professional program freshman year. Deadline for freshmen and transfers: July 26. Notification date for freshmen and transfers: September 2. Required: high school transcript, college transcript(s) for transfer students, minimum 2.0 high school GPA, SAT or ACT test scores, minimum 2.0 college GPA for transfer students, portfolio for scholarship consideration and for transfers. Recommended: minimum 3.0 high school GPA, 3 letters of recommendation, interview, portfolio. Portfolio reviews held by appointment on campus; the submission of slides may be substituted for portfolios whenever needed.

Web Site http://www.montevallo.edu

Undergraduate Contact Dr. Clifton Pearson, Chair, Department of Art, University of Montevallo, Station 6400, Montevallo, Alabama 35115; 205-665-6400, fax: 205-665-6383, e-mail address: pearsonc@montevallo.edu

University of Nebraska–Lincoln

Lincoln, Nebraska

State-supported, coed. Urban campus. Total enrollment: 22,106. Art program established 1918.

Degrees Bachelor of Fine Arts in the area of studio art. Majors and concentrations: art history, ceramics, drawing, graphic design, illustration, painting, photography, printmaking, sculpture, studio art. Graduate degrees offered: Master of Fine Arts in the area of studio art. Cross-registration with

University of Nebraska–Lincoln (continued)

University of Nebraska at Omaha, University of Nebraska at Kearney. Program accredited by NASAD.

Enrollment 337 total; 250 undergraduate, 33 graduate, 54 nonprofessional degree.

Art Student Profile 58% females, 42% males, 8% minorities, 2% international.

Art Faculty 21 total (full-time), 10 total (part-time). 100% of full-time faculty have terminal degrees. Graduate students teach a few undergraduate courses. Undergraduate student–faculty ratio: 14:1.

Student Life Student groups/activities include Annual Juried Undergraduate Exhibition, Rotunda Gallery Exhibitions, Fame Awards.

Expenses for 2007–2008 Application fee: $45. State resident tuition: $5085 full-time. Nonresident tuition: $15,105 full-time. Mandatory fees: $1130 full-time. Full-time tuition and fees vary according to course load. College room and board: $6523. College room only: $3441. Room and board charges vary according to board plan and housing facility. Special program-related fees: $15–$150 per semester for lab fees.

Financial Aid Program-specific awards: 38 endowed scholarships for program majors ($3000).

Application Procedures Students admitted directly into the professional program freshman year. Deadline for freshmen and transfers: June 30. Required: high school transcript, college transcript(s) for transfer students, minimum 2.0 high school GPA, SAT or ACT test scores (minimum composite ACT score of 22). Recommended: interview, portfolio.

Web Site http://www.unl.edu

Undergraduate Contact Admission Office, University of Nebraska–Lincoln, Alexander Building, 1410 O Street, Lincoln, Nebraska 68588-0417; 402-472-2023, fax: 402-472-0670.

Graduate Contact Prof. Santiago Cal, Chairperson, Graduate Committee, Department of Art and Art History, University of Nebraska–Lincoln, 120 Richards Hall, Lincoln, Nebraska 68588-0114; 402-472-2102, fax: 402-472-9746.

University of New Mexico

Albuquerque, New Mexico

State-supported, coed. Urban campus. Total enrollment: 26,172.

Degrees Bachelor of Fine Arts in the area of studio art; Bachelor of Arts in Fine Arts in the areas of studio art, art history. Majors and concentrations: art history, studio art. Graduate degrees offered: Master of Arts in the area of art history; Master of Fine Arts in the area of studio art. Doctor of Philosophy in the area of art history.

Enrollment 394 total; 185 undergraduate, 85 graduate, 124 nonprofessional degree.

Art Student Profile 63% females, 37% males, 28% minorities.

Art Faculty 30 total (full-time), 15 total (part-time). 100% of full-time faculty have terminal degrees. Graduate students teach about a quarter of undergraduate courses. Undergraduate student–faculty ratio: 35:1.

Student Life Student groups/activities include Art Student Association Gallery.

Expenses for 2007–2008 Application fee: $20. State resident tuition: $4571 full-time. Nonresident tuition: $14,942 full-time. College room and board: $6800. College room only: $4100. Room and board charges vary according to board plan and housing facility. Special program-related fees: $33–$150 for studio/art history courses for materials/technology fee.

Financial Aid Program-specific awards: 20–35 art scholarships for juniors in College of Fine Arts ($500–$1000).

Application Procedures Students apply for admission into the professional program by junior year. Deadline for freshmen and transfers: June 15. Required: high school transcript, SAT or ACT test scores, minimum 2.5 high school GPA, portfolio for transfer students. Recommended: essay. Portfolio reviews held continuously by appointment on campus; the submission of slides may be substituted for portfolios.

Web Site http://www.unm.edu/~artdept2/

Undergraduate Contact Office of Admissions, University of New Mexico, Albuquerque, New Mexico 87131-0001; 505-277-2446.

Graduate Contact Ms. Kat Heatherington, Graduate Advisor, Department of Art and Art History, University of New Mexico, Albuquerque, New Mexico 87131-0001; 505-277-6672, fax: 505-277-5955.

University of North Alabama

Florence, Alabama

State-supported, coed. Urban campus. Total enrollment: 6,810. Art program established 1930.

Degrees Bachelor of Fine Arts in the area of art. Majors and concentrations: ceramics, digital media, painting, photography, sculpture. Cross-registration with other institutions in Alabama (specific courses only). Program accredited by NASAD.

Enrollment 158 total; 78 undergraduate, 80 nonprofessional degree.

Art Student Profile 47% females, 53% males, 5% minorities, 6% international.

Art Faculty 8 undergraduate (full-time). 100% of full-time faculty have terminal degrees. Graduate students do not teach undergraduate courses. Undergraduate student–faculty ratio: 9:1.

Student Life Student groups/activities include Student Art Association, FLORALA (student newspaper) and Diorama (yearbook), Lights and Shadows "Magazine."

Expenses for 2006–2007 Application fee: $25. State resident tuition: $3768 full-time. Nonresident tuition: $7536 full-time. Mandatory fees: $883 full-time. Full-time tuition and fees vary according to course load. College room and board: $4372. College room only: $2060. Room and board charges vary according to board plan and housing facility. Special program-related fees: $30 per semester for studio lab fee.

Financial Aid Program-specific awards: 1 endowed scholarship for program majors ($900).

Application Procedures Students apply for admission into the professional program by sophomore year. Deadline for freshmen and transfers: August 30. Notification date for freshmen and transfers: continuous. Required: high school transcript, college transcript(s) for transfer students, SAT or ACT test scores, portfolio after 45 hours for entry into BFA program. Recommended: minimum 2.0 high school GPA. Portfolio reviews held twice on campus.

Web Site http://www.una.edu

Undergraduate Contact Dr. Sue Wilson, Dean of Enrollment Management, Admissions Office, University of North Alabama, Box 5058, Florence, Alabama 35632-0001; 256-765-4680, fax: 256-765-4329, e-mail address: swilson@ unanov.una.edu

The University of North Carolina at Charlotte

Charlotte, North Carolina

State-supported, coed. Suburban campus. Total enrollment: 21,519. Art program established 1965.

Degrees Bachelor of Fine Arts in the area of art. Majors and concentrations: art history, ceramics, cross-discipline studies, fibers, graphic design, illustration, painting, photography, print media, sculpture. Cross-registration with NC consortium.

Enrollment 550 total; all undergraduate.

Art Student Profile 54% females, 46% males, 11% minorities, 2% international.

Art Faculty 26 undergraduate (full-time), 10 undergraduate (part-time). 100% of full-time faculty have terminal degrees. Graduate students do not teach undergraduate courses. Undergraduate student–faculty ratio: 16:1.

Student Life Student groups/activities include National Art Education Association Student Chapter, Art Student Association.

Expenses for 2006–2007 Application fee: $50. State resident tuition: $2344 full-time. Nonresident tuition: $12,756 full-time. Mandatory fees: $1551 full-time. Full-time tuition and fees vary according to course load. College room and board: $5790. College room only: $2940. Room and board charges vary according to board plan and housing facility.

Financial Aid Program-specific awards: 7 Mull Scholarships for freshmen ($1000–$2000).

Application Procedures Students apply for admission into the professional program by sophomore year. Deadline for freshmen and transfers: continuous. Required: essay, college transcript(s) for transfer students, portfolio, SAT or ACT test scores. Portfolio reviews held on campus; the submission of slides may be substituted for portfolios for freshmen and transfers.

Web Site http://www.uncc.edu/art/

Visual Arts

The University of North Carolina at Charlotte (continued)

Undergraduate Contact Prof. Malena Bergmann, Undergraduate Advisor, Department of Art and Art History, The University of North Carolina at Charlotte, 173 Rowe Building, Charlotte, North Carolina 28223; 704-687-2473, fax: 704-687-2591.

The University of North Carolina at Greensboro

Greensboro, North Carolina

State-supported, coed. Urban campus. Total enrollment: 16,728. Art program established 1936.

Degrees Bachelor of Arts in the areas of studio art, art history combined with museum studies; Bachelor of Fine Arts in the areas of studio art, art education. Majors and concentrations: art education, art history and museum studies, ceramics, design, painting/drawing, photography, printmaking, sculpture, studio art. Graduate degrees offered: Master of Fine Arts in the area of studio art. Cross-registration with Guilford College, Greensboro College, North Carolina Agricultural and Technical State University. Program accredited by NCATE.

Enrollment 450 undergraduate, 15 graduate.

Art Student Profile 68% females, 32% males, 30% minorities.

Art Faculty 12 undergraduate (full-time), 5 undergraduate (part-time), 24 graduate (full-time). 100% of full-time faculty have terminal degrees. Graduate students do not teach undergraduate courses. Undergraduate student–faculty ratio: 21:1.

Student Life Student groups/activities include Student Art League, Coraddi Art Magazine. Special housing available for art students.

Expenses for 2007–2008 Application fee: $45. State resident tuition: $2458 full-time. Nonresident tuition: $13,726 full-time. Mandatory fees: $1571 full-time. College room and board: $6051. College room only: $3427.

Financial Aid Program-specific awards: Pierce Memorial Scholarship for North Carolina residents, Maud F. Gatewood Scholarships for for painting majors demonstrating merit, Peter Agostini and Andrew Martin Scholarship for art majors with financial need, Reeves Scholarship for art majors, Mary Cochrane Austin Scholarships for art education majors, Elizabeth Jastrow Scholarship for junior art history majors.

Application Procedures Students admitted directly into the professional program freshman year. Deadline for freshmen: March 1; transfers: August 1. Required: high school transcript, college transcript(s) for transfer students, minimum 3.0 high school GPA, SAT or ACT test scores, portfolio for transfer students and for scholarship consideration. Recommended: 3.5 GPA for freshman, 1044 SAT scores (math and critical reading sections only). Portfolio reviews held continuously by appointment on campus; the submission of slides may be substituted for portfolios.

Web Site http://www.uncg.edu/art

Undergraduate Contact Undergraduate Advisor, Department of Art, The University of North Carolina at Greensboro, PO Box 26170, Greensboro, North Carolina 27402-6170; 336-334-5909, fax: 336-334-5270.

Graduate Contact Niki Blair, Associate Professor, Department of Art, The University of North Carolina at Greensboro, PO Box 26170, Greensboro, North Carolina 27402-6170; 336-334-5248, fax: 336-334-5270, e-mail address: nblair1@yahoo.com

University of North Dakota

Grand Forks, North Dakota

State-supported, coed. Urban campus. Total enrollment: 12,834. Art program established 1978.

Degrees Bachelor of Fine Arts in the area of visual arts. Majors and concentrations: ceramic art and design, fibers, jewelry and metalsmithing, new media, painting/drawing, photography, printmaking, sculpture. Graduate degrees offered: Master of Fine Arts in the area of visual arts. Program accredited by NASAD.

Enrollment 114 total; 65 undergraduate, 14 graduate, 35 nonprofessional degree.

Art Student Profile 60% females, 40% males, 3% minorities, 1% international.

Art Faculty 11 undergraduate (full-time), 8 undergraduate (part-time), 11 graduate (full-time). 100% of full-time faculty have terminal degrees. Graduate students teach about a quarter of undergraduate courses. Undergraduate student–faculty ratio: 6:1.

Student Life Student groups/activities include Ceramic Arts Organization, Art Student Collective, League of Metalsmiths.

Expenses for 2006–2007 Application fee: $35. State resident tuition: $4786 full-time. Nonresident tuition: $12,780 full-time. Mandatory fees: $1006 full-time. Full-time tuition and fees vary according to degree level, program, and reciprocity agreements. College room and board: $5085. College room only: $2137. Room and board charges vary according to board plan and housing facility. Special program-related fees: $55 per course for art materials (average fee).

Financial Aid Program-specific awards: 2 Beverly Bushaw Gulmon Scholarships ($750), 2 Stephanie Prepioria Memorial Scholarships ($600), 1 M. Anderson Scholarship ($600), 2 Friedmen Scholarships ($300–$500), 1 Mary Ellen Rogers Scholarship for sculpture students ($300), 1 Alma Anderson Scholarship ($500), 2 Haugen Scholarships ($650), 2 Rod and Carmen Gergstrom Thorpe Scholarships ($1000).

Application Procedures Students apply for admission into the professional program by sophomore year. Deadline for freshmen and transfers: continuous. Required: high school transcript, college transcript(s) for transfer students, portfolio, ACT test score only. Portfolio reviews held by appointment on campus; the submission of slides may be substituted for portfolios for large works of art or when distance is prohibitive.

Web Site http://www.und.edu/dept/arts2000

Undergraduate Contact Dr. Arthur F. Jones, Chair, Department of Art, University of North Dakota, Box 7099, Grand Forks, North Dakota 58202fax: 701-777-2903, e-mail address: art.jones@und.nodak.edu

Graduate Contact Ms. Anita Monsebroten, Associate Professor, Department of Art, University of North Dakota, Box 7099, Grand Forks, North Dakota 58202fax: 701-777-2903, e-mail address: anita_monsebroten@und.nodak.edu

University of Northern Iowa
Cedar Falls, Iowa

State-supported, coed. Small town campus. Total enrollment: 12,327. Art program established 1895.

Web Site http://www.uni.edu/

University of North Florida
Jacksonville, Florida

State-supported, coed. Urban campus. Total enrollment: 15,954. Art program established 1972.

Web Site http://www.unf.edu/

University of North Texas
Denton, Texas

State-supported, coed. Suburban campus. Total enrollment: 33,443. Art program established 1894.

Degrees Bachelor of Arts in the area of art history; Bachelor of Fine Arts in the areas of studio art, visual art studies, interior design, communication design, fashion design. Majors and concentrations: art history, ceramics, communication design, fashion design, fibers, interior design, jewelry and metalsmithing, new media, painting/drawing, photography, printmaking, sculpture, visual arts, watercolors. Graduate degrees offered: Master of Arts in the areas of art history, art education; Master of Fine Arts in the areas of art education, art history, ceramics, communication design, drawing and painting, fashion design, fibers, interior design, metalsmithing and jewelry, photography, printmaking, sculpture. Doctor of Philosophy in the area of art education. Program accredited by CIDA.

Enrollment 2,443 total; 2,295 undergraduate, 148 graduate.

Art Student Profile 62% females, 38% males, 19% minorities, 4% international.

Art Faculty 39 total (full-time), 54 total (part-time). 95% of full-time faculty have

University of North Texas (continued)

terminal degrees. Graduate students teach about a quarter of undergraduate courses. Undergraduate student–faculty ratio: 25:1.

Student Life Student groups/activities include Clay Guild, National Art Education Association (NAEA) Student Chapter, Interior Design Student Chapter. Special housing available for art students.

Expenses for 2007–2008 Application fee: $40. State resident tuition: $4335 full-time. Nonresident tuition: $12,675 full-time. Mandatory fees: $1937 full-time. Full-time tuition and fees vary according to course load. College room and board: $5940. Room and board charges vary according to board plan and housing facility. Special program-related fees: $25–$75 per course for materials fee.

Financial Aid Program-specific awards: 1 John D. Murchison Sr. Scholarship for undergraduate art majors with a minimum 3.0 GPA ($1000), 3 Helen Voertman Memorial Scholarships for full-time undergraduate (sophomore level or higher) art majors with minimum 3.0 GPA ($1000), 1 Cora E. Stafford Scholarship for full-time undergraduate (sophomore level or higher) art majors with minimum 3.0 GPA ($500), 1 Roger Thomason Scholarship for full-time undergraduate (sophomore level or higher) fibers majors with minimum 3.0 GPA ($1000), 6 Jean Andrews Scholarships for undergraduate art majors with a minimum 3.0 GPA ($1000–$1500), 1 Edward and Betty Mattil Scholarship for undergraduate art majors with a minimum 3.0 GPA ($500), 1 J. Robert Egar Scholarship for undergraduate photography majors with a minimum 3.0 GPA ($750), 3 Mack Mathes Scholarships for full-time undergraduate (sophomore level or higher) art majors with minimum 3.0 GPA ($500), 1 Barney Budow Scholarship for undergraduate fashion design majors with a minimum 3.0 GPA ($1000), 1 William J. Lee Scholarship for undergraduate fashion design majors with a minimum 3.0 GPA ($500), 4 SOVA Bloggers awards for full-time students ($1000).

Application Procedures Students apply for admission into the professional program by freshman, sophomore year. Deadline for freshmen and transfers: June 15. Required: high school transcript, college transcript(s) for transfer students, SAT or ACT test scores, minimum 2.5 high school GPA, portfolio for entry into BFA program. Portfolio reviews held on campus; the submission of slides may be substituted for portfolios (electronic media may also be used).

Web Site http://www.art.unt.edu

Undergraduate Contact Ms. Marian O'Rourke-Kapla, Associate Dean for Academic and Student Affairs, School of Visual Arts, University of North Texas, PO Box 305100, Denton, Texas 76203-5100; 940-565-2216, fax: 940-565-4717.

Graduate Contact Ms. Marian O'Rourke-Kaplan, Associate Dean for Academic and Student Affairs, School of Visual Arts, University of North Texas, PO Box 305100, Denton, Texas 76203-5100; 940-565-2216, fax: 940-565-4717.

University of Notre Dame
Notre Dame, Indiana

Independent Roman Catholic, coed. Suburban campus. Total enrollment: 11,603. Art program established 1842.

Degrees Bachelor of Fine Arts in the areas of studio art, design. Majors and concentrations: art/fine arts, ceramic art and design, computer graphics, graphic arts, industrial design, painting/drawing, photography, printmaking, sculpture, studio art. Graduate degrees offered: Master of Arts in the area of art history; Master of Fine Arts in the areas of studio art, design. Program accredited by NASAD.

Enrollment 292 total; 42 undergraduate, 24 graduate, 226 nonprofessional degree.

Art Student Profile 76% females, 24% males, 21% minorities, 30% international.

Art Faculty 17 total (full-time), 7 total (part-time). 100% of full-time faculty have terminal degrees. Graduate students teach about a quarter of undergraduate courses. Undergraduate student–faculty ratio: 2:1.

Student Life Student groups/activities include student exhibitions.

Expenses for 2007–2008 Application fee: $50. Comprehensive fee: $44,477 includes full-time tuition ($34,680), mandatory fees ($507), and college room and board ($9290). Special program-related fees: $15–$100 per course for studio materials.

Application Procedures Students apply for admission into the professional program by sophomore year. Deadline for freshmen and transfers: January 4. Notification date for freshmen and transfers: April 10. Required: essay, high school transcript, minimum 3.0 high school GPA, 2 letters of recommendation. Recommended: interview, slide portfolio. Portfolio reviews held by request on campus; the submission of slides may be substituted for portfolios (slides or CD preferred).

Web Site http://www.nd.edu/~art

Undergraduate Contact Admissions Office, University of Notre Dame, 113 Main Building, Notre Dame, Indiana 46556; 574-631-7505.

Graduate Contact Ms. Martina Lopez, Graduate Director, Department of Art, Art History, and Design, University of Notre Dame, 306 Riley Hall of Art, Notre Dame, Indiana 46556; 574-631-4272, fax: 574-631-6312, e-mail address: lopez.29@nd.edu

University of Oregon

Eugene, Oregon

State-supported, coed. Urban campus. Total enrollment: 20,348. Art program established 1929.

Degrees Bachelor of Fine Arts in the areas of painting, sculpture, ceramics, fibers, metalsmithing and jewelry, printmaking, photography, digital arts. Majors and concentrations: animation, ceramics, computer graphics, digital art, fibers, jewelry and metalsmithing, multimedia, painting/drawing, photography, printmaking, sculpture. Graduate degrees offered: Master of Fine Arts in the areas of painting, sculpture, ceramics, fibers, metalsmithing and jewelry, printmaking, photography, digital arts. Program accredited by NASAD.

Enrollment 665 total; 70 undergraduate, 45 graduate, 550 nonprofessional degree.

Art Student Profile 50% females, 50% males, 10% minorities, 3% international.

Art Faculty 18 total (full-time), 20 total (part-time). 90% of full-time faculty have terminal degrees. Graduate students teach a few undergraduate courses. Undergraduate student–faculty ratio: 4:1.

Student Life Special housing available for art students.

Expenses for 2006–2007 Application fee: $50. State resident tuition: $4341 full-time. Nonresident tuition: $16,755 full-time. Mandatory fees: $1497 full-time. Full-time tuition and fees vary according to class time, course load, program, and reciprocity agreements. College room and board: $7827. Room and board charges vary according to board plan and housing facility. Special program-related fees: $5–$80 per course for material fees, $25 per course for studio fees, $125 per term for major program fee.

Financial Aid Program-specific awards: 1 Eugene Weavers' Guild Scholarship for continuing weaving students ($150), 4 Phillip Johnson Scholarships for continuing painting and printmaking students ($200–$400), 1 LaVerne Krause Scholarship for continuing printmaking students ($300–$750), 4 David McCosh Painting Scholarships for continuing painting students ($200–$400), 1 Jack Wilkinson Paint Award for continuing painting students ($200–$400), 1 Molly Muntzel Award for continuing painting students ($200–$400).

Application Procedures Deadline for freshmen and transfers: March 1. Notification date for freshmen and transfers: April 1. Required: letter of recommendation, portfolio, statement of interest, college transcript(s) for 2nd degree students. Portfolio reviews held once (digital arts), 3 times (all others) on campus; the submission of slides may be substituted for portfolios (slides preferred).

Web Site http://art-uo.uoregon.edu

Undergraduate Contact Ms. Heidi Howes, Admissions, Department of Art, University of Oregon, 5232 University of Oregon, Eugene, Oregon 97403-5232; 541-346-3610, fax: 541-346-3626, e-mail address: hhowes@uoregon.edu

Graduate Contact Ms. Bonnie Lawrence, Graduate Program Coordinator, Department of Art, University of Oregon, 5232 University of Oregon, Eugene, Oregon 97403-5232; 541-346-3618, fax: 541-346-3626, e-mail address: blawrenc@uoregon.edu

University of Regina

Regina, Saskatchewan, Canada

Province-supported, coed. Urban campus. Total enrollment: 12,056. Art program established 1915.

Web Site http://www.uregina.ca/

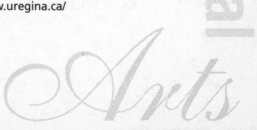

University of South Carolina

Columbia, South Carolina

State-supported, coed. Total enrollment: 27,390.
Web Site http://www.sc.edu/

Roski School of Fine Arts
University of Southern California

Los Angeles, California

Independent, coed. Urban campus. Total enrollment: 33,389. Art program established 1895.

Degrees Bachelor of Fine Arts in the area of studio arts. Majors and concentrations: advertising design and communication, art, art and business, art and design, art/fine arts, ceramics, clay, communication design, computer imaging, digital media, digital photography, drawing, fine art photography, fine art studio, game art and design, graphic design, intaglio, multimedia, new genres, painting, painting/drawing, photography, photography/digital media, printmaking, public art studies, sculpture, studio art, video art. Graduate degrees offered: Master of Fine Arts in the area of studio arts; Master of Public Art Studies; Master of Public Art Studies/Master of Planning; Master of Public Art Studies/Master of Arts in Jewish Communal Service.

Enrollment 350 total; 100 undergraduate, 50 graduate, 200 nonprofessional degree.

Art Student Profile 60% females, 40% males, 20% minorities, 16% international.

Art Faculty 20 undergraduate (full-time), 40 undergraduate (part-time), 6 graduate (full-time), 8 graduate (part-time). 85% of full-time faculty have terminal degrees. Graduate students do not teach undergraduate courses. Undergraduate student–faculty ratio: 4:1.

Student Life Student groups/activities include American Institute of Graphic Arts, Animation Club, Students of Fine Arts Association. Special housing available for art students.

Expenses for 2006–2007 Application fee: $65. Comprehensive fee: $44,036 includes full-time tuition ($33,314), mandatory fees ($578), and college room and board ($10,144). College room only: $5580. Full-time tuition and fees vary according to program. Room and board charges vary according to board plan and housing facility. Special program-related fees: $55 per course for lab/studio materials fee.

Financial Aid Program-specific awards: 30 Fine Art Talent Scholarships for program majors ($2000).

Application Procedures Students admitted directly into the professional program freshman year. Deadline for freshmen: January 10; transfers: February 1. Notification date for freshmen: April 1; transfers: June 1. Required: essay, high school transcript, college transcript(s) for transfer students, portfolio, SAT or ACT test scores, 2 letters of recommendation for transfer applicants, minimum 3.3 college GPA for transfer applicants. Recommended: interview, minimum 3.5 high school GPA. Portfolio reviews held continuously on campus and off campus in various; the submission of slides may be substituted for portfolios (or digital images on CD).

Web Site http://roski.usc.edu

Contact Ms. Penelope Jones, Director of Admissions, Roski School of Fine Arts, University of Southern California, Watt Hall 104, Los Angeles, California 90089-0292; 213-740-9153, fax: 213-740-8938, e-mail address: finearts@usc.edu

University of Southern Maine

Portland, Maine

State-supported, coed. Suburban campus. Total enrollment: 10,478. Art program established 1976.

Degrees Bachelor of Arts in the area of studio art and entrepreneurial studies; Bachelor of Fine Arts in the areas of studio art, art education. Majors and concentrations: art education, ceramics, digital art, drawing, painting, photography, printmaking, sculpture. Cross-registration with Maine College of Art,

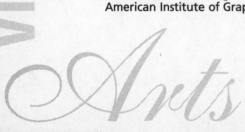

University of New England, St. Joseph's College, Westbrook College, Southern Maine Technical College. Program accredited by NASAD.

Enrollment 290 total; all undergraduate.

Art Faculty 12 undergraduate (full-time), 12 undergraduate (part-time). 100% of full-time faculty have terminal degrees. Graduate students do not teach undergraduate courses. Undergraduate student–faculty ratio: 13:1.

Student Life Student groups/activities include Union of the Visual Arts, Union of Art Students, Printmaking Collective. Special housing available for art students.

Expenses for 2006–2007 Application fee: $40. State resident tuition: $5400 full-time. Nonresident tuition: $14,640 full-time. Mandatory fees: $926 full-time. Full-time tuition and fees vary according to course load, degree level, and reciprocity agreements. College room and board: $7444. College room only: $3834. Room and board charges vary according to board plan, housing facility, and location. Special program-related fees: $10–$120 per semester for supplies for some studio and lecture courses.

Application Procedures Students apply for admission into the professional program by freshman year. Deadline for freshmen: August 1; transfers: continuous. Notification date for freshmen and transfers: July 15. Required: essay, high school transcript, college transcript(s) for transfer students, letter of recommendation, portfolio, SAT or ACT test scores. Recommended: minimum 2.0 high school GPA, interview. Portfolio reviews held twice on campus.

Web Site http://www.usm.maine.edu

Undergraduate Contact Dee Gardner, Director of Admissions, University of Southern Maine, 37 College Avenue, Gorham, Maine 04038; 207-780-5670, fax: 207-780-5640.

University of Southern Mississippi

Hattiesburg, Mississippi

State-supported, coed. Suburban campus. Total enrollment: 14,777. Art program established 1947.

Degrees Bachelor of Arts in the area of museum studies; Bachelor of Fine Arts in the area of art; Bachelor of Science in the area of interior design. Majors and concentrations: art education, graphic communication, museum studies, painting/drawing, three-dimensional studies. Graduate degrees offered: Master of Art Education. Program accredited by NASAD, CIDA, NCATE.

Enrollment 296 total; 280 undergraduate, 9 graduate, 7 nonprofessional degree.

Art Student Profile 60% females, 40% males, 13% minorities, 1% international.

Art Faculty 12 undergraduate (full-time), 5 undergraduate (part-time), 3 graduate (full-time). 100% of full-time faculty have terminal degrees. Graduate students do not teach undergraduate courses. Undergraduate student–faculty ratio: 23:1.

Student Life Student groups/activities include Student Art Club, American Institute of Graphic Arts Student Chapter, Student Chapter: ASID, IIDA, & NKBA, National Council for Accreditation of Teacher Education (NCATE) Student Chapter. Special housing available for art students.

Expenses for 2006–2007 Application fee: $0. State resident tuition: $4594 full-time. Nonresident tuition: $10,622 full-time. Mandatory fees: $120 full-time. College room and board: $5070. College room only: $3010. Room and board charges vary according to board plan and housing facility. Special program-related fees: $35–$40 per course for expendable materials.

Financial Aid Program-specific awards: 7 endowed scholarships for program majors ($1250), 1 Mississippi Gulf Coast Scholarship for program majors ($600–$900), 1 Maude Sherrod Scholarship for program majors ($700).

Application Procedures Students apply for admission into the professional program by freshman year. Deadline for freshmen and transfers: continuous. Notification date for freshmen and transfers: continuous. Required: high school transcript, college transcript(s) for transfer students, ACT test score only (minimum composite ACT score of 18), portfolio for scholarship consideration. Portfolio reviews held by appointment on campus; the submission of slides may be substituted for portfolios (slides preferred).

Web Site http://www.arts.usm.edu/

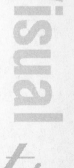

University of Southern Mississippi (continued)

Undergraduate Contact Jara Naquin, Executive Secretary, Department of Art, University of Southern Mississippi, Box 5033, Hattiesburg, Mississippi 39406-5011; 601-266-4972, fax: 601-266-6379, e-mail address: jara.naquin@usm.edu

Graduate Contact Dr. Carley Causey, Director of Art Education, Graduate Admissions, University of Southern Mississippi, Box 10066, Hattiesburg, Mississippi 39406; 601-266-5137, fax: 601-266-5138, e-mail address: carley.causey@usm.edu

The University of Tennessee

Knoxville, Tennessee

State-supported, coed. Urban campus. Total enrollment: 28,901. Art program established 1947.

Degrees Bachelor of Fine Arts in the areas of studio art, graphic design. Majors and concentrations: art history, ceramics, drawing, graphic design, media arts, painting, printmaking, sculpture, watercolors. Graduate degrees offered: Master of Fine Arts in the area of studio art. Cross-registration with Arrowmont School of Art and Crafts. Program accredited by NASAD.

Enrollment 635 total; 450 undergraduate, 35 graduate, 150 nonprofessional degree.

Art Student Profile 58% females, 42% males, 2% minorities, 2% international.

Art Faculty 27 total (full-time), 12 total (part-time). 100% of full-time faculty have terminal degrees. Graduate students teach a few undergraduate courses. Undergraduate student–faculty ratio: 17:1.

Student Life Student groups/activities include University of Tennessee Potters, Student Art History Association, Sculpture Club, University of Tennessee Print Club, AIGA-American Institute of Graphic Arts Student Group.

Expenses for 2007–2008 Application fee: $30. State resident tuition: $5072 full-time. Nonresident tuition: $16,638 full-time. Mandatory fees: $792 full-time. College room and board:

$6358. College room only: $3348. Special program-related fees: $10–$100 per course for lab fees.

Financial Aid Program-specific awards: 1–3 Orin B. and Erma G. Graff Scholarships for freshmen ($2000), 1–2 Buck Ewing Undergraduate Scholarships for juniors and seniors ($2000), Mary Louise Seilaz Awards for program students ($1000), T. H. Jeanette Gillespie Awards for juniors and seniors ($500), 1 Mary Lynn Glustoff Memorial Scholarship for program students ($1000), 1 Rod Norman Memorial Scholarship for program students ($500), 1–3 Dorothy Dille Materials/Travel Awards ($1000), 1–2 freshmen scholarships ($2000).

Application Procedures Students apply for admission into the professional program by freshman year. Deadline for freshmen and transfers: June 2. Required: high school transcript, college transcript(s) for transfer students, minimum 3.0 high school GPA, SAT or ACT test scores.

Web Site http://art.utk.edu

Undergraduate Contact Dr. Suzanne E. Wright, Associate Director, School of Art, The University of Tennessee, 1715 Volunteer Boulevard, Knoxville, Tennessee 37996-2410; 865-974-3407, fax: 865-974-3198, e-mail address: swright5@utk.edu

Graduate Contact Tom Riesing, Graduate Coordinator, School of Art, The University of Tennessee, 1715 Volunteer Boulevard, Knoxville, Tennessee 37996-2410; 865-974-3407, fax: 865-974-3198, e-mail address: triesing@utk.edu

The University of Tennessee at Martin

Martin, Tennessee

State-supported, coed. Small town campus. Total enrollment: 6,893. Art program established 1999.

Degrees Bachelor of Fine Arts in the area of fine and performing arts. Majors and concentrations: art education, graphic design, visual arts.

Enrollment 110 total; all undergraduate.

Art Student Profile 60% females, 40% males, 12% minorities, 3% international.

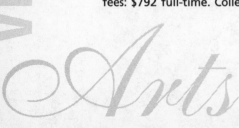

Art Faculty 5 undergraduate (full-time), 3 undergraduate (part-time). 100% of full-time faculty have terminal degrees. Graduate students do not teach undergraduate courses. Undergraduate student–faculty ratio: 16:1.

Student Life Student groups/activities include Visual Arts Society.

Expenses for 2006–2007 Application fee: $30. State resident tuition: $3916 full-time. Nonresident tuition: $13,388 full-time. Mandatory fees: $749 full-time. College room and board: $4410. College room only: $2100. Room and board charges vary according to board plan and housing facility.

Financial Aid Program-specific awards: 2 Endowment for the Arts Scholarships for art design majors ($1000), 1 David Wechsler Scholarship for art/design majors ($1000).

Application Procedures Students admitted directly into the professional program freshman year. Deadline for freshmen and transfers: continuous. Required: high school transcript, college transcript(s) for transfer students, SAT or ACT test scores, ACT score of 21 and high school GPA of 2.50 or ACT score of 18 and high school GPA of 2.85.

Web Site http://www.utm.edu/departments/finearts/music

Undergraduate Contact Mr. Douglas J. Cook, Chair, Department of Visual and Theatre Arts, The University of Tennessee at Martin, 102 Fine Arts Building, Martin, Tennessee 38238; 731-881-7400, fax: 731-881-7415, e-mail address: dcook@utm.edu

The University of Texas at Arlington

Arlington, Texas

State-supported, coed. Urban campus. Total enrollment: 24,825.

Degrees Bachelor of Arts in the area of art history; Bachelor of Fine Arts in the area of art. Majors and concentrations: art history, ceramic art and design, film, glass, graphic arts, jewelry and metalsmithing, painting/drawing, photography, printmaking, screenwriting, sculpture, teacher certification.

Graduate degrees offered: Master of Fine Arts in the area of art. Program accredited by NASAD.

Enrollment 601 total; all undergraduate.

Art Student Profile 55% females, 45% males, 37% minorities, 2% international.

Art Faculty 29 undergraduate (full-time), 16 undergraduate (part-time). 93% of full-time faculty have terminal degrees. Graduate students do not teach undergraduate courses. Undergraduate student–faculty ratio: 20:1.

Student Life Student groups/activities include Student Art Association, Student Film and Video Organization, Art History Student Union, Eye Candy Visual Communication.

Expenses for 2006–2007 Application fee: $35. State resident tuition: $6400 full-time. Nonresident tuition: $14,650 full-time. Full-time tuition varies according to course level, course load, and program. College room and board: $5553. College room only: $3046. Room and board charges vary according to board plan and housing facility. Tuition includes required fees. Special program-related fees: $25–$100 per course for materials fee.

Financial Aid Program-specific awards: 9 Ideas in Art Awards for all students ($1000), 4 Wishful Wings Awards for all students ($500), 3 Arlington Arts League Awards for all students ($400), 3 Mark Baum Awards for all students ($1500).

Application Procedures Students apply for admission into the professional program by sophomore year. Deadline for freshmen and transfers: continuous. Required: high school transcript, college transcript(s) for transfer students, minimum 2.0 high school GPA, SAT or ACT test scores.

Web Site http://www.uta.edu/art

Undergraduate Contact Office of Admissions, The University of Texas at Arlington, Box 19111, Arlington, Texas 76019-0111; 817-272-2118, fax: 817-272-3435.

Graduate Contact Ms. Nancy Palmeri, Graduate Advisor, Associate Professor, Art and Art History, The University of Texas at Arlington, Box 19089, Arlington, Texas 76019; 817-272-2871, fax: 817-272-2805, e-mail address: art@uta.edu

The University of Texas at Austin

Austin, Texas

State-supported, coed. Urban campus. Total enrollment: 49,697. Art program established 1938.

Degrees Bachelor of Fine Arts in the areas of studio art, design. Majors and concentrations: design, studio art. Graduate degrees offered: Master of Fine Arts in the areas of studio art, design. Program accredited by NASAD.

Enrollment 766 total; 432 undergraduate, 45 graduate, 289 nonprofessional degree.

Art Student Profile 70% females, 30% males, 33% minorities, 4% international.

Art Faculty 61 total (full-time), 5 total (part-time). 97% of full-time faculty have terminal degrees. Graduate students teach a few undergraduate courses.

Student Life Student groups/activities include Fine Arts Student Council, Art Students Association, Undergraduate Art History Association.

Expenses for 2006–2007 Application fee: $60. State resident tuition: $7630 full-time. Nonresident tuition: $20,364 full-time. Full-time tuition varies according to course load and program. College room and board: $8176. Room and board charges vary according to board plan, housing facility, and location. Special program-related fees for to maintain studio labs, for to supplement course instruction.

Financial Aid Program-specific awards: 6 department scholarships for currently enrolled students ($1000).

Application Procedures Students admitted directly into the professional program freshman year. Deadline for freshmen: February 1; transfers: March 1. Notification date for freshmen and transfers: April 15. Required: essay, high school transcript, college transcript(s) for transfer students, SAT or ACT test scores, portfolio for transfer applicants. Recommended: minimum 3.0 high school GPA, 3 letters of recommendation, portfolio, portfolio for freshman applicants. Portfolio reviews held 4 times on campus and off campus; the submission of slides may be substituted for portfolios (we only accept slide portfolio, not acutal work).

Web Site http://www.finearts.utexas.edu/aah/

Undergraduate Contact Mr. Shane Sullivan, Undergraduate Coordinator, Department of Art and Art History, The University of Texas at Austin, ART 3.340, Austin, Texas 78712-1285; 512-475-7718, fax: 512-471-7801, e-mail address: shanesullivan@mail.utexas.edu

Graduate Contact Ms. Judy Clack, Graduate Coordinator, Department of Art and Art History, The University of Texas at Austin, ART 3.320, Austin, Texas 78712-1285; 512-471-3377, fax: 512-471-7801, e-mail address: jclack@mail.utexas.edu

The University of Texas at El Paso

El Paso, Texas

State-supported, coed. Urban campus. Total enrollment: 19,842. Art program established 1958.

Web Site http://www.utep.edu/

The University of Texas at San Antonio

San Antonio, Texas

State-supported, coed. Suburban campus. Total enrollment: 28,380. Art program established 1974.

Degrees Bachelor of Fine Arts in the area of art. Majors and concentrations: art. Graduate degrees offered: Master of Arts in the area of art history and criticism; Master of Fine Arts in the area of art. Program accredited by NASAD.

Enrollment 436 total; 284 undergraduate, 28 graduate, 124 nonprofessional degree.

Art Faculty 13 undergraduate (full-time), 13 undergraduate (part-time), 13 graduate (full-time), 13 graduate (part-time). 100% of full-time faculty have terminal degrees. Graduate students teach a few undergraduate courses. Undergraduate student–faculty ratio: 12:1.

Student Life Student groups/activities include Photo Exposure Club, Clay Bodies, Fine Arts Association.

Expenses for 2007–2008 Application fee: $40. State resident tuition: $4530 full-time. Nonresident tuition: $12,780 full-time. Mandatory fees: $2169 full-time. College room and board: $8169. College room only: $5616. Special program-related fees: $35 per course for studio materials.

Financial Aid Program-specific awards: 3 art scholarships ($500).

Application Procedures Students admitted directly into the professional program freshman year. Deadline for freshmen and transfers: July 1. Required: high school transcript, college transcript(s) for transfer students, minimum 2.0 high school GPA, SAT or ACT test scores (minimum composite ACT score of 20), Texas Academic Skills Program test, portfolio for transfer students with junior standing and above. Portfolio reviews held as needed on campus; the submission of slides may be substituted for portfolios when original work is not available or for large works of art.

Web Site http://art.utsa.edu

Undergraduate Contact Mr. Kent T. Rush, Chair, Department of Art and Art History, The University of Texas at San Antonio, One UTSA Circle, San Antonio, Texas 78249; 210-458-4352, fax: 210-458-4356, e-mail address: kent-rush@utsa.edu

Graduate Contact Mr. Ken Little, Graduate Advisor of Record, Department of Art and Art History, The University of Texas at San Antonio, 6900 North Loop 1604 West, San Antonio, Texas 78249-1130; 210-458-4352, fax: 201-458-4356, e-mail address: klittle@utsa.edu

The University of the Arts

Philadelphia, Pennsylvania

Independent, coed. Total enrollment: 2,315. Art program established 1876.

Degrees Bachelor of Fine Arts in the areas of graphic design, painting, printmaking, sculpture, illustration, photography, animation, ceramics, wood, multimedia, writing for film and television; Bachelor of Science in the areas of industrial design, communication. Majors and concentrations: animation, digital art, film and video production, film studies, graphic design, illustration, industrial design, multimedia, painting, painting/drawing, photography, printmaking, sculpture. Graduate degrees offered: Master of Arts in the areas of art education, museum education, museum communication; Master of Arts in Teaching in the area of visual art; Master of Fine Arts in the areas of museum exhibition planning and design, book arts/printmaking, painting, sculpture, ceramics; Master of Industrial Design in the area of industrial design. Cross-registration with schools sponsored by American Independent Colleges of Art and Design. Program accredited by NASAD, IDSA.

Enrollment 1,327 total; 1,146 undergraduate, 181 graduate.

Art Student Profile 56% females, 44% males, 18% minorities, 3% international.

Art Faculty 36 undergraduate (full-time), 118 undergraduate (part-time), 20 graduate (full-time), 25 graduate (part-time). 82% of full-time faculty have terminal degrees. Graduate students do not teach undergraduate courses. Undergraduate student–faculty ratio: 7:1.

Student Life Student groups/activities include Student Government. Special housing available for art students.

Expenses for 2006–2007 Application fee: $60. Tuition: $24,730 full-time. Mandatory fees: $950 full-time. College room only: $6300. Room charges vary according to housing facility. Special program-related fees for various lab fees (depending on the curriculum).

Financial Aid Program-specific awards: 50 merit scholarships for program students ($500–$10,000).

Application Procedures Students apply for admission into the professional program by sophomore year. Deadline for freshmen and transfers: continuous. Notification date for freshmen and transfers: September 1. Required: essay, high school transcript, college transcript(s) for transfer students, minimum 2.0 high school GPA, letter of recommendation, portfolio, SAT or ACT test scores. Recommended: minimum 3.0 high school GPA, interview. Portfolio reviews held continuously by appointment on campus and off campus at National Portfolio Days; the submission of slides may be substituted for portfolios when distance is prohibitive.

Web Site http://www.uarts.edu

Contact Susan Gandy, Director of Admission, The University of the Arts, 320 South Broad Street, Philadelphia, Pennsylvania 19102; 800-616-ARTS ext. 6049, fax: 215-717-6045, e-mail address: admissions@uarts.edu

Visual Arts

The University of the Arts (continued)

More About the University

The University of the Arts (UArts) is unique among the nation's leading colleges and universities. Located in Center City Philadelphia, UArts is the only school in the country devoted to all the arts and communication. Composed of the College of Art and Design, the College of Performing Arts, and the College of Media and Communication, UArts offers intensive concentration within each major as well as other creative opportunities for further artistic exploration and growth.

More than 2,200 undergraduate and graduate students from forty states and thirty countries are enrolled. UArts educates professional artists, performers, and communicators—people who make their living creating, designing, communicating, and performing. The active Internship Program offers students opportunities to gain hands-on experience in their field during the academic year.

The College of Art and Design offers a full range of programs in the visual arts. It includes dynamic programs in animation, crafts, film/animation, film/digital video, graphic design, illustration, industrial design, painting/drawing, photography, printmaking/book arts, and sculpture. These programs share both exceptionally high standards and a supportive, personal environment to explore and grow as a creative individual.

The College of Performing Arts combines both the exhilaration of performance and the diligent commitment to practice and rehearsal to sharpen technique and shape vision. It includes the Schools of Dance, Music, and Theater Arts. The College offers outstanding opportunities to perform as well as the chance to grow as an artist through rigorous training.

The College of Media and Communications explores new ideas and concepts in a changing world. Video games, the Internet, CD-ROM technology, interactive television, and virtual reality are just a few examples of the emerging forms that are featured in the challenging and exciting curriculum. Offering majors in writing for film and television, multimedia, and communication, the College celebrates the interdisciplinary nature of these new forms of creative expression. Now, students who want to learn more about media and communication before choosing a major can enroll in the UArts Discovery Year, giving them time to explore where their passions lie.

Program Facilities UArts offers excellent facilities to support all of its programs in an environment rich with opportunities to encounter art and artistic inspiration. The studios, shops, theaters, recital halls, labs, galleries, and libraries are housed nearby in Hamilton Hall, the Terra Building, the Merriam Theater, the Arts Bank, and Anderson Hall, the nine-story studio building.

The facilities in the College of Art and Design include a broad range of studios and equipment: woodworking and metal shops, including a foundry; printmaking shops and digital pre-press labs; fine arts, crafts, design, and film/animation studios; and digital imaging labs. Four gas and several electric kilns are available for work in ceramics, as is a forge for sculpture. A large weaving shop offers dozens of looms and a dyeing room. Facilities supporting work in film, video, photography, and animation are extensive and first-class. UArts is one of the first academic institutions to acquire a 3-D printer and scanner for student use. It is used primarily by industrial design and jewelry design students to develop mock-ups of their ideas faster and less expensively than the traditional way of hand molding wax or foam.

The School of Dance offers a rigorous studio experience, and its home is the newly renovated Terra Building. Dance studios are bright, well-lit, and fully equipped with barres and mirrors, responsive suspension floors, beautiful windows, ceiling fans, pianos, and audio systems. Visiting artists, including Mikhail Baryshnikov and members of the Twyla Tharp Company, teach master classes and meet informally with students. In addition to the 1,600-seat Merriam Theater, student performances are held in the 240-seat UArts Dance Theater. The Alfred M. Greenfield Library houses an extensive collection of dance books and videotapes.

The School of Music at UArts has three big bands, thirty-five small jazz ensembles, seven vocal ensembles, and ten traditional ensembles. In addition to performance opportunities in recital halls and theaters, facilities include fully equipped music studios, practice rooms, and a class piano laboratory. The MIDI and Recording Studio is a modern recording and music technology facility with a complete 32-input recording studio, MIDI and computer labs, computer and synthesizer workstation labs, and an audio-for-video dubbing and editing room. Most practice rooms are equipped with grand pianos, and a suite of fully equipped percussion studios is also available for student practice.

Students in the College of Media and Communication have ready access to state-of-the-art audio and video systems; highly portable equipment; preproduction and postproduction studios; PC-, Mac-, and UNIX-based systems; and industry-standard software used for audio, video, and Web work. The College supports a student-run Webzine and Web radio and hosts a number of student- and alumni-produced Web sites. UArts is a member of the New Media Centers (NMC), an organization of leading universities and corporations dedicated to innovative uses of technology.

Faculty, Residential Artists, and Alumni Numbering 476 full- and part-time members, the faculty is the driving force of the UArts programs. They are practicing professionals, most with advanced degrees, who are committed to both their own creative expression and the development of their students. The student-faculty ratio is 10:1, so students can be assured of individual attention and guidance.

Visiting artists have included these fine professionals: dance: Suzanne Farrell, Edward Villelo, Mikhail Baryshnikov, Donna McKechnie, Oleg Eriansky, Gabriella Darvash, James Truitt, Meredith Monk, and Ronnie Favors; music: Andre Watts, Jack Elliott, Wynton Marsalis, Pierre Boulez, Billy Joel, George Crumb, Eddie Gomez, Placido Domingo, Klaus Tennstedt, Ricardo Muti, Thad Jones, Mel Lewis, Peter Erskine, and Stanley Clarke; and theater: Elizabeth Ashley, Laurie Anderson, Tommy Hicks, and David Henry Hwang.

Proud alumni include Philadelphia Orchestra violinist Michael Ludwig, Alvin Ailey Dance member Antonio Carlos Scott, artist Sidney Goodman, Tony Award–nominated dancer/actress Rhonda LaChanze Sapp, illustrator Arnold Roth, jazz artist/composer Stanley Clarke, director Joe Dante, illustrator Charles Santore, dancer/choreographer Judith Jamison, actress Irene Bodard, concert pianist Lydia Artymiw, children's book authors/illustrators Jan and Stan Berenstain, and the Quay Brothers.

Student Performance/Exhibit Opportunities

Events include exhibitions in UArts galleries, ensemble productions, student composition concerts featuring original choreography, repertory concerts, an annual freshmen inter-arts project, recitals, and appearances with visiting artists.

Special Programs Programs include student exchanges with other schools and colleges, foreign and summer studies, pre-College Summer Institute for talented and motivated high school students, career planning and placement, personal counseling, academic support, professional and peer tutoring, services for students with disabilities, and international student services. Students in the UArts Colleges of Performing Arts and Media and Communication benefit from an exciting partnership with the Liverpool Institute for the Performing Arts (LIPA) in England. Initiatives between the schools include class-abroad opportunities, student exchanges, recordings, performance workshops, and joint master's degree programs.

University of the Pacific
Stockton, California

Independent, coed. Suburban campus. Total enrollment: 6,251. Art program established 1980.

Degrees Bachelor of Fine Arts in the areas of graphic design, studio arts. Majors and concentrations: graphic design, studio art. Program accredited by NASAD.

Enrollment 90 total; 65 undergraduate, 25 nonprofessional degree.

Art Student Profile 65% females, 35% males, 45% minorities, 5% international.

Art Faculty 8 undergraduate (full-time), 3 undergraduate (part-time). 100% of full-time faculty have terminal degrees. Graduate students do not teach undergraduate courses. Undergraduate student–faculty ratio: 8:1.

Student Life Student groups/activities include Undergraduate Research Conference, Associated Student Union of Pacific, AIGA-American Institute of Graphic Arts Student Chapter.

Expenses for 2007–2008 Application fee: $60. Comprehensive fee: $38,190 includes full-time tuition ($28,480), mandatory fees ($500), and college room and board ($9210). College room only: $4610. Room and board charges vary according to board plan and housing facility. Special program-related fees: $25–$100 per course for studio materials.

Financial Aid Program-specific awards: 10–20 endowed scholarships for art majors: studio arts graphic design ($2000–$5000).

Application Procedures Students admitted directly into the professional program freshman year. Deadline for freshmen: March 1. Notification date for freshmen: April 15. Required: essay, high school transcript, minimum 2.0 high school GPA, letter of recommendation, SAT or ACT test scores. Recommended: minimum 3.0 high school GPA, portfolio. Portfolio reviews held continuously for transfer students on campus; the submission of slides may be substituted for portfolios (or CD ROM with detailed list).

Web Site http://www.pacific.edu/cop/art/

University of the Pacific (continued)

Undergraduate Contact Office of Admissions, University of the Pacific, 3601 Pacific Avenue, Stockton, California 95211-0197; 800-959-2867, fax: 209-946-2413, e-mail address: admissions@uop.edu

University of Utah

Salt Lake City, Utah

State-supported, coed. Urban campus. Total enrollment: 28,619. Art program established 1890.

Degrees Bachelor of Fine Arts in the area of art. Majors and concentrations: art education, ceramics, digital imaging, graphic design, illustration, intermedia, painting/drawing, photography, printmaking, sculpture. Graduate degrees offered: Master of Fine Arts in the area of art.

Enrollment 610 total; 460 undergraduate, 26 graduate, 124 nonprofessional degree.

Art Student Profile 50% females, 50% males, 12% minorities, 10% international.

Art Faculty 21 total (full-time), 21 total (part-time). 100% of full-time faculty have terminal degrees. Graduate students do not teach undergraduate courses. Undergraduate student–faculty ratio: 13:1.

Student Life Student groups/activities include cross-discriminary classes and fine arts technology events, intercollegiate and interregional traveling exhibitions, Carmen Morton Christensen Visiting Artist/Scholar Lecture Series. Special housing available for art students.

Expenses for 2007–2008 Application fee: $35. State resident tuition: $4269 full-time. Nonresident tuition: $14,945 full-time. Mandatory fees: $717 full-time. Full-time tuition and fees vary according to course level, course load, degree level, program, reciprocity agreements, and student level. College room and board: $5778. College room only: $2890. Room and board charges vary according to board plan and housing facility. Contact university directly for part-time tuition costs. Special program-related fees: $30–$75 per course for tools and equipment maintenance, materials.

Financial Aid Program-specific awards: 5 departmental tuition scholarships for freshmen and continuing students ($4000), 2 Ann Can-non Scholarships for continuing students ($1000), 1 Ethel A. Rolapp Award for graduating students ($2000), 1 E. J. Bird Memorial Scholarship for continuing students ($4000), 14 C. M. Christensen Scholarships for freshmen and continuing students ($1800), 1 Florence Ware Scholarship for continuing students ($1500), 1 freshman tuition scholarship for freshmen ($4000), 1 Grace Durkee Meldrum Scholarship for continuing students ($2500), 1 Paul Davis Travel Award for continuing students ($500), 1 outstanding high school award for incoming high school students ($500), 2 Howard Clark Scholarships for continuing students ($1500), 1 Jack and Florence Sears Scholarship for continuing students ($1500), 1 Antista-Fairclough Scholarship for continuing students ($2000).

Application Procedures Students apply for admission into the professional program by freshman year. Deadline for freshmen and transfers: continuous. Required: high school transcript, college transcript(s) for transfer students, minimum 2.0 high school GPA, SAT or ACT test scores (minimum composite ACT score of 18), portfolio for transfer students and for scholarship consideration. Recommended: minimum 3.0 high school GPA. Portfolio reviews held as needed on campus; the submission of slides may be substituted for portfolios for large works of art.

Web Site http://www.art.utah.edu/

Undergraduate Contact Ms. Nevon Bruschke, Undergraduate Advisor, Department of Art and Art History, University of Utah, 375 South 1530 E Room 161, Salt Lake City, Utah 84112-0380; 801-581-8677, fax: 801-585-6171, e-mail address: n.bruschke@utah.edu

Graduate Contact Prof. John O'Connell, Graduate Director of MFA Program, Department of Art and Art History, University of Utah, 375 South 1530 E Room 161, Salt Lake City, Utah 84112-0380; 801-581-8677, fax: 801-585-6171, e-mail address: j.oconnell@utah.edu

University of Washington

Seattle, Washington

State-supported, coed. Urban campus. Total enrollment: 39,524. Art program established 1867.

Degrees Bachelor of Arts in the areas of design studies, art history; Bachelor of Fine Arts in the areas of art, design. Majors and concentrations: art history, ceramics, design art, fibers, industrial design, interdisciplinary studies, painting/drawing, photography, sculpture, visual communication design. Graduate degrees offered: Master of Arts in the area of art history; Master of Fine Arts in the areas of art, design. Doctor of Philosophy in the area of art history.

Enrollment 1,450 total; 800 undergraduate, 100 graduate, 550 nonprofessional degree.

Art Student Profile 65% females, 35% males, 10% minorities, 10% international.

Art Faculty 38 total (full-time), 2 total (part-time). 94% of full-time faculty have terminal degrees. Graduate students teach a few undergraduate courses. Undergraduate student–faculty ratio: 14:1.

Student Life Student groups/activities include MFA Thesis Exhibit, School of Art Open House, Career Discovery Week.

Expenses for 2006–2007 Application fee: $50. State resident tuition: $5988 full-time. Nonresident tuition: $21,286 full-time. Full-time tuition varies according to course load. College room and board: $6561. Room and board charges vary according to board plan and housing facility. Special program-related fees: $35–$110 per course for materials fee.

Financial Aid Program-specific awards: 56 School of Art Scholarships for program majors ($1000).

Application Procedures Students apply for admission into the professional program by freshman, sophomore, junior year. Deadline for freshmen: February 1; transfers: April 1. Notification date for freshmen: March 15. Required: essay, high school transcript, college transcript(s) for transfer students, SAT or ACT test scores, portfolio for transfer applicants (for some majors). Portfolio reviews held continuously on campus; the submission of slides may be substituted for portfolios whenever needed.

Web Site http://art.washington.edu

Undergraduate Contact Admissions Office, University of Washington, Box 355840, Seattle, Washington 98195-5840; 206-543-9686.

Graduate Contact Autumn Yoke, Adviser, School of Art, University of Washington, Box 353440, Seattle, Washington 98195-3440; 206-543-0646, fax: 206-685-1657, e-mail address: gradart@u.washington.edu

University of West Florida

Pensacola, Florida

State-supported, coed. Suburban campus. Total enrollment: 9,819. Art program established 1980.

Web Site http://uwf.edu/

University of Wisconsin–Madison

Madison, Wisconsin

State-supported, coed. Urban campus. Total enrollment: 41,466.

Degrees Bachelor of Fine Arts in the area of art; Bachelor of Science in the areas of art, art education. Majors and concentrations: art education, art/fine arts, graphic design. Graduate degrees offered: Master of Arts in the areas of art, art education; Master of Fine Arts in the area of art. Doctor of Philosophy in the area of art education. Program accredited by NASAD.

Enrollment 475 total; 375 undergraduate, 100 graduate.

Art Student Profile 60% females, 40% males, 10% minorities, 1% international.

Art Faculty 30 total (full-time), 4 total (part-time). 100% of full-time faculty have terminal degrees. Graduate students teach a few undergraduate courses. Undergraduate student–faculty ratio: 10:1.

Student Life Student groups/activities include Arts Night Out, Student Art Exhibit, Student art organizations.

Expenses for 2006–2007 Application fee: $35. State resident tuition: $6000 full-time. Nonresident tuition: $20,000 full-time. Mandatory fees: $726 full-time. Full-time tuition and fees vary according to degree level and reciprocity agreements. College room and board: $6920. Room and board charges vary according to board plan, housing facility, and location. Special program-related fees: $10–$300 per course for expendable supplies.

Financial Aid Program-specific awards: 4 Edith Gilbertson Scholarships for continuing pro-

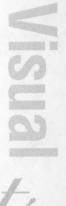

University of Wisconsin–Madison (continued)

gram students ($5000), 2 Ethel Odegaard Scholarships for continuing program students ($3000), 1 Carrie Jones Cady Scholarship for continuing program students/applied art ($7500), 2 Butor Scholarships for continuing program students ($2000), 2 Frazier Scholarships for continuing program students ($1250), 2 Hokin Scholarships for continuing program students ($2000), 1 Regan Scholarship for continuing program students ($500), 2 Austin Scholarships for continuing program students from Milwaukee High School ($7500), 1 Ebling Scholarship for continuing program students from Wisconsin ($1500), 1 Faculty Scholarship for continuing program students ($800), 1 Krug Scholarship for continuing program students ($1000), 1 Marten Scholarship for continuing program students/art education ($1000), 1 Logan Scholarship for continuing program students/art education ($4500), 1 Hooper Scholarship for continuing program students/printmaking ($1500), 1 Wartmann Scholarship for continuing program students/printmaking ($3500), 3 Art Metals Scholarships for continuing program students/printmaking ($7500).

Application Procedures Students admitted directly into the professional program freshman year. Deadline for freshmen and transfers: February 1. Required: essay, high school transcript, college transcript(s) for transfer students, minimum 3.0 high school GPA, SAT test score only.

Web Site http://art.wisc.edu

Undergraduate Contact Julie Ganser, Undergraduate Advisor, Art Department, University of Wisconsin–Madison, 455 North Park Street, 6241 Humanities C, Madison, Wisconsin 53706; 608-262-8831, e-mail address: ganser@education.wisc.edu

Graduate Contact Ms. Teri Van Genderen, Student Status Examiner, Art Department, University of Wisconsin–Madison, 455 North Park Street, 6241 Humanities, Madison, Wisconsin 53706; 608-262-1660.

Peck School of the Arts
University of Wisconsin–Milwaukee
Milwaukee, Wisconsin

State-supported, coed. Urban campus. Total enrollment: 28,309. Art program established 1961.

Degrees Bachelor of Fine Arts in the areas of art, art with teacher certification. Majors and concentrations: art education, ceramics, digital art, fibers, graphic design, jewelry and metalsmithing, painting/drawing, photography, printmaking, sculpture. Graduate degrees offered: Master of Arts in the area of art; Master of Fine Arts in the area of art.

Enrollment 865 total; 775 undergraduate, 30 graduate, 60 nonprofessional degree.

Art Student Profile 61% females, 39% males, 8% minorities, 1% international.

Art Faculty 20 undergraduate (full-time), 47 undergraduate (part-time), 20 graduate (full-time). 100% of full-time faculty have terminal degrees. Graduate students teach a few undergraduate courses. Undergraduate student–faculty ratio: 39:1.

Expenses for 2006–2007 Application fee: $35. State resident tuition: $6630 full-time. Nonresident tuition: $16,232 full-time. Mandatory fees: $762 full-time. Full-time tuition and fees vary according to location, program, and reciprocity agreements. College room and board: $5314. College room only: $3304. Room and board charges vary according to board plan and housing facility. Special program-related fees: $35–$75 per course for art supplies, $60 per course for infrastructure, technology, instruction.

Financial Aid Program-specific awards: 10 Layton Scholarships ($500–$1000), 1–2 Harold A. Levin Memorial Scholarships for program majors ($500–$1000), 10 Visual Arts Scholarships ($500–$1000), 3–4 Elsa Ulbricht Memorial Scholarships for program majors ($500–$1000), 1 Rorabeck Memorial Scholarship for painting and drawing majors ($1000), 1 Clarice George Logan Travel Scholarship for juniors only ($2500), 1 Racine Art Guild Scholarship for program majors who are residents of Racine, WI ($500), 2–3 Mary E. Van Deven Scholarships for juniors (renewable in senior year) ($500–

$1000), 1 Lawrence Rathsack Scholarship for painting and drawing majors ($1000), 1–2 Ester C. Waldheim Scholarships for graphic design majors ($900).

Application Procedures Students apply for admission into the professional program by sophomore year. Deadline for freshmen and transfers: continuous. Required: essay, high school transcript, college transcript(s) for transfer students, 2 letters of recommendation, portfolio, ACT score for state residents, SAT or ACT score for out-of-state residents. Recommended: minimum 3.0 high school GPA. Portfolio reviews held on campus; the submission of slides may be substituted for portfolios with permission of graphic design faculty for graphic design program; slides or CD required for freshmen.

Web Site http://www.uwm.edu/Dept/SFA/

Undergraduate Contact Ms. Kelly Beisbier, Administrative Program Manager, Department of Visual Art, University of Wisconsin–Milwaukee, PO Box 413, 2400 East Kenwood Boulevard, Milwaukee, Wisconsin 53201; 414-229-6054, fax: 414-229-2973, e-mail address: beis@uwm.edu

Graduate Contact Prof. Marna Brauner, Director, Graduate Studies, Department of Visual Art, University of Wisconsin–Milwaukee, PO Box 413, 2400 East Kenwood Boulevard, Milwaukee, Wisconsin 53201; 414-229-6053, fax: 414-229-2973, e-mail address: marnab@uwm.edu

University of Wisconsin–Oshkosh

Oshkosh, Wisconsin

State-supported, coed. Suburban campus. Total enrollment: 11,080.

Degrees Bachelor of Fine Arts in the areas of art education, studio/fine arts, graphic communications. Majors and concentrations: applied design, art education, ceramics, drawing, fibers, graphic communication, metals, painting, photography, printmaking, sculpture.

Enrollment 370 total.

Art Faculty 13 total (full-time), 7 total (part-time). 100% of full-time faculty have terminal degrees. Graduate students do not teach undergraduate courses. Undergraduate student–faculty ratio: 20:1.

Student Life Student groups/activities include Priebe Gallery Board, SOFA (Students Organized for Art).

Expenses for 2006–2007 Application fee: $35. State resident tuition: $5364 full-time. Nonresident tuition: $12,838 full-time. College room and board: $5164. College room only: $3034. Special program-related fees: $10–$30 per course per semester for lab fees.

Financial Aid Program-specific awards: 2 Pride of Oshkosh Art Student Scholarships for any art majors, 1 Joann Kindt Scholarship for female non-traditional art students, 1 Charles Charonis Scholarship for junior or senior art education majors, 1 Milton Gardener Sculpture Scholarship for junior or senior sculpture students, 1 Bill Neiderberger Scholarship for junior or senior art students, Willcockson Scholarships for incoming freshmen, 1 William Leffin Scholarship for program majors.

Application Procedures Students admitted directly into the professional program freshman year. Deadline for freshmen and transfers: continuous. Notification date for freshmen and transfers: continuous. Required: high school transcript, college transcript(s) for transfer students, standing in top half of graduating class or minimum ACT score of 22.

Web Site http://www.uwosh.edu

Undergraduate Contact Chair, Department of Art, University of Wisconsin–Oshkosh, 900 Algoma Boulevard, Oshkosh, Wisconsin 54901; 920-424-0492, fax: 920-424-1738.

University of Wisconsin–Stevens Point

Stevens Point, Wisconsin

State-supported, coed. Small town campus. Total enrollment: 8,842.
Web Site http://www.uwsp.edu/

University of Wisconsin–Stout

Menomonie, Wisconsin

State-supported, coed. Small town campus. Total enrollment: 8,327.

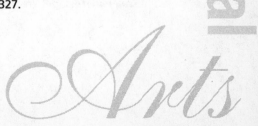

University of Wisconsin–Stout (continued)

Degrees Bachelor of Fine Arts in the area of art; Bachelor of Science in the area of art education. Majors and concentrations: art education, graphic design, industrial design, interior design, multimedia design, studio art. Program accredited by NASAD, CIDA.

Enrollment 802 total; all undergraduate.

Art Student Profile 61% females, 39% males, 5% minorities, 1% international.

Art Faculty 28 undergraduate (full-time), 8 undergraduate (part-time). 95% of full-time faculty have terminal degrees. Graduate students do not teach undergraduate courses. Undergraduate student–faculty ratio: 15:1.

Student Life Student groups/activities include Industrial Design Society of America Student Chapter (IDSA), American Society of Interior Designers (ASID) Student Chapter, Graphic Design Association Student Chapter (GDA), International Interior Design Association, Fine Arts Association, SIGGRAPH Student Chapter.

Expenses for 2007–2008 Application fee: $35. State resident tuition: $5087 full-time. Nonresident tuition: $12,737 full-time. Mandatory fees: $1876 full-time. College room and board: $4884. College room only: $2990.

Financial Aid Program-specific awards: 1 John and Frances Furlong Art Scholarship for art/art education majors ($1000), 2 Bud and Betty Micheels Student Artist-in-Residence Grants for undergraduates ($1500), 1 Larsen Design Scholarship for art/graphic design or multimedia design majors ($1000).

Application Procedures Students admitted directly into the professional program freshman year. Deadline for freshmen and transfers: continuous. Notification date for freshmen and transfers: continuous. Required: portfolio.

Web Site http://www.uwstout.edu/programs/bfaa

Undergraduate Contact Dr. Cynthia Gilberts, Director of Admissions, University of Wisconsin–Stout, 124 Bowman Hall, Menomonie, Wisconsin 54751; 715-232-1232, fax: 715-232-1667, e-mail address: gilbertsc@uwstout.edu

University of Wisconsin–Superior

Superior, Wisconsin

State-supported, coed. Suburban campus. Total enrollment: 2,924. Art program established 1922.
Web Site http://www.uwsuper.edu/

Utah State University

Logan, Utah

State-supported, coed. Urban campus. Total enrollment: 14,444. Art program established 1908.
Web Site http://www.usu.edu/

Valdosta State University

Valdosta, Georgia

State-supported, coed. Small town campus. Total enrollment: 10,888.

Degrees Bachelor of Fine Arts in the areas of art, art education, interior design. Majors and concentrations: art education, art/fine arts, interior design. Graduate degrees offered: Master of Art Education. Program accredited by NASAD.

Enrollment 300 total; 270 undergraduate, 30 nonprofessional degree.

Art Student Profile 74% females, 26% males, 19% minorities, 3% international.

Art Faculty 16 total (full-time), 5 total (part-time). 100% of full-time faculty have terminal degrees. Graduate students do not teach undergraduate courses. Undergraduate student–faculty ratio: 16:1.

Student Life Student groups/activities include National Art Education Association Student Chapter, American Society of Interior Designers (ASID).

Expenses for 2007–2008 Application fee: $40. State resident tuition: $2560 full-time. Nonresident tuition: $10,242 full-time. Mandatory fees: $930 full-time. College room and board: $5680. College room only: $2880. Special program-related fees: $20 per course for materials purchase in lab classes.

Financial Aid Program-specific awards: 3 freshman art scholarships for incoming majors ($700–$1000), 2 Fortner Scholarships for continuing majors ($1275), 1–5 Art Department Assistantships for program majors ($1000), 1 Lee Bennet Scholarship for continuing majors ($2800).

Application Procedures Students admitted directly into the professional program freshman year. Deadline for freshmen and transfers: continuous. Required: high school transcript, college transcript(s) for transfer students, SAT or ACT test scores, completion of college preparatory curriculum or equivalent, minimum re-centered SAT scores of 440 verbal and 410 math or ACT English 18 and ACT Math 17. Recommended: minimum 2.0 high school GPA, portfolio. Portfolio reviews held once on campus; the submission of slides may be substituted for portfolios whenever needed.

Web Site http://www.valdosta.edu/art/

Undergraduate Contact Mr. Walter Peacock, Director, Admissions Office, Valdosta State University, 1500 North Patterson Street, Valdosta, Georgia 31698; 229-333-5791, e-mail address: wpeacock@valdosta.edu

Graduate Contact Dr. J. Stephen Lahr, Professor/Art Education, Department of Art, Valdosta State University, 1500 North Patterson Street, Valdosta, Georgia 31698-0110; 229-333-5835, fax: 229-259-5121, e-mail address: jslahr@valdosta.edu

Virginia Commonwealth University

Richmond, Virginia

State-supported, coed. Urban campus. Total enrollment: 30,381. Art program established 1928.

Degrees Bachelor of Arts in the areas of fashion merchandising, cinema, art history; Bachelor of Fine Arts in the areas of film, art education, communication arts, crafts/material studies, fashion design, interior design, painting/printmaking, sculpture, photography, graphic design, kinetic imaging. Majors and concentrations: animation, art education, art history, communication arts, communication design, craft/material studies, crafts, digital imaging, fashion design, fashion merchandising, film, furniture design, glassworking, graphic arts, graphic design, illustration, interior design, jewelry and metalsmithing, kinetic imaging, medical illustration, painting/drawing, photography, printmaking, sculpture, textile arts, video art, woodworking design. Graduate degrees offered: Master of Arts in the area of art history; Master of Art Education; Master of Fine Arts in the areas of glass, jewelry/metal, interior environments, ceramics, fiber, painting/printmaking, photography, sculpture, film, kinetic imaging, furniture design, visual communication. Doctor of Philosophy in the areas of art history (media, art and text). Program accredited by NASAD, NCATE, CIDA.

Enrollment 3,323 total; 3,022 undergraduate, 301 graduate.

Art Student Profile 66% females, 34% males, 28% minorities, 17% international.

Art Faculty 132 total (full-time), 160 total (part-time). 97% of full-time faculty have terminal degrees. Graduate students teach a few undergraduate courses. Undergraduate student–faculty ratio: 13:1.

Student Life Student groups/activities include Annual Juried Student Exhibitions at the Anderson Gallery. Special housing available for art students.

Expenses for 2006–2007 Application fee: $30. State resident tuition: $4227 full-time. Nonresident tuition: $15,904 full-time. College room and board: $7473. College room only: $4273. Room and board charges vary according to board plan. Special program-related fees: $257 per semester for comprehensive arts fee.

Financial Aid Program-specific awards: 15–16 Visual Arts Scholarships for current students ($500–$1000), 1–2 Doris Lansing Scholarships for entering freshmen ($1000–$2500), university scholarship for entering freshmen ($500–$3000).

Application Procedures Students apply for admission into the professional program by freshman year. Deadline for freshmen and transfers: February 1. Notification date for freshmen and transfers: continuous. Required: high school transcript, college transcript(s) for transfer students, letter of recommendation, portfolio, SAT or ACT test scores, 12-16 images of art created in the past 2 years or 10 projects - exercises described in application. Recommended: essay, minimum 2.0 high school GPA.

Virginia Commonwealth University (continued)

Portfolio reviews held continuously on campus and off campus; the submission of slides may be substituted for portfolios.

Web Site http://www.vcu.edu/arts

Undergraduate Contact Ms. Carolyn Henne, Assistant Dean for Student Affairs, School of the Arts, Virginia Commonwealth University, PO Box 842519, Richmond, Virginia 23284-2519; 866-534-3201, fax: 804-828-6469, e-mail address: chenne@vcu.edu

Graduate Contact Mr. Joseph Seipel, Senior Associate Dean for Academic Affairs and Director of Graduate Studies, School of the Arts, Virginia Commonwealth University, PO Box 842519, Richmond, Virginia 23284-2519; 804-828-6827, fax: 804-828-6469, e-mail address: jseipel@vcu.edu

Virginia Intermont College

Bristol, Virginia

Independent, coed. Small town campus. Total enrollment: 916.

Web Site http://www.vic.edu/

Washburn University

Topeka, Kansas

City-supported, coed. Urban campus. Total enrollment: 7,153. Art program established 1897.

Degrees Bachelor of Fine Arts. Majors and concentrations: art education, art history, visual arts. Program accredited by NASAD.

Enrollment 110 total; 50 undergraduate, 60 nonprofessional degree.

Art Student Profile 56% females, 44% males, 2% minorities, 2% international.

Art Faculty 6 undergraduate (full-time), 7 undergraduate (part-time). 100% of full-time faculty have terminal degrees. Graduate students do not teach undergraduate courses. Undergraduate student–faculty ratio: 9:1.

Student Life Student groups/activities include Washburn Art Student Association, Mulvane Art Museum.

Expenses for 2006–2007 Application fee: $20. State resident tuition: $5250 full-time. Nonresident tuition: $11,910 full-time. Mandatory fees: $62 full-time. College room and board: $5170. College room only: $2910. Room and board charges vary according to board plan and housing facility.

Financial Aid Program-specific awards: 20 Art Department Scholarship Awards for art majors ($1200–$1800), 1 Pollak Art Purchase Award for junior or senior art majors ($1300).

Application Procedures Students apply for admission into the professional program by sophomore year. Deadline for freshmen and transfers: continuous. Required: high school transcript, college transcript(s) for transfer students, ACT test score only (minimum composite ACT score of 17), minimum 2.0 high school GPA for out-of-state applicants. Recommended: portfolio for transfer applicants. Portfolio reviews held twice during sophomore year on campus; the submission of slides may be substituted for portfolios for transfer applicants.

Web Site http://www.washburn.edu/cas/art/index.html

Undergraduate Contact Ms. Glenda Taylor, Chair, Department of Art, Washburn University, 1700 College Street, Topeka, Kansas 66621; 785-670-2238, fax: 785-670-1089, e-mail address: glenda.taylor@washburn.edu

Washington State University

Pullman, Washington

State-supported, coed. Rural campus. Total enrollment: 23,655. Art program established 1910.

Degrees Bachelor of Fine Arts in the areas of painting, sculpture, printmaking, ceramics, photography, computer art, drawing. Majors and concentrations: art/fine arts, ceramics, computer graphics, painting/drawing, photography, printmaking, sculpture, studio art. Graduate degrees offered: Master of Fine Arts in the areas of painting, sculpture, printmaking, ceramics, photography, computer art, drawing. Cross-registration with institutions in the state of Washington, University of Idaho.

Enrollment 470 total; 300 undergraduate, 20 graduate, 150 nonprofessional degree.

Art Student Profile 60% females, 40% males, 30% minorities, 10% international.

Art Faculty 9 total (full-time), 8 total (part-time). 100% of full-time faculty have terminal degrees. Graduate students teach more than half of undergraduate courses. Undergraduate student–faculty ratio: 25:1.

Student Life Student groups/activities include Art Student Union, Undergraduate Exhibition Hall.

Expenses for 2006–2007 Application fee: $50. State resident tuition: $5432 full-time. Nonresident tuition: $15,072 full-time. Mandatory fees: $1015 full-time. College room and board: $6890. College room only: $3390. Room and board charges vary according to board plan, housing facility, and location. Special program-related fees: $25–$60 for materials.

Financial Aid Program-specific awards: 1 John Ludwig Memorial Scholarship for program majors ($300–$500), 2–3 James Balyeat Awards for program majors ($200–$300), 3 Fine Arts Development Fund Scholarships for program majors ($200–$500), 2 Fine Arts Faculty Fund Scholarships for program majors ($200–$300).

Application Procedures Students apply for admission into the professional program by sophomore, junior year. Deadline for freshmen and transfers: continuous. Required: high school transcript, college transcript(s) for transfer students, minimum 2.0 high school GPA. Portfolio reviews held whenever needed on campus.

Web Site http://www.wsu.edu/~finearts

Contact Kathy Parkins, Support Supervisor, Fine Arts Department, Washington State University, 5072 Fine Arts Center, Pullman, Washington 99164-7450; 509-335-8686, fax: 509-335-7742, e-mail address: lparkins@wsu.edu

Washington University in St. Louis

St. Louis, Missouri

Independent, coed. Suburban campus. Total enrollment: 13,355.

Web Site http://www.wustl.edu/

Watkins College of Art and Design

Nashville, Tennessee

Independent, coed. Urban campus. Total enrollment: 393. Art program established 1978.

Degrees Bachelor of Fine Arts in the areas of film, fine arts, graphic design, interior design, photography. Majors and concentrations: ceramics, cinematography, directing, drawing, editing, graphic design, interior design, painting, photography, printmaking, producing, screenwriting, sculpture. Program accredited by NASAD, CIDA.

Enrollment 360 undergraduate.

Art Student Profile 57% females, 43% males, 19% minorities, 2% international.

Art Faculty 18 undergraduate (full-time), 21 graduate (full-time). 98% of full-time faculty have terminal degrees. Graduate students do not teach undergraduate courses. Undergraduate student–faculty ratio: 11:1.

Student Life Student groups/activities include Screenwriters Association, AISD, Nashville Advertising Association.

Expenses for 2007–2008 Application fee: $50. Tuition: $12,000 full-time. Mandatory fees: $960 full-time. College room only: $5600.

Financial Aid Program-specific awards: 100 Institutional Scholarships for students demonstrating merit ($1500), 50 Cent. Student Awards for those students demonstrating merit and need ($1000).

Application Procedures Students admitted directly into the professional program freshman year. Deadline for freshmen and transfers: July 15. Notification date for freshmen and transfers: August 1. Required: essay, high school transcript, college transcript(s) for transfer students, minimum 2.0 high school GPA, letter of recommendation, portfolio, SAT or ACT test scores (minimum combined SAT score of 1500, minimum composite ACT score of 20). Recommended: minimum 3.0 high school GPA, interview. Portfolio reviews held as needed on campus and off campus; the submission of slides may be substituted for portfolios if requested by applicant.

Web Site http://www.watkins.edu

Undergraduate Contact Ms. Linda Schwab, Admissions, Watkins College of Art and De-

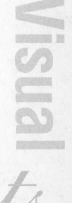

Watkins College of Art and Design (continued)

sign, 2298 MetroCenter Boulevard, Nashville, Tennessee 37228; 615-383-4848, fax: 615-383-4849, e-mail address: admissions@watkins.edu

Wayne State University

Detroit, Michigan

State-supported, coed. Urban campus. Total enrollment: 33,137 (2006).

Degrees Bachelor of Arts in the areas of fashion design and merchandising, art history, art; Bachelor of Fine Arts in the area of art; Bachelor of Science in the area of fashion design and merchandising. Majors and concentrations: apparel design, art history, ceramic art and design, drawing, electronic arts, fashion design, fashion merchandising, fibers, graphic design, industrial design, interior design, jewelry and metalsmithing, painting, painting/drawing, photography, printmaking, sculpture. Graduate degrees offered: Master of Arts in the areas of fine arts, art history, fashion design and merchandising; Master of Fine Arts in the area of art. Cross-registration with University of Windsor (Canada).

Enrollment 926 total; 875 undergraduate, 51 graduate.

Art Student Profile 60% females, 40% males, 25% minorities, 5% international.

Art Faculty 32 total (full-time), 39 total (part-time). 100% of full-time faculty have terminal degrees. Graduate students teach a few undergraduate courses. Undergraduate student–faculty ratio: 23:1.

Student Life Student groups/activities include Fashion Design and Merchandising Club, Art Student Art Organization.

Expenses for 2006–2007 Application fee: $30. State resident tuition: $6012 full-time. Nonresident tuition: $13,770 full-time. Mandatory fees: $800 full-time. College room and board: $6575. Room and board charges vary according to housing facility. Special program-related fees: $15–$275 per course for materials, model fees, special course expenses.

Financial Aid Program-specific awards: 4 talent awards for program majors ($1600), 1 Becker Award for program majors ($1500), 10 en-dowed scholarships for program majors ($1300), 2 endowed travel scholarships for program majors ($2000).

Application Procedures Students admitted directly into the professional program freshman year. Deadline for freshmen and transfers: continuous. Required: high school transcript, college transcript(s) for transfer students, minimum 2.0 high school GPA, SAT or ACT test scores (minimum composite ACT score of 21), possible portfolio review for graphic design, interior design, or industrial design for transfer students.

Web Site http://www.art.wayne.edu

Undergraduate Contact Michele Porter, Academic Services Officer II, Department of Art and Art History, Wayne State University, 150 Art Building, Detroit, Michigan 48202; 313-577-2980, fax: 313-577-3491, e-mail address: aa2961@wayne.edu

Graduate Contact Stanley Rosenthal, Graduate Advisor, Department of Art and Art History, Wayne State University, 150 Art Building, Detroit, Michigan 48202; 313-577-2980, fax: 313-577-3491.

Weber State University

Ogden, Utah

State-supported, coed. Urban campus. Total enrollment: 18,303. Art program established 1965.

Web Site http://weber.edu/

Leigh Gerdine College of Fine Arts
Webster University

St. Louis, Missouri

Independent, coed. Suburban campus. Total enrollment: 7,840. Art program established 1960.

Degrees Bachelor of Arts in the areas of studio art, art history and criticism, art education K-12 certification; Bachelor of Fine Arts in the areas of studio art, graphic design. Majors and concentrations: art education, art history, art therapy, ceramic art and design, ceramics, graphic design, media arts, media performance, painting/drawing, photography, printmaking, sculpture. Graduate degrees offered: Master of Arts in the areas of studio art, art history and criticism. Cross-registration with various colleges in St. Louis.

Enrollment 195 total; 180 undergraduate, 15 graduate.

Art Student Profile 60% females, 40% males, 11% minorities, 4% international.

Art Faculty 10 total (full-time), 21 total (part-time). 100% of full-time faculty have terminal degrees. Graduate students do not teach undergraduate courses. Undergraduate student–faculty ratio: 10:1.

Student Life Student groups/activities include Art Council, Graduate Art Council.

Expenses for 2007–2008 Application fee: $25. Comprehensive fee: $27,550 includes full-time tuition ($19,330) and college room and board ($8220). College room only: $4100. Full-time tuition varies according to program. Room and board charges vary according to board plan and housing facility. Special program-related fees: $50–$150 per course for studio lab fee.

Financial Aid Program-specific awards: Sr. Gabriel Mary Hoare Scholarship for visual arts students.

Application Procedures Students apply for admission into the professional program by junior year. Deadline for freshmen and transfers: continuous. Notification date for freshmen and transfers: August 15. Required: essay, high school transcript, college transcript(s) for transfer students, minimum 2.0 high school GPA, 2 letters of recommendation, interview, portfolio, SAT or ACT test scores (minimum combined SAT score of 1500, minimum composite ACT score of 21). Recommended: minimum 3.0 high school GPA. Portfolio reviews held 12 times on campus and off campus in Vienna, Austria; the submission of slides may be substituted for portfolios when distance is prohibitive.

Web Site http://www.webster.edu/depts/finearts/art

Undergraduate Contact Carrie Indelicato, Portfolio Review Coordinator, Office of Admissions, Webster University, 470 East Lockwood Avenue, St. Louis, Missouri 63119-3194; 314-968-7001, fax: 314-968-7115, e-mail address: cgeorge@webster.edu

Graduate Contact Dr. Jeffrey A. Hughes, Graduate Program Coordinator, Department of Art, Webster University, 470 East Lockwood Avenue, St. Louis, Missouri 63119-3194; 314-968-7159, fax: 314-968-7139, e-mail address: hughes@webster.edu

West Chester University of Pennsylvania

West Chester, Pennsylvania

State-supported, coed. Suburban campus. Total enrollment: 12,882.

Degrees Bachelor of Arts in the area of art; Bachelor of Fine Arts in the area of studio art. Majors and concentrations: art/fine arts, ceramics, computer graphics, painting/drawing, sculpture.

Enrollment 225 total; all undergraduate.

Art Student Profile 60% females, 40% males.

Art Faculty 12 undergraduate (full-time), 3 undergraduate (part-time). 100% of full-time faculty have terminal degrees. Graduate students do not teach undergraduate courses. Undergraduate student–faculty ratio: 10:1.

Student Life Student groups/activities include Print Club, Art Association, American Institute of Graphic Arts.

Expenses for 2006–2007 Application fee: $35. State resident tuition: $5038 full-time. Nonresident tuition: $12,598 full-time. Mandatory fees: $1255 full-time. Full-time tuition and fees vary according to course load. College room and board: $6342. College room only: $4220. Room and board charges vary according to board plan and housing facility.

Financial Aid Program-specific awards: 2 McKinney Scholarships for junior painting majors ($1000), 1 Bessie Grubb Scholarship for junior graphic design majors ($1000), 1 Hawthorne Scholarship for painting majors ($1000).

Application Procedures Students admitted directly into the professional program freshman year. Deadline for freshmen and transfers: continuous. Required: essay, high school transcript, college transcript(s) for transfer students, minimum 2.0 high school GPA, SAT or ACT test scores. Recommended: minimum 3.0 high school GPA.

Web Site http://www.wcupa.edu/

Undergraduate Contact Mr. John Baker, Chair, Art Department, West Chester University of

West Chester University of Pennsylvania (continued)

Pennsylvania, Mitchell Hall, West Chester, Pennsylvania 19383; 610-436-2755, e-mail address: jbaker@wcupa.edu

Western Carolina University

Cullowhee, North Carolina

State-supported, coed. Rural campus. Total enrollment: 8,861. Art program established 1964.

Degrees Bachelor of Fine Arts in the areas of studio art, graphic design. Majors and concentrations: book arts, ceramic art and design, graphic design, painting/drawing, photography, printmaking, sculpture. Graduate degrees offered: Master of Art in Education; Master of Arts in Teaching; Master of Fine Arts in the area of fine arts. Cross-registration with Penland School of Crafts.

Enrollment 313 total; 296 undergraduate, 4 graduate, 13 nonprofessional degree.

Art Student Profile 50% females, 50% males, 3% minorities, 1% international.

Art Faculty 15 total (full-time), 13 total (part-time). 100% of full-time faculty have terminal degrees. Graduate students teach a few undergraduate courses. Undergraduate student–faculty ratio: 15:1.

Student Life Student groups/activities include Annual Student Exhibition, Nomad (student art and literature publication), Art Students League.

Expenses for 2006–2007 Application fee: $40. State resident tuition: $1,972 full-time. Nonresident tuition: $11,487 full-time. Mandatory fees: $2637 full-time. College room and board: $5210. College room only: $2660. Room and board charges vary according to board plan and housing facility.

Financial Aid Program-specific awards: 1 Lorraine Stone Scholarship for non-traditional students ($1000), 4 departmental scholarships for program students ($500).

Application Procedures Students admitted directly into the professional program freshman year. Deadline for freshmen and transfers: continuous. Notification date for freshmen and transfers: August 1. Required: high school transcript, college transcript(s) for transfer students, minimum 2.0 high school GPA, 3 letters of recommendation, SAT or ACT test scores. Recommended: interview, portfolio. Portfolio reviews held continuously on campus; the submission of slides may be substituted for portfolios (slides preferred).

Web Site http://www.wcu.edu/as/arts

Undergraduate Contact Mr. Richard Tichich, Director, Department of Art, Western Carolina University, Cullowhee, North Carolina 28723; 828-227-2464, fax: 828-227-7505, e-mail address: rtichich@wcu.edu

Graduate Contact Mr. Richard Tichich, Director, School of Art and Design, Western Carolina University, Cullowhee, North Carolina 28723; 828-227-2464, fax: 828-227-7505, e-mail address: rtichich@wcu.edu

Western Illinois University

Macomb, Illinois

State-supported, coed. Small town campus. Total enrollment: 13,602. Art program established 1938.

Degrees Bachelor of Arts in the area of teacher education; Bachelor of Fine Arts in the area of art. Majors and concentrations: art education, ceramics, graphic design, metals, painting/drawing, printmaking, sculpture, studio art, watercolors. Cross-registration with Spoon River College.

Enrollment 149 total; 52 undergraduate, 97 nonprofessional degree.

Art Student Profile 58% females, 42% males, 11% minorities, 1% international.

Art Faculty 16 undergraduate (full-time), 2 undergraduate (part-time). 100% of full-time faculty have terminal degrees. Graduate students do not teach undergraduate courses. Undergraduate student–faculty ratio: 10:1.

Student Life Student groups/activities include Student Art League, National Art Education Association Student Chapter, Clay Club. Special housing available for art students.

Expenses for 2007–2008 Application fee: $30. State resident tuition: $5895 full-time. Nonresident tuition: $8843 full-time. Mandatory fees: $2184 full-time. Full-time tuition and fees vary according to course load, location, and student level. College room and board: $6808.

College room only: $4148. Special program-related fees: $75–$100 per semester for material fees.

Financial Aid Program-specific awards: 4 Bulkeley Scholarships for program majors ($600), 10 talent grants for program majors ($3300), 20 tuition waivers for program majors ($1400), 4 freshman scholarships for incoming freshmen program majors ($500), 1 Purdum Scholarship for art education majors ($1000).

Application Procedures Students admitted directly into the professional program freshman year. Deadline for freshmen and transfers: August 10. Notification date for freshmen and transfers: continuous. Required: high school transcript, college transcript(s) for transfer students, SAT or ACT test scores (minimum combined SAT score of 920, minimum composite ACT score of 20), ACT score of 18, SAT score of 850, if in upper 40% of high school graduating class, minimum 2.5 high school GPA. Recommended: portfolio. Portfolio reviews held continuously on campus; the submission of slides may be substituted for portfolios when distance is prohibitive or for large work.

Web Site http://www.wiu.edu

Undergraduate Contact Ms. Jan Clough, Chair, Department of Art, Western Illinois University, 32 Garwood Hall, Macomb, Illinois 61455; 309-298-1549, fax: 309-298-2605, e-mail address: jb-clough@wiu.edu

Frostic School of Art
Western Michigan University

Kalamazoo, Michigan

State-supported, coed. Urban campus. Total enrollment: 24,841.

Degrees Bachelor of Fine Arts in the areas of painting, ceramics, sculpture, photography, graphic design, printmaking. Majors and concentrations: art education, art history, art/fine arts, ceramics, graphic design, metals and jewelry, painting, photography, photography and intermedia, printmaking, sculpture. Graduate degrees offered: Master of Arts in the area of art education. Cross-registration with Michigan colleges and universities and community colleges. Program accredited by NASAD.

Enrollment 668 total; 385 undergraduate, 8 graduate, 275 nonprofessional degree.

Art Student Profile 70% females, 30% males, 10% minorities, 1% international.

Art Faculty 21 total (full-time), 18 total (part-time). 100% of full-time faculty have terminal degrees. Graduate students teach a few undergraduate courses. Undergraduate student–faculty ratio: 25:1.

Student Life Student groups/activities include Students in Design, Michigan Art Education Association.

Expenses for 2006–2007 Application fee: $35. State resident tuition: $6176 full-time. Nonresident tuition: $16,116 full-time. Mandatory fees: $690 full-time. Full-time tuition and fees vary according to course load, location, and student level. College room and board: $6877. College room only: $3638. Room and board charges vary according to board plan. Special program-related fees: $25–$150 per class for studio fees.

Financial Aid Program-specific awards: 1 departmental scholarship for freshmen with outstanding portfolios ($500), 5 James Kerr and Rose Netzorg Kerr Awards for outstanding students ($400), 9 Art Star Awards for junior/senior art majors ($200), 2 Elizabeth Smutz Awards for outstanding art education majors ($600), 2 Haig and Janette Tashjian Scholarships for outstanding art education majors demonstrating need ($1100), 2 Walter F. Enz Memorial Awards for outstanding art students ($1000), 7 Angie Gayman Carmer Art Scholarships for art students with minimum 3.5 GPA demonstrating financial need ($1400), 4 foundation scholarships for outstanding students in foundation courses ($375), 20 enrichment grants for full-time art students ($600).

Application Procedures Students apply for admission into the professional program by freshman, sophomore year. Deadline for freshmen and transfers: March 14. Notification date for freshmen and transfers: April 1. Required: essay, high school transcript, college transcript(s) for transfer students, minimum 2.0 high school GPA, letter of recommendation, portfolio, ACT test score only. Recommended: minimum 3.0 high school GPA. Portfolio reviews held once for graphic design majors and 2 times for other program majors on

Western Michigan University (continued)

campus; the submission of slides may be substituted for portfolios on a case-by-case basis.

Web Site http://www.wmich.edu/art

Undergraduate Contact John Kollig, Academic Advisor, Department of Art, Western Michigan University, 2104 Richmond Center, Kalamazoo, Michigan 49008-5213; 269-387-2440, fax: 269-387-2477, e-mail address: john.kollig@wmich.edu

Graduate Contact Ellen Armstrong, Academic Advisor, Department of Art, Western Michigan University, 2104 Richmond Center, Kalamazoo, Michigan 49008-5213; 269-387-2440, fax: 269-387-2477, e-mail address: ellen.armstrong@wmich.edu

West Texas A&M University

Canyon, Texas

State-supported, coed. Small town campus. Total enrollment: 7,412. Art program established 1953.

Degrees Bachelor of Fine Arts in the areas of studio art, graphic design. Majors and concentrations: ceramics, computer art, glassworking, graphic design, jewelry and metalsmithing, painting/drawing, printmaking, sculpture. Graduate degrees offered: Master of Arts in the area of art; Master of Fine Arts in the area of studio art.

Enrollment 106 total; 80 undergraduate, 21 graduate, 5 nonprofessional degree.

Art Student Profile 48% females, 52% males, 10% minorities, 3% international.

Art Faculty 5 total (full-time), 3 total (part-time). 100% of full-time faculty have terminal degrees. Graduate students teach a few undergraduate courses. Undergraduate student–faculty ratio: 16:1.

Student Life Student groups/activities include Art This.

Expenses for 2007–2008 Application fee: $25. State resident tuition: $3516 full-time. Nonresident tuition: $11,856 full-time. Mandatory fees: $1404 full-time. College room and board: $5506. College room only: $2886. Room and board charges vary according to board plan. Special program-related fees: $7–$30 per course for lab fees.

Financial Aid Program-specific awards: 2 Levi Margaret Cole Endowment Awards for program majors ($200–$500), 1 Charles Hohmann Endowment Award for graphic design majors ($400), 1 Mary Moody Northen Endowment Award for program majors ($200–$500), 1 Isabel Robinson Scholarship for program majors ($200–$500), 1 Emmit Smith Art Scholarship for studio art students ($200–$500), 12 Foundation for Fine Arts Awards for program majors ($200–$500), 6 Sybil Harrington Scholarships for program majors ($500–$1000), 4 Harrington Bequest Awards for program majors ($200–$500), 1 Georgia O'Keefe Scholarship for program majors ($500–$600).

Application Procedures Students admitted directly into the professional program freshman year. Deadline for freshmen and transfers: continuous. Required: high school transcript, college transcript(s) for transfer students, SAT or ACT test scores. Recommended: 2 letters of recommendation, interview, portfolio. Portfolio reviews held once and as needed on campus; the submission of slides may be substituted for portfolios when distance is prohibitive.

Web Site http://www.wtamu.edu

Undergraduate Contact Mr. Royal Brantley, Head, Department of Art, Theater and Dance, West Texas A&M University, WTAMU Box 60747, Canyon, Texas 79016; 806-651-2799, fax: 806-651-2818, e-mail address: rbrantley@mail.wtamu.edu

Graduate Contact Mr. David Rindlisbacher, Graduate Program Coordinator, Department of Art, Theater and Dance, West Texas A&M University, WTAMU Box 60747, Canyon, Texas 79016; 806-651-2792, fax: 806-651-2818, e-mail address: drindlisbacher@mail.wtamu.edu

West Virginia University

Morgantown, West Virginia

State-supported, coed. Small town campus. Total enrollment: 27,115. Art program established 1897.

Degrees Bachelor of Fine Arts. Majors and concentrations: art education, ceramics, graphic design, intermedia, painting/drawing, printmaking, sculpture. Graduate degrees offered: Master of Arts in the areas of art education, studio art; Master of Fine Arts in the areas of painting, printmaking, sculpture, ceramics, intermedia graphic design. Program accredited by NASAD.

Enrollment 328 total; 310 undergraduate, 18 graduate.

Art Student Profile 55% females, 45% males, 6% minorities, 4% international.

Art Faculty 16 total (full-time), 3 total (part-time). 98% of full-time faculty have terminal degrees. Graduate students teach a few undergraduate courses. Undergraduate student–faculty ratio: 17:1.

Student Life Student groups/activities include Student Art Association, National Art Education Association Student Chapter. Special housing available for art students.

Expenses for 2007–2008 Application fee: $25. State resident tuition: $4722 full-time. Nonresident tuition: $14,600 full-time. Full-time tuition varies according to location, program, and reciprocity agreements. College room and board: $7046. College room only: $3728. Room and board charges vary according to board plan, housing facility, and location. Special program-related fees: $75 per 3 credit hours for expendable supplies for studio courses.

Financial Aid Program-specific awards: 12 Fine Arts Awards for program students ($2000–$6000), 3 Loyalty Permanent Endowment Awards for state residents ($1000), 1 Gabriel Fellowship for state residents ($1000), 6 Mesaros Scholarships for junior and senior art majors ($500–$2000).

Application Procedures Students apply for admission into the professional program by sophomore year. Deadline for freshmen and transfers: February 1. Notification date for freshmen and transfers: March 1. Required: high school transcript, college transcript(s) for transfer students, minimum 2.0 high school GPA, letter of recommendation, portfolio, SAT or ACT test scores, minimum combined SAT scores 910 (state residents), minimum combined SAT scores 950 (non-residents), minimum composite ACT scores-19 (state residents), minimum composite ACT scores-20 (non-residents). Recommended: interview. Portfolio reviews held 3 times on campus; the submission of slides may be substituted for portfolios if original work is not available or distance is prohibitive.

Web Site http://www.wvu.edu/~ccarts
Undergraduate Contact Ms. Kristina Olson, Associate Chair, Division of Art, West Virginia University, College of Creative Arts, PO Box 6111, Morgantown, West Virginia 26506-6111; 304-293-4841 ext. 3210, fax: 304-293-5731, e-mail address: kristina.olson2@mail.wvu.edu
Graduate Contact Ms. Alison Helm, Interim Chair, Division of Art, West Virginia University, College of Creative Arts, PO Box 6111, Morgantown, West Virginia 26506-6111; 304-293-4841 ext. 3138, fax: 304-293-5731.

Williams Baptist College
Walnut Ridge, Arkansas

Independent Southern Baptist, coed. Rural campus. Total enrollment: 629. Art program established 1994.

Degrees Bachelor of Arts in the area of studio art. Majors and concentrations: ceramics, painting, printmaking.

Enrollment 5 total; all undergraduate.

Art Student Profile 100% females.

Art Faculty 1 undergraduate (full-time), 1 undergraduate (part-time). 100% of full-time faculty have terminal degrees. Graduate students do not teach undergraduate courses. Undergraduate student–faculty ratio: 3:1.

Student Life Student groups/activities include museum trips.

Expenses for 2007–2008 Application fee: $20. Comprehensive fee: $15,070 includes full-time tuition ($9700), mandatory fees ($670), and college room and board ($4700). Special program-related fees: $75 per course for studio fee.

Financial Aid Program-specific awards: 4 art scholarships for program majors ($500).

Application Procedures Students admitted directly into the professional program freshman year. Deadline for freshmen and transfers: continuous. Required: high school transcript, college transcript(s) for transfer students, portfolio, SAT or ACT test scores. Recommended: interview, minimum 2.5 high school GPA. Portfolio reviews held once per semester after completion of foundation courses on campus; the submission of slides may be substituted for portfolios when distance is prohibitive.

Williams Baptist College (continued)

Web Site http://www.wbcoll.edu

Undergraduate Contact Dr. David Midkiff, Chairman, Department of Art, Williams Baptist College, PO Box 3681 WBC, Walnut Ridge, Arkansas 72476; 870-759-4141, fax: 870-886-3924, e-mail address: dmidkiff@wbcoll.edu

Wright State University

Dayton, Ohio

State-supported, coed. Suburban campus. Total enrollment: 16,207. Art program established 1964.

Degrees Bachelor of Fine Arts in the areas of art education, fine arts. Majors and concentrations: art education, painting, photography, printmaking, sculpture.

Enrollment 206 total; 139 undergraduate, 67 nonprofessional degree.

Art Student Profile 70% females, 30% males, 21% minorities, 4% international.

Art Faculty 11 undergraduate (full-time), 7 undergraduate (part-time). 100% of full-time faculty have terminal degrees. Graduate students do not teach undergraduate courses. Undergraduate student–faculty ratio: 8:1.

Student Life Student groups/activities include Graphic Arts Club.

Expenses for 2007–2008 Application fee: $30. State resident tuition: $7278 full-time. Nonresident tuition: $14,004 full-time. College room and board: $7180. Special program-related fees: $35–$120 per course for materials fee.

Financial Aid Program-specific awards: 10–20 Art Department Merit Scholarships for program majors ($1800), 1–2 Arts Gala Scholarships for entering program majors ($5000).

Application Procedures Students apply for admission into the professional program by sophomore year. Deadline for freshmen and transfers: continuous. Required: high school transcript, college transcript(s) for transfer students, SAT or ACT test scores.

Web Site http://www.wright.edu

Undergraduate Contact Dr. Linda Caron, Chair, Department of Art and Art History, Wright State University, Creative Arts Center A-226, Colonel Glenn Highway, Dayton, Ohio 45435; 937-775-2896, fax: 937-775-3049, e-mail address: linda.caron@wright.edu

York University

Toronto, Ontario, Canada

Province-supported, coed. Urban campus. Total enrollment: 50,691. Art program established 1969.

Degrees Bachelor of Design in the area of communications design; Bachelor of Fine Arts in the area of visual arts. Majors and concentrations: design, drawing, new media, painting, photography, printmaking, sculpture. Graduate degrees offered: Master of Fine Arts in the area of visual arts; Master of Design in Designed Objects in the areas of graphic, communications design. Mandatory cross-registration with Sheridan College (BDes program only).

Enrollment 1,256 total; 1,037 undergraduate, 35 graduate, 184 nonprofessional degree.

Art Student Profile 77% females, 23% males, 3% international.

Art Faculty 39 total (full-time), 39 total (part-time). 88% of full-time faculty have terminal degrees. Graduate students teach a few undergraduate courses. Undergraduate student–faculty ratio: 12:1.

Student Life Student groups/activities include Visual Arts Student Council, Creative Arts Students Association, Design Students Association.

Expenses for 2006–2007 Application fee: $90 Canadian dollars. Tuition, fee, and room and board charges are reported in Canadian dollars. Comprehensive fee: $11,258 includes full-time tuition ($5065) and college room and board ($6193). College room only: $3793. Full-time tuition varies according to course load, degree level, and program. Room and board charges vary according to board plan and housing facility. International student tuition: $15,065 full-time. Special program-related fees: $15–$150 per semester for lab fees for photography, sculpture, printmaking, and new media.

Financial Aid Program-specific awards: 6 talent awards for applicants with outstanding portfolios ($1000), 5 Harry Rowe Bursaries for those demonstrating achievement or potential in artistic or scholarly work ($1000–$2000), Fine Arts Bursaries for academically qualified applicants demonstrating financial need, 6 Jack Bush Scholarships for those demonstrating merit in studio work ($800), 1 L.L. Odette

Sculpture Scholarship for juniors or seniors showing excellence in sculpture ($2000), 2 Michael Plexman Awards for juniors or seniors demonstrating creative innovation and need ($2000), 1 Department of Visual Arts Award for those demonstrating financial need and with B average ($1000), Joseph Drapell Award for those demonstrating financial need and academic and artistic excellence.

Application Procedures Students admitted directly into the professional program freshman year. Deadline for freshmen and transfers: March 1. Notification date for freshmen: June 30; transfers: July 15. Required: high school transcript, college transcript(s) for transfer students, minimum 3.0 high school GPA, portfolio, SAT, ACT or Canadian equivalent, interview for applicants within a reasonable distance, questionnaire. Recommended: interview. Portfolio reviews held 15 times on campus; the submission of slides may be substituted for portfolios when distance is prohibitive or for large works of art.

Web Site http://www.yorku.ca/finearts/visa/

Undergraduate Contact Susan Wessels, Coordinator, Recruitment and Liaison, Student and Academic Services, York University, 201R Goldfarb Centre for Fine Arts, Toronto, Ontario M3J 1P3, Canada; 416-736-2100 ext. 77141, fax: 416-736-5447, e-mail address: swessels@yorku.ca

Graduate Contact Yvonne Singer, Graduate Director, Department of Visual Arts, York University, 235 GCFA, 4700 Keele Street, Toronto, Ontario M3J 1P3, Canada; 416-736-5533, fax: 416-736-5875.

Youngstown State University

Youngstown, Ohio

State-supported, coed. Urban campus. Total enrollment: 13,178. Art program established 1927.

Degrees Bachelor of Arts in the area of art history; Bachelor of Fine Arts in the area of studio art; Bachelor of Science in the area of art education. Majors and concentrations: art and technology, art education, art history, general studio, graphic design, individualized major, painting, photography, printmaking, spatial arts. Program accredited by NASAD.

Enrollment 313 total; 307 undergraduate, 6 graduate.

Art Student Profile 55% females, 45% males, 9% minorities, 2% international.

Art Faculty 16 undergraduate (full-time), 20 undergraduate (part-time). 95% of full-time faculty have terminal degrees. Graduate students do not teach undergraduate courses. Undergraduate student–faculty ratio: 13:1.

Student Life Student groups/activities include Student Art Association, American Institute of Graphic Arts Student Chapter, Spatial Arts Alliance.

Expenses for 2007–2008 Application fee: $30. State resident tuition: $6492 full-time. Nonresident tuition: $12,165 full-time. Mandatory fees: $229 full-time. Full-time tuition and fees vary according to course load. College room and board: $6740. Room and board charges vary according to board plan and housing facility. Special program-related fees: $45 per course for art history classes, $60 per course for studio lab fees.

Financial Aid Program-specific awards: Beecher Talent Scholarships for freshmen (renewable) ($1000), Scholastics Portfolio Award for freshmen (renewable) ($2000), Trumbull County Scholarship for freshmen (renewable) ($300), Cubbison Painting Award for freshmen ($2500).

Application Procedures Students apply for admission into the professional program by sophomore year. Deadline for freshmen and transfers: continuous. Required: high school transcript, college transcript(s) for transfer students, portfolio for scholarship consideration. Recommended: SAT or ACT test scores. Portfolio reviews held twice on campus; the submission of slides may be substituted for portfolios.

Web Site http://www.fpa.ysu.edu/art/index.html

Undergraduate Contact Chair, Department of Art, Youngstown State University, 1 University Plaza, Youngstown, Ohio 44555; 330-941-3627, fax: 330-941-7183, e-mail address: art@cc.ysu.edu

Appendixes

Summer Programs in Art

ABBEY ROAD OVERSEAS PROGRAMS

Abbey Road Overseas Programs-Pre-College: Art History, Studio Art, and Italian-Florence

Dr. Arthur Kian
Managing Director
8904 Rangely Avenue
West Hollywood, CA 90048
Phone: 888-462-2239
Fax: 866-488-4642
E-mail: info@goabbeyroad.com
Web site:
www.goabbeyroad.com/florence.htm

APPEL FARM ARTS AND MUSIC CENTER

Appel Farm Summer Arts Camp

Ms. Jennie Quinn
Camp Director
PO Box 888
Elmer, NJ 08318-0888
Phone: 856-358-2472
Fax: 856-358-6513
E-mail: appelcamp@aol.com
Web site: www.appelfarm.org

ATELIER DES ARTS

Francia Tobacman
Director
55 Bethune Street, B645
New York, NY 10014
Phone: 212-727-1756
Fax: 212-691-0631
E-mail: info@atelierdesarts.org
Web site: www.atelierdesarts.org

BELVOIR TERRACE

Summer Contact
Ms. Nancy S. Goldberg
Director
80 Cliffwood Street
Lenox, MA 01240
Phone: 413-637-0555
Fax: 413-637-4651
E-mail: belvoirt@aol.com
Web site: www.belvoirterrace.com

Winter Contact
Ms. Nancy S. Goldberg
Director
101 West 79th Street
New York, NY 10024
Phone: 212-580-3398
Fax: 212-579-7282
E-mail: info@belvoirterrace
Web site: www.belvoirterrace.com

CALIFORNIA STATE SUMMER SCHOOL FOR THE ARTS/INNER SPARK

Shelly Reyes
Office Technician
1010 Hurley
Suite 185
Sacramento, CA 95825
Phone: 916-274-5815
Fax: 916-274-5814
E-mail: application@innerspark.us
Web site: www.innerspark.us

CAPITOL REGION EDUCATION COUNCIL

Center for Creative Youth

Nancy Wolfe
Director
Wesleyan University
350 High Street
Middletown, CT 06459
Phone: 860-685-3307
Fax: 860-685-3311
E-mail: ccy@wesleyan.edu
Web site: www.crec.org/ccy

CARNEGIE MELLON UNIVERSITY

Carnegie Mellon University Pre-College Program in the Fine Arts

Office of Admission, Pre-College Programs
5000 Forbes Avenue
Pittsburgh, PA 15213-3890
Phone: 412-268-2082
Fax: 412-268-7838
E-mail: precollege@andrew.cmu.edu
Web site: www.cmu.edu/enrollment/pre-college

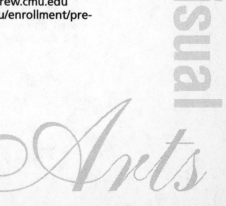

Visual *Arts*

CHAUTAUQUA INSTITUTION

Chautauqua School of Art

Sarah Malinoski, Coordinator of
Student Services
PO Box 1098
Chautauqua, NY 14722
Phone: 800-836-ARTS
716-357-6233
Fax: 716-357-9014
E-mail: art@ciweb.org
Web site: www.ciweb.org

CHOATE ROSEMARY HALL

Choate Rosemary Hall Summer Arts Conservatory-Visual Arts Program

Mrs. Randi J. Brandt
Admissions Director, Arts Conservatory
Paul Mellon Arts Center
333 Christian Street
Wallingford, CT 06492
Phone: 203-697-2423
Fax: 203-697-2396
E-mail: rbrandt@choate.edu
Web site:
www.choate.edu/summerprograms

DUKE YOUTH PROGRAMS-DUKE UNIVERSITY CONTINUING STUDIES

EXPRESSIONS! Duke Fine Arts Camp

Youth Program Director
203 Bishop's House
Box 90702
Durham, NC 27708
Phone: 919-684-6259
Fax: 919-681-8235
E-mail: youth@duke.edu
Web site: www.learnmore.duke.edu/youth

THE EXPERIMENT IN INTERNATIONAL LIVING

France, Four-Week Homestay and Photography

Chris Frantz
Deputy Director
Summer Abroad, Kipling Road
PO Box 676
Brattleboro, VT 05302-0676
Phone: 800-345-2929
Fax: 802-258-3428
E-mail: eil@worldlearning.org
Web site: www.usexperiment.org

United Kingdom Filmmaking Program and Homestay

Annie Thompson
Enrollment Director
Summer Abroad, Kipling Road
PO Box 676
Brattleboro, VT 05302-0676
Phone: 800-345-2929
Fax: 802-258-3428
E-mail: eil@worldlearning.org
Web site: www.usexperiment.org

HOLLINS UNIVERSITY

Hollinsummer

Admissions Office
PO Box 9707
Roanoke, VA 24020
Phone: 800-456-9595
Fax: 540-362-6218
E-mail: huadm@hollins.edu
Web site: www.hollins.edu/

THE HOTCHKISS SCHOOL

Hotchkiss School Summer Music Studies

Christie Gurney Rawlings
Admission and Student Life Director
PO Box 800
Lakeville, CT 06039
Phone: 860-435-3173
Fax: 860-435-4413
E-mail: crawling@hotchkiss.org
Web site: www.hotchkiss.org/
AboutHotchkiss/SummerProg.asp

IDYLLWILD ARTS FOUNDATION

Idyllwild Arts Summer Program-Youth Arts Center

Diane Dennis
Registrar, Summer Program
PO Box 38
Idyllwild, CA 92549
Phone: 951-659-2171 Ext. 2365
Fax: 951-659-4552
E-mail: summer@idyllwildarts.org
Web site: www.idyllwildarts.org

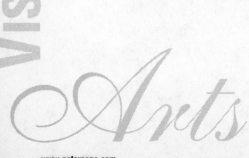

INTERLOCHEN CENTER FOR THE ARTS

Interlochen Arts Camp

Kelye Modarelli
Director of Admissions
PO Box 199
Interlochen, MI 49643
Phone: 231-276-7472
Fax: 231-276-7464
E-mail: admissions@interlochen.org
Web site: www.interlochen.org/

INTERN EXCHANGE INTERNATIONAL, LTD.

IEI-Digital Media Plus Programme

IEI-Fashion and Design Plus Programme

IEI-Fine Arts Plus Programme

IEI-Photography Plus Programme

IEI-Theatre Plus Programme

Nina Miller Glickman
Director
1858 Mallard Lane
Villanova, PA 19085
Phone: 610-527-6066
Fax: 610-527-5499
E-mail: info@internexchange.com
Web site: www.internexchange.com

LEYSIN AMERICAN SCHOOL IN SWITZERLAND

Summer in Switzerland

Mr. Tim Sloman
Director of Summer in Switzerland
Admissions Office
Leysin American School
Leysin 1854, Switzerland
Phone: 41-24-493-3777
Fax: 41-24-494-1585
E-mail: admissions@las.ch
Web site: www.las.ch/summer

MASSACHUSETTS COLLEGE OF ART

Creative Vacation

Summer Studios

Lin Lufkin
Program Administrative Assistant
621 Huntington Avenue
Boston, MA 02115
Phone: 617-879-7170
Fax: 617-879-7171
E-mail: llufkin@massart.edu
Web site: www.massartplus.org

NEW YORK FILM ACADEMY

The New York Film Academy, Disney-MGM Studios, FL

The New York Film Academy, Harvard University, Cambridge, MA

The New York Film Academy in Florence, Italy

The New York Film Academy/Saint Catherine's College at Oxford University

The New York Film Academy in Paris

The New York Film Academy, Universal Studios, Hollywood, CA

Admissions
100 East 17th Street
New York, NY 10003
Phone: 212-674-4300
Fax: 212-477-1414
E-mail: film@nyfa.com
Web site: www.nyfa.com

NEW YORK UNIVERSITY, TISCH SCHOOL OF THE ARTS

Tisch School of the Arts-International High School Program-Dublin

Tisch School of the Arts-International High School Program-Paris

Tisch School of the Arts-Summer High School Programs

Mr. Josh Murray
Assistant Director of Recruitment
Special Programs
721 Broadway
12th Floor
New York, NY 10003
Phone: 212-998-1500
Fax: 212-995-4610
E-mail: tisch.special.info@nyu.edu
Web site:
http://specialprograms.tisch.nyu.edu

OXFORD MEDIA SCHOOL

Oxford Media School-Film

Oxford Media School-Film Master Class

Oxford Media School at New College
110 Pricefield Road
Toronto, ON M4W 1Z9, Canada
Phone: 416-964-0746
Fax: 416-929-4230
E-mail: newsco@sympatico.ca
Web site: www.oxfordmediaschool.com

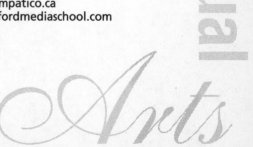

Visual *Arts*

PARSONS THE NEW SCHOOL FOR DESIGN

Parsons Pre-College Academy

Parsons Summer Intensive Studies-New York

Parsons Summer Intensive Studies-Paris

Charlotte Rice
Director, Pre-Enrollment Programs
66 Fifth Avenue
New York, NY 10011
Phone: 212-229-8925
Fax: 212-229-8975
E-mail: summer@newschool.edu
Web site: www.parsons.edu/summer

THE PUTNEY SCHOOL

The Putney School Summer Arts Program

Maria Ogden
Administrative Coordinator
Elm Lea Farm
418 Houghton Brook Road
Putney, VT 05346
Phone: 802-387-6297
Fax: 802-387-6216
E-mail: summer@putneyschool.org
Web site: www.putneyschool.org/summer

RENSSELAER POLYTECHNIC INSTITUTE

Summer@Rensselaer

Mr. Michael L. Gunther
Program Manager for Recruitment
CII Low Center, Suite 4011
110 8th Street
Troy, NY 12180-3590
Phone: 518-276-8351
Fax: 518-276-8738
E-mail: gunthm@rpi.edu
Web site: www.summer.rpi.edu

RHODE ISLAND SCHOOL OF DESIGN

**Rhode Island School of Design
Pre-College Program**

Mr. Marc Torick
Continuing Education Office/Summer
   Programs
2 College Street
Providence, RI 02903-2787
Phone: 401-454-6200
Fax: 401-454-6218
E-mail: cemail@risd.edu
Web site: www.risd.edu/precollege.cfm

RINGLING SCHOOL OF ART AND DESIGN

**Ringling School of Art and Design Pre-
College Perspective**

Director of Continuing Studies and Special
   Programs
2700 North Tamiami Trail
Sarasota, FL 34234
Phone: 941-955-8866
Fax: 941-955-8801
E-mail: cssp@ringling.edu
Web site: www.ringling.edu/precollege

SARAH LAWRENCE COLLEGE

**Sarah Lawrence College Summer High
School Programs**

Liz Irmiter
Director of Special Programs
1 Mead Way
Bronxville, NY 10708
Phone: 914-395-2693
Fax: 914-395-2694
E-mail: specialprograms@sarahlawrence.edu
Web site: www.sarahlawrence.edu/summer

SAVANNAH COLLEGE OF ART AND DESIGN

**Savannah College of Art and Design
Rising Star**

**Savannah College of Art and Design SCAD
Summer Seminars**

Admission Department
PO Box 2072
Savannah, GA 31402-2072
Phone: 800-869-7223
Fax: 912-525-5986
E-mail: admission@scad.edu
Web site: www.scad.edu/summer

**SCHOOL OF THE MUSEUM OF FINE
ARTS, BOSTON**

**School of the Museum of Fine Arts, Boston-
Pre-College Summer Studio**

Debra Samdperil
Director of Continuing Education and the
   Artist's Resource Center
230 The Fenway
Boston, MA 02115
Phone: 617-267-1219
Fax: 617-369-3679
E-mail: coned@smfa.edu
Web site: www.smfa.edu/precollege

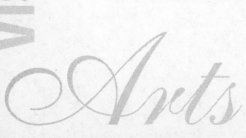

SKIDMORE COLLEGE

Skidmore College-Pre-College Program in the Studio Arts

Ms. Marianne Needham
Coordinator
Saisselin Art Building
815 North Broadway
Saratoga Springs, NY 12866
Phone: 518-580-5052
Fax: 518-580-5029
E-mail: mneedham@skidmore.edu
Web site: www.skidmore.edu/academics/
art/summersix/

SUFFIELD ACADEMY

The Summer Academy at Suffield

Tony O'Shaughnessy
Director, Summer Academy Admissions
185 North Main Street
Suffield, CT 06078
Phone: 860-386-4475
Fax: 860-386-4476
E-mail: summer@suffieldacademy.org
Web site: www.suffieldacademy.org

SYRACUSE UNIVERSITY

Syracuse University Summer College

Program Manager
111 Waverly Avenue
Suite 240
Syracuse, NY 13244-1270
Phone: 315-443-5297
Fax: 315-443-3976
E-mail: sumcoll@syr.edu
Web site: www.summercollege.syr.edu/

UCLA SUMMER SESSIONS AND SPECIAL PROGRAMS

UCLA Summer Experience: Institutes

Dr. Susan Pertel Jain
Director of Academic Program
    Development
Box 951418
Los Angeles, CA 90095
Phone: 310-825-4101
Fax: 310-825-1528
E-mail: spjain@summer.ucla.edu
Web site: www.summer.ucla.edu

UNIVERSITY OF MARYLAND, OFFICE OF SUMMER AND WINTER TERMS

The Arts! at Maryland

Student Services
Mitchell Building, 1st Floor
University of Maryland
College Park, MD 20742
Phone: 301-314-8240
Fax: 301-314-1282
Web site: www.summer.umd.edu/s/taam

UNIVERSITY OF PENNSYLVANIA

University of Pennsylvania-Penn Summer Art Studio

Ms. Heather Haseley
Youth Programs Coordinator
3440 Market Street, Suite 100
Philadelphia, PA 19104-3335
Phone: 215-746-6901
Fax: 215-573-2053
E-mail: hsprogs@sas.upenn.edu
Web site: www.sas.upenn.edu/cgs/highschool/

THE UNIVERSITY OF THE ARTS

Pre-College Summer Institute, The University of the Arts

Erin Elman
Director, Pre-College Programs
320 South Broad Street
Philadelphia, PA 19102
Phone: 215-717-6430
Fax: 215-717-6433
E-mail: precollege@uarts.edu
Web site: www.uarts.edu/precollege

WASHINGTON UNIVERSITY IN ST. LOUIS, SCHOOL OF ART

Washington University in St. Louis, School of Art-Portfolio Plus

Katerina Papageorgio
Assistant Dean of Undergraduate
    Programs
Washington University in St. Louis, School
    of Art
Box 1031
One Brookings Drive
St. Louis, MO 63130
Phone: 314-935-6500
Fax: 314-935-4643
E-mail: cpapageo@art.wustl.edu
Web site: www.arch.wustl.edu/art

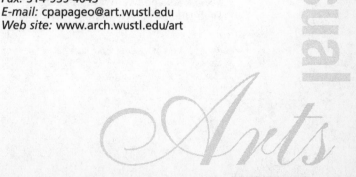

Scholarships for Artists

AACE INTERNATIONAL
AACE International Competitive Scholarship
Charla Miller, Staff Director-Education and
Administration
AACE International
209 Prairie Avenue, Suite 100
Morgantown, WV 26501
Phone: 304-296-8444 Ext. 113
Fax: 304-291-5728
E-mail: cmiller@aacei.org
Web site: http://www.aacei.org

ACADEMY FOUNDATION OF THE ACADEMY OF MOTION PICTURE ARTS AND SCIENCES
Academy of Motion Picture Student Academy Award-Honorary Foreign Film
Academy of Motion Pictures Student Academy Awards
Richard Miller, Awards Administration
Director
Academy Foundation of the Academy of
Motion Picture Arts and Sciences
8949 Wilshire Boulevard
Beverly Hills, CA 90211-1972
Phone: 310-247-3000 Ext. 129
Fax: 310-859-9619
E-mail: rmiller@oscars.org
Web site: http://www.oscars.org/saa

ACADEMY OF TELEVISION ARTS AND SCIENCES FOUNDATION
Academy of Television Arts and Sciences College Television Awards
Nancy Robinson, Programs Coordinator
Academy of Television Arts and Sciences
Foundation
5220 Lankershim Boulevard
North Hollywood, CA 91601
Phone: 818-754-2839
Fax: 818-761-8524
E-mail: collegeawards@emmys.org
Web site: http://www.emmys.tv/foundation

ACI INTERNATIONAL/CONCRETE RESEARCH AND EDUCATION FOUNDATION (CONREF)
Kumar Mehta Scholarship
Peter D. Courtois Concrete Construction Scholarship
V. Mohan Malhotra Scholarship
W.R. Grace Scholarship Award
Jessie Bournay, Fundraising and
Scholarship Assistant
ACI International/Concrete Research and
Education Foundation (CONREF)
38800 Country Club Drive
Farmington Hills, MI 48331
Phone: 248-848-3832
Fax: 248-848-3740
E-mail: scholarships@concrete.org
Web site: http://www.concrete.org

ADC RESEARCH INSTITUTE
Jack Shaheen Mass Communications Scholarship Award
Marvin Wingfield, Director of Education
and Outreach
ADC Research Institute
4201 Connecticut Avenue, NW Suite 300
Washington, DC 20008
Phone: 202-244-2990
Fax: 202-244-3196
E-mail: marvinw@adc.org
Web site: http://www.adc.org

ADVERTISING FEDERATION OF FORT WAYNE, INC.
Advertising Federation of Fort Wayne, Inc., Scholarship
Scholarship Committee
Advertising Federation of Fort Wayne, Inc.
PO Box 10066
Fort Wayne, IN 46850
Phone: 260-427-9106
Web site: http://www.adfedfortwayne.org

Visual *Arts*

ALLIANCE FOR YOUNG ARTISTS AND WRITERS, INC.

Scholastic Art and Writing Awards— Art Section

Alliance for Young Artists and Writers, Inc.
557 Broadway
New York, NY 10012-1396
Phone: 212-343-6493
Web site: http://www.artandwriting.org

ALPHA DELTA KAPPA FOUNDATION

Apha Delta Kappa Foundation Fine Arts Grants

Dee Frost, Scholarships and Grants
    Coordinator
Alpha Delta Kappa Foundation
1615 West 92nd Street
Kansas City, MO 64114-3296
Phone: 816-363-5525
Fax: 816-363-4010
E-mail: headquarters@alphadeltakappa.org
Web site: http://www.alphadeltakappa.org

AMERICAN ARCHITECTURAL FOUNDATION

American Institute of Architects Minority/Disadvantaged Scholarship

Mary Felber, Director of Scholarship
    Programs
American Architectural Foundation
1735 New York Avenue, NW
Washington, DC 20006-5292
Phone: 202-626-7511
Fax: 202-626-7509
E-mail: mfelber@archfoundation.org
Web site: http://www.archfoundation.org

AMERICAN INSTITUTE OF ARCHITECTS

American Institute of Architects/American Architectural Foundation Minority/Disadvantaged Scholarships

Mary Felber, Scholarship Chair
American Institute of Architects
1735 New York Avenue, NW
Washington, DC 20006-5292
Phone: 202-626-7511
Fax: 202-626-7509
E-mail: mfelber@aia.org
Web site: http://www.aia.org

AMERICAN INSTITUTE OF ARCHITECTS, NEW YORK CHAPTER

The Douglas Haskell Award for Student Journalism

Women's Architectural Auxiliary Eleanor Allwork Scholarship Grants

Marcus Bleyer
American Institute of Architects, New York
    Chapter
536 LaGuardia Place
New York, NY 10012
Phone: 212-358-6117
E-mail: mbleyer@aiany.org
Web site: http://www.aiany.org

AMERICAN INSTITUTE OF ARCHITECTS, WEST VIRGINIA CHAPTER

AIA West Virginia Scholarship Program

Roberta Guffey, Executive Director
American Institute of Architects,
    West Virginia Chapter
PO Box 813
Charleston, WV 25323
Phone: 304-344-9872
Fax: 304-343-0205
E-mail: roberta.guffey@aiawv.org
Web site: http://www.aiawv.org

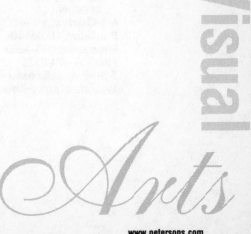

Visual *Arts*

AMERICAN LEGION AUXILIARY, DEPARTMENT OF WASHINGTON

Florence Lemcke Memorial Scholarship in Fine Arts

Crystal Lawrence, Department Secretary
American Legion Auxiliary, Department
    of Washington
3600 Ruddell Road
Lacey, WA 98503
Phone: 360-456-5995
Fax: 360-491-7442
E-mail: alawash@qwest.net
Web site: http://www.walegion-aux.org

AMERICAN LEGION, PRESS CLUB OF NEW JERSEY

American Legion Press Club of New Jersey and Post 170 Arthur Dehardt Memorial Scholarship

Jack W. Kuepfer, Scholarship Chairman
American Legion, Press Club of New Jersey
68 Merrill Road
Clifton, NJ 07012-1622
Phone: 973-473-5176
Web site: http://www.alpcnj.org/

AMERICAN PHILOLOGICAL ASSOCIATION

Minority Student Summer Scholarship

Adam Blistein, Executive Director
American Philological Association
292 Logan Hall
University of Pennsylvania
249 South 36th Street
Philadelphia, PA 19104-6304
Phone: 215-898-4975
Fax: 215-573-7874
E-mail: apaclassics@sas.upenn.edu
Web site: http://www.apaclassics.org

AMERICAN SCHOOL OF CLASSICAL STUDIES AT ATHENS

ASCSA Summer Sessions Open Scholarships

Timothy F Winters, Chair, Committee of
    Summer Sessions
American School of Classical Studies
    at Athens
6-8 Charlton Street
Princeton, NJ 08540
Phone: 609-683-0800
Fax: 609-924-0578
E-mail: ascsa@ascsa.org
Web site: http://www.ascsa.edu.gr

AMERICAN SOCIETY OF INTERIOR DESIGNERS (ASID) EDUCATION FOUNDATION, INC.

ASID Educational Foundation/Irene Winifred Eno Grant

ASID Educational Foundation/Joel Polsky Academic Achievement Award

ASID Educational Foundation/Yale R. Burge Competition

American Society of Interior Designers
    (ASID) Education Foundation, Inc.
608 Massachusetts Avenue, NE
Washington, DC 20002-6006
Phone: 202-546-3480
Fax: 202-546-3240
E-mail: education@asid.org
Web site: http://www.asid.org

ANGELUS AWARDS STUDENT FILM FESTIVAL

Angelus Awards Student Film Festival

Monika Moreno, Director, Angelus Awards
Angelus Awards Student Film Festival
7201 Sunset Boulevard
Los Angeles, CA 90046
Phone: 323-874-6633 Ext. 24
Fax: 323-874-1168
E-mail: monika@angelus.org
Web site: http://www.angelus.org

ART INSTITUTES

National Art Honor Society Scholarship

Bill McAnulty, National Art Honor Society
    Scholarship
Art Institutes
c/o The Art Institute of Pittsburgh
420 Boulevard of the Allies
Pittsburgh, PA 15219-1328
Phone: 800-275-2470
Web site: http://www.artinstitutes.edu

National Poster Design Contest

Michael Maki, Vice President for Academic
    Affairs
Art Institutes
210 Sixth Ave, 32nd Floor
Pittsburgh, PA 15222-2598
Phone: 888-624-0300
Web site: http://www.artinstitutes.edu

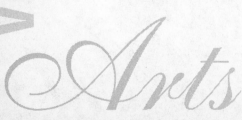

ARTIST-BLACKSMITH'S ASSOCIATION OF NORTH AMERICA, INC.

Artist's-Blacksmith's Association of North America, Inc. Scholarship Program

Artist's-Blacksmith's Association of North America, Inc. Affiliate Visiting Artist Grant Program

Lee Ann Mitchell, Central Office
    Administrator
Artist-Blacksmith's Association of North
    America, Inc.
PO Box 816
Farmington, GA 30638-0816
Phone: 706-310-1030
Fax: 706-769-7147
E-mail: abana@abana.org
Web site: http://www.abana.org

ARTIST'S MAGAZINE

Artist's Magazine's Annual Art Competition

Terri Boes, Customer Service
    Representative
Artist's Magazine
4700 East Galbraith Road
Cincinnati, OH 45236
Phone: 513-531-2690 Ext. 1328
Fax: 513-531-0798
E-mail: arts-competition@fwpubs.com
Web site: http://www.artistsmagazine.com

ASIAN AMERICAN JOURNALISTS ASSOCIATION

Asian American Journalists Association Scholarship

Brandon Sugiyama, Student Programs
    Coordinator
Asian American Journalists Association
1182 Market Street, Suite 320
San Francisco, CA 94102
Phone: 415-346-2051 Ext. 102
Fax: 415-346-6343
E-mail: programs@aaja.org
Web site: http://www.aaja.org

ASPRS, THE IMAGING AND GEOSPATIAL INFORMATION SOCIETY

Robert E. Altenhofen Memorial Scholarship

Space Imaging Award for Application of High Resolution Digital Satellite Imagery

Jesse Winch, Program Manager
ASPRS, The Imaging and Geospatial
    Information Society
5410 Grosvenor Lane, Suite 210
Bethesda, MD 20814-2160
Phone: 301-493-0290 Ext. 101
Fax: 301-493-0208
E-mail: scholarships@asprs.org
Web site: http://www.asprs.org

ASSOCIATION FOR WOMEN IN ARCHITECTURE FOUNDATION

Association for Women in Architecture Scholarship

Nina Briggs, Scholarship Chair
Association for Women in Architecture
    Foundation
386 Beech Avenue, Unit B4
Torrance, CA 90501-6203
Phone: 310-533-4042
E-mail: ninabriggs@earthlink.net
Web site: http://www.awa-la.org

AUTHOR SERVICES, INC.

L. Ron Hubbard's Illustrators of the Future Contest

Judy Young, Contest Administrator
Author Services, Inc.
PO Box 3190
Los Angeles, CA 90078
Phone: 323-466-3310
Fax: 323-466-6474
E-mail: contests@authorservicesinc.com
Web site: http://www.writersofthefuture.com

BEINECKE SCHOLARSHIP PROGRAM

Beinecke Scholarship for Graduate Study

Thomas Parkinson, Program Director
Beinecke Scholarship Program
PO Box 125
Fogelsville, PA 18051-0125
Phone: 610-395-5560
Fax: 610-625-7919
E-mail: beineckescholarship@earthlink.net
Web site:
    http://www.beineckescholarship.org/

Visual *Arts*

BMI FOUNDATION, INC.

BMI Student Composer Awards

Mr. Ralph N. Jackson, Director, BMI
 Student Composer Awards
BMI Foundation, Inc.
320 West 57th Street
New York, NY 10019
Phone: 212-586-2000
Fax: 212-245-8986
E-mail: classical@bmi.com
Web site: http://www.bmi.com

CALIFORNIA ALLIANCE FOR ARTS EDUCATION (CAAE)

Emerging Young Artist Awards

Peggy Burt, Project Manager
California Alliance for Arts Education
 (CAAE)
495 East Colorado Boulevard
Pasadena, CA 91101
Phone: 626-578-9315 Ext. 102
Fax: 626-578-9894
E-mail: peggy@artsed411.org
Web site: http://www.artsed411.org

CALIFORNIA CHICANO NEWS MEDIA ASSOCIATION (CCNMA)

Joel Garcia Memorial Scholarship

Julio Moran, Executive Director
California Chicano News Media Association
 (CCNMA)
300 South Grand Avenue, Suite 3950
Los Angeles, CA 90071-8110
Phone: 213-437-4408
Fax: 213-437-4423
E-mail: ccnmainfo@ccnma.org
Web site: http://www.ccnma.org

CENTRAL INTELLIGENCE AGENCY

Central Intelligence Agency Undergraduate Scholarship Program

Van Patrick, Chief, College Relations
Central Intelligence Agency
Recruitment Center
L 100 LF7
Washington, DC 20505
Phone: 703-613-8388
Fax: 703-613-7676
E-mail: ivanilp0@ucia.gov
Web site: http://www.cia.gov

CHARLES & LUCILLE KING FAMILY FOUNDATION, INC.

Charles and Lucille King Family Foundation Scholarships

Michael Donovan, Educational Director
Charles & Lucille King Family Foundation,
 Inc.
366 Madison Avenue, 10th Floor
New York, NY 10017
Phone: 212-682-2913
Fax: 212-949-0728
E-mail: info@kingfoundation.org
Web site: http://www.kingfoundation.org/

THE CIRI FOUNDATION

CIRI Foundation Susie Qimmiqsak Bevins Endowment Scholarship Fund

The CRI Foundation
3600 San Jeronimo Drive Suite 256
Anchorage, AK 99508-2870
Phone: 907-263-5582
Fax: 907-263-5588
Web site: http://www.thecirifoundation.org

COLLEGEBOUND FOUNDATION

Janet B. Sondheim Scholarship

April Bell, Associate Program Director
CollegeBound Foundation
300 Water Street, Suite 300
Baltimore, MD 21202
Phone: 410-783-2905 Ext. 208
Fax: 410-727-5786
E-mail: abell@collegeboundfoundation.org
Web site:
 http://www.collegeboundfoundation.org

CONNECTICUT CHAPTER OF SOCIETY OF PROFESSIONAL JOURNALISTS

Connecticut SPJ Bob Eddy Scholarship Program

Debra Estock, Scholarship Committee
 Chairman
Connecticut Chapter of Society of
 Professional Journalists
71 Kenwood Avenue
Fairfield, CT 06430
Phone: 203-255-2127
E-mail: destock963@aol.com
Web site: http://www.ctspj.org

Visual *Arts*

COSTUME SOCIETY OF AMERICA

Adele Filene Travel Award

Stella Blum Research Grant

Kim Righi, Program Contact
Costume Society of America
203 Towne Center Drive, PO Box 73
Hillsborough, NJ 08844
Phone: 800-272-9447
E-mail:
national.office@costumesocietyamerica.com
Web site:
http://www.costumesocietyamerica.com

CULTURE CONNECTION

Culture Connection Foundation Scholarship

Anna Leis, National Program Director
Culture Connection
8888 Keystone Crossing, Suite 1300
Indianapolis, IN 46240
Phone: 317-547-7055
E-mail:
annaleis@thecultureconnection.com
Web site:
http://www.thecultureconnection.com

DALLAS ARCHITECTURAL FOUNDATION-HKS/ JOHN HUMPHRIES MINORITY SCHOLARSHIP

Dallas Architectural Foundation—Harrell and Hamilton Scholarship Fund

Dallas Architectural Foundation-HKS/John
Humphries Minority Scholarship
1444 Oak Lawn Avenue, Suite 600
Dallas, TX 75207
Phone: 214-742-3242
Web site: http://www.dallasfoundation.org

DALLAS-FORT WORTH ASSOCIATION OF BLACK COMMUNICATORS

Future Journalists Scholarship Program

Ira Hadnot, DFW/ABC Scholarship Chair
Phone: 469-330-9696
E-mail: scholarship@dfwabc.org
Web site: http://www.dfwabc.org

DAYTON FOUNDATION

American Institute of Architecture (AIA) Dayton Architectural Scholarship Fund

Larry Fullerton Photojournalism Scholarship

Diane Timmons, Director of Grants and
Programs
Dayton Foundation
2300 Kettering Tower
Dayton, OH 45423
Phone: 937-222-0410
Fax: 937-222-0636
E-mail: dtimmons@daytonfoundation.org
Web site:
http://www.daytonfoundation.org

ELECTRONIC DOCUMENT SYSTEMS FOUNDATION

Electronic Document Systems Foundation Scholarship Awards

Jeanne Mowlds, Executive Director
Electronic Document Systems Foundation
24238 Hawthorne Boulevard
608 Silver Spur Road, Suite 280
Rolling Hills Estates, CA 90274-3616
Phone: 310-265-5510
Fax: 310-265-5588
E-mail: jcmowlds@aol.com
Web site: http://www.edsf.org

ELIZABETH GREENSHIELDS FOUNDATION

Elizabeth Greenshields Award/Grant

Diane Pitcher, Applications Coordinator
Elizabeth Greenshields Foundation
1814 Sherbrooke Street West, Suite 1
Montreal, QC H3H IE4
Canada
Phone: 514-937-9225
Fax: 514-937-0141
E-mail: greenshields@bellnet.ca

FISHER BROADCASTING COMPANY

Fisher Broadcasting, Inc., Scholarship for Minorities

Annnarie Hitchcock, Human Resources
Administrator
Fisher Broadcasting Company
100 4th Avenue North, Suite 510
Seattle, WA 98109
Phone: 206-404-6050
Fax: 206-404-6760
Web site:
http://www.fisherbroadcasting.com

Visual *Arts*

FLORIDA EDUCATIONAL FACILITIES PLANNERS' ASSOCIATION

FEFPA Assistantship

Bob Griffith, FEFPA Assistantship, Selection Committee Chair
Florida Educational Facilities Planners' Association
Florida International University
University Park, CSC 236
Miami, FL 33199
Web site: http://www.fefpa.org

GENERAL FEDERATION OF WOMEN'S CLUBS OF MASSACHUSETTS

General Federation of Women's Clubs of Massachusetts Pennies For Art

Kay Doody, Art Chairman
General Federation of Women's Clubs of Massachusetts
PO Box 679
Sudbury, MA 01776-0679
Phone: 978-443-4569
E-mail: kdoody1890@aol.com
Web site: http://www.gfwcma.org/

GEORGE BIRD GRINNELL AMERICAN INDIAN FUND

Al Qoyawayma Award

Paula Mintzies, President
George Bird Grinnell American Indian Fund
PO Box 59033
Potomac, MD 20859
Phone: 301-424-2440
Fax: 301-424-8281
Web site: http://www.grinnellfund.org/

GETTY GRANT PROGRAM

Library Research Grants

Kathleen Johnson, Program Associate
Getty Grant Program
1200 Getty Center Drive, Suite 800
Los Angeles, CA 90049-1685
Phone: 310-440-7320
Fax: 310-440-7703
E-mail: researchgrants@getty.edu
Web site: http://www.getty.edu/grants

GOLDEN KEY INTERNATIONAL HONOUR SOCIETY

Visual and Performing Arts Achievement Awards

Scholarship Program Administrators
Golden Key International Honour Society
PO Box 23737
Nashville, TN 37202
Phone: 800-377-2401
Web site: http://www.goldenkey.org

GREAT LAKES COMMISSION

Carol A. Ratza Memorial Scholarship

Christine Manninen, Program Manager
Great Lakes Commission
Eisenhower Corporate Park, 2805 South Industrial Highway, Suite 100
Ann Arbor, MI 48104-6791
Phone: 734-971-9135
Fax: 734-971-9150
E-mail: manninen@glc.org
Web site: http://www.glc.org

HALLMARK GRAPHIC ARTS SCHOLARSHIP

Hallmark Graphic Arts Scholarship

Robert Sheridan, Director of Development
Hallmark Graphic Arts Scholarship
c/o Gravure Education Foundation
107 East Sutton Place
Wilmington, DE 19810
Phone: 315-589-8879
E-mail: rbsheridan@gaa.org
Web site:
http://www.gaa.org/GEF/scholarships.htm

HAWAIIAN LODGE, F. & A. M.

Hawaiian Lodge Scholarships

Chairman, Scholarship Committee
Hawaiian Lodge, F. & A. M.
1227 Makiki Street
Honolulu, HI 96814
Phone: 808-979-7809
E-mail: secretary@hawaiianlodge.org
Web site: http://www.hawaiianlodge.org/

Visual

Arts

HELLENIC UNIVERSITY CLUB OF PHILADELPHIA

The Dimitri J. Ververelli Memorial Scholarship for Architecture and/or Engineering

Zoe Tripolitis, Scholarship Chairman
Hellenic University Club of Philadelphia
PO Box 42199
Philadelphia, PA 19101
Phone: 215-483-7440
E-mail: zoe.tripolitis@arkemagroup.com
Web site: http://www.hucphila.org

HERB SOCIETY OF AMERICA

Herb Society Research Grants

The Herb Society of America, Inc.
Research Grant
Herb Society of America
9019 Kirtland-Chardon Road
Kirtland, OH 44094
Phone: 440-256-0514
Fax: 440-256-0541
E-mail: herbs@herbsociety.org
Web site: http://www.herbsociety.org

HISPANIC COLLEGE FUND, INC.

Denny's/Hispanic College Fund Scholarship

El Nuevo Constructor Scholarship Program

Stina Augustsson, Program Manager
Hispanic College Fund, Inc.
1717 Pennsylvania Avenue, NW, Suite 460
Washington, DC 20006
Phone: 202-296-5400
Fax: 202-296-3774
E-mail: hcf-info@hispanicfund.org
Web site: http://www.hispanicfund.org

ILLUMINATING ENGINEERING SOCIETY OF NORTH AMERICA

Robert W. Thunen Memorial Scholarships

Chairperson (Thunen Scholarship Committee)
Illuminating Engineering Society of North America
IESNA Golden Gate Section
1514 Gibbons Drive
Alameda, CA 94501-4001
Phone: 510-864-0204
Fax: 510-864-8511
E-mail: mrcatisbac@aol.com
Web site: http://www.iesna.org

ILLUMINATING ENGINEERING SOCIETY OF NORTH AMERICA–GOLDEN GATE SECTION

Alan Lucas Memorial Educational Scholarship

Robert W. Thunen Memorial Scholarships

Phil Hall, Coordinator
Illuminating Engineering Society of North America–Golden Gate Section
1514 Gibbons Drive
Alameda, CA 94501
Phone: 510-208-5005 Ext. 3030
E-mail: information@iesgg.org
Web site: http://www.iesgg.org

INDIANAPOLIS ASSOCIATION OF BLACK JOURNALISTS

Lynn Dean Ford IABJ Scholarship Awards

Courtenay Edelhart, Scholarship Committee Chair
Indianapolis Association of Black Journalists
PO Box 441795
Indianapolis, IN 46244-1795
Phone: 317-388-8163
E-mail: courtenay.edelhart@indystar.com
Web site: http://www.iabj.net

INSTITUTE FOR HUMANE STUDIES

Film and Fiction Scholarship

Institute for Humane Studies
3301 North Fairfax Drive, Suite 440
Arlington, VA 22201-4432
Phone: 703-993-4880
Fax: 703-993-4890
E-mail: ihs@gmu.edu
Web site: http://www.theihs.org

INTERNATIONAL COMMUNICATIONS INDUSTRIES FOUNDATION

ICIF Scholarship for Dependents of Member Organizations

International Communications Industries Foundation AV Scholarship

Duffy Wilbert, Vice President, Membership
International Communications Industries Foundation
11242 Waples Mill Road, Suite 200
Fairfax, VA 22030
Phone: 703-273-7200 Ext. 3470
Fax: 703-278-8082
E-mail: dwilbert@infocomm.org
Web site: http://www.infocomm.org/foundation

Visual *Arts*

INTERNATIONAL FACILITY MANAGEMENT ASSOCIATION FOUNDATION

IFMA Foundation Scholarships

Mr. William Rub, Foundation Manager
International Facility Management
    Association Foundation
1 East Greenway Plaza
Suite 1100
Houston, TX 77046-0194
Phone: 713-623-4362 Ext. 158
Fax: 713-623-6124
E-mail: william.rub@ifma.org
Web site: http://www.ifmafoundation.org

INTERNATIONAL FOODSERVICE EDITORIAL COUNCIL

International Foodservice Editorial Council Communications Scholarship

Carol Lally, Executive Director
International Foodservice Editorial Council
PO Box 491
Hyde Park, NY 12538-0491
Phone: 845-229-6973
Fax: 845-229-6993
E-mail: ifec@aol.com
Web site: http://www.ifec-is-us.com

INTERNATIONAL FURNISHINGS AND DESIGN ASSOCIATION

Charles D. Mayo Scholarship

IFDA Student Scholarship

Ruth Clark Scholarship

Joan Long, Director of Grants
International Furnishings and Design
    Association
191 Clarksville Road
Princeton Junction, NJ 08550
Phone: 919-847-3064
Fax: 919-847-3064
E-mail: jlongdesigns@yahoo.com
Web site: http://www.ifdaef.org

JACK J. ISGUR FOUNDATION

Jack J. Isgur Foundation Scholarship

Charles Jensen, Attorney at Law
Jack J. Isgur Foundation
c/o Charles F. Jensen, Stinson, Morrison,
    Hecker LLP
1201 Walnut Street, 28th Floor
Kansas City, MO 64106
Phone: 816-691-2760
Fax: 816-691-3495
E-mail: cjensen@stinsonmoheck.com

JOHN C. SANTISTEVAN MEMORIAL SCHOLARSHIP

John C. Santistevan Memorial Scholarship

Ivan Houston, President
John C. Santistevan Memorial Scholarship
419 North Larch Mont Boulevard,
    Number 98
Los Angeles, CA 90004
Web site: http://www.santistevanart.org

JOHN F. AND ANNA LEE STACEY SCHOLARSHIP FUND

John F. and Anna Lee Stacey Scholarship Fund

Ed Muno, Art Curator
John F. and Anna Lee Stacey Scholarship
    Fund
1700 Northeast 63rd Street
Oklahoma City, OK 73111
Phone: 405-478-2250
Fax: 405-478-4714
Web site:
    http://www.nationalcowboymuseum.org

JUNIOR ACHIEVEMENT

Walt Disney Company Foundation Scholarship

Scholarship Coordinator
Junior Achievement
1 Education Way
Colorado Springs, CO 80906
Phone: 719-535-2954
Fax: 719-540-6175
Web site: http://www.ja.org

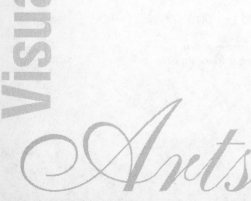

LA KELLEY COMMUNICATIONS

Artistic Endeavors Scholarship

Sandy Aultman
LA Kelley Communications
1405 W. Pinhook Road, Suite 101
Lafayette, LA 70503
Phone: 337-261-9787
Fax: 337-261-1787
Web site: http://www.kelleycom.com

LINCOLN COMMUNITY FOUNDATION

Haymarket Gallery Emerging Artists Scholarship

Debra Shoemaker, Director of Program
  and Distribution
Lincoln Community Foundation
215 Centennial Mall South, Suite 200
Lincoln, NE 68508
Phone: 402-474-2345
Fax: 402-476-8532
E-mail: debs@lcf.org
Web site: http://www.lcf.org

LIQUITEX ARTIST MATERIALS

Liquitex Excellence in Art Purchase Award Program

11 Constitution Avenue
PO Box 1396
Piscataway, NJ 08855-1396
Phone: 888-422-7954
          732-562-0770
E-mail: renee@liquitex.com
Web site: http://www.liquitex.com

MAINE GRAPHICS ARTS ASSOCIATION

Maine Graphics Art Association Scholarship

Angie Dougherty, Director
Maine Graphics Arts Association
PO Box 874
Auburn, ME 04212-0874
Phone: 207-883-3083
Fax: 207-883-3158
E-mail: edpougher@maine.rr.com
Web site: http://www.megaa.org

MEDIA ACTION NETWORK FOR ASIAN AMERICANS

MANAA Media Scholarships for Asian American Students

MANAA Scholarship
Media Action Network for Asian
  Americans
PO Box 11105
Burbank, CA 91510
E-mail: manaaletters@yahoo.com.
Web site: http://www.manaa.org

METAVUE CORPORATION

The FW Rausch Arts and Humanities Paper Contest

Michael Rufflo
Metavue Corporation
1110 Surrey Drive
Sun Prairie, WI 53590
Phone: 608-577-0642
Fax: 512-685-4074
E-mail: rufflo@metavue.com
Web site: http://www.metavue.com

MIDWEST ROOFING CONTRACTORS ASSOCIATION

MRCA Foundation Scholarship Program

MRCA Foundation
Midwest Roofing Contractors Association
4840 Bob Billings Parkway, Suite 1000
Lawrence, KS 66049-3862
Phone: 800-497-6722
Fax: 785-843-7555
Web site: http://www.mrca.org

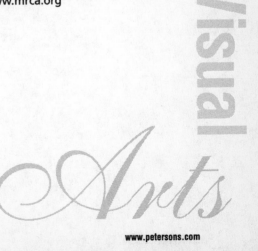

Visual *Arts*

NATIONAL ART MATERIALS TRADE ASSOCIATION

National Art Materials Trade Association Art Major Scholarship

Katharine Coffey, Scholarship Coordinator
National Art Materials Trade Association
15806 Brookway Drive, Suite 300
Huntersville, NC 28078
Phone: 704-892-6244
Fax: 704-892-6247
E-mail: kcoffey@namta.org
Web site: http://www.namta.org

NATIONAL ASSOCIATION OF BLACK JOURNALISTS

National Association of Black Journalists Non-Sustaining Scholarship Awards

Ryan Williams, Program and Exposition
Coordinator
National Association of Black Journalists
8701-A Adelphi Road
Adelphi, MD 20783-1716
Phone: 301-445-7100 Ext. 109
Fax: 301-445-7101
Web site: http://www.nabj.org

Visual Task Force Scholarship

Program and Exposition Coordinator
National Association of Black Journalists
8701-A Adelphi Road
Adelphi, MD 20783-1716
Phone: 301-445-7100
Fax: 301-445-7101
Web site: http://www.nabj.org

NATIONAL ASSOCIATION OF WOMEN IN CONSTRUCTION

NAWIC Undergraduate Scholarships

Scholarship Administrator
National Association of Women in
Construction
327 South Adams Street
Fort Worth, TX 76104
E-mail: nawic@nawic.org
Web site: http://nawic.org

NATIONAL FEDERATION OF THE BLIND

Howard Brown Rickard Scholarship

Peggy Elliot, Chairman, Scholarship
Committee
National Federation of the Blind
805 5th Avenue
Grinnell, IA 50112
Phone: 641-236-3366
Web site: http://www.nfb.org

NATIONAL FOUNDATION FOR ADVANCEMENT IN THE ARTS

Arts Recognition and Talent Search (ARTS)

Programs Department
National Foundation for Advancement in
the Arts
444 Brickell Avenue, Suite R14
Miami, FL 33133
Phone: 800-970-2787
Fax: 305-377-1149
E-mail: nfaa@nfaa.org
Web site: http://www.artsawards.org

NATIONAL INSTITUTE OF BUILDING SCIENCES, MULTIHAZARD MITIGATION COUNCIL

Architecture, Construction, and Engineering Mentor Program Scholarships

Pamela Mullender, Acting Executive
Director, ACE Mentor Program
National Institute of Building Sciences,
Multihazard Mitigation Council
National Institute of Building Sciences,
1090 Vermont Avenue, NW, Suite 700
Washington, DC 20005
Phone: 202-898-6396
Fax: 202-289-1092
Web site: http://www.nibs.org

NATIONAL LEAGUE OF AMERICAN PEN WOMEN, INC.

NLAPW Virginia Liebeler Biennial Grants for Mature Women (Arts)

NLAPW Virginia Liebeler Biennial Grants
for Women
National League of American Pen
Women, Inc.
1300 17th Street, NW
Washington, DC 20036-1973
Web site:
http://www.americanpenwomen.org

Visual

Arts

NATIONAL OPERA ASSOCIATION

NOA Vocal Competition/Legacy Award Program

Robert Hansen, Executive Secretary
National Opera Association
PO Box 60869
Canyon, TX 79016-0869
Phone: 806-651-2857
Fax: 806-651-2958
E-mail: hansen@mail.wtamu.edu
Web site: http://www.noa.org

NATIONAL PRESS PHOTOGRAPHERS FOUNDATION, INC.

Bob East Scholarship

Chuck Fadely
National Press Photographers
    Foundation, Inc.
The Miami Herald, One Herald Plaza
Miami, FL 33132
Phone: 305-376-2015
E-mail: info@nppa.org

National Press Photographers Foundation Still Photographer Scholarship

Bill Sanders, Photo Editor
E-mail: wsanders@citizen-times.com
Web site: http://www.nppa.org

National Press Photographers Foundation Television News Scholarship

Ed Dooks
National Press Photographers
    Foundation, Inc.
5 Mohawk Drive
Lexington, MA 02421-6217
E-mail: dooks@verizon.net
Web site: http://www.nppa.org

Reid Blackburn Scholarship

Jeremiah Coughlan, Staff Photographer
National Press Photographers
    Foundation, Inc.
The Columbian, 701 West 8th Street
Vancouver, WA 98660
Phone: 360-694-3391
E-mail: coughlan@attbi.com
Web site: http://www.nppa.org

NATIONAL SCULPTURE SOCIETY

National Sculpture Competition for Young Sculptors

National Sculpture Society Scholarships

Gwen Pier, Executive Director
National Sculpture Society
237 Park Avenue
New York, NY 10017
Phone: 212-764-5645 Ext. 15
Fax: 212-764-5651
E-mail: gwen@nationalsculpture.org
Web site: http://www.nationalsculpture.org

NATIONAL WRITERS ASSOCIATION FOUNDATION

National Writers Association Foundation Scholarships

Sandy Welchel, Executive Director
National Writers Association Foundation
10940 South Parker Road, Suite 508
Parker, CO 80134
Phone: 303-841-0246
Fax: 303-841-2607
E-mail: info@nationalwriters.com
Web site: http://www.nationalwriters.com

NEBRASKA PRESS ASSOCIATION

Nebraska Press Association Foundation, Inc., Scholarship

Allen Beermann, Executive Director
Nebraska Press Association
845 S Street
Lincoln, NE 68508-1226
Phone: 402-476-2851
Fax: 402-476-2942
E-mail: nebpress@nebpress.com
Web site: http://www.nebpress.com

NETWORK OF EXECUTIVE WOMEN IN HOSPITALITY

Network of Executive Women in Hospitality, Inc. Scholarship

Scholarship Director
NEWH, Inc.
PO Box 322
Shawano, WI 54166
Phone: 800-593-6394
Fax: 800-693-6394
Web site: http://www.newh.org

Visual *Arts*

NEW ENGLAND FILM AND VIDEO FESTIVAL

New England Film and Video Festival Awards

Sandra Sullivan, Festival Co-director
New England Film and Video Festival
119 Braintree Street, Box 159, Suite 104
Boston, MA 02134
Phone: 617-783-9241 Ext. 12
Fax: 617-783-4368
E-mail: festival@bfvf.org
Web site: http://www.nefvf.com

NEW ENGLAND PRINTING AND PUBLISHING COUNCIL

New England Graphic Arts Scholarship

Kurt Drescher, Scholarship Chair
New England Printing and Publishing
Council
PO Box 593
Reading, MA 01867-0218
Phone: 781-944-1116
Fax: 781-944-3905
Web site: http://www.ppcne.org

NEW JERSEY SOCIETY OF ARCHITECTS/AIA NEW JERSEY SCHOLARSHIP FOUNDATION

New Jersey Society of Architects Scholarship

Robert Zaccone, President
New Jersey Society of Architects/AIA New
Jersey Scholarship Foundation
212 White Avenue
Old Tappan, NJ 07675
Phone: 201-767-9575
Fax: 201-767-5541
Web site: http://www.aia-nj.org/about/
scholarship.shtml

NEW YORK STATE EDUCATION DEPARTMENT

Regents Professional Opportunity Scholarship

Lewis J. Hall, Coordinator
New York State Education Department
Room 1078 EBA
Albany, NY 12234
Phone: 518-486-1319
Fax: 518-486-5346
Web site: http://www.highered.nysed.gov

ORANGE COUNTY COMMUNITY FOUNDATION

Architecture and Engineering Scholarship Program

Arts Scholarship Program

Rose Garris, Hispanic Education
Endowment Fund
Orange County Community Foundation
30 Corporate Park, Suite 410
Irvine, CA 92606
Phone: 949-543-4202 Ext. 23
Fax: 949-553-4211
Web site: http://www.heef.org

OREGON STUDENT ASSISTANCE COMMISSION

Glenn R. and Juanita B. Struble Scholarship II

Homestead Capital Housing Scholarship

Director of Grant Programs
Oregon Student Assistance Commission
1500 Valley River Drive, Suite 100
Eugene, OR 97401-7020
Phone: 800-452-8807 Ext. 7395
Web site: http://www.osac.state.or.us

OUTDOOR WRITERS ASSOCIATION OF AMERICA

Outdoor Writers Association of America Bodie McDowell Scholarship Award

Executive Director
Outdoor Writers Association of America
121 Hickory Street, Suite 1
Missoula, MT 59801
Phone: 406-728-7434
Fax: 406-728-7445
E-mail: owaa@montana.com
Web site: http://www.owaa.org/

PARK PEOPLE

The Park People $2000 Scholarship

Scholarship Chair
Park People
3015 Richmond, Suite 210
Houston, TX 77098
Phone: 713-942-8429
Fax: 713-942-7275
E-mail: annem@parkpeople.org
Web site: http://www.parkpeople.org

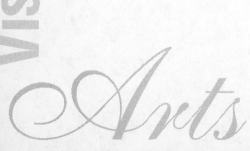

PHI DELTA THETA EDUCATIONAL FOUNDATION

Francis D. Lyon Scholarships

Carmalieta Jenkins, Assistant to the President
Phi Delta Theta Educational Foundation
2 South Campus Avenue
Oxford, OH 45056-1801
Phone: 513-523-6966
Fax: 513-523-9200
E-mail: carmalieta@phideltatheta.org
Web site: http://phideltatheta.org

PLUMBING-HEATING-COOLING CONTRACTORS ASSOCIATION EDUCATION FOUNDATION

Bradford White Corporation Scholarship

Program Assistant
Plumbing-Heating-Cooling Contractors Association Education Foundation
PO Box 6808
Falls Church, VA 22040
Phone: 703-237-8100
Web site: http://www.phccweb.org

Delta Faucet Company Scholarship Program

PHCC Educational Foundation Need-Based Scholarship

PHCC Educational Foundation Scholarship Program

Scholarship Administrator
Plumbing-Heating-Cooling Contractors Association Education Foundation
PO Box 6808
Falls Church, VA 22040
Phone: 800-533-7694
Fax: 703-237-7442
E-mail: naphcc@naphcc.org
Web site: http://www.phccweb.org

POLISH ARTS CLUB OF BUFFALO SCHOLARSHIP FOUNDATION

Polish Arts Club of Buffalo Scholarship Foundation Trust

Ann Flansburg, Selection Chair
Polish Arts Club of Buffalo Scholarship Foundation
PO Box 1362
Williamsville, NY 14231-1362
Phone: 716-626-9083
E-mail: donflans123@aol.com
Web site: http://pacb.bfn.org/about/constitution.html

PRINT AND GRAPHIC SCHOLARSHIP FOUNDATION

Print and Graphics Scholarships

Bernadine Eckert, Program Administrator
Print and Graphic Scholarship Foundation
Printing Industries of America/Graphic Arts Technical Foundation
200 Deer Run Road
Sewickley, PA 15143-2600
Phone: 412-741-6860
Fax: 412-741-2311
E-mail: pgsf@gatf.org
Web site: http://www.gain.net

PRINTING AND IMAGING ASSOCIATION OF MIDAMERICA

Clampitt Paper/Henry Phillips Memorial Scholarship

Clampitt Paper/Henry Phillips Memorial Scholarship
Printing and Imaging Association of MidAmerica
c/o PIA-MidAmerica
8828 North Stemmons, Suite 505
Dallas, TX 75247
Phone: 214-630-8871 Ext. 205
E-mail: dodier@piamidam.org
Web site: http://www.piamidam.org

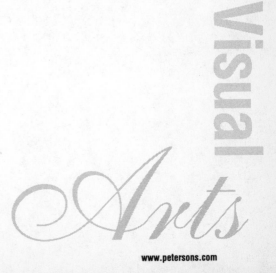

Visual *Arts*

PRINTING INDUSTRIES OF MICHIGAN, INC. SCHOLARSHIP

Printing Industries of Michigan Scholarship Fund

Scholarship Committee
Printing Industries of Michigan, Inc.
    Scholarship
23815 Northwestern Highway, Suite 2700
Southfield, MI 48075-7713
Phone: 248-354-9200
Fax: 248-354-1711
Web site: http://www.print.org

PRINTING INDUSTRIES OF WISCONSIN EDUCATION FOUNDATION SCHOLARSHIPS

Madison Area Club of Printing House Craftsmen Scholarship

Doug Mackenzie
Printing Industries of Wisconsin Education
    Foundation Scholarships
Stoughton High School
600 Llincoln Avenue
Stoughton, WI 53589
Phone: 608-877-5781
Fax: 608-877-5619
E-mail: mackedo@mail.stoughton.k12.wi.us
Web site: http://www.piw.org

PRINTING INDUSTRY OF MINNESOTA EDUCATION FOUNDATION

Printing Industry of Minnesota Education Foundation Scholarship Fund

Carla Steuck, Director of Education
    Services
Printing Industry of Minnesota Education
    Foundation
2829 University Avenue SE, Suite 750
Minneapolis, MN 55414-3248
Phone: 612-379-6012
Fax: 612-379-6030
E-mail: csteuck@pimn.org
Web site: http://www.pimn.org

QUILL AND SCROLL FOUNDATION

Edward J. Nell Memorial Scholarship in Journalism

Quill and Scroll International Writing/ Photo Contest

Richard Johns, Executive Director
Quill and Scroll Foundation
312 WSSH, School of Journalism
Iowa City, IA 52242-1528
Phone: 319-335-3321
Fax: 319-335-5210
E-mail: quill-scroll@uiowa.edu
Web site: http://www.uiowa.edu/~quill-sc

RADIO-TELEVISION NEWS DIRECTORS ASSOCIATION AND FOUNDATION

Carole Simpson Scholarship

Karen Jackson-Bullitt, Project Coordinator
Radio-Television News Directors
    Association and Foundation
1600 K Street, NW, Suite 700
Washington, DC 20006
Phone: 202-467-5218
Fax: 202-223-4007
E-mail: karenb@rtndf.org
Web site: http://www.rtndf.org/

RHODE ISLAND FOUNDATION

Constant Memorial Scholarship for Aquidneck Island Residents

Libby Monahan, Scholarship Coordinator
Rhode Island Foundation
1 Union Station
Providence, RI 02903
Phone: 401-274-4564
Fax: 401-272-1359
E-mail: libbym@rifoundation.org
Web site: http://www.rifoundation.org

J.D. Edsal Advertising Scholarship

Scholarship Coordinator
Rhode Island Foundation
1 Union Station
Providence, RI 02903
Phone: 401-274-4564
Fax: 401-272-1359
Web site: http://www.rifoundation.org

ROBERT H. MOLLOHAN FAMILY CHARITABLE FOUNDATION, INC.

Mary Olive Eddy Jones Art Scholarship

Teah Bayless, Program Manager
Robert H. Mollohan Family Charitable
 Foundation, Inc.
1000 Technology Drive, Suite 2000
Fairmont, WV 26554
Phone: 304-333-2251
Fax: 304-333-3900
E-mail: tmbayless@wvhtf.org
Web site:
 http://www.mollohanfoundation.org

SAN FRANCISCO FOUNDATION

Phelan Art Award in Filmmaking

Phelan Art Award in Video

Art Awards Coordinator
San Francisco Foundation
225 Bush Street, Suite 500
San Francisco, CA 94104
Phone: 415-733-8500
Web site: http://www.sff.org

SISTER KENNY REHAB

International Art Show for Artists with Disabilities

Laura Swift, Administrative Assistant
Sister Kenny Rehabilitation Institute
800 East 28th Street
Minneapolis, MN 55407-3799
Phone: 612-863-4466
Fax: 612-863-8942
E-mail: laura.swift@allina.com
Web site: http://www.allina.com/

SOCIETY OF AMERICAN MILITARY ENGINEERS—VIRGINIA PENINSULA POST

The Virginia Peninsula Post of the Society of American Military Engineers (S.A.M.E.) Scholarship

Jeffrey B. Merz, Scholarship Chair
Society of American Military Engineers—
 Virginia Peninsula Post
129 Andrews Street, Suite 102
Langley AFB, VA 23665-2769
Phone: 757-764-6579
E-mail: jeffrey.merz@langley.af.mil
Web site:
 http://posts.same.org/vapeninsula/

SOCIETY OF AMERICAN REGISTERED ARCHITECTS

SARA Student Design Competition

Cathie Moscato, Program Administrator
Society of American Registered Architects
PO Box 280
Cosby, TN 37822
Phone: 423-487-0365
Fax: 423-487-0365
E-mail: cathiemoscato@hotmail.com
Web site: http://www.sara-national.org

SOCIETY OF MOTION PICTURE AND TELEVISION ENGINEERS

Lou Wolf Memorial Scholarship

Student Paper Award

Sally-Ann D'Amato
Society of Motion Picture and Television
 Engineers
3 Barker Avenue
White Plains, NY 10601
Phone: 914-761-1100
E-mail: sdamato@smpte.org
Web site: http://www.smpte.org

SOUTH DAKOTA RETAILERS ASSOCIATION

South Dakota Retailers Association Scholarship Program

Donna Leslie, Communications Director
South Dakota Retailers Association
PO Box 638
Pierre, SD 57501
Phone: 800-658-5545
Fax: 605-224-2059
E-mail: dleslie@sdra.org
Web site: http://www.sdra.org

TAG AND LABEL MANUFACTURERS INSTITUTE, INC.

TLMI 4-Year Colleges/Full-Time Students Scholarship

Karen Planz
Tag and Label Manufacturers Institute, Inc.
40 Shuman Boulevard, Suite 295
Naperville, IL 60563
Phone: 800-533-8564
E-mail: office@tlmi.com
Web site: http://www.tlmi.com

Visual *Arts*

TELETOON

Teletoon Animation Scholarship Award Competition

Denise Vaughan, Senior Coordinator, Public Relations
Teletoon
BCE Place
181 Bay Street, PO Box 787
Toronto M5J 2T3
Canada
Phone: 416-956-2060
Fax: 416-956-2070
E-mail: scholarship@teletoon.com
Web site: http://www.teletoon.com

TEXAS ARTS AND CRAFTS EDUCATIONAL FOUNDATION

Emerging Texas Artist Scholarship

Texas Arts and Crafts Educational Foundation
PO Box 291527
Kerrville, TX 78029-1527
Phone: 830-896-5711
E-mail: info@tacef.org
Web site: http://www.tacef.org

TEXAS GRAPHIC ARTS EDUCATIONAL FOUNDATION SCHOLARSHIPS

Texas Graphic Arts Educational Foundation Scholarships

Jim Weinstein, Director
Texas Graphic Arts Educational Foundation
1720 Regal Row, Suite 150
Dallas, TX 75235
Phone: 214-630-8277
Fax: 214-637-1508

TEXAS GRIDIRON CLUB, INC.

Texas Gridiron Club Scholarships

Angie Summers, Scholarships Coordinator
Texas Gridiron Club, Inc.
709 Houston Street
Arlington, TX 76012
E-mail: asummers@star.telegram.com
Web site: http://www.spjfw.org

TURNER CONSTRUCTION COMPANY

YouthForce 2020 Scholarship Program

Stephanie V. Ansari, Community Affairs Coordinator
Turner Construction Company
375 Hudson Street, 6th Floor
New York, NY 10014
Phone: 212-229-6480
E-mail: sansari@tcco.com
Web site: http://www.turnerconstruction.com

U.S. FISH AND WILDLIFE SERVICE

Federal Junior Duck Stamp Conservation and Design Competition

Pat Fisher, Chief
U.S. Fish and Wildlife Service
The Federal Duck Stamp Program
4401 North Fairfax Drive
Mail Stop: MBSP-4070
Arlington, VA 22203-1622
Phone: 703-358-2000
Fax: 703-358-2009
E-mail: duckstamps@fws.gov
Web site: http://www.fws.gov/duckstamps/

UNICO NATIONAL, INC

Theodore Mazza Scholarship

UNICO National, Inc
UNICO National, Inc
271 US Highway 46 West, Suite A-108
Fairfield, NJ 07004
Phone: 973-808-0035
Fax: 973-808-0043
Web site: http://www.unico.org

UNITED METHODIST COMMUNICATIONS

Leonard M. Perryman Communications Scholarship for Ethnic Minority Students

Amelia Tucker-Shaw, Coordinator
United Methodist Communications
810 12th Avenue, South
Nashville, TN 37202-4744
Phone: 888-278-4862
E-mail: atucker-shaw@umcom.org
Web site: http://www.umcom.org/

UNITED NEGRO COLLEGE FUND

Houston Symphony/ Top Ladies Scholarship

Rebecca Bennett, Director, Program
Services
United Negro College Fund
8260 Willow Oaks Corporate Drive
Fairfax, VA 22031-8044
Phone: 800-331-2244
E-mail: rbennett@uncf.org
Web site: http://www.uncf.org

UNIVERSITY FILM AND VIDEO ASSOCIATION

University Film and Video Association Carole Fielding Student Grants

Prof. Robert Johnson, Jr., Chair, Carole
Fielding Grants
University Film and Video Association
Framingham State College, 100 State
Street
Framingham, MA 01701-9101
Phone: 508-626-4684
Fax: 508-626-4847
E-mail: rjohnso@frc.mass.edu
Web site: http://www.ufva.org

VALLEY PRESS CLUB

Valley Press Club Scholarships, The Republican Scholarship; Photojournalism Scholarship, Channel 22 Scholarship

Robert McClellan, Scholarship
Committee Chair
Valley Press Club
PO Box 5475
Springfield, MA 01101
Phone: 413-783-3355
Web site: http://www.valleypressclub.com/

VARIAZIONE MIXED MEDIA ARTISTS' COLLECTIVE

Learning Scholarship

Zen Learning Scholarship
VariaZioNE Mixed Media Artists' Collective
1152 Crellin Road
Pleasanton, CA 94566
Web site: http://www.zneart.com

W. EUGENE SMITH MEMORIAL FUND, INC.

W. Eugene Smith Grant in Humanistic Photography

Suzanne Nicholas, c/o ICP
W. Eugene Smith Memorial Fund, Inc.
1133 Avenue of Americas
New York, NY 10036
Phone: 212-857-9720
Web site: http://www.smithfund.org

WATERBURY FOUNDATION

Lois McMillen Memorial Scholarship Fund

Josh Carey, Program Officer
Waterbury Foundation
43 Field Street
Waterbury, CT 06702-1216
Phone: 203-753-1315
Fax: 203-756-3054
E-mail: jcarey@conncf.org
Web site: http://www.conncf.org/

WAVERLY COMMUNITY HOUSE, INC.

F. Lammot Belin Arts Scholarship

Chairperson
Waverly Community House, Inc.
1115 North Abington Road
PO Box 142
Waverly, PA 18471
Phone: 570-586-8191
Fax: 570-586-0185
E-mail: info@waverlycomm.com
Web site: http://www.waverlycomm.com

WEST VIRGINIA SOCIETY OF ARCHITECTS/AIA

West Virginia Society of Architects/ AIA Scholarship

Roberta Guffey, Executive Director
West Virginia Society of Architects/AIA
223 Hale Street
Charleston, WV 25323
Phone: 304-344-9872
Fax: 304-343-0205
E-mail: Roberta.Guffey@aiawv.org
Web site: http://www.aiawv.org

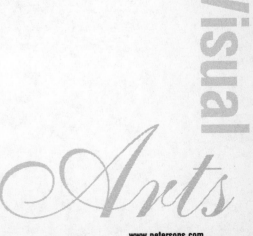

WOMEN IN FILM AND TELEVISION (WIFT)

WIF Foundation Scholarship

Gayle Nachlix, WIF Foundation Scholarship
  Coordinator
Women in Film and Television (WIFT)
8857 West Olympic Boulevard, Suite 201
Beverly Hills, CA 90211
Phone: 310-657-5144
Web site: http://www.wif.org

WORLDFEST INTERNATIONAL FILM AND VIDEO FESTIVAL

Worldfest Student Film Award

Hunter Todd, Executive Director
Worldfest International Film and
  Video Festival
PO Box 56566
Houston, TX 77256-6566
Phone: 713-965-9955
Fax: 713-965-9960
E-mail: mail@worldfest.org
Web site: http://www.worldfest.org

WORLDSTUDIO FOUNDATION

Worldstudio AIGA Scholarships

Worldstudio Foundation Scholarship Program

Scholarship Coordinator
Worldstudio Foundation
200 Varick Street, Suite 507
New York, NY 10014
Phone: 212-366-1317 Ext. 18
Fax: 212-807-0024
E-mail: scholarships@worldstudio.org
Web site: http://www.worldstudio.org

Visual

Arts

Additional Resources

AMERICAN SOCIETY OF INTERIOR DESIGNERS (ASID)

608 Massachusetts Ave., NE
Washington, DC 20002-6006
Phone: 202-546-3480
Fax: 202-546-3240
Web site: www.asid.org

FOUNDATION FOR INTERIOR DESIGN EDUCATION RESEARCH (FIDER)

146 Monroe Center NW, Suite 1318
Grand Rapids, MI 49503-2822
Phone: 616-458-0400
Fax: 616-458-0460
E-mail: fider@fider.org
Web site: www.fider.org

NATIONAL ART HONOR SOCIETIES

A Program of the National Art Education
    Association
1916 Association Drive
Reston, VA 20191-1590
Phone: 703-860-8000
Fax: 703-860-2960
Web site: www.naea-reston.org

NATIONAL ASSOCIATION OF SCHOOLS OF ART AND DESIGN (NASAD)

11250 Roger Bacon Drive, Suite 21
Reston, VA 20190-5248
Phone: 703-437-0700
Fax: 703-437-6312
E-mail: info@arts-accredit.org
Web site: http://nasad.arts-accredit.org

NATIONAL FOUNDATION FOR ADVANCEMENT IN THE ARTS (NFAA)

Arts Recognition and Talent Search®
    (ARTS)
444 Brickell Avenue, P-14
Miami, FL 33131
Phone: 305-377-1140
Fax: 305-377-1149
Web site: www.artsawards.org

NATIONAL PORTFOLIO DAY ASSOCIATION (NPDA)

Web site: www.npda.org

THE SOCIETY OF ILLUSTRATORS

128 East 63rd Street
New York, NY 10021-7303
Phone: 212-838-2560
Fax: 212-838-2561
E-mail: info@societyillustrators.org
Web site: www.societyillustrators.org

VISUAL AND PERFORMING ARTS COLLEGE FAIRS

National Association for College Admission
    Counseling (NACAC)
1631 Prince Street
Alexandria, Virginia, 22314
Phone: 703-836-2222
Fax: 703-836-8015
Web site: www.nacacnet.org/memberportal/
    events/collegefairs/

Indexes

Majors and Concentrations

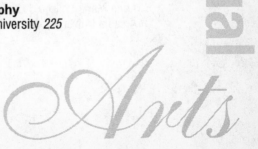

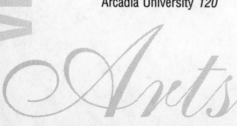

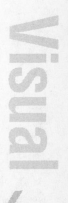

CAD/CAM
Temple University *281*

Cartooning
School of Visual Arts *265*

Ceramic art and design
Abilene Christian University *111*
Alberta College of Art & Design *114*
Arcadia University *120*
California College of the Arts *140*
California State University, Chico *145*
College for Creative Studies *152*
East Carolina University *169*
Grand Valley State University *174*
Illinois Wesleyan University *178*
Indiana State University *179*
Indiana University Bloomington *180*
Kansas State University *188*
Lehman College of the City University of New York *190*
Louisiana Tech University *193*
Maryland Institute College of Art *200*
Massachusetts College of Art *203*
Memphis College of Art *204*
Miami University *207*
New Mexico State University *219*
Pratt Institute *241*
Saint Mary's College *254*
School of the Art Institute of Chicago *260*
Southern Illinois University Carbondale *270*
Southern Illinois University Edwardsville *271*
Temple University *281*
Truman State University *280*
The University of Akron *282*
The University of Alabama *283*
The University of Arizona *284*
University of Montevallo *303*
University of North Dakota *306*
University of Notre Dame *308*
The University of Texas at Arlington *313*
Wayne State University *326*
Webster University *326*
Western Carolina University *328*

Ceramics
Alfred University *115*
Arizona State University *121*
Arkansas State University *122*
Austin Peay State University *134*
Ball State University *134*

Barton College *135*
California State University, Fullerton *146*
Clarke College *149*
The Cleveland Institute of Art *150*
Columbia College *156*
Corcoran College of Art and Design *160*
Edinboro University of Pennsylvania *169*
Emporia State University *170*
Guilford College *175*
Jacksonville State University *183*
Johnson State College *184*
Kansas City Art Institute *185*
Kent State University *189*
Lindenwood University *191*
Long Island University, C.W. Post Campus *192*
Maharishi University of Management *195*
Maine College of Art *196*
Manhattanville College *198*
Marshall University *199*
Metropolitan State College of Denver *206*
Michigan State University *208*
Minnesota State University Mankato *211*
Mississippi State University *211*
Missouri State University *212*
Murray State University *217*
New Hampshire Institute of Art *217*
New Mexico Highlands University *218*
Northern Illinois University *224*
Northern Kentucky University *225*
NSCAD University *227*
The Ohio State University *228*
Oregon College of Art & Craft *230*
Plymouth State University *239*
Radford University *245*
Rhode Island School of Design *246*
Rockford College *251*
Roger Williams University *252*
Rutgers, The State University of New Jersey, Mason Gross School of the Arts *203*
St. Cloud State University *253*
Salisbury University *255*
School of the Museum of Fine Arts, Boston *264*
Shorter College *269*
Southern Methodist University *272*
Southern Oregon University *272*
State University of New York at Fredonia *274*
Syracuse University *276*
Tennessee Technological University *119*
Texas A&M University–Commerce *277*
Texas Christian University *278*

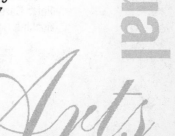

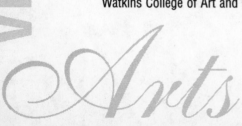

Visual *Arts*

Visual *Arts*

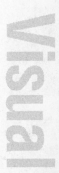

Visual

Arts

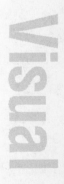

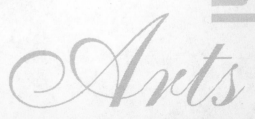

Graphic design and interactive media

Graphic design/letterform

Historical preservation

History and theory of contemporary art

History of decorative arts

Illustration

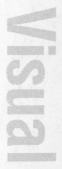

Visual *Arts*

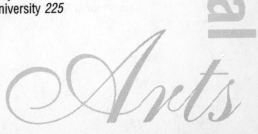

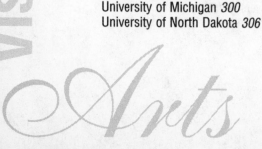

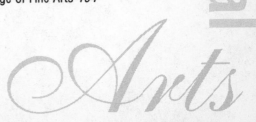

Painting (continued)

Maine College of Art *196*
Manhattanville College *198*
Marshall University *199*
Maryland Institute College of Art *200*
Milwaukee Institute of Art and Design *209*
Minneapolis College of Art and Design *210*
Minnesota State University Mankato *211*
Mississippi State University *211*
Missouri State University *212*
New Hampshire Institute of Art *217*
New Mexico Highlands University *218*
New World School of the Arts *219*
Old Dominion University *229*
Otis College of Art and Design *230*
Pennsylvania Academy of the Fine Arts *235*
Plymouth State University *239*
Queen's University at Kingston *245*
Radford University *245*
Rhode Island School of Design *246*
Rockford College *251*
Roger Williams University *252*
St. Cloud State University *253*
St. John's University *254*
San Francisco Art Institute *255*
Savannah College of Art and Design *257*
School of the Museum of Fine Arts, Boston *264*
Sonoma State University *269*
Southern Methodist University *272*
State University of New York at Fredonia *274*
Tennessee Technological University *119*
Texas A&M University–Commerce *277*
Truman State University *280*
University of Arkansas *285*
University of Evansville *290*
University of Hartford *292*
University of Illinois at Urbana–Champaign *294*
University of Kansas *296*
University of Massachusetts Dartmouth *298*
University of Missouri–Columbia *301*
University of Nebraska–Lincoln *303*
University of North Alabama *305*
The University of North Carolina at Charlotte *305*
University of Southern California *310*
University of Southern Maine *310*
The University of Tennessee *312*
The University of the Arts *315*
University of Wisconsin–Oshkosh *321*
Watkins College of Art and Design *325*

Wayne State University *326*
Western Michigan University *329*
Williams Baptist College *331*
Wright State University *332*
York University *332*
Youngstown State University *333*

Painting/drawing

Abilene Christian University *111*
Academy of Art University *111*
Alberta College of Art & Design *114*
Alfred University *115*
Arcadia University *120*
Arkansas State University *122*
Brooklyn College of the City University of New York *140*
California College of the Arts *140*
California State University, Chico *145*
California State University, Fullerton *146*
College for Creative Studies *152*
Columbia College *156*
Cornell University *162*
Cornish College of the Arts *165*
East Carolina University *169*
Emporia State University *170*
Grand Valley State University *174*
Guilford College *175*
Indiana State University *179*
Indiana University Bloomington *180*
Jacksonville State University *183*
Kansas City Art Institute *185*
Lehman College of the City University of New York *190*
Lindenwood University *191*
Louisiana Tech University *193*
Maharishi University of Management *195*
Massachusetts College of Art *203*
Memphis College of Art *204*
Metropolitan State College of Denver *206*
Miami University *207*
Michigan State University *208*
Montserrat College of Art *213*
Mount Allison University *216*
Murray State University *217*
New Mexico State University *219*
Northern Illinois University *224*
Northern Kentucky University *225*
Notre Dame de Namur University *226*
The Ohio State University *228*
Oregon College of Art & Craft *230*

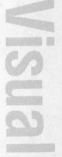

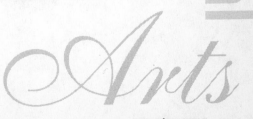

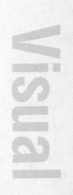

Visual *Arts*

Visual

Arts

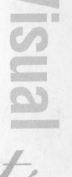

Visual *Arts*

Sculpture (continued)

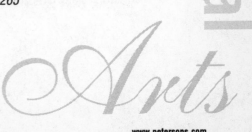

Visual **Arts**

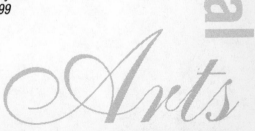

Visual Arts

Alphabetical Listing of Schools

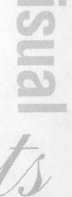

393

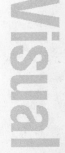

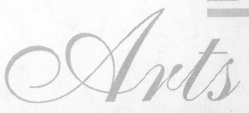

Visual *Arts*

NOTES

NOTES

NOTES

NOTES

NOTES

NOTES

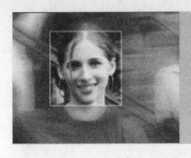

Peterson's
Book Satisfaction Survey

Give Us Your Feedback

Thank you for choosing Peterson's as your source for personalized solutions for your education and career achievement. Please take a few minutes to answer the following questions. Your answers will go a long way in helping us to produce the most user-friendly and comprehensive resources to meet your individual needs.

When completed, please tear out this page and mail it to us at:

Publishing Department
Peterson's, a Nelnet company
2000 Lenox Drive
Lawrenceville, NJ 08648

You can also complete this survey online at **www.petersons.com/booksurvey.**

1. **What is the ISBN of the book you have purchased? (The ISBN can be found on the book's back cover in the lower right-hand corner.)** _____

2. **Where did you purchase this book?**
   ❏ Retailer, such as Barnes & Noble
   ❏ Online reseller, such as Amazon.com
   ❏ Petersons.com
   ❏ Other (please specify) _____

3. **If you purchased this book on Petersons.com, please rate the following aspects of your online purchasing experience on a scale of 4 to 1 (4 = Excellent and 1 = Poor).**

	4	3	2	1
Comprehensiveness of Peterson's Online Bookstore page	❏	❏	❏	❏
Overall online customer experience	❏	❏	❏	❏

4. **Which category best describes you?**
   ❏ High school student
   ❏ Parent of high school student
   ❏ College student
   ❏ Graduate/professional student
   ❏ Returning adult student

   ❏ Teacher
   ❏ Counselor
   ❏ Working professional/military
   ❏ Other (please specify) _____

5. **Rate your overall satisfaction with this book.**

Extremely Satisfied	Satisfied	Not Satisfied
❏	❏	❏

6. Rate each of the following aspects of this book on a scale of 4 to 1 (4 = Excellent and 1 = Poor).

	4	3	2	1
Comprehensiveness of the information	❑	❑	❑	❑
Accuracy of the information	❑	❑	❑	❑
Usability	❑	❑	❑	❑
Cover design	❑	❑	❑	❑
Book layout	❑	❑	❑	❑
Special features (e.g., CD, flashcards, charts, etc.)	❑	❑	❑	❑
Value for the money	❑	❑	❑	❑

7. This book was recommended by:
❑ Guidance counselor
❑ Parent/guardian
❑ Family member/relative
❑ Friend
❑ Teacher
❑ Not recommended by anyone—I found the book on my own
❑ Other (please specify) _____

Would you recommend this book to others?

Yes	Not Sure	No
❑	❑	❑

Please provide any additional comments.

_____

_____

_____

_____

_____

you can tear out this page and mail it to us at:

ishing Department
son's, a Nelnet company
Lenox Drive
nceville, NJ 08648

plete the survey online at **www.petersons.com/booksurvey.**

important to us at Peterson's, and we thank you for your time!

us to keep in touch with you about new products and services, please include your
re: _____